648-4627-

MW01592150

Assessment of Children

Fundamental Methods and Practices

———

Assessment of Children

Fundamental Methods and Practices

Joseph C. Witt
Louisiana State University

Stephen N. Elliott
University of Wisconsin – Madison

Jack J. Kramer
University of Nebraska, Lincoln

Frank M. Gresham
University of California, Riverside

WCB Brown & Benchmark
PUBLISHERS

Madison, Wisconsin • Dubuque, Iowa

Book Team

Managing Editor *Sue Pulvermacher-Alt*
Production Editor *Karen A. Pluemer*
Permissions Freelancer *Karen Dorman*
Visuals/Design Developmental Consultant *Marilyn A. Phelps*
Visuals/Design Freelance Specialist *Mary L. Christianson*
Marketing Manager *Elizabeth Haefele*
Advertising Manager *Nancy Milling*

WCB Brown & Benchmark

A Division of Wm. C. Brown Communications, Inc.

Executive Vice President/General Manager *Thomas E. Doran*
Vice President/Editor in Chief *Edgar J. Laube*
Vice President/Sales and Marketing *Eric Ziegler*
Director of Production *Vickie Putman Caughron*
Director of Custom and Electronic Publishing *Chris Rogers*

Wm. C. Brown Communications, Inc.

President and Chief Executive Officer *G. Franklin Lewis*
Corporate Senior Vice President and Chief Financial Officer *Robert Chesterman*
Corporate Senior Vice President and President of Manufacturing *Roger Meyer*

Cover and interior designs by Matthew Doherty Design.

Interior illustrations by Publishers Services, Inc., unless noted otherwise.

Copyedited by Laurie McGee

The credits section for this book begins on page 501 and is considered
an extension of the copyright page.

For my daughter, Sarah Anne
J. C. W.

To the memory of Ed Argulewicz, who always reminded me of the importance of individual differences; to my loving wife, Anita; and to my two "special" children, Dustin Rhodes and Andrew Taylor.
S. N. E.

To Jeannie, Jamie, and Jessica—my best friend and our special contributions
J. J. K.

To my parents, Metz and Julia Gresham
F. M. G.

Brief Contents

Alternative Assessment Techniques and Approaches   396

Contents

Chapter 3
Assessment and the Law 43

Preface

Purpose of the Text

How is it possible to convey fully the degree to which the assessment of special children is a rich, rewarding process? As authors we wanted to write an interesting and readable text. We were concerned that an encyclopedic listing of tests and an overemphasis on the technology (e.g., statistics) of assessment might overshadow the more important and interesting features of the field. We wanted to present stories of children like Rhonda K., who, because of cerebral palsy, had very poor control of her arms and legs and was thought to be mentally disabled. However, skillful testing with nontraditional methods indicated she was a bright young girl who could benefit from a much higher level of instruction than traditional tests had suggested. This practical focus, based on our experience, is interwoven with a clear, accurate, and readable description of all the essential information one would expect to find in an introductory text on assessment in special education.

We have stressed the application of assessment in two ways. First, there is a strong emphasis on the linking of assessment with intervention and instruction through a problem-solving process. In fact, this book evolved out of a perception that specialists wanted a source of information that would link assessment to intervention and the solution of important educational problems. The goals, therefore, are to describe how assessment data can be obtained and used by individuals engaged in the problem-solving process within educational settings and to integrate the assessment process typically used in schools with test instruments. Application also has been stressed through the frequent discussion of actual case studies, examples, and special sections entitled "Focus on Practice" that show real people dealing with real problems.

To describe a field as broad and diverse as assessment and still convey that it is an organized and coherent body of knowledge, it was necessary to maintain uniformity from chapter to chapter by emphasizing the following common themes.

Linking Assessment and Intervention

The book is based on the assumption that when a child is referred for assessment, the goal is to solve the child's problem by developing appropriate academic or social interventions. Thus, the focus is on using tests within a problem-solving process. For too long, giving tests has been equated with problem solving, but the link between assessment and intervention must be explicitly planned and practiced. The text first details the assessment process and then examines several areas of concern, such as reading, math, language, and preschool readiness, to illustrate how to understand a child experiencing problems in each of these domains.

Using and Interpreting Tests

The text also helps test users master assessment fundamentals so that instruments can be administered and interpreted correctly. Because assessment data play a major role in determining how children will be educated, they can be harmful as well as helpful, depending on their use. Irrevocable damage can be done by individuals misinformed about the limitations of tests; thus, every test user is responsible for knowing what tests can and cannot do.

Audience for This Book

Special education professionals taking their first course in assessment are the audience for this book. We have assumed no previous knowledge of or work in educational measurement or statistics. The book is designed for individuals who will be working with special needs children and who must be able to use and interpret both standardized and informal tests. This text will also benefit counselors, school psychologists, educational administrators, speech and language pathologists, social workers, and others directly or indirectly involved in the education of preschool children, children with behavior problems, and those with mild or severe disabilities.

Learning Aids Accompanying the Book

Students using this book will have the opportunity to access reviews of some of the best tests published in the United States. As part of the Instructor's Manual, we have provided a computer disk with reviews of 10 tests (Child Behavior Checklist, Iowa Test of Basic Skills, Test of Early Reading, Wechsler Preschool and Primary Scale of Intelligence-Revised, Adaptive Behavior Inventory, BRIGANCE® Preschool Screen, ENRIGHT® Diagnostic Inventory of Basic Arithmetic Skills, The Instructional Environment Scale, Kaufman Test of Educational Achievement, Stanford-Binet Intelligence Scale-4th Edition) published in recent editions of the Buros

Mental Measurements Yearbooks. Reviews of these tests provide excellent evaluative models based on content expertise and use of knowledge about the essential qualities of a reliable and valid test. Students can learn much from reading a sample of these reviews!

The instructor using this book will have access to a comprehensive Instructor's Manual. This manual includes detailed summaries of each of the 18 chapters in the text, lists of key terms used in each chapter, ideas for lectures on critical or controversial issues in assessment, and a variety of test questions (i.e., multiple-choice, true or false, and short answer essay) that can be used to facilitate studying or to evaluate learning. The Instructor's Manual also includes blackline masters for nearly 50 of the key tables or figures from the text and a hard copy of the reviews of tests from the *Mental Measurements Yearbooks.*

Acknowledgments

A number of people have been extraordinarily generous with their time, energy, and wisdom during the writing of this book. We are hopelessly in debt to these individuals.

Joseph Witt would like to acknowledge several people who contributed to his work on this book. Kevin Jones merits special attention for his extensive research and input into several chapters, and for indexing the book. Michael Bigalke is acknowledged for his expert editorial assistance and his facile use of every electronic medium available to rush this book into print. Discussions with and assistance from Wayne Stewart, Angela Vaughn, Katherine Wickstrom, Bill McKee, Ed Lentz, and Brian Martens also benefited the book immea-surably. Finally, acknowledgment must also be given to colleagues at LSU who granted me a sabbatical during completion of the book. I am also extremely grateful to John Reid and the Oregon Social Learning Center where I spent Fall 1992 in a stimulating, yet contemplative atmosphere.

Stephen Elliott would like to acknowledge the unnamed hundreds of teachers and parents he has worked with over the past decade who have children with learning or behavior problems. They served to provide the context for his writing and a reminder that *assessment is communication*—it involves looking, listening, and questioning! As the point man on this project, Steve would also like to acknowledge the contributions of Paul Tavenner and Steve Lehman, both Brown and Benchmark editors who made a difference and were great to work with.

Jack Kramer would like to acknowledge the seminal contributions of his parents, Emma and Joseph Kramer, to this book.

Several professionals provided thoughtful and helpful reviews. We gratefully acknowledge Louis P. Messier, College of William and Mary; William R. Reid, University of Florida; Roy L. Smith, Long Island University; and John C. Van Vactor, University of Nevada–Las Vegas.

Finally, but most especially, we want to thank our families for their patience, understanding, and encouragement during the completion of this book.

Assessment of Children

Fundamental Methods and Practices

Part One

Foundations of Assessment

Whether one is building a house or teaching fifth-grade math, it is both necessary and important to set a proper foundation. A good foundation is also important to school-based assessment of children for special education, and this first part of the book introduces basic assumptions and terminology upon which the remainder of the book is based. This part also provides a context within which assessment can be placed.

This book is mostly about children—children who are experiencing problems of one type or another. Individuals working directly with these children both want and demand solutions to the problems. In Chapter 1, assessment is presented as a vital source of the information needed to address these problems. More specifically, assessment should yield information that helps identify the nature of the problems, the factors that may be contributing to them, and, most important, possible remedies.

Chapter 2 provides a conceptual and theoretical basis essential to the conduct of assessment procedures and introduces additional terminology used throughout the book.

In Chapter 3, problem solving is placed within the context of the laws and regulations that govern the education of handicapped children. These laws govern not only the day-to-day functioning of the special education assessment process but also its very existence. The application of the various laws and regulations is described to explain how the assessment process works. By the time you complete this section, you should have a richer understanding of why we assess, the legal foundation of the assessment process, and the context within which that process exists.

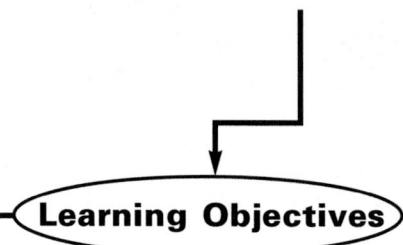

Chapter 1

Assessment and the Solving of Problems

Learning Objectives

1. Distinguish between the content and process of assessment.
2. Describe and be able to apply a problem-solving model to the process of assessment.
3. Explain the use of the Centra and Potter model of school learning in the identification of factors to consider when planning an assessment.
4. Explain how the assessment process should function like a funnel.
5. List and describe the five major decisions for which assessment data are used.

The ability to solve complex problems is critical to the successful functioning of teachers, psychologists, and others involved in the schooling of children. Central to the process of problem solving is **assessment,** the collecting and synthesizing of information about a problem.

Assessment means different things to different people. Many laypersons as well as professional educators believe standardized testing and assessment are synonymous terms. Assessment, however, involves much more than testing. Most teachers will tell you they assess students by observing classwork, asking questions, and evaluating performances on classroom tests. Speech clinicians may argue that the best way to assess children is to listen to them talk. Psychologists tend to emphasize testing, yet they also use direct observations, rating scales, and clinical interviews as common means of assessment. All these perceptions of what assessment involves are accurate yet incomplete.

Effective communication about tests and the assessment process requires us to also introduce the concept of measurement along with the terms testing and assessment. To measure means to quantify or to place a number value on a student's performance. Not all performances can be or need to be quantified; however, most tests will result in some numerical value that serves to summarize a student's functioning. Thus, tests are measurement tools used to gather assessment information. The science of measurement in itself includes many important concepts—reliability, validity, norms, standard scores—about which test users and consumers need to have a basic understanding. We will consider these and many related concepts that influence the selection and meaningful use of tests and numerous other assessment techniques.

Assessment should be viewed as an ongoing process that involves the use of an array of materials, techniques, and tests across a variety of time periods and situations. Teachers, parents, counselors, psychologists, speech clinicians, and even children can be involved actively in the process of assessing the strengths and weaknesses of a child experiencing a problem at school or home. Thus assessment, particularly for purposes of special or remedial education, is multifaceted and should be a team process whereby professionals and laypersons work cooperatively toward the solution of a problem.

Any study of assessment theory and practice must take into account inherent unknowns, inconsistencies, and ambiguities. One must be prepared to take a cautious approach to the use and interpretation of assessment instruments, because some very practical consequences can result from the problems intrinsic to our measuring systems, as the following four examples illustrate.

1. A speech clinician and a special education teacher have each evaluated a five-year-old boy but disagree on the source of his difficulty. The speech clinician feels that the child has a language delay, whereas the special education teacher insists that he is disabled. The speech clinician suggests the child only appeared disabled on the tests because of his language problems. The special education teacher insists that the language delay is indicative of the disability. How can two individuals evaluate the same child, review essentially identical assessment information, and reach such different conclusions?

2. Following a recent district desegregation, 15 third-grade students newly transferred to Bailey School are referred for reading evaluations because they are struggling in the basal reading series. According to their records, they all had been functioning at grade level in reading at their old schools. What could account for this discrepancy in the students' ability between schools? Is something wrong with all 15 students, the teacher, or the curriculum?

3. A group of specialists in a suburban school district have been asked to assess the effectiveness of special education classes. Part of the group believes that the goal of the classes is the academic progress of the students, which therefore is the only factor that should be assessed. The remainder of the group argues that any assessment of effectiveness should consider an array of factors, including teacher experience, type of student disability, and length of special program. What should be done to resolve these differing viewpoints and to assess the programs?

4. The parents of a young girl are becoming increasingly confused. They suspect their child is having difficulties in math but when the child was given a math test at school, her scores indicated she was progressing normally. The parents then had their child tested by a private consultant who reported that her math ability was at least one grade level behind that of her peers. The parents wonder how two tests claiming to measure "math ability" could yield such discrepant results.

A major goal of this chapter is to emphasize that assessment practices can and should vary according to the type of problem that precipitated assessment. Assessment is a tool that is useful if, and only if, it contributes to the solution of problems.

➡ *Assessment and Schooling*

The assessment process, and in particular the use of standardized tests in schools to identify children who are at-risk and disabled, has attracted much attention from educators, professional groups such as psychologists and counselors, parents, and occasionally lawyers and state and federal legislators. For example, the National Association of Early Childhood Teacher Educators (NAECTE) stated they "encourage the replacement of current questionable testing practices with those more consonant with the knowledge base on how young children demonstrate what they learn and know" (NAECTE, 1989). Albert Shanker (1989), then president of the American Federation of Teachers, stated, "I would call for an immediate end to standardized tests as they are now." Shanker was talking about group standardized achievement tests, which are commonly administered to all students in grades 4, 8, and 12 as a means of assessing academic progress of students and maintaining some accountability of educators. Data collected in the late 1980s by the National Center for Fair and Open Testing (1989) indicated that more than 100 million standardized tests were administered annually to public school students. Finally, during the 1970s and 1980s there were more than 10 major court cases (which we will discuss in chapter 3) in the United States concerning the alleged mis-use of tests and poor assessment practices with minority and/or students who may be disabled.

The list of concerns raised by parents, educators, and others about tests, the assessment process, and the education of children could go on for several more pages. Why all the concern about tests and the assess-ment of children? The answer to this simple question is not simple, but through the course of reading this book you will become familiar with many of the substantive concerns about tests and testing practices with children in schools today. Many of these concerns revolve around the misuse of tests and incomplete assessment practices by persons employed by schools! Fortunately, most all the concerns with standardized tests can be overcome with knowledge of the limitations of tests, an awareness of complementary alternative assessment methods, and an understanding of the "best professional practices" for conducting and interpreting assess-ments. Thus the reason for this book and supervised study of tests and assessment practices.

"AFTER 20 YEARS OF SCHOOLING, YOUR APTITUDE TEST SHOWS THAT YOU'RE SKILLED AT JUST ONE THING--TAKING TESTS."

Courtesy of Harley Schwadron.

Many individuals, whether handicapped or not, are tested repeatedly throughout their educational lifetimes. Unfortunately, many of the tests do not provide useful results *or* users do not use the results wisely.

➔ *The Processes of Assessment and Decision Making*

Assessment requires the collection and interpretation of many pieces of information. A primary goal of any assessment is to determine what a student can and cannot do and how that student learns best in order that successful interventions can be designed. To accomplish this goal efficiently and effectively, a systematic plan is needed for the collection and interpretation of data. Such a plan functions like a road map, since it can provide direction and landmarks for moving from the problem state to the intervention state in the delivery of psychoeducational services.

The activities and decisions that occur during assessment can be thought of as *process* components, while the information collected represents *content* components. For example, the decision to use interview and direct observation techniques instead of a test to assess a disruptive student represents a process component, whereas the information derived from the interview and observation would represent a content component. This chapter focuses on the process components of assessment. We will explore the steps involved in an individual assessment and how to use the assessment information to make decisions about students. Later chapters focus on the content components of assessment relating to intelligence, reading, math, and adaptive behavior. Knowledge of the process of assessment may be used or generalized across all types of assessment situations. Thus, knowledge of the assessment process, from our perspective, is prerequisite to knowledge of the various content domains for it serves as the framework to organize assessment activities.

➔ *Problem Solving and the Role of Assessment*

Assessment is never an end in itself. Rather, as part of the problem-solving process, assessment is used in screening, classifying and placing, progress monitoring, programming, and determining program effectiveness. Numerous psychologists and educators have written about problem-solving strategies; however, less has been written about how such strategies or schemes apply to assessment.

Before examining a general model of problem solving, we must define the term "problem." Most people think of a problem as something negative, subaverage, or at least bothersome. Although this is often true, there are numerous situations in which individuals are functioning well above average but still have problems or concerns. For example, a student may be functioning several grades above average in math yet experience significant difficulties when placed in an accelerated math program. In addition, the student's self-concept may be influenced negatively because of the failures in the accelerated program. "Problem" is thus a relative

Focus on
Practice

The Problem Identification Interview

The identification and definition of a problem is the first and probably the most important step in problem solving. Therefore, Witt and Elliott (1983) outlined a series of objectives that can be used to guide a consultant's interview with a parent or teacher, which is intended to define a problem. These objectives are described briefly below:

1. *Explanation of problem definition purposes.* The parent or teacher should be told what is to be accomplished during the interview and why problem identification is important. (Example statement: "I would like to talk with you a few minutes about John and his behaviors that bother you most. In order to help you, we will need to assess his behaviors, when and how often they occur, and what factors in your classroom (or home) influence them.")

2. *Identification and selection of target behaviors.* The parent or teacher should be asked to focus his or her attention on the problematic aspects of a student's difficulties. (Example statement: "Please describe exactly what John is doing that has caused you concern.") When individuals identify multiple problems, it is necessary to determine which to address. (Example statement: "Which of these concerns is most pressing to you now?")

3. *Identification of problem frequency, duration, and intensity.* After a target behavior has been defined, it is helpful to assess its basic characteristics: How often does it occur (*frequency*), how long does it last (*duration*), and how strong is it (*intensity*)? (Example statements: "How many times did John cry last week?" "How long does each crying session last?" "Does he cry loud enough for everyone in the room to hear him?") To interpret descriptions of frequency, duration, and intensity, we usually ask the parent or teacher to compare the target child's behavior with that of other children. In addition, a consultant should have knowledge of normative expectations to which the child's behavior can be compared.

4. *Identification of the conditions under which the target behavior occurs.* The assessment of environmental factors that occur in conjunction with a target behavior often helps to understand the problem. (Example statement: "How do you and the class react to John's crying?") Use of a simple model of behavior, such as the ABC model, can help unravel many problems. This model construes behavior (B) to be a function of antecedent (A) and/or consequent (C) events. Thus, once a behavior has been identified, a consultant looks at events that chronologically precede and follow it.

5. *Identification of the required level of performance.* Obtaining a description of the behavior required of a student is as important as obtaining a description of the student's problem behavior. (Example statement: "What would you consider to be an acceptable frequency for this out-of-seat behavior?") Once a desired or expected level of performance is identified, it serves as a goal to work toward.

6. *Identification of the student's strengths.* Learning what a child does well is often more useful than learning what a child does not do or does poorly. (Example statement: "What does John do best when interacting with his classmates?") Developing interventions that use a student's strengths helps to increase the probability of a successful treatment.

7. *Identification of behavioral assessment procedures.* All interventions require some assessment or recording of behavior. Thus, a consultant should help a teacher or parent decide what, how, when, and where behavior will be recorded and who will do the recording.

8. *Summary of the interview.* The final step should include a summary of the important points discussed and a review of individuals' responsibilities. This can be accomplished by reviewing or restating the definition of the target behavior, the method of recording behavior, and the person responsible for data collection.

The eight objectives outlined should not be viewed as steps through which the consultant should rigidly or mechanically progress. To do so could be detrimental to the interpersonal processes between a consultant and the parent or teacher with whom the consultant is working.

Adapted from J. C. Witt and S. N. Elliott, "Assessment in Behavioral Consultation: The Initial Interview" in *School Psychology Review*, 1:42–49. Copyright © 1983 by the National Association of School Psychologists. Reprinted by permission of the publisher.

concept and can be said to exist when an individual (child, teacher, or parent) reports a significant discrepancy between a target person's current level of performance and a desired level of performance.

A number of aspects of this definition require elaboration. First, although the person reporting the problem may or may not be the target person, the reporter in most cases would be considered a component of the problem. Second, the determination of whether a problem involves a "significant discrepancy" is initially not questioned; however, once the current and desired levels of performance are defined operationally, this significant discrepancy becomes the focal point of assessment. This approach to problem definition is based on the belief that such problems grow out of the unsuccessful or discrepant interactions between persons (e.g., child and peers, child and teacher, child and parent, and parent and teacher). Thus, the person targeted as having a problem and his or her interactions with the environment must be examined first to understand and then to change the problem behavior. Several models have been developed for problem solving by professionals in educational settings.

➡ *A General Model of Problem Solving*

Many special educators and psychologists have used a general problem-solving model that has been conceptualized as a seven-step process by Gutkin and Curtis (1982, 1990):

1. Define and clarify the problem.
2. Analyze factors that may be causing the problem.
3. Brainstorm alternative strategies for solving the problem.
4. Evaluate and choose among the alternatives.
5. Specify responsibilities of those involved in solving the problem.
6. Implement the chosen remedial strategy.
7. Evaluate the effectiveness of the solution and repeat the process if necessary.

Within this process the first step is to achieve a clear, objective definition of the problem. Once a problem has been identified and defined, the helper or consultant and the referral agent are ready to analyze factors that may be influencing the targeted problem. After a comprehensive assessment of the problem and the factors influencing it, some intervention designed to treat the problem must be developed and implemented. Finally, after a suitable time period, the intervention plan is evaluated to determine its effectiveness.

Assessment plays a central role in this model in that assessment data are used in several steps to assist in decision making. This model also illustrates that a comprehensive assessment should result in an intervention designed to resolve the problem. Adherence to this process does not ensure a successful problem solution, but it does increase the chances that one will be reached.

➡ *Problem Solving Within the Assessment Phase*

In the problem analysis stage, one must examine the nature of the problem and the environmental factors that may influence it. Then one must decide what specific questions one needs to ask to help solve the problem. For example, if a student is having difficulty in reading, one question could be, "Is the student's visual acuity adequate?" This is then stated as a hypothesis: "The student has poor visual acuity that interferes with reading." This hypothesis is tested and action taken. If it is incorrect (i.e., if testing reveals the student has good vision), another hypothesis is generated. Additional hypotheses concerning the reading problem legitimately could be generated concerning the teacher's instructional approach, the instructional materials in use, the student's effort or attending skills, and the possible interaction of two or more of these factors. Hypotheses can be tested by observational techniques, standardized norm-referenced and criterion-referenced tests, behavioral checklists, and informal tests using curriculum material. This process can be thought of as a funnel. Such an analogy is instructive because the assessment process progresses from a wide perspective on a problem to a narrower, more well-defined perspective. The various hypothesis testing techniques flow through the funnel differently and aid in making screening, diagnostic, and programming decisions at three critical or structural points.

Elliott and Piersel's (1982) depiction of the assessment process as a funnel is illustrated in figure 1.1. Assessment techniques are arranged in order of specificity of instructional information provided and types of decisions for which the techniques contribute information. As the assessor continues to refine hypotheses, data collection techniques become more specific to a focal child and his or her particular learning environment. Therefore, assessment becomes more direct and serves as a link to intervention.

Operationalizing the Assessment Funnel

The assessment of students often ends prematurely at the diagnostic or classification phase. Consequently, service providers, whether teachers, psychologists, or counselors, are left with little more than a label (such as "learning disabled") and general information about a student's strengths and weaknesses. The formulation of an intervention or Individualized Educational Plan (IEP) remains to be done, and it may become a very subjective task when it should be quite objective. Too often it seems that testers test and teachers teach but they do not share meaningful information. The basic point is that service providers want to know specifically what to do for and with children!

An example of a reading problem may help to illustrate the assessment process. Experienced educators and psychologists may hypothesize accurately about a given reading problem on the basis of data collected from interviews, classroom observations, or referral forms. However, since reading is a complex process, most professionals will probably need to initiate some systematic observation and testing before really knowing the sources of a student's reading difficulties. A good place to start any assessment is with an investigation of a student's sensory capabilities, particularly vision and hearing, and prerequisite learning skills and behaviors.

Figure 1.1 The Assessment Funnel

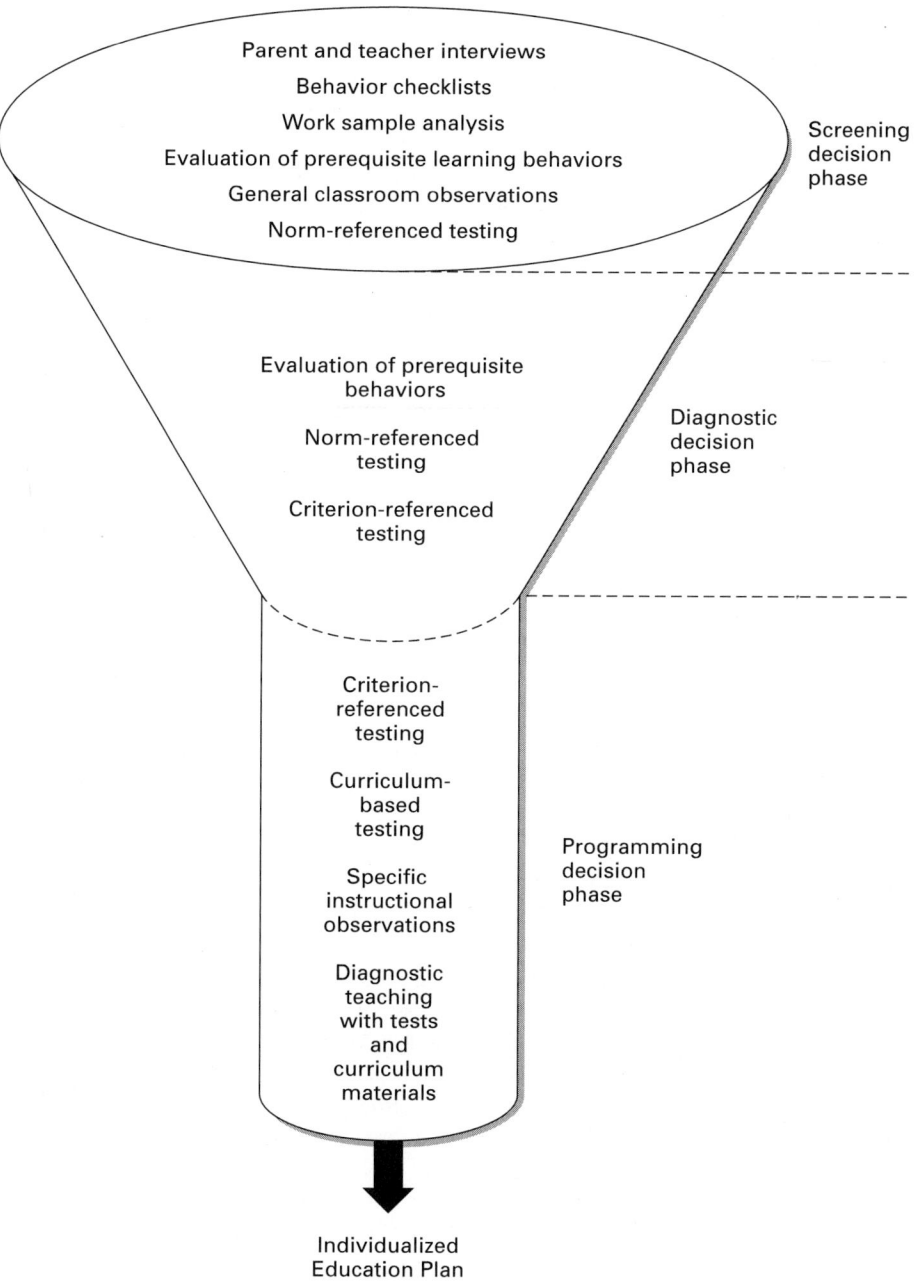

Parent and teacher interviews
Behavior checklists
Work sample analysis
Evaluation of prerequisite learning behaviors
General classroom observations
Norm-referenced testing

Screening
decision
phase

Evaluation of prerequisite
behaviors

Norm-referenced
testing

Criterion-referenced
testing

Diagnostic
decision
phase

Criterion-
referenced
testing

Curriculum-
based
testing

Specific
instructional
observations

Diagnostic
teaching
with tests
and
curriculum
materials

Programming
decision
phase

Individualized
Education Plan

Important prerequisite behaviors include attending to a task, following directions, and correcting oneself. Such characteristics are fundamental to educational progress and are often the source of faulty learning or inappropriate behavior. Such behaviors can be assessed with classroom observations and individualized testing.

Following the assessment of sensory capabilities and prerequisite learning behaviors, the assessor is ready to examine a student's basic reading skills. This can be accomplished by a combination of standardized tests and classwork samples. The assessor's task is facilitated by looking for an error pattern (i.e., frequent mistakes resulting from a knowledge or skill deficit) on tests of reading and classwork samples. Once an error pattern is detected, the assessor needs to determine the **reliability** and **generalizability** of the errors. Reliability refers to the consistency with which an error occurs, whereas generalizability involves the presence of an error in various forms and across types of tasks and materials. In determining the reliability (test-retest) and generalizability of any given error pattern, an assessor answers important questions such as: Are errors due to a lack of knowledge (e.g., that the vowel *a* says its name when it is long as in the word *make*)? Are errors specific to unfamiliar words or do they also occur with familiar words of similar structure or meaning? Do the same errors occur when words are isolated, as when presented in the context of a sentence?

Techniques that are used to determine the reliability and generalizability of an error are referred to as **testing the limits** and **diagnostic** or **trial teaching.** In our model of assessment, these techniques are used sequentially. That is, once testing is completed, high-frequency errors such as vowel confusion, inappropriate syllabification, incorrect sound-symbol relations, and failure to apply the rule of the final e are identified, and items similar to missed representative test items are administered in at least two fashions: according to the way the test item was administered initially and with some additional coaching. This combination of procedures helps to determine whether the error is reliable (consistent) and whether it can be removed with minimal additional structure from an instructor. When a student is unable to solve a reading task correctly after several attempts and with minimal instruction, trial teaching should be initiated.

In trial teaching, an assessor's goal is to teach the student skills to solve new problems from curriculum materials similar to those missed on the initial tests. Trial teaching usually is brief (10 to 15 minutes), intensive, individualized instruction on the correct application of a skill. It is characterized by task analysis techniques, instructor modeling, instructor guidance in problem-solving strategies, and reinforcement of success. As a result of trial teaching, the assessor should be able to comment on the generalizability of a skill or knowledge deficit (i.e., which words or conditions are affected) and instructional factors and materials that can or cannot be used with the student in future remedial activities.

Based on the funnel analogy of assessment and the brief example concerning reading, it should be clear that meaningful assessment is time-consuming and requires an assessor or team of assessors to possess collective knowledge of learning and behavior beyond that necessary to score and interpret standardized tests. Knowledge of variables that may influence learning and behavior is critical to a comprehensive and flexible approach to assessment. In the next section, we examine two general models for understanding students' behavior that are useful during the problem analysis phase of assessment. Other models specific to various content areas of assessment such as reading or math are explored in later chapters.

Conceptual Aids for Analyzing a Problem

A comprehensive analysis of a student's problem requires the use of several methods to collect data about the relationship between student and environment (including school, teacher, class materials, and types of tasks). Centra and Potter (1980) developed a model for investigating school and teacher variables that influence students' achievement (see figure 1.2). This model, although now more than a decade old, is still relevant and includes examples of teacher and school variables and their expected relationships to each other and to student learning outcomes. Such a model provides a valuable framework for hypothesizing about students' school performances. Examine figure 1.2 and see how many viable hypotheses about a young boy with behavior problems or a high school girl with reading problems you can generate. Without spending much time, we are sure you can propose at least a dozen hypotheses about variables influencing each of these two students' problems. The model developed by Centra and Potter, along with your own experiences with school, serve to stimulate many viable hypotheses that could guide problem solving and meaningful assessment actions.

In the Centra and Potter model, school factors include differences between schools and school districts and conditions within an individual school. Teacher factors include characteristics such as experience, verbal aptitude, and classroom behavior. Although this model highlights school and teacher factors, it does not disregard peer group and parental influences. Three student-oriented factors complete the model: student behavior, student characteristics, and student learning outcomes.

The model contains two types of relationships: causal and correlational. A **causal** relationship exists if one variable or factor is thought to cause another. A **correlational** relationship is present when two variables occur together but one does not cause the other. For example, a child's height and reading ability are usually correlated because as children get taller, they also tend to become better readers. However, this is only a correlational relationship because neither variable causes the other. Instead both variables are probably related to some third variable, such as aging.

Figure 1.2 Structural Model of School and Teacher Variables Influencing Student Learning Outcomes

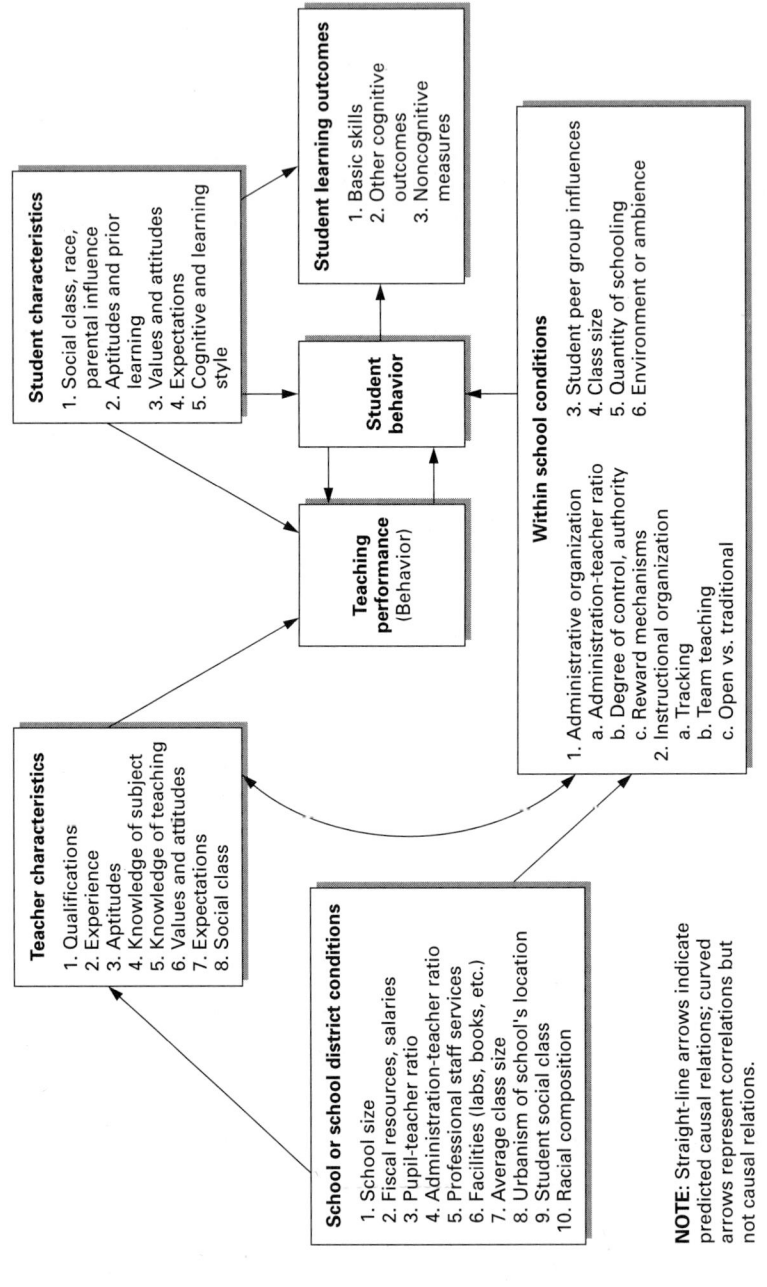

Student characteristics

1. Social class, race, parental influence
2. Aptitudes and prior learning
3. Values and attitudes
4. Expectations
5. Cognitive and learning style

Student learning outcomes

1. Basic skills
2. Other cognitive outcomes
3. Noncognitive measures

Student behavior

Teaching performance (Behavior)

Within school conditions

1. Administrative organization
   a. Administration-teacher ratio
   b. Degree of control, authority
   c. Reward mechanisms
2. Instructional organization
   a. Tracking
   b. Team teaching
   c. Open vs. traditional
3. Student peer group influences
4. Class size
5. Quantity of schooling
6. Environment or ambience

Teacher characteristics

1. Qualifications
2. Experience
3. Aptitudes
4. Knowledge of subject
5. Knowledge of teaching
6. Values and attitudes
7. Expectations
8. Social class

School or school district conditions

1. School size
2. Fiscal resources, salaries
3. Pupil-teacher ratio
4. Administration-teacher ratio
5. Professional staff services
6. Facilities (labs, books, etc.)
7. Average class size
8. Urbanism of school's location
9. Student social class
10. Racial composition

NOTE: Straight-line arrows indicate predicted causal relations; curved arrows represent correlations but not causal relations.

From J. A. Centra and D. A. Potter, "School and Teacher Effects: An Interrelational Model" in *Review of Educational Research,* 50:277. Copyright © 1980 by the American Educational Research Association.

(This will be discussed in depth in chapter 4.) In figure 1.2, expected causal relationships are indicated by the straight arrows. The curved arrow between teacher characteristics and within-school conditions represents a correlational rather than a causal relation. The double arrows going in opposite directions signify a causal relationship in either direction. For example, not only does teaching performance affect student behavior but also the reverse is true: Student behavior in response to teacher behavior probably causes many teachers to adjust their own behavior.

According to Centra and Potter (1980), their model indicates that "student behavior and student learning outcomes are most directly affected by student characteristics, teaching performance, and within-school conditions" (p. 275). Thus, when trying to solve a student's learning or behavior problem, an assessor would be wise to investigate the relationship among student characteristics, performance of the student's teachers, and within-school conditions such as class size and rules.

Goslin (1963) developed a useful model for understanding factors that may influence a person's test performance (see figure 1.3). In this enduring model, a test score is viewed as the end product of constitutional and environmental factors as well as of intervening variables such as personality, situation, test demands, and random variation factors.

The Goslin model provides an assessor with a framework for hypothesizing about a person's test performance. When used with other models, such as that of Centra and Potter, an assessor can maximize the probability that the assessment is sensitive to the many factors that can affect human behavior. In the following section, we discuss another major influence on the decision-making process: the type of decision that must be made.

➡ *Purposes of Assessment*

The overriding purpose of all assessments is to gather information to facilitate effective decision making. Within education, assessment is used to help people (i.e., teachers, administrators, psychologists, parents, and students) make at least five kinds of decisions: screening, classification and placement, student progress, programming or instruction, and program effectiveness decisions (Hawkins, 1979; Salvia & Ysseldyke, 1991; Ysseldyke, 1979). Each type of decision requires the collection of a variety of data on students' backgrounds, interests, and abilities as well as the environmental conditions and expectations of their families and school. The type of data collected to make any of these decisions can be very similar. In other words, academic achievement data (such as scores on standardized achievement tests, grades, or classwork samples) or behavior rating data can be used to help make any of the five kinds of decisions. It is the criteria and standards used to interpret the data that vary across the five kinds of decisions. In addition, as highlighted in figure 1.4, different

Figure 1.3   Paradigm for the Analysis of Variables that may Influence Learning and Behavior

Innate factors	Background and environment	Personality	Situation	Test demands	Random variation	Test score
Input	Input	Intervening	Intervening	Intervening	Intervening	Output

1. General inherited ability
2. Special inherited abilities
3. Cultural background and informal learning
4. Formal training
5. Experience with similar tests
6. General health (and special handicaps)
7. Achievement motivation
8. Interest in test problems
9. Anxiety
10. Perceived importance of test
11. Morale of the individual
12. Physical condition of examinee at time of test
13. Interference from environment
14. Influence of the tester
15. Specific abilities required
16. Speed of response required
17. Misleading items
18. Guessing
19. Clerical errors

Background   Personality   Situation   Test demands   Random variation   Test score

Reprinted from *The Search for Ability: Standardized Testing in Social Perspective* by David A. Goslin, © 1963 the Russell Sage Foundation. Reprinted with the permission of the Russell Sage Foundation.

**Figure 1.4   The Many Purposes of Assessment from the
Viewpoints of Parents, Students, Teachers,
Administrators, and Policymakers**

Policymakers need
assessments to:

- Set standards
- Focus on goals
- Monitor the quality of education
- Reward/sanction various practices
- Formulate policies
- Direct resources including
  personnel and money

Administrators need
assessments to:

- Monitor program effectiveness
- Identify program strengths and
  weaknesses
- Designate program priorities
- Assess alternatives
- Plan and improve programs

Teachers and administrators
use assessment for:

- Grouping decisions
- Individual diagnosis and
  prescription
- Monitoring student progress
- Curriculum evaluation and
  refinement
- Fostering
  mastery/promotion/grading and
  other feedback
- Motivating students
- Grading

Parents and student can
use assessments to:

- Gauge student progress
- Assess student strengths and
  weaknesses
- Evaluate school accountability

---

consumers of assessment information use it for a wide array of purposes,
all of which are subsumed under the five basic decisions facilitated by
assessment. We examine each of these next.

Screening Decisions

Screening is a procedure in which an entire population of students, such
as those entering kindergarten, are evaluated to determine whether they
may need additional assessment from educational, psychological, or medical specialists. Abilities and skills assessed during a screening process are
generally considered to be basic or prerequisite to success in regular

education settings. Therefore, individuals who cannot or do not perform at least at a specified level of competency on screening tasks are labeled "at risk" and are usually targeted for a more detailed, individualized examination of their abilities.

Assessment for educational screening purposes is generally carried out by teachers and involves brief tests, skill inventories, and behavioral checklists. These instruments are characterized by ease of administration, brevity, and only moderate levels of reliability. In addition to teachers, speech, vision, and hearing specialists are routinely involved in screening. Many school systems also require regular health screenings of students.

Classification and Placement Decisions

Students whose abilities or behaviors seem to differ significantly from those of "normal" peers are often targeted by teachers or parents for consideration for placement in special instructional programs. Some of these students have persistent learning difficulties, others have behavioral or emotional disorders, and still others are intellectually gifted or talented. Of course, assessment will indicate that some of the students referred have no serious difficulties and do not require special services. Regardless of the reason for the referral, if an appropriate referral is made, it becomes the collective responsibility of educators, parents, and specialists to gather data on which to base informed decisions.

A classification decision technically is separate from a placement decision and in fact must precede it with regard to special education actions. Historically, psychologists have been responsible for the classification or, more specifically, the diagnosis of individuals' learning and behavior problems, whereas educators have decided where to teach such individuals. However, with the passage of the Individuals with Disabilities Education Act (IDEA; originally referred to as the Education for All Handicapped Children Act of 1975, Public Law No. 94–142), eligibility, classification, and placement decisions must now be made by teams of knowledgeable professionals and parents. Such a legal requirement provides a strong rationale for the development of assessment knowledge and skills in all teachers.

Although a classification decision is a very serious action intended to help students obtain needed services, it can have adverse effects if improperly used (Edelbrock, 1988; Hobbs, 1975). Therefore, for intelligent classification and placement decisions to be made, specific and accurate data must be gathered concerning a student's ability and present educational setting (e.g., materials, seating arrangement, and teacher's methods and learning expectations). Assessment information typically used to make such decisions includes direct behavior observations, results from individually administered intelligence and achievement tests, behavior rating scales, and class performance indicators such as work samples.

Student Progress Decisions

The educational development of a student c
ally is of much interest to parents, teachers,
fact, an effective teacher continuously monito
gress in numerous areas. On a daily basis,
classroom performances provide information f
ever, since the learning of many concepts and
time, most progress decisions can be made or
elapsed. Data concerning student progress are
dardized group achievement tests, curriculum-
tives accomplished, and teachers' subjective re .... students
receiving special or remedial services often are given the same test at the
beginning and end of each school year to enable educators to document
their progress more accurately.

Programming or Instructional Decisions

Teachers need information about a student's abilities, curriculum content,
and teaching methods to make intelligent programming or instructional
decisions, for such decisions are complex and cannot be made automat-
ically because students with similar abilities do not always learn in the
same way (Cronbach & Snow, 1977; Travers, Elliott, & Kratochwill, 1993;
Ysseldyke, 1977). Therefore, a student's progress within a particular curriculum, and under given instructional methods, must be assessed regularly if effective programming decisions are to be reached.

Standardized intelligence and achievement tests often have been used
to develop instructional programs for exceptional students, but unless
these tests correspond well with the content of a given curriculum, such
use must be questioned. Instead, direct assessment of a student's performance on classroom materials and teacher-prepared tests can provide detailed, reliable information for specific programming decisions.

Program Effectiveness Decisions

Assessing the effectiveness of an educational program is difficult, because
generally more than one student or educator is involved and the criteria
for determining effectiveness are often undefined. Nevertheless, educators
must be accountable for their programs. Hence, program evaluation has
become a major activity of educational administrators and psychologists.
Assessment data such as those used to make decisions about students'
progress are particularly helpful in making decisions about a given program's effectiveness. Of course, data from individual students must be integrated to obtain an overall picture of the educational impact of a
program. Published investigations of the effectiveness of various special

...tion programs have appeared recently in several major educational ...d psychological journals and provide interesting reading (see e.g., Kavale, 1990). Since assessment for classification and placement is likely to be the goal of most readers of this text, we examine a typical school-based referral process in some detail in the next chapter.

Chapter Summary

This chapter, like this entire text, is based on a relatively simple premise: The purpose of assessment is to facilitate problem solving. In schools this problem-solving process is usually applied to children who are not progressing at an expected level or rate. Special education services have been developed as a primary method by which problems are solved. It is important to keep in mind, however, that the original purpose of special education is to solve problems. In too many cases, determining whether a child qualifies for special education is the beginning and end of this problem solving. The teacher who refers a child for assessment but is told the child does not qualify for special education services may be left with no alternative solutions. The problem is not solved. It still exists. The method of solving the problem (the special education refer-test-place sequence) has become an end in itself. But the goal is always to solve the problem. Assessment can provide information to accomplish this goal, but assessment is not an end in itself.

Chapter 2

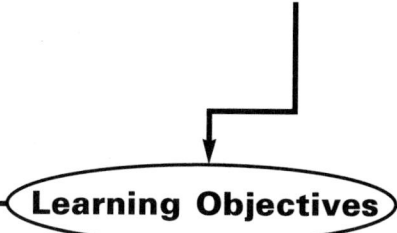

Assessment Models, Approaches, and Assumptions

Learning Objectives

1. Compare and contrast the medical and behavioral-ecological models of child behavior.

2. List the strengths and weaknesses of each major approach to educational assessment.

3. Discuss the meaning and importance of each of the major assumptions of assessment.

4. Describe the importance of the linkage between assessment and intervention.

5. Describe how working on an assessment team can be made more difficult by different theoretical orientations.

Professionals in various fields develop frameworks or theories for understanding their highly specialized worlds. Different frameworks or theories lead to different decisions about assessment methods and different interpretations of data. One's theoretical orientation may dictate whether to test, which tests to give, what to test, and how to interpret the tests. Consider, for example, a situation in which a child is referred by a teacher for evaluation because of hyperactivity. The child is evaluated by a team of specialists with different types of training and frameworks for viewing behavior. The basic questions are "What is causing the hyperactivity?" and "What can be done to reduce the problem?" A social worker may see the problem as a result of difficulties in the home. A behavioral consultant may review her observations and suggest the child is overly active because of insufficient teacher control in the classroom. The school nurse may recall that the child eats chocolate "all day long" and attributes the problem to poor nutrition. The psychologist may consider the problem a result of minimal brain dysfunction.

One solution to the lack of consensus among the specialists about the cause of the child's hyperactivity would be for the specialists to acknowledge their own respective frameworks and try to understand the child's functioning from a variety of perspectives. Such an approach is necessary because the same professional frameworks that give order to our decision making can cause a failure to consider all variables for a given case objectively. If you have only one way of viewing the world, you will attempt to mold the world to be consistent with your view.

This chapter introduces several theoretical perspectives on human behavior and subsequent approaches to assessment. In addition, we consider the different types of assessment information that can be collected, the various purposes for which they can be used, and the major methods of assessment.

➡ *Perspectives on Human Behavior*

Human behavior is quite predictable. Determining, for example, why Sarah behaves "appropriately" one day but not the next can be accomplished through a systematic assessment process, if you understand the factors that influence human learning and behavior. Psychologists and educators have contributed significantly to the understanding of human behavior by developing theories or models that help to explain an individual's behavior in a given situation. In this section, we use two general models of human behavior to illustrate the importance of theory for assessment: the **medical** model and the **behavioral-ecological** model.

A useful model of human behavior should provide a theoretical framework for increasing our understanding of individuals' past actions and predicting their future behaviors. A study of models of human behavior is important because they can influence one's beliefs about why people behave as they do. Consider the now-humorous example of a phrenologist who believes that behavior is determined by the size and location of bumps on the head. This view of behavior dictates the subject matter for assessment (bumps on the head); the phrenologist would thus see no benefit in administering a personality test. Fortunately, this model of behavior and its corollary assessment strategy has been categorically rejected by the scientific community!

It is useful for purposes of assessment to categorize human behavior into three broad categories: motoric, cognitive, or physiological. Clearly, these categories are not entirely separate and distinct, nor should it be inferred that one category of behavior can occur without a corresponding action in the other two categories. These three categories, however, do provide a framework for focusing on different types of behavior. The two models of human behavior we have chosen to discuss focus on these categories differentially, with motor and cognitive behavior receiving the most attention.

The Medical Model

The traditional medical model of behavior is illustrated by the psychoanalytic theory of Sigmund Freud and other later analysts. A central postulate of this model is that actions or behaviors are best understood through the intensive study of intrapsychic states. According to the theory, one's intrapsychic state is significantly influenced by early life events, particularly those in the first five years of life. The medical model focuses on an individual's thoughts or cognitions as they influence deviant behavior. It assumes (a) that behavior which deviates negatively from normative standards is a reflection of a personal disease, or disturbance, disorder, or dysfunction; and (b) that treatment/intervention must bring about changes within the individual (Johnson, Rasbury, & Seigel, 1986; Reger, 1972). The first assumption implies that children who cannot be maintained or accommodated in a regular education program are suffering from an internal psychological disorder. The second assumption implies that such children are deviant and that educational treatments should be designed to modify them. Educational "cures" seem most frequently to take the form of special classes that tend to isolate the "diseased" child from normal or healthy children. The utility of the medical model for education has been seriously challenged for more than 30 years (Szasz, 1960; Zubin, 1967), yet for some educators it apparently still holds value. Reger (1972) succinctly summarized some of the problems with the model:

> When a child is seen as a "patient" in school, when he [she] is looked at as a carrier of a medical-model illness (or deviation, etc.), then the teacher and the school are relieved of much of the responsibility for the child. If he [she] makes little or no progress, it is because of him [her] and his [her] condition rather than the school teacher. (pp. 11–12)

Several alternatives to a medical-model approach to problem conceptualization exist, such as a family model, a limited-capacities model, and a cognitive model (Levine & Sandeen, 1985). Each of these models has its advantages and advocates; however, when it comes to understanding children and school-based problems of learning and behaving, we have found the behavioral-ecological model of functioning to be the most powerful and informative.

The Behavioral-Ecological Model

The behavioral-ecological model of human behavior acknowledges the impact of other people and environmental factors in shaping a child's behavior.

Figure 2.1   The S-O-R-K-C Model

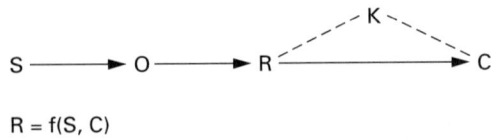

$$R = f(S, C)$$

The major assumption of this model is that human behavior is primarily a function of the interaction between environmental events and individual characteristics of people (Lewin, 1951; Skinner, 1953). With this model, deviant behavior is viewed as inappropriate or maladaptive rather than as an illness or intrapsychic disturbance. Assessors subscribing to this model would probably assess all three categories of behavior but focus primarily on observable motoric behavior.

Various forms of the behavioral-ecological model have been developed; however, Kanfer's (1973) S-O-R-K-C formula serves as the most clearly described model (see figure 2.1). In this characterization of behavior, the S stands for stimulus, the O for the biological state of the organism, the R for the response, the K for the ratio of consequence frequency to response, and the C for consequence. This formula describes the smallest unit of analysis for a behavior episode and summarizes the major components acting at a time of a response that affects the probability of the occurrence of the response. Target problems in a behavioral model generally are characterized as either a deficit or excess in the client's (student's) behavior, inappropriate client-generated stimulus control, and/or inappropriate reinforcement contingencies. This model also offers a substantial number of environmental (S, K, and C) and personal (O and R) components that are hypothesized to influence behavior and could become the focus for intervention. Common classroom examples of S, or stimuli, are a teacher's verbal directives, another student teasing a classmate, a math worksheet, or a test. Examples of K, or consequence frequency to a response, include being praised every time a student raises his or her hand, students being scolded frequently for being out of their seats, or students occasionally receiving free time when the entire class has been successful. Examples of C, or consequences, abound and include receiving praise, getting attention, going to time-out, or getting free time. Examples of O, or the organism's reactions, include statements of being anxious or happy, signs of being tired or sleepy, or being attentive. Finally, examples of R, or responses, common to classrooms include providing an answer to a question, taking a test, reading a book, helping a classmate, or following a teacher's directions. In summary, an assessor's goal in the problem-solving process using the S-O-R-K-C model of behavior is to functionally analyze the various components of the model and to select one or more components to change, assuming that these actions will result in changes in the problem behavior.

Obviously, a behavioral-ecological model would cause one to examine different variables than a medical model. Assessment procedures selected within this framework would focus on environmental variables rather than on internal child variables. Given the complexity of the learning and adjustment problems of schoolchildren, behavior is clearly a function of many factors, and a comprehensive assessment thus requires that one have substantial knowledge and skills as well as the ingenuity of a good detective. In the next section, several approaches to this assessment "mystery" are described.

➡ *Approaches to Assessment*

A theory determines the types of variables that will be measured during the assessment process. The assessment of different types of variables in turn leads to the use of different approaches to assessment. Major traditional approaches to assessment include **norm-referenced** assessment, **criterion-referenced** assessment, **informal** assessment, and **ecological** assessment. They differ not only with respect to what is measured but also with respect to how it is measured. This section provides a critical analysis of the various approaches to assessment, including a discussion of the strengths and weaknesses of each.

Norm-Referenced Assessment

Perhaps the most common approach to testing is norm-referenced assessment. It derives its name from the method in which test scores get their meaning by comparison to a representative group of scores. For example, a test score of 86 is considered good if it is higher than 95 percent of the scores with which it is compared, but it is not so good if it is lower than 70 percent of the other scores. In other words, norm-referenced assessments compare one child's behavior or performance with other children's behavior or performances. Thus, other children play a major role in providing a standard for interpreting the target child's performance.

Typically, in the development of norm-referenced tests, a large, collectively representative sample of the general population is tested. These people are referred to as the **norm group.** On one of the most common children's intelligence tests, such as the Wechsler Intelligence Scale for Children-Revised (WISC-R and more recently the WISC-III), the norm group has an average score of 100 (this is the result of a rather complex transformation process whereby raw scores are transferred to a scale with a mean of 100). The properties of this test have been extensively studied, and the test manual suggests, for example, that less than 5 percent of the population score above 130. Because it is norm-referenced, any WISC-R score can be meaningfully interpreted by comparing it to the norm group. Norm-referenced assessment can be used to answer the following types of questions: How does Sarah compare in reading comprehension to the rest of the class? Does Dustin have the math aptitude needed for a college engineering program? Are Julie's SAT scores high enough to qualify her for admission to the university of her choice?

Advantages of Norm-Referenced Assessment

Norm-referenced tests are widely used in special and remedial education for several reasons. First, many decisions involve categorizing children as "exceptional" or "special." These are essentially norm-referenced decisions because information is needed (and sometimes is required by law) on who is legally eligible for special services and who will probably be in greatest need of such services. Second, norm-referenced assessment provides information that is easily communicated to parents and others unfamiliar with tests. Telling parents that their child is in the lower 5 percent of the population with respect to hearing ability is usually more meaningful than providing data about their child's decibel (loudness) levels. Third, norm-referenced tests have received the most attention in terms of technical data and research. They have a long history, and their usefulness for a wide range of purposes (such as problem identification and screening) is well documented.

Disadvantages of Norm-Referenced Assessment

A major difficulty with norm-referenced assessment is that it typically provides information that may be too general to be useful in everyday classroom teaching activities. Many educators disregard the prognostic and interpretative types of data provided by standardized tests because the information is often not directly applicable to developing daily instructional activities or interventions. What does knowing a child's WISC-III score or grade equivalent in reading specifically tell a teacher about what and how to teach? Does the child need to learn initial consonants or is he or she having difficulty with comprehension?

Another problem is that because most norm-referenced tests are designed for a broad national use, often a discrepancy exists between what is taught in an individual classroom and what is tested. For example, the spelling subtest of the Peabody Individual Achievement Test-Revised (PIAT-R) requires the respondent to choose the one word out of a list of four that is spelled incorrectly. The problem with this test is that most classroom spelling tests require the respondent to write words from memory as they are dictated by a teacher. Thus, the PIAT-R would provide information that not only lacks the specificity to guide remediation but also would probably be inaccurate unless a child's ability to recognize a correctly spelled word corresponded perfectly to his or her ability to recall and write spelling words from memory.

Another form of the problem concerning the discrepancy between what is taught and what is tested reveals itself in the form of content differences that frequently exist between published tests and the curriculum content taught in any given classroom. For example, the numerous norm-referenced achievement tests on the market today differentially sample the many curricula used in schools (Jenkins & Pany, 1978; Marston, 1989). Without careful attention to the potential testing-teaching overlap, or lack thereof, test scores do not truly index students' skill levels, since they do not adequately sample what the students have learned.

A fourth problem with norm-referenced tests is that, because their primary purpose is to compare one student with another, they tend to promote and reinforce the belief that the locus of the problem is within the child. However, although a child may differ from the norm, the real problem may not be within the child but in the teaching, placement, or curriculum. Educational specialists must begin to assess teacher's behaviors, curriculum content and sequencing, and other variables not measured by norm-referenced tests.

Criterion-Referenced Assessment

Whether a child can perform a particular skill is the question that criterion-referenced assessment seeks to answer. In contrast to norm-referenced assessment, which compares, or references, one person's performance with others', criterion-referenced assessment seeks to determine which individuals have reached some preestablished level or standard of performance. Typically, skills within a subject are hierarchically arranged so that those that must be learned first are tested first. In math, for example, addition skills would be evaluated (and taught) before multiplication skills. These tests usually are criterion-referenced because a student must achieve competence at one level before being taught at a higher level; criterion-referenced tests help to determine if a person is ready to move on to the next level. No effort is made to determine how much better or worse than the criterion a student performs but merely to assess, in a pass-fail manner, if a student possesses a certain skill.

Criterion-referenced assessment can be further illustrated by referring to differences in the methods used by some graduate and professional schools to evaluate students. A medical school, for example, may be concerned that everyone achieve surgery skills at some established criterion level (e.g., the patient must recover in a minimal amount of time with no complications). However, some professional schools may use a norm-referenced approach in which they admit more students than they expect to graduate and then "weed out" the weaker ones by administering difficult tests and passing only those with the highest scores.

Conceptually, much of what is occurring in the recent authentic assessment and outcome-based education movements is consistent with criterion-referenced assessment (Elliott, 1991; Gresham, 1991). That is, educators are reacting against the use of norm-referenced tests and arguing for the use of assessment methods that compare a student's performance or products to some agreed-upon standard. This approach to assessment is discussed later in this chapter, but it clearly is consistent with the notion that standards or criteria for performing can be identified in advance of the performance and can be used to judge a performance in an objective manner.

Advantages of Criterion-Referenced Assessment

The primary usefulness of criterion-referenced assessment is in identifying a child's specific skills. Since most skills have been extensively studied and broken down into a series of steps or hierarchies, the test results could be used to determine the next most logical skill to teach. Thus, the implications for teaching are more direct with criterion-referenced tests than with norm-referenced tests.

A related advantage is the ability to use criterion-referenced tests in formative evaluation, which means assessing a child regularly, usually daily, when skills are being learned. This makes it possible to note student progress, determine if instruction is effective, and help plan the next skill to be taught. Since the focus is on skills instead of comparison with others, knowing what to teach and how to measure it becomes simplified.

Disadvantages of Criterion-Referenced Assessment

The primary problem with this form of assessment is establishing a suitable criterion. If a test were needed to determine whether students had mastered high school mathematics, for example, there is the challenge of determining exactly which skills should be included in the test. Some may feel that geometry must be included, but others may disagree. After it is decided to measure a particular skill, the level at which the skill must be performed for the student to pass must be determined. Should a student pass the test if 90 percent of the questions are answered correctly or only if 100 percent are correct? These decisions must be carefully considered, because setting inappropriate criteria may cause a student to struggle unnecessarily with a concept. Currently, many more educators are demonstrating an interest in determining the essential learning outcomes of schooling, so it is likely that there will be increased use of criterion-referenced assessments in the schools of the 1990s (e.g., Spady & Kit, 1991).

Advocates of criterion-referenced testing assume that a child who fails to master a concept does so because of lack of exposure to the material. It is further assumed that additional instruction related to the concept will enable a child to pass the test. However, these assumptions may be inaccurate for some youngsters in special education, because additional instruction of the wrong type may not benefit some children and may result in repeated failures.

A potentially troublesome aspect of this form of test, for some educators, is that the skills assessed may become the goals of instruction rather than selected samples exemplifying what the child should know (Ebel, 1975). Teachers may then narrow the focus of their instruction and simply teach in accordance with what is measured on the test, which can result in a loss of the richness and variety that characterize good instruction.

Informal Assessment

Watching grandparents interact with their grandchildren is a good opportunity to see a wide range of assessment activities. For example, a three-year-old might be asked to count to 10, to follow simple directions, to color with crayons, or to name the animals in a book. Such tasks may or may not be present at that age, but grandparents derive a great deal of satisfaction whatever the outcome. This type of assessment is ongoing and occurs in a very flexible and open social atmosphere. The tasks are obviously not standardized.

Similarly, teachers who analyze a child's writing for error patterns, special education teachers who observe a child in the regular classroom, speech therapists who just listen to a child talk, and psychologists who look at a child's mannerisms during oral reading may all be using informal assessment. Informal in this instance refers to the fact that this form of assessment is not a standardized and prespecified process but rather is adapted to the individual child and situation. Such techniques tell how a child learns and what a child knows. The selection of the word "informal" to describe a model of assessment may be problematic, for it may lead to some unfortunate misunderstandings. The term is intended to refer to the content of assessment (i.e., the type of measures used and the way in which they are used) and the use of such content rather than the process. Since the late 1980s many authors have referred to informal assessment as **authentic** or **performance** assessment (Airasian, 1991). The process is really basic behavioral assessment and represents a very structured and systematized problem-solving approach (see, e.g., the systems suggested by Eaves & McLaughlin, 1977; Elliott, 1991; Elliott & Piersel, 1982). Specifically, the intent is to emphasize the use of curriculum-based tests, behavioral observations, and trial teaching in the assessment of children.

Individuals who utilize informal assessment seem to view themselves as detectives. If a child is experiencing failure, assessment consists of collecting clues and facts about what contributes to the problem. Is it a problem with the child, such as a lack of ability or low motivation, or with the task being too difficult, insufficiently explained, or not worth learning? Or is it a problem with the setting, such as poor teaching or the lack of a quiet place to study? A good detective attempts to evaluate every area that might possibly contribute to the problem. A major assumption of this approach is that the closer the evaluation is to the actual situation in which the child is experiencing difficulty, the more accurate the identification processes and remedial interventions.

Advantages of Informal Assessment

The primary benefit of informal assessment over either norm-referenced or criterion-referenced assessment is its relevance to developing instructional or intervention activities. In general, norm-referenced tests can be used to select those who need instruction, and criterion-referenced tests help to determine what needs to be taught. Informal assessment practices also provide information about what a child needs to learn, but they do so using the actual materials and stimuli that the child encounters daily. Additionally, informal assessment is unique in providing information about *how* instruction should be given. By experimenting and playing detective, one can determine whether a child should be seated at the front or back of the room, what reinforces him or her, and when performance is best and worst.

Another reason that informal assessment is so applicable to instruction is that only very small inferences are needed to use the test data for instruction. Compare, for example, the degree of inference required to apply data from a nationally standardized norm-referenced test of reading ability versus information from a test derived from the reading book the child uses in class. Naturally the use of classroom materials increases the applicability of assessment results to instructional activities. Since informal assessment typically occurs in the child's natural environment, assessors do not have the problem of generalizing the results from one situation to another. For example, consider a child who is being evaluated for a behavior problem. One evaluator may take the child into a quiet place for interviewing and formal testing. Another person may choose to observe the child in the classroom and on the playground under a variety of conditions. It is easy to question the degree to which the formal testing generalizes, since it was conducted in a small, quiet room on a one-to-one basis. Even the informal aspects of this situation are suspect because whether the child behaves normally during the individual session may have little relevance to how he or she may behave in a classroom with 25 other children who may encourage and reinforce the child's behavior. The observations, on the other hand, may easily be generalized because they took place in the child's actual environment.

Another major advantage of informal assessment is its flexibility. It can be utilized nearly any time, any place, and with any problem. Virtually the only limits are the users' knowledge of specific subjects or behaviors and the means of gathering reliable data. Little problems occur very frequently when working with children. It is usually best to check out such difficulties before they become big problems. The flexibility of informal assessment enhances its use over other types of assessment because users can take whatever materials are available and obtain a quick and simple check in a problem area. In general, fast and economical assessment procedures are preferred to those that are equally effective but require more personnel and material resources. The acceptability of informal or authentic assessment methods is attested to by the plethora of articles published in major education journals and presentations given at national conventions during the past several years.

Disadvantages of Informal Assessment

One drawback to informal assessment is that it places a great deal of burden on a teacher or an examiner to select appropriate tasks, be a good detective, and to correctly interpret the results in the absence of a test manual or formal guidelines. Informal assessment also requires good training in the content area in which assessment occurs and good problem-solving skills. For example, if a teacher notices that a kindergarten child consistently is reversing the letters *b* and *d,* does this mean that the child might have a learning disability? In this case, a little knowledge (that *b* and *d* reversals are bad) might cause problems, because *b* and *d* reversals are relatively common among kindergarten and first-grade children and reflect developmental immaturity rather than a learning disability. Users of norm-referenced tests do not have this problem of interpretation because standards are provided.

A related problem with informal assessment is that the values and biases of the assessor can influence testing. For example, most people believe that boys are more aggressive and create more problems in school than girls. The difficulty with this and other biases is that judgment does not always correspond to reality. Observations of primary-grade children, for example, indicate that girls display as many deviant behaviors as boys but that teachers are more likely to respond to boys' misbehavior in a negative way (Patterson, 1982). Similar biases affect how informal assessment methods are chosen, implemented, and interpreted. Systematically approaching informal assessment and being aware of personal biases may help reduce bias as much as possible.

Finally, informal assessment does not have the long history of supportive research and theory enjoyed by criterion-referenced and norm-referenced assessment. Consequently, informal assessment has seldom been included in teacher or psychologist training programs. Although many practitioners use it on an ongoing basis, few have received any formal training in informal assessment. Its outward simplicity compared with the grand statistical underpinnings of formal testing cause some individuals to question its adequacy. Although researchers suggest that educational programming can be accomplished just as effectively with informal assessment as with standardized testing (Lovitt & Fantasia, 1980; Wiggins, 1990), some practitioners are still reluctant to adopt informal, authentic assessment procedures.

Ecological Assessment

Anyone who has ever worked with children is aware of some of the complex interrelationships that exist between student and teacher, student and student, student and environment, teacher and community, and the like. Children are affected by other children, approaching holidays, the subject matter they are learning, the social mores of their community, their family situations, and even world economic conditions, especially if their parents are unemployed. It may be impossible to assess every factor that can influence student learning and behavior, but it is possible to move beyond an almost exclusive focus on the child. Ecological assessment must include an analysis of the teacher as well as the child (e.g., does the teacher use appropriate feedback and instructional techniques?), the teacher's expectations (e.g., does the teacher expect the child to be perfectly still and docile?), the environment (e.g., is the temperature at the proper level and are the desks arranged in a manner consistent with what the teacher wants to accomplish?), and the task (e.g., was the material worth learning and related to the content?).

Consider a teacher who is concerned about the number of students who have begun to turn in incomplete assignments during the last month. Previously, the rate of assignment completion had been excellent for the entire class. An analysis of the situation suggests the problem really began when construction was initiated on a new wing of the school. The building activities were clearly visible to the students through an open window, and many enjoyed watching the progress. An easy solution would be to close the curtains or turn the students' desks away from the window. However, a less complete, child-centered analysis may have resulted in the time-consuming and possibly less successful remedy of modifying student behavior in spite of an environment that encouraged off-task behavior.

Ecological assessment is not a category of tests or even a theory of assessment. Instead, it is more of a viewpoint of assessment. Virtually any type of criterion-referenced, norm-referenced, or informal test could be used in an ecological approach, for it offers the freedom to use assessment devices in unique and creative ways. The Centra and Potter model (see figure 1.2) illustrates the wide range of variables that can influence student learning and behavior, many of which can be measured using a variety of assessment approaches.

Recently, Ysseldyke and Christenson (1987) developed a formal systematic procedure that can be used to gather data on the nature of an instructional environment for an individual student. After reviewing the research and conceptual literature on effective instruction, models of schooling, and instructional psychology, Ysseldyke and Christenson developed The Instructional Environment Scale or TIES. TIES provides an excellent illustration of the components in a comprehensive education-focused ecological assessment. Specifically, TIES is a qualitative observation scale

Figure 2.2   The 12 Variables of an Instructional Environment as Conceptualized on TIES

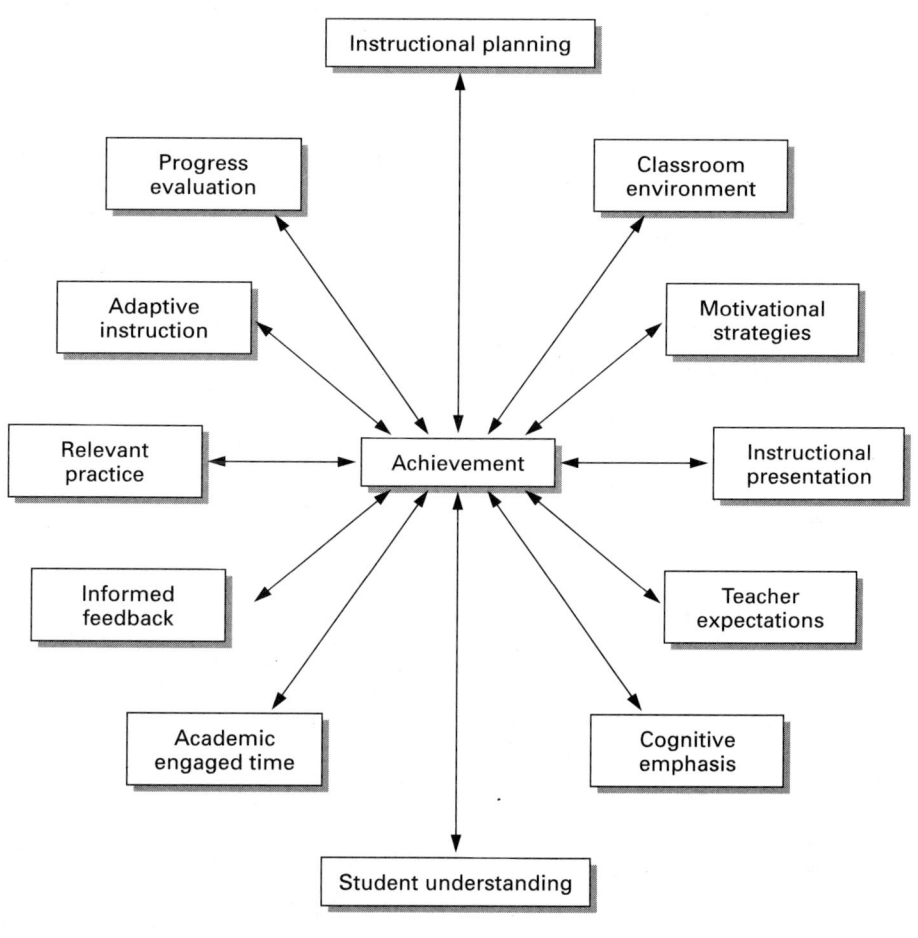

From Ysseldyke, J. E., and Christenson, S. L. (1987). The Instructional Environmental Scale. Austin, TX: PRO–ED. Reprinted by permission.

that provides information on 12 descriptive indicators of a student's learning environment (see figure 2.2). These include information on instructional presentation (e.g., lesson development, clarity of directions, checking for student understanding), classroom environment (e.g., management, time use, climate), teacher expectations, cognitive emphasis, motivational strategies, relevant practice (e.g., opportunity, task relevance, materials), academic engaged time (e.g., student involvement, maintenance), informed feedback (e.g., feedback, corrections), adaptive instruction, and progress evaluation (e.g., monitoring, follow-up planning). More will be said about TIES in later chapters.

Advantages of Ecological Assessment

The ecological model has four major advantages over other forms of assessment. First, because it is a process of assessment, it is more than a collection of tests: It is a way of viewing all forms of assessment. Second, it has helped to expand the focus of assessment. Rather than simply focusing on the child, an intensive study of the student is made in relationship to his or her environment. Third, ecological assessment increases our awareness of the complexity of human behavior. Finally, this model causes us to question the validity of simplistic and mechanical assessment practices that diagnose a child's problem on the basis of only one or two standardized tests.

Disadvantages of Ecological Assessment

The most obvious problem in using ecological assessment is its complexity. Instead of administering a test or observing one or two behaviors, an evaluator is faced with the additional possibilities of interviewing other adults, observing the child in multiple situations, and collecting and synthesizing a large amount of information. This process may be too time-consuming or impractical for many situations. Professionals using the ecological approach must be careful to collect enough information so that the problem can be understood, yet not so much that it cannot be used or comprehended.

A second problem with this form of assessment is the lack of adequate instruments. To a large extent, assessors are left on their own to determine what and how to assess, although tools like TIES certainly provide some useful structure to one's ecological assessment. A related problem is the lack of research into factors, such as the seating arrangement or the type of instruction, that significantly affect learning.

An Integration of Assessment Models and Approaches

Each of the models of human behavior and the various approaches to the assessment of children has some advantages and disadvantages for professionals entrusted to assess children experiencing difficulties in school. There is no perfect or fool-proof assessment approach; however, when confronted with the task of assessing a child who is experiencing academic or behavior difficulties, we have found it helpful to focus assessment activities on six general variables: the target child, his/her teacher(s), his/her parent(s), the school materials, the task(s), and his/her peers. We have found that for most cases, we need to collect information about each of these six variables (child, teacher, parent, materials, tasks, and peers) to discern how they relate to the target child's problems. The collection of information often involves the use of direct observations, standardized and informal tests, interviews, and examination of products produced by the student. Thus, these six variables organize most of our assessment efforts.

In addition, we have found that by changing aspects of one or more of these six variables, we are likely to improve the target child's functioning.

In summary, by using the best features of the various assessment models and approaches and by focusing one's activities on six practical variables, one generally can conduct a meaningful assessment—one that leads to changes in instructional tactics and outcomes. Let's now examine the assumptions that guide assessment activities and the conclusions one draws from assessment results.

➡ *General Assumptions in the Assessment of Children*

Some of the ambiguity surrounding assessment practices can be directly attributed to the fact that various individuals approach assessment with differing assumptions concerning how and when tests can be utilized. This problem is complicated further by the lack of any one universally accepted theory guiding the development, use, and interpretation of tests. However, despite the many different perceptions of assessment, a set of five common assumptions still exists. A review of these assumptions provides a basis for the examination of assessment in content areas that follows in later chapters.

Assumption 1: Individual Differences Among Children Derive Their Meaning from the Situation in Which They Occur

In assessing the many attributes and behaviors of a particular child, it is very likely that the child will differ, perhaps markedly, from his or her peers on at least one dimension. It must be determined if we should be concerned about such differences. That determination depends on the child's situation, acculturation, and the expectations placed upon the child in that situation. Behaviors considered normal in one setting may be considered abnormal in another, and skills considered adequate in one school may cause problems in another school. The point is that tests can determine if a child is different from the norm but not if this difference is a problem.

Children differ on innumerable attributes, some of which are important while others are not. For example, a child's hearing is measured frequently during the school years, and those with a hearing loss are identified because this is a problem that may interfere with learning. However, some children have a quite different hearing abnormality: They are able to perceive extremely high-pitched sounds (i.e., those in excess of 20,000 cycles per second). At present, this capability has no practical importance in our society (except perhaps to people who test dog whistles). Children who cannot hear sounds in this range are not considered hearing impaired because there is no expectation that they should be able to hear sounds at such high frequencies. Suppose, however, that it suddenly became important for children to be able to hear sounds of 20,000 cycles per second. Children who could hear at such frequencies would be valued highly by our culture, whereas those who could not probably would be viewed as less capable and possibly marked for placement in classrooms for the hearing impaired.

Consider the more realistic example of a child who moves from the Watts neighborhood of Los Angeles (an inner-city environment) to Scarsdale, a suburb of New York City (an upper-class, professional community). According to a nationally standardized reading test, the child's reading ability would be approximately a half-year below grade level, yet when he was in Watts his reading ability was not considered a problem. In fact, there he was a good student. However, in Scarsdale he is immediately referred for specialized programming because perhaps the average child in that community scores more than one year above grade level on the national test. The obvious conclusion is that a test score becomes most meaningful when the conditions and expectations under which the child must operate are known. With the growing number of children from different cultures—different environments, different expectations for behavior, and different values—the task of meaningful and unbiased assessment will be an ongoing challenge for professionals.

Assessment data must also be interpreted in terms of developmental norms, which evaluate a child's performance relative to what other children that age are doing. For example, an interview with a mother indicates that she is concerned about her five-year-old son who is frequently disobedient at home. Reference to developmental norms suggests that such behavior is relatively normal for children that age. In fact, 56 percent of normal boys are considered disobedient at one time or another. Similarly, kindergarten and first-grade children are referred frequently to speech clinicians because of problems articulating the letters s and r. Generally, however, speech therapy is not initiated with such young children because the problems often disappear with another year or two of experience in the natural environment.

It is important to assume that test data derive their meaning from the social context, because viewing test scores as meaningful by themselves can lead to their misuse. It is important to state this explicitly because all too often tests that are interpreted naively and mechanically do more harm than good. Simply because a child may score in the impaired range on a particular test should not be sufficient evidence to label the child as handicapped. Most importantly, a test score in the impaired range does not always correspond to impaired performance in other situations.

Assumption 2: Tests Are Samples of Behavior and Only Aids to Decision Making

The assumption that test data will be only a portion of the information used to make a decision about a child is related to the first assumption and pertains to how test data are used. Unfortunately, in practice, test data are frequently the only information considered. Children are placed in programs based upon very specific criteria often operationalized by exact scores on tests. For example, a score of 130 or above on an intelligence test may be needed for placement in a program for gifted youngsters, and a score of 129 simply will not suffice. Perhaps if other criteria were examined, a child with a 129 IQ may be more suited to the program than a child with an IQ in the 140 range. Tests are simply not accurate enough, nor do they measure a wide enough range of variables, to be used as the sole criterion for most decisions. They are only samples of behavior, and common sense must be used in judging their contribution to decisions.

A simple decision, such as placement in the proper reading group, may be fraught with difficulty if a test score is the major determiner. Two children with scores indicating they read at the third-grade level may have quite different reading abilities, especially if they were given different tests or were tested in different aspects of reading. One child may have approached the task with a cavalier attitude and, because of carelessness, responded incorrectly in some relatively minor areas. Another child may have approached the test very anxiously and struggled all the way through, as evidenced by grimacing, stammering, and statements suggesting self-doubt. A test score may suggest that the two children should be in the same reading group, yet it may be very difficult to teach them in the same manner and at the same rate. In addition to knowing a test score and the manner in which it was achieved, it may be helpful to have information that is not in any test (e.g., whether the child learns best in a group or one-to-one situation, whether the child responds best in written form or orally, and whether the child could be taught more effectively by a teacher or a peer). Good educational programming is seldom based on test scores alone but instead considers the complex array of variables that influence student learning.

This problem can be partially overcome by making sure an adequate sample of behavior is included in assessment. For example, the assessment of intelligence should measure a wide range of behaviors that have been associated with the construct of intelligence. In addition, it is important that the child is properly motivated and puts forth an optimal or nearly optimal effort. By doing this, it is possible to predict more accurately what the child can do given proper motivation in the classroom.

Assumption 3: A Primary Reason to Conduct an Assessment Is to Improve Instructional or Intervention Activities

What are the goals of assessment? To find out how to eliminate a problem? To find out why a child performs as he or she does? To determine the appropriate placement for a child? Some may argue that determining etiology and finding the cause of a problem are primary reasons for conducting an assessment. In ordinary educational practice, this is true, however, only to the extent that assessment also points to an effective intervention for the child's problem. Knowing a child's educational classification may help decide how to teach or work with the child, but such classifications do not provide information for planning daily lessons. For example, knowing a child has a learning disability does not lead to the same level of treatment specificity as does knowing the child has a medical problem, such as phenylketonuria (PKU). On this topic, Howell, Kaplan, and O'Connell (1979) noted:

> When the problem is academic deficiency, the variables for classification are less specific. . . . Yet educators have tended to treat students who fail academically as if they have enzyme deficiencies. That is, they have sought to label students and then make treatment statements from the label. . . . Of course, our educational levels are far from precise. (p. 16)

Consider a teacher or a psychologist who knows only that a child completes his assignments in a sloppy fashion because he is "impulse-ridden" or a youngster frequently displays aggressive and inappropriate behavior because he or she is "socially maladjusted." Labels are useful only to the extent that they lead to a successful intervention. If there is a prescribed treatment for the "impulse-ridden" child, then using that label is advantageous; however, if no such prescription is available, such a label may actually interfere with treatment by clouding the variables that influence the problem.

All too often educational specialists have considered their job to be completed when they have labeled the child to determine the classification and made some general recommendations. This attitude may be partially attributable to the categorical system of special education established in most states and the heavy demands on specialists to conduct large numbers of assessments. By law a child must be classified as eligible to receive special education services. Thus, some specialists may communicate only the appropriate categorical label and leave teachers and therapists, who do most of the direct, daily work with the child, to develop the individualized educational programming.

Assumption 4: The Assessor Is Properly Trained

Since many potential sources of error exist in administering and interpreting tests and other assessment devices, it is extremely important that they be administered by individuals who are knowledgeable about both assessment and human behavior. For example, an acquaintance of the authors told of a college student who was gaining experience administering tests to children in a small rural school. In discussing the results of the testing with the college student, our friend learned that two Native American students would not respond to any test questions. Our friend then readministered the test but allowed more time than usual for answering each question. Although perhaps 30 seconds were required for the students to respond to each question, they did eventually respond, and very accurately. They simply needed more time to respond than white middle-class children. A person less familiar with the response times of individuals from some Native American tribes may have assumed a lack of knowledge on their part. Thus, skill in administering an assessment device encompasses more than the simple mechanics of test giving and requires knowledge and training in many aspects of human behavior.

The lack of highly skilled assessors has been a major problem in special education because of the sudden and dramatic demand for individuals in this field after the passing of P.L. 94–142. As a result, states allowed people to become "provisionally" or temporarily certified. Master's degree programs in speech pathology, school psychology, and special education sprang up to meet the demand for practitioners. Some of these programs have provided adequate training, but others have not.

Ample evidence exists that many in the field of special education are inadequately trained in assessment practices. Bennett and Shepard (1982), for example, reported that on the average, a sample of learning disability specialists missed 50 percent of the items on a test reflecting their knowledge of basic measurement (such as reliability, validity, and use of norms). This lack of skill often translates into the misuse of tests and misinterpretation of assessment information.

The assumption that a person doing an assessment is properly trained implies that people can be trained at different levels. At one level, regular classroom teachers are well trained to administer a number of assessment instruments. In fact, in many cases they are the persons of choice to conduct an assessment, for they are familiar with the classroom materials and the demands that will be placed on the child, have access to almost unlimited samples of the child's behavior, and have more contacts with the child than almost any other individual (Moran, 1978; Wiggins, 1989). At a more complex level, more specialized tests, such as individually administered intelligence tests, require supervised training to learn to administer. Most professional codes of ethics admonish individuals to administer only those tests for which they have the training and skills.

Assumption 5: All Forms of Assessment Contain Error

Information provided by lie detectors is inadmissible as evidence in court because of an error rate of between 10 percent and 25 percent (Bersoff, 1983). Unfortunately, many of the tests administered to schoolchildren contain even greater error. It is simply not possible to measure such variables as anxiety, motivation, intelligence, and self-concept without some degree of error.

Error is introduced into the assessment of children by several factors. First, tests themselves often have low reliability and validity. A common and frustrating example is that different reading and math achievement tests provide different grade equivalent scores. Second, the same test may indicate different results when administered to the same child on different occasions. Test scores should be expected to fluctuate slightly because the child will remember some of the items and may feel more at ease when the test is repeated. Marked variations in scores can result because of other factors as well. For example, a child may feel more motivated on one occasion than another or the conditions under which the test is given may change from one testing to another.

The assumption that error is present in all forms of evaluation influences practice in two primary ways. First, it mandates that we be aware of and try to minimize factors that might contribute to inaccurate test scores. Every effort should be made to see that an assessment reflects the attribute being measured to the fullest possible extent. Second, the presence of errors makes it all the more necessary to use and interpret test data in a cautious and professional manner. Fortunately, with standardized tests we can statistically estimate error. This point provides a convenient springboard to chapters 4 and 5, in which technical procedures used in determining the worth of a test will be introduced.

Chapter Summary

This chapter introduced some terms that are used throughout the text and showed how one's theoretical orientation and assumptions influence the testing process. It would be worthwhile to take a few minutes and characterize your own thinking about human behavior in general. It is important to recognize that one's own view of the world may differ markedly from those of others with whom you must work. A person who believes that children's behavior is caused by intrapsychic forces is likely to develop different assessment plans and interventions than someone who believes behavior is a function of environmental influence. We suggested in this chapter that students' behavior is an interaction of internal and external factors and when organizing an assessment one should focus on six domains: child, teacher, materials, task(s), parents, and peers. Assessment information from each of these domains should provide valuable insights into most school-based problems and pathways to instructional interventions.

How do we go about settling differences between people with contrasting points of view about human behavior? An obvious choice would be to examine research relevant to each position. If the effectiveness of various interventions has been evaluated, one then has a basis for recommending an assessment or intervention procedure. In many cases, however, a person's belief system will not be altered by data or any other form of persuasion. In working with others this is a problem not easily resolved.

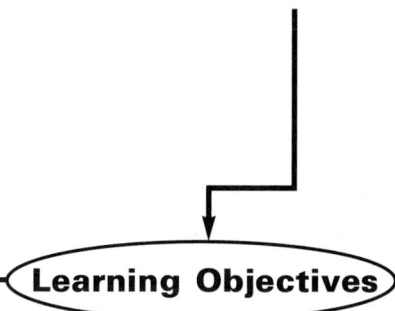

Chapter 3

Assessment and the Law

Learning Objectives

1. Identify major legal decisions that form the basis for the Individuals with Disabilities Education Act (IDEA).

2. Describe major provisions of IDEA that prescribe activities prior to and during the assessment phase of the special education process.

3. Describe major provisions of IDEA that control the process of making classification and placement decisions.

4. Describe the major components to be included in an Individualized Education Plan.

5. List the major steps that a school district would take when applying IDEA on a day-to-day basis.

Most school districts currently provide a relatively wide array of special education services for children with mild to severe disabilities. We do not have to go back much more than 10 years, however, to discover that this level of service to children with disabilities did not always exist. In fact, at one time most children with disabilities were denied any type of education. Parents were encouraged to find an institutional setting for the child or do what they could at home. Now, schools have elaborate procedures not only to admit and educate all children with disabilities but also to search for such children whose parents may not be aware that services are available.

What has brought about this marked change in school attitudes in such a short period? Could it be that benevolent school districts have suddenly become aware of the learning potential of children with even the most severe disabilities? Have school districts proactively taken steps to ensure that all children receive the education to which they are entitled?

Unfortunately most school systems have been neither benevolent nor proactive in responding to the needs of children with disabilities. Instead, parents of children with disabilities have argued successfully in one law-suit after another that it is illegal to deny children with disabilities their basic right to an education. Thus, school systems have been required to provide an education to all children. In this chapter we describe how the law has influenced how we conduct assessment, classification, and intervention activities with potentially disabled children.

➡ *Legal Influences on Assessment and Special Education*

Court Decisions Establishing a Free and Appropriate Public Education

The issue at the heart of all the litigation between parents of children with disabilities and school systems has been that all children have a basic right to an education. The legal basis used by parents to establish this right is the Fourteenth Amendment to the United States Constitution, which forbids any state from denying "to any person within its jurisdiction the equal protection of the laws." This is frequently referred to as the equal protection clause and has been interpreted by the courts as directing schools to provide equal educational opportunities to all students.

The first and most significant court decision invoking the equal protection clause was *Brown v. Board of Education* (1954). Although *Brown* was filed in behalf of black students without disabilities, the logic behind the case has been subsequently used in defending the rights of children with disabilities. *Brown* was filed because it was believed that black children were not receiving an education equivalent to that given to white children. In its ruling, the U.S. Supreme Court agreed with this argument and stipulated that black students must receive an equivalent education using equivalent resources. This decision is relevant to children with disabilities because in this case the Court considered students to be a class of persons in society. According to the Constitution, all members of a class must be treated equally. In cases involving children with disabilities, *Brown* has been used as a precedent to argue that both students with and without disabilities should be defined as a class and must therefore be treated equally. Just as the Court indicated in *Brown* that black children had been denied equal protection because of an unalterable and unchosen trait, their race, in subsequent cases involving children with disabilities the Court has stipulated that such children have been denied an equal education because of an unalterable and uncontrollable trait, their disability.

Among the major post-*Brown* cases that helped gain equal education for children with disabilities, the most important were *Pennsylvania Association for Retarded Children (PARC) v. Commonwealth of Pennsylvania* (1972) and *Mills v. Board of Education of the District of Columbia* (1972).

In *PARC* the suit was filed because Pennsylvania state law relieved a board of education "from any obligation to educate a child whom a public school psychologist certified as uneducable or untrainable" and permitted "an indefinite postponement of admission to public school of any child who has not obtained a mental age of 5 years" (*PARC,* 1972, p. 282). The U.S. Supreme Court struck down this state law, stipulating that all children with mental disabilities are capable of benefiting from an education and the state has the responsibility to provide all such children between the ages to 6 and 21 years access to a free education.

After the *PARC* decision, the Court heard the *Mills* case, in which the school system did not deny that all children had the right to a free education but rather argued that the system lacked the financial resources to fulfill its obligation to handicapped children. Although the Court acknowledged that the education of children with severe disabilities can be very expensive, it did not accept this as an excuse for failing to provide an education to children with disabilities, ruling that if sufficient funds are not available to finance all of the services and programs needed and desirable in the system then the available funds must be expended equitably in such manner that no child is entirely excluded from a publicly supported education that is consistent with the child's needs and ability to benefit from it. The inadequacies of the District of Columbia public school system, whether occasioned by insufficient funding or administrative inefficiency, certainly cannot be permitted to bear more heavily on the child who is "exceptional" or disabled than on the normal child (*Mills,* 1972).

In both the *PARC* and *Mills* cases, the Court went beyond establishing that children with disabilities had a right to a free and appropriate public education, for it imposed many procedural and due process requirements on school systems. Due process is a means of ensuring that schools perform as the law mandates. For example, in the *PARC* decision, the court declared that the state must locate all children with mental disabilities in the state, that those children should be placed in as normal an environment as possible, and that their progress should be reviewed yearly or at the parents' request. In both *PARC* and *Mills,* the Court recognized that the advances granted to parents by the law would be meaningless if due process procedures were not also specified. These procedures make it clear to school systems that parents are to be involved and may challenge decisions about their children made by the system.

The Education of All Handicapped Children Act of 1975

The *PARC* and *Mills* cases as well as many subsequent decisions have had a profound effect on who is educated, how they are educated, and which due process procedures are available to safeguard the children and their parents. The most obvious result was the recognition by Congress that federal legislation and funding would be necessary to guarantee a free and appropriate public education for all children. Congress accordingly enacted the Education of All Handicapped Children Act of 1975, Public Law 94–142, which goes far beyond simply establishing each child's right to an education by specifying the process through which education must occur (e.g., describing the steps in the assessment process and declaring that children must be educated in the least restrictive environment).

P.L. 94–142 was amended by P.L. 101–476 in 1990 and is now called the Individuals with Disabilities Education Act (IDEA). Although P.L. 94–142 and IDEA are similar, Congress did revise and extend the law in some important ways (see table 3.1 for a summary). Seven major provisions of this law are summarized in table 3.2. Its importance for individuals concerned with the assessment and placement of children with disabilities cannot be overstated, because it literally directs practitioners' daily activities.

The law has been a two-edged sword in the field of special education. On one hand, it has created a vast network of services for children with disabilities who were often denied any publicly supported education prior to the 1970s. On the other hand, it has made the assessment of children more complex. Generally, this increased complexity is not unnecessarily constricting. In fact, in most cases what was once simply good educational practice is now the law.

Table 3.1   Summary of Major Changes from P.L. 94–142 to IDEA

- New programs for transition
- New programs for children with serious emotional disturbance
- New research and information dissemination program on Attention Deficit Disorder
- Added transition and assistive technology services
- Included rehabilitation counseling and social work as related services
- Services expanded to more fully include children with autism and traumatic brain injury

---

From time to time, concern is focused on the expense of educating children with disabilities, and there are calls within U.S. Congress to repeal IDEA. This often causes fear among those whose employment in special education depends on the existence of the law. However, such fear is probably unfounded for three reasons. First, IDEA is based directly on case law, which in turn is influenced by the U.S. Constitution. Thus, as long as a free education is offered to children without disabilities, a free and appropriate public education must also be granted to children with disabilities. Congress cannot alter this right unless it amends the Constitution. Second, many states have adopted laws that are highly similar to

Table 3.2   Major Provisions of IDEA

Free and Appropriate Public Education

All children are entitled to a free and appropriate public education, regardless of the nature or severity of their disability.

Nondiscriminatory Assessment

Requires the establishment of procedures to ensure that testing and evaluation materials and procedures utilized for evaluation and placement of children with disabilities will be selected and administered so as not to be culturally or racially discriminatory.

Development of an Individual Education Plan (IEP)

Requires the development of a written IEP for each child with a disability that will include a statement of current levels of educational achievement, annual and short-term goals, specific educational services to be provided, dates of initiation and duration of services, and criteria for evaluating the degree to which the objectives are achieved.

Due Process

Requires an opportunity to present complaints with respect to any matter relating to the identification, evaluation, or educational placement of a child. Specific due process procedures include: (a) written notification to parents before evaluation, (b) written notification when initiating or refusing to initiate a change in educational placement, (c) opportunity to obtain an independent evaluation of the child, and (d) an opportunity for an impartial due process hearing.

Privacy and Records

Requires that educational and psychological records pertaining to a child remain confidential except to those individuals who are directly involved in a child's education and who have a specific reason for reviewing the records. Further, the law provides an opportunity for the parents or guardian of a child with a disability to examine all relevant records with respect to the identification, evaluation, and educational placement of the child.

Least Restrictive Environment

Requires to the maximum extent appropriate that children with disabilities be educated with children who are not disabled in as normal an environment as possible.

Related Services

Required support services (e.g., psychological, audiology, occupational therapy, music therapy) are required to assist the child with a disability to benefit from special education.

Source: Adapted from Individuals with Disabilities Education Act, P.L. 101–476.

IDEA. Many are even more procedurally specific than the federal law and would remain in effect if the latter were changed. Finally, there is still considerable support in Congress for IDEA. Originally, the bill passed by a margin of 87 to 7 in the Senate and 404 to 7 in the House. Evidence of the continued support for the law in Congress is provided by the passage in October 1986 of the Education of the Handicapped Amendments, Public Law 99–457, which serves to amend IDEA by requiring states to provide special education services to not only school-aged children but also preschoolers as young as three years. Thus, it seems likely that the fundamental philosophy of IDEA will influence the profession of special education and the delivery of psychoeducational services for years to come.

P.L. 99–457, Handicapped Infants and Toddlers

P.L. 99–457 extended the Education of the Handicapped Act (i.e., IDEA, Part H), which targeted primarily school-age children, to include infants and toddlers. The law provides governmental support for early intervention and was viewed by Congress as cost effective because problems that are targeted and perhaps resolved early minimize the need for more intensive and costly services later.

Infants and toddlers who are eligible for services include those who (a) experience a measured developmental delay in areas such as cognitive, physical, psychosocial, or language functioning, (b) have a diagnosed physical or mental condition such as Down's syndrome, or (c) are "at risk" for having developmental delays if early intervention services are not provided. Factors that may place an infant at risk include poverty, teenage parentage, low birth weight, physical abuse or neglect, malnutrition, and environmental poisoning (Garwood and Sheehan, 1989).

Parent involvement is a major factor incorporated into P.L. 99–457. Specifically, there is a requirement that an Individualized Family Services Plan (IFSP) be developed for each child and family. The emphasis on family needs, in name and intent, comes from a recognition that children with disabilities are better served when parents are actively involved and served as well. Hence, P.L. 99–457 moved away from the more or less exclusive focus on the child found in IDEA and provided a mechanism where parents could receive mental health services, parent training, and other services to help them be more effective caretakers of their infant or toddler with a disability.

An IFSP is to be based on a multidisciplinary evaluation that includes an assessment of the child's current developmental levels as well as the family's strengths and weaknesses. The content of the IFSP should include:

1. Statement of assessment results relative to six major areas of functioning.

2. Statement of the family's strengths and weaknesses relating to enhancing the development of the family's infant or toddler with a disability.

3. A statement of major outcomes expected.

4. A statement of specific early intervention services necessary to meet the unique needs of the child or the family.

5. The projected dates of services and the name of the case manager, from the profession most immediately relevant to the specified needs, who will coordinate services.

P.L. 99–457 appears to come from a theoretical and research base that is on the cutting edge. Unfortunately, for those involved in the assessment process, what the law requires is ahead of the available technology. That is, the quality and availability of tests and other assessment procedures for infants and toddlers leaves a lot to be desired. In addition to problems with the reliability and validity of tests, there are problems inherent in obtaining a stable assessment of young children. Also, the idea of assessing the family is a relatively new one and quality assessment instruments need to be developed and refined.

Section 504 of the Rehabilitation Act of 1973

Typically, children in school settings are classified as disabled under IDEA because it pertains directly to educational settings. Increasingly, however, schools are being required to provide special services to children classified as "disordered" or "disabled" by other professions (e.g., physicians, private psychologists) using classification systems such as the *Diagnostic and Statistical Manual of the American Psychiatric Association, Third Edition (DSM-III-R)*. The basis in law for obtaining services for children who do not qualify for services under IDEA but who have a disorder according to some other diagnostic scheme has typically been Section 504 of the Rehabilitation Act of 1973. Section 504 is an antidiscrimination law that grants equal access for all. The law is far-ranging and does everything from requiring wheelchair ramps in buildings to ensuring that individuals are not discriminated against on the basis of race.

Section 504 has been used increasingly in schools to get services for children classified as having a disorder under DSM-III-R. For example, a child diagnosed as depressed by a psychiatrist may not qualify for services under IDEA but may be eligible under Section 504. The U.S. Office of Civil Rights (OCR) has been relatively vigorous in enforcing this new interpretation of Section 504. Like IDEA, schools have a duty to inform parents that their child with, for example, Attention Deficit-Hyperactivity Disorder, may be eligible for special education services. Unlike IDEA, school districts can be found liable for civil damages for not serving children with disabilities in a timely and appropriate manner.

The potential influence of Section 504 is great because educational institutions, guided by each state's department of education, have been relatively self-contained in deciding who is disabled, and under IDEA it was possible to legally tell parents their child did not fit one of the IDEA "pigeonholes." Under Section 504 all public institutions must provide equal access to all and as Hackola (in press) has indicated: "OCR has found that students with conditions such as sleep disorders, allergies/asthma, AIDS/HIV, dyslexia, mental illness, arthritis, and obesity that do not fit with an IDEA category may be entitled under Section 504 to special education services and procedural safeguards."

Schools who expel or suspend students without due process are particularly vulnerable under Section 504 because, unlike IDEA, a formal evaluation must be conducted prior to any change in placement, including exclusion from school (Hackola, in press). Hence, a child who has been diagnosed as being conduct disordered, depressed, alcoholic, and so on would appear to need a formal evaluation by the school to determine if the problem for which he or she was being suspended was due to the disorder. Section 504 appears to require this even though the school has not diagnosed the problem or even made any formal recognition of it.

Historically, many schools have only done as much for children with disabilies as they have been forced to do. Because of the "teeth" in Section 504 they will probably adhere to the procedures closely and quickly. In addition to the potential loss of federal funds for noncompliance, Hackola has indicated there is increasing support for the award of monetary damages that is "more than a special education dispute about the adequacy of services; it may allege violations of federal constitutional and civil rights laws, laws which have historically served as a basis for money damages to compensate for the individual's injuries" (Hackola, in press).

➡ *Legal Influences in the Assessment Phase*

Parental Consent

Legal regulation of the education of children with disabilities starts even before assessment begins. The law requires that parental approval is necessary before the evaluation of any child for potential placement in special education. Under ordinary circumstances, a regular classroom teacher who is administering tests to the entire class for the purpose of improving educational programming within the classroom does not need to obtain parental permission to give the tests. Likewise, permission is not usually required for a school district to administer routine educational tests to all children. In general, parental permission is usually not required if a test is administered to all children, if it does not reveal information that is educationally irrelevant (e.g., questions about drug use), and if the test it not used to change a child's educational placement.

According to IDEA, parental permission is required when an educational agency proposes to initiate (or refuses to initiate) or change the classification, evaluation, or educational placement of a child or the

```
                    ┌─────────────────────┐
                    │     Focus on        │
         ┌──────────►    Practice    ◄────────────┐
```

How Does the Prudent School-Based Specialist Steer Clear of Problems with Section 504?

The following recommendations were offered by Stuart Hackola, (in press) an attorney, with respect to Attention Deficit Disorder (ADD). Although this model policy is most relevant to ADD, the general process to comply with Section 504 is applicable to other disorders.

Identification Procedures

1. Ensure that the identification mechanism includes referral for evaluation of suspected ADD and other disorders and that children receive the formal multidisciplinary evaluations mandated by the IDEA, with consent to evaluate and full notice of parental rights. Conducting "prescreening" for eligibility without parental consent and involvement is legally questionable.

2. Have the evaluation team first consider the student's eligibility under the IDEA and address eligibility under Section 504 only if the student does not meet IDEA criteria. Note, however, that students found eligible under the IDEA criteria still have Section 504 rights, including the right to an evaluation prior to long-term suspension/expulsion or any other significant change in placement.

3. Convene an IEP Committee within the required timelines. If the IEP Committee finds the student ineligible under the IDEA, the same group of persons should immediately reconstitute itself as a "Section 504 Committee" to consider eligibility under the broader criteria. If the Section 504 Committee finds the student eligible under Section 504, a written plan of service is required. Again, using the existing IEP form will assure compliance.

4. Provide parents and guardians with full notice of rights under both IDEA and Section 504; for example, if a student is found eligible under the IDEA to challenge the IDEA eligibility denial via independent educational evaluations and/or impartial due process hearings.

Provision of Services

5. Ensure that the decision-making team, whether constituted as an IEP Committee or as a "Section 504 Committee," considers the entire range of special education and related services needed to meet the student's unique needs. For students with ADD, such may include medical evaluations (including ongoing monitoring of medication), counseling/ psychotherapy, and behavioral management plans. Consideration should also be given to securing parental consent to any behavior management plan and/or to the administration of medication by school personnel.

6. Provide guidance to the IEP Committee/Section 504 Committee in implementing the legal mandate that children be placed in the most normal or least restrictive environment possible. For children with ADD, the team should consider support services and modification of the regular education classroom environment and/or curriculum.

Behavioral Control

7. Ensure that the IEP Committees or Section 504 Committees proactively address the behavioral needs of students with ADD by establishing adequate behavior plans and services.

8. Ensure that the school's code of conduct provides for the detailed procedures required for disciplining handicapped students and that these special procedures extend to students protected by Section 504.

9. Ensure proper evaluation prior to long-term suspension/expulsion. This evaluation should precede IEPC consideration of whether the misconduct is a manifestation of disability. The evaluation and the IEP Committee should be completed within 10 days of the initial exclusion. There should also be provisions for disciplining students who have not yet been evaluated for special education but who are suspected of having a disability. Such students may be entitled to remain in school pending full and immediate evaluation of their eligibility under the IDEA and Section 504.

10. Ensure adequate compliance with the special protections of special education laws and with the constitutional right of due process.

provisions of a free and appropriate public education for the child. Thus, parental permission is a legal necessity when a child is singled out and removed from the classroom to be tested by a psychologist, speech clinician, or special education teacher, regardless of whether the child eventually is placed in special education. Parents have a right to know when a potential change is being considered.

It is not enough simply to tell parents that an evaluation of their child is planned. The notice must also meet the legal requirements of informed consent, which means that parents must be informed in writing, in their primary language, of the purpose of the evaluation, the specific tests that will be administered, what they measure, how the information will be used, and the likely outcomes of such an assessment.

Nondiscriminatory Assessment

By far the most intense involvement in assessment by courts and legislatures has been to establish procedures to ensure that assessment materials and procedures utilized for the evaluation and placement of children with disabilities will be selected and administered so as not to be culturally or racially discriminatory. The impetus for the development of law in this area has its roots in the civil rights struggles of the 1950s, when minorities fought for and won the right for their children to have the same education as white children, as in *Brown*. Many schools, however, sought to circumvent the rights of minority children by placing them in "special" classrooms on the basis of their performance on standardized tests. The courts (see, e.g., *Larry P. v. Wilson Riles, et al.*, 1979) have often concluded that the intelligence and achievement tests used to place these children are biased or discriminatory and result in a disproportionate number of minority children in special education classrooms. Many tests have been considered discriminatory because of the lack of minority group children in the sample on which they were standardized and because children from minority cultures tend to achieve lower scores than middle-class white children (cf. Reynolds, 1982).

The issue of discriminatory assessment has not always received a fair appraisal in the courts because many of the individuals responsible for making decisions have appeared to ignore the scientific evidence concerning assessment instruments and have instead relied upon intuition and inference. The problem of deciding intuitively whether a test is biased has been examined by Reschly and Sabers (1979), who argued that evaluating a test without reference to research can lead to inaccurate conclusions. They pointed out, for example, that the widely criticized item from the Wechsler Intelligence Scale for Children-Revised, "What is the thing to do if a boy (girl) much smaller than yourself starts to fight with you?" may actually be easier for black children to answer than for white children. Without consulting the research on this particular question, it would be easy to conclude that it was biased against poor children because turning your back on anyone who hits you in the ghetto would not be an intelligent thing to do. Determining whether a test is biased is a complex social and psychometric issue that has challenged researchers from many scientific disciplines.

Larry P. concerned the overrepresentation of minority students in special education classrooms. The plaintiffs portrayed the "culturally biased" intelligence test as the primary reason that black children were placed in "isolating," "inferior," "deadened," and "stigmatizing" classes for those with mild mental disabilities. The logic of this statement has been questioned, and the court has been faulted for not inquiring as to why so many black children are even brought into the referral process (MacMillan & Meyers, 1980).

The question of why so many minority children are referred in the first place played a central role in *Marshall et al. v. Georgia* (1984) (Reschly, Kicklighter, & McKee, 1988). In *Larry P.* the court pointed an accusing finger at IQ tests, blaming these instruments for many of the problems surrounding minority children, including and especially their overrepresentation in special education. However in *Marshall,* it was argued that referral occurs not because children come from a minority culture but because children often are not able to learn from standard curricula and teaching practices and because schools may lack sufficient educational options for remedying children's deficits. Although defendant school districts in the *Marshall* case did have an overrepresentation of minority children in special education, they argued that this was simply because more minority children exhibit severe achievement problems and need help.

Marshall is an important case for school-based professionals because it provides specific recommendations for providing quality services to children. According to Reschly and colleagues (1988), a critical difference between *Marshall* and previous cases, such as *Larry P.,* where schools had been criticized for placing disproportionate numbers of minority children in special education, was the ability of the schools in *Marshall* to show positive outcomes for minority students. In *Larry P.* and cases before it, schools appeared to be using IQ tests as a rationale for first segregating minority children and then educating them in an inferior fashion. However, in *Marshall*, school districts were able to prove that placement of children was related to low achievement and that placement resulted in positive outcomes.

IDEA contains a good summary of the legalities influencing assessment. This law emphasizes the use of a wide range of assessment information that is collected by a variety of professionals so as to be as culturally fair as possible. Table 3.3 provides an overview of portions of the law relevant to testing and assessment.

Table 3.3   Major Requirements Concerning Testing and Assessment in IDEA

1. Each state educational agency shall ensure that each public agency establishes and implements procedures that meet the requirements of this law.
2. Testing and evaluation materials and procedures used for the purposes of evaluation and placement of children with disabilities must be selected and administered so as not to be racially or culturally discriminatory.
3. Before any action is taken with respect to the initial placement of a child with a disability in a special education program, a full and individual evaluation of the child's educational needs must be conducted in accordance with the requirements of this law.
4. State and local educational agencies shall ensure, at a minimum, that tests and other evaluation materials:

   a. Are provided and administered in the child's native language or other mode of communication, unless it is clearly not feasible to do so;
   b. Have been validated for the specific purpose for which they are used; and
   c. Are administered by trained personnel in conformance with the instructions provided by their producer.
   d. No single procedure shall be the sole criterion for determining an appropriate educational program for a child.

Table 3.3—*Continued*

---

5. Tests and other evaluation materials include those tailored to assess specific areas of educational need and not merely those designed to provide a single general intelligence quotient.
6. Tests are selected and administered so as best to ensure that when a test is administered to a child with impaired sensory, manual, or speaking skills, the test results accurately reflect the child's aptitude or achievement level or whatever other factors the test purports to measure, rather than reflecting the child's impaired sensory, manual, or speaking skills (except when those skills are the factors that the test purports to measure).
7. No single procedure is used as the sole criterion for determining an appropriate educational program for a child.
8. The evaluation is made by a multidisciplinary team or group of persons, including at least one teacher or other specialist with knowledge in the area of suspected disability.
9. The child is assessed in all areas related to the suspected disability, including, where appropriate, health, vision, hearing, social and emotional status, general intelligence, academic performance, communicative status, and motor abilities.
10. In interpreting evaluation data and in making placement decisions, each public agency shall:

    a. Draw upon information from a variety of sources, including aptitude and achievement tests, teacher recommendations, physical condition, social or cultural background, and adaptive behavior.
    b. Ensure that information obtained from all of these sources is documented and carefully considered.
    c. Ensure that the placement decision is made by a group of persons, including persons knowledgeable about the child, the meaning of the evaluation data, and the placement options.
    d. Ensure that the placement decision is made in conformity with the least restrictive environment rules.

11. If a determination is made that a child is disabled and needs special education and related services, an Individualized Education Program must be developed for the child.

Source: Adapted from IDEA.

Access to Records

IDEA as well as another federal law, the Family Educational Rights and Privacy Act (FERPA) of 1977 (often referred to as the Buckley Amendment), govern the handling of records in educational settings. These laws require that all public educational institutions:

1. Allow parents access to all official educational records related to their child and provide an interpretation of the records if necessary;

2. allow parents to challenge records that may be inaccurate or misleading; and

3. obtain the written consent of parents before releasing a child's records to a third party.

Basic to understanding the regulations contained within these laws is the legal definition of "educational records." Simply stated, educational records are any records directly related to a student that are maintained by an educational institution. Stated even more simply by Trachtman (1972), a record is "anything put in writing for others to see" (p. 45). Obviously all reports and other official documentation of evaluation, classification, and placement should be open for parental inspection. Frequently school districts appoint an individual to review the records with parents so that explanations and interpretations can be offered if needed.

To follow the law is not always a straightforward matter, and the issue of access to records provides an excellent example of the problems that may be encountered. The fact that FERPA allows parents to see the educational records of their child runs counter to the rights of some test publishers, who argue that test forms and test protocol must not be shown to anyone except qualified professionals because to do so would jeopardize test security. Since many of these test protocols contain actual test items, publishers are concerned that parents might tell others about test content, thus jeopardizing the validity of the test. Individuals who provide interpretations of test results to parents can usually avoid problems by telling parents the general type of items on the test and giving examples that are similar but not identical to the ones actually on the test.

Although FERPA allows parents wide latitude in having access to records, it is quite specific in denying access to all other persons except those who have a "legitimate educational interest" in the child. For example, if a child moves from one school system to another, the new system may want to know the results of special education evaluations conducted by the former district. However, no records can be released unless the parents give written permission. Parents have the right to know what records are being disclosed and to whom and the purposes of the disclosure. In addition, parents have the right to a copy of all records being disclosed. An issue that arises with some frequency involves telephone requests for information about a child with whom an educational specialist has had some contact. The caller may or may not have permission to see the records and could be an individual from another school district or the private sector (such as a speech pathologist or psychologist) or even a relative of the child. According to FERPA, it is clearly not prudent to provide information over the telephone. First, it is difficult to be completely certain to whom you are talking. Second, although the caller may have the child's best interests in mind, the law requires parental permission be obtained before information is released. Third, the specialist must exercise reasonable care in ensuring that information is disclosed to parties who have obtained such permission.

➜ Legal Influences in the Classification and Placement Phase

Multidisciplinary Decision Making

After the assessment phase has been completed, the classification phase typically begins with a group of professionals meeting to make decisions about classification and placement. IDEA requires that the evaluation be made by a multidisciplinary team or group of persons, including at least one teacher or other specialist with knowledge in the area of suspected disability. The law further requires each school to ensure that the placement decision is made by a group of persons, including persons knowledgeable about the child, the meaning of the evaluation data, and the placement options. Thus, educational decision-making teams composed of teachers, parents, and support personnel (e.g., psychologists, counselors, nurses, physical and occupational therapists, speech pathologists, and social workers) have been required to ensure such a mandate is carried out. Children can also be a part of this team, although they are rarely present during formal team meetings.

According to Fenton, Yoshida, Maxwell, and Kaufman (1979), teams should try to accomplish 11 goals for every student with special needs:

1. Determine the student's eligibility for special education.
2. Determine whether sufficient information about the student exists before the placement team makes decisions affecting the student's instructional program.
3. Evaluate the educational significance of such data.
4. Determine the student's placement.
5. Formulate appropriate year-long educational goals and objectives for the student.
6. Develop specific short-term instructional objectives for the student.
7. Communicate with the parents about changes in the student's educational program.
8. Decide which information is needed for the future review of the student's program and progress.
9. Establish the date for the placement team's review.
10. Review the continued appropriateness of the student's educational program.
11. Review the student's educational progress.

The implicit rationale for a team approach to special education decision making is the belief that a group decision provides safeguards against individual errors in judgment while enhancing adherence to due process requirements (Pfeiffer, 1980). According to Pfeiffer (1981), "the key elements of a multidisciplinary team are a common purpose, cooperative problem-solving by different professionals who possess unique skills and orientation, and a coordination of activities" (p. 330). Thus, multidisciplinary teams provide a number of benefits beyond those provided by a single individual, including:

1. greater accuracy in assessment, classification, and placement decisions;

2. a forum for sharing differing views;

3. provisions for specialized consultative services to school personnel, parents, and community groups; and

4. the resources for developing and evaluating Individualized Educational Programs for exceptional students.

Classification and Diagnosis

A major goal of the multidisciplinary decision-making process is to determine if a child is disabled and qualifies for placement in special education. Although they are often used interchangeably, the terms "classification" and "diagnosis" refer to different processes. Within an educational setting, classification involves the ordering or grouping of the attributes, characteristics, or behaviors of children into distinct categories. Effective classification systems use objective criteria or rules to decide whether a particular child belongs in a specific category. For example, to be classified as mentally disabled a child must have a score that is less than 70 (or 2 standard deviations below the mean) on a comprehensive intelligence test and significantly subaverage adaptive behavior. In this case, test scores provide relatively objective criteria upon which to base a decision to classify a child as mentally disabled. Classification is thus the system used to categorize the characteristics and behaviors of children.

Diagnosis follows from classification and is the process of assigning a child to a particular category within the classification system. In education, the development of the classification system has involved the establishment of a series of categories such as mentally disabled, learning disabled, and behavior disordered. The diagnostic process that evolves from this classification scheme requires that the attributes of a particular child be compared with the criteria that define each category. Diagnosis is thus simply the process of assigning a child to one of the classification categories (such as mentally disabled).

Classification in Educational Settings

Although a number of educational classification systems are available, one derived from the federal guidelines (i.e., IDEA) is used almost without exception throughout the United States. This system, which is typically interpreted in a slightly different manner by each state's department of education, is widely used because funding from the federal government to state governments and from state governments to local school districts is based on the system. Thus, local school districts are reimbursed by state governments for each child classified as disabled. Typically, children with the more severe disabilities entitle their school district to more funding than do children with mild disabilities.

As mentioned previously, schools are increasingly being required to serve children diagnosed as "disabled" under classification systems other than those derived from IDEA. Diagnoses derived from DSM-III-R, in particular, are being used more frequently in connection with Section 504.

Evaluation of the Educational Classification System

Ysseldyke and Thurlow (1984) collected considerable data on how well the educational classification system works. They found that approximately 5 percent of the elementary school population is referred for evaluation during any given year. Once a student is referred, 92 percent are evaluated, and 73 percent of the students who are evaluated are actually placed in special education. Thus, teachers who refer a student for evaluation appear to have an astoundingly high prediction rate; that is, most students who are referred for testing are diagnosed as disabled and placed in special education. Ysseldyke and Thurlow (1984) attribute this phenomenon not to the keen eye of teachers but instead to negative features of the diagnostic process itself. They characterize the multidisci- plinary decision-making process as a "search for pathology" during which it is "assumed that *if* a teacher refers a student, then the student must have a problem; it is assumed that the task of the decision-making team is to find the problem" (Ysseldyke & Thurlow, 1984, p. 125). This perspective, although probably true in many cases, is quite pessimistic and fails to acknowledge the ability that teachers develop for identifying children experiencing problems (Hoge, 1983).

Children diagnosed as disabled are most frequently placed in situations involving part-day services in a resource room with the remainder of their time in school being spent in the regular classroom. According to Ysseldyke and Algozzine (1982), the overall outcome of the educational classification process, which often involves the use of psychometrically inadequate tests, is the overinclusion of children on a one-way street into special education programs.

Needless to say, the educational classification system has been a matter of intense debate. Critics have strongly suggested that it has a number of serious shortcomings and that classification of children in this way should be abandoned. Although proponents of the system recognize that it could be improved, they also argue that it offers a number of advantages, including several administrative necessities, not the least of which are record keeping and a means for funding. Readers interested in an extensive discussion of issues surrounding the classification of children should consult other sources, including the Project on the Classification of Exceptional Children, a comprehensive and systematic analysis of the educational classification system. This project, coordinated by Nicholas Hobbs and funded by the federal government, was eventually published as *Issues in the Classification of Children* (Hobbs, 1975), and, although somewhat dated, should be required reading for anyone involved with children with disablities.

➡ *Legal Influences in the Intervention Phase*

Individualized Education Plan

After a child has been assessed and classified, IDEA requires that a team of individuals, including the child's parents, develop an Individualized Education Plan, or IEP, which is a written document describing the goals, objectives, and procedures that will be used to provide an appropriate education for the child with a disability. The plan must contain at least the following types of information:

1. a statement of the child's present levels of educational performance;
2. a statement of annual goals, including short-term instructional objectives;
3. a statement of the specific special education and related services to be provided and the extent to which the child will be able to participate in regular education programs;
4. the projected dates of the initiation of services and the anticipated duration; and
5. objective criteria and evaluation procedures for determining, at least annually, whether the short-term instructional objectives are being achieved.
6. A statement of the needed transition services for students beginning no later than age 16 including, when appropriate, a statement of the interagency responsibilities or linkages (or both), before the student leaves the school setting.

After the IEP is developed, the special education and related service personnel who will implement the objectives are given copies of the final document to guide their interventions. There are at least two major problems with a follow-up evaluation of an IEP. First, the review of an IEP is required only annually. Although it is possible to review goals more frequently, the process of meeting with a number of different professionals can be time-consuming and expensive. The problem, however, with only a yearly review is that the needs of and goals for a child can change several times during that period. Although IDEA calls for the specification of short-term objectives, it provides no formal mechanism for monitoring the realization of these objectives or changing them as they are determined to be ineffective or inappropriate. Therefore, a high probability exists that problems with an IEP will not be discovered until an entire year has passed and it is time for the annual review of the IEP. Of course, active parental involvement in their child's education enhances the accountability of educators and increases the probability the objectives are accomplished or adjusted when needed.

A second major problem with the review of the IEP is that school personnel are often concerned that their professional credibility will be damaged if a child's educational objectives are *not* achieved. They have this concern despite explicit statements in the regulations governing special education that educational personnel will not be held accountable if educational objectives are not met. This fear among school personnel can lead to the establishment of only minimal annual goals that can be easily attained.

Least Restrictive Environment

In making placement and intervention decisions, multidisciplinary teams must take care to ensure that education occurs in the least restrictive environment, which is best defined within the context of a continuum of educational services for children with disabilities. One such continuum is illustrated in figure 3.1. The figure is organized from top to bottom, with services at the top (i.e., those provided in the regular classroom) being less restrictive than those at the bottom (i.e., those provided in a residential school). The idea behind the principle of least restrictive environment is that children must be educated in as normal an environment as their disability allows. Thus, children with minor disabilities, such as a minor reading problem, can be educated in their home school where they socialize with their neighborhood friends. Children with very severe disabilities, such as autism, may require placement in a school that specializes in that disability.

Education in the least restrictive environment is sometimes referred to as **mainstreaming** because many children with mild disabilities are pulled out of their regular education classes for part of the day and placed in a resource room where they receive specialized services for impairments such as learning disabilities or mild mental disabilities. The

Figure 3.1   Continuum of Special Education Services along Three Dimensions

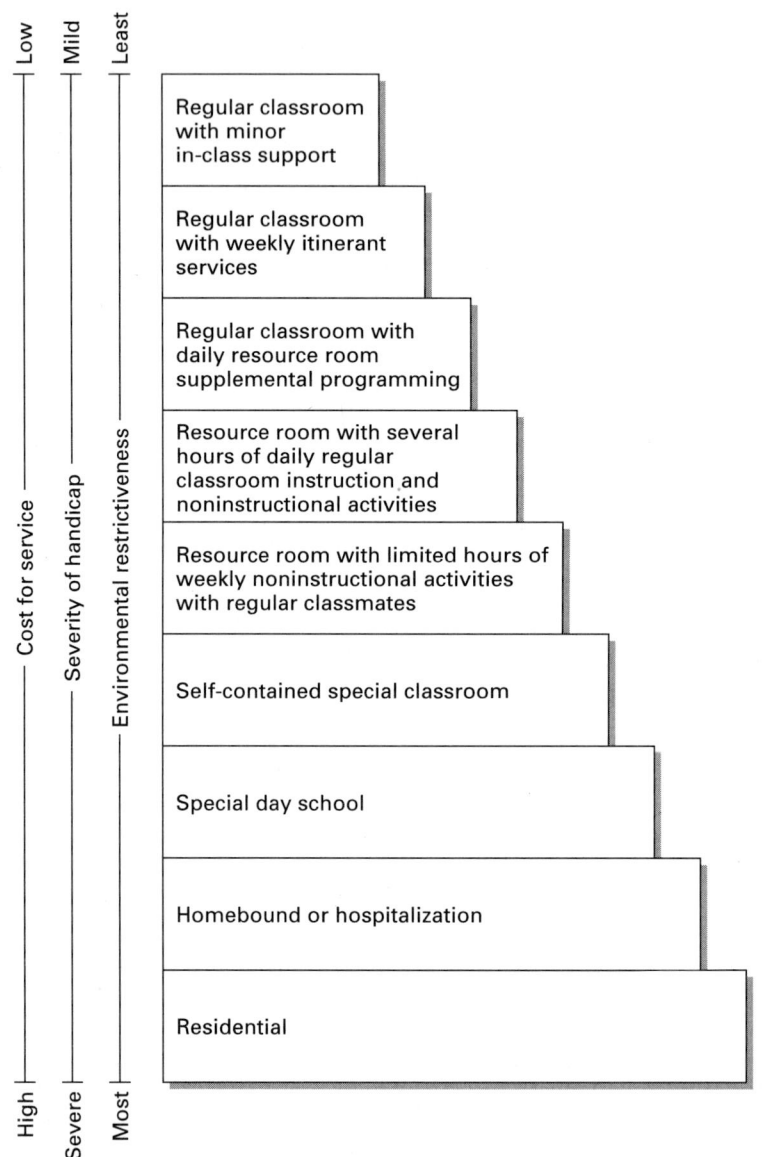

From C. R. Reynolds and L. Mann, *Encyclopedia of Special Education*. Copyright © 1987 John Wiley & Sons, New York. Reprinted by permission of John Wiley & Sons, Inc.

remainder of the day they are "mainstreamed," or placed with children without disabilities for socialization and instruction in subjects in which their deficits do not interfere with their ability to benefit from the teaching.

Appropriate Education

The major purpose of the entire special education referral, assessment, and placement process is to ensure that children with disabilities receive an *appropriate* education. Typically, this is a straightforward process, and the multidisciplinary team designs a program individualized for a child's unique strengths and weaknesses. Occasionally, however, as in all decision-making processes, disagreement arises about what represents the most appropriate educational services. The definition of the term "appropriate" has thus become a major issue in the placement process.

Such disagreements have usually been between parents and the school system. Parents, for example, may want their child to be placed in a special school in another state that has an excellent reputation for handling problems similar to the ones their child is experiencing. The local school system may refuse to pay for placement in such a setting, saying they can provide an appropriate education within the district. Does a school system have an obligation to provide the best possible education for a child or only an appropriate education?

In response to this question, the U.S. Supreme Court sided with the school system in the case of *Hendrick Hudson District Board of Education v. Rowley* (1982). The Court ruled that a school system must provide an appropriate but not necessarily an ideal educational program for a child and that "the requirement that a state provide specialized services to handicapped children generated no additional requirement that the services so provided be sufficient to maximize each child's potential 'commensurate with the opportunity provided to other children' " (*Hendricks,* p. 198).

➡ *Psychoeducational Assessment Procedures in Schools*

From the preceeding discussion it should be obvious that the special education referral, classification, and placement process has become a highly regulated process due to federal legislation such as IDEA. The question remains, however, as to how the various aspects of the law can be translated into step-by-step procedures whereby the needs of children and teachers are provided for within an orderly process that takes into account the legal issues bearing upon special education. In the remainder of this chapter we describe a generic process, typical of those used in many school districts throughout the United States, for the accomplishment of these goals. Figure 3.2 depicts a flow chart that describes the procedural steps typically taken by psychologists and special educators in the evaluation and treatment of students. A brief discussion of each step provides

Figure 3.2   Flow Chart of Consultation-Assessment-Intervention Service System

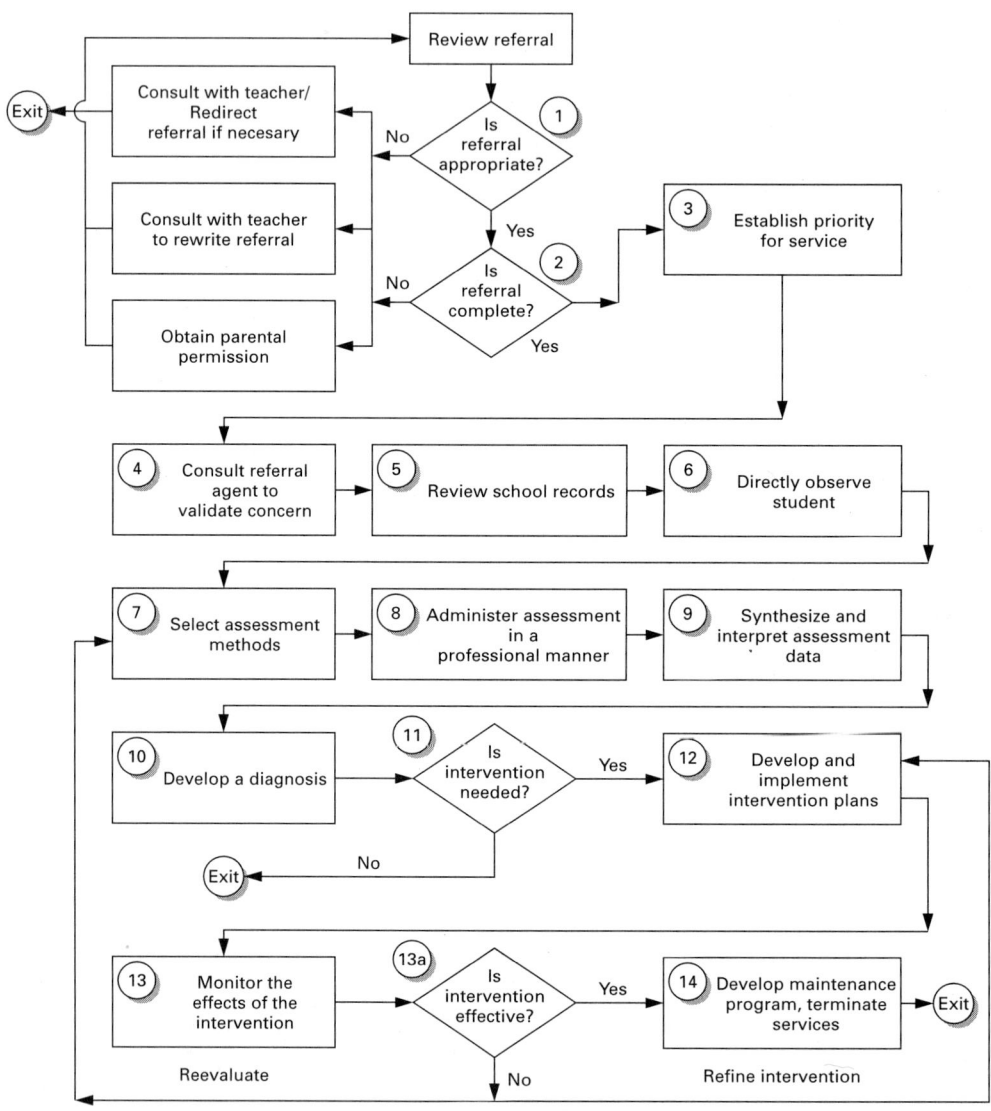

From Reynolds, C. R., Gutkin, T. B., Elliott, S. N., and Witt, J. C. (1984). *School Psychology: Essentials of Theory and Practice.* New York: Wiley. Reprinted by permission of the authors.

an overview of a complete psychoeducational service model, thus highlighting the interrelationships among consultation, assessment, and intervention services.

Step 1: Determine appropriateness of referral. A referral, whether formal or informal, signals to an assessor that a student is perceived to be experiencing a problem. The assessor's task is to determine whether the referral is "appropriate." The definition of an "inappropriate" referral will vary. However, some documentation of the perceived problem or concern as well as an enumeration of previous teacher- or parent-directed interventions is usually necessary before an assessor should get involved. If the referral is deemed inappropriate and does not warrant direct or indirect involvement by school district personnel, it should be either referred back to the person making the request or directed to another service system or agency. If no service is needed, an explanation should be made to the person who made the referral.

Step 2: Review referral for essential components. If the referral is judged to be appropriate, the assessor must determine whether it has all the essential components applicable to psychoeducational services, including a clear, behavioral statement of the problem and the written permission of the student's parents or legal guardians if a psychologist or educational diagnostician will be working directly with the student.

If the referral is incomplete, the assessor should initiate the steps needed to secure the necessary information. This will most likely involve returning the referral to the referring agent for revision. In the interim, consultation with teachers or parents, record reviews, and classroom observations could be initiated.

Step 3: Establish service priority. The demands for psychoeducational services are usually such that some individual or group of individuals must decide who receives priority in acquiring services. Some systems utilize a severity-of-problem scale, whereas others use the date of referral to prioritize potential recipients. Typically, the assessor reviews referrals and other time investments with a principal or special education coordinator before prioritizing cases. When an appreciable delay between initial referral and expected date of service is anticipated, it is advisable to notify parents and teachers involved in the case.

Step 4: Consult with referral agents. The assessor should meet at least once with the individual who referred a student to clarify and validate the child's problem before further interactions take place. This step is particularly necessary when there has been a significant delay between the referral date and the assessor's initial involvement. When the referral agent is not a parent, the assessor might also contact the parents or legal guardians to ensure cooperation and to gather information. If nothing more, this step provides for enhanced communication among assessors, parents, and teachers, all of whom are critical in the assessment and intervention phases.

Step 5: Review school records. Prior to an evaluation or intervention, the assessor should review and analyze a student's cumulative records. Information gleaned from such records can be classified as relating to the student's (a) sensory system (such as vision and hearing) integrity, (b) academic progress, (c) history of physical health, (d) history of emotional health, and (e) family or social history. A review of school records should be supplemented by interviews with parents, school personnel, or other significant individuals.

Step 6: Direct student observations. Observations of a student in different settings and by different observers provide valuable information for decision making, whether one actually records specific behaviors or simply attempts to better understand a student interacting within a particular setting. When testing is likely to occur, unobtrusive observation may be impossible unless it takes place prior to working with the student directly. Thus, conducting observations prior to meeting a student reduces the probability of the student behaving differently because of your presence and thereby enhances the meaningfulness of the observation.

Step 7: Select assessment methods. Selection of assessment instruments and strategies should be based on the student's stated problem and the assessor's competencies. If a student requires an assessment beyond the competencies of a given assessor, that professional is ethically obligated to refuse to use procedures beyond his or her level of competence and to refer the case to someone skilled in using the methods or tests.

Step 8: Administer assessment professionally. The assessor should administer all tests and collect observations or ratings according to recommended procedures. In other words, when administering and scoring standardized instruments or using nonstandardized assessment methods, assessors should adhere to the procedures outlined in test manuals or documented in the professional literature.

Step 9: Synthesize and interpret assessment data. Once all the assessment data have been collected and quantified, the assessor is responsible for analyzing and interpreting the results with respect to the stated problems. The results usually are communicated in a written report and a verbal summary at a multidisciplinary staff meeting. Assessors should be aware of their colleagues' knowledge so as to write reports in an understandable and meaningful manner. Oral or written reports laden with technical terms and jargon may confuse or even antagonize others. Communication to all parties is facilitated by providing objective and concrete evidence to support interpretations. Information and interpretations also should account for measurement error and recognize the limitations of particular instruments. Finally, assessors should not rely solely on their written reports or verbal summaries if behavior change in a student is a desired outcome of the evaluation; follow-up discussions or notes to those who will provide direct services are often necessary to ensure understanding and correct implementation of such recommendations.

Step 10: Develop a diagnosis. At the conclusion of the interpretation of assessment data, the assessors are responsible for formulating a psychological-educational diagnosis whenever classification or eligibility for services is a consideration. In most states, guidelines for determining disabling conditions (such as learning disabilities, behavioral impairments, and mild mental disabilities) have been developed by state departments of education or mental health agencies that assist psychologists and educators in determining classification criteria.

Step 11: Decide if intervention is needed. Decisions about interventions usually follow a comprehensive consultation or assessment of a student. An assessor formulates an opinion regarding the need for intervention, whether functioning as an assessment team member or individual consultant. When a team is involved, other members of the team should have input about intervention plans. When the assessor is the primary or only person consulting with a teacher, parent, or other individual on a case, responsibility for determining the need for intervention effectively rests with the assessor and referring adult. In every case, *not* to implement an intervention must be considered a viable option, because some problems will solve themselves if left alone. Determining which problems demand attention and which do not is one of the most difficult of lessons for professionals eager to help.

Step 12: Develop and implement intervention plans. The assessor, along with others (assessment team members or consultees), develops potential intervention plans for implementation in the least restrictive environment. These intervention plans should (a) correspond to the student's problem statement and diagnosis, (b) be practical, (c) contain behavioral objectives, and (d) be communicated in sufficient detail for implementation. If a student is to be enrolled in special education, the intervention plan would be included in an IEP.

Step 13: Monitor effects of intervention. Assessors should try to measure the results of interventions that they have helped to develop. Periodic monitoring allows for corrections or adjustments in services and provides valuable feedback about diagnosis and intervention plans. According to IDEA and most state special education regulations, follow-up in the form of a psychological reevaluation must occur at least every three years. Reviews of students' IEPs are to occur annually, and thus provide another opportunity for assessors to receive feedback and have input into the refinement of services. However, three-year reevaluations and annual IEP reviews are insufficient for maximal use of follow-up information, so we suggest weekly monitoring of interventions initially after implementation and monthly contacts thereafter to monitor a client's progress.

Step 14: Determine if psychoeducational services should be terminated. After an intervention has been in place for a reasonable period and improvement has been documented, the assessor should formulate an opinion concerning the necessity of continuing the intervention. Although a decision may be made to develop a generalization and maintenance plan, if generalization has occurred already, termination of services may be in order.

This 14-step procedural model of psychoeducational services for referred students should be viewed as a flexible process. It is an attempt to organize typical services in a logical sequence. In addition, feedback or refinement loops are available at each major decision point, allowing for redefinition of a problem, further assessment of a student, or redesigning of an intervention.

Chapter Summary

The law has been a double-edged sword for individuals providing services to children with disabilities. For the most part, the laws have been very helpful in securing services for these children. However, they sometimes cause the system to become rigid and inflexible and provide services in ways that may not be optimal. In the present system, children must be evaluated in specific ways and labeled as disabled before they can receive services. Some who need services still do not qualify under the existing guidelines. Many critics of the present system insist that all children who need help should receive it. Opponents of that proposal say a system is necessary to account for the money spent on special education. The prudent psychoeducational specialist will remember that the laws governing special education are useful tools for problem solving and advocating an appropriate education. It is important to understand the laws so that they may be used and applied to one's advantage.

Part Two

Technical Issues in Assessment

After reading material that was similar to what follows in this section of the book, a student remarked, or more accurately complained, that her goal—her only goal—was to help people and that the technical issues surrounding assessment seemed to offer little that was relevant to that goal. This student, along with many others, equates helping with working directly with children who have special needs. To some, the specialized technology that often accompanies these efforts seems antithetical to such a goal. However, given the structure of the system through which children are helped, providing quality assistance without a strong grounding in the technical issues is an impossibility. Measurement and statistics can be used either for or against children. Those who want to help children must understand such concepts to argue their side in the inevitable battles over the needs of children versus the needs of the system.

Part Two extends the discussion of foundational concepts begun in Part One but is presented separately because of its specialized and technical nature. Chapter 4 discusses the basic statistical concepts needed to understand, utilize, and interpret tests and test results. Chapter 5 can be viewed as a consumer's guide to the selection of tests because it discusses the three key ingredients to any test: reliability, validity, and norms.

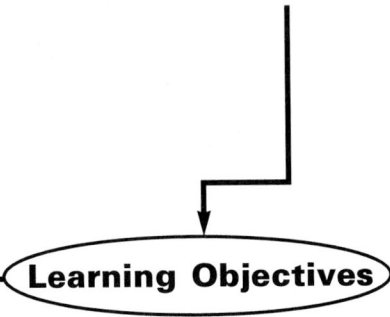

Chapter 4

Basic Statistical Concepts

Learning Objectives

1. Describe the four types of measurement scales.
2. Describe and interpret the following measures of central tendency: mean, median, mode.
3. Define variability and interpret both the range and standard deviation.
4. Interpret the meaning of standard scores and percentiles.
5. Interpret the type and degree of association between two variables.

During the early 1980s millions of people throughout the world spent countless hours almost oblivious to events occurring around them. The focus of their rapt attention was the Rubik's Cube, which outsold virtually every other puzzle or game in existence. The Rubik's Cube heightened interest in puzzles of all types, and prompted *Psychology Today* magazine to commission Dr. Robert Sternberg and Janet Davidson (1982) of Yale University to study the types of people who spend their time solving these puzzles. They tested the hypothesis that people who are good at puzzles and brainteasers are more intelligent than those who are not good at solving puzzles.

Sternberg and Davidson discovered that puzzle solving and intelligence (as defined by IQ) were highly correlated, thus indicating that people who solve certain types of puzzles are more intelligent than people who cannot solve the puzzles. Even more unusual was the fact that the time it took to solve the puzzles had a higher correlation (i.e., a stronger relationship) with IQ than did the number of puzzles solved correctly. The unusual aspect of this finding was that more intelligent people took *longer* to solve the puzzles than less intelligent people. Thus, the higher their IQ, the longer the individual took to solve a puzzle. This certainly seems to go against common sense, because one would expect that bright people solve problems more quickly than individuals with lower intelligence.

What do these results mean? Can we say that practice in solving puzzles causes you to be more intelligent? If someone is a poor problem solver, can we predict that the person is less intelligent? Should we recommend that a course in puzzle solving be introduced in every high school in the country? Why does it take smart people longer to solve puzzles? These and many more important questions can be asked about the findings. This chapter introduces the methods and techniques test developers and statisticians use to answer questions of this kind.

➡ *The Methods of Data Analysis*

One of Mr. Barton's high school students brought Sternberg and Davidson's *Psychology Today* article to class. Students questioned whether a test of puzzle solving could really be indicative of intelligence and whether more intelligent people really took longer to solve problems, so Mr. Barton decided to launch an investigation. As a first step, he constructed a 25-item test composed of brain twisters taken from Sternberg and Davidson's article. (Sample items are displayed in table 4.1.) He then administered the test to 20 students and noted the number of puzzles they were able to

---

Table 4.1   Sample Items from Mr. Barton's Test Questions

1. Water lilies double in area every 24 hours. At the beginning of the summer there is one water lily on a lake. It takes 60 days for the lake to become covered with water lilies. On what day is the lake half-covered?
2. If you have black socks and brown socks in your drawer, mixed in the ratio of 4 to 5, how many socks will you have to take out to make sure of having a pair of the same color?
3. How could two men play five games of checkers and each win the same number of games without any ties?
4. A bottle of wine costs $10. The wine was worth $9 more than the bottle. How much was the bottle worth? (Hint: The answer is not $1.)

Answers

1. Fifty-ninth day
2. Three socks
3. They were not playing with each other.
4. The bottle was worth $0.50, and the wine was worth $9.50.

Adapted from R. J. Sternberg and J. E. Davidson, "The Mind of the Puzzler" in *Psychology Today*, 16:37–44, 1982. Reprinted with permission from Psychology Today Magazine Copyright © 1982 (Sussex Publishers, Inc.)

Table 4.2   Data from Mr. Barton's Test

Student	Number of Puzzles Solved Correctly	Average Amount of Time Spent on Each Puzzle (in seconds)	IQ Score
Tommy	6	101	111
Jane	4	69	90
Linda	5	65	92
Larie	8	114	115
Anita	8	100	108
Sarah	7	64	99
Dustin	8	107	102
Bob	7	90	100
Mary	7	87	107
Katie	6	62	94
Ron	8	105	103
Deb	10	161	121
Mitzi	10	141	141
Wade	7	88	106
Wes	8	106	107
Brendon	8	89	99
Megan	9	121	110
Edna	9	110	118
Bunny	11	161	136
Flo	12	170	182

solve correctly. In addition, he recorded the time required by each student to solve the puzzles. Finally, he obtained the students' IQ scores. All of this information is displayed in table 4.2.

At first glance table 4.2 is a confusing array of numbers. What do all these scores mean? Is IQ related to puzzle-solving ability? Are Mr. Barton's results similar to Sternberg and Davidson's original findings? How do you tell? Some way of summarizing these scores must be found so that we can get an overall picture. In the following sections we introduce some terminology and a process for summarizing and understanding these data. The information will be useful in learning to apply statistical concepts to your own data and for reading research reports, but it is even more important in interpreting the statistical terminology found in tests and test manuals. The discussion begins with an overview of scales of measurement.

Measurement Scales

As a first step in clarifying the data it is important to determine what kinds of measurement scales were used. **Measurement** can be defined as assigning numbers to objects or events according to a set of rules. Clearly, not all types of measurement are the same. Measuring the size of an atom, for example, requires a vastly different type of measurement than measuring a student's knowledge about spelling rules. The types of measurement can be classified within a hierarchy according to the precision of the measurement and the types of arithmetical operations that can be performed. The four types of measurement scales are **nominal** scales, **ordinal** scales, **interval** scales, and **ratio** scales.

Nominal Scales

Sometimes the scores assigned to people have a qualitative rather than a quantitative meaning. Qualitative measurement is referred to as nominal scale measurement and represents the least sophisticated level of measurement because the scores are simply used for grouping people, objects, or events into categories. Examples of nominal scales are Democrat-Republican, Chevy-Ford-Chrysler, and girl-boy. Some statisticians claim that nominal measurement is not measurement at all, because the only measurement operation is the judgment of whether something is equal to (=) or not equal to (≠) other members of the category.

Many times nominal data are in the form of numbers, but the numbers still do not imply that something has been measured. For example, a researcher may say Female = 1 and Male = 2. In this case the numbers are much like the numbers on football players' jerseys, and they possess no numerical qualities. It would be inaccurate to say that it takes two females to equal one male. It would be equally inaccurate to average the numbers on football players to determine the winning team. With nominal level measurement, numbers simply refer to the names of objects or people.

Ordinal Scales

The term "ordinal" implies a rank ordering of the characteristic being measured. In a horse race, for example, we indicate which horses came in first, second, and third; the higher the ranking, the faster the horse. Here the relative magnitude is meaningful in that numbers are assigned according to the amount of the characteristic being measured (e.g., speed in a horse race). If Stefan Edberg, Jimmy Connors, Martina Navratilova, and Ann Landers would play in an imaginary tennis tournament, their rank order of finish should reflect their tennis skill. If Edberg finished first, he would do so because he performed better than Connors, who came in second. If Connors finished second it is likely that he did so because he played better than Navratilova, who finished third. Because Ann Landers is not known for her tennis ability, she would likely finish fourth. Thus, when these individuals are assessed according to their tennis skills, the fact that one received a higher ranking is based on ability. Contrast this with nominal scales, in which the numbers on the football jerseys did not have any meaning in terms of magnitude.

It should be noted that equal intervals do not usually exist between rankings. In the tennis tournament described above, a much greater difference in tennis ability exists between Landers and Navratilova (ranked fourth and third, respectively) than between Connors and Navratilova (ranked second and third, respectively). Similarly, the interval between kindergarten and 2nd grade is greater in terms of the number of basic academic skills learned in that time period than between 10th and 12th grades.

Measurements on an ordinal scale, however, tell us nothing about how much better Edberg was than Connors, only their relative ranking. Ordinal measurements thus may yield deceptive results when manipulated arithmetically. For example, if the director of a tennis tournament decided to make pairings for doubles based on the average ranking of the partners, he might pair ranks 2 and 3 against ranks 1 and 4, giving both teams an average ranking of 2.5. Unfortunately, the magnitude of the difference between Ann Landers (fourth place) and Martina Navratilova (third place) is so great that the pairings would not be equal. The team of Connors and Navratilova would probably be far superior to the Edberg and Landers team.

Interval Scales

Unlike the ordinal scale, equal differences between scores can be treated as equal units when using an interval scale. Interval scale measurement is rare in educational assessment and most common in the physical sciences, when measuring temperature with an ordinary thermometer. The 10-degree difference between the temperatures of 30°F and 40°F is assumed to be the same as the difference between 0°F and 90°F. The zero point in interval measurement, which indicates that zero amount of the attribute exists, is arbitrary. With temperature, for example, the zero point is not the beginning of the scale. Further, when the thermometer reads zero, it is incorrect to say that there is a total absence of temperature.

Ratio Scales

Like the interval scale, in the ratio scale there is equal distance between the variables being measured. The major difference is that with a ratio scale a true or real zero point exists. Measurements of height, weight, and length exemplify ratio scales that have a zero point and equal units.

Table 4.3   Characteristics of Measurement Scales

Scale	Characteristics
Nominal scale	Mutually exclusive categories
Ordinal scale	Mutually exclusive categories
	Magnitude
Interval scale	Mutually exclusive categories
	Magnitude
	Equal intervals
Ratio scale	Mutually exclusive categories
	Magnitude
	Equal intervals
	Absolute zero point

A second difference between ratio and interval scales is the computation of arithmetical operations. Addition and subtraction produce meaningful results with both types of scales. However, multiplication and division yield understandable results only when a true zero point exists, and these operations are appropriate only for ratio level measurement. Thus, it would not be accurate to say that 10°C (Centigrade) is twice as hot as 5°C because temperature is an interval scale. However, it would be correct to say that 10 feet is twice as long as 5 feet, because length is a ratio scale. Table 4.3 summarizes the major characteristics of each of the four kinds of scales. The scores on Mr. Barton's test would most likely be ordinal data. It would be wrong to say that a child who scores 120 on an IQ test is twice as smart as a child who scored 60. Also, there is no evidence for equal intervals between ranks.

Frequency Distributions—Organizing the Data

Now that we have some understanding of the type of data with which Mr. Barton was dealing, we can discuss some statistical procedures that will help us interpret the data. The next step in trying to summarize the puzzle-solving data might be for Mr. Barton to construct **frequency distributions** and **graphs.**

The frequency distribution for the number of puzzles solved correctly is presented in table 4.4. First, the scores were ranked from highest to lowest, and then the number of students who achieved each score was tallied. Already the scores are becoming easier to understand. For example, it is apparent that most students tend to score around the middle of the distribution, with a score of 8 being about average.

Table 4.4   Frequency Distribution of Puzzles Solved Correctly in Mr. Barton's Test

Score	Number of Students
4	I
5	I
6	II
7	IIII
8	IIIII
9	III
10	II
11	I
12	I

For an even clearer picture of the score distribution, we can draw graphs to represent the data visually. Figure 4.1 displays the number of puzzles solved correctly in the form of a bar graph, or histogram, and figure 4.2 presents the same data using a frequency curve polygon. By looking at the graphs it is easy to compare scores.

Central Tendency—The Mean, Median, and Mode

Three different statistics are used to describe the **central tendency,** or average, of the frequency distribution: the **mean, median,** and **mode.** A measure of central tendency is needed because it is useful to have one point that is representative of the distribution. Perhaps the best-known measure of central tendency is the mean. To calculate the mean you add all the scores and divide by the total number of scores. The procedure used to calculate the mean number of puzzles solved correctly and mean IQ in Mr. Barton's class is presented in table 4.5, which also introduces some basic statistical symbols. Each puzzle-solving score is represented by the letter X. When the 20 Xs are added, this summing process is shown as ΣX; the Greek capital letter sigma, Σ, is a symbol for "sum of the scores that follow." In table 4.5, IQ is represented by the letter Y, and thus ΣY means to add the Y scores. N simply refers to the number of people in each group, and when divided into ΣX yields the mean (M). Now if the students were to ask Mr. Barton how the class performed on the test, he could simply report the mean, which was 7.9 puzzles solved.

Although the mean is by far the most frequently used measure of central tendency, the median and mode are also reported, especially when data are ordinal or nominal. The mode is the score that occurs most frequently in the distribution. In table 4.2, for example, the score of 8 is the

Figure 4.1   Bar Graph of the Frequency Distribution of Puzzles Solved Correcly in Mr. Barton's Test

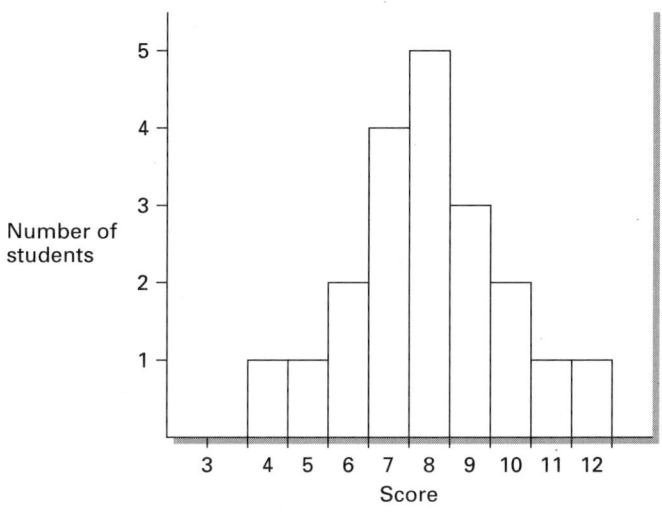

Figure 4.2   Frequency Curve Polygon of Puzzles Solved Correctly in Mr. Barton's Test

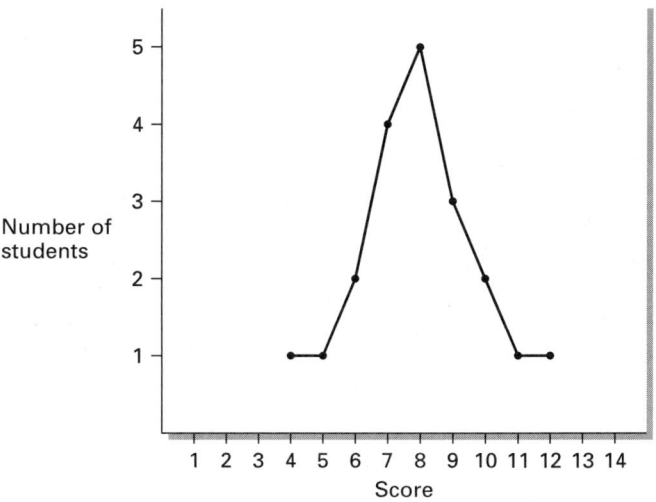

Table 4.5   Computation of the Mean Number of Puzzles Solved Correctly and Mean IQ in Mr. Barton's Test

Student	Number of Puzzles Solved Correctly (X)	IQ (Y)
Tommy	6	111
Jane	4	90
Linda	5	92
Larie	8	115
Anita	8	108
Sarah	7	99
Dustin	8	102
Bob	7	100
Mary	7	107
Katie	6	94
Ron	8	103
Deb	10	121
Mitzi	10	141
Wade	7	106
Wes	8	107
Brendon	8	99
Megan	9	110
Edna	9	118
Bunny	11	136
Flo	12	182
	$\Sigma X = 158$	$\Sigma Y = 2241$
	$N = 20$	$N = 20$
	$M = 7.9^{a}$	$M = 112.05^{b}$

$$^{a}M = \frac{\Sigma X}{N} = \frac{158}{20} = 7.9$$

$$^{b}M = \frac{\Sigma Y}{N} = \frac{2241}{20} = 112.05$$

mode, for it occurs most often. The median is the middle score—the one that divides the distribution in half: 50 percent of the scores fall above it and 50 percent fall below it. For example, suppose a test was administered to seven students who obtained the following scores: 12, 5, 10, 4, 9, 2, 6. If we reorder the scores from low to high (2, 4, 5, 6, 9, 10, 12), it is clear that the median is 6 because as many scores fall below it (2, 4, 5) as above it (9, 10, 12). It is the middle score and represents the 50th percentile.

Variability—The Range and Standard Deviation

To know only a person's raw score is of little value. Knowing where that score falls in relation to the mean is a little more helpful but can still be misleading. Scores are much easier to interpret if both the central tendency and the **variability** of the distribution are determined.

Variability refers to the extent to which scores differ from one another. If a test were given and the resulting scores were all the same, as would occur if everybody scored a perfect score, the distribution would have no variability. Suppose that you have two sets of data: A = 3, 5, 7 and B = 1, 5, 9. Notice that distributions A and B each have the same mean (5) but that they differ in the amount of variability. Distribution A is less variable around the mean than distribution B. Figure 4.3 displays ways in which the relationship between variability and central tendency can vary. Descriptions of two common measures of variability follow.

Range

The easiest way to calculate the variability of a distribution, or the **range,** is to subtract the lowest score from the highest score. To calculate the range of IQ scores in Mr. Barton's class (see table 4.5), you would subtract the lowest IQ, 90, from the highest IQ, 182. This yields a range of 92. The range is limited in its ability to reflect the variability of a distribution.

Standard Deviation

An index of the degree of variability in a distribution without the limitations of the range is the **standard deviation.** Understanding standard deviation is prerequisite to understanding and interpreting virtually all standardized tests. Conceptually, the standard deviation is a logical way to measure the variability of a distribution. If we want to assess the degree to which scores in a distribution differ from one another, it seems logical to base our assessment upon the extent to which scores deviate from the central value of the distribution. That is, one subtracts each score from the mean of the distribution. Table 4.6 shows how this is accomplished for the puzzle scores of the children in Mr. Barton's class.

The first step is to calculate the mean (M). Next, each student's score (X) is subtracted from the mean. These new scores, symbolized by the lowercase letter x, measure the distance of each score from the mean. At this point it may seem plausible simply to find the average variability by adding all of the x scores and dividing by the total number of scores. Unfortunately, when you add the distance scores for an average distance score, you will always get a sum of zero, because the mean is the

Figure 4.3   Variations in Normal Distributions

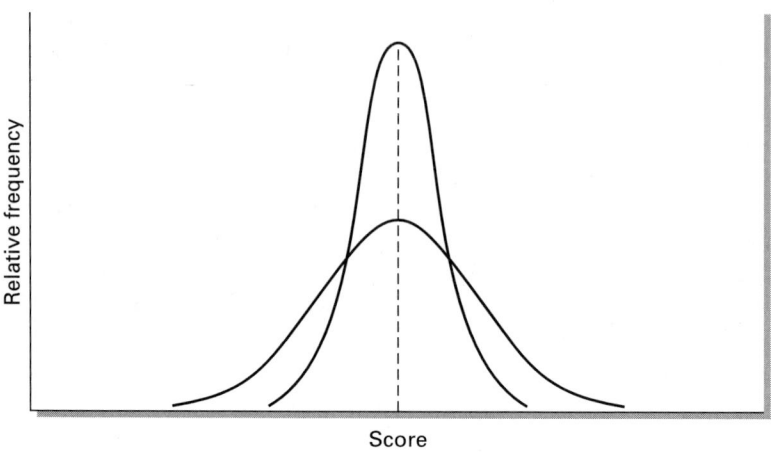

Score

(a) Equal means, unequal standard deviations

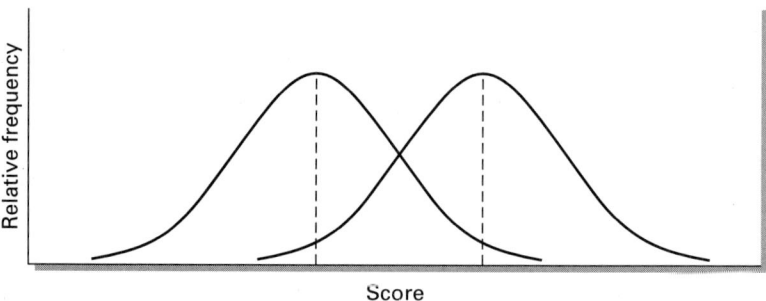

Score

(b) Unequal means, equal standard deviations

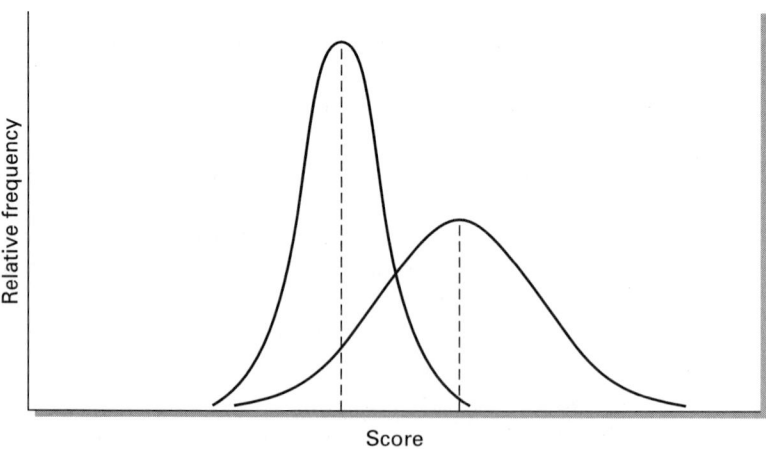

Score

(c) Unequal means, unequal standard deviations

Table 4.6   Computation of the Standard Deviation of the Puzzle Scores in Mr. Barton's Class

Student	Number of Puzzles Solved Correctly (X)	Mean Number of Puzzles Solved Correctly (M)	X − M = x	x^2
Tommy	6	7.9	−1.9	3.61
Jane	4	7.9	−3.9	15.21
Linda	5	7.9	−2.9	8.41
Larie	8	7.9	.1	.01
Anita	8	7.9	.1	.01
Sarah	7	7.9	−.9	.81
Dustin	8	7.9	.1	.01
Bob	7	7.9	−.9	.81
Mary	7	7.9	−.9	.81
Katie	6	7.9	−1.9	3.61
Ron	8	7.9	.1	.01
Deb	10	7.9	2.1	4.41
Mitzi	10	7.9	2.1	4.41
Wade	7	7.9	−.9	.81
Wes	8	7.9	.1	.01
Brendon	8	7.9	.1	.01
Megan	9	7.9	1.1	1.21
Edna	9	7.9	1.1	1.21
Bunny	11	7.9	3.1	9.61
Flo	12	7.9	4.1	16.81

$$SD = \sqrt{\frac{\Sigma x^2}{N}} = \sqrt{\frac{71.8}{20}} = 1.89$$

algebraic middle of the distribution. Instead, the distance scores must first be squared and then summed, thus eliminating the negative values. The average deviation of the squared distance scores (x^2) is then calculated as

$$\frac{\Sigma x^2}{N}$$

Since the distance scores were originally squared, this result is in the form of squared units. To return to regular units you calculate the square root. Thus, the standard deviation (SD) is determined as

$$\sqrt{\frac{\Sigma x^2}{N}}$$

The standard deviation for the number of puzzles solved correctly is 1.89. The meaning of this number will become more apparent as you read the next section on the normal curve.

The Normal Curve

The standard deviation is a particularly useful tool when used in conjunction with the normal distribution, or **normal curve.** For example, IQ test scores in the general population tend to conform to a normal distribution (see figure 4.4) with a mean of 100 and a standard deviation of 15. Since IQ scores form a normal distribution, we know that approximately 34 percent of the scores fall between the mean and one standard above the mean. Thus, approximately 68 percent of the population scores between 85 and 115 on IQ tests and approximately 96 percent scores between 70 and 130.

The normal or bell-shaped curve seen in figure 4.4 represents the distribution of such a large number of human attributes that it is used frequently in psychoeducational work, especially in educational measurement. If we were to examine the distribution of people on many physical or psychological attributes (e.g., height, weight, intelligence, and graduate school aptitude), a natural pattern would appear. This pattern is such that most people are about average, a few are moderately above or below average, and even fewer have extremely high or extremely low scores. If we plotted such a distribution it would resemble the familiar normal curve (see figure 4.5). Every normal curve has a single peak near the middle of the distribution, indicating frequently occurring scores, and then trails off in each direction, indicating that as we move away from the mean, we encounter fewer scores. We can take this a step further and say that the likelihood of obtaining a score near the middle of the distribution is very good but that it is much less likely that people will score at the extreme ends of the distribution. Hence, IQ scores of 100 are fairly common but not many people have scores above 140. Flo, in Mr. Barton's class, whose IQ is 182, is an extremely rare individual.

Standard Scores

One of the most frequent uses of the normal curve is to determine the degree to which an individual's score is unusual by comparing it to those of others. For example, many parents of preschoolers believe firmly that their child is "gifted." One such child, Megan, was recently tested with a popular preschool "intelligence" test. She earned a score of 600. Her parents were sure that any child who could score 600 must surely be gifted, and they eagerly awaited an interpretation of the test.

Figure 4.4 The Normal Distribution of IQ Scores

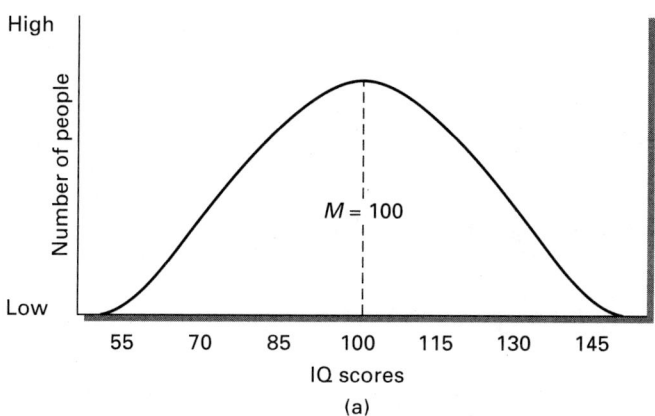

(a)

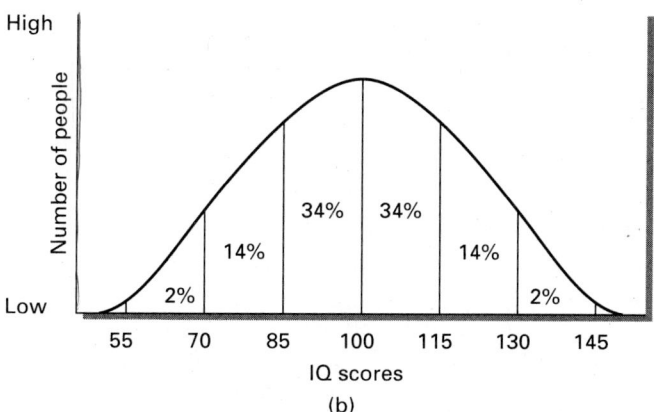

(b)

Since intelligence is normally distributed in the population, we can use the theoretical properties of the normal curve to determine whether Megan is in fact gifted. This is most easily accomplished through the use of a **standard score,** or z-score, which indicates the number of standard deviation units a particular raw score is either above or below the mean. Recall that approximately 16 percent of people score one or more standard deviations above the mean. We can convert a raw score to a z-score by the following formula:

$$\frac{X - M}{SD}$$

Figure 4.5   The Normal Curve

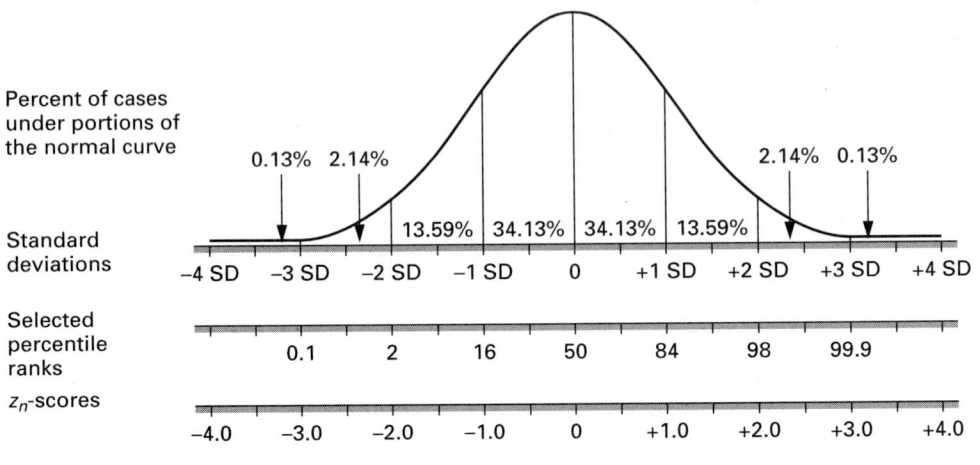

Percent of cases under portions of the normal curve

0.13% 2.14%   13.59% | 34.13% | 34.13% | 13.59%   2.14% 0.13%

Standard deviations

−4 SD   −3 SD   −2 SD   −1 SD   0   +1 SD   +2 SD   +3 SD   +4 SD

Selected percentile ranks

0.1   2   16   50   84   98   99.9

z_n-scores

−4.0   −3.0   −2.0   −1.0   0   +1.0   +2.0   +3.0   +4.0

---

where X = child's score, M = mean of distribution, and SD = standard deviation of distribution. On the test given to Megan, the mean is 500 and the standard deviation is 100. Thus, Megan's z-score is determined as follows:

$$z = \frac{600 - 500}{100} = 1.00$$

From her z-score it would appear that Megan is above average but not gifted. Since the z-score is in standard deviation units, a score of 1.00 indicates that Megan is one standard deviation above the mean. The normal curve (figure 4.5) shows that one standard deviation above the mean is better than the scores of about 84 percent of the population and thus not really rare. If only those in the top 2 percent of the population are defined as gifted (as is fairly common in education), a z-score of 2.00 would be needed for a child to be labeled "gifted." To have a z-score of 2.00, Megan would need a raw score of 700:

$$z = \frac{700 - 500}{100} = 2.00$$

By using a similar procedure with other scores, even though they may have different means and standard deviations, it is possible to determine exactly how extreme a particular score is. If we return to Mr. Barton's data, we can see that Mitzi's z-score for the number of puzzles solved correctly (z = 1.06) is an above-average score. This score is calculated as follows:

$$z = \frac{10 - 8}{1.89} = 1.058 = 1.06$$

Figure 4.6   Mary's Scores on Two Tests

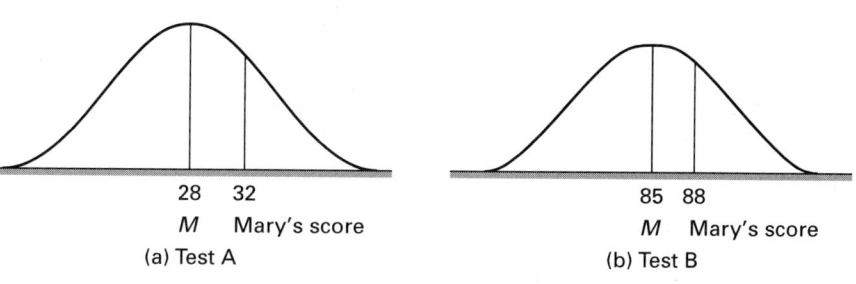

28 32	85 88
M Mary's score	*M* Mary's score
(a) Test A	(b) Test B

Standard scores are also useful if we have a person's scores on two tests and want to know on which test the individual performed better. The use of standard scores allows us to convert the two tests to a common scale. For example, if Mary scored 32 on Test A, with a mean of 28 and a standard deviation of 4, and she scored 88 on Test B, with a mean of 85 and a standard deviation of 6, which was the relatively better score? Figure 4.6 displays her scores graphically. We can see that her score on Test A is relatively farther from the mean than her score on Test B; that is, a greater percentage of persons scored lower than Mary on Test A than on Test B. Thus, Mary did relatively better on Test A. It would be inefficient to plot distributions of scores on both tests to answer questions of this type. Standard scores can be used to answer such questions more effectively:

$$z\text{-score on Test A} = \frac{32 - 28}{4} = \frac{4}{4} = 1$$

$$z\text{-score on Test B} = \frac{88 - 85}{6} = \frac{3}{6} = .5$$

Since her z-score is higher for Test A, it is apparent that she did relatively better on that test.

Percentiles

Percentiles are a more common and understandable way of expressing a person's relative position in a distribution than are standard scores. A percentile is the point on a distribution below which a given percentage of the scores are found. For example, the 44th percentile is the point on the distribution below which 44 percent of the cases fall. By definition, the percentile rank for the median is 50 because 50 percent of the cases fall at or below the median. As another example, a score of 36 on a given

Figure 4.7   Illustration of a Percentile

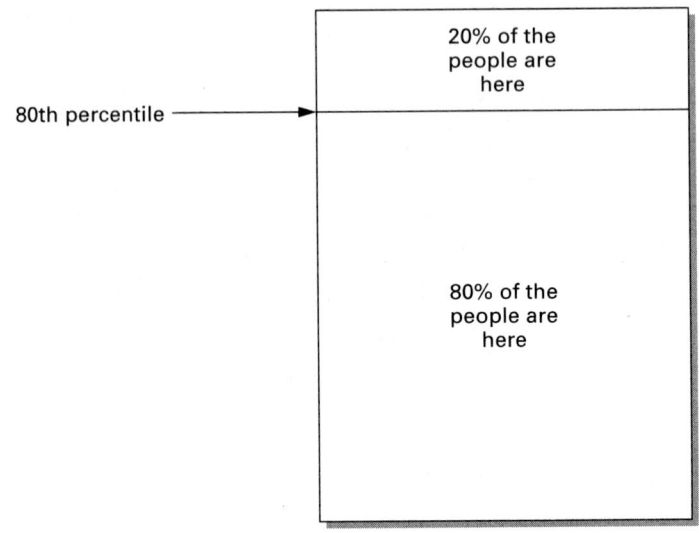

80th percentile ⟶

20% of the people are here

80% of the people are here

test is at the 60th percentile if 60 percent of the scores are below it. On a different test, a score of 36 might be at the 20th percentile because only 20 percent of the cases fall at or below it (see figure 4.7).

Percentiles are popular because they appear easy to understand and interpret and are relatively easy to calculate. However, one problem in understanding and interpreting percentiles is that they are frequently confused with percentages, especially by parents and students. In testing, percentages usually refer only to the percentage of correct or incorrect answers.

Correlation—A Measure of the Relationship Between Two Variables

Let's return to Sternberg and Davidson's (1982) findings that puzzle-solving ability is related to intelligence and that the higher the IQ, the more time taken for puzzle solving. Sternberg and Davidson used **correlation** to assess the relationship between puzzle solving and intelligence. Correlation is simply a measure of how things are related to one another. In this context, "related" means that people who score one way on the puzzle-solving test tend to score in a predictable way on the IQ test. If high scores on one test tend to correspond with high scores on the other test, the two tests are said to have a *positive correlation*. If high scores on one test tend to correspond with low scores on the other test, the tests are said to have a *negative correlation*. If scores on one test have no relationship to scores on the other test, we say there is *no correlation* between the tests.

The Pearson product moment correlation, symbolized by *r*, is the most common method of assessing the correlation between variables. The correlation coefficient can range from −1.00 to +1.00. The smaller the correlation coefficient, whether positive or negative, the weaker the relationship between variables. Correlations close to zero would mean that little or no relationship exists between variables. Positive numbers, such as +.87, denote positive relationships and negative numbers, such as −.87, indicate a negative correlation. The positive or negative *sign* of the correlation does not indicate the strength of the relationship, only the direction. Two variables that have a negative correlation coefficient of −.92 would thus be more strongly related than two variables that have a +.36 correlation.

The correlation data for Mr. Barton's experiment are presented in table 4.7. Examine the table closely and try to determine the type of relationship, if any, between puzzle solving and IQ. Those with a sharp eye may be able to detect that a positive relationship exists. However, when analyzing a large number of scores, it is usually difficult to tell by visual inspection the type of relationship between two variables. **Scatterplots** are often used for this purpose. To construct a scatterplot of the data of table 4.7, we plot each pair of *X* and *Y* scores as a geometric point (see figure 4.8). This scatterplot represents the puzzle-solving and IQ scores for the 20 students in Mr. Barton's class. It is apparent from the scatterplot that a positive relationship does exist. If the relationship were negative, it would resemble the scatterplot in figure 4.9. Notice that as scores on one test increase, those on the other decreased. However, in figure 4.8, as scores on the IQ test increased, so did puzzle-solving scores.

Sternberg and Davidson reported the relatively high positive correlation of .66 between number of puzzles solved correctly and IQ. How would we compute a similar correlation for Mr. Barton's data? Table 4.7 shows the steps for calculating the Pearson product moment correlation, which describes the relationship between the two sets of scores. Note that there *r* = .84, which is higher than the correlation of .66 obtained by Sternberg and Davidson. Mr. Barton was also interested in knowing if those students with higher IQ scores took longer to solve puzzles. Try figuring this out on your own from the data in table 4.2. You should discover that the correlation is .85.

Correlation takes some time and work to understand, but it will help you grasp other concepts in this book. Therefore, although it is not essential to know how to calculate a correlation coefficient, it is important to understand what a correlation means.

Table 4.7   Computation of Pearson Product Moment Correlation (r) for Mr. Barton's Test

Number of Puzzles Solved Correctly (X)	X^2	IQ (Y)	Y^2	XY
6	36	111	12,321	666
4	16	90	8,100	360
5	25	92	8,464	460
8	64	115	13,225	920
8	64	108	11,664	864
7	49	99	9,801	693
8	64	102	10,404	816
7	49	100	10,000	700
7	49	107	11,449	749
6	36	94	8,836	564
8	64	103	10,609	824
10	100	121	14,641	1,210
10	100	141	19,881	1,410
7	49	106	11,236	742
8	64	107	11,449	856
8	64	99	9,801	792
9	81	110	12,100	990
9	81	118	13,924	1,062
11	121	136	18,496	1,496
12	144	182	33,124	2,184
$\Sigma X = 158$	$\Sigma X^2 = 1{,}320$	$\Sigma Y = 2{,}241$	$\Sigma Y^2 = 259{,}525$	$\Sigma XY = 18{,}358$

$$r = \frac{N\,\Sigma XY - \Sigma X\,\Sigma Y}{\sqrt{[N\,\Sigma X^2 - (\Sigma X)^2]\,[N\,\Sigma Y^2 - (\Sigma Y)^2]}}$$

$$r = \frac{20 \times 18{,}358 - 158 \times 2{,}241}{\sqrt{[[20 \times 1{,}320 - (158)^2][20 \times 259{,}545 - (2{,}241)^2]]}}$$

$$r = \frac{13{,}082}{15{,}551.52} = .84$$

Figure 4.8   Scatterplot of the IQ and Puzzle-Solving Scores of Mr. Barton's Students

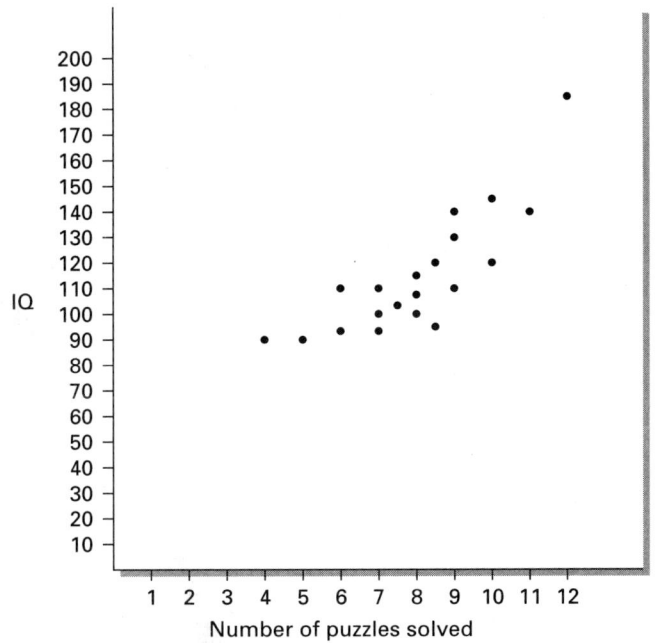

Figure 4.9   Scatterplot of a Fictitious Negative Relationship

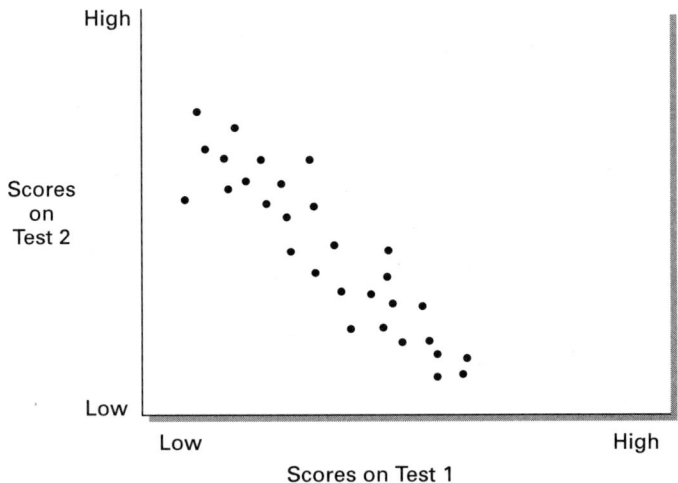

Chapter Summary

In this chapter we described a variety of techniques for organizing test scores and other data. Data management techniques are dictated to some extent by the level of measurement used: nominal, ordinal, interval, or ratio. The first step in organizing data is to develop a frequency distribution that specifies how many people received a particular score. Techniques for describing the frequency distribution include those that describe its central tendency (mean, median, and mode) and those that reflect the variability in the distribution (range and standard deviation). Standard scores and percentiles tell how a particular person scored relative to others. The chapter concluded with a discussion of correlation, which assesses the relationship between two variables.

Some people feel that statistics makes everyone the same, that is, it reduces people to numbers and these numbers do not convey the uniqueness of any one person. Although it is true that statistics can be misused, it is important to keep in mind that statistical analyses would not be needed if everyone were the same. It is because of the rich variety among individuals that statistics, when properly understood and used, can be helpful.

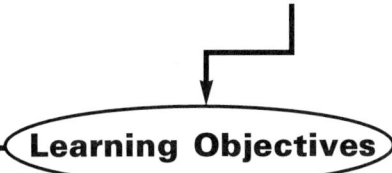

Chapter 5

Essential Characteristics of Tests: Reliability, Validity, and Norms

Learning Objectives

1. List sources of error in test scores.
2. Define each major type of reliability.
3. Define each major type of validity.
4. List the major criteria by which a normative sample can be evaluated.
5. List and describe sources of information for use in the evaluation of tests.

The Department of Mathematics at Johns Hopkins University in Baltimore conducted a talent search a few years ago to locate 11th-grade students who showed exceptional promise in math. Teachers in the area were contacted and invited to send their brightest math students to the contest. Julian C. Stanley, director of the Study of Mathematically Precocious Youths at Johns Hopkins University heard about the contest and asked to nominate some children. His was a special case, because the students he had in mind were not in any of his classes and he was obviously not an 11th-grade teacher. His only prior dealings with students had been three years earlier, when he had administered the mathematical part of the College Entrance Examination Board's Scholastic Aptitude Test (SAT-M). Stanley received permission to submit nominees, and eventually 10 of his nominees took the math department's test. The results of the contest were astonishing:

Among the 51 people who entered the contest, the 10 chosen by Stanley [based on their scores] SAT-M ranked 1, 2, 3, 5.5, 7, 8, 12, 16.5, 19, 23.5. Points earned by the top three were 140, 112, and 91. The highest scoring person nominated only by a teacher scored 83. Just 3 of 10 ranks, 2, 5.5, and 19, had also been nominated by their teachers. The No. 1 contestant was not nominated by his teacher. He is quite able mathematically but had been far from the top of the 396 entrants in my March 1972 SAT-M contest. Most of the higher scorers from that testing had already skipped beyond the 11th grade and therefore were not eligible to enter the math department's contest. (The ablest of them, a 16-year-old Hopkins student, had already completed a junior-year course in mathematical analysis with a final grade of A.) (Stanley, 1976, p. 313)

The results were so astounding because teachers who had known their students for almost an entire year could not compete with three-year-old SAT-M scores in selecting the best math talent. In fact, one of the teacher nominees received only two points, whereas the lowest rank of the SAT-M nominees was 23.5 out of 51.

This represents a striking example of the value of tests. However, before we conclude that the test was far superior to the teacher in determining talent, let's keep in mind that the contest was really just another test. A cynic would say that the only math talent identified by the test was the ability to take another test.

Not all tests are as good as the SAT-M; some have inadequate norms and poor standardization, and many do not have any demonstrated validity. How can you distinguish between good tests and poor tests? How can you select a test that is suitable for your purposes? What are some of the characteristics of good tests? This chapter discusses three technical components that contribute to the quality of a test: reliability, validity, and norms.

➡ *Reliability*

At the Olympics in Mexico City during the summer of 1968, Bob Beamon won a gold medal by broad jumping over 28 feet. This was about 3 feet further than any human being had ever jumped. Some sports authorities now recognize that jump as the single greatest athletic accomplishment ever. Until much later, no one, including Beamon himself, even came close to equaling that record. If the event is examined objectively, the question must be asked, "Did the jump represent Beamon's true jumping ability or was it a rare fluke?" Since Beamon's jumps before and after the record setter were nowhere close to 28 feet, we may assume the jump was a fluke; that is, a rare combination of factors may have combined and resulted in the record-setting performance. We might conclude that the jump was not an accurate representation of Beamon's jumping ability because it could not be repeated.

An only slightly less rare event occurred in the 1976 Olympics, when Nadia Comenich of Romania scored a perfect 10 points in the gymnastics competition. However, her score did appear to be a much more reliable indicator of her true athletic ability, because the 14-year-old performer repeatedly received ratings of 10 in various other competitions.

Whether we are measuring athletic ability or spelling skill, concern arises about the degree to which the result is a true measure of a person's ability. In the terminology of educational and psychological measurement, this is a concern about **reliability.** Reliability involves the degree to which we get the same result when repeatedly measuring the same thing. Since Nadia Comenich's achievements were repeated and Bob Beamon's were not, we would say that her score was a reliable measure of her gymnastics skill but that his broad jump was not a reliable measure of his jumping ability.

The same kind of logic can be applied to educational and psychological tests. For example, Jill and Toni studied together for a midterm physics exam, and both seemed to know the material equally well. However, when the test was given, Toni scored much higher than Jill. In talking, they discovered some reasons for the difference in scores. Jill had had a cold and did not sleep well the night before. Further, she had had a bad case of test anxiety and said she had not been able to think clearly. Toni, on the other hand, was feeling great the day of the test. In addition, some of the examples on the test involved the application of physics problems to automobiles. Since Toni is in an automotive repair class this term and Jill is not, her score, relative to Jill's, could have been enhanced. They both said that they had had to guess at some of the answers, but Toni had evidently guessed correctly more often. This illustrates a case in which both students had about the same true ability in physics but extraneous factors caused them to receive different scores.

Learning some basic terminology will allow us to explain what happened to Jill and Toni more precisely. We can divide each of their scores into two parts. The first, and preferably the major, part of their score reflects their knowledge about physics. This score is referred to as a **hypothetical true score.** It is called hypothetical because there is really no way we can determine their actual knowledge of physics. The other part of their scores, or the **error score,** consists of all factors that caused their scores to fluctuate, including guesses, fatigue, and anxiety. Theoretically, it is impossible ever to know a person's true score because some error factor is always present.

Symbolically, we represent a person's score, X, as follows:

$$X = T + E$$

where

$$X = \text{test score}$$
$$T = \text{true score}$$
$$E = \text{error score}$$

This equation, while quite theoretical, represents a most essential concept for the practitioner: *Every score obtained while assessing a child contains some degree of error.* Even the best test may over- or underestimate a child's true ability. This is a critical piece of information if important educational decisions are made on the basis of the obtained score. In many states, one criterion for classifying a student as mentally disabled is an IQ score of 69 or below. What if the child scored exactly 69? Given that there is some error in the test score, caution must be exercised in deciding to label the child as retarded. Certainly the error could have worked in the child's favor, and the true IQ may be only 63. However, if the error worked against the child, the true IQ may be closer to 75. In a problem-solving process involving a child's placement, factors such as illness or motivation, which could have affected the test performance and thus inflated or deflated the error component, should be considered. Test scores are not unalterable facts but instead are subject to error, just as a teacher's judgments are liable to fluctuate.

Tests are not the only form of assessment for which reliability must be a concern. Simply observing a child in class is also subject to such problems. If two people were to observe the same child, would they see the same things? Would they agree that a certain behavior occurred or failed to occur? Unless observations are highly structured, two people are likely to disagree about what they saw. Although this chapter will primarily focus on reliability as it applies to standardized tests, the reader should bear in mind that reliability is *always* a concern, whether the assessment takes the form of standardized tests, informal tests, interviews, or observations.

Types of Reliability

You are likely to encounter many of the numerous methods for computing test reliability as you read test manuals. The more common methods include test-retest, equivalent form, split-half, and internal consistency.

Test-Retest Reliability

Recall that reliability refers to the extent to which we get the same result when repeatedly measuring the same thing. A logical way to establish the reliability of a test would then be to measure the same person twice and compare the results. This is precisely what is done in the **test-retest** procedure. Table 5.1 illustrates this process using a kindergarten screening test that was administered to the same 20 children on a Monday and again on the following Friday. (*Note:* Reliabilities are rarely, if ever, computed on only five scores, but only five are utilized here.) Correlations are computed for both sets of scores, yielding the reliability coefficient r_{xx}. This symbol is used to designate reliability because the Pearson product moment correlation r is often used for assessing reliability. The subscript $_{xx}$ refers to the correlation of a test x with itself.

Table 5.1   Test-Retest Reliability of a Kindergarten Screening Test

Student	Number of Answers Correct	
	Test	Retest
1	9	10
2	7	6
3	5	1
4	3	5
5	1	3

$$r_{xy} = \frac{N\,\Sigma XY - (\Sigma X)(\Sigma Y)}{\sqrt{[N\,\Sigma X^2 - (\Sigma X)^2][N\,\Sigma Y^2 - (\Sigma Y)^2]}}$$

$$r = \frac{150}{\sqrt{(200)(230)}}$$

$$r = .70$$

Although the test-retest method is useful, it is used very seldom in the actual computation of reliability, because it can over- or underestimate the reliability coefficient. A spuriously high reliability coefficient may be obtained when the second test is given too soon following the initial testing, because students may recall their first responses and tend to respond in the same way (Blood & Budd, 1972). If the test-retest interval is too long, however, the reliability coefficient may be artificially low, because a person's true score may change during that time as, for example, additional skills may be learned. Another problem with the test-retest method is that having students take the same test twice is an inefficient use of time.

If a test-retest reliability coefficient is reported in a test manual, the interval between testings must also be reported. The evaluation of the length of the interval is a subjective process. If a relatively stable trait, such as intelligence, is being measured, a longer interval may be used. However, when assessing a skill such as arithmetic ability, which can change relatively quickly when learning new material, the value of r_{xx} is likely to be reduced with long intervals.

Equivalent-Form Reliability

If a test of math aptitude is being constructed, one way to assess a person's true ability would be to construct a test using all possible math questions. Of course this is impractical because such a test would contain millions of questions beginning with simple number recognition and continuing through advanced mathematical theory. Most math tests thus sample only a few of all possible items. If the sample is representative of the larger domain of items, we can generalize from the sample to the domain. Given the extremely large number of potential tests measuring math aptitude, it should be possible to construct several equivalent tests. Each would be a measure of math aptitude, and although they would have different items, each should provide equally good estimates of a person's true score.

Using this example, it seems logical to determine correlations between the two alternative forms of the same test as a measure of reliability. This method of reliability computation is referred to as **equivalent-** or **parallel-form reliability.** If the test is reliable, the scores on separate tests should be relatively consistent. Figure 5.1 illustrates this process using an analogy suggested by Gleitman (1981). The bull's-eye represents a person's true score. Each shot aimed at the bull's-eye symbolizes an attempt at measuring a person's true score. When the instrument firing the shots is reliable, each measure will be close to the bull's-eye. However, much more scatter is present when the measurements come from an unreliable source.

Although the use of equivalent forms as a measure of reliability can be more easily justified from a theoretical perspective, this method shares some of the shortcomings of the test-retest method, including requiring students to sit through two test sessions, and determining the appropriate length of the interval between testings. In addition, it is difficult to construct a second form that is truly equivalent, because both tests should have identical means and standard deviations.

Split-Half Reliability

In one sense, the split-half method is identical to the equivalent forms method. **Split-half reliability** is determined by dividing one test into two parts of equal lengths. One common method of dividing the test is by odd- and even-numbered questions. Each person then receives a score for both sets of questions. The "equivalent forms" in this case are the halves of the same test. The reliability coefficient is derived by determining the correlation between the halves.

A primary difference between this method and equivalent-form reliability is that with this method the length of the test is halved. This can be a problem because longer tests are generally more reliable than shorter ones, because they are less affected by factors that can increase measurement error, such as guessing. The Spearman-Brown formula has been developed to correct for the shorter test length and is reported frequently in test manuals.

Compared to the test-retest and equivalent-form methods of calculating reliability, the split-half approach has the advantage of requiring only one test administration. Because the data are thus available even if the test-retest procedure is used, most test manuals that report reliability will give a split-half reliability coefficient, regardless of other methods used.

**Figure 5.1   Analogy of Equivalent-Form Reliability
Using Shots at a Bull's-Eye**

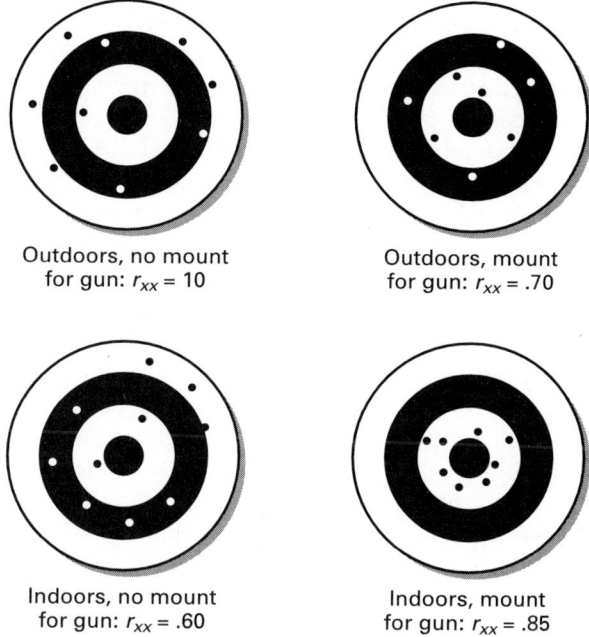

Outdoors, no mount
for gun: r_{xx} = 10

Outdoors, mount
for gun: r_{xx} = .70

Indoors, no mount
for gun: r_{xx} = .60

Indoors, mount
for gun: r_{xx} = .85

Adapted from *Psychology* by Henry Gleitman, by permission of W. W. Norton &
Company, Inc. Copyright © 1981 by W. W. Norton & Company, Inc.

However, split-half reliabilities may be inflated somewhat because these
estimates do not reflect errors of measurement due to changes in the student over time. For example, error related to a student's particularly bad
mood on test day would not be reflected with the split-half procedure,
because the entire test would probably be affected by the mood.

Internal Consistency

Although split-half reliability measures the **internal consistency** of a test,
it is used less often today than the Kuder-Richardson formula 20 (KR-20)
and coefficient alpha, which are also derived from a single test. These
procedures reflect the degree to which an individual's test performance is
consistent from item to item. Under most conditions, both procedures
yield roughly consistent results (Lindeman & Merenda, 1979).

The Standard Error of Measurement

The preceding methods of calculating the reliability coefficient help to answer the question, "How consistently do we get the same result when repeatedly measuring the same thing?" Another reliability question deals with the amount of variation expected in a score, or "How much confidence can we place in this score?" This is an important issue in interpreting the meaning of a score. If a person's score is 69, are we reasonably sure that it represents a true score?

The **standard error of measurement** can answer these questions, as the example of Bob Beamon's Olympic broad jump can illustrate. Recall that Beamon made one jump of over 28 feet, a distance much further than he jumped before or since. If we examine his feat more closely, we can see that it was not a reliable measure of how well he could routinely jump. Table 5.2 presents data on 10 hypothetical jumps Beamon could have made prior to his record jump and 10 jumps he might have made following the Olympics. Figure 5.2 displays a graph of these data. Note that there is some variability in the jumps, perhaps related to factors such as motivation, anxiety, illness, and weather. Notice also that the higher scores in the distribution are statistically rarer. It is thus clear that the 28-foot jump is not representative of his jumping ability. Which distance is representative? Measurement theory dictates that the mean of this distribution is the most logical reflection of Beamon's true jumping ability. Excluding the 28-foot jump, Beamon's mean from table 5.2 is 24.5 feet. Any of the jumps that deviate from this measure of his true jumping ability would be attributable to error. In other words, if Beamon were in perfect condition each time he jumped and if all other factors remained constant, he would always jump the same distance.

If we wanted to measure the variability of Beamon's jumps, the standard deviation would be the appropriate means. In this case the standard deviation would be a measure of the degree to which Beamon's jumps deviated from his true jumping ability. In measurement terminology, the extent to which a particular jump deviates from his true jumping ability is considered error, because Beamon would jump the same distance each time if sources of error did not cause variations. In a sense, the standard deviation would characterize the amount of error in the distribution. This special type of standard deviation is called the **standard error of measurement,** although it is really a standard deviation of measurement error. The standard error of measurement, or SEM, is directly related to the reliability of a test and is calculated as follows:

$$SEM = SD_x \sqrt{1 - r_{xx}}$$

where

SD_{xx} = standard deviation of obtained scores

r_{xx} = test reliability

Table 5.2	Bob Beamon's Broad Jumps Before and After His Olympic Jump	

Hypothetical Jumps before Olympics (feet)	Hypothetical Jumps after Olympics (feet)
24	26
23	23
24	24
25	25
25	24
25	24
23	25
26	25
24	26
24	25

Figure 5.2   Graph of Bob Beamon's Olympic Broad Jump and Jumps Before and After

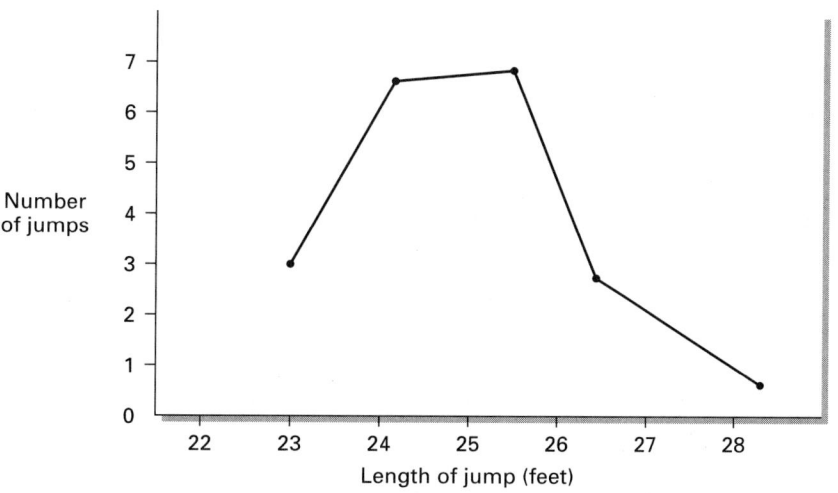

Tests that have higher reliability coefficients have a lower SEM. This means that more confidence can be placed on scores from reliable tests because they have less error. In other words, there is less variability of obtained scores around the true score. However, a relatively larger standard deviation tends to increase the standard error of measurement.

A Practical Use of the Standard Error of Measurement

All test scores contain some degree of error. It is difficult to communicate the concept of test error to laypeople who try to interpret educational and psychological tests. Many tend to believe that a person's obtained score is the true score. In actuality, the person is likely to obtain a *different* score if given the test again. To the extent that a test is reliable, the magnitude of the difference between the two test scores will be small. The SEM can be used to communicate this rather complex array of information to others in a relatively straightforward manner using **confidence intervals.**

A confidence interval provides a range of scores rather than an exact score. Instead of indicating that John has an IQ of 110, we would say that John's IQ is between 105 and 115. In this way, we indicate that his score is probably within 5 points of 110 but not exactly 110.

We can increase the precision of our communication by indicating our degree of confidence that the true score will be within the interval. For example, we might say that we are 68 percent confident that John's score is between 105 and 115. We are able to make this type of statement by applying our knowledge of the normal curve. Recall that 68 percent of the cases in a distribution fall within one standard deviation of the mean. When using the SEM, we can say that 68 percent of the time the true score will fall within one SEM of the obtained score (and about 16% of the score would be above and another 16% below the confidence interval).

To establish a confidence interval, the first step is to select the degree of confidence desired. The most commonly used intervals are the 68-percent and the 95-percent confidence levels, because they correspond with one and two standard deviations, respectively. Next, the z-score associated with the particular level of confidence is selected. For example, the z-score corresponding to the 95-percent confidence level is 1.96. This z-score is then multiplied by the SEM to yield one-half of the confidence interval. This one-half interval is then added to and subtracted from the obtained score. An example from the Wechsler Intelligence Scale for Children (WISC-R) (Wechsler, 1974) will illustrate. On the WISC-R the SEM for children 11 1/2 years old is 2.96. If a child of that age obtains an IQ score of 100 on the test, the 95-percent confidence level is derived by multiplying the z-score corresponding to the 95 percent level (1.96) by the SEM (2.96) to obtain a value of 5.8. Typically, this value is rounded off and then both added to and subtracted from the obtained score. In this example, we would say that we are 95 percent confident the student's score is 100, plus or minus 6. Alternatively, we could say that we are 95 percent certain that the *range* of scores from 94 to 106 contains the child's true IQ.

It should be noted that as the confidence interval increases, the band of scores must become wider. However, it is not possible to establish 100-percent confidence boundaries.

Some test users may resist the use of confidence intervals because they make for unduly tenuous statements. However, people do change, and our assessment procedures have not reached a level of precision that enables us to communicate more precisely. To do otherwise misinforms the recipient of test information. The use of confidence intervals may prevent such nonsense as rigidly adhering to a single criterion of 130 IQ for placement in a program for the "gifted" that puts one child who has an IQ of 131 in such a program and denies admission to another child with an IQ of 129. In actuality, the range of true scores for both children overlaps markedly.

Factors Affecting Reliability

The reliability of a test can be affected by a variety of factors. Table 5.3 lists the more common factors that can influence test scores and thus the reliability of a test. Some factors, such as whether a child guesses on questions, are not under the control of the person giving the test. Others, such as ambiguous instructions, can be eliminated by careful test design and administration. In reporting test results to others, it is important to note factors that may have influenced the reliability of the test scores. Motivational lapses in those being tested, for example, are some of the more common reasons given for poor test performances.

➡ *Validity*

Validity, or the extent to which a test fulfills its function, is the sine qua non of educational and psychological tests. Put another way, a test is valid if it measures what it is supposed to measure. Reliability, you will recall, refers to how consistently and accurately a test measures *something*. What the "something" is really does not matter in determining reliability. Thus, a test can have high reliability and yet not be valid for your particular purpose. Reaction time, for example, can be very reliably measured, but it is not a valid measure of intelligence. Reliability is a necessary, but not a sufficient, condition for validity. This means that a test *must* be measuring a trait or skill consistently *before* it can be considered to measure what it is supposed to measure.

When we measure height, there is little question about the validity of a tape measure for this purpose. However, other concepts are not so easily defined. For example, suppose we want to measure a child's motivation. Most people would agree that motivation is an important determinant of how a child functions in school. If you think of various children with whom you are acquainted, you can probably categorize some as "motivated" and others as "unmotivated." Now comes the tricky part. What is it about these children that causes you to give them such labels? What specific kinds of behaviors did you think about when you evaluated

---

Table 5.3   Factors Affecting Test Reliability

I. Lasting and general characteristics of the individual
   1. General skills (e.g., reading)
   2. General ability to comprehend instructions, testwiseness, techniques of taking tests
   3. Ability to solve problems of the general type presented in this test
   4. Attitudes, emotional reactions, or habits generally operating in situations like the test situations (e.g., self-confidence)
II. Lasting and specific characteristics of the individual
   1. Knowledge and skills required by particular problems in the test
   2. Attitudes, emotional reactions, or habits related to particular test stimuli (e.g., fear of high places brought to mind by an inquiry about such fears on a personality test)
III. Temporary and general characteristics of the individual (systematically affecting performance on various tests at a particular time)
   1. Health, fatigue, and emotional strain
   2. Motivation, rapport with examiner
   3. Effects of heat, light, ventilation, etc.
   4. Level of practice on skills required by tests of this type
   5. Present attitudes, emotional reactions, or strength of habits (insofar as these are departures from the person's average or lasting characteristics—e.g., political attitudes during an election campaign)
IV. Temporary and specific characteristics of the individual
   1. Changes in fatigue or motivation developed by this particular test (e.g., discouragement resulting from failure on a particular item)
   2. Fluctuations in attention, coordination, or standards of judgment
   3. Fluctuations in memory for particular facts
   4. Level of practice on skills or knowledge required by this particular test (e.g., effects of special coaching)
   5. Temporary emotional states, strength of habits, etc., related to particular test stimuli (e.g., a question calls to mind a recent bad dream)
   6. Luck in the selection of answers by "guessing"

From R. L. Thorndike, *Personal Selection.* John Wiley & Sons, New York, 1949. Reprinted by permission.

motivation? How fast the child completes assigned work? Previous work habits? Attitude? How would you construct a test to measure motivation? Would it be capable of measuring motivation in every situation and circumstance? Could it tell you if a child would be motivated in both math and reading?

Obviously, constructing a test to measure a concept such as motivation is a difficult task, and not everyone will agree on the best method for measuring motivation. At the outset, we wish to reinforce Cronbach's (1970) assertion that we cannot ask the general question, "Is this a valid test?" Instead, the question should be rephrased: "Is this a valid test for the purpose for which it is intended?" A test that has been validated for assessing intelligence may be totally useless when used to diagnose neurological problems even though neurological functioning and intelligence may both utilize cognitive processes.

In 1974, a joint committee of the American Psychological Association, the American Educational Research Association, and the National Council on Measurement in Education met to grapple with some of these issues and identified three separate methods for evaluating the validity of a test: content validity, criterion-related validity, and construct validity.

Content Validity

A test is said to have **content validity** to the extent that it is an adequate sample of the attribute, trait, or skill being assessed. The process of content validation consists of the test developer's decision that the items on the test are representative of a specified skill or ability domain. Obviously, an item requesting students to calculate the speed of the moon would be inappropriate on a test of third-grade math ability. A third-grade math test with good content validity should include a representative sample of the types of problems that third-grade children normally encounter. Thus, if a test contains too few items, omits some important aspects of math functioning (e.g., no word problems), or contains subject matter irrelevant to math functioning, its content validity would be reduced. Most of the commercially available achievement tests are reviewed by experts in the particular subject areas of the tests to determine if their content validity is adequate. Still, each user must determine if the test appropriately measures content for each particular use. If a skill is omitted on a test that is important in a particular situation, then the test may not be valid in that instance.

For some tests, such as the BRIGANCE® Inventory of Basic Skills, content validity was a major objective in designing the test (BRIGANCE®, 1977). Such criterion-referenced tests are designed to assess major skills within a content area. Table 5.4 illustrates the various skills measured by the BRIGANCE®.

Cronbach (1970) suggested that "the most general maxim to ensure content validity is this: *no irrelevant difficulty*" (p. 147, italics in original). For example, a student may be perfectly capable of computing the math problems on a test but fail certain items because they are embedded in lengthy paragraphs. Such a test might be more a measure of reading comprehension than computational skill. Test users should be alert to such instances in which irrelevant difficulties may unnecessarily influence test results.

Test users cannot rely on the test name to guide them in selecting an instrument that is valid for their purposes. Three problems that arise in using the test name to judge content validity are called the "jingle fallacy,"

Table 5.4 Detailed Range of Skills Assessed by the BRIGANCE® Inventory of Basic Skills

I. Readiness

Test	Title	Test	Title
1	Color recognition	17	Numeral recognition
2	Visual discrimination	18	Number comprehension
3	Visual-motor skills	19	Recognition of lower case letters
4	Visual memory	20	Recognition of upper case letters
5	Body image	21	Writing name
6	Gross motor coordination	22	Numbers in sequence
7	Identification of body parts	23	Lower case letters by dictation
8	Directional/positional skills	24	Upper case letters by dictation
9	Fine motor skills		
10	Verbal fluency		
11	Verbal directions		
12	Articulation of sounds		
13	Personal data response		
14	Sentence memory		
15	Counting		
16	Alphabet		

II. Reading

Test	Title	Test	Title
A. Word recognition		C-2	Initial consonant sounds auditorily
A-1	Word recognition grade level	C-3	Initial consonant sounds visually
A-2	Basic sight vocabulary	C-4	Substitution of initial consonant sounds
A-3	Direction words	C-5	Ending sounds auditorily
A-4	Abbreviations	C-6	Vowels
A-5	Contractions	C-7	Short vowel sounds
A-6	Common signs	C-8	Long vowel sounds
B. Reading		C-9	Initial clusters auditorily
B-1	Oral reading level	C-10	Initial clusters visually
B-2	Reading comprehension level	C-11	Substitution of initial cluster sounds
B-3	Oral reading rate	C-12	Digraphs and diphthongs
C. Word analysis		C-13	Phonetic irregularities
C-1	Auditory discrimination	C-14	Common endings of rhyming words
		C-15	Suffixes
		C-16	Prefixes
		C-17	Meaning of prefixes
		C-18	Number of syllables auditorily
		C-19	Syllabication concepts
		D. Vocabulary	
		D-1	Context clues
		D-2	Classification
		D-3	Analogies
		D-4	Antonyms
		D-5	Homonyms

BRIGANCE® *Diagnostic Inventory of Basic Skills,* © 1976, 1977, Curriculum Associates, Inc. Adapted by permission. BRIGANCE® is a registered trademark of Curriculum Associates, Inc.

106

the "jangle fallacy," and the "jungle fallacy" (Kelly, 1927; Messick, 1984). Test users fall victim to the jingle fallacy when they assume two tests with the same name are measuring similar things. A case in point is the Illinois Test of Psycholinguistic Ability (ITPA) (Kirk, McCarthy, & Kirk, 1968), which is assumed to measure something called "psycholinguistic ability," or, more simply, language functioning. However, as Carroll (1972) pointed out in his analysis of the ITPA,

> it requires some stretching of the meaning to call the ITPA a measure of "psycholinguistic abilities." The title is a misnomer, and users should be cautioned to look carefully at the true nature of the test, which might less misleadingly have been named the "Illinois Diagnostic Test of Cognitive Functioning." From the present title, a potential user might feel justified in expecting it to cover such language skills as reading, writing, and spelling. Actually, tests of these skills were deliberately excluded. (p. 442)

A second example of the jingle fallacy involves two tests that contain measures of spelling ability: the Wide Range Achievement Test-Revised (WRAT-R) (Jastak & Wilkinson, 1984) and the Peabody Individual Achievement Test (PIAT-R) (Dunn & Markwardt, 1970). The WRAT-R spelling test consists of dictating a word and requiring the examinee to write the word from memory. In contrast, the spelling subtest of the PIAT-R requires the child to select the correctly spelled word from four choices. If the technical characteristics of these tests were equal, teachers wishing to predict how well a child will actually spell would choose the WRAT-R because in reality children seldomly encounter a multiple-choice spelling situation. Thus even though the two tests purport to measure spelling achievement, they do not measure the same skills.

A companion to the jingle fallacy is the jangle fallacy, which causes a test user to assume incorrectly that two tests with different names are measuring different things. Close examination of the Devereux Child Behavior Rating Scale (McDaniel, 1973), which purports to measure child behavior, and the Inferred Self-Concept Scale (Spivack & Seift, 1967), which is supposed to reflect self-concept, will illustrate this fallacy. Both instruments ask someone familiar with the child to rate that child's behavior. In addition, both contain a list of behaviors that the rater is to check if applicable to the child being examined. Although these tests have different names, their content is very similar, and in fact the Inferred Self-Concept Scale appears to be more a measure of overt behavior than self-concept.

The jungle fallacy is one to which many test developers fall victim. In this fallacy, two tests that are supposed to measure different things are found to be highly statistically correlated. The correlation is taken as evidence that the two tests are measuring the same thing. The fallacy is in not distinguishing between what is being measured and the instruments used for measuring. Thus, though a test of self-concept and a test of intelligence may be highly correlated, this should not be seen as proof that they are both measuring intelligence or self-concept. Although either of these possibilities *may* be true, a third explanation is that both tests are measuring still another construct, such as social acceptability. When asked to define the concept of intelligence, some individuals have responded that it is what intelligence tests measure. We must draw a distinction between the test, the name of the test, and that which the test is supposed to measure. If the test has construct validity, it defines that construct, although the test developer names it.

Criterion-Related Validity

For a test to have **criterion-related validity,** it must be highly correlated with some other measure or event (i.e., future or concurrent criterion). For example, when tests are given to candidates for medical school admission, there should be a high correlation between test scores and the criterion of success in medical school, because predicting such success is the reason for the test. The criterion validity of such a test would be assessed by computing correlations between the applicants' scores with their actual grades in medical school a year or two later or with another criterion of medical school success.

Most intelligence tests are designed to have good criterion-related validity. With intelligence tests given to children, the most frequent goal is to predict success in school. Jensen (1980) has reported that correlations between intelligence tests and measures of school achievement are generally in the range of .50 to .70, which is relatively high for a single test predicting a complex set of skills.

A criterion measure may be available at the time the test is taken, but administering the test is more efficient than measuring the criterion behavior directly. For example, a behavioral measure of neurological dysfunction may not be nearly as accurate as examining the brain directly through a CAT scan, but it is much more time and cost efficient. If the behavioral test and other factors suggest some organic problem, additional testing may be warranted. In such situations, the test serves to predict a criterion (in this case, brain functioning) that is not readily and directly observed.

How successfully do tests predict behavior? In the field of special education, one does not have to look very far to find a very capable individual who was misdiagnosed, on the basis of tests, as someone who would never be a success in school. Predictive validity is not easy to establish; tests that are used to predict behaviors are sometimes wrong, just as predictions of the stock market, longevity, and athletic game results are sometimes wrong. Tests with good predictive validity only help to improve accuracy, not to ensure it.

Construct Validity

Construct validity reflects the extent to which a test is capable of measuring a hypothetical trait, or construct. Tests have been designed to measure a number of constructs, including intelligence, motivation, anxiety, and self-concept. These traits are considered hypothetical because they do not represent observable behaviors that can be seen or measured directly.

To determine if a test has construct validity, we must rely on the theory behind the construct or statistical analyses of test scores. For example, psychological theory holds that there is a strong relationship between anxiety and scores on college exams. This theory predicts that people with a moderate level of anxiety perform best; extremely low levels of anxiety apparently do not provide motivation sufficient to perform well, and high levels of anxiety can interfere with test performance. Tests measuring anxiety could be validated against this prediction if students with high, medium, and low levels of anxiety should perform in the hypothesized ways on college tests. The problem with a test lacking construct validity is that it may not be measuring the underlying trait. The Peabody Picture Vocabulary Test-R (Dunn & Dunn, 1981), for example, was once used to yield IQ scores. However, since the test measured only receptive vocabulary, we would not be too surprised if people who scored high IQs on the test did not perform as theory says those with high intelligence should perform, because the construct of intelligence is defined narrowly.

➡ *Normative Procedures*

The third major factor we will consider in the evaluation of tests is the procedures for establishing test norms. Recall that in chapter 4 we used percentiles and z-scores to compare one person's score with those of others who had taken the same test, which is necessary because the interpretation of any score on a norm-referenced test requires some means of comparing it with an established point of reference. Test manuals facilitate such interpretation by providing a set of **norms** for use in comparing an individual's scores with those of a representative sample. Tables usually allow a raw score to be converted to one derived in reference to the norm group. A norm table from the Wide Range Achievement Test–Revised is displayed in figure 5.3. From the table it can be determined that a raw score of 45 on the reading subtest is consistent with the performance of a sixth-grader. People discussing this score would probably say that the student is reading at the sixth-grade level, since reporting a score of 45 will have little meaning to most people. Because the scores from the norm group are the ones reported most frequently, the characteristics of the normative sample are extremely important in evaluating a test for possible use.

Figure 5.3   Normative Table for Translating Raw Score (RS) to Grade-Equivalent Score (GE) from the Level 2 Test Form of the Wide Range Achievement Test–Revised

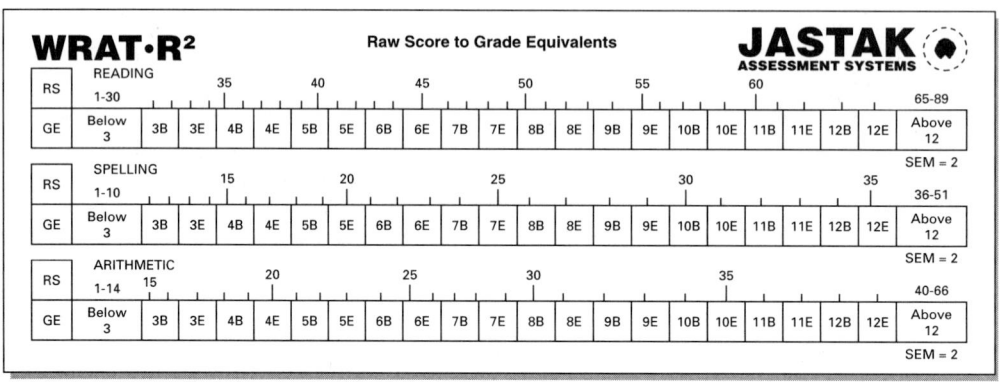

To use the table an examiner enters with a child's RS and determines grade-level score. From S. Jastak and G. Wilkinson, *Wide Range Achievement Test.* Copyright © 1984 Jastak Associates, Inc., Wilmington, DE.

Criteria for Evaluating the Normative Sample

To evaluate the representativeness of the normative sample, one should first determine that the individuals in the norm group are reasonably comparable to those being tested. According to Hills (1976),

> the best clue for [someone] . . . who does not know a lot about sampling procedures is to look for a clear statement of the population, some description of how samples were drawn from the population, and a description of how closely the sample fits the characteristics of the population. If all these things are provided, the user is reasonably safe in assuming that the norms adequately represent the population and were obtained from sound sampling procedures. If the publisher does not give details of how the sample was drawn, how well it fits the population, and so on, but merely speaks of the size of the sample or gives a vague description perhaps based on equating this test through another test, etc., be careful. If the results seem strange it may be because the norms are not sound. (p. 130)

This means that information given in the test manual should be quite specific. For example, more than six pages of the Wechsler Intelligence Scale for Children–Revised (WISC-R) manual describe the normative sample alone. Table 5.5 is from this manual and represents the type of detailed information to which Hills was referring. Contrast this level of specificity with the Jordan Left-Right Reversal Test (Jordan, 1980), which contains only the statement that the standardization sample included children from "rural and urban areas, public and private schools, all socioeconomic levels," with little documentation of the precise characteristics of the sample, such as the number of children tested from rural and urban schools.

The representativeness of the sample can be inferred by noting the number of people in each of the following categories: sex, age, community size, geographic location, acculturation, primary language, and socioeconomic status. Certainly, it would affect the interpretation of a test of learning abilities if the norm group consisted only of Nashville children or only of children with learning disabilities. A common limitation is the failure to report the ages of the sample. For example, a test may be designed for children from two to ten years of age. However, the test authors may have been unable to test any two-year-olds. In this situation it is possible to extrapolate statistically how two-year-olds *might* have scored, although this is a much less accurate method of predicting performance.

In addition to being representative, the normative sample must also be *recent*. The decline of SAT scores of the last decade shows why it is necessary to review and reinterpret norm-referenced scores. When tests are revised or translated into a new language, new norms must be gathered. Since our culture is changing at a rapid pace, we would expect that the way in which people respond to tests would also change.

Should you make comparisons even if the sample is probably unrepresentative? After all, isn't it better to use a poorly normed test than to make decisions without *any* comparative information? Salvia and Ysseldyke (1978) suggest that the answer is a resounding NO!

> It is occasionally argued that inadequate norms are better than no norms at all. This argument is analogous to the argument that even a broken clock is correct twice a day. With 86,400 seconds in a day, remarking that a clock is right twice a day is an overly optimistic way of saying that the clock is wrong 99.99 percent of the time. Inadequate norms do not allow meaningful and accurate inferences about the population. If poor norms are used, misinterpretation follows. (p. 122)

Cronbach (1970) suggests that norms are unimportant only if one is concerned simply with identifying individual differences within a group or a person's absolute performance. Thus, if the goal is to select the three students in each class most in need of remedial reading, national norms are not needed, for the purpose here is to choose those with the lowest absolute performances.

Table 5.5   WISC-III Standardization Sample by Age, Race/Ethnicity, and Geographic Region

Age	n	White				Black				Hispanic				Other			
		North-east	North Central	South	West	North-east	North Central	South	West	North-east	North Central	South	West	North-east	North Central	South	West
6	200	14.5	21.5	23.5	10.0	1.0	4.0	9.5	0.5	1.0	0.5	4.5	5.0	0.0	1.5	1.5	1.5
7	200	13.0	24.5	19.0	13.0	2.5	4.0	7.5	2.0	1.0	0.5	5.0	5.0	0.5	0.5	0.0	2.0
8	200	14.0	21.0	22.0	12.5	2.5	3.0	8.5	0.5	2.0	0.5	5.0	4.0	1.0	0.5	0.0	3.0
9	200	15.5	21.5	20.5	13.0	1.0	3.5	0.0	1.0	2.0	1.0	4.0	3.5	0.5	0.0	1.5	1.5
10	200	15.5	22.5	19.0	13.5	2.0	3.5	9.0	0.5	1.5	1.5	4.5	3.0	1.0	0.5	1.0	1.5
11	200	16.0	19.5	20.0	15.0	3.0	3.5	8.0	1.0	0.5	1.0	6.0	3.5	0.5	1.0	0.5	1.0
12	200	15.5	22.0	22.0	11.5	2.0	3.5	7.0	0.5	1.0	0.5	5.0	4.5	2.0	0.5	1.0	1.5
13	200	15.0	23.5	18.5	12.5	2.5	2.0	9.5	2.0	0.5	0.5	6.5	4.0	0.5	0.0	0.5	2.0
14	200	15.0	21.5	21.0	12.5	2.5	1.5	10.0	2.0	0.0	1.0	4.5	6.0	0.5	0.5	0.5	1.0
15	200	11.5	23.5	22.0	14.0	1.5	3.0	11.5	0.5	0.5	0.5	4.5	4.5	0.0	0.5	0.5	1.5
16	200	3.0	20.0	23.0	14.0	0.5	3.5	11.5	0.5	0.5	0.5	3.5	6.5	0.0	0.5	0.5	2.0
Total	2200	14.4	21.9	21.0	12.8	1.9	3.2	9.3	1.0	1.0	0.7	4.8	4.5	0.6	0.5	0.7	1.7
U.S. Population[a]		14.0	20.8	22.3	13.0	2.2	3.0	8.9	1.2	1.8	0.8	3.4	4.8	0.6	0.6	0.7	1.9

Alternatives to National Norms

As an alternative to national norms, some test users have developed local norms when the situation dictates the use of a particular test but the norms for that test are not representative of the locale or population being tested. Instances in which a local group is not adequately represented by national norms are not uncommon. Individuals familiar with school districts are aware that even *within* a particular district, the achievement levels of students vary from school to school. Local norms may be helpful when there is a reason to believe national norms should not be applied to a local group. The interested reader is referred to an article by Elliott and Bretzing (1980) for information on the procedures to use in constructing local norms.

Grade-Equivalent Scores

One of the most popular methods of using norms is to translate a person's score into a grade-equivalent. This popularity stems from the fact that grade-equivalent scores seem to be simple and easily interpreted by persons unfamiliar with tests. If we say that Tim scored at the third-grade level on a particular test of reading comprehension, people understand our words very quickly but may not have much real understanding. There are numerous such disadvantages to the use of grade-equivalent scores that mitigate against their use. In fact, in June 1980 the Board of Directors of the International Reading Association recommended that test authors and publishers eliminate grade-equivalent scores from their tests.

Critics of grade-equivalent scores have identified three major limitations to their use. First, these scores do not provide equal units of measurement (i.e., they are ordinal rather than interval level measurements). This means that an increase in reading achievement from grade 5.0 to grade 6.0 on a particular test is probably not the same amount of growth as an increase from grade 2.0 to grade 3.0 on the same test. On the original Test of Written Language (Hammill & Larsen, 1990), for example, raw scores on the handwriting subtest range from 0 to 10. A student who earns a raw score of 5 obtains a grade-equivalent score of 4.6. If that test were given one month later and that same student were to earn *one* additional point, the grade-equivalent score for a raw score of 6 would be 7.2. Such a result would give the superficial impression that the student had made nearly three years growth in handwriting ability in only one month!

The second problem with grade-equivalent scores is that the same score may not have the same meaning for students of different ages. For example, a first-grade student and a seventh-grade student who have a grade score of 4.0 may not be equivalent in reading ability. Perhaps the test required only the ability to recognize words. If the task had been reading comprehension, the seventh-grade student, who may have a richer variety of experiences, may be able to comprehend the material at a higher level and thus outperform the first-grade student on the more complex task.

Another problem with grade-equivalent scores is that they are misrepresented by critics of education (Mehrens & Lehmann, 1978). For example, a local school board candidate may alarm parents by indicating that fully 50 percent of the children in the district are functioning below grade level. The truth is that *by definition,* 50 percent of the students *should* be below grade level. A score of 5.0 is used to describe the *average* fifth-grader. On a national basis, about 50 percent of the students will be below average and about half will be above average. Some local districts may have a larger percentage above or below average depending on the composition of their student populations.

➔ *Sources of Information to Aid in Test Selection*

The bulk of this chapter has been devoted to the three most important characteristics to consider when selecting a test: reliability, validity, and norms. Careful attention to these characteristics should increase the likelihood of selecting a good test. In addition to analyzing a test yourself, it is possible to obtain information from other sources.

Without any question the most highly regarded source when evaluating tests is the *Buros Mental Measurements Yearbook.* The *Yearbook* functions as a *Consumer Reports* for the testing industry. When selecting a stereo or automobile, many individuals do the best they can to evaluate the potential purchase but then, to be completely sure, they consult experts, who can determine the advisability of the choice by application of their advanced knowledge. This information is often already available in the form of such publications as *Consumer Reports,* which annually assigns experts to evaluate a large number of products. The *Buros Mental Measurements Yearbook* contains experts' reviews of virtually every test marketed in the English-speaking world. The *Yearbook* series, which was initiated by Oscar Buros in 1938, has three primary objectives:

1. To provide comprehensive and up-to-date bibliographies of recent tests published in all English-speaking countries.

2. To provide comprehensive and accurate bibliographies of references on the construction, validation, use, and limitations of specific tests.

3. To provide frankly critical test reviews, written by persons of outstanding ability representing various viewpoints, which will help test users to make more discriminating selections of the standardized tests that will best meet their needs.

Yearbook test reviews are indeed "frankly critical," as can be seen in the following Focus on Practice. The quality of the reviews is extremely high for two primary reasons. First, only specialists and scholars of the highest caliber are selected to write the reviews. Second, each review is carefully edited, and every fact is checked before it is published. Statements made by reviewers for or against a test are carefully evaluated.

In addition to the reviews, the *Yearbook* also lists virtually every article that investigates the technical qualities of a particular test. For some of the more widely used tests, this can amount to several hundred references. The *Yearbook* can also be used as a catalog to locate various types of tests and their cost. One drawback is that the *Yearbook* is not really a yearbook and in fact is only published every five to seven years. This can mean that a newly published test is not reviewed until several years after it appears. This problem has been partially corrected by putting all test reviews on a national computer network so that they can be obtained through a computer terminal and a telephone hookup at most university libraries.

Reviews of tests are also available in other sources, particularly professional journals such as the *Journal of Educational Measurement, Measurement and Evaluation in Guidance, Journal of Educational Research,* and *Journal of School Psychology.* In choosing a test, one should not rely solely on the advice of experts. Rather, expert advice is most useful concerning the technical adequacy of a test. Whether the test is relevant and valid for the intended purpose can only be decided by the test user.

Chapter Summary

Beginning students in a testing course are often surprised to learn about the shortcomings of commercially available tests. The lesson is similar to learning that many car manufacturers are more often concerned with efficiency than with quality. Thus, the consumer must be prepared to evaluate the quality of tests, rather than relying upon the claims of test publishers or the opinions of those who may be less than objective, by assessing a test's reliability and validity and the procedures for establishing test norms.

This chapter also stressed that the entire assessment process contains various degrees of error that may be based in the examiner, the test, the examinee, the teacher observations, the parent reports, and the thinking of the people who use the tests to make decisions. It is the wise student who takes from this chapter a sense of humility born of an awareness of the insufficiency of knowledge.

Focus on
→ Practice ←

Sample Review from Mental Measurements Yearbook
Borman-Sanders Science Test

Carl J. Olson, Assistant Professor of Medical Education, University of Illinois at the Medical Center; Chicago, Illinois.

This test, containing 75 multiple-choice and 25 matching items, allegedly measures the achievement of "elementary principles and facts of physical science with which the elementary school pupil should be familiar."

Despite the catalog claims, the Borman-Sanders is a prime example of a test that measures practically nothing of consequence but does it with high reliability. The failure of the test authors to provide important technical information—such as the distribution of the norming population, the methods used in computing reliabilities, and substantiating evidence to support claims of validity—is important, but it becomes secondary when one reviews the test content.

While the format is awkward and difficult to read, it may be the best feature of the test. It certainly helps to conceal the fact that most of the test items suffer from the molehill-out-of-the-mountain syndrome, asking for what may be the least important information about significant science concepts. In addition to being obsolete, the remainder of the test items are insignificant (e.g., "Inflate a balloon and release it, open end toward you. The principle it exemplifies was worked out by: 1. Sir Isaac Newton 2. Henri Becquerel 3. Alexander Graham Bell 4. J. Bjerknes"), provincial (e.g., "A wild flower sometimes called the 'Kansas City Feather' is really a: 1. sunflower 2. smartweed 3. spiked blazing star 4. snow on the mountain"), and trivial (e.g., "The space capsule of the Redstone rocket that carried the United State's [sic] second astronaut was named: 1. Monarch 2. Angel 3. Liberty Bell 4. Trieste").

In all fairness, it must be noted that the multiple-choice items as exemplified above are superior to the matching section of the test.

There is not a single item that requires student cognition above the level of recall or which appears to be relevant to modern science curricula. If the Borman-Sanders has any use, it is as a convenient compendium for instructors of measurement courses. In it they will find examples of nearly every error in test development and construction that it is possible to commit, all arranged in one convenient unattractive package.

From O. K. Buros (Ed.), *Seventh Mental Measurements Yearbook.* Copyright © 1972 Buros Institute of Mental Measurements, Lincoln, NE.

Three

The Practice of School-Based Assessment

Teachers have numerous behavioral and academic expectations for children. Consequently, an array of assessment techniques has been developed to measure the many types of behaviors and abilities exhibited by children. In Part Three we examine nine major behavior domains, evaluate frequently used tests and assessment techniques for each domain, and discuss the linking of assessment information to classroom interventions. Five of the nine chapters in this section cover the traditional areas of cognitive ability (intelligence), academic achievement, reading, math, and language. The remaining chapters cover topics of burgeoning interest to educators and psychologists alike: preschool screening and academic readiness, behavior and adjustment problems, and adaptive behavior. Also included is a chapter on the assessment of perceptual-motor skills. Tests for this later domain have been conceptually and technically limited, but because of its persistent popularity, we believe an enlightened examination of this assessment practice is necessary.

Given the number of tests available, only the most frequently used or most reliable are reviewed. Many of the most commonly used tests, however, are inadequate and should never have been published. We discuss why such tests are conceptually, technically, or functionally flawed and constructively suggest alternatives. We have worked hard in selecting tests for discussion and have developed several extensive tables that directly compare tests on critical indexes. By the time you complete Part Three you should have an appreciation for the relationships among the development of children's behavior, the process of identifying and testing important skills and abilities, and the planning of instructional interventions for children.

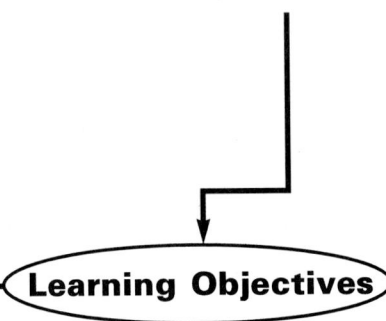

Chapter 6

Cognitive Abilities

Learning Objectives

1. Discuss the major historical approaches to the measurement of intelligence.
2. Cite two reasons for the widespread use of intelligence tests.
3. Describe appropriate and inappropriate uses of intelligence tests in educational settings.
4. Explain different approaches to the measurement of bias in mental tests.
5. Discuss the strengths and weaknesses of major tests of cognitive ability.

A young school psychologist, Dr. Bailey, approaches a fifth-grade classroom. She knocks on the door and is greeted warmly by the teacher. The teacher turns toward her class and asks Ted to come to the door. Ted knows Dr. Bailey is there to see him. He worked with her last Wednesday, and she has come back to work with him again this week. During the next 60 minutes Ted and Dr. Bailey will be together in a quiet room adjoining the school library. During this time Ted is asked to answer a number of questions (e.g., What is the capital of France? From what animal do we get veal? What is $(6 \times 5) - 11$? How are concrete and asphalt alike?) and to complete a variety of timed tasks (e.g., Put these pictures in the correct order to tell a good story; Copy these designs; Tell me what important part is missing from this picture; Put this puzzle together).

At the end of the testing session, Ted is tired. He has tried to do his best, and Dr. Bailey congratulates him for his effort. Ted knows that he answered some questions correctly and that he missed some of the harder ones. Dr. Bailey accompanies Ted back to his classroom, thanks him and his teacher, and then returns to her office to score Ted's responses. In approximately 15 minutes she will have calculated Ted's IQ score according to the directions provided by the developer of the test she administered.

Scenes similar to the one described occur many thousands of times across this country every year. Intelligence tests are just one of many different kinds of tests administered to schoolchildren during the typical evaluation process. Is IQ testing a worthwhile exercise? Here is what some noted scholars have had to say about intelligence and IQ tests:

> The IQ test has also played an important part in the American school system—especially in assigning lower class and minority children to dead-end classes for those with mild mental disabilities. (Kamin, 1981)

> A person's level of g [i.e., *general* intelligence] has ramifications for everyday life—in school, at work, and in personal matters. Because a standard IQ score is usually a good measure of g, it efficiently tells us something important. (Herrnstein, 1982)

> IQ is a questionable measure of general intelligence and a minor determination of success. (Robinson, 1973)

> IQ jointly with scholastic performance predicts more of the variance among persons in adult occupational status and income than any other known combination of variables, including race and social class or origin. (Jensen, 1980)

> If . . . the impression takes root that these tests really measure intelligence, that they constitute a sort of last judgment on the child's capacity, that they reveal "scientifically" his predestined ability, then it would be a thousand times better if all the intelligence testers and all their questionnaires were sunk without warning in the Sargasso Sea. (Lippmann, 1976)

> The outstanding success of scientific measurement of individual differences has been that of the general mental test. Despite occasional overenthusiasm and misconceptions and the fact that the established tests are rendered obsolescent by recent conceptual advances, the general mental test stands today as the most important technical contribution psychology has made to the practical guidance of human affairs. (Cronbach, 1970)

Who is correct? Should these tests that purport to measure cognitive abilities and general intelligence be abolished or are they useful tools for understanding people? Why is the debate so intense? Although there is much debate among experts about the value of intelligence tests, the general public appears to believe that intelligence does play a role in the behavior and decision making of individuals.

The tests discussed in this chapter have sometimes been referred to as "mental tests," tests of "general ability" or "academic aptitude," "intelligence tests," or tests of "cognitive abilities." We will attempt to make clear the many important issues related to intelligence testing through careful review and analysis of fact and fiction. Toward that end we examine the origins and current status of the mental testing movement, explore many of the issues surrounding the use of these tests in our society, discuss a number of the most widely used measures of intelligence, and conclude with a brief discussion of the future directions.

➔ Historical Approaches to the Definition and Measurement of Intelligence

Early Efforts

The study of intelligence can be clearly traced to 19th-century attempts to measure individual differences in a wide variety of human characteristics. It has been claimed that this testing movement was an essential part of the establishment of psychology as a separate discipline (see, e.g., Sattler, 1988). Three major contributors to these early efforts were Sir Francis Galton in England, Wilhelm Wundt in Germany, and J. McKeen Cattell in the United States. Galton developed psychophysical measurements such as strength of push and pull, breathing capacity, keenness of the senses, and mental imagery. His efforts in the study of individual differences led to the development of a psychometric laboratory at the International Exposition in England in 1884 and to his designation as the "father" of the testing movement (Shouksmith, 1970).

Wundt opened the first psychological testing laboratory in Leipzig, Germany, in 1879. He utilized the early work of Galton and others but took a slightly different approach. He attempted to identify general laws governing behavior rather than to measure the extent of individual variation among humans. Cattell, who gave us the term "mental tests," imported these techniques to the United States. Procedures to measure factors such as sensory acuity, strength of grip, sensitivity to pain, and memory for dictated consonants characterized his efforts to assess individual differences and later to measure individual mental skills. The tests used by these pioneers were not very useful in predicting behavior (e.g., a good sensory acuity score did not translate to good academic achievement) and seem primitive by today's standards. These early approaches did, however, serve as a foundation for future research and moved intellectual measurement out of the realm of speculation and clinical judgments and into the world of scientific measurement.

Early 20th-Century Approaches: The Search for Relevance

Around the turn of the century in France, Alfred Binet became interested in studying complex mental processes. His findings were similar to those previously cited and supported the notion that simple sensory discriminations and physical attributes had little relation to general mental functioning. In 1905 the Minister of Public Instruction in France wanted a test that would assist school personnel in determining which students were *not* capable of achieving in the regular classroom. In response to the Minister's request, Binet and his associate, Theodore Simon, developed and published the Binet-Simon Scale. Revised in 1908, the scale's major contributions were that it was pragmatic in development, used complex tasks as test items, ranked items in order of difficulty and grouped them according to age levels, measured general mental ability rather than separate mental faculties, included careful instructions for administration, and exhibited some concern with normative data. Further, student test scores were shown to be related to academic performance. The Binet-Simon Scale was designed to predict school achievement and did a fairly good job of it. Today, one of the primary reasons that tests like the Binet (or Stanford-Binet as it is often referred to today) continue to be so widely used is that they remain among the best (although imperfect) predictors of school achievement. Following the introduction of this scale in the United States, the testing movement began to flourish.

Although a significant advance over previous efforts, the Binet-Simon Scale and its subsequent revisions had problems. One of the most persistent criticisms was related to its age-scale format; that is, tests were selected for inclusion at various age levels based on the difficulty of the tests, and different tasks were included at different age levels. The result was a great deal of heterogeneity of item content (see figure 6.1) for representative items across age levels. Thus, interpretation of an individual's performance on the Binet was difficult because of the varied item content and because measurements of individuals of different ages were not strictly comparable. (If all this talk about the structure and design of the Binet is a little fuzzy, don't be discouraged. This test has been confusing people for years!)

Enter David Wechsler, who took a different approach to the development of an intelligence test. Wechsler wanted to find tasks that would measure various cognitive abilities and could be used across a wide range of age levels. He studied a variety of tests available and developed 11 subtests, which he used to form the Wechsler Bellevue Intelligence Scale, designed for use with adults. The same subtests were administered to all individuals, making interpretation of performance and comparison across individuals (or intraindividual comparisons across time, etc.) easier. This

Figure 6.1   Stanford-Binet Intelligence Scale: Representative Year Levels and Subtests

Year III
Credit—6 tests × 1 month or 4 tests × 1 1/2 months

1. Stringing Beads—the examiner models the stringing of beads on a shoestring and the child is asked to "play this game."
2. Picture Vocabulary—naming pictures of common objects.
3. Block Building—bridge-building a bridge of three blocks modeled by the examiner.
4. Picture Memories—finding animal pictures hidden by the examiner.
5. Copying a Circle—three trials of copying a circle.
6. Drawing a Vertical Line—one trial drawing a vertical line just like the one drawn by the examiner.
A. Repeating 3 Digits—repeating 3 digits in sequence.

Year VIII
Credit—6 tests × 2 months or 4 tests × 3 months

1. Vocabulary—children are asked to provide the definitions of words.
2. Memory for Stories: The Wet Fall—children are asked a series of questions based on a story read by the examiner.
3. Verbal Absurdities I—a series of absurd or foolish situations are presented and the child asked to tell, "What's foolish about this?"
4. Similarities and Differences—describing the similarities and differences of two things.
5. Comprehension IV—a series of general comprehension questions to which the examinee must respond.
6. Naming the Days of the Week—naming the days of the week.
A. Problem Situation I—incomplete situations are presented, followed by questions which require the child to infer what is happening in the scene.

Superior. Adult III
Credit—6 tests × 6 months or 1 test × 9 months

1. Vocabulary—providing definitions of words.
2. Proverbs III—explaining the meaning of words..
3. Opposite Analogies IV—analogies are provided with the final word in the analogy supplied by the subject.
4. Orientation: Direction III—analyzing distance and direction based on information provided by the examiner.
5. Reasoning II—individual is presented brief problem and given 5 minutes to solve it (without pencil and paper).
6. Passage II: Tests—repeating the main ideas of a brief passage read by the examiner.
A. Opposite Analogies—same as above.

From *Stanford-Binet Intelligence Scale: 1973, Norms Edition* by L. M. Terman and M. A. Merrill, 1973, Boston: Houghton Mifflin. These Stanford-Binet materials are also included in the Fourth Edition, Copyright 1986 by the Riverside Publishing Company. Reproduced by permission of the publisher. Authors of this revision are Elizabeth Hagen, Jerome M. Sattler, and Robert L. Thorndike.

test led to the development of the Wechsler series of intelligence tests (Wechsler Primary and Preschool Scale of Intelligence [WPPSI], Wechsler Intelligence Scale for Children [WISC], Wechsler Adult Intelligence Scale [WAIS]). Today, the current revisions of the Wechsler tests are the most widely used measures of cognitive functioning in educational and clinical settings. Later we will examine one of these instruments, the WISC-III, and the subtest format that Wechsler developed.

verbal & non verbal.

Recent Developments

Both Binet and Wechsler wanted to develop a test instrument that would be useful in the clinical and educational assessment of individuals. Although both men conceptualized intelligence as a very complex and multifaceted phenomenon, their tests yielded global intelligence scores that suggested a more unified view of intelligence. Many individuals lost sight of the fact that the Binet-Simon and Wechsler scales contained a variety of tasks tapping many different abilities and instead focused on the comprehensive IQ scores these tests yielded. The question of whether intelligence is a single ability or a collection of multiple abilities has received the attention of theorists and researchers during the last 50 years.

The best-known proponent of the former approach was Charles E. Spearman (1927), who set forth a **two-factor theory** of intelligence. He hypothesized that performance on intelligence tests resulted from a general factor (g) and a group of specific factors that varied from test to test. Spearman is sometimes viewed as a single-factor theorist due to his emphasis on the importance of g, which he said is involved in all problem solving and is especially important in complicated mental activities. Specific factors, on the other hand, are unique to a particular activity or test. A major implication of this theory was that although specific factors must be considered, the primary goal of intellectual measurement should be the construction of tests that measure g. Why? Because if we develop tests that are good measures of this general factor that influences performance on all tasks, we should be better able to predict how an individual will do on tasks in the future.

Louis L. Thurstone (1938) and J. P. Guilford (1967) have been more closely identified with the **multifactor theory** approach. Both believed that intelligence could not be reduced to a unitary factor such as g. Thurstone developed the Primary Mental Abilities Test to measure what he felt to be the primary mental abilities (such as verbal skills, perceptual speed, inductive reasoning, word fluency, and rote memory), and Guilford developed a three-dimensional Structure of Intellect Model (see figure 6.2) that organized intellectual factors hierarchically. Both approaches assumed that a model of intellectual functioning must include a variety of fairly broad factors if it is to account for the complexity of mental activity.

Figure 6.2   Guilford's Three-Dimensional Structure of Intellect Model

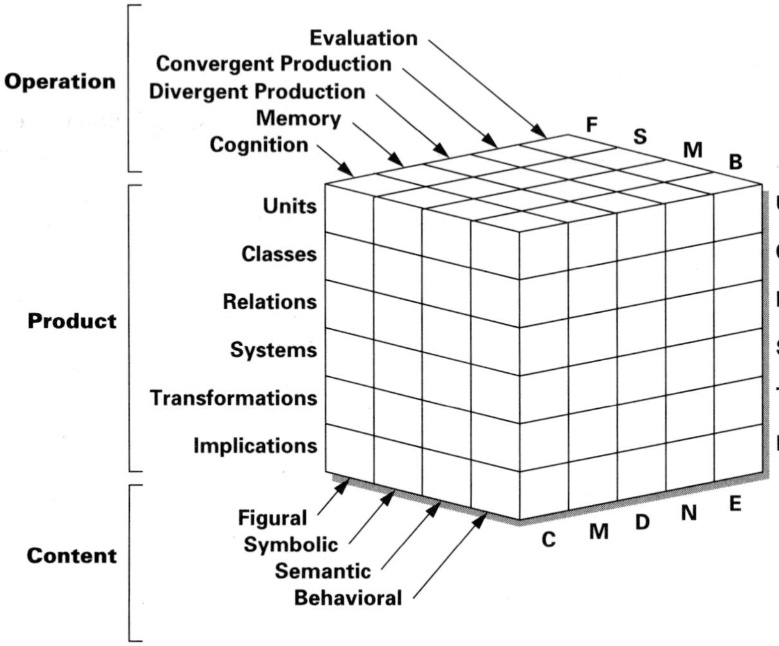

From J. P. Guilford, *The Nature of Human Intelligence.* Copyright © 1967 McGraw-Hill, New York. Reprinted with permission.

Within the last decade, two other explanations of intelligence have gained increased attention. The first is based on the work of Alexsadr Luria and has been expanded by J. P. Das and his colleagues (Das, Kirby, & Jarman, 1979; Jarman & Das, 1977). This model has been referred to as simultaneous/successive processing, and later in the chapter we look at a new test based on this theoretical model. Simply stated, this model suggests that individuals process information primarily in one of two ways—simultaneously or successively. In the former, problem solving and decision making involve the simultaneous integration of a variety of stimuli. Information is processed in a holistic manner, as when people are asked to recognize faces, solve mazes, and complete puzzles. In the successive mode, stimuli are arranged in sequence and dealt with one at a time. Decisions are reached by processing information in an orderly, sequence-dependent fashion (e.g., remembering a series of digits or words in the proper order). The usefulness of this model and its ability to increase our understanding of human behavior remain to be determined.

More recently, Sternberg (1984) has postulated a "triarchic theory" of intelligence that is composed of three components. The first component emphasizes the ability of individuals to organize, plan, and carry out activities (these skills have sometimes been referred to as metacognitive abilities); the second component focuses on the individual's experience with novel, complex problems; and the third component concentrates on intelligence as it relates to the external world. Sternberg believes that conventional intelligence tests have worked as well as they have because the tasks represented on them involve a good deal of the abilities emphasized in his first two subtheories. He suggests, however, that intelligence tests are imprecise measures of these abilities and further, that we must take into account the ability of individuals to adapt to their particular environment to have a complete definition of intelligent behavior.

Summary

As we indicated at the beginning of this section, questions about the nature of intelligence have occupied the thoughts and research efforts of many people during the last century. We do not mean to imply that this concern began in the late 19th century, for the quest began long before. Furthermore, we have only touched upon the work of some of the most important contributors to this effort. Next we examine certain crucial issues related to the application of measures of cognitive ability by professionals in educational and mental health settings.

➡ *The Assessment of Cognitive Ability: Critical Issues and Concerns*

Intelligence testing has gained widespread acceptance in the United States. This is true among not only measurement experts, many psychologists, and educators, but also the general public. For example, parents have become increasingly concerned with providing the optimal environment for their infants and preschoolers to maximize intellectual potential, and as children grow older teachers and parents often want to know their child's IQ score. A trip to your favorite bookstore is likely to reveal a number of books concerned with "increasing your child's IQ" or "testing your own intelligence in 15 minutes by asking yourself only four simple questions." This growing fascination with IQ measurement has not occurred without concern. Before analyzing the most widely used tests of cognitive ability, let's first explore a few of the most critical issues associated with the measurement of intelligence.

Stability of IQ

As a result of the popularization of intelligence tests and the intelligence testing movement, numerous misconceptions about the nature of intelligence developed and were fed by overzealous testers and a misinformed public. One of the most pervasive ideas, which became solidly entrenched in public opinion, was the notion that an infant was born with a certain amount of "intelligence" that did not change as the child grew older. As with many myths, this one was supported with a grain or two of truth. In general, most research has suggested that IQ tests do *tend* to yield scores that are *fairly* stable. However, this same research indicates that IQs are more stable over shorter as opposed to longer periods and more stable for older children and adults than for children under six years of age. A good deal of evidence indicates that IQ scores obtained before children enter kindergarten or first grade are not highly reliable. No one knows exactly to what extent intelligence scores can be altered through environmental manipulation. Although studies of the late 1960s and early 1970s (e.g., the Milwaukee Project) reported that intensive early intervention in children's lives was capable of producing incredible increases in measured IQ, such studies have been severely criticized (see, e.g., Sommer & Sommer, 1983). Despite this criticism, most experts would agree that enriched environments are better than impoverished ones for fostering intellectual development.

Data on the relative stability of IQ can be deceiving and must be interpreted with care. When looking at the IQ scores of large groups of individuals, we can make the general statement that most of those within the group would receive similar scores if retested. However, it is not at all unusual for particular individuals to show a great deal of variability in their scores. Changes of 8, 10, 15, or even 30 IQ points are not unheard of, and each author of this text has tested children who exhibited these types of changes. This potential for intraindividual difference in IQ scores during different testing sessions means that when examining test results, we must not assume that a child who obtained an IQ in a certain range of intelligence will always remain in that range.

Bias in Cognitive Ability Testing

No issue related to the assessment of cognitive abilities has generated as much or as heated debate as the question of whether IQ tests are biased against individuals from minority cultures. Discussions in the popular press have vehemently assailed most aptitude and achievement tests as being unfair to children from backgrounds that are different from those of most middle-class white Americans (Herrnstein, 1982). Although we have no data other than our perceptions, we believe that most students enter our classes convinced that standardized tests are unfair, inaccurate indicators of the abilities of individuals from minority populations. Numerous researchers have investigated the issue of bias in mental tests, with the greatest amount of attention focused on the differences between the performance of blacks and whites (e.g., Jensen, 1980). Some have turned to the courts for help in determining whether IQ tests are biased and whether they should be used in the assessment of minority children, but the courts have not been consistent in their findings (*Larry P. v. Riles,* 1986; *PASE v. Hannon,* 1980).

Many different types of test bias have been identified, and these have been discussed at length by both proponents and opponents of cognitive ability testing. Table 6.1 lists and defines the most common types of test bias that have been studied. As Brown (1983) has indicated, there is no universally accepted definition of bias but most definitions hold that:

> a test can be considered biased if it differentiates between members of various groups (for example, between men and women or between blacks and whites) on bases other than the characteristic being measured. That is, a test is biased if its content, procedures, or use result in a systematic advantage or disadvantage to members of certain groups over other groups and if the basis of this differentiation is irrelevant to the test purpose. (p. 224)

An examination of the research and writings related to bias in cognitive ability testing reveals that the issues are very complex, not easily resolved, and complicated by the emotional intensity with which individuals have advanced their arguments in this area. Consider the factors listed below, and you will understand why testing bias has come to be such an emotional topic:

1. Our society has long discriminated against African Americans and members of other minority groups through a variety of overt and covert mechanisms. Slavery, exclusionary voting laws, separate educational systems, racial slurs, and the like have all occupied a place in this abhorrent, unfortunate history. Although discrimination continues to exist at unacceptable levels, many public and private institutions have committed themselves to the establishment of equal opportunity for all.

2. Intelligence testing has been popular in this country since the introduction of the Binet scales. African Americans, for example, have consistently obtained average scores that are approximately one standard deviation (15–16 IQ points) below the average score of whites. Some have used this type of information to argue for the existence of genetic differences between the races (e.g., Jensen, 1980). Others have suggested that environmental factors are more crucial in the development of intelligence (e.g., Kamin, 1981), but there is little disagreement with the fact that average scores do differ among racial and ethnic groups.

Table 6.1   Types of Test Bias

Type	Definition
Mean Differences	Average scores for various groups (such as black, white, and Hispanic or rich and poor) are different
Item/Content Bias	Portions of test content are biased in a manner that differentially affects the performance of certain groups (such as black and white, or men and women)
Factor Analysis	The factors (for example, verbal abilities or attention) being measured are different for various racial, cultural, or economic groups
Predictive Validity	Scores predict with varying levels of confidence for different groups
Social Consequences	Tests are misused or misinterpreted to justify restrictive social policies
Selection Ratios	Test results are used in ways that cause particular groups to be over- or underrepresented in special classes or certain diagnostic categories (for example, mentally disabled)

Adapted from D. Reschly, "Concepts of Bias in Assessment and WISC-R Research with Minorities" in H. Vance and L. F. Wallbrown (Eds.), *WISC-R: Research and Interpretation,* pp. 87–94. Copyright © 1980 by the National Association of School Psychologists. Adapted by permission of the publisher.

3. The most widely used tests of cognitive ability have been developed by whites, published by whites, and made money for whites. Furthermore, these tests are used to estimate and predict performance in a society that is dominated by the white culture. A good deal of evidence indicates that white society has used the results of these tests to justify discriminatory laws and practices (McPherson, 1985).

Given society's attention to the issue of equality, the different performances on IQ tests by different groups, and the fact that the history of these tests has been dominated by whites, it is not surprising that so many believe so strongly that these tests must be biased against minorities and in favor of whites.

In fact, there is little evidence to support the belief of bias in intelligence tests. First, although it is true that blacks average lower intelligence scores than whites, this is not enough information to conclude that the tests are biased, especially when socioeconomic status is considered. The tests may be biased, but first we must determine if the differences in scores reflect true differences in the ability being measured. Tests are designed to discriminate—to tell good spellers from poor ones, to predict success or failure in graduate school or in a job as a bank teller, and to determine those who have learned the material in history class and those who have not. Simple differences in average scores alone do not prove that bias exists. The fact that you may consistently obtain lower scores than a friend in history class does not mean that the instructor or the tests are biased. Other factors must be studied to reach that conclusion. In the case of intelligence tests, we must investigate their content, construct, and predictive validity. That is, we have to examine whether the test items are biased in favor of one group, whether the test measures the same abilities for all groups, and whether the test predicts equally well for all groups.

The technical evidence overwhelmingly indicates that the vast majority of items used on tests such as the Wechsler and Binet are not biased, that these tests tend to measure the same factors (verbal, perceptual, performance, quantitative, or the like) and predict success equally well for all racial groups (Reynolds, 1982). This last point is critical. It is important to remember that IQ tests do not measure the amount of some innate, immutable ability that we all possess, but do provide a general measure of expected school achievement, just as they were designed to do in the early 1900s. The evidence on predictive validity suggests that whether someone is black, white, or Hispanic does not really matter: An individual with an IQ score of 60 from a reliable test is at risk of failing in most every public educational system, and an individual with a score of 140 is likely to do well in that same system. The research indicates that these tests, although not perfect predictors, are not biased and that race has nothing to do with the accuracy with which these tests predict. Therefore, when we say that the difference in the average IQ scores of blacks and whites is not due to test bias, we are not asserting that blacks are less intelligent but that they are more likely to experience problems in our educational system. Nor does the failure to find bias in these tests explain why one group obtains higher scores than another, and whether that difference is due to a biased school system, cultural deprivation (or advantages), or, as some have asserted, genetic differences. We only know that the tests do a fair job of what they were designed to do—predict school achievement.

Although we conclude that most intellectual or cognitive ability tests are not biased, these instruments have clearly not always been used in a nonbiased fashion. Many have argued that early immigration restrictions were in part based on the data showing that certain ethnic groups scored lower than others on IQ tests (McPherson, 1985). Because the term "intelligence" has been misused by so many people and because there is such widespread misunderstanding of what these tests are designed to do, it has been easy for some individuals to use differences in the average scores of various racial groups as confirmation of racist ideology.

It may be true that most intelligence tests are free of bias; it is also true that these tests have been used to discriminate. To see that these tests are used fairly and judiciously, they must be revised frequently to make sure that they reflect the most advanced understanding of the nature of cognitive abilities and that they utilize appropriate methodologies for assessing cognitive skills. As we will soon see, however, bias may not be the biggest problem facing tests of cognitive abilities.

Treatment Validity and Educational Applications

Our review of the measurement of cognitive abilities has uncovered a number of positive aspects of the testing instruments that have been developed. We have concluded that most measures of intellectual or cognitive ability yield reliable results, that they are reasonably good predictors of achievement levels, and that they are essentially free of bias. This last factor has been especially satisfying to those who have suggested that most of these tests validly estimate the cognitive abilities of minority populations.

We cannot help but wonder, however, if there is not a more subtle, more damaging problem in the manner in which these tests have been used in educational, clinical, and vocational settings (Witt & Gresham, 1985). We are specifically speaking of the question of **treatment validity,** of the ability of a test to lead to better treatments, such as more effective educational programs or better counseling or teaching strategies (Gresham, 1992). Although many have tried, there simply is no clear evidence that test results yielded by general measures of intelligence can be directly translated into effective educational or clinical programs (Kramer, Henning-Sout, Ullman, & Schellenberg, 1987).

It is important to remember that although these types of tests were developed to provide educators with general predictions of success in the educational system, they were not designed to enable educators or psychologists to design effective remedial strategies for individual children. Although we can be relatively confident that children who score in the superior (or gifted) range of intelligence will do better in school than those who score in the intellectually disabled range, we cannot design individualized educational programs for either gifted or mentally disabled children based on their particular pattern of scores or their overall intelligence test performance. The tests were not designed for that purpose, and attempts to make them into tools for specific instructional planning have failed miserably (Kramer et al., 1987).

Throughout this book we have emphasized the need for direct, effective, and unbiased approaches to the process of assessment and treatment validity. Tests of cognitive ability can be a valuable part of the assessment process because they allow for the observation of children in a structured situation and provide an additional sample of behavior for analysis. However, these tests have been misused and overinterpreted and problems continue to exist. We do not recommend the abandonment of the use of measures of cognitive ability simply because they have been mishandled in the past, but we must keep in mind the purposes for which they have been developed and the practices for which they have been validated.

→ *Measures of Cognitive Ability*

What we have called "measures of cognitive ability" have typically been referred to as "tests of intelligence." Instruments developed early in the history of the testing movement (e.g., the Wechsler series of tests) retain the term intelligence in their titles. Newer instruments are titled somewhat differently. Is the search for a new name a reaction to all the controversy over intelligence tests and the true meaning of the term intelligence, or the result of the realization that we must move beyond attempts to measure the hypothetical construct of intelligence? Both explanations are probably at least partly true, as is the realization by publishers that tests that do not mention intelligence in their titles have a better chance of being effectively marketed. Whatever the reason, many different tests purport to measure cognitive abilities: short tests, long tests; individual tests, group tests; comprehensive tests, specific tests; tests for infants, tests for children and adolescents, tests for adults, and so on.

Wechsler Intelligence Scale for Children-III

Overview and Purpose

In recent years the most widely administered test of cognitive ability with school-age children has been the Wechsler Intelligence Scale for Children-Revised (WISC-R) (Wechsler, 1974). The original WISC was designed as a downward extension of the adult intelligence scale that David Wechsler had developed (the Wechsler Bellevue Intelligence Scale) while working at Bellevue State Hospital. Originally published in 1949, the WISC was first revised in 1974 and became the WISC-R following the revision. In 1991 the WISC-R was revised and reappeared as the WISC-III. The general format and item content on the WISC-III remain similar to earlier editions of this test. This is not to suggest, however, that there have not been numerous changes with the current version of the WISC. For example, the pictures used are larger, updated, and better reflect ethnic diversity. Symbol Search is a new subtest and new rules for subtest administration (e.g., establishing ceilings) have been introduced on many subtests.

The WISC-III is individually administered by a qualified examiner (who is usually a psychologist with several advanced assessment courses and more than 500 hours of supervised experience) in 60 to 90 minutes. The WISC-III is designed for children from 6 to 17 years of age and aims to provide a global measure of intelligence that taps "many different mental abilities, which all together reflect a child's general intellectual ability" (Wechsler, 1991, p. 1). The test is comprised of 13 subtests, 6 in the Verbal Scale and 7 in the Performance Scale. All instructions are given orally and all subtests on the Verbal Scale require oral responses. Performance subtests have time limits, and in some cases bonus points are provided for quick, accurate responses. Arithmetic is the only timed sub-test on the Verbal Scale. The 13 subtests are examined in more detail in the following sections.

Verbal Scale

1. Information—30 questions requiring general knowledge of facts
2. Similarities—19 pairs of words requiring an indication of how the items are similar
3. Arithmetic—24 (timed) arithmetic problems requiring a response without the aid of paper and pencil
4. Vocabulary—30 words, requiring definitions or synonyms
5. Comprehension—18 problem situations requiring solutions or an understanding of social rules
6. Digit Span—forward and backward repetition of digits

Performance Scale

1. Picture Completion—30 drawings of common objects, all of which require the identification of a missing essential element
2. Coding—symbols such as vertical lines and circles are to be matched to specific numbers according to a key available for the subject to review and examine
3. Picture Arrangement—a series of pictures requiring placement in a logical, ordered sequence
4. Block Design—12 abstract designs to be copied using two-colored blocks
5. Object Assembly—5 jigsaw puzzles of common objects requiring assembly
6. Symbol Search—a series of paired groups of symbols with the child scanning each group to assess whether or not a target symbol appears in the search group
7. Mazes—8 mazes requiring a child to mark the way out without being blocked

Verbal and Performance subtests are to be administered in alternating order unless the needs of the child dictate otherwise. Mazes, Symbol Search, and Digit Span are considered supplemental tests and generally are not included in the calculation of the IQ scores, unless one of the regular subtests is omitted or "spoiled" because of improper administration or disruption. Symbol Search may only be substituted for the Coding subtest.

Not all items on the WISC-III are administered to each subject. Each subtest has specific rules about where to begin and end, depending on the age or assumed ability of the subject. The specificity of administration and scoring directions provided in the manual generally are considered assets of the Wechsler series of tests (in addition to the WISC-III, the Wechsler Preschool and Primary Scale of Intelligence-Revised, and the Wechsler Adult Intelligence Scale-Revised). Wechsler originally divided his tests into verbal and performance sections based on his conceptualization of intelligence, and he placed subtests that he believed involved primarily verbal or performance abilities into each domain. Many subsequent factor analytic studies (see, e.g., Kaufman, 1975) have generally supported the verbal/performance organization of the test.

Standardization Sample and Norms

The WISC-III remains a model of standardization procedures. It was standardized on 2,200 children selected to be representative of the U.S. population based on data gathered in 1988 by the U.S. Bureau of the Census. The sample was stratified on the basis of geographic region, age, gender, parent education, and race/ethnicity. Data were gathered in 31 states. Two hundred children (100 boys and 100 girls) wee tested at each of 11 different ages, with the median age at each age level being the sixth month of that age range.

Data Obtained

Raw scores on each subtest are first changed into normalized standard scores (scaled scores) with a mean of 10 and a standard deviation of 3. Tables of scaled scores and their raw score equivalents are provided for each four-month age interval (e.g., 6–0 to 6–3, 6–4 to 6–7, 6–8 to 6–11 all the way to 16–8 to 16–11). The scaled subtest scores are then added and converted into deviation IQs (standard scores) for the Verbal, Performance, and Full Scales. Verbal Scale IQ, Performance Scale IQ, and Full Scale IQ each has a mean of 100 and a standard deviation of 15. A child's "test-age" for each subtest can be obtained, and a mean or median test-age for each of the scales can be calculated. With this revision, the examiner is also able to calculate four "factor-based scores," including Verbal Comprehension, Perceptual Organization, Freedom From Distractability, and Processing Speed. These scores also have a mean of 100 and a standard deviation of 15. The factor-based scores are the result of previous analyses with the WISC-R (e.g., Kaufman, 1979) and factor analysis of the standardization data from the WISC-III. Although the author attempts to validate a four-factor solution as indicated above, only the Verbal Comprehension and Perceptual Organization factors receive strong empirical support (e.g., Little, 1992). New norms have been introduced to allow examiners to determine strengths and weaknesses among individual subtests.

Reliability and Validity

Subtest reliabilities (split-half and test-retest) are very good, ranging from .69 to .87 and .57 to .89, respectively. Average Verbal Scale, Performance Scale, and Full Scale IQ reliability estimates are all above .90. Retest coefficients (with a range of 12–63 days between testing) were obtained by testing 353 individuals across 6 of the 11 different age groups. Average gains of 2 to 3 IQ points on the Verbal Scale, 12 to 13 points on the Performance Scale, and 7 to 8 points on the Full Scale were reported for the test-retest sample. The manual includes, for each age level, the standard error of measurement for each subtest as well as for the Verbal, Performance, and Full Scale scores. Interscorer agreement for the subtests is very high, with reliability coefficients above .90 for all subtests evaluated.

Much of the information related to validity presented in the WISC-III manual has to do with earlier research on the WISC-R. For example, correlations between the WISC-R and other tests in the Wechsler series (Wechsler Preschool and Primary Scale of Intelligence [WPPSI] and Wechsler Adult Intelligence Scale [WAIS]) yield similar correlation coefficients (a range of .70–.90) for age ranges in which the tests overlap. Studies comparing WISC-R scores and other intellectual tests such as the Stanford Binet IV and the K-ABC have yielded correlation coefficients in the .70 to .90 range.

Scores on the WISC-III have also been compared to the more recent revisions of the tests in the Wechsler series (i.e., the WPPSI-R, the WAIS-R, and the WISC-R). As might be expected, most correlations are above .85 between these similar tests. The correlations between the Performance Scales on these tests provide the smallest correlation coefficients whereas the Full Scale scores generate the highest coefficients. Intercorrelations among the individual subtests and the correlations of each subtest with the IQ scores also are reported in the manual. The WISC-III is similar to the WISC-R in that IQ scores appear to be moderately related to achievement based on correlations between the WISC-III and measures of academic achievement. Scaled scores (Verbal, Performance, and Full Scales) obtained from the WISC-III can be expected to be lower than the same scores obtained from the WISC-R. Examiners can expect differences of about 5 points for the Full Scale score and from 2 to 7 points for the Verbal and Performance Scale scores, respectively.

Summary

From a technical perspective, the WISC-III is a sound instrument. Although recently revised, preliminary information suggests that it will be widely used and that obtained scores will be moderately related to school achievement. The Wechsler tests are the standard against which other measures of cognitive abilities have been judged for the last three decades. Revised and restandardized in 1974 and again in 1991, the format and many items on the WISC-III are unchanged from the original WISC published in 1949. Pictures and some items have been updated and new norms provided. Much has been learned about the nature of cognitive abilities in the last 30 years and yet the design and purpose of the WISC-III has changed little. Many of the problems associated with earlier editions do not seem to have been addressed with the current revision of this test.

Stanford-Binet Intelligence Scale IV

Overview and Purpose

The original Binet-Simon Scale discussed earlier in the chapter has gone through a number of revisions during the last half century. Most practitioners were familiar with the 1973 edition of the test, the Stanford-Binet Intelligence Scale (SBIS), which served as the standard for intelligence testing for so many years (Terman & Merrill, 1973). Recently, the SBIS has undergone substantial modification and restandardization (Thorndike, Hagen, & Sattler, 1986). The following Focus on Practice and figure 6.3 detail certain ways that the test has been altered through the years. Although many item types that were present in previous editions have been retained, the current organization differs radically from previous editions. This difference is made more apparent by comparing the descriptions in the Focus on Practice and figure 6.3 with figure 6.1.

According to its authors (Thorndike, Hagen, & Sattler, 1986, p. 2), the SBIS is designed to meet the following objectives:

1. To help differentiate between students who are mentally disabled and those who have specific learning disabilities.
2. To help educators and psychologists understand why a particular student is having difficulty in school.
3. To help identify gifted students.
4. To study the development of cognitive skills of individuals from ages two to adult.

The test is individually administered, covers ages two to adult, and includes items that are grouped into 15 tests assessing four broad areas of cognitive functioning: Verbal Reasoning, Quantitative Reasoning, Abstract/Visual Reasoning, and Short-Term Memory. Descriptions of the subtests and their appropriate age ranges follow.

Verbal Reasoning

1. Vocabulary (2–0 through adult)—46 items, the first 14 being picture vocabulary with the remainder requiring oral responses
2. Comprehension (2–0 through adult)—42 items, the first six requiring the identification of various body parts on a picture card of a child (see Focus on Practice and figure 6.3), with subsequent questions requiring verbal responses

Focus on
➤ **Practice** ◄

Stanford-Binet—Past and Present

Although the scales and most of the items in the 1986 edition of the Stanford-Binet are new, users will recognize some familiar items that have been revised to be in accord with current test standards and to improve testing procedures. For example, figure 6.3 shows the evolution of two item types. The card used to measure the examinee's knowledge of parts of the body illustrates an increased sensitivity to issues of ethnicity and gender. The rosy-cheeked boy used in the 1937 edition wore a short red jacket, shorts, and black patent-leather shoes. The blue-eyed girl in the 1973 edition had blond hair tied with a pretty pink ribbon. By contrast, the child in the 1985 edition is drawn with facial features, dress, and hair that *minimize* gender and racial characteristics. The Bead Memory subtests, which also originated in the 1937 edition, required the examiner to create sample bead chains. The new test uses photographs as the stimuli, which eliminates the need for examiners to create sample chains and results in increased standardization of administrative conditions.

Figure 6.3   The Development of Two Stanford-Binet Subtests

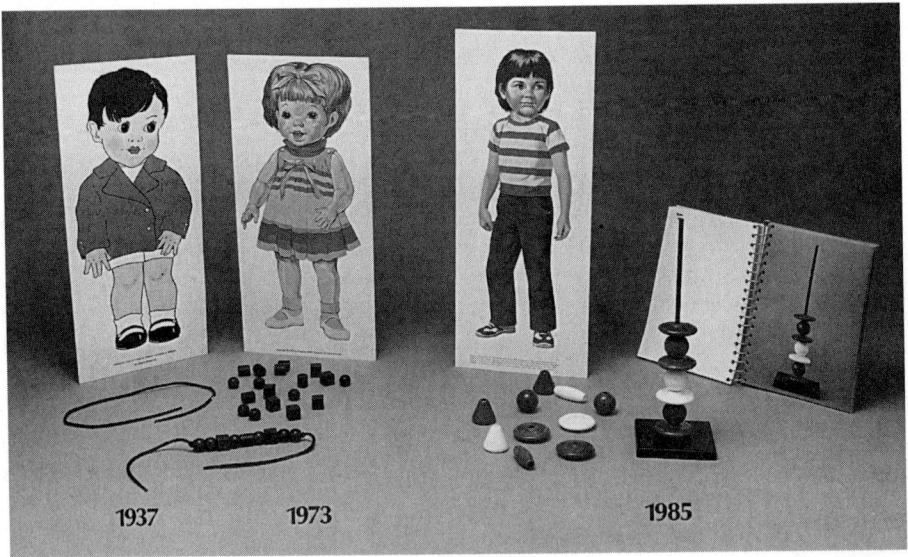

1937   1973   1985

From Elizabeth Hagen, Jerome M. Sattler, and Robert L. Thorndike, *Stanford-Binet Intelligence Scale,* 4th edition. Riverside Publishing Company, Chicago, IL., 1986. Reproduced with permission of The Riverside Publishing Company, Chicago, IL.

3. Absurdities (2–0 through 17–11)—32 items requiring the determination of what is wrong or silly in each picture

4. Verbal Relations (10–0 through adult)—18 items requiring a description of how the first three of four words are related but different from the fourth word

Quantitative Reasoning

1. Quantitative (2–0 through adult)—40 items assessing a broad range of arithmetic skills through tasks ranging from counting blocks to orally presented word problems

2. Number Series (5–0 through adult)—26 items requiring the discovery of the "certain rule," according to which a number sequence is arranged and the naming of the numbers that come next

3. Equation Building (10–0 through adult)—18 items requiring rearranging numbers and arithmetic signs into a true equation

Abstract/Visual Reasoning

1. Pattern Analysis (2–0 through adult)—42 items requiring duplication of patterns presented via either a form board, an examiner's model, or pictured cube patterns

2. Copying (2–0 through 17–11)—28 items requiring the use of blocks to copy block designs or pencil and paper to copy line drawings

3. Matrices (5–0 through adult)—26 items requiring the determination of an appropriate shape, design, letter, or the like to fill a blank spot in a matrix

4. Paper Folding and Cutting (10–0 through adult)—18 items requiring the study of pictures describing a paper-folding and cutting sequence to determine how a piece of paper would look after being folded and cut

Short-Term Memory

1. Bead Memory (2–0 through adult)—42 items requiring the identification of colored bead shapes exposed by the examiner for two seconds or the duplication of bead designs depicted on stimulus cards exposed for five seconds

2. Memory for Sentences (2–0 through adult)—42 items requiring the repetition of orally presented phrases or sentences or both

3. Memory for Digits (6–0 through adult)—26 items requiring the repetition of a series of digits either as stated (11 items) or in reverse order (12 items)

4. Memory for Objects (5–0 through adult)—14 items in which examinees are shown a number of pictures of common objects, one at a time. Examinees are then shown a picture containing many different pictures and asked to identify the pictures shown previously, in the correct order.

As indicated previously, not all items within a particular test nor all tests are administered to each individual. The starting point for each examinee is determined by the results of the vocabulary test, and all tests are to be administered in a prescribed order depending on the subject's age and ability.

Standardization Sample and Norms

The standardization sample was stratified on the basis of data from the 1980 U.S. census and included the following variables: geographic region, community size, ethnic group, age, and gender. The manual indicates that socioeconomic status was monitored through indexes of parental occupation and educational attainment. Approximately 200 to 300 (range of 194 to 460) individuals were tested within each of 17 age groups.

Data Obtained

Raw scores for each test are converted to Standard Age Scores (SAS), which have a mean of 50 and a standard deviation of 8. The SAS within each area are summed and an Area SAS derived. The Area SAS can be summed to determine a Composite SAS score. Both Area SAS and Composite SAS have a mean of 100 and a standard deviation of 16. If fewer than four areas are used to determine the Composite SAS, the examiner is cautioned to calculate a Partial Composite score.

Reliability and Validity

Data related to internal consistency estimates and test-retest reliability are presented in the SBIS technical manual. Median KR-20 reliabilities for the individual tests range from .94 (Paper Folding and Cutting) to .73 (Memory for Objects). Standard error of estimate (SEM) figures generally range between 2 and 3 for each age group. Internal consistency estimates are usually lower for (a) younger children and (b) the Short-Term Memory tests. Reliability estimates for the Area SAS generally were above .80, with most above .90 (SEM 2.8–7.2). Composite score reliabilities were all above .95 (SEM 1.6–3.6). Two groups (five-year-olds and eight-year-olds), totaling 112 children, were retested within two to eight months of the original testing to determine test-retest reliability. Test-retest estimates for five-year-olds and eight year-olds were as follows: individual tests: .56 to .78 and .28 to .86, respectively, Area SAS: .71 to .91 and .51 to .90, respectively, and Composite SAS: .91 and .90, respectively.

The only validity information presented with the SBIS is related to construct validity. Factor analytic studies tend to support the test as a measure of general cognitive ability. The rationale for the placement of each of the subtests within separate areas is sound, with the least amount of support for those within the Abstract/Visual Reasoning subtest. Correlations with other measures of cognitive ability also tend to support the construct validity of the SBIS (most correlation coefficients were above .60). The highest correlations were obtained with older samples (such as the Wechsler Adult Intelligence Scale Revised [WAIS-R]) and the lowest generally with younger samples (such as the Wechsler Preschool and Primary Scale of Intelligence [WPPSI]). The manual suggests that the SBIS will not be a useful measure with two- and three-year-old children of below average abilities due to floor effects on a number of tests. Data from samples of exceptional children indicate that the SBIS does yield Composite SAS consistent with the children's identified areas of exceptionality (e.g., high scores for gifted children). No information related to the use of the SBIS in educational planning or treatment is presented in the manual.

Summary

For many years the SBIS was synonymous with the very notion of intelligence testing in the United States (Boring, 1950). The reasons given for the reorganization and the inclusion of specific tests are not substantial, and the descriptions of specific tests and the presumed abilities involved in each are inadequate. Although the authors do occasionally provide cautions regarding the limitations of the current SBIS, there is little evidence that it meets any of the four original objectives of the test. Research that has appeared since the publication of the test appears to support the test as a reliable measure of general cognitive ability (i.e., intelligence) (e.g., Lamp & Kron, 1990; Rothlisberg & McIntosh, 1991), although the specific factor structure of the test is less clear (e.g., Gridley & McIntosh, 1991; Thorndike, 1990). Much more study is required before its strengths and limitations can be adequately assessed.

Kaufman Assessment Battery for Children

Overview and Purpose

The Kaufman Assessment Battery for Children, or K-ABC (Kaufman & Kaufman, 1983) is an individually administered, multisubtest battery designed to provide information on the intellectual and achievement abilities of preschool and elementary school children between the ages of 2 1/2 and 12 1/2. Appropriate interpretation of the results requires an understanding of the Das/Luria theoretical perspective (discussed earlier in the chapter) and extensive training and supervised experience. The K-ABC breaks intellectual functioning into two distinct styles of information processing: sequential and simultaneous. In the sequential (or successive) mode, stimuli are arranged in sequence, and decisions are reached by processing information in an orderly (i.e., one at a time), sequence-dependent fashion. In the simultaneous mode, information is arranged in a simultaneous fashion, and the decision-making process proceeds in an integrated, holistic manner. The K-ABC, at least as it relates to mental processing, is not designed to measure what or how much a child knows but rather how that child goes about knowing. Stated differently, the K-ABC attempts to assess intellectual ability by asking questions about how a child approaches problem solving and information processing and places less importance on previously learned information. The K-ABC Mental Processing subtests (the Sequential and Simultaneous Scales combined) were designed to minimize the importance of verbal skills to make the test as fair as possible for individuals from diverse cultural backgrounds. In fact, smaller black-white discrepancies in standard scores (3–8 points) have been reported for the K-ABC than for most popular intelligence tests.

The K-ABC is composed of three scales (Sequential Processing, Simultaneous Processing, and Achievement) and 16 subtests. The specific composition of each scale and the design and age range of each subtest is as follows:

Sequential Processing Scale

1. Hand Movements (2 through 12–5)—21 items requiring the repetition of a series of hand movements in the correct order
2. Number Recall (2–6 through 12–5)—19 items requiring recall of numbers from 2 to 8 in sequence
3. Word Order (4–0 through 12–5)—20 items requiring subjects to point to pictures of common objects in the same order as the objects were named by the examiner

Simultaneous Processing Scale

1. Magic Window (2–6 through 4–11)—15 pictures presented by rotating a wheel so that only a portion is visible at any one time. Children are required to name the object pictured
2. Face Recognition (2–6 through 4–11)—15 items requiring the identification of one or two faces from those in a group
3. Gestalt Closure (2–6 through 12–5)—25 items requiring the identification of incomplete ink-blot drawings of common objects
4. Triangles (4–0 through 12–5)—18 items requiring the copying of abstract designs using several rubber triangles

5. Matrix Analogies (5–0 through 12–5)—20 items requiring the selection of a picture or design that best completes an analogy

6. Spatial Memory (5–0 through 12–5)—21 items requiring recall of the location of pictures on a page

7. Photo Series (6–0 through 12–5)—17 items asking subjects to organize an array of photographs illustrating an event and then to order the photographs in their proper time sequence

Achievement Scale

1. Expressive Vocabulary (2–6 through 4–11)—14 pictures requiring identification

2. Faces and Places (3–0 through 12–5)—35 pictures of famous persons, places, or fictional characters requiring identification

3. Arithmetic (3–0 through 12–5)—38 items requiring number identification, multiplication, division, and rounding

4. Riddles (3–0 through 12–5)—32 items requiring the identification of the items or concepts referred to in riddles

5. Reading/Decoding (5–0 through 12–5)—38 items ranging from letter identification to word recognition

6. Reading/Understanding (7–0 through 12–5)—24 items requiring the acting out of commands given in sentences

No child takes more than 13 subtests, and not all items within a subtest are administered. Explicit instructions are provided to determine where to begin testing as well as the criteria for discontinuing a subtest.

Standardization Sample and Norms

Two thousand children, (100 for each six-month age group between the ages of 2 1/2 and 12 1/2) were in the standardization group. Stratification variables included age, sex, geographic region, socioeconomic status (determined by parental education), race or ethnic group, community size, and educational placement (to ensure adequate representation of children with disabilities). In addition, to allow specific race and parental education comparisons, sociocultural norms were established by the additional testing of 496 black and 119 white children.

Data Obtained

Raw scores on each subtest are first changed into normalized standard scores. Subtests on the Sequential and Simultaneous Scales have a mean of 10 and a standard deviation of 3. Subtests on the Achievement Scale have a mean of 100 and a standard deviation of 15. The scores from the subtests on each scale are then totaled and transformed into a Sequential Processing Scale score, a Simultaneous Processing Scale score, a Mental Processing Composite score (Sequential plus Simultaneous scores), and an Achievement Scale score, each with a mean of 100 and a standard deviation of 15. A Nonverbal Scale score, with a mean of 100 and a standard deviation of 15, can be calculated as an estimate of the intellectual potential of individuals with language or communication problems. In addition to these scores, tables allow the examiner to generate information such as national percentile rank, sociocultural percentile rank, age equivalents, confidence intervals, and subtest (or scale) strengths and weaknesses for most of the subtest and scale scores.

Reliability and Validity

Internal consistency reliabilities (presented for both preschool and school-age children, respectively) for the subtests (.72–.89 and .71–.92, respectively) and global scales (Sequential: .90 and .89, respectively; Simultaneous: .86 and .93, respectively; Mental: .91 and .84, respectively; Achievement: .93 and .97, respectively; and Nonverbal: .87 and .93, respectively) are very good. Test-retest reliabilities were obtained by retesting a portion of the standardization sample at each of three different ages (2–6 to 4–11: $N = 84$; 5–0 to 8–11: $N = 92$; 9–0 to 12–5: $N = 70$) for the subtests (.62–.87; .61–.98; and .59–.94, respectively) and global scales (median coefficient = .88).

Extensive information, covering more than 40 pages, related to construct, predictive, and concurrent validity accompanies the K-ABC. Evidence for construct validity is good, with factor analytic studies typically identifying two separate factors (interpreted as simultaneous and sequential factors). In addition, moderate correlations (.36–.76) between K-ABC standard scores and WISC-R Full Scale IQ scores have been obtained (with the K-ABC Achievement Scale–WISC-R Full Scale correlation generally the highest). Both predictive and concurrent validity studies suggest the relationship of the K-ABC with various achievement scales. Regardless of whether there was a delay of 6 to 12 months between the administrations of tests (predictive validity) or whether the tests were administered at the same time (concurrent validity), the results indicate moderate correlations between the Simultaneous, Sequential, and Nonverbal Scales and achievement test scores (typically .30s–.50s); and slightly higher correlations when the Mental or Achievement Scales were reported (.40s–.80s). Although no long-term predictive validity studies are currently available, they will be important in evaluating the test's usefulness. It will be especially interesting to see if the K-ABC predicts achievement equally well for blacks and whites in light of the small black-white differences in obtained test scores.

Summary

The K-ABC has received widespread attention since its introduction. Hailed by its publishers as the most innovative and useful entrant into the cognitive assessment arena in the last half-century, the test has not avoided substantial and pointed criticism (Bracken, 1985; Page, 1985). The K-ABC is psychometrically sound, has very good standardization, is attractively presented, and is relatively easy to learn and use. However, the major questions remain to be resolved over whether the theoretical model upon which the test is based is sound and whether the test ultimately aids in the treatment process. To date, there is no sound evidence that the results from this test can be used to plan educational programming.

Columbia Mental Maturity Scale

Overview and Purpose

The third edition of the Columbia Mental Maturity Scale, or CMMS (Burgemeister, Blum, & Lorge, 1972) was originally designed to estimate the "general reasoning ability" of physically disabled and nonverbal children between the ages of three years, six months, and nine years, eleven months. The CMMS contains 92 items, each printed on a 6 × 19-inch card that features three to five color or black-and-white drawings of figural and pictorial symbols such as shapes, common objects, abstract designs, dots, and body parts. Children are asked to examine each card and identify the one image that does not relate to any of the others. Correct responses require the formulation of an explicit rationale for determining the relationships among the pictures. No time limit is imposed upon the child; however, the examiner is instructed to encourage a response after 20 to 25 seconds.

The CMMS is individually administered and takes approximately 15 to 20 minutes to complete. It differs from the other individually administered instruments we have examined in that it assesses a very limited range of cognitive abilities: classifying, discriminating, and perhaps reasoning. However, since it requires only nonverbal, pointing responses, it has been useful in the assessment of children with a variety of disabilities.

Standardization Sample and Norms

The 1972 CMMS was standardized on 2,600 children from 25 states. The sampling procedure was designed to ensure a representative national sample based on the 1960 census data, with the stratification variables including geographic region, race, parental occupation, age, and sex. The design and execution of the norming process for the CMMS is excellent.

Data Obtained

An Age Deviation Score (ADS) with a mean of 100 and a standard deviation of 16 can be calculated for each child completing the CMMS. In addition, a Maturity Index, or mental age score, can be obtained by determining the age group in the standardization sample that most closely corresponds to a child's performance.

Reliability and Validity

Test-retest reliability and internal consistency estimates (split-half reliability) are provided in the CMMS manual. Test-retest figures were calculated on a group of approximately 100 children at each of three ages, and ranged from .84 to .86. Split-half estimates ranged from .86 to .91. The standard error of measurement is given as 5 to 6 ADS points (depending on the age group).

Validity for the CMMS was established by correlating scores with results from achievement and ability tests. Correlations with achievement scores ranged from .31 to .61 (Stanford Achievement Test) and with mental tests from .62 to .69 (Otis-Lennon Mental Ability Test) and .67 (SBIS).

Summary

As a test of cognitive abilities, the CMMS is limited because it does not sample a broad range of skills. The test, however, has traditionally been used to estimate the intellectual potential of individuals who have difficulty responding verbally, and it has proved to be an excellent adjunct when used in this manner. It is easily administered, simple to score, psychometrically sound, and a worthwhile addition to one's assessment repertoire.

McCarthy Scales of Children's Abilities

Overview and Purpose

The McCarthy Scales of Children's Abilities, or MSCA (McCarthy, 1972) was developed to measure general intellectual development in children between the ages of two and a half and eight and a half. Before this test, psychologists and educators wanting to assess the abilities of this age group had been limited in their choices to the SBIS or the WPPSI. With the publication of the MSCA it was hoped that psychologists and educators would have a single instrument for measuring several aspects of cognitive and motor abilities in pre-and early elementary school children.

The MSCA is individually administered, like the WISC-III, SBIS, and K-ABC, and requires training and supervised experience for proper use. It has a wide variety of "gamelike and nonthreatening" tasks that are organized into 18 subtests and six scales. The six scales, Verbal, Perceptual-Performance, Quantitative, General Cognitive, Memory, and Motor are discussed in greater detail below.

1. **Verbal Scale.** As on the WISC-III, this scale is designed to assess the ability of the subject to understand, process, remember, and problem solve with the English language. Subtests include Pictorial Memory, Word Knowledge, Verbal Memory, Verbal Fluency, and Opposite Analogies. In addition to measuring an individual's receptive and expressive language abilities, the Verbal Scale assesses attentional, short-term memory, and reasoning abilities.

2. **Perceptual-Performance Scale.** The seven subtests on this scale are designed to evaluate an individual's nonverbal problem-solving skills and visual-motor coordination. Subtests include Block Building, Puzzle Solving, Tapping Sequence, Right-Left Orientation (ages five and above), Draw-A-Design, Draw-A-Child, and Conceptual Grouping.

3. **Quantitative Scale.** A unique feature of the MSCA is the Quantitative Scale, which is designed to provide an index of the ability to use and remember numerical symbols and concepts. Its subtests include Number Questions, Numerical Memory, and Counting and Sorting. In addition to math skills, the ability of children to attend, concentrate, and hold material in short-term memory are important on this scale.

4. **General Cognitive Index (GCI).** This index includes the 15 subtests that are part of the Verbal, Perceptual-Performance, and Quantitative Scales. Although not referred to as an IQ score, the GCI is defined as an overall measure of a child's "cognitive functioning" (McCarthy, 1972).

5. **Memory Scale.** This scale is composed of four subtests aimed at assessing auditory and visual short-term memory—Pictorial Memory, Tapping Sequence, Verbal Memory, and Numerical Memory—which all appear on other MSCA scales.

6. **Motor Scale.** This scale includes five subtests designed to measure fine and gross motor skills: Leg Coordination, Arm Coordination, Imitative Action, Draw-A-Design, and Draw-A-Child (the last two also appear on the Perceptual-Performance Scale).

Standardization Sample and Norms

The standardization group was based on a national sample, stratified on the following variables: age, sex, color, geographic region, and father's occupation. Urban-rural residence was also included as an "informal selection variable." The standardization sample size at each of 10 ages (each half-year from two and a half to seven and a half, plus eight and a half), ranged from 100 to 106, making a total of 1,032 cases. In general, the design and execution of the standardization process for the MSCA are considered excellent.

Data Obtained

Standard scores (referred to as Indexes) are computed for each scale. The GCI has a mean of 100 and a standard deviation of 16. Each of the remaining scale indexes has a mean of 50 and a standard deviation of 10.

Reliability and Validity

The manual provides internal consistency measures as well as stability co-efficient and standard errors of measurement for each of the six scales (at all 10 age levels in the standardization sample). Split-half reliability for the GCI ($r = .93$) and the other scales (.79–.88) is very good. The average standard error of measurement for the GCI is 4 points. Stability coefficients of the MSCA, with a 30-day test-retest interval, are .90 for the GCI and range from .69 to .89 for the other scales.

Both concurrent and predictive validity are referred to in the manual. Concurrent validity was established by correlating the MSCA Scale Indexes with IQ scores obtained on the WPPSI and SBIS. Correlations ranged from .45 to .91 (median $r = .75$), if one excludes the scores from the Motor Scale Index (r ranged from .02–.10). Predictive validity was established by comparing the MSCA scores of 35 children with their scores obtained four months later on the Metropolitan Achievement Test; correlations ranged from .34 to .54. A number of other validity studies have been published in recent years, and the concern has been raised that the MSCA seems to underestimate the intellectual abilities of children identified as learning disabled.

Summary

The MSCA is a well-designed, psychometrically sound instrument for as-sessing the cognitive abilities of young children. Most children find the test interesting and enjoyable, although the material on the test is becom-ing somewhat dated. A good deal of evidence suggests that the MSCA yields lower scores for children with learning disabilities and who are mentally disabled (Nagle, 1979) than do other frequently administered tests of cognitive ability. Perhaps a more significant concern is that the MSCA's design is based on a rather traditional conceptualization of intelli-gence (i.e., verbal-performance) that seems dated by today's standards.

Cognitive Abilities Test

Overview and Purpose

The Cognitive Abilities Test (Thorndike & Hagen, 1986) differs from other tests examined in this chapter in that it is group administered. As with most group tests, the Cognitive Abilities Test is often used for general school administration planning for all children and as a screening device to help identify individuals who may need further diagnostic assessment (e.g., to determine eligibility for educational programs). There are 10 levels of the Cognitive Abilities Test, 2 in the Primary Battery (PB: Kindergarten–Grade 2) and 8 in the Multilevel Edition (ME: Grades 3–12). Extensive training is not required to administer this test.

The PB yields Verbal, Quantitative, and Nonverbal scores, is untimed, and allows the examiner to pace the examination according to individual circumstances. Two levels of the PB are available to provide maximum discrimination among the skill levels of children in this age range. The eight levels of the ME are also divided into tests that yield Verbal, Quantitative, and Nonverbal reasoning ability scores. The nonverbal test is suggested to be especially useful in the assessment of disadvantaged children and poor readers. No reading is required on the nonverbal test—all items involve either pictures or diagrams.

Standardization Sample and Norms
The Cognitive Abilities Test was standardized in 1984 and 1985 in conjunction with the Iowa Test of Basic Skills (ITBS) and the Tests of Achievement and Proficiency (TAPS) (all published by Riverside Press). Stratification variables included the size of school district enrollment, geographic region, and community socioeconomic status. An attempt also was made to include representative samples of students from nonpublic schools and various racial and ethnic groups. More than 150,000 children participated in the standardization.

Data Obtained
Raw scores are converted into scale scores, which can then be converted to any of the following: standard age scores (with a mean of 100 and a standard deviation of 16), percentile ranks for standard age scores, stanines corresponding to standard age scores, normal curve equivalents of standard age scores, percentile ranks for grades, and stanines by grade. It is recommended that the three scores on the PB and ME should *not* be averaged to yield an overall score.

Reliability and Validity
Internal consistency estimates for the various levels of both the PB and the ME are provided and are within acceptable limits (.82–.94). Information related to content, criterion, and construct validity of the Cognitive Abilities Test is available in the manual. The description of its content validation is essentially a verbal explanation of the rationale for the inclusion of certain types of items. Criterion-related validity is assessed by correlating Cognitive Abilities Test scores with results from the ITBS, TAPS, and end-of-year grade point averages. All correlations support the general

notion that the test successfully discriminates across ability and achieve-ment levels and is measuring something similar to but different than achievement.

Summary

The current version of the Cognitive Abilities Test is very similar to earlier forms. Among the several new features are shorter directions for adminis-tration and expanded information on the interpretation of scores. The Pri-mary Battery has been expanded to yield three scores as does the MultiLevel Battery. Although the Cognitive Abilities Test is psychometri-cally sound, results should only be used for general screening purposes. As with many group tests of cognitive abilities, this test is standardized on a very large sample, and standardization procedures were carefully executed.

Chapter Summary

What is this thing called intelligence? Is it a single ability that affects all cognitive activity? Is it something we all have to a greater or lesser extent? Or is it a collection of abilities and thus more appropriate for us to con-sider its relationship to specific skills like verbal and performance abilities or simultaneous and successive processing? Or, is it time for a new definition?

Sternberg (1979) argues that it is indeed time for a novel approach, some new ideas, a little fresh air. He suggests that we view intelligence as a prototype, an ideal model. This approach would argue that instead of formulating theories, developing tests to fit our theories, and testing indi-viduals on our measures of cognitive ability (to confirm our theories!), we should move in a different, almost opposite direction. Sternberg would have us start by asking: What are the characteristics of intelligent people? How do they behave? How do they think? As we proceed, we would first answer the questions intuitively, based on our observations and experi-ence (the intelligent person is a good planner and organizer, has excellent abstract reasoning skills, and is able to think logically), and only after we have developed some ideas about the intelligent person (our prototype) should we begin to research the nature of the abilities we have identified.

At this point Sternberg would have us ask: What is abstract reasoning? How do people demonstrate it? What are its components? What is the nature of logical thinking and what are the psychological mechanisms that underlie it? Are the types of people we have identified as intelligent really better planners, and if so, on what types of tasks? He would also have us ask how these skills relate to an individual's ability to adapt to the envi-ronment. Are the same skills important in all environmental settings, or are there important interactions between environment and ability of which we must remain aware? This approach has been referred to as **compo-nential analysis** because it is designed to identify the critical components of intelligence that relate to performance as well as knowledge acquisition,

Defining Intelligence

There is an intuitive appeal to the method used by Robert Sternberg of Yale University in New Haven to define and describe intelligence. He began with the assumption that the usual definitions developed by and for experts were often "rarefied abstractions, unconnected with real people or real life. And formal IQ tests seem unfair or beside the point" (Sternberg, 1982, p. 30). His approach was simply to ask laypeople how they define intelligence or intelligent behavior.

Sternberg first asked people to list behaviors that were embodied in the terms "intelligence," "academic intelligence," "everyday intelligence," and "unintelligence." From the responses he developed a master list of 250 relatively unique behaviors that characterize either intelligent or unintelligent people. Next, Sternberg and his associates had another group of individuals rate each of the 250 behaviors on a 1-to-9 scale to indicate relative importance of each characteristic to an "ideally intelligent person." To determine whether laypeople differed from experts in their notions of intelligence, the behaviors were also rated by a number of university professors who specialized in the study of intelligence or intelligence testing.

Laypeople viewed intelligence as composed of three broad facets: practical problem-solving ability, verbal ability, and social competence. Surprisingly, the laypeople and the experts did not differ a great deal in their views of intelligence. There were, however, three areas of difference. First, laypeople tended to have a broader view of intelligence. What experts study in terms of intelligence and the content of IQ tests comprises only a portion of the broad array of characteristics that laypeople associate with the concept of intelligence. Second, laypeople tended to emphasize the importance of intelligence in *inter*personal relationships in a *social* situation, whereas the experts tended to stress *intra*personal competence in an *individual* context. For example, laypeople were more likely to associate "acts politely" with intelligence, and experts stressed behaviors such as "reasons logically and well." Third, the scientists considered motivation to be much more central to the concept of intelligence than did laypeople. Thus characteristics such as "displays dedication and motivation in chosen pursuits" were rated highly by the experts.

A remarkable aspect of this research was the use of the 250 behaviors as a measure of intelligence. The list of behaviors was used as a means for individuals to rate themselves. People were instructed to rate the degree to which each of the 250 behaviors was characteristic of themselves. The scoring was based upon how closely a person's responses resembled those of someone considered to be ideally intelligent. Thus, it was not possible to falsify the results by rating oneself high on the desirable characteristics. Results of the rating scale correlated about as well with IQs as other more traditional tests of intelligence, which suggests a kind of validity.

The appeal of this approach is that it allows society or the culture, not so-called experts or intelligence tests, to define intelligence. Obviously, Sternberg's method is but one of hundreds of approaches to defining and measuring intelligence.

transfer, and retention (Sternberg, 1984). Componential analysis has received a great deal of attention and has been the focus of intensive research. Will componential analysis improve our ability to develop educational interventions for children? How will the psychologists of the next century view our efforts? Will our work seem as primitive to them as the efforts to Galton and Wundt seem to us?

Finally, it should be apparent that we believe there are many potential problems with the use of intelligence tests. As part of a comprehensive battery of tests, intellectual tests can provide limited information of use. When interpreted inappropriately or as a sole measure of a person's abilities, test results can easily be misinterpreted and mistakes can lead to unfortunate and even disastrous consequences for children. Many of these tests seem outdated in terms of current understanding of how best to help children achieve and learn. As Cantor (1990) has stated, "Regardless of the sophistication of theory and structure, modern measures of intelligence lack treatment utility and thus, fail to address the desired outcomes of psychoeducational assessment-potential intervention strategies" (p. 443). Although intelligence tests continue to play a substantial role in the assessment of children, these tests are likely to continue to fade in importance unless it can be shown that they possess treatment validity and are important tools in making a difference in the lives of children.

Chapter 7

Academic Achievement

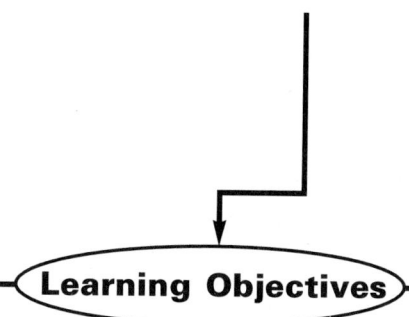

Learning Objectives

1. Describe the differences between an achievement battery and an achievement test in reading, mathematics, or spelling.
2. Differentiate between survey and diagnostic tests and provide a rationale for the use of each.
3. Describe reasons for choosing either an individually- or a group-administered achievement battery.
4. List and describe the various uses of achievement batteries.
5. Discuss the strengths and weaknesses of four of the achievement batteries examined in this chapter.

The scene is a familiar one. A teacher stands at the front of the classroom, a packet of test booklets held firmly in hand. In a few minutes she will break the seal on the packet of booklets and hand one to each student. She has placed a small clock on her desk so that students will be aware of how much time they have left on each section of the test. During the administration of the test she will also record the time remaining on the chalkboard. The students are sitting quietly, their pencils primed for action. They have been told that during the next few days they will be taking a number of different kinds of tests in reading, mathematics, and language arts. Although they may suspect that the test results will be reported to their parents, they are unaware of the many other uses for the results of standardized achievement batteries.

School districts all across the country set aside a certain number of days each year to administer achievement batteries. Indeed, many large school districts have separate departments that devote a great deal of time to the administration, interpretation, and dissemination of the results of such tests (see Focus on Practice: The National Association of Test Directors). Although these tests are given routinely, there is considerable misunderstanding about their appropriate use and the effective application of the data obtained from them.

Criticism of achievement batteries has focused on their validity (Wright & Piersel, 1987). A frequent complaint concerns their potential for underestimating the ability of individuals from minority cultures. These are important criticisms and similar to the issues discussed in chapter 6.

The manner in which achievement batteries have been used (and abused) has also come under close scrutiny. For example, suppose in the case cited at the beginning of the chapter, the teacher worked within a school district that in the past year had taken a good deal of criticism because the students' average test scores were the lowest in five years and were lower than those in most other districts in the state. Administrators, feeling the pressure to "do something," met behind closed doors to discuss two plans for raising the scores. One of the strategies is designed to elevate individual scores while the other will eliminate some low scores; in both cases the score of the "average" student will go up. More specifically, the tactics include:

1. Coaching students in the weeks before the test. This coaching, or "teaching to the test," would involve using class time to practice answering items similar to those on the actual test. Although school officials do not know the exact items that will appear on the test, they do have a good idea of the types that will be sampled as a result of studying the publisher's objectives for the test.

2. Excluding special education students from the testing. The school officials argue that these students have already been extensively tested to qualify for special services and that little can be gained from further testing.

These strategies would most probably increase the average scores for each grade level, and thus the average score for the entire district would be higher than those from previous years. What is to be gained, however, if test scores are raised but no longer accurately reflect the knowledge level of a particular child or the average performance of children within the district? As Anastasi (1981) states, "a test score is invalidated . . . when a particular experience raises the score without appreciably affecting the behavior domain that the test samples" (p. 1087). In the preceding example, the school officials would be raising scores without modifying students' knowledge, thus invalidating the test.

Although activities similar to those just described have taken place in some schools, they are certainly not standard practice. Although there are potential problems, achievement batteries can be valuable aids in the

---

Focus on
Practice

The National Association of Test Directors

Although the example of a fictional school district's approach to achievement batteries is not very flattering, most school districts do use data obtained from such tests in an appropriate fashion. The National Association of Test Directors (NATD) is a group of individuals (typically the coordinators of evaluation or assessment from large school districts) interested in learning the best ways to use tests within the public schools. They are exploring which tests have been found useful across the nation, the desirability of testing every student every year, and the most effective means of reporting scores to parents. During a recent meeting of the NATD (which took place at the 1987 annual meeting of the American Education Research Association) the agenda of items for future study included:

1. The desirability of developing a national, cooperative item bank for school systems designing their own achievement tests.
2. The effects of competency testing.
3. The merits of the national standardization of tests.
4. Methods of reporting district test results to the public.
5. Use of grade-equivalent scores by publishers, educators, and the public.
6. Strategies for test selection.
7. Methods of evaluating achievement in social studies and science.
8. Computer scoring of tests.
9. Use of standardized tests to determine school effectiveness, teacher effectiveness, and principal effectiveness.

Thus, although our example focused on the misuse of testing practices, clearly, individuals and groups such as the NATD are working to improve their use in the schools.

---

educational process. In this chapter, we examine the foundations of achievement batteries, methods of utilizing the data obtained from them, and a small sample of these tests. The tests presented are designed to measure more than one achievement area (e.g., reading and math, social studies and science) and in that way differ from the domain-referenced achievement tests discussed elsewhere (e.g., see chapters 9 and 10).

➔ *The Development and Use of Achievement Batteries*

An **achievement battery** is a collection of tests from different subject areas that have been integrated into one test battery. Achievement batteries are often confused with aptitude tests, and both tests do measure, to some extent, prior learning. However, achievement tests differ from aptitude tests in two important ways (Anastasi, 1982). First, achievement tests typically are samples of rather well-defined knowledge domains such as elementary mathematics, geography, and/or American history before 1865, whereas aptitude tests have a much broader pool of information from which to choose. Second, achievement tests are intended to measure the result of *previous* instruction; aptitude tests are designed to assess a student's potential to benefit from *future* instruction. It is important to remember, however, that both types of tests involve measurement of what an individual has learned. An aptitude test is not administered in a vacuum and the things that someone has learned/not learned in the past (e.g., the importance of double-checking an answer) cannot help but influence how they will do on a test of "aptitude" or "intelligence."

The principles that guide the construction of achievement batteries are the same as those that guide the development of specific-subject tests (see chapters 9 and 10). Selection of an appropriate instrument depends on careful analysis of (a) the purpose of the assessment, (b) the content and technical properties of the instruments being considered, and (c) the match between them. In other chapters we have emphasized the necessity of evaluating the technical adequacy of tests and the extent to which a variety of instruments meet this need. However, no understanding of reliability or validity will compensate for a failure to analyze carefully the purpose of the assessment. Questions related to the goals and objectives of a testing program must be answered before, not after, testing. For example, why is an achievement battery being considered? How will the results be used? Are you interested in receiving diagnostic information for students in special programs or only in reporting the results from a reliable, norm-referenced test to state and federal agencies? Do you want to know which subject areas in your curriculum are being successfully taught and which need improvement? Has the match between the content of the school district's curriculum and the content of the test been evaluated? This type of planning must be completed before one begins to consider specific instruments: No test is capable of correcting for insufficient or inadequate planning.

It is also important to note that the label a test author or publisher applies to an achievement battery (e.g., The All-Purpose Achievement Test) or a particular subtest (e.g., reading) is, in and of itself, not an indication of the validity of that test for measuring the variable indicated by the title. A thorough analysis of the content is the only sure method of determining whether a test really qualifies as "all-purpose," measures "reading," or meets your needs. Later in this chapter a number of achievement batteries are discussed, but we now turn to a closer examination of the specific issues that must be considered before beginning an evaluation of achievement batteries.

Survey versus Diagnostic Tests

Achievement batteries generally fall into one of two categories: screening or diagnostic tests. Many group tests designed for use with all students are used as screening tests in special education. Screening batteries are designed to provide a general estimate of current levels of academic achievement across a wide range of skill levels. Often, these tests contain a limited sample of problems from a particular content area. Survey tests typically are norm-referenced and administered to determine an individual's relative standing within a group. These tests generally are not designed to be aids in the development of specific educational programs. Instead, survey batteries provide a gross, overall picture of an individual's current level of achievement and as such are a reasonable first step in the assessment of academic skills.

Sometimes, because of prior testing or background information, an examiner may need more specific information about an individual's skills. Diagnostic achievement batteries are designed to identify specific strengths and weaknesses in a variety of academic skills, such as reading, arithmetic, and spelling. A particular content area (e.g., reading) is typically subdivided into skill areas (in this case, word recognition, word analysis, and vocabulary). This process makes possible a more detailed interpretation of an individual's mastery of the basic skills in a certain area. Many diagnostic tests are criterion-referenced, although some also are norm-referenced. Diagnostic tests are intended to be useful in the development of specific educational programs.

Group versus Individual Administration

Achievement batteries can also be categorized as either group or individually administered. Group tests are typically given to entire classes at one time, making them an efficient tool for the cost-effective collection of a great deal of information in a relatively short period. In contrast, individual tests require one-to-one administration but allow the examiner greater opportunity to observe the behavior of a particular individual. Group tests also require less training in administration techniques than do most individual tests. Although individual tests cannot routinely be given to groups, a group test may be administered to one student, provided that it is administered in the standardized fashion.

Individual administration is considered better than group administration for making placement and classification decisions about individual students because it allows for more direct observation of behavior and because one can select a group of tests that are directly related to an individual's situation (or problem). Some individual tests, however, are poorly constructed or sample only a limited amount of content (e.g., the Wide Range Achievement Test-Revised), whereas some group tests have been meticulously developed and sample from an extensive variety of academic areas (see table 7.1). The importance of the information gathered from a well-constructed group test of achievement should not be overlooked. Anastasi (1982) has suggested also that an advantage of group achievement batteries that are administered on a regular basis is that they permit both *horizontal* and *vertical* comparisons among large numbers of students. That is, a teacher can compare an individual's performance across academic areas (such as mathematics, reading, spelling, and social studies) in terms of a consistent standardization group (a horizontal comparison) and also evaluate the progress that the individual is making from year to year (a vertical comparison).

Potential Uses of Achievement Battery Data

As indicated earlier, we have sometimes lost sight of the fact that achievement batteries are designed to aid in the instructional process. School personnel may be concerned with getting the highest scores rather than the most representative. Or, in the rush to meet federal mandates for the assessment of disabled children, educators have occasionally made sure that achievement test data are in the files of students with disablities without first examining all of the implications of the data. Luckily, such practices are less common today than they were only a few years ago. Two valuable ways of using the information collected from achievement batteries are in the evaluation of individuals and the evaluation of programs.

Evaluation of Individuals

Achievement batteries often play an important role in the selection and placement of individuals in the educational system. For example, schools commonly conduct preschool screenings to determine a child's readiness for kindergarten. Sometimes these decisions are based on informal, locally constructed batteries, but in most cases professionals may choose to use commercially published tests. Data from achievement batteries may be used to make initial decisions about which children qualify for special programs (e.g., for the gifted). In such cases, the results from the current year's districtwide group testing program (perhaps the Iowa Test of Basic Skills) will be examined, and all children with scores above the 95th percentile will be referred for individual testing to determine whether they qualify for placement in a program for talented and gifted students.

Table 7.1   Widely Used and Highly Regarded Group-Administered Comprehensive Achievement Batteries

Battery	Grades	Subject Areas
Iowa Tests of Basic Skills (Forms G and H) (Hieronymus et al., 1986)	K.1–1.5	Listening, Vocabulary, Word Analysis, Language, Mathematics
	K.8–1.9	Listening, Vocabulary, Word Analysis, Reading, Language, Mathematics
	1.7–2.6	Vocabulary, Word Analysis, Reading Comprehension, Spelling, Mathematics Concepts, Mathematics Problems, Mathematics Computation, Listening, Capitalization, Punctuation, Usage and Expression, Visual Materials Reference Materials, Social Studies, Science
Note: At older grade levels not all subject areas need be administered to all children as subtests are divided into Basic, Complete, and Complete Plus Supplemental batteries of tests. Schools may choose whichever battery they believe best meets their need.	2.5–3.5	Vocabulary, Word Analysis, Reading Comprehension, Spelling, Mathematics Concepts, Mathematics Problems, Mathematics Computation, Listening, Capitalization, Punctuation, Usage and Expression, Visual Materials, Reference Materials, Social Studies, Science
	3–9	Vocabulary, Word Analysis, Reading Comprehension, Spelling, Mathematics Concepts, Mathematics Problems, Mathematics Computation, Listening, Capitalization, Punctuation, Usage and Expression, Visual Materials, Reference Materials, Supplemental Social Studies/Science Test
Metropolitan Achievement Tests (Sixth Edition) (Prescott, Balow, Hogan, & Farr, 1987) (Survey Battery)	K.0–K.5	Reading, Mathematics, Language, Total
	K.5–1.9	Reading, Mathematics, Language, Total
	1.5–2.9	Reading, Mathematics, Language, Basic Total, Science, Social Studies, Complete Total
	2.5–3.9	Reading, Mathematics, Language, Basic Total, Science, Social Studies, Complete Total
Note: At older grade levels some subject areas (e.g., Reading) contain a number of different subtests (e.g., at grades 3.5–4.9 Reading consists	3.5–4.9	Reading, Mathematics, Language, Basic Total, Science, Social Studies, Complete Total, Research Skills
	5.0–6.9	Reading, Mathematics, Language, Basic Total, Science, Social Studies, Complete Total, Research Skills

Table 7.1—*Continued*

Battery	Grades	Subject Areas
of vocabulary, word recognition, reading comprehension, and total reading).	7.0–9.9	Reading, Mathematics, Language, Basic Total, Science, Social Studies, Complete Total, Research Skills
	10.0–12.9	Reading, Mathematics, Language, Basic Total, Science, Social Studies, Complete Total, Research Skills
SRA Achievement Series (Forms 1 and 2) Science Research Associates, 1987)	K.5–1.5	Reading, Mathematics, Composite, Verbal, Nonverbal, Total
	1.5–2.5	Reading, Mathematics, Composite, Verbal, Nonverbal, Total
	2.5–3.5	Reading, Mathematics, Language Arts, Composite, Verbal, Nonverbal, Total
	3.5–4.5	Reading, Mathematics, Language Arts, Composite, Verbal, Nonverbal, Total
Note: At all age levels some subject areas (e.g., Mathematics) contain a number of different subtests (e.g., at grades 6.5–8.5 Math consists of math computations, math concepts, math problem solving). The Verbal, Nonverbal, and Total tests are referred to as Educational Ability Scales.	4.5–6.5	Reading, Mathematics, Language Arts, Reference Materials, Social Studies, Science, Composite, Verbal, Nonverbal, Total
	6.5–8.5	Reading, Mathematics, Language Arts, Reference Materials, Social Studies, Science, Composite, Verbal, Nonverbal, Total
	8.5–10.5	Reading, Mathematics, Language Arts, Reference Materials, Social Studies, Science, Composite, Verbal, Nonverbal, Total
	9.0–12.9	Reading, Mathematics, Language Arts, Reference Materials, Social Studies, Science, Survey of Applied Skills, Composite, Verbal, Nonverbal, Total
Stanford Achievement Test (Eighth Edition) (The Psychological Corporation, 1990)	1.5–2.5	Reading, Mathematics, Language, Spelling, Listening, Environment, Basic Battery, Complete Battery
	2.5–3.5	Reading, Mathematics, Language, Spelling, Listening, Environment, Basic Battery, Complete Battery
Note: At all grade levels some subject areas (e.g., Language) contain a number of different subtests (e.g., at grades 3.5–4.5 Language consists of mechanics, expression, and total scores).	3.5–4.5	Reading, Mathematics, Language, Listening, Spelling, Study Skills, Science, Social Studies, Listening, Using Information, Thinking Skills, Basic Battery, Complete Battery
	4.5–5.5	Reading, Mathematics, Language, Listening, Spelling, Study Skills, Science, Social Studies, Listening, Using Information, Thinking Skills, Basic Battery, Complete Battery

Table 7.1—Continued

	5.5–6.5	Reading, Mathematics, Language, Listening, Spelling, Study Skills, Science, Social Studies, Listening, Using Information, Thinking Skills, Basic Battery, Complete Battery
	6.5–7.5	Reading, Mathematics, Language, Listening, Spelling, Study Skills, Science, Social Studies, Listening, Using Information, Thinking Skills, Basic Battery, Complete Battery
	7.5–8.5	Reading, Mathematics, Language, Listening, Spelling, Study Skills, Science, Social Studies, Listening, Using Information, Thinking Skills, Basic Battery, Complete Battery
	8.5–9.9	Reading, Mathematics, Language, Listening, Spelling, Study Skills, Science, Social Studies, Listening, Using Information, Thinking Skills, Basic Battery, Complete Battery

Achievement batteries also play an important role in the instructional planning process. Although we maintain that achievement tests may provide useful information about *all* students, special educators use the tests in planning for special needs students. Earlier we presented a model for a funnel approach to assessment (see figure 1.1) that also illustrates how information from achievement batteries can be integrated with other assessment data to develop an educational program for disabled as well as other children.

Finally, achievement batteries are receiving increased attention as educators, legislators, and the public become concerned with measuring "minimal competency," or the extent to which individuals have mastered the content of a particular area. Within the public schools, such attention has generally been focused on the testing of high school seniors and teachers, not to make a comprehensive assessment of their knowledge but rather to make sure that they have obtained a minimal level of competency to function in society or in the classroom. Achievement batteries will continue to play a part in this process.

Evaluation of Programs
Given that two instructional programs for teaching mathematics cost the same, are equally well liked by students and teachers, and match the content objectives of the district, achievement batteries are one method of

assessing their relative effectiveness. However, we must be aware of the many factors that may confound the results of such studies. When comparing instructional programs it would not be fair to claim that one was better than another if the "better" program was used in a school with students who were more completely prepared for learning (as in a suburban school with highly educated residents). Other factors such as cost and the satisfaction of students, parents, and teachers must also be assessed before making final decisions about the effectiveness of a particular program.

➡ *Representative Achievement Batteries*

Many different achievement batteries are available for inspection and use. Some of the most widely used tests of achievement are discussed next, although options from which to choose are extensive and growing (see e.g., Kramer & Conoley, 1992).

BRIGANCE® Diagnostic Inventory of Basic Skills

Overview and Purpose

The Diagnostic Inventory of Basic Skills, or DIBS (BRIGANCE®, 1977), was the first of a series of individually administered, criterion-referenced diagnostic tests (e.g., Diagnostic Inventory of Early Development-Revised, Diagnostic Comprehensive Inventory of Basic Skills, and Diagnostic Inventory of Essential Skills) originally developed by Albert H. Brigance. The inventories are similar in purpose and format but differ in the assumptions about the performance level of the individual being assessed. The specific skills tested on each inventory differ, although there is some overlap. The DIBS is designed for students achieving in the kindergarten through sixth-grade levels, and its author has identified its five specific purposes:

1. to assess basic readiness and academic skills in key subject areas from the kindergarten to sixth-grade level;

2. to provide a systematic performance record, expressed in grade-level terms, for diagnosis and evaluation;

3. to define instructional objectives in precise terms to measure a student's performance in a given subject area;

4. to determine a student's level of achievement, readiness to advance, or need for improvement; and

5. to guide the teacher in designing an instructional program to meet the specific needs of the student (Brigance, 1977).

The DIBS assesses skills in four general areas: readiness, reading, language arts, and math. Each of these domains is broken into a number of skill (and subskill) areas, with the items arranged in order of difficulty.

Focus on
Research

The National Assessment of Educational Progress

How does student achievement today compare with that of previous generations, and what changes will occur during the next few decades? How good is the American educational system? There appears to be as many answers to these queries as there are people to ask. In just the last few years numerous groups (e.g., the Carnegie Foundation National Commission on Excellence in Education) have filed reports on the current status of the American educational system.

The National Assessment of Educational Progress (NAEP) was developed to monitor how the knowledge and skills of American schoolchildren changed over time (Ebel, 1966; Merwin, 1966; Tyler, 1966). In addition to written tests in 10 areas, (literature, science, social studies, writing, citizenship, music, mathematics, reading, art, and vocational education), interviews, observations, questionnaires, and performance items have been included in the NAEP assessment strategy. The tests were first administered in 1969 at four age levels: 9, 13, 17, and 23 to 35. Plans were for the tests to be readministered to new groups periodically.

Over the last two decades the NAEP has undergone significant changes (Johnson, 1992). Current goals for the NAEP include both providing a national census on academic performance *and* trying to identify reasons for changes in scores. Innovative assessment strategies were developed with plans for the 1992 testing to include more extensive use of writing samples, oral interviews, and portfolio assessment (Mullis, 1992).

During the past few years, ETS and numerous professional journals (e.g., *Journal of Educational Measurement*) have published thousands of pages detailing the strategies and results of previous NAEP testing. Although it is beyond the scope of this brief report to summarize all of the findings, it is fair to say that these data have not indicated that American education should be a model for the world. NAEP results are often cited as evidence that American schoolchildren know less than children in most other developed countries. Deficiencies in math and science education have been of special concern to those who see America falling behind in the race to be a leader in new technology and innovation. Many reasons have been proposed for the apparent failure of American education to keep pace with the rest of the world and much disagreement about the cause and cure of this problem exists. One thing that is clear, however, is that the NAEP provides information about the achievement of American schoolchildren in an ongoing, systematic manner that is not available from other sources.

**Table 7.2   Readiness and Reading Skills Assessed in the BRIGANCE®
Diagnostic Inventory of Basic Skills**

Readiness

Color recognition
Visual discrimination
Visual-motor skills
Visual memory
Body image
Gross motor coordination
Identification of body
  parts
Directional/positional
  skills
Fine motor skills
Verbal fluency
Verbal directions
Articulation of sounds
Personal data response
Sentence memory
Counting
Alphabet
Number recognition
Number comprehension
Recognition of lowercase
  letters
Recognition of uppercase
  letters
Writing name
Numbers in sequence

Lowercase letters in
  sequence
Uppercase letters in
  sequence

Reading

Word recognition
Word recognition grade
  level
Basic sight vocabulary
Direction words
Abbreviations
Contractions
Common signs

Reading
Oral reading list
Reading comprehension
  level
Oral reading rate

Vocabulary
Context clues
Classifications
Analogies
Antonyms
Homonyms

Word analysis
Auditory discrimination
Initial consonant sounds
  auditorily
Initial consonant sounds
  visually
Substitution of initial
  consonant sounds
Endiing sounds auditorily
Vowels
Short vowel sounds
Long vowel sounds
Initial clusters
  auditorily
Initial clusters
  visually
Substitution of initial
  cluster sounds
Digaphs and dipthongs
Phonetic irregularities
Common endings of
  rhyming words
Suffixes
Prefixes
Meaning of prefixes
Number of syllables
  auditorily
Syllabication concepts

BRIGANCE® *Diagnostic Inventory of Basic Skills,* © 1976, 1977, Curriculum Associates, Inc.
Adapted by permission. BRIGANCE® is a registered trademark of Curriculum Associates, Inc.

Table 7.2 presents the skill areas in the readiness and reading domains. As
this table indicates, the DIBS attempts to provide comprehensive diagnostic information on a variety of skills.

The comprehensive nature of the DIBS has contributed to its widespread use, as has its ease and flexibility of administration. Directions are
clear and are printed on each page of the examination material. Examiners are encouraged to modify the procedures in any manner they deem
appropriate to determine whether students have mastered particular skills.
Depending on the age, skill level, distractibility of the child, and the
amount of information desired, administration can take from 10 minutes to a

few hours spread across a couple of days. The DIBS can be used to supplement data obtained from other sources or to provide a comprehensive assessment of an individual's proficiency level in a number of academic skill areas.

Standardization Sample and Norms
The DIBS is criterion-referenced, and little normative data are reported in the manual.

Data Obtained
Based on their performance, individuals are considered to have either mastered or not mastered the skill assessed in each sequence. In addition, grade-level information is provided for many of the subtests based on the author's attempts to "text-reference" the DIBS. That is, many commonly used texts, word lists, developmental scales, and the like were examined to determine the level at which a particular skill is typically first introduced or expected. No summary or overall achievement level scores are provided.

Reliability and Validity
No information related to the reliability and little validity data are reported in the test materials. Although the content validity of the DIBS appears excellent, specific details about its development and refinement are not included.

Summary
Perhaps the greatest disadvantage to the DIBS is the lack of specific information about the development of the scale and the author's failure to provide any reliability data. Beyond these shortcomings, the DIBS appears to be an excellent criterion-referenced achievement battery for teachers who are primarily concerned with what skill to teach next. The comprehensive sampling of content across the various domains assessed makes it easy to translate results from the DIBS into educational plans and programs.

California Achievement Tests

Overview and Purpose
The California Achievement Tests, or CAT (CTB/McGraw-Hill, 1985), is one of a number of widely used and highly regarded group-administered, comprehensive achievement batteries currently available for use in public schools (see table 7.1).

The CAT (Forms E and F) is a series of comprehensive tests that measure skills in seven areas: Reading, Spelling, Language, Mathematics, Study Skills, Science, and Social Studies. Not all tests are administered at all levels and some tests (e.g., science and social studies) are optional (Airasian, 1989). The CAT assesses skills at eleven overlapping grade levels (K–12). In table 7.1 it can be seen that many group achievement tests have divided their tests into grade levels that overlap. The overlap in grade levels makes it easy to assess children at their functional level rather than their assigned grade level. There are two forms of the CAT (E and F) for the eight oldest age groups. Brief, optional pretests are available for teachers who want to obtain an accurate reading of a particular child's functional level prior to the administration of a form of the CAT. Both norm-referenced (national and local) and criterion-referenced information are available with the CAT.

Standardization Sample and Norms
The CAT was standardized on a stratified national sample of approximately 300,000 students in grades K to 12 during the fall and spring of the 1984–85 school year. Stratification variables included type of school (public or Catholic), geographic region, social class/SES, and size of school district and community type (rural, urban, suburban). An attempt was made to provide adequate representation of disabled and minority populations.

Data Obtained
The CAT may be hand scored or returned to the publisher for scoring. A variety of derived scores are available: grade equivalents, percentiles, normal curve equivalents, scale scores, anticipated achievement scores, and category objective scores. Information provided by the test publisher to assist in the interpretation of results appears adequate, although the test publisher has been criticized for not having enough information available for users who need to understand appropriate uses of test scores (Wardrop, 1989).

Reliability and Validity
Reliability estimates are provided for each subtest at each level. Extensive information is presented on the internal consistency (KR-20) of the CAT, and these estimates appear to be uniformly high. Test-retest figures for the subtests are consistent with internal consistency estimates (generally .86 or above). Most validity data on the CAT are related to content validity. Objectives for the CAT were developed following a review of curriculum guides from various state departments of education and large cities as well as the objectives of other achievement tests. Test items were developed by professional item writers and care was taken to eliminate those items that appeared to be biased in any fashion.

Summary
The CAT is a well-standardized, reliable achievement battery for testing school-age children. Its development began approximately a half-century ago, and the current edition of the battery is an excellent example of a well-constructed, group-administered test. Although billed as a comprehensive test, the CAT focuses on the evaluation of basic academic skills (reading,

mathematics, and language arts). The adequacy of the test's category objectives and the value of criterion-referenced results in helping teachers plan instruction remain unknown.

Kaufman Test of Educational Achievement (Comprehensive Form)

Overview and Purpose

The Kaufman Test of Educational Achievement, or K-TEA (Kaufman & Kaufman, 1985) is designed to measure school achievement of children from 6 years, 0 months, to 18 years, 11 months. It is individually administered and is available in two forms. The Brief Form assesses the global areas of reading, mathematics, and spelling; a Battery Composite score is also available. The Comprehensive Form assesses the areas of Mathematics Applications, Reading Decoding, Spelling, Reading Comprehension, and Mathematics Computation; Reading Composite, Mathematics Composite, and Battery Composite scores are also available. Although there are a number of similarities between the two forms (e.g., in how they are presented to subjects and the information in their manuals), the content does not overlap. A decision about whether the Brief or the Comprehensive Form is used depends on the amount and type of information desired on an individual child (e.g., screening versus diagnostic). A description of the Comprehensive Form follows.

According to the K-TEA manual, the administration of the test takes from 20 to 30 minutes for first-graders and from 55 to 65 minutes for eleventh- and twelfth-graders. The K-TEA may be administered by educational and psychological personnel skilled in testing as well as "technicians" and paraprofessionals with proper training. It is suggested that the interpretation of the results requires more skill than does the administration and that interpretation should be the responsibility of trained personnel.

The subtests on the Comprehensive Form include:

1. Mathematics Applications—60 items presented orally and assessing a wide variety of concepts and applications of mathematical principles

2. Reading Decoding—60 items involving identification of letters and pronunciation of words

3. Spelling—50 items that the examiner reads aloud and uses in a sentence, with the student then writing the word

4. Reading Comprehension—50 items requiring oral answers to questions related to paragraphs the subjects have read. Some items also require gestural or oral responses to printed sentences

5. Mathematics Computation—60 written items ranging from simple addition and subtraction to algebraic computations

The Comprehensive Form allows for extensive error analysis of an individual's mistakes on any of the five subtests. For example, in Mathematics Computation, the subskill areas include Basic Addition, Regrouping Addition, Basic Subtraction, Regrouping Subtraction, Multiplication, Division, Fractions, Advanced Addition, Advanced Subtraction, Algebraic Equations, and Square Roots and Exponents. In Reading Comprehension there are two subskill areas, Literal Comprehension and Inferential Comprehension.

Standardization Sample and Norms

Standardization of the Comprehensive Form took place during two separate nationwide administrations in the spring and fall of 1983. Approximately 2,500 students (1,400+ in the spring and 1,000+ in the fall) participated in the standardization. An attempt was made to select a representative national sample based on U.S. Census Bureau data. The samples were stratified within each grade level (approximately 100 per grade for both spring and fall) by race or ethnic group, sex, socioeconomic status (educational attainment of parents or other adults living in the household), and geographic region. No systematic attempt to include special education students was made, although permission slips for participating in the standardization were given to special education students. That is, these students were provided an opportunity to participate, but no record was kept of the number returning permission slips.

Data Obtained

The K-TEA provides standard scores, with a mean of 100 and a standard deviation of 15 (although there is some variability in the exact means and standard deviations on each subtest and composite at each grade), grade equivalents, age equivalents, percentile ranks, stanines, and normal curve equivalents.

Reliability and Validity

Mean split-half reliability coefficients ranged from .90 (Mathematics Computation) to .95 (Reading Decoding) for the subtests and .94 (Mathematics Composite) to .98 (Battery Composite) for the composites. Test-retest reliability estimates ($N = 172$, retest interval of 1 to 35 days) are reported for grades 1 to 6 and 7 to 12. For the lower grades, estimates ranged from .83 (Mathematics Computation) to .95 (Spelling/Reading Decoding) for the subtests and .93 (Mathematics Composite) to .97 (Battery Composite) for the composites. For the higher grades, estimates ranged from .90 (Reading Comprehension) to .96 (Spelling) for the subtests and .94 (Reading Composite) to .97 (Battery Composite) for the composites.

Standard errors of measurement (SEM) are reported and generally range from about 2 standard score points for the Battery Composite to 3 to 5 points for the individual subtests. Reading Composite SEMs are generally about 3 points, whereas Mathematics Composite SEMs generally are 3 to 4 points.

Validation of the K-TEA was a sequential process involving assessment of content validity, construct validity, and concurrent validity. A content blueprint for the K-TEA was developed by its authors, members of the publisher's staff, and curriculum consultants. The large number of items originally considered were reduced through various types of analyses (both conventional as well as the Rasch-Wright item response techniques). After national samplings some items were eliminated either because they failed to fit the Rasch-Wright model or because of evidence of bias.

Evidence for construct validity is provided in that as children grow older and experience more schooling, their K-TEA scores tend to improve. Internal consistency estimates for the five subtests ranged from .77 to .85 (by grade level).

Evidence of concurrent validity is provided through correlations between the K-TEA scores of some of the standardization sample with either the Kaufman Assessment Battery for Children (K-ABC), Wide Range Achievement Test (WRAT), Peabody Individual Achievement Test (PIAT), or Peabody Picture Vocabulary Test-Revised (PPVT-R). Comparisons also were made between K-TEA scores and three group achievement batteries: Stanford Achievement Test, Metropolitan Achievement Tests, and Comprehensive Tests of Basic Skills. The large amount of information collected in these comparisons indicate that, in general, the K-TEA subtests and composites appear to measure the same abilities as similar subtests and composites on other academic tests.

Summary

The K-TEA appears to be a psychometrically sound achievement battery. The standardization process is exemplary in its attention to detail. The test provides both norm- and criterion-referenced information, which should prove to be a valuable aid in the assessment of children. The extent to which the K-TEA will be adopted as a measure of academic achievement remains to be seen, but it seems to have much promise.

Peabody Individual Achievement Test-Revised

Overview and Purpose

The Peabody Individual Achievement Test-Revised, or PIAT-R (Markwardt, 1989), is an individually administered, norm-referenced achievement battery. The Peabody Individual Achievement Test was originally published in 1970. Designed as a screening or survey measure, the PIAT-R provides an overview of scholastic attainment in six content areas: Mathematics, Reading Recognition, Reading Comprehension, Spelling, Written Expression, and General Information. The test takes approximately 60 minutes to administer and is normed for grades K to 12. Only the written expression subtest is timed; however, on the other subtests examiners are warned to give individuals enough time to respond but not to wait an "unlimited time" for subjects to answer. The subtests include:

1. Mathematics—100 multiple-choice items ranging from matching and visual discrimination at the lower levels to trigonometry at the upper levels

2. Reading Recognition—100 items including 16 multiple-choice "readiness" questions (e.g., matching letters) and 84 words to be read aloud

3. Reading Comprehension—82 questions requiring the subject to read a sentence silently and to pick the one picture from four different choices that best illustrates the meaning of the sentence

4. Spelling—100 multiple-choice items requiring a range of skills from identification of printed letters to the spelling of words ready by the examiner

5. Written Expression

- Level 1 assesses writing readiness skills with 19 items requiring writing your name, copying letters, and writing letters, words, or sentences in response to dictation;

- Level 2 consists of a 20-minute period in which the subject is asked to write a story about a picture

6. General Information—100 open-ended questions testing general knowledge in science, social studies, fine arts, humanities, and recreation

The manual is clearly written, and the record booklet is easily used. The administration of the PIAT-R is generally easy to learn, although individuals familiar with the original PIAT will need to acquaint themselves with the changes and additions before attempting to administer this test.

Standardization Sample and Norms

The original standardization sample consisted of 1,563 students kindergarten through 12th grade, most of whom attended public schools (91.4%). An additional 175 kindergarten children were tested the following fall to provide data for beginning kindergarten students. The sample was stratified according to geographic region, race/ethnic group, and socioeconomic status based on the "most current Census information available." Between 98 and 148 children were sampled at each of the 13 grade levels in the sample. Children in special education classes were not included in the standardization.

Data Obtained

The PIAT-R provides grade equivalents, age equivalents, percentile ranks, stanine scores, normal curve equivalents, and standard scores by grade or age (with a mean of 100 and a standard deviation of 15) for each of the subtests and composite scores (Total Reading and Total Test) except for those in the written language area. For written language, grade-based stanines are provided and a developmental scaled score is available for Level II. An optional written language composite score (Spelling + Written Expression) is also available.

Reliability and Validity

Test-retest, split-half, Kuder-Richardson, and item response estimates of reliability were obtained for the PIAT-R (except for the written expression subtest and scores). The median split-half reliabilities for all subtests evaluated were above .90 (range .92–.98). Both Kuder-Richardson (KR-20) and item response estimates of reliability were high, with median estimates above .94 for all subtests at all ages and grades. Fifty individuals in kindergarten as well as grades 2, 4, 6, and 8 were retested at intervals of two to four weeks after original testing to assess test-retest reliability. Median test-retest reliabilities are reported as .96 for the Total Test, .84 for Mathematics, .96 for Reading Recognition, .88 of Reading Comprehension, .88 for Spelling, and .91 for General Information. The median standard error of measurement for standard scores (mean of 100 and standard deviation of 15) is reported for both grade and age norms. These figures indicate median SEM estimates as approximately 2.0 points for the total test and range from 2.4 to 4.1 for the subtests. Reliability for the Written Expression-Level 1 subtest was calculated using interrater, internal consistency, and test-retest procedures. Although interrater reliabilities were high (.88–.95), more modest estimates were obtained with internal consistency (.61–.69) and test-retest (.56) procedures. Written Expression-Level 2 reliabilities were determined using interrater, internal consistency, and alternate form estimates for the two forms (i.e., the two different picture prompts—A/B). Median interrater reliabilities were .58/.67 for the two prompts, internal consistency estimates of .86/.88 were obtained for the total sample, and test-retest estimates ranged from .44 to .61.

Two types of validity information are presented in the PIAT manual: content and construct. Content validity was established by extensive review of curriculum materials to aid in item development. In addition, experts in the various areas were asked to evaluate the extent to which the test material was representative of the curricula of various grade levels and the specific content domain (e.g., mathematics) to be tested. The use of time review, item analysis, and content experts in the test development process is detailed in the test manual and appears very thorough. Construct validity was based on correlations between scores on the PIAT-R and both the original PIAT and the PPVT-R. These results suggest moderate overlap between these tests as would be expected. Factor analysis was also used to assess construct validity and yielded a three-factor solution, generally supportive of test validity (Benes, 1992; Rogers, 1992).

Summary

The PIAT-R continues to be widely used in screening academic skill development and is a significant improvement on the original PIAT. The multiple-choice format is especially useful for children with language or physical disabilities. The reliability and validity information is impressive, although more data assessing concurrent validity need to be collected. The vast amount of research with the original edition of this test suggests that this test does what it purports to: provide a rough measure of academic competence across a number of important academic skill areas.

Wide Range Achievement Test-Revised

Overview and Purpose

According to the authors of the Wide Range Achievement Test-Revised, or WRAT-R (Jastak & Wilkinson, 1984), this test is designed to measure the "codes" that are essential to learning basic skills in arithmetic, spelling, and reading. There are two levels (or forms) of the test. Level 1 is intended for subjects between the ages of 5-0 and 11-11 years; Level 2 is for those from 12-0 years through adulthood. The specific number and type of items on each subtest vary between the levels. The test is designed to minimize the importance of comprehension skills in order to separate those whose problems are related to the "codes . . . necessary to acquire the skill" (Jastak & Wilkinson, 1984, p. 1) from those with comprehension problems. No definition of the term "codes" is provided. The subtests include:

1. Reading—naming and recognizing letters as well as reading words in isolation (i.e., word recognition)

2. Spelling—copying symbols, writing the subject's name, and spelling dictated words

3. Arithmetic—counting, reading numbers, and solving oral problems and written computations

Standardization Sample and Norms

The WRAT-R was standardized on 5,600 individuals, with 250 subjects tested in each of 28 age groups between 5 years and 74 years, 11 months. The sample was stratified on the basis of five factors: age, sex, race, geographic region, and metropolitan/nonmetropolitan residence. Most populations with disabilities were excluded from the standardization, although an attempt was made to include individuals with mental disabilities (2% of the sample). Some difficulty in obtaining a representative adult sample was indicated.

Data Obtained

Raw scores from the WRAT-R can be translated into standard scores, grade equivalents, and percentiles.

Reliability and Validity

Reliability data are briefly presented on one page of the WRAT-R manual, and figures for test-retest (the retest interval is not specified) and standard errors of measurement are provided. Test-retest figures are: Level 1 (N = 81)—Reading (.96), Spelling (.97), Arithmetic (.94); Level 2 (N = 67)—Reading (.90), Spelling (.89), Arithmetic (.79). Standard error of measurement (SEM) calculations are provided at five points across the ability range. No details on the method of dividing the sample or the number of subjects in any of the ability level groups are provided. Further, these calculations were made on the raw scores rather than any of the derived scores (e.g., standard scores). The range of raw score SEM figures for the WRAT-R are: Level 1—Reading (1.55–2.55), Spelling (1.61–1.77), Arithmetic (1.22–1.89); Level 2—Reading (1.96–2.52), Spelling (1.40–2.05), Arithmetic (1.92–2.12).

Information on content, construct, and concurrent validity is presented in the WRAT-R manual. According to its authors, the content validity of the WRAT-R "is apparent," although details are not provided. As evidence of construct validity the authors cite the fact that the test becomes easier as children get older and for concurrent validity the reader is referred to earlier studies with the WRAT. Although the authors should be congratulated for their desire to include data about the test's validity, the discussions are very minimal. It would be helpful to know, for example, how items were originally selected for inclusion on the WRAT-R. Were experts consulted? Were textbooks analyzed? Knowing that earlier editions of the WRAT yielded scores that were moderately correlated with other achievement tests is not sufficient evidence of the concurrent validity of the revised WRAT. Also, the discussions of validity often are difficult to follow, which appears to support Thorndike's (1972) comments about the description of validity procedures in an earlier edition of the WRAT: "The exact nature of the procedure is apparently known only to the authors and God, and He may have some uncertainty" (p. 68).

Summary

The WRAT-R has been a most durable achievement battery, probably because it is easy and quickly administered. First available in 1936, the standardization of its current version is an improvement over earlier editions with their many problems (see Thorndike, 1972). Indeed, the

WRAT-R spelling test appears to be one of the most ecologically valid available. On this subtest the examiner says a word, reads a sentence using the word, and then repeats the word. Only then does the examinee attempt to write the word. There are many problems with the WRAT-R, among the most important of which is that it assesses a very narrow range of skills, by far the narrowest of any instrument examined in this chapter. To describe the word recognition task of the WRAT-R as reading is a misnomer, and the arithmetic test provides no sample applications of arithmetic skills. Except as a screening device or a supplement to other instruments, the WRAT-R cannot be recommended.

Woodcock-Johnson Psychoeducational Battery-Revised

Overview and Purpose

The Woodcock-Johnson Psychoeducational Battery-Revised, or WJ-R (Woodcock & Johnson, 1991), is a comprehensive, multiple-skill battery designed to assess cognitive skills and achievement. The WJ-R is individually administered to subjects from 3 to 80 years of age. The complete battery contains 39 tests or measures organized into two parts: Cognitive Ability and Academic Achievement. There are 21 tests for evaluating cognitive ability and 18 tests for assessing academic achievement. Both the cognitive and achievement parts of the test are further divided into standard and supplemental batteries. The achievement battery has two alternate forms (A and B). The number of tests administered to a particular individual is a function of the subject's age and the purpose of the assessment (e.g., reading comprehension would not be administered to a typical three-year-old, or an examiner may wish to test only cognitive abilities or achievement or a subsection of these skills). As would be expected, the time needed to administer the WJ-R depends on the purpose of the assessment, the age and responsiveness of the examinee, and the number of tests to be administered.

The WJ-R is both a revised and an expanded version of the original Woodcock-Johnson. For example, changes include new tests added to the cognitive and achievement batteries, individual items revised and reordered on some subtests, and more sample items added to some subtests. As mentioned, the achievement battery now has two parallel forms (A and B). Individuals familiar with the previous edition will note that the WJ-R no longer includes tests of interests. According to the authors, the uses of the revised Woodcock-Johnson include diagnosis, determination of discrepancies among academic and cognitive abilities, program placement, planning individual programs, guidance, assessment of growth, program evaluation, research, and psychometric training.

Standardization Sample and Norms

The WJ-R was standardized on 6,359 subjects (the majority, or 3,245, were in school at the time) in more than 100 communities throughout the United States. The sample was stratified on the basis of 1980 and later census data according to the following subject and community variables: sex, race, geographic region, and community size. For adults these variables were also considered: funding source of college and university being attended (for the college sample), type of college, education, occupational status, and occupation. The manual states that "Severely handicapped students" were not included in the sample; however, the term was not defined. Nor were students with less than one year of experience with English included in the sample.

Data Obtained

Although the WJ-R is organized into subtests, the basic units of analysis are the cluster scores, or scores earned on groups of subtests. The WJ-R yields a variety of derived scores including cluster scores, percentile rankings, age and grade equivalents, and relative mastery indexes.

Scoring the WJ-R may be the most difficult task associated with the test. According to Cummings (1985), in his review of the original Woodcock-Johnson Psychoeducational Battery:

> once the instrument has been administered, the process of obtaining derived scores is somewhat arduous. There are numerous score transformations and sums to be added. Consider the process of obtaining a percentile rank for a child's verbal ability cluster. The raw score is transformed to a part score, the part scores are totalled to obtain a cluster score, the average age score for the child's chronological age is found in a table and then subtracted from the obtained cluster score in order to arrive at the cluster difference score, and finally a table is consulted to determine the examinee's percentile rank. For Parts I and II of the battery, this procedure must be completed 13 times. (p. 1760)

Scoring of the current revision is just as difficult and examiners are encouraged to use the computer-based scoring system available from the test publisher (written expression must be hand scored).

Reliability and Validity

Split-half reliabilities for subtest scores and cluster scores are reported and are generally excellent. Median reliabilities on the achievement battery are all above .86 for subtests and .94 for clusters. No test-retest comparisons are reported (except for Writing Fluency, in which split-half estimates were inappropriate), and thus no evidence on the effects of stability over time is available.

Extensive concurrent and predictive validity data are reported in the manual. The WJ-R serves as an excellent model for the reporting of test validity data. Correlations with a number of intellectual measures (e.g., the K-ABC), achievement tests (e.g., K-TEA, PIAT, WRAT-R), and related tests are reported. These data all tend to support the validity of the WJ-R and indicate that the test measures what it claims to measure: cognitive abilities and achievement. A major shortcoming is that no specific information is presented to support the uses of the WJ-R that have been identified by the authors.

Summary

The WJ-R is a useful individually administered battery of tests. It is relatively easy to administer, adequately standardized, reliable, and valid, but difficult to score. Our experience with the written language subtests suggests that these subtests can be especially difficult to score reliably. In a relatively short period this test has had a significant impact on achievement testing and today is one of the most popular individually administered batteries with school-age populations. The inclusion of measures of cognitive ability and achievement within an individually administered battery is an innovative and positive feature. Coverage of such a broad age range also makes the WJ-R an attractive instrument.

Chapter Summary

Earlier in the chapter we referred to certain issues involved in minimal competency testing. This area will continue to be an important one as schools and states attempt to develop evaluation programs to ensure that students have learned and teachers can teach. Achievement batteries will most certainly play a significant role in such evaluations, although many questions about their use have been raised. Many have even questioned whether *any* tests can measure competence. The movement toward curriculum-based assessment techniques discussed elsewhere in this text (e.g., see chapter 17) also offers hope for a better understanding of what it means to be competent in a particular academic skill area. Debates will continue, but in the interim many states already have mandated that teachers and students must be tested to determine minimal competence.

Unfortunately, in the haste to develop programs to test minimal competence, many poor tests and testing practices have been used. One of the most persistent problems facing individuals has been how to establish the cutoff scores that determine who passes and who fails the test (Livingston & Zieky, 1982). In the past, three basic approaches have been used (Wise, 1985). The first is to adopt cutoff scores used at other locations for the same test. The second is to collect preliminary scores for a limited period and then to use them to establish a cutoff. The third approach is to form a panel of "experts" in the area you are evaluating (e.g., teacher education) and have them systematically assess the test items to determine cutoff scores.

The first approach is clearly the simplest. However, this will not work if a test has been developed for local use, if others have not used the test, or if different cutoffs have been used in different places. Finally, this approach may cause legal problems if you cannot justify the score you have established. Imagine trying to justify your decision not to let students graduate from high school because their scores fell below a cutoff that was established in another state or part of the country!

In the second approach, local data could be used to establish the cutoff scores, although there remains the problem of establishing the number of individuals who should pass and fail. For example, it may be decided that the lowest 20 percent of the examinees will fail a given test. But what happens if the quality of the people passing and failing the test changes from year to year? In the first year you may be content that the lowest 20 percent failed, but in subsequent years you may feel that the 20 percent cutoff is discriminating against people who are truly competent or letting incompetent people slip through. In either case, how do you know what level of performance signifies competence?

In the third approach, the use of a panel of experts has the advantage of requiring panel members to directly judge the minimal level of basic skills required to pass certain test items. There is, however, no guarantee that the experts will arrive at an acceptable or useful cutoff.

The development of basic competency tests and the establishment of cutoff scores are not easy tasks. Although the answers are not simple, we can be assured that with the push for excellence in education, minimal competency tests will be with us for the foreseeable future. Achievement batteries have proved to be useful tools in the assessment of behavior, although they are not without the potential for abuse. In the future we will undoubtedly discover improved techniques for developing such tests and expand the number of uses for them. Remember, however, that no test will help you if you have not planned carefully and systematically defined your reasons for giving a test in the first place.

Chapter 8

Preschool Screening, Kindergarten Readiness, and Early Identification of At-Risk Students

Learning Objectives

1. Describe the typical course of cognitive, motor, and social-emotional development during early childhood.
2. List typical expected learner outcomes for kindergarten students.
3. Identify at least five major preschool screening measures.
4. Discuss preschool screening procedures and identify at least two target behaviors in each of five major areas of development.
5. Cite and discuss three major concerns in the assessment of preschool children.

If you want to teach someone, does it matter whether the person is two or eight years old? Of course it does. Even if you have not had much firsthand experience with young children, you know that they differ in many ways that influence how they learn and how they are taught. For example, given normal development, we expect two- and eight-year-olds to differ significantly in language and other cognitive skills, motor performance, and social-emotional functioning. Developmental differences in such skill domains influence when children are ready to learn, or when their skills best match the instructional expectations or demands of formal educational systems.

In this chapter, we explore the concept of educational readiness, the burgeoning area of preschool screening, and the use of tests to make decisions about young children. Such an examination is needed because a substantial number of young children are struggling and even failing in school. Some of these children are physically or cognitively disabled, others have come from impoverished environments that did not facilitate their growth, and still others simply started school too early. This chapter focuses on three topics: (a) early childhood development and typical entry expectations of schools, (b) issues in preschool screening, and (c) methods for assessing young children's development and readiness for school. These topics have a rich and extensive history, particularly in the disciplines of education and developmental psychology (Biber, 1984; Bruner, 1960; Kelley & Surbeck, 1983).

➡ *Early Childhood Development and Educational Readiness*

Early childhood, which we rather arbitrarily consider to occur between the ages of two and six, is typically a period of rapid physical, cognitive, and emotional growth. For example, during this time, children usually acquire the ability to ride tricycles and bicycles, draw pictures, print their names, speak in complete sentences, feed and toilet themselves, and play "appropriately" with other children. The abilities or skills underlying such tasks are the result of a complex interaction of a child's inherited and acquired characteristics with the environment. Jean Piaget has provided a viable model for understanding the development of many important cognitive and emotional attributes and has significantly influenced the concept of readiness. A brief examination of his work provides the theoretical background for conceptualizing human development and some benchmarks of normalcy.

Piaget's Theory of Cognitive Development

Piaget (1954, 1963, 1970) developed an interactive model to describe the process by which human beings go about making sense of their world. According to his model, people are adaptive, information-seeking beings with an internal set of principles that are used to organize knowledge about their environment. Piaget believed that from birth a person begins to look for ways to adapt to the environment. Two basic processes hypothesized to be involved in this adaption are assimilation and accommodation. **Assimilation** is the process of relating new information to existing ways of thinking. **Accommodation** is the process of modifying existing cognitive structures so that new information can be understood. It is imperative to think of assimilation and accommodation as occurring together. Consider the following example. A three-year-old is on a ride in the countryside with her parents and sees a cow for the first time. She promptly points toward the cow and says, "Big doggy!" Her mother, however, politely corrects her by saying, "That's a cow, honey, not a dog." In this brief example, the little girl has taken new information (seeing a cow) and assimilated it into her scheme for a dog. For this assimilation to occur, however, the dog scheme requires some modification (accommodation). By repeatedly seeing a cow and hearing it called a cow, she will differentiate her dog scheme into dog and cow schemes, thus allowing for rapid, accurate assimilation of both dogs and cows in future interactions with such animals.

Piaget believed humans strive for balance, or **equilibrium,** between assimilation and accommodation. Obviously, if we always assimilated information, we would end up with a few, very large schemes and thus have difficulty detecting differences in things. Conversely, if we always accommodated information, we would end up with a huge number of schemes and then have difficulty detecting similarities in the things we perceive. The desire for equilibrium is an overriding principle of mental growth that allows us to develop more and more complex but stable schemes.

Piaget hypothesized that **equilibration** (the act of searching for balance between assimilation and accommodation) was the major process of cognitive development. He identified the forces causing equilibration as biological maturation, activity with the physical environment, and experience with the social environment. Although the process of equilibration or cognitive development was theorized to take place throughout a person's life, the most significant growth was believed to occur between birth and 15 or 16 years of age. According to Piaget, the major changes in cognitive development could best be characterized by a sequential model of four stages: the sensorimotor, preoperational, concrete operational, and formal operational stages. Table 8.1 identifies the approximate ages and major characteristics associated with each stage. Since this chapter focuses on children between the ages of two and six, we will be interested primarily in the preoperational stage. A brief overview of the stages coming immediately before and after preoperations, however, is necessary for a more complete understanding of early childhood developmental changes.

Sensorimotor Stage

This first major stage of cognitive development earns its name from the fact that infants gain information from their senses and their actions or body movements. An important acquisition during the first two years of life is the realization that objects in the environment are permanent, or in other words, stable and separate from the infant. This knowledge, referred to as **object permanence** by Piaget, arises from repeated activities and observations in which objects and people appear, disappear, and reappear.

A second major accomplishment during this initial period of development is the beginning of logical goal-directed actions. Through repeated trial-and-error interactions, infants begin to organize their behavior to manipulate toys and other objects successfully. Random, uncoordinated interactions with familiar objects diminish in number as they are replaced by more systematic, intentional motor actions.

Table 8.1   Piaget's Stages of Cognitive Development

Stage	Approximate Age	Characteristics
Sensorimotor	0–2 years	Begins to make use of imitation, memory, and thought Begins to recognize that objects do not cease to exist when they are hidden Moves from reflex actions to goal-directed activity
Preoperational	2–7 years	Gradual language development and ability to think in symbolic form Able to think operations through logically in one direction Has difficulties seeing another person's point of view
Concrete Operational	7–11 years	Able to solve concrete (hands-on) problems in logical fashion Understands laws of conservation and is able to classify and seriate Understands reversibility
Formal Operational	11–15 years	Able to solve abstract problems in logical fashion Thinking becomes more scientific Develops concerns about social issues, identity

From *Piaget's Theory of Cognitive and Affective Development* by Barry J. Wadsworth. Copyright © 1971, 1979, 1984, 1989 by Longman Publishing Group.

Preoperational Stage

This stage spans the period commonly referred to as early childhood and generally is characterized by tremendous growth in the internalization of operations. According to Piaget, operations are actions that are first carried out mentally rather than physically. To internalize actions, it is hypothesized that symbols representative of objects are used. For adults, written and spoken language provides the primary set of symbols. Preoperational children, however, have just begun to acquire language. In fact, language acquisition, which begins with physically mimicking others' actions and progresses to speaking in complete subject-verb expressions, is the most important development in the preoperational stage. Language provides the symbolic basis for internalizing thoughts and actions, thus allowing the child to interact with the surroundings in many ways that foster the equilibration process.

Piaget found that even though preoperational children are able to internalize actions using symbols, they are unable to reverse an operation; that is, they are able to model an action or image in the fashion shown but cannot work consistently backward or in a reverse process from that shown. Reversible thinking requires the ability to keep an entire action in mind and to grasp the concept of **conservation,** or the understanding that the amount of something (e.g., clay and water) remains the same even if its appearance is changed, as long as nothing is actually added or taken away. Piaget developed several simple tasks to assess conservation. He concluded that the ability to understand conservation is a complex task that few children younger than seven can consistently accomplish.

In addition to being unable to reverse their thinking and being confused by changes in appearance, preoperational children are very egocentric. This does not mean that they think a lot of themselves but rather that they are not able to see the world from a perspective other than their own. **Egocentrism** is predominant in preoperational children because of their inability to mentally manipulate their environment and their general lack of experience with the world.

In sum, the preoperational child is grappling with the ability to internalize actions. Language development provides a symbolic medium for this internalization, yet the child's cognitive skills are not developed sufficiently to permit mental reversibility or conservation of objects. An egocentric window on the world can be expected given the relative paucity of experiences and attention allocated to the task of language acquisition. Guidelines for successfully working with children in the preoperational stage include:

1. Make instructions relatively short (in two parts) and use actions accompanied by words to model the instructions.

2. Use concrete props and visual aids whenever possible to illustrate desired actions.

3. Do not expect the children to see the world from someone else's perspective easily.

4. Allow children much practice with facts and skills so that they establish fundamental building blocks for later development.

Concrete Operational Stage

The basic characteristics of this stage, which spans the ages of approximately 7 to 11 years, are that children recognize that (a) the physical world is logically stable, (b) elements can be changed or transformed and still retain many of their original characteristics, and (c) these changes are reversible. Probably the most basic of all concrete operational skills is the ability to conserve quantity. The reasoning skills underlying this ability are typically referred to as identity, conservation, and reversibility. **Identity** is the concept that if nothing is added or taken away, the material is unchanged. **Conservation** is the concept that an apparent change in one direction can be conserved or counterbalanced by a change in another direction. Finally, **reversibility** is the concept that a change that has been made can be mentally canceled. The combination of these three concepts allows the concrete operational child to master the two-way thinking unavailable to the preoperational child.

Two other important operations typically mastered in this stage of cognitive development are classification and seriation. **Classification** requires a child to assess and compare details of objects so they can be grouped according to similarities. **Seriation** is the process of orderly arranging objects according to size or quantity. With the ability to conserve, classify, and seriate, a child has developed a rather sophisticated system of thinking that allows for many varied interactions with the environment. The ability to deal with complex abstract problems and to think scientifically remains to be developed in Piaget's fourth and final development stage, formal operations.

As a means of reviewing many of the important cognitive developments of children, table 8.2 summarizes the relationship between cognitive concepts and readiness to complete mathematical operations in children from two to seven years old. This table also highlights the practical impact of Piaget's work on early childhood education.

Despite much theoretical and empirical support, Piaget's theories of cognitive development have received criticism. Perhaps the most serious criticisms have been offered by neo-Piagetians such as Case (1974), who depart from Piaget's theory in assuming that stage transition takes place by a set of processes oriented toward problem solving. Thus, the neo-Piagetians seem to represent a middle position between information-processing theorists and Piagetian developmentalists. In brief, the neo-Piagetians readily acknowledge that knowledge is a critical factor in cognitive development, yet they perceive mental processes such as short-term memory to be more important. To date, the impact of this viewpoint primarily has been theoretical. Regardless of one's emphasis on cognitive processes, however, the stages of intellectual development described by Piaget have stood the rigorous test of time and still prevail today.

With this review of the highlights of Piaget's work and brief discussion of the neo-Piagetian position on early childhood cognitive development, we are ready to focus on nine areas of development traditionally assessed in a preschool evaluation.

Table 8.2   Mathematical Readiness According to Piaget's Preoperational Stage of Cognitive Development   (Children from Two to Seven Years Old)

Readiness of Child

Cognitive Concept	Stage I (2 to 5 years)	Stage II (5 to 7 years)
Spatial Relations The ability to perceive and compare spatial forms and patterns accurately. The ability to visualize size, depth, and distance.	Can discriminate between similar objects, if distinction is obvious.	Can discriminate difference in pattern if shape is similar.
Object permanence Size	Well established. Can distinguish differences.	Well established. Can begin to discriminate using two characteristics. Can recall differences from own experiences.
Distance	Knows distance within own experience.	Can think about distance using concrete experiences.
Time	Remembers what comes first. Can wait according to own daily activities. Understands: today, tomorrow, morning, afternoon.	Can anticipate and plan on the basis of own experiences. Understands relative length of "minute," "hour," "day." Realizes birthdays are repeated, and how old will be on next birthday. Can tell time to hour.
Classification The ability to group objects according to certain defined characteristics.	Most often cannot classify because child forgets the characteristic to identify the class.	Can classify using some definite property, i.e., redness, but cannot put into more general category because does not understand the concept of inclusion: i.e., bananas, apples, and oranges are all fruit.
One-to-One Correspondence The child's ability to understand that one object is *one*, regardless of its characteristics and that the number concept of *one* child is the same as *one* apple. The ability to count meaningfully is related to this concept.	Rarely understands. Can count by rote but is usually reciting a memorized list of words and will skip items or "count" when no object is present.	Can do with some assistance. Spatial concepts are not well developed, so child will have tendency to assume that other characteristics influence numerosity. Has difficulty with such games as Musical Chairs.

184

Readiness of Child

Cognitive Concept	Stage I (2 to 5 years)	Stage II (5 to 7 years)
Seriation The ability to order objects in relation to one or more of the characteristics, i.e., length, weight, or volume.	Cannot do, because cannot consider all the characteristics of an object.	Can do with objects that are equally separate from each other, i.e., line up sticks that are one inch, two inches, three inches, etc., but has more difficulty with such items as stones that are of random shapes and weights.
Reversibility The ability to recognize that objects, when changed and rearranged can return to their original condition.	Cannot do.	Cannot do. Can perform an experiment such as pouring water from two beakers back into one larger one to prove the same amount of water is present, but does not understand concept.
Conservation The ability to recognize that number, size, weight, and volume remain the same regardless of the arrangement or shape of the object or objects.	Cannot do. Concentrates on only characteristics and centers on how object "looks."	Can do with some help. If shown that there are equal number of cups to saucers, will remember even when they are separated and rearranged. Understands conservation of quantity.
Language The ability to use words describing the concepts of number, comparing, contrasting, and problem solving.	Uses names for size, although there is some confusion, i.e., "big" for "tall" or "larger."	Uses words correctly to describe size, weight, depth, distance. Increasing vocabulary to correspond to increasing ability to classify. Can easily identify and label "biggest," "littlest."

From *Informal Assessment in Education* (pp. 260–261) by Gilbert R. Guerin and Arlee S. Maier, 1983, Palo Alto, CA: Mayfield Publishing Company. Copyright © 1983 Mayfield Publishing Company. Reprinted by permission.

Focus on
Research and Practice

Early Identification of Developmentally Disabled and At-Risk Preschoolers

Attempts to identify children at risk for developmental disabilities were initially reported more than a century ago (Little, 1861). Since that time, many researchers have attempted to isolate prenatal and perinatal traumata that negatively affect the developmental pathways of infants and toddlers. Researchers that examined isolated factors such as anoxia concluded that models which attempt to predict school-age functioning on the basis of a single factor were plagued by unacceptably high rates of error and misclassification. What has become apparent from all the research is that a child's development cannot be predicted independent of caretaking experiences (Werner & Smith, 1982). Significant cross-cultural evidence also underscores the impact of social environment on mental performance (Susser, Hauser, & Kelly, 1985). Given this perspective, Kochanek, Kabacoff, and Lipsitt (1990) asked the question, Which child and parental attributes accurately predict adolescent status, and how do these factors change over time? The answer to this question is clearly of interest to developmental researchers, as well as to persons working across the United States to implement a comprehensive child-find system for P.L. 99–457. Let's examine a method for answering this question and the answer that Kochanek and his colleagues provided.

Using a sample of 513 adolescent students (268 disabled and 268 non-disabled) from the original National Collaborative Perinatal Project in Rhode Island who were all judged as disabled at school entry, Kochanek and his colleagues examined child-centered data (i.e., cognitive, motor, physical, language) over the course of the children's first seven years and familial factors (i.e., pregnancy history, maternal childhood diseases, labor data, maternal education). Results of the study indicated that parental traits (i.e., maternal education) were more accurate predictors of adolescent status than the child's own behavior from birth to three years, whereas child-centered skills assessed at four and seven years of age are better predictors than familial factors. Overall, the data suggested that early identification models which focus upon developmental delay or adverse medical events from birth to three years of age are inadequate in fully identifying children eventually judged to be disabled. The researchers recommended practitioners develop screening initiatives that are both child and family focused and account for differential weights of risk factors over time.

Based on this research conducted by Kochanek, Kabacoff, and Lipsitt, one can see the need to assess both the child and the environment (i.e., family) is empirically wise practice and now the law given the implementation of P.L. 99–457.

Source: Based on T. T. Kochanek, R. I. Kabacoff, and L. P. Lippsitt, "Early Identification of Developmentally Disabled and At-Risk Preschool Children" in *Exceptional Children*, 56(6): 528–538, 1990.

➡ *Areas of Development Targeted for Assessment*

Many different sets of developmental categories or skills have been identified as important targets of assessment. However, none of the sets is ideal because it is difficult to separate abilities into nonoverlapping categories. Lichtenstein and Ireton (1984) proposed an appealing taxonomy of nine broad areas: perceptual processing, cognitive, language, speech/articulation, gross motor, fine motor, self-help, social-emotional, and school readiness. In the remainder of this section, we define and discuss behaviors typically observed in each of these categories.

Perceptual Processing

A normal child develops the ability to perceive and act upon increasingly complex perceptual stimuli over several years. Visual and auditory information from the environment is received by the child's sensory system and must be neurologically transmitted and interpreted. Such processing of information requires a well-coordinated, intact neurological system. The typical preschool child will not have fully developed information-processing capacities and thus may have difficulty copying simple shapes (e.g., triangles, squares, diamonds), distinguishing left and right consistently, discriminating between letter symbols, or blending sounds together to form words.

Perceptual-processing difficulties are not easily distinguished from other developmental areas because the perception process is prerequisite to the functioning of virtually all behavior. Clearly, auditory perceptual processes are central to receptive language, and visual-motor processes are essential to fine motor and gross motor functioning.

In most cases, poor perceptual processing results from developmental immaturity and limited stimulation. A very small percentage of preschoolers, however, have some fundamental dysfunction in their neurological system and do not benefit from increased stimulation experiences.

Cognitive

In general, cognition encompasses a wide range of mental abilities that are often referred to as intelligence. In practice, subsets of cognitive abilities, namely attention, memory, comprehension, and reasoning, are of primary concern to educators and psychologists. Activities such as classifying objects according to color, shape, or size; identifying similarities and differences; repeating phrases or sets of numbers; and naming letters and numbers are examples of tasks requiring basic cognitive skills.

Language

Language and cognitive abilities are interrelated and thus illustrate overlapping categories. Nevertheless, certain tasks, such as defining words, supplying words to complete a sentence, and labeling an object, place greater emphasis on language than other cognitive abilities.

Language abilities can be divided into receptive language and expressive language. Receptive language involves the ability to understand what is said and is often assessed in young children by observing motor responses such as nodding or pointing. Expressive language requires speaking and involves knowledge of syntax and grammar. It is assessed by analyzing language samples on dimensions of sentence length and complexity, word use, and grammatical features. In general, oral expressive language abilities develop later than receptive language; children thus often understand the meaning of a word long before they say that word.

Speech/Articulation

Although speech and language are highly related, they are distinct aspects of verbal communication. Speech involves the generation of sound in a coherent pattern. It is the process of using language. Important components of speech are articulation (formation of sounds), voice (pitch and intensity of vocal production), and rhythm (integration of sounds in a comprehensible manner).

In the preschool years, the assessment of speech is at a basic level. For example, are the child's verbalizations intelligible? Minor articulation errors are common. The most active period of speech-sound development is from 18 months to four years, by which time all the vowel sounds and many consonant sounds are mastered by normal children. Acquisition of vowel sounds is normally completed by age three, whereas all consonant sounds often are not accomplished until age eight (Lamberts, 1979).

Gross Motor

The years from two to six are considered the "golden years" for motor development. During this period, most children acquire a basic repertoire of manipulative and locomotor skills, develop goal-directed motor behaviors, and learn to connect two or three movement sequences (Cratty, 1970). The major gross motor skills to develop during these years are body projection, body manipulation, and object manipulation (Williams, 1983). Typical body projection skills include running, jumping, hopping, skipping, and sliding. All require coordination among large muscle masses to move one's total body. Body manipulation skills, on the other hand, involve moving one's body or body parts in a well-defined but small area. Typical body manipulation skills include stretching, curling, rolling, bending, and balancing. Object manipulations universally observed in young children include throwing, catching, striking, kicking, and ball bouncing (De Oreo, 1980). It is not uncommon for this array of gross motor skills to be developed unevenly in preschoolers.

Fine Motor

Fine motor skills involve control over fine muscles. In regard to school functioning, these skills primarily involve eye-hand coordination. This is readily apparent in tasks such as drawing, coloring, cutting, and manipulating small objects. The skills required to accomplish these tasks successfully range from fundamental to more complex visual-spatial or perceptual-motor abilities, which in turn are important indicators of readiness for reading and writing. In chapter 12 we will discuss perceptual-motor skills and assessment in detail, but we have provided table 8.3 to illustrate a typical pattern of perceptual–fine motor skill development during the period from two to seven years.

Self-Help

Feeding, toileting, washing, and dressing are examples of basic self-help skills expected of preschoolers. They are commonly thought of as adaptive behaviors (see chapter 14 for details) and are clearly prerequisites for entry to a mainstream school setting. Attitudes of independence from adults and control over one's environment accompany the development of self-help skills in preschoolers.

Social-Emotional

By two years of age most children display a unique personality. They exhibit emotions and are becoming increasingly social with peers and adults. The ability to separate from a parent without anxiety, follow rules and develop a sense of right and wrong, and relate to others are important social-emotional developments for preschoolers. Of all the areas of development, this one is possibly characterized by the greatest number of individual differences and thus is the hardest to describe in terms of a "normal" pattern.

The identification of social-emotional problems in young children is particularly difficult, because it is normal for children to demonstrate some problems (such as temper tantrums, withdrawal from people, crying, and a high activity level) some of the time. The differences between children with serious social-emotional problems and normal children are often differences in the frequency, intensity, and duration of an undesirable behavior.

**Table 8.3   Typical Perceptual–Fine Motor Development
in Children from Two to Seven Years Old**

---

2 years

Rotates forearm (supinates), turns
   knobs
Turns pages singly
Strings several beads
Unwraps piece of candy
Imitates vertical stroke
Crudely imitates circular stroke
Imitates a V stroke
Aligns 2 or more blocks for a train
Makes 6–7 block tower
Can match 2 or more simple shapes
Places blocks on formboard separately
   with demonstration

2J* years

Grasps too strongly with overextension
Places blocks in formboard with no
   demonstration
May imitate H in drawing
Imitates horizontal line
Holds crayon with fingers
Builds 8-block tower
Adds 1-block chimney to block train
Matches 1 color form
Dries own hands

3 years

Good rotation of wrist
Builds 9–10 block tower
Imitates cross
Copies circle from a model
Cuts with scissors
Matches 3 color forms
Puts on socks and shoes
Unbuttons medium shirt buttons
Places 10 pellets in bottle in 30 sec (1
   at a time)

3J* years

Traces a diamond
Builds 3-block bridge from model
Washes and dries hands and face
Feeds self well
Matches simple colors

4 years

Throws overhand
Cuts with scissors
Copies cross from a model
Draws crude pictures of familiar things
Builds with large blocks
Copies a diagonal line
Buttons large buttons
Knows front from back on clothes
Brushes teeth
Places 10 pellets into bottle in 25 sec
Performs serial opposition of thumb to
   fingers

4J* years

Copies a square
Draws a person with several body parts
Draws pictures of familiar objects
Identifies simple objects by feeling, such
   as ball, block, or crayon
Catches a bounced ball
May name several colors

5 years

Prehends precisely and releases well
Tries to color within lines
May copy an X
May copy a triangle
Enjoys coloring, cutting, and pasting
Laces shoes without tying
Can dress and undress alone except for
   small buttons and bows
Draws a house with windows and doors
Draws a person with arms, legs, feet, and
   facial features

Table 8.3—*Continued*

6 years

Ties shoelaces loosely in a bow
Throws ball with follow-through
Can print some letters and numbers
    (may be reversed)
Draws person with detailed body parts
    and some clothing
Imitates inverted triangle
May imitate horizontal diamond

Buttons small buttons on shirt or blouse
May know right and left on self
May have stable hand preference

7 years

Copies a Maltese cross
Cuts with knife
No longer has *b–d* confusion
Draws human figure with clearly
    represented clothing

*J means the skill/behavior is *just* beginning to appear.

From Bruce A. Bracken, *The Psychoeducational Assessment of Preschool Children,* Second Edition. Copyright © 1991 by Allyn and Bacon. Reprinted with permission. Compiled from Gesell & Amatruda (1947); Gesell & Ilg (1946); Hartlage and Lucas (1973); Kaufman (1978); and Werner (1980).

School Readiness

Technically, school readiness is not an area of development but rather subsumes a wide range of skills and behavior related to success in school. School readiness primarily cuts across areas of cognitive, language, and fine motor development. Skills or behaviors typically considered important to school readiness include copying shapes and figures, identifying numbers and letters, knowing left and right orientation, and understanding basic concepts such as same-different, top-bottom, first-last, and before-after. Most educators believe attentional abilities and interpersonal characteristics such as working and playing cooperatively and following teachers' directions are also important prerequisites for success in school.

The concept of readiness has been an important issue for developmental psychologists for years and is a major concern of early childhood educators. Its essence is the match between the skills or abilities of a child and the skill demands of the tasks required at school. When these two variables match, learning is expected to advance more easily, meaningfully, and with less negative affect. Today there are nearly 100 tests and assessment procedures designed specifically to chart early childhood development and make decisions about school readiness. A sample of such tests is examined in the next section.

➡ *Developmental and Preschool Screening Instruments*

The development and use of tests for preschoolers has rapidly increased during the past 15 years. Much of this increase can be attributed to federal legislation directed at improving early childhood education, especially for "at risk" and disabled children (see the Focus on Law later in this chapter). However, simply having a large number of tests does not guarantee that good tests exist or that they are appropriately used. Our goal is to provide a rather extensive list of basic indexes of many tests and a detailed critique of three screening instruments. Readers interested in more comprehensive test reviews are referred to Lichtenstein and Ireton's (1984) book on preschool screening or Bagnato and Neisworth's (1991) book on assessment for early intervention.

Although nearly 100 tests are available for preschool screening, the viable alternatives can be readily reduced to a manageable few when selection criteria include adequate coverage of a specific domain of behavior and empirical evidence of reliability and validity. For our discussion we have selected individually administered tests appropriate for children between the ages of two and six and have categorized tests as multidimensional, language, speech/articulation, perceptual-motor, social-emotional, or observational.

Multidimensional Tests

Instruments covering multiple areas of functioning, such as cognition, language, and perceptual-motor skills, are traditionally referred to as multidimensional tests. Lichtenstein and Ireton (1984) compiled a list of 32 tests that they considered multidimensional preschool measures. Many of these are identified in table 8.4, along with basic selection information about their age range, administration time, nature, developmental areas covered, and availability of technical data.

Developmental Indicators for the Assessment of Learning-Revised (DIAL-R)

The Developmental Indicators for the Assessment of Learning-Revised or DIAL-R (Mardell-Czudnowski & Goldenberg, 1990) is an individually administered screening test designed to identify young children (ages 2–0 to 5–11 years) in need of further diagnostic assessment or curricular intervention. The DIAL-R is a revision of the Developmental Indicators for the Assessment of Learning developed by Mardell and Goldenberg in 1975 and originally revised in 1983. The present edition uses the 1983 standardization sample; however, the norms were entirely reanalyzed in 1990 to adjust for score inaccuracies that occurred in the original norms development.

The DIAL-R is an untimed assessment administered by a team of four adults and requires between 20 and 30 minutes to evaluate the motoric, conceptual, and language behaviors of children. Observations of several social/emotional indicators are also encouraged during the assessment of the three basic domains of functioning. In addition, a Parent Information Form is available so that a parent or guardian can provide documentation of a child's health history, interests, and home-related behaviors.

Table 8.4 Multidimensional Preschool Screening Instruments

Name of Instrument	Age Range	Administration Time	T = Test	P = Parent Record	E = Professional Examiner	Cognitive	Language	Speech	Fine Motor	Gross Motor	Self-Help	Social-Emotional	Reliability Data	Validity Data	Normative Data
ABC Inventory	3-6 to 6-6	10 min.	T			x	x		x	x			–	+	+
BRIGANCE® Diagnostic Inventory of Basic Skills	4-5 to 12-0	15 min.	T			x	x		x	x			–	–	–
BRIGANCE® Diagnostic Inventory of Early Development	0-1 to 6-0	30–15 min.	T	P		x	x	x	x	x	x	x	–	–	–
Comprehensive Identification Process	2-6 to 5-6	30 min.	T	P		x	x	x	x	x	x		–	–	–
Cooperative Preschool Inventory, Revised Edition	3-0 to 6-0	15–20 min.	T			x	x		x	x			+	+	+
Daberon: A Screening Device for School Readiness	4-0 to 6-0	20–40 min.	T			x	x		x	x			+	+	+
Dallas Preschool Screening Test	3-0 to 6-0	15 min.	T			x	x	x	x	x		x	+	+	+
Denver Developmental Screening Test	0-1 to 6-0	15–20 min.	T			x	x		x	x	x		+	+	+
Denver Prescreening Developmental Questionnaire	0-3 to 6-0	5 min.		P		x	x		x	x	x		–	+	+
Developmental Indicators for the Assessment of Learning (DIAL-R)	2-0 to 5-1	25–30 min.	T	P	E	x	x	x	x	x		x	+	+	+
Developmental Profile II (Developmental Profile)	0-0 to 9-0	30–40 min.		P		x	x		x	x	x	x	+	+	+
Developmental Tasks for Kindergarten Readiness	4-6 to 6-2	20–30 min.	T			x	x	x	x	x		x	+	+	+
Early Detection Inventory	3-6 to 7-6	15–30 min.	T	P		x	x	x	x	x		x	–	–	+
Early Screening Inventory (Eliot-Pearson Screening Inventory)	4-0 to 6-0	15 min.	T			x	x	x	x	x			+	+	+
Hannah-Gardner Test of Verbal and Nonverbal Language Functioning	3-6 to 5-6	25–35 min.	T			x	x	x	x	x			+	+	+
Kaufman Infant and Preschool Scale	0-1 to 4-0	25–30 min.	T	P		x	x		x	x	x	x	–	–	–
Kindergarten Questionnaire	4-0 to 6-0	20–30 min.	T	P		x	x		x	x	x	x	–	+	+
Lexington Developmental Scale, Short Form	0-3 to 6-0	30–45 min.	T			x	x		x	x	x	x	+	+	–
Lollipop Test: A Diagnostic Screening Test of School Readiness	4-0 to 6-0	15–20 min.	T		E	x	x		x	x			+	+	–
McCarthy Screening Test	4-0 to 6-5	20 min.	T			x	x		x	x			+	+	+
Minneapolis Preschool Screening Instrument	3-7 to 5-1	10–15 min.	T			x	x	x	x	x			+	+	+
Minnesota Preschool Inventory	4-8 to 5-7	15 min.		P		x	x	x	x	x	x	x	+	+	+
Preschool Attainment Record, Research Edition	0-6 to 7-0	20–30 min.		P	E	x	x		x	x	x	x	–	–	–
Preschool Screening Instrument	4-0 to 5-0	5–10 min.	T	P		x	x		x	x	x	x	–	+	+
Preschool Screening System (PSS Field Trial Edition)	2-6 to 5-9	15–20 min.	T	P		x	x	x	x	x	x	x	+	+	+
Riley Preschool Developmental Screening Inventory	3-0 to 6-0	5–10 min.	T			x	x	x	x	x		x	–	–	–
School Readiness Checklist—Ready or Not?	4-0 to 7-0	10–15 min.		P		x	x		x	x	x	x	–	+	+
School Readiness Survey	4-0 to 6-0	25–35 min.	T	P		x	x	x	x	x			+	+	+
Slosson Intelligence Test	0-1 to adult	10–20 min.	T			x	x	x	x	x			–	+	+

From Robert Lichtenstein and Harry Ireton, *Preschool Screening: Identifying Young Children with Developmental and Educational Problems*. Copyright © 1984 by Allyn and Bacon. Reprinted with permission.

Focus on
Law

Federal Legislation and Preschoolers

Federal legislation beginning in the 1960s served as the impetus for widespread preschool programming. This government involvement was fueled by the belief that early intervention programs could offset the negative effects of cultural deprivation. As a result, several major pieces of legislation have been passed during the past 20 years. These include the Handicapped Children's Early Education Assistance Act of 1968, P.L. 90–538; the Early and Periodic Screening, Diagnosis and Treatment Program of 1968; the Education Amendments of 1974, P.L. 93–380; and the Education for All Handicapped Children Act of 1975, P.L. 94–142.

The Handicapped Children's Early Education Assistance Act called for the development of experimental programs for educating disabled preschool children. Specifically, it facilitated the development and dissemination of model programs for disabled preschoolers throughout the country.

The Early and Periodic Screening, Diagnosis and Treatment Program was designed to ensure that persons under 21 who are eligible for Medicaid would receive necessary medical services. This program was responsible for stimulating several new screening instruments and subsequent data on the incidence of disabilities among infants and preschoolers.

The Education Amendments of 1974, better known as P.L. 93–380, required the development of state plans for the provision of full educational opportunities to all disabled children from birth to age 20, with priority for disabled preschoolers not receiving any services. This law was supportive of preschool education but did not mandate such programs. It was left to individual states to decide which programs were actually developed.

With the passage of the Education for All Handicapped Children Act (P.L. 94–142), the provision of educational services enacted under P.L. 93–380 was ensured. This act further defined program requirements, procedural safeguards, and due process requirements with regard to identification, placement, and continuing education services. However, the law did not mandate services to children up to 3 years of age and only required services be provided to children aged 3 to 5 years and 18 to 21 years in states in which school attendance laws included these children.

In October 1986, the Education of the Handicapped Amendments to P.L. 94–142, P.L. 99–457, provided new federal incentives for the education of disabled infants and young children. This bill has two major provisions: The first part requires states to provide special education services to eligible children aged three and older, and the second part establishes a grant program for the development of early intervention services for disabled infants (from birth through two years). This law amends sections of

P.L. 94–142 to include the term "developmentally delayed" for children aged three to five years, inclusive, in definitions of disabled children. This term can thus be used to identify and serve preschool children without labeling them by disability. To serve these children, a multidisciplinary team must determine that the child has a "significant delay in one or more areas of development such as speech/language, cognition, motor, or social/emotional development."

P.L. 99–457 further specifies the following characteristics of the evaluation and assessment of a child. It must:

1. Be conducted by personnel trained to utilize appropriate methods and procedures.
2. Be based on informed clinical opinion; and
3. Include the following:
   (i) A review of the pertinent records related to the child's current health status and medical history.
   (ii) An evaluation of the child's level of functioning in each of the following developmental areas:
      (a) Cognitive development.
      (b) Physical development, including vision and hearing.
      (c) Language and speech development.
      (d) Psychosocial development.
      (e) Self-help skills (Federal Register, 1989, p. 26320)

Another critical element of the law is the 45-day timeline during which the evaluation and initial assessment of each child must be completed. In addition, any family assessment must be completed within the same timeline and according to the criteria specified in the law.

P.L. 99–457 is quite flexible concerning where assessment can occur. Multidisciplinary teams can test children in environments selected with the child and family in mind. The law is far more specific regarding the nondiscriminatory assessment procedures that must be followed. Specifically, it states that (a) all tests and other procedures must be administered in the child's or the parent's native language or their preferred mode of communication, (b) test procedures must not be culturally or racially discriminatory, (c) more than one procedure must be used for determining a child's eligibility, and (d) assessments must be completed by qualified personnel.

In the past three years, a number of excellent books have been published on the topic of infant and toddler assessment and intervention (e.g., Bagnato & Neisworth, 1991; Bailey & Wolery, 1989). These books along with the ever-growing professional literature (see, e.g., *Exceptional Children,* vol. 58–2, 1991) are providing educators and mental health professionals needed guidance for working effectively with preschool children who may be at risk for later academic, social-emotional, or physical problems.

The authors stress the instrument is not a measure of innate abilities nor is it designed to identify children with brain dysfunction. Rather, the DIAL-R is intended as a first step in identifying young children at either end of the functioning continuum of developmental skills who may be in need of additional educational or health services.

The 1990 or AGS revision of the DIAL resulted in three basic changes: (1) the instrument was standardized on a national sample in place of a sample restricted to Illinois; (2) the instrument was modified to assess a wider age range of children from 2–0 to 5–11 instead of 2–6 through 5–5 years; and (3) the Gross Motor and Fine Motor items were combined into one domain.

Content

Each of these three areas of assessment, motoric, conceptual, and language, contains eight items that are further subdivided into tasks that sample typical developmental behaviors. Figure 8.1 illustrates the behaviors and the underlying abilities assumed to be assessed by the DIAL-R items. The authors suggest that children's social/emotional behavior also can be assessed concurrently with screening of motor, conceptual, and language skills. To facilitate this social/emotional assessment, examiners are provided a brief behavior checklist that focuses on behaviors such as separation from adult, unwillingness to answer, and hyperactive or restless.

Of the 24 items in the DIAL-R, 18 are revised from the DIAL, 3 are unchanged from the DIAL, and 3 are new. All the new items and most of the revised items were designed to accommodate the extended age range covered on the DIAL-R. The authors used a systematic approach to item development whereby they selected examples of behaviors expected of children in regular classrooms. The items successfully meet standards of content and social validity.

Administration

As noted earlier, the DIAL-R is a team-administered assessment device, thus allowing three or four children to be evaluated simultaneously during a 30-minute period. The DIAL-R Manual provides detailed materials for training examiners and specific guidance in setting up the assessment environment. Figure 8.2 is the model floor plan provided in the DIAL-R Manual. This floor plan, although for the DIAL-R administration, nicely illustrates a typical preschool screening set-up.

Based on our review of the materials and scoring requirements, considerable coordination and training of examiners (or operators as labeled in the DIAL-R Manual) is needed to ensure a consistent and meaningful administration of the DIAL-R. The team administration format has the advantage of time efficiency; however, such an arrangement can have problems unless managed extremely well. For example, the large group format can have negative effects on shy and distractible children and the inter-rater reliabilities across operators and test situations appear subject to problems.

Figure 8.1   DIAL-R Area Code Illustrating the Abilities Assessed by the Items

Motor Items

	Perceptual	Memory	Previous learning association	Kinesthetic awareness & coordination	Language
Catching	•			•	
Jumping, Hopping, & Skipping				•	
Building	•	•		•	
Touching Fingers	•	•		•	
Cutting	•			•	
Matching	•			•	
Copying	•			•	
Writing Name	•	•	•	•	•

Concepts Items

	Perceptual	Memory	Previous learning association	Kinesthetic awareness & coordination	Language
Identifying Body Parts		•	•		•
Naming Colors		•	•		•
Counting (Rote)		•	•		•
Counting (Meaningful)		•	•		•
Positioning		•	•		•
Identifying Concepts		•	•		•
Naming Letters		•	•		•
Sorting Chips	•				

Language Items

	Perceptual	Memory	Previous learning association	Kinesthetic awareness & coordination	Language
Articulating		•			•
Giving Personal Data		•	•		•
Remembering	•	•		•	•
Naming Nouns		•	•		•
Naming Verbs		•	•		•
Classifying Foods		•	•		•
Problem Solving		•	•		•
Sentence Length					•

Standardization and Scoring

All DIAL-R standardization testing took place between fall of 1981 and spring of 1983. A total of 2,447 children were actually tested. The final sample for norming totaled 2,227 (49% female, 51% male) and can be characterized as representative of all regions of the United States. The norming sample was nearly 55% caucasians and 45% minority, with more than 86% of the minority children speaking English.

The 1990 reanalysis of the standardization data changed the norms and resulted in the sample performing better than had been indicated in

Figure 8.2   Floor Plan Indicating Placement of Areas During DIAL-R Screening

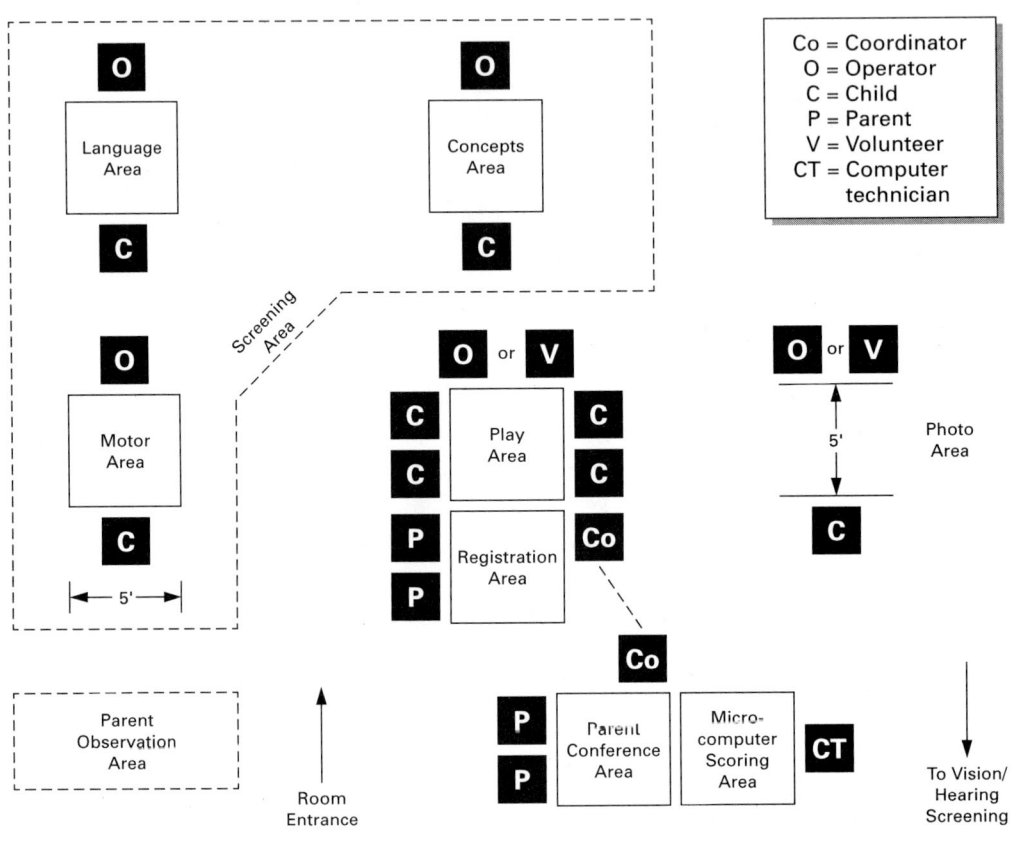

the earlier DIAL manuals. To arrive at an overall screening decision from the DIAL-R, a child's total score is compared to cutoff scores. In most cases a cutoff score based on a ± 1.5 standard deviation should be used, thus creating an average range of scores between a −1.5 SD and +1.5 SD. The manual, however, provides scores under several different cutoff criteria. Regardless of cutoff criteria, the result is one of three decision statements: Potential Problem (a performance that is outside and below the average range of scores for same-aged peers), OK (a performance that is within the average range of scores for same-aged peers), or Potential Advanced (a performance that is outside and above the average range of scores for same-aged peers). Of course, the number of children characterized by each of the statements will depend on the cutoff criteria selected. The higher the SDs selected as cutoff criteria the fewer the number of children identified in the two extreme groups.

Reliability and Validity

In general, the 1990 revision of the DIAL-R has impressive reliability and validity. The authors report detailed information on the test-retest reliability (mean $r = .87$ for total score), internal consistency ($r > .80$ for almost all subscales and total scale), and interrater agreement (range of 81% to 99% across different examiners). With regard to validity information, the authors provide extensive documentation of their and others research examining the DIAL-R's construct and criterion-related (both concurrent and predictive) validity. It is difficult to summarize the validity of this instrument given the range of tests that it has been validated with and the varying samples of children examined. It is fair to say that the DIAL-R measures what it says it measures and relates to other well-accepted tests in predictable ways. In summary, the DIAL-R is one of the most comprehensive screening measures of school readiness.

AGS Early Screening Profiles

The *AGS Early Screening Profiles,* or ESP (Harrison et al., 1990), is a nationally normed screening battery for children 2–0 through 6–11 years of age. It provides a brief method of testing large numbers of children to identify possible disabilities or giftedness. The ESP incorporates a flexible, ecological approach to early childhood screening. The battery measures development in several domains, including cognitive/language, motor, and self-help/social. Direct, individual testing of children is accompanied by parent or teacher surveys concerning a child's articulation, health history, home environment, and behavior. The resulting information reflects multiple sources and a variety of settings in which young children participate. The ESP was authored by a team of experienced test developers (P. Harrison, A. Kaufman, N. Kaufman, R. Bruininks, J. Rynders, S. Llmer, S. Sparrow, and D. Cicchetti) who have made the battery compatible with more inclusive instruments that are recommended for follow-up assessment, including the *Kaufman Assessment Battery for Children,* the *Bruininks-Oseretsky Test of Motor Proficiency,* and the *Vineland Adaptive Behavior Scales.*

Content

The ESP consists of seven parts. The Cognitive/Language Profile, Motor Profile, and Self-Help/Social Profile measure major areas of young children's development. The Articulation Survey, Home Survey, Health History Survey, and Behavior Survey complement the Profiles by focusing on information from additional parents and teachers who are familiar with a child. These components can be used independently or in any combination,

---

Table 8.5   Components of the AGS Early Screening Profiles

PROFILES

Cognitive/Language Profile

Source: direct testing
of child
Time: 5 to 15 minutes

Cognitive Subscale
Visual Discrimination
Subtest (14 items)
Logical Relations Subtest
(14 items)
Language Subscale
Verbal Concepts Subtest
(25 items)
Basic School Skills Subtest
(25 items)

Motor Profile

Source: direct testing
of child
Time: 5 to 15 minutes

Gross Motor Subtest
(5 items)
Fine Motor Subtest
(3 items)

Self-Help/Social Profile

Source: parent, teacher
questionnaires
Time: 5 to 10 minutes

Communication Domain
(15 items)
Daily Living Skills Domain
(15 items)
Socialization Domain
(15 items)
Motor Skills Domain
(15 items)

SURVEYS

Articulation Survey

Source: direct testing
of child
Time: 2 to 3 minutes
Articulation of Single
Words (20 items)
Intelligibility During
Continuous Speech
(1 rating)

Home Survey

Source: parent
questionnaire
Time: 5 minutes
(12 items)

Health History Survey

Source: parent
questionnaire
Time: 5 mintues
(12 items)

Behavior Survey

Source: examiner
questionnaire
Time: 2 to 3 minutes
Cognitive/Language
Observations
(9 items)
Motor Observations
(13 items)

From *AGS Early Screening Profiles* (ESP) by Patti Harrison et al. © 1990 American Guidance
Service, Inc., 4201 Woodland Road, Circle Pines, Minnesota 55014–1796. All rights reserved.

according to the needs of the screening program. Table 8.5 provides a
summary of the seven ESP components by indicating subparts and number of items for each component and an estimate of the time needed to
administer the various parts.

Administration

The administration of the ESP generally involves a variety of professionals
and nonprofessionals in roles of coordinators, interdisciplinary team members, and examiners. The duties and qualifications of persons assuming
each of these roles are described clearly in the test manual. The manual
also provides well-designed materials for training personnel to reliably
administer the various components and to manage a large group screening
effort. A room arrangement plan is provided, as is a comprehensive list of
tips for testing young children. We have reproduced the ESP "Guidelines
for Testing Young Children" as table 8.6 because of their general relevance to working with all types of children.

Table 8.6   Guidelines for Testing Young Children

The battery is administered to children as young as age 2. To obtain meaningful test results, examiners must use special patience and sensitivity to make these children as comfortable as possible. This must be done without giving the child any additional help, training, or practice.

Whenever possible, test the child without the parent being present. If this is not possible, have the parent sit behind the child and far enough away to prevent distraction. Tell the parent to remain quiet and to give the child no help or encouragement.

Establishing Rapport

1. When you meet, use the child's name and tell the child your name.
2. Do not *ask* the child whether he or she wants to come with you, since that may invite refusal. *Tell* the child, in a friendly, confident manner, to accompany you.
3. Try to put the child immediately at ease. Do not talk too loudly or be too formal.
4. Be honest, open, and friendly.
5. Use language that is at an appropriate level for the child.
6. At the beginning of testing, engage the child in a brief conversation that focuses on the child. Do not, however, bombard the child with questions.
7. Express genuine interest in the child and in his or her needs.
8. Have a few age-appropriate toys or games (never test materials) available to arouse the interest of a shy or hesitant child.
9. Make sure that the child's physical needs (hunger, thirst, restroom, sleep) are met before beginning testing. Do not test a child who is upset or unable to concentrate.
10. Do not appear hesitant, nervous, or apprehensive. Interact confidently with the child.
11. Avoid suggesting to the child that the activity will be an ordeal. For example, do not say "Let's get this over with quickly."
12. Briefly explain to the child what is going to happen. Tell the child that he or she is expected to do his or her best, but not to get all of the answers right or to do everything perfectly. Say, for example, "We are going to do some things that are fun. Work really hard and do your very best, but don't worry if there are some things you can't do."
13. Avoid using the word *test* with young children, because it may frighten them.
14. If a child is so frightened or uncooperative that no useful results will be obtained that day, reschedule that child's screening for another day.

Table 8.6—Continued

Maintaining Rapport

1. Treat the child with respect, enthusiasm, warmth, reassurance, and support, but do not be overly playful.
2. Use the child's name often.
3. Maintain good eye contact with the child and smile often.
4. Although the test is standardized and you will sometimes read directions word-for-word to the child, do not be stilted or mechanical in your actions, and do not sound as if you are reading. Administer the test in a relaxed manner, using a light, conversational tone.
5. If the child's attention wanders, warmly but firmly redirect the child to the task.
6. Convey to the child that the tasks are fun and interesting, and that *you* are having fun.
7. Give appropriate, sincere, and varied praise and encouragement to maintain the child's attention and motivation. Say, for example, "You're really working hard," "Good work," or "Nice try." Praise the child for his or her effort, *not* for the correctness of the response. But remember: praise that is too repetitive, perfunctory, insincere, or frequent may defeat its purpose.
8. Be sensitive to the child's needs and feelings and to signs of fatigue, boredom, distress, and restlessness. Remember that children have different needs and feelings. For example, a pat on the shoulder might reassure one child who is anxious or afraid but embarrass another child.
9. Be alert to the child's need for breaks. Young children may need a drink of water, a restroom visit, or just a brief pause during testing.
10. Be sensitive to your own feelings. Examiners may need periodic breaks to maintain optimal alertness in testing conditions. And don't ignore your own physical discomfort. If you are hot or tired, the child may be feeling the same way.
11. Establish a steady, smooth, and lively pace for testing. Never ignore the child's questions or comments, but limit conversation unless the child is experiencing discomfort, anxiety, or other feelings that may interfere with optimal performance.
12. Do not be too ready to accept "I don't know," "I can't," or silence for a response. These responses may mean "I don't want to" or "I'm afraid." In these cases, tactfully encourage the child to respond by saying, for example, "Give it a try" or "I bet you can do it." Do not apply excessive pressure.
13. Know the materials so well that you can give full attention to the child rather than fumbling with the test materials or looking up information in the test directions.

From *AGS Early Screening Profiles* (ESP) by Patti Harrison et al. © 1990 American Guidance Service, Inc., 4201 Woodland Road, Circle Pines, Minnesota 55014–1796. All rights reserved.

Standardization and Scoring

The standardization of the ESP took place in 1987 and 1988 at 42 sites in 26 states, resulting in a standardization sample of 1,149 children. Of these children, 50.4 percent were female and 49.6 percent male. The sample closely represented the racial census of the United States with 69.4 percent of the children being white, 17.1 percent black, 10.1 percent Hispanic, and 3.4 percent being characterized as other. This nationally representative sample of children ages 2–0 through 6–11 years provided the data for developing the norm-referenced scores of the *Early Screening Profiles.*

The ESP yields five types of scores: screening indexes (or general performance levels), standard scores (mean = 100, sd = 15), bands of error for standard scores, national percentile ranks, and age equivalents. These scores are part of a two-level scoring system: Level I scores are the screening indexes for the Cognitive/Language Profile, Motor Profile, Self-Help/Social Profile, and Total Screening; Level II scores are composed of the normative scores (i.e., standard scores, percentile ranks, age equivalents). The Screening Indexes represent six broad ranges of performance (1 = below –2 sd, 2 = between –1 and –2 sd, 3 = between the mean and –1 sd, 4 = between the mean and +1 sd, 5 = between +1 and +2 sd, and 6 = above +2 sd) and gives a quick picture of the general functioning of a child. This two-level scoring system is designed to save scoring time and to facilitate making different types of decisions. Level I scores can all be gleaned from tables packaged with the test components; Level II scores require accessing several tables in the test manual.

Reliability and Validity

An examination of the ESP test manual reveals an extensive report of reliability and validity. Detailed evidence is provided for virtually all types of reliability (i.e., internal consistency, test-retest, and interrater). The correlations used to support each of these forms of reliability all exceed commonly accepted standards and in most cases are in the .90 range. The standard errors of measurement for the various subscales are in the 3- to 4-point range, which also is indicative of a reliable test.

Evidence for the validity of the ESP is impressive. The authors detail a strong rationale for the test's content validity and provide reports of numerous investigations by them, as well as other researchers, attesting to the construct and criterion-related (concurrent and predictive) validity for the ESP. The instrument correlates moderately to strongly with several comprehensive instruments (e.g., K-ABC, Standford-Binet, Bruininks-Oseretsky, Social Skills Rating System, Stanford Achievement) commonly used to assess children identified as having problems in schools. This is exactly what a good preschool screening instrument must be able to do.

In summary, the *AGS Early Screening Profiles* offers educators a reliable and valid instrument for identifying children who may be at risk for school problems or who may be potentially gifted. The ESP can be

administered efficiently but requires professional coordination and interpretation for Level II scoring. The instrument has been designed with clear
links to more comprehensive assessment tools in basic domains of functioning and illustrates many best practices in the assessment of young children.

Denver Developmental Screening Test (DDST)

The *Denver Developmental Screening Test,* or DDST (Frankenburg &
Dodds, 1967), is an individually administered test designed for the identification of developmental and behavioral problems in infants and children
up to six years of age. It was intended for use by physicians and nurses
with no background in psychological testing, yet many educators and psychologists have used it. Since the publication of the original version, there
have been some revisions and variations of the DDST. Presently, there is
a Spanish-language edition and a brief parent report form entitled the
Denver Prescreening Developmental Questionnaire (Frankenburg, Van
Doorninck, Liddell, & Dick, 1976), although they will not be examined here.

Content

The DDST consists of 105 items standardized on 1,036 boys and girls from
Denver ranging in age from two weeks to six years. The items are clus-
tered into four areas: gross motor, language, fine motor, and personal-social. The item content varies with age, as might be expected in a test
covering a period of such rapid development. A preponderance of items
(75, or more than 70%) are associated with development from birth to age
two; this reflects the original intent of the DDST: to alert pediatricians to
serious developmental deviations or medical problems.

Administration

The DDST was designed for easy administration in a short time (approximately 20 minutes). According to the manual, only those items at or
below a child's chronological age are to be administered. It is even acceptable, according to the manual, to score many items without direct
assessment if a parent reports observing the required behavior. This test is
widely used because it is easily and quickly administered and scored.

Scoring and Interpretation

Each item on the DDST is represented by a bar that spans several months.
The left end of the bar represents the age at which 25 percent of the
Denver sample passed the item. The right end of the bar represents the
age at which 90 percent of the sample passed the item. A child who fails
an item that 90 percent of younger children passed is considered to exhibit
"delayed" development. The test manual provides classification criteria
(abnormal, questionable, normal, and untestable) based on the number of
delays in each area and the specific areas of delayed development.

Reliability and Validity

Several reliability and validity studies of the DDST have been published during its 20-year history. Most researchers have concluded the DDST has adequate interrater reliability (approximate mean r = .96), test-retest reliability (approximate mean r = .78), and content and concurrent validity.

Lindquist (1982) investigated the predictive validity of the DDST with respect to reading achievement in first, second, and third grades. The DDST was administered in the spring prior to kindergarten, and the *Gates-MacGinite Reading Test* was given as a measure of reading achievement. A statistically significant correlation of .46 was found between prekindergarten DDST results and reading achievement in first grade. However, an examination of the total sample of 351 children revealed that of 55 children characterized as "at risk" by the DDST results, only 26 were actually below the 25th percentile in reading. This study indicates the DDST may have limited use in preschool screening decisions. Rather, its strengths are in the assessment of developmentally delayed children between the ages of two weeks and three and a half years.

The availability of multidimensional tests, such as the DIAL-R and ESP, seems to be decreasing the use of the DDST in preschool screening work, but the DDST will likely continue to be popular in medical settings and in assessing severely disabled toddlers. Thus, educators should be aware of its content and limitations.

Minnesota Preschool Inventory (MPI)

The *Minnesota Preschool Inventory*, or MPI (Ireton & Thwing, 1974), is a standardized form used for inventorying a parent's observations about a child's kindergarten readiness skills and development. The MPI thus quantifies an important perspective, parent observations, in the assessment of school readiness.

Content

The MPI consists of two parts, 87 statements about developmental behaviors of children aged two to six and 63 statements about adjustment problems and symptoms of children this age. The developmental items were taken directly from the *Minnesota Child Development Inventory* (Ireton & Thwing, 1974), whereas the adjustment items were derived primarily from research on elementary school children by Quay and Werry (1972). The 87 developmental items are grouped into seven scales: self-help (21 items), fine motor (17 items), expressive language (18 items), comprehension (4 items), memory (15 items), letter recognition (7 items), and number comprehension (9 items). In practice, memory, letter recognition, and number comprehension are all part of the comprehension scale. The 63 adjustment problem and symptom items are grouped into four adjustment problem scales—immaturity (18 items), hyperactivity (8 items), behavior problems (20 items), and emotional problems (11 items)—and four symptom scales—motor (4 items), language (5 items), somatic (4 items), and sensory (2 items). Item groups were derived clinically rather than empirically through factor or item analyses.

The normative sample for this inventory consisted of 60 white children and their mothers in a suburb of Minneapolis. The children ranged in ages from 4–8 to 5–7 years. The parents' socioeconomic status can best be characterized as upper middle class. Such a standardization sample is quite restrictive and meets only minimal standards, even for a screening test.

Administration and Scoring

When the MPI is administered, a parent is instructed to complete all items, first, reporting any problems or disabilities he or she observes in the child, and second, simply marking "yes" or "no" to indicate if certain statements describe the child. Most parents complete this brief inventory in less than 15 minutes.

The parents' responses are easily scored and transferred to a score profile sheet that converts raw scores to percentiles for each of the developmental and adjustment subscales. Items within the four symptom clusters are ordered from mild to severe and rather broadly ascribed to either the 0 to 5th percentile, 5th to 10th percentile, or above the 10th percentile. All percentiles are based on the normative sample of 60 white middle-class children. Because they serve as normative comparisons, children falling below the 5th and 10th percentiles are considered to be "at risk" of severe developmental delays or maladjustment.

The test authors wisely recommend that users construct local norms to accompany those derived from the Minneapolis standardization sample. Little interpretative information or advice is provided for users. The successful use of this inventory depends on a parent's ability to observe and accurately report observations of a child. (See the following Focus on Research for more information on parents' ratings of children's behavior.)

Reliability and Validity

To date, no reliability studies and only one validity study (Ireton, Lun, & Kampen, 1981) have been published on the MPI. The one validity study reported positive agreement between the prekindergarten MPI scores of 287 children and their teachers' ratings at the end of kindergarten. Specifically, the comprehension, letter recognition, and memory subscales were the best predictors of kindergarten performance. When the final classifications of "developmentally delayed" or "normal" based on the prekindergarten MPI results were tested against reality, only 9 (or 3%) of the 287 were "mislabeled." Such a correlation is very good for a parent rating scale; however, one must remember that work in first grade rather than kindergarten will provide a better test of the predictive strength of the MPI.

Focus on
Research

Parents' Predictions of Their Children's Preschool Performance

Parent report measures, such as the *Minnesota Preschool Inventory,* have appeared increasingly attractive as a cost-effective means of obtaining a broad range of relevant developmental screening information. Concerns, however, are raised frequently about the objectivity and accuracy of parent reports. For example, how comparable are judgments by different parents, given that some are better observers than others and that most have a limited sample of children against which to measure their own child? Do parents tend to be biased in reporting on their children due to their own personal needs?

Researchers have shown that structured interviews or questionnaires addressing current and observable behaviors that involve low inferences yield more reliable data. The validity of using parent-reported information to supplement or replace direct testing and other preschool screening measures, however, has not been demonstrated.

Lichtenstein (1984) recently investigated how well parent reports about their preschool children predicted school performance. Parents of 91 preschoolers between the ages of 49 and 64 months completed a brief developmental inventory as part of the screening program of an urban school district. The 28-item inventory assessed adaptive behavior and language development. In addition, the children were administered the *Minneapolis Preschool Screening Instrument.* Teacher ratings of their kindergarten performance the following year provided criteria to validate the screening measures. Correlations with the overall teacher ratings (the mean of 9 ratings) were .40 for the adaptive behavior scale and .57 for the language scale. Validity figures for the developmental inventory were significantly higher for children with low socioeconomic status than for those with high status, for older children (57 to 64 months) than for younger children (49 to 56 months), and for firstborns than for younger siblings. No effects were found by sex. While a positive relationship between parent reports of developmental functioning and early school performance was clearly established, validity levels did not justify the use of parent information as a sole source of preschool screening information.

Source: From Robert Lichtenstein, "Predicting School Performance of Preschool Children from Parent Reports" in *Journal of Abnormal Psychology,* 1:79–94, 1984.

In sum, the MPI can be a valuable supplement to a battery of preschool screening instruments. It involves a parent in the assessment process and provides a general picture of a child's current development. The normative data for the instrument, however, should be complemented by the construction of local norms.

Selected Other Tests

As noted, preschool developmental tests can be categorized in several ways. We elected to focus on multidimensional tests in this chapter because of their popularity in preschool screening programs and because areas such as language, perceptual-motor, and speech/articulation are covered in detail in other chapters. We have, however, compiled a list of tests in these and other developmental areas appropriate for use with young children, along with basic selection indexes (see table 8.7). Interested readers again are referred to a recent practitioner-oriented book by Bagnato and Neisworth (1991). This book provides information on numerous additional preschool tests and screening tools.

➡ *Issues in Preschool Assessment*

Preschoolers can be difficult to assess. They often do not have well-developed verbal skills, are not likely to sit attentively for 20 minutes, and are not very concerned about compliance with an examiner's directives. The rapid development of abilities and skills during the preschool years can result in assessment data of questionable value when it is based on only one brief time or cross-sectional sampling of a child's behavior. Finally, the relative paucity of psychometrically sound tests places a premium on direct, repeated observations of a child across settings and learning situations. Placement decisions should never be based on results of screening tests alone. In the final section of this chapter, we examine several practical issues central to preschool assessment and educational readiness.

Assessing Young Children

Assessing young children demands excellent test administration skills, foresight, and ability to communicate effectively. Not everyone is good at dealing with young, active children or severely disabled children. There is no substitute for supervised experience combined with a basic concern for the testing environment, skill in establishing rapport, and sensitivity to a child's needs. Many of the important skills needed to assess young children were listed in table 8.6. Let's now examine some of these points further.

Ideally, testing should occur in a quiet, well-lighted, distraction-free room equipped with a table and chairs appropriate for small children. The child's comfort is more important than the examiner's comfort.

Table 8.7 Selected Unidimensional Preschool Screening Measures

Name of Instrument	Age Range	Administration Time	T = Test	P = Parent Report	E = Professional Examiner	Reliability Data	Validity Data	Normative Data
Language and Vocabulary Measures								
Assessment of Children's Language Comprehension[a]	3-0 to 6-6	10–20 min.	T		E	–	–	+
Bankson Language Screening Test[c]	4-1 to 8-0	25 min.	T			+	+	+
Del Rio Language Screening Test[c]	3-0 to 6-11		T			–	+	+
Peabody Picture Vocabulary Test-Revised[a]	2-6 to adult	10–20 min.	T		E	+	+	+
Pictorial Test of Bilingualism and Language Development[b]	4-0 to 8-0	15 min.	T			+	–	–
Preschool Language Assessment Instrument[c]	3-0 to 6-0	20 min.	T			+	–	+
Screening Test for Auditory Comprehension of Language[a]	3-0 to 6-0	5–10 min.	T		E	+	–	+
Test of Early Language Development[c]	3-0 to 7-11	15–20 min.	T		E	+	+	+
Verbal Language Development Scale[c]	0-1 to 16-0	20 min.		P		+	+	–
Social-Emotional Measures								
Burks' Behavior Rating Scales: Preschool and Kindergarten	3-0 to 6-11	10 min.			E	+	–	–
Child Behavior Rating Scale	4-0 to 9-0	10 min.		P		+	+	+
Children's Self-Social Construct Tests: Preschool Form	3-6 to 10-0	10–15 min.		P		–	–	–
Joseph Preschool and Primary Self Concept Screening Test	3-6 to 9-11	5–7 min.	T			+	+	+
Speech/Articulation Measures								
Denver Articulation Screening Test	2-6 to 7-0	5 min.	T			+	+	+
Photo Articulation	3-0 to 12-0	5 min.	T		E	+	+	+
Perceptual-Motor Measures								
Developmental Test of Visual-Motor Integration	2-0 to 15-0	5–10 min.	T			+	+	+
Riley Motor Problems Inventory	4-0 to 9-0	10 min.	T			+	+	–
Tree/Bee Test of Auditory Discrimination	3-0 to adult	10–15 min.	T		E	+	+	+
Observational Instruments for Classroom Use								
Basic School Skills Inventory-Screen	4-0 to 6-11	5–10 min.				+	+	+
Preschool Behavior Rating Scale	3-0 to 5-11	5–10 min.				+	+	+
Classroom Behavior Inventory, Preschool Form	2-0 to 6-0	10–15 min.				–	+	–

From Robert Lichtenstein and Harry Ireton, *Preschool Screening: Identifying Young Children with Developmental and Educational Problems.* Copyright © 1984 by Allyn and Bacon. Reprinted with permission.

[a]Measures receptive language only.
[b]Measures expressive language only.
[c]Measures both expressive and receptive language.

Whenever possible, assess a child without the parents present. This is often difficult with children younger than two years and magnifies the importance of the examiner's rapport-building skills. To set a child at ease and to encourage cooperation, the examiner should portray a warm, friendly, and reassuring demeanor. The use of a well-recognized and familiar toy of a character such as Big Bird or Mickey Mouse may facilitate child's transition to a strange room and unfamiliar adult. Novice examiners often make the mistake of being too playful or cute, and consequently create a situation in which testing is difficult.

Sensitivity to signs of boredom, fatigue, or distress in a child are very important if an optimal testing situation is to be maintained. As a rule, young children are not intrinsically motivated to achieve in a new testing situation. Rather, it seems the responses of the examiner are frequently more important in determining success. Therefore, we encourage examiners to praise children's work efforts such as attention, persistence, and cooperation.

In sum, the test administration skills and interpersonal style of an examiner are critical influences on the test performance of a young child. A well-organized, time-efficient evaluation plan is likewise very important given the behavioral characteristics of preschoolers. When such an evaluation is accomplished, the personal rewards and job satisfaction are great.

Developmental Scores

Many tests, particularly those designed to assess young children, transform raw scores into age or grade equivalents. These scores are commonly referred to as developmental scores, for they provide comparisons to easily understood developmental landmarks. For example, an age equivalent of 4–2 means a child's raw score is the average (or mean) score for children four years and two months old who participated in the standardization of the test. Similarly, a grade equivalent of 1–5 is a test performance equal to that of the average child in the fifth month of first grade who participated in the standardization of the test.

Although conceptually meaningful, developmental scores are inferior to standard scores and subject to several problems. First, they tend to be ordinal rather than interval. Thus, when plotting the number of items correct by ages or grades, the result is generally a curved prediction line for young children with a flattening of the line for higher ages or grades. Second, the developmental scores of many tests are only estimates. In other words, children at all age or grade increments did not actually participate in the standardization of the test, and thus scores were interpolated or extrapolated based on those who did take part. Consequently, a child could earn an age equivalent of 4–1 when in fact no individual of that age even participated in the standardization of the test. Finally, perhaps the most common problem with developmental scores concerns developmental comparisons. When a four-year-old and a six-year-old both earn an age score of 5–0, for example, it only means they both correctly answered the same number of questions as the average of the children exactly five years old. The two children did not necessarily attack the questions identically, nor did they necessarily function like the average 5–0 child. In summary, the interpretation of age and grade equivalents requires caution. Whenever possible, it is wise to report standard scores along with developmental scores.

School Readiness

Throughout this chapter, we have interchangeably discussed school readiness and developmental instruments as if they were synonymous. However, although they are similar, as they both often focus on basic areas of development, they have at least two major distinctions: the purposes of the user and the scope of assessment. With school readiness tests, the user wants to predict whether a child's functioning is adequate for success in school. Thus, the major outcome of an assessment of school readiness is a "go" or "no go" decision. Developmental instruments, on the other hand, are not intended for use in placement or instructional decisions. Rather, they provide a normative standard of behavior in basic areas of development to which a child is compared. In essence, school readiness tests are best conceptualized as criterion-referenced, whereas developmental screening instruments are best viewed as norm-referenced.

The second distinction, the scope of assessment, is more pragmatic than the first. School readiness tests generally are designed to assess a narrower skill level or difficulty range than developmental instruments. To ensure good predictive validity, skills measured on a school readiness test should be drawn from kindergarten and first-grade curricula. Skills assessed by developmental screening instruments necessarily are more diverse because they represent a greater span of development. Consequently, the point between being "ready" or "not ready" for school is at a much higher level of functioning than the point distinguishing between being "at risk" or "not at risk" for developmental problems.

The conceptual and pragmatic distinctions between school readiness and developmental instruments are not always obvious for a variety of reasons, such as the publisher's advertising and the name of the test. Regardless of the reason for ambiguity, one should always consult teachers familiar with the curriculum and demands of the potential receiving educational institution. In many cases, the teachers' reviews of the test content will provide valuable information about the extent of overlap between what is tested and what is taught.

Preschool Screening

Throughout this book, we repeatedly note that the primary purpose of assessment is to determine if a problem exists and how it should be solved. In other words, assessment is only a means to an end. In theory, preschool screening should aim to recognize early problem warning signs in order to make a comprehensive assessment for purposes of identification and treatment. The utility of preschool screening, however, is contingent on several factors, including the accuracy of screening procedures, provision of follow-up services, timing of screening, and involvement of parents.

Accuracy of Screening Procedures

Inaccurate screening procedures pose serious problems because they result in identification and treatment errors. These errors include not identifying and treating a child who actually has a problem and, conversely, identifying and treating a child as if a problem exists but actually does not. Such errors, which cause inconvenience and anxiety for parents and children, occur in preschool screening because of a combination of factors. Specifically, screening procedures generally are administered in one setting during a rather brief interaction with children who lack experience with tests. In addition to setting demands and test-taking characteristics of children, most preschool screening measures are not refined psychometric instruments. Thus, some identification errors are to be expected. It is hoped that when errors do occur, they are in the direction of identifying more children as "at risk" than really exist. Such identifications necessitate follow-up services that include direct, ongoing monitoring of the progress of the identified children.

Provision of Follow-Up Services

Implementation of a screening program without the provision of follow-up assessment and treatment services is an irresponsible policy and poor educational practice. We believe the development of preschool screening procedures should be concurrently coordinated with a comprehensive assessment and treatment program. In fact, the instructional objectives of a treatment program provide the primary basis for determining the content validity of assessment procedures. Finally, as mentioned previously, follow-up services that are coordinated with screening play a valuable role in confirming the identification of children as "at risk."

Timing of Screening

The issue of timing of screening has two components: (a) the age of the child and (b) the time of year when screening is done. A guiding principle in all assessment activities is that the more recent an assessment, the more accurately it predicts behavior. This is particularly true with preschoolers because in a couple of months, a child may demonstrate quantitative and

Focus on
Practice

Kindergarten ELOs

A common trend among school districts is to establish expected learner outcomes (ELOs) for each primary grade. Part of the basic competency movement in education, ELOs are used to communicate a school district's learning expectations to parents, teachers, and students. Well-written ELOs list curriculum-referenced cognitive and behavior objectives that can be empirically assessed.

Many school districts use their ELOs in making decisions about school entry and grade retentions. Ideally, preschool screening tests should be highly congruent with a school's kindergarten ELOs. Thus, when selecting preschool screening measures, you can assess their content validity by systematically comparing them to the ELOs developed by the schools the children will attend.

A representative set of kindergarten ELOs for reading, writing, and mathematics follows:

Kindergarten ELOs—Reading*

1. Identify common objects in the environment and pictures.
2. Identify these positions: above-below, behind-in front, top-bottom, and left-right.
3. Distinguish likenesses and differences.
4. Identify lowercase manuscript letters.
5. Identify uppercase manuscript letters.
6. Identify rhyming pictures.
7. Match upper- and lowercase manuscript letters.
8. Sequence pictures.
9. Select pictures that show story endings.
10. Recognize words that begin with the same sound.

Kindergarten ELOs—Writing

1. Identify these positions: above-below, behind-in front, top-bottom, and left-right.
2. Distinguish likenesses and differences.
3. Identify lowercase manuscript letters.
4. Identify uppercase manuscript letters.
5. Match upper- and lowercase manuscript letters.
6. Sequence pictures.

Kindergarten ELOs—Mathematics

1. Identify elements of a set.

2. Identify the smaller or larger object.

3. Identify these simple closed figures: circle, triangle, and square.

4. Compare the number of elements in two sets and indicate which is greater.

5. Classify objects or pictures according to color and shape.

6. Count concrete objects.

7. Count to ten by ones.

8. Identify one-half of a concrete object.

9. Identify these coins: penny, nickel, dime, and quarter.

10. Identify sets with an equal number of elements.

11. Identify the cardinal number of a set of not more than ten elements.

12. Identify the primary colors.

Source: Modeled after the New Orleans' Public Schools Kindergarten ELOs, Fall, 1984.

qualitative advances in development across several domains. A corollary principle of preschool assessment is that identification must be made soon enough to permit early intervention, especially for sensory problems and "disadvantaged" children. Thus, the critical question becomes, At what age can reliable and valid measures of skills and abilities that are relevant to successful performance in school first be obtained?

Generally, research indicates that by the ages of four and five, developmental gains in language, fine motor, and cognitive skills begin to stabilize and correlate significantly with school-age measures of achievement. Earlier assessments, except in cases of severe handicaps, generally do not have substantial predictive validity. Thus, the dilemma is wanting to intervene as early as possible but being confronted with the limitations of the reliability and validity of one's assessment tools.

Several schedules for preschool screening programs exist, including testing children (a) once in the spring or fall prior to school entry, (b) more than once during the years preceding school entry, or (c) once immediately before or during the first few weeks of kindergarten. Each schedule has its advantages and disadvantages. In general, periodic, repeated assessments offer several important advantages over a one-time, annual approach, for they have the potential for greater reliability and flexibility. Ideally, a combination of screening procedures whereby children are evaluated several times prior to and immediately upon school entry will be used to develop a flexible and comprehensive system.

Involvement of Parents

Although parent involvement is one of the last topics discussed in this chapter, it is by no means the least important. In fact, parents play an instrumental role in the assessment and treatment of young, disabled children and, accordingly, have been granted many rights and procedural safeguards by major special education legislation (i.e., P.L. 94–142 and P.L 99–457). Working cooperatively with parents is thus not only the law but also good practice!

New Trends in Assessment of Preschoolers

As more individuals have become interested in the assessment and treatment of preschool children, several new approaches to assessment have begun to emerge. Fewell (1991) characterized six such emerging trends as follows: (a) play, (b) ecological assessment, (c) arena assessment, (d) judgment-based assessment, (e) adaptive assessment, and (f) social interaction assessment. Fewell noted that several of these approaches share common traits. For example, play, arena assessment, and ecological assessment all use naturalistic formats in which a child is an active partner in the testing. In the *Play Assessment Scale* (Fewell, 1991), the child selects a toy and interacts with it in his or her preferred way. It is the examiner's task to score interactions, making a quick clinical interpretation of the interaction and determining where the action or its equivalent appears in a sequenced scale of play behavior. Arena assessment is an observational assessment in which staff from several disciplines focus on their particular domains with the context of play (Linder, 1990). Adaptive assessment refers to an array of techniques ranging from modifications in the administration of standardized tests to the use of new technologies, such as computers, assistive devices, and interactive laser discs (Schlater, Fewell, & Sandall, 1987). In all of these new approaches to assessment there appears to be a shift from product-oriented testing to process-oriented testing that will enable examiners to be more sensitive to individual differences and to incorporate more of a child's environment into the process.

Another significant new trend in the assessment of preschoolers has been the development of decision-making systems or tools that help professionals integrate assessment information and identify possible interventions for children. Such decision-making systems are consistent with the spirit of P.L. 99–457 and especially useful when professionals from several disciplines (e.g., education, school psychology, nursing, physical therapy, medicine, social work) are trying to work together to coordinate school and home services for a young child. Bagnato and Neisworth (1990) designed the first such published decision-making tool, the *System to Plan Early Childhood Services* or SPECS. A brief overview of SPECS will provide a fitting conclusion to this chapter for it reminds us that collaboration across professional disciplines is a key to quality assessment and treatment for young children both at home and at school.

Figure 8.3   Steps to Follow in Using the SPECS System

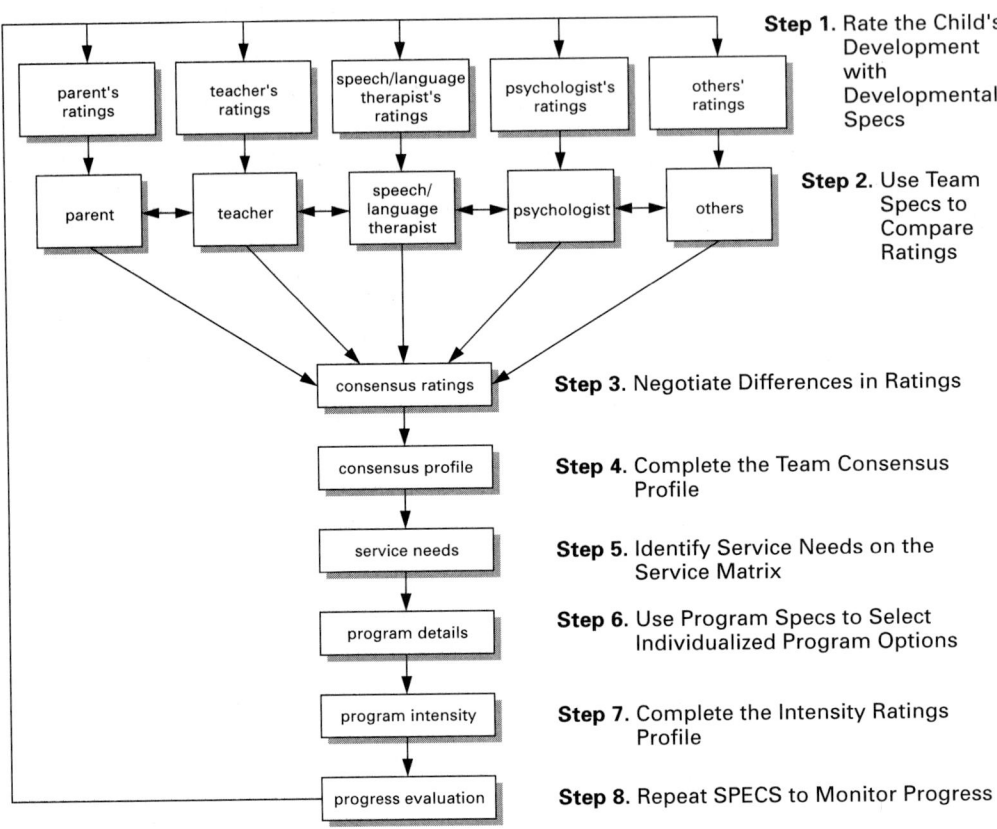

The *System to Plan Early Childhood Services* comprises three main components, referred to as Developmental Specifications, Team Specifications, and Program Specifications. Developmental Specifications (called Developmental Specs) contains a series of 19 judgment-based rating scales to appraise a child's status on 19 developmental and behavioral dimensions that are subsumed in six domains of functioning (i.e., communication, sensorimotor, physical, self-regulation, cognition, and self/social). These scales are to be rated independently by multidisciplinary team members. Team Specifications (called Team Specs) is an organizer that facilitates interdisciplinary team meetings, consensus-building, and service planning. Ratings from the Developmental Specs are integrated into Team Specs to gain a picture of consensus points. Program Specifications (called Program Specs) is used to plan details of a child's intended program and to document both the child's progress and the selected program's effectiveness. This component of SPECS has some unique aspects that focus on the type and intensity of the program needed to help a child. Program options built into SPECS include early education, adaptive services, behavior therapy, speech/language therapy, physical therapy, occupational therapy, vision services, hearing services, medical services, and transition services. Figure 8.3 provides a flowchart for using SPECS, and, more important, illustrates the multirater, interdisciplinary, assessment-to-intervention focus of preschool services today.

Chapter Summary

In this chapter, we have concentrated on the development and assessment of children between the ages of two and six years. Piagetian theory concerning cognitive development was briefly reviewed along with the development of perceptual and motor skills to establish some normative benchmarks. The major focus of the chapter was an examination of developmental and school readiness screening tests. Four tests were reviewed in detail: the *Developmental Indicators for the Assessment of Learning-Revised (DIAL-R)*, the *AGS Early Screening Profiles (ESP)*, the *Denver Developmental Screening Test (DDST)*, and the *Minnesota Preschool Inventory (MPI)*. Basic information on more than 40 other tests and a decision-making system called the *System to Plan Early Childhood Services* was also provided in a summary fashion. The chapter concluded with an examination of four issues relevant to successful preschool screening and a peek at some new trends in preschool assessment. You should now be ready to complete the five learning objectives that guided the writing of this chapter. Are you also ready to make informed decisions about educational readiness?

Chapter 9

Reading

<table>
<tr><td>

Learning Objectives

1. Describe the process of reading and identify major developmental milestones in the acquisition of reading skills.
2. Identify and discuss individual and environmental factors that influence reading performance.
3. Identify and select methods to assess decoding and comprehension skills.
4. Identify the types of reading errors a child could make.
5. Describe the salient features of an IRI and note the benefits of using IRIs to access reading.

</td></tr>
</table>

Notbeingabletoreadisafrustratingexperience. Being able to read but not understanding what you have read is also frustrating. The development of reading skills is a complex process that typically evolves over many years and is influenced by personal and environmental factors. Virtually everyone experiences some problems in learning to read and in learning from reading, and at least 25 percent of elementary school children experience moderate to severe difficulties that result in below grade-level performances (Aaron & Joshi, 1992). In this chapter, we provide an overview of the normal development of reading skills, identify typical reading problems, and then focus on the assessment of such probelms.

➡ *What is Reading?*

Asking "What is reading?" may seem simplistic, but numerous definitions of reading have been proposed by experts (see, e.g., Chall, 1967; Gibson & Levin, 1975). For example: Reading is recognizing letters that make words; reading is sounding out a sequence of sounds to make words; reading is identifying words and understanding what the author is trying to say (Guerin & Maier, 1983). For our purposes, *reading is defined as a self-directed process of extracting information from written or printed symbols.* This definition is narrower than many and is influenced by the writings of Harris (1970), Gibson and Levin (1975), and Gillet and Temple (1990).

Gillet and Temple (1990), in their comprehensive volume on reading, discussed the "many sides" of reading and in so doing emphasize the critical role that reading plays in the development of a person and a country.   For example, they see reading as: a language ability, a set of perceptual abilities, a literary act, an automatized psychomotor act, a political issue, a matter of self-worth, a pressing economic issue, a critical instructional concern, and an outcome of self-directed discovery learning. We cannot

Chronicle Features. 1982

"Wait! Wait! . . . Cancel that, I guess it says 'help.' "

Reading is More Than Looking At Written Words!

investigate all these perspectives on reading here. We, however, agree that reading is one of the most important aspects of schooling and when a student has trouble reading, it requires expert assessment and remedial attention.

➡ *The Development of Reading*

Learning to read occurs in three general stages labeled **prereading, decoding,** and **comprehension.** Each of these stages is characterized by the acquisition of several subskills that collectively contribute to efficient reading.

Prereading Stage

Broadly defined, the prereading stage occurs between birth and the time a child can recognize and decode words. In normal children, the latter usually begins around five or six years of age. Sensory skills such as hand-eye coordination and sound discrimination are considered prerequisites to reading. A narrower and more practical approach to identifying prereading skills has been advocated by Venesky (1976), who suggested that the following five actions are involved in decoding:

1. attending to letter order
2. attending to letter orientation
3. attending to word detail
4. matching sounds
5. blending sounds

Once children master these skills, they should be able to recognize words and thus move developmentally into the decoding stage.

Decoding Stage

This stage or period of reading development usually is the focus of reading instruction during the first three or four years of school. Often referred to as the "learning to read" stage, it primarily involves the refinement of sound blending skills and the acquisition of rules concerning word structure such as silent letter conventions, vowel conventions, and syllabification.

Current approaches to teaching decoding skills stress a combination of phonics and language experience methods. Phonics emphasizes letter sound relationships, and the language experience approach emphasizes the relationship of decoding words to a child's general language experiences. Basal reading materials typically combine these two approaches to the task of teaching reading. Table 9.1 illustrates abbreviated instructional objectives by grade level for a typical basal reading series.

Table 9.1   Curriculum Sequence Chart for a Typical Basal Reading Series

Grade	Skills Acquired
Kindergarten	Identify sounds and pictures Express ideas in complete verbal sentences Understand meaning of words such as *above* and *far* Understand concepts of size, small, etc. Recognize and identify colors Organize objects into groups Match forms Understand beginning concepts of number
Grade 1	Recognize letters of alphabet; can write and give sound Auditory and visual perception and discrimination of initial and final consonants Observe left to right progression Recall what has been read Aware of medial consonants, consonant blends, digraphs Recognize long sound of vowels; root words; plural forms; verb endings *-s, -ed, -d, -ing;* opposites; pronouns *he, she* Understand concept of synonyms, homonyms, antonyms Understand simple compound words Copy simple sentences, fill-ins
Grade 2	Comprehension and analysis of what has been read Identify vowel digraphs Understand variant sounds of *y* Identify medial vowels Identify diphthongs Understand influence of *r* on preceding vowel Identify three-letter blends Understand use of suffix *-er* Understand verb endings (for example, *stop, stopped*)
Grade 3	Recognize multiple sounds of long *a* as in *ei, ay, ey* Understand silent *e* in *-le* endings Understand use of suffix *-est* Know how to change *y* to *i* before adding *er, est* Understand comparative and superlative forms of adjectives Understand possessive form using *s* Use contractions Identify syllabic breaks
Grade 4	Recognize main and subordinate parts Recognize unknown words using configuration and other word attack skills Identify various sounds of *ch* Recognize various phonetic values of *gh* Identify rounded *o* sound formed by *au, aw, al* Use and interpret diacritical markings Discriminate among multiple meaning of words

Table 9.1—*Continued*

Grade	Skills Acquired
Grade 5	Read critically to evaluate
	Identify digraphs *gn, mb, bt*
	Recognize that *augh* and *ough* may have round *o* sound
	Recognize and pronounce muted vowels in *el, al, le*
	Recognize secondary and primary accents
	Use of apostrophe
	Understand suffixes *-al, -hand, -ship, -ist, -ling, -an, -ian, -dom, -ern*
	Understand use of figures of speech: metaphor, simile
	Ability to paraphrase main idea
	Know ways paragraphs are developed
	Outline using two or three main heads and subheadings
	Use graphic material
Grade 6	Develop ability for critical analysis
	Recognize and use Latin, Greek roots, such as *photo, tele, graph, geo, auto*
	Develop generalization that some suffixes can change part of speech, such as *-ure* changing an adjective to noun (*moist-moisture*)
	Understand meaning and pronunciation of homographs
	Develop awareness of shifting accents

From *Informal Assessment in Education* (pp. 245–246), by Gilbert R. Guerin and Arlee S. Maier, 1983, Palo Alto, CA: Mayfield Publishing Company. Copyright © 1983 Mayfield Publishing Company. Reprinted by permission.

Comprehension Stage

The ultimate goal of reading is comprehension, or extracting meaning from what is read. Thus, this last, broad stage of reading development is often referred to as the "learning from reading" stage. The reading skills and activities in this stage can be classified as literal or direct comprehension and inferential or indirect comprehension. Literal comprehension involves remembering written information. Inferential comprehension is much more complex and requires a reader to piece together information and go beyond what is written to make it meaningful. Both literal and inferential comprehension require good attention skills, memory ability, and some prior knowledge of a topic.

➡ *A Model of Reading*

Understanding the reading process is essential to conducting meaningful assessments of children with reading problems. Just and Carpenter (1980) as well as several others (e.g., Aaron & Joshi, 1992; Carnine & Silbert,

Figure 9.1   A Cognitive Model of the Reading Process

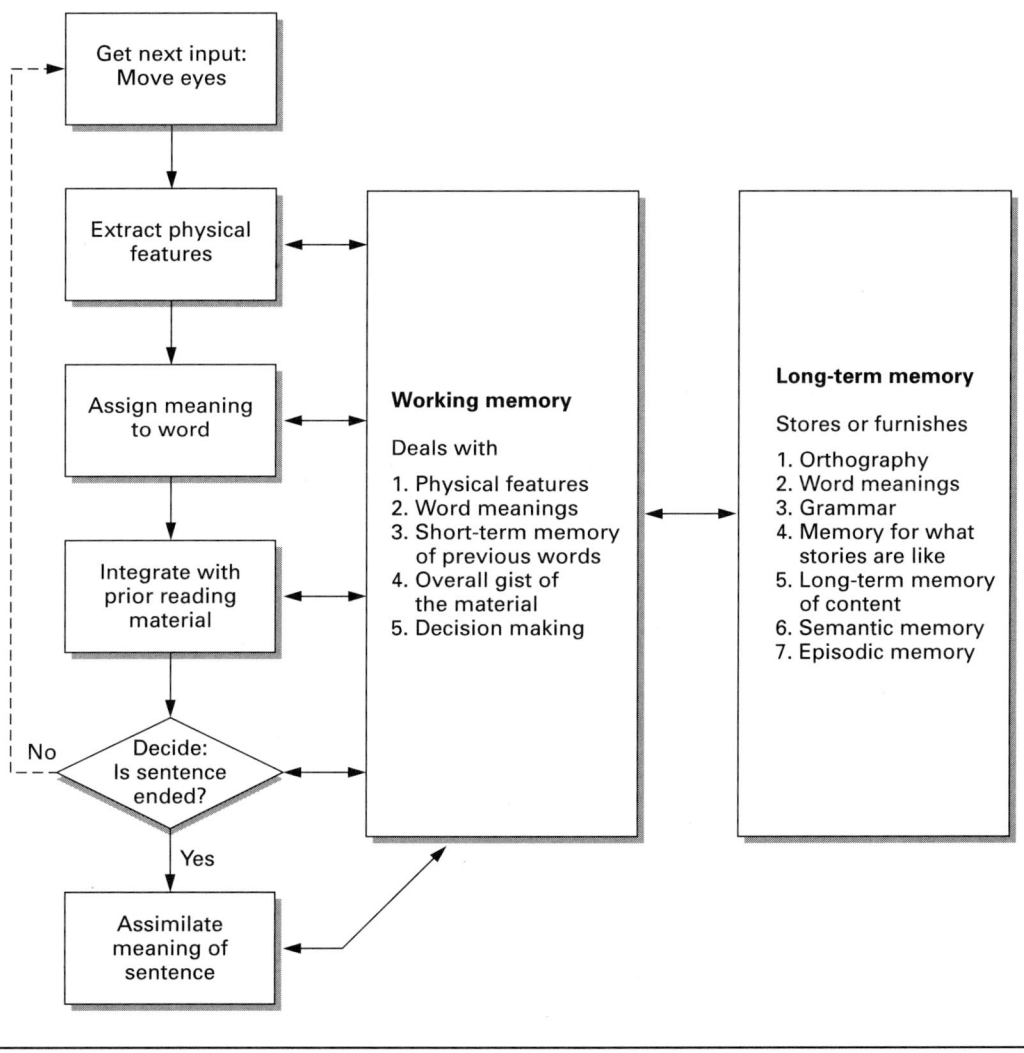

From M. Just and P. Carpenter, "A Theory of Reading: From Eye Fixations to Comprehension," in *Psychological Review,* 87:329–354, 1980. Copyright © 1980 by the American Psychological Association. Adapted by permission of the publisher and the authors.

1979; LaBerge & Samuels, 1974), have integrated information ranging from eye fixations to comprehension into a cognitive model of the reading process (see figure 9.1). The Just and Carpenter model characterizes reading as a dynamic, interactive process whereby written stimuli are processed at several levels to extract meaning. As readers gain competence, most decoding skills become automatic, thus allowing for attention and memory to focus on comprehension.

➔ *Factors That Influence the Development of Reading*

The research on reading indicates that numerous factors influence the development of reading. In this section, we identify and briefly review the effect of major noninstructional and instructional factors, both of which should be considered in any assessment of a reading problem.

Noninstructional Factors

Noninstructional factors are those that cannot be controlled by a teacher, including characteristics of the learner such as sex or auditory ability. A sex difference has historically been identified in reading achievement, with girls outperforming boys (Dwyer, 1973). Such assertions, however, are based on published reports at least 20 years old. Fry and Lagomarsino (1982), however, believe that the sex difference in reading achievement in regular classrooms is rather meager and is disappearing. More boys than girls may be labeled "reading disabled," but sex will not account for much of the difference in first-grade or third-grade reading achievement.

The relation between reading achievement and auditory acuity, however, is fairly strong. Deaf children rarely learn to read well (Gibson & Levin, 1975). Correctly identifying letters by name involves visual discrimination, and many researchers have found that a child's ability to recognize and name letters before or during kindergarten is a very good predictor of first-grade and primary reading achievement (see e.g., deHirsch, Jansky, & Langford, 1966). On the other hand, intelligence, as typically measured, is a rather weak predictor of progress in learning to read.

Instructional Factors

Time on task, classroom management, and size of reading group are all instructional factors that influence learning to read. Wyne and Stuck (1979) worked with second- and third-grade students who were reading below grade level. After an eight-week program to increase task-oriented behavior during reading, they found that reading achievement was positively influenced by the amount of time a student spent actively learning to read. In a more recent investigation by Gaskins (1988), it was reported that poor readers spent "an alarming amount of time in unproductive ways" (p. 751). Gaskins noted that it was not uncommon for teachers to allow 5 to 10 minutes of reading group time to elapse before instruction began and to use a significant portion of reading time dealing with disciplinary and management tasks. Anderson, Evertson, and Brophy (1979) found that a teacher who can structure, maintain, and monitor classroom activities will facilitate higher reading performances. Good (1979) reported that small group instruction, compared to individualized programs, appears to yield higher reading achievement for first- and second-grade students.

➡ *Typical Reading Problems*

Reading problems usually are manifested in children in three ways: (a) ineffective decoding or word attack strategies, (b) inconsistent comprehension, and (c) a negative attitude toward reading. Clearly, problems in any of these areas will likely affect the others. Therefore, early and ongoing evaluation of reading progress is desirable.

Word attack problems often are evidenced by mispronunciations of letter sounds, omissions of syllables, and substitutions of sounds. Some of the most pervasive problems are the result of the failure to learn the long and short vowel sounds and the rules of word construction that provide cues to syllabification. In addition, efficient word attack ability requires a large sight-word vocabulary (e.g., *the, on, at, to, out, go*) and knowledge of prefixes (e.g., *pre-, post-, a-, re-,*) and suffixes (e.g., *-ing, -ed, -ly, -ish, -ful*) .

Difficulties with comprehension directly follow from flawed word attack skills. However, even when one can accurately read every word in a sentence, comprehension is not assured. Reading rate, memory, background knowledge, and perspective are all critical influences on reading comprehension. For young readers, among whom literal comprehension is usually stressed, reading rate and memory are probably the most salient. However, as readers mature, the importance of background knowledge and perspective increases. For example, read the following paragraph:

> Rocky slowly got up from the mat, planning his escape. He hesitated a moment and thought. Things were not going well. What bothered him most was being held, especially since the charge against him had been weak. He considered his present situation. The lock that held him was strong but he thought he could break it. He knew, however, that his timing would have to be perfect. Rocky was aware that it was because of his early roughness that he had been penalized so severely—much too severely from his point of view. The situation was becoming frustrating; the pressure had been grinding on him far too long. He was being ridden unmercifully. Rocky was getting angry now. He felt he was ready to make his move. He knew his success or failure would depend on what he did in the next few seconds. (Anderson, Reynolds, Schallert, & Goetz, 1977, p. 372)

Depending on your background and experience, you probably understood this passage to be about either a convict planning his escape or a wrestler plotting his moves to break a tough hold. A reader's background, which is largely measured through language proficiency and fund of words, thus plays an important role in comprehension. Obtaining such basic information is fundamental to administering and interpreting reading tests. If you believe you have a good command of this basic knowledge, you are ready to begin an examination of reading tests.

Focus on
→ **Practice** ←

Sight-Word Vocabulary

The English language is made up of thousands of words, yet, quite logically, beginning readers generally are exposed to a subset of 300 to 400 high-frequency words. Such a corpus of words is often referred to as a sight-word vocabulary. Regardless of the reading series and instructional approach used to teach reading, almost all young readers are exposed to words such as *to, we, up, big, dog,* and *girl.* Several published lists of high-frequency words from the first, second, and third grades exist, such as the Dolch Basic Sight Vocabulary List, the BRIGANCE® Basic Sight Vocabulary, and the Durrell Word Frequency List. Below are 50 words extracted from these lists:

to	that	like	father	run
the	are	did	come	name
in	up	her	from	over
and	they	baby	here	day
at	me	but	just	ride
we	go	with	if	where
see	mother	will	or	look
on	was	dog	make	home
not	box	what	blue	school
said	had	no	green	pets

For most children, the identification of these words requires practice and illustrative examples. By third grade these words should be read rapidly with very few errors. You might informally assess several young children to determine the development of their sight-word vocabulary.

➡ Reading Tests

More than 175 published reading tests were in circulation as of early 1989, according to *The Tenth Mental Measurements Yearbook* (Conoley & Kramer, 1989). Because it would be impossible to discuss each of these tests here, we have selected 10 to examine in detail either because of their popularity or because they represent a particular type of test (such as group administered/individually administered, norm-referenced/criterion-referenced, and standardized/informal). We first document the various reading skills each test purports to measure and then discuss their technical adequacy.

Reading Skills and Selected Reading Tests

Carnine and Silbert (1979) developed a three-part model of reading instruction that is useful for examining the content of reading tests. Specifically, they hypothesized that the important elements of reading could be described as units, skills, and knowledge base. *Units* form a hierarchy beginning with single words and continuing to entire passages. *Skills* begin with sounding out letters and increase in complexity to include inferential comprehension and evaluation actions. The hierarchy for *knowledge base* begins with simple vocabulary and increases to sophisticated vocabulary. This three-part model can be used to describe and compare the content of the 10 reading tests selected (see table 9.2). Table 9.2 indicates that no single test samples all reading behaviors. For example, the California Achievement Tests (CTB/McGraw-Hill, 1985), and the Metropolitan Achievement Tests, Sixth Edition (Prescott, Balow, Hogan, & Farr, 1987) are both widely used group tests that cannot assess oral reading but rather sample a broad range of decoding and comprehension behaviors. Tests such as the Gates-McKillop-Horowitz Reading Diagnostic Tests (Gates, McKillop, & Horowitz, 1981) and the Nelson-Denny Reading Test (Brown, Bennett, & Hanna, 1981), which were developed for two very different age groups, focus on decoding and comprehension, respectively.

The Technical Adequacy of Reading Tests

As emphasized in chapter 5, reliability, validity, and norms are important indicators of the quality and utility of a test. However, table 9.3 reveals that not one of our 10 selected standardized reading tests provides data on all seven of the basic evaluative indexes. This should cause you to choose any reading test with caution, given that these 10 are some of the best available. In all cases, users must consult a test's technical manual for details about its psychometric characteristics.

In the remainder of this section, we examine the content and outcomes of two tests, the Test of Early Reading and the Woodcock Reading Mastery Tests-Revised, which were selected because of their frequent use with young children with reading problems.

TERA: Test of Early Reading Ability

The TERA or the Test of Early Reading Ability is an individually administered test for assessing preschool children's prereading and beginning reading abilities. Items were constructed to assess children's efforts at (a) finding meaning in print, (b) learning the alphabet and its use, and (c) discovering conventions of reading and writing English. The TERA is most appropriate for English-speaking children who are between 4–0 and 7–11 years of age and can follow simple directions. Its authors recommend its use in

Table 9.2 Reading Skills Sampled by Selected Reading Tests

	Decoding																Comprehension																
	Units						Skills						Knowledge				Units					Skills							Knowledge				
	Letter Sounds	Letters	Letter combination	Syllables	Words	Phrases	Sounding out	Sight reading	Breakdown of large words	Accuracy	Fluency	Oral reading	Silent reading	Oral language	Word familiarity	Syntax	Words	Phrases	Sentences	Paragraphs	Passages	Literal	Inferential	Sequencing	Summarization	Simplification	Critical reading	Study skills	Syntax	Semantics	Facts	Logic	Schema
California Achievement Tests (CTB/McGraw-Hill, 1985)	X	X	X	X	X	X	X	X	X				X	X	X	X	X	X	X	X	X	X	X				X	X		X	X	X	X
Metropolitan Achievement Tests (Prescott, Balow, Hogan & Farr, 1987)																																	
Surveys	X	X	X	X	X	X	X	X					X	X	X	X	X	X	X	X	X	X	X		X	X			X	X	X	X	X
Instructional	X	X	X	X	X	X	X	X					X	X	X	X	X	X	X	X	X	X	X		X	X			X	X	X	X	
Peabody Individual Achievement Tests Revised (Markwardt, 1989)					X				X			X	X	X	X	X	X	X	X	X	X	X	X										
Gates-McKillop-Horowitz Reading Diagnostic Tests (Gates & McKillop, 1981)	X	X	X	X	X	X	X	X	X	X	X	X	X	X	X	X	X	X	X	X	X	X	X							X		X	X
Diagnostic Reading Scales (Spache, 1972)	X	X	X	X	X	X	X			X	X	X	X	X	X	X	X	X	X	X	X	X	X							X			
Nelson-Denny Reading Test (Brown, Bennett, & Hanna, 1981)				X	X	X				X	X	X	X	X	X	X	X	X	X	X	X	X	X						X	X	X	X	X
TERA: Test of Early Reading Ability (Reid, Hvesko, & Hammill, 1981)	X																											X					
Degrees of Reading Power (The College Board, 1981)													X		X	X	X	X	X	X	X	X											
Woodcock Reading Mastery Tests-Revised (Woodcock, 1987)	X			X	X		X						X	X	X	X	X	X	X	X	X	X		X					X	X	X		
Gates-MacGinite Reading Tests (MacGinite, 1978)			X	X	X	X	X						X	X	X	X	X	X	X	X	X	X	X						X	X	X	X	X

Table 9.3 Reliability, Validity, and Norms for Selected Reading Tests

Test*	Reliability				Validity	Norms	
	Test-Retest	Parallel Form	Internal Consistency	Standard Error of Measurement	Criterion Validity	Sample	Representativeness
California Achievement Tests	None	.54–.90	.76–.97	Yes	None	200,000: grades K–12; national representation	Excellent
Metropolitan Achievement Tests Survey	N/A	N/A	.85–.96	Yes	.55–.82	550,000: grades K–12; national representation	Excellent
Instructional	N/A	N/A	.88–.95	Yes	N/A	1,563 ages 5–18, national representation	Excellent
Peabody Individual Achievement Tests-Revised	.95	None	.97	Yes	None		Adequate
Gates-McKillop-Horowitz Reading Diagnostic Tests	.94	None	None	No	.68–.96	600: grades 1–6	Inadequate
Diagnostic Reading Scales	.30–.96	None	.87–.96	Yes	.13–.77		
Nelson-Denny Reading Tests	None	.69–.92	None	Yes	None	25,000: grades 9–16	Excellent
Test of Early Reading Ability	.82–.94	None	.87–.96	Yes	.52–.66	1,184: ages 3–7; national representation	Excellent
Degrees of Reading Power	None	.86–.91	None	Yes	.70–.84	34,000: grades 4–12; national representation	Excellent
Woodcock Reading Mastery Tests-Revised	None	.16–.94	.84–.99	Yes	None	6,089: grade K through 75 yrs	Adequate
Gates-MacGinitie Reading Tests	.77–.89	.77–.94	.88–.94	No	.88–.91	6,500: grades 1–12; national representation	Adequate

*For sources of tests see Table 9.2.

Note: "None" means the information is relevant and desired but not provided, whereas "N/A" means the information is not applicable.

identifying children who are significantly behind age peers in the development of basic reading skills, in research, and in instructional planning. Based on our examination of the TERA, use for instructional planning is questionable.

The TERA was standardized on performances of 1,184 children from 11 states and one Canadian province. This sample was reported to be representative of the U.S. population in 1979.

Content

The TERA is a 50-item test developed according to a three-factor conceptual model comprised of Meaning, Alphabet Knowledge, and Conventions of Written Language. Items measuring ability to construct meaning from print were of three types: (a) awareness of print in an environmental context, (b) knowledge of relations among vocabulary items, and (c) comprehension or awareness of print in connected discourse. To assess awareness of print in an environmental context, a child is asked to identify common signs, logos, or small words. To measure knowledge of relational vocabulary items, a child is required to select two words that relate to a stimulus word. To assess awareness of print in discourse, a child is told to retell a well-formed story or to supply missing words in a sentence during reading (cloze procedure). Items on Alphabet Knowledge include naming letters, reading short words, and proofreading. To assess the Conventions of Written Language factor, items tap book-handling skills and responses to print conventions such as punctuation, left-right orientation, and spatial presentation of a story on a page. Our examination of item difficulties and discriminating power indicates that the TERA is most appropriate for five- and six-year-olds.

Reliability and Validity

The authors of the TERA provide basic information on its internal consistency and test-retest reliabilities. As noted in table 9.3, the internal consistency reliabilities range from .87 to .96, depending on the age of the individuals. Such reliabilities are good and indicate consistent item content. The stability of the TERA over approximately two weeks was tested with a restricted subsample ($N = 177$, from the Dallas area only) of children varying in age. The test-retest reliability for this entire subsample was .97, although for some age levels within the small subsample the reliabilities were in the .82 to .85 range. Overall, the TERA has demonstrated very good stability, given that it is designed for use with young children.

The primary evidence for the validity of the TERA consists of correlational data with other reading tests and with tests of intelligence, language, and school readiness. Specifically, the authors reported correlations between TERA total scores and the Reading subtest of the Metropolitan Achievement Tests of .66 and the Test of Reading Comprehension of .52. These correlations were again based on a limited sample of children and are lower than desirable for the criterion validity of a diagnostic test.

Evidence for the construct validity was sought by correlating TERA total scores with several tests, including the Slosson Intelligence Test ($r = .66$), the Test of Language Development ($r = .62$), and the Metropolitan Achievement Tests listening subtest ($r = .79$). Although the authors have provided more information than most, the data are not particularly compelling because of the noticeable omission of validity evidence with other *reading* measures. From the present correlational data it seems that the TERA has a significant verbal ability emphasis. This, however, is only part of the development of early reading skills, as Venesky noted (1976). A final bit of validity evidence concerning group differentiation is discussed in the manual, although it cannot be seriously considered (and may even be misleading) because both the research methods and sample of children were limited.

Administration and Scoring

According to the test manual, the TERA can be administered by anyone with basic competencies in the administration of individualized tests after the manual has been thoroughly reviewed. The TERA requires approximately 20 minutes to administer. The manual provides a specific procedural script for each item but allows the examiner to improvise directions. Scoring the responses is a fairly objective task. Each of the 50 items is worth 1 point, and scoring criteria accompany the administrative scripts for each item. The basal point is where a child passes five consecutive items, and a ceiling is reached when five consecutive items are missed.

A child's performance on the TERA is reported in terms of three kinds of normative scores: the Reading Quotient (RQ), Percentile, and Reading Age (RA). The RQ is a standard deviation score (with a mean of 100 and a standard deviation of 15) based on the cumulative frequency distributions of the raw scores of the standardization population. The Percentile is simply a conversion of raw scores with respect to the individual performances of the standardization sample. Finally, the RA was developed by plotting raw scores against ages in months. Because this score suffers from several statistical and interpretative problems, only the RQ and Percentile should be used.

At the time this book was going to press, a revised version of the TERA was being released. The second edition of TERA appears to cover the same content; however, it was standardized on children ages 3–0 through 9–11 years.

Woodcock Reading Mastery Tests-Revised

The Woodcock Reading Mastery Tests-Revised (WRMT-R), a revised version of the 1973 WRMT, is a comprehensive battery of tests measuring several important aspects of reading ability. The WRMT-R consists of six tests and a two-part supplementary checklist that all can be individually administered to persons kindergarten through age 75 years. Two alternate forms of the test are available (Forms G and H), both of which are accompanied by a comprehensive and well-organized test manual.

Content

The most comprehensive form (G) of the WRMT-R consists of 905 items that are the result of a validation process, which started with expert nominations and ended with a systematic statistical examination. The items are organized into six subtests that are divided into three clusters: Readiness Cluster, Basic Skills Cluster, and Reading Comprehension Cluster.

The Readiness Cluster includes a Visual-Auditory Learning Subtest (134 items that measure how well an individual can form associations between visual stimuli and oral responses) and a Letter Identification Subtest (51 items that measure an individual's ability to name various forms of uppercase and lowercase letters). A Supplementary Letter Checklist that presents letters in the style of many beginning reading materials is also included in the Readiness Cluster.

The Basic Skills Cluster includes Word Identification and Word Attack Subtests. The Word Identification Subtest includes 106 items arranged in increasing difficulty and is designed to measure a person's ability to identify words in isolation. The Word Attack Subtest consists of 45 items also arranged in order of difficulty. The items on the subtest are either nonsense words (e.g., *wug*) or words with a very low frequency of usage. The goal of the subtest is to measure a person's ability to apply phonic and structural analysis skills with unfamiliar words. Figure 9.2 is a copy of the Word Attack Error Inventory that can be used to facilitate interpretation of a person's performance on the Word Attack subtest. An examination of the Pronunciation column provides an overview of the sounds students will be tested on.

The Reading Comprehension Cluster is composed of two tests: Word Comprehension and Passage Comprehension. The Word Comprehension test consists of three subtests: Antonyms, Synonyms, and Analogies. Each of these subtests is designed to measure a person's reading vocabulary at a different level of processing. The Antonyms subtest measures ability to read a word (e.g., *good*) and then respond orally with a word opposite in meaning (e.g., *bad*). The Synonym subtest requires reading a word (e.g., *pretty*) and then stating another word similar in meaning to the presented word (e.g., *beautiful*). The Antonyms and Synonyms combined contain 67 items. The Analogies subtest is the most difficult of the Word Comprehension subtests. It requires reading a pair of words and ascertaining the relationship between the words and then reading the first word of a second pair and using the same relationship to supply a new word to complete the analogy appropriately. For example, *he-she boy-_____* or *milk-drink apple-_____* . The Passage Comprehension test contains 68 items that measure a person's ability to study a short passage—usually two or three sentences long—and to identify a key word missing from the passage. This type of task is referred to as a **modified cloze procedure** and requires a variety of comprehension and vocabulary skills. Figure 9.3 illustrates the skills assessed by two subtests from the WRMT-R.

Figure 9.2   Word Attack Error Inventory Completed on the Woodcock Reading Mastery Tests–Revised for Rosa, a Sixth-Grade Student

WORD ATTACK ERROR INVENTORY

Directions: Circled numbers refer to item numbers in the Word Attack test. For each Sound Category or Syllable, shade the circles representing the subject's errors on the target sound or target syllable. (Include as errors any items that the subject was administered, but did not respond to.) Draw a line through the circles for any items that were not administered.

Final Word Attack item administered __36__

	Sound Category	Pronun-ciation	Spellings	Additional Spelling Examples[a]
Single Consonants and Digraphs	1	b	● b- ● -b	㉑ buf- ㉟ -bet ㊳ baf
	2	ch	㉔ ch- ● -ch	㊺ cher
	3	d	① d- ⑯ d- ㉔ -d ● -d-	㉖ tad- ㉙ ad-
	4	f	④ -ff ⑧ f-	㉑ buf- ㊱ -ful ㊳ baf
	5	g	⑨ g- ⑫ -g ● g- ● g-	● cig-
	6	h		⑲ -hip
	7	hw	⑱ wh-	
	8	j	㊹ -ge	㉙ -jex ㉚ sodge
	9	k		㉝ -k-d ㉞ -nk
	10	kw	㊸ qu-	
	11	l	㉘ l-	㊱ -ful ㊴ lib
	12	m	● -m ● -m	㊱ man- ㊳ -mot ㊳ bem
	13	n	⑤ n- ⑥ -n ⑦ -n ⑳ n- ㉞ kn- ㊸ gn-	⑲ vun- ㊺ pno-
	14	ŋ	㉛ -ng	㉖ -ing ㊱ -cing-
	15	p	② -p ● p- ⑬ p- ⑮ -p ㉘ -p	⑲ -hip
	16	r	④ r- ⑩ r- ㊲ wr-	
	17	s	⑪ -ss ㉒ s- ㊹ c-	㉟ cig- ㊱ -cing- ㊳ sodge
	18	sh	⑰ sh-	
	19	t	⑨ -t ⑭ -t	㉑ -ty ㉖ tad- ㉟ -bet
	20	th	㉕ th- ㊷ the	
	21	v	㊹ v-	⑲ vun-
	22	w	⑭ w-	㉗ tw-
	23	ks		㉙ -jex
	24	y	㉛ y-	
	25	z	● z-	㊳ trans- ㊸ -c-s

	Sound Category	Pronunciation	Spelling (Individual pronunciations are enclosed in parentheses.)
Consonant Blends	26	Two-consonant blends	③ -ft ⑮ pl- ⑯ -d's (dz) ㉓ -c-d (st) ㉕ -n't ㉗ tw- ● -n't ● -k-d (kt) ● -nk (ŋk) ㊸ -c-s (kz)
	27	Three-consonant blends	㉓ str-

	Sound Category	Pronun-ciation	Spellings	Additional Spelling Examples[a]
Vowels	28	a	② a- ④ -a- ⑥ -a- ● -a- ● -a- ㉔ -a- ● -a-	㉖ tad- ㉙ ad- ㊱ man-
	29	e	● -e- ● -e-	㉙ -jex ㉟ -bet ㊳ bem
	30	i	③ i- ● -i- ● -i-	● -hip ㉖ -ing ● cig-
	31	o	⑪ o- ⑫ -o-	㊳ mot ㊳ sodge ㊵ mon-
	32	u	⑦ u- ⑯ -u-	⑲ vun- ㉑ buf- ㊵ glus-
	33	ā	⑧ -ay ㉓ -a-e- ● -ai- ㉝ -a-e- ㊲ ey	
	34	ē	① -ee ⑭ -ea-	㉑ -ty
	35	ī	⑱ -ie ● -igh ㉒ -y ㊸ -i-e	
	36	ō	⑬ -oe	㊺ pno- ㊺ -mo-
	37	aw	㊹ -au-	
	38	oi	● -oi-	
	39	oo	⑩ -oo	
	40	ou	● -ou- ㊸ -ou-	
	41	er	● -ir- ㊹ -yr-	㊵ -mer ㊺ -cher

	Syllable	Pronun-ciation	Spelling	Syllable	Pronun-ciation	Spelling	Syllable	Pronun-ciation	Spelling
Multisyllable Words	42	vun	⑲ vun-	52	man	㊱ man-	61	mon	㊵ mon-
	43	hip	● -hip	53	sin	㊱ -cing-	62	glus	㊵ -glus-
	44	buf	㉑ buf-	54	fel	● -ful	63	te	㊵ -ta-
	45	tē	㉑ -ty	55	baf	㊳ baf	64	mer	㊵ -mer
	46	tad	㉖ tad-	56	mot	㊳ -mot	65	nō	㊺ pno-
	47	iŋ	㉖ -ing	57	bem	㊳ -bem	66	mō / mŏk	㊺ -mo- / -moch-
	48	ad	㉙ ad-	58	tranz	㊳ -trans-			
	49	jeks	㉙ -jex	59	lib	㊴ -lib-	67	cher / er	㊺ -cher / -er
	50	sig	● cig-	60	soj	㊳ -sodge			
	51	bet	● -bet						

[a]Shade the circles for the additional examples only if the subject makes an error on the *target sound*.

Figure 9.3 Sample Items from the Word Comprehension and Word Attack Subtests of the Woodcock Reading Mastery Tests–Revised

**WORD COMPREHENSION SAMPLE ITEMS—
DO NOT RECORD ON THE RESPONSE FORM**

Point to the first sample item and say: **Listen carefully and finish what I say** (point to each of the three words and the blank space, in turn, while reading the item).
A dog walks; a bird . . . (pause). (*flies*) If the subject gives an incorrect response or does not respond, read the item again, completing it with the correct word.
Continue with the remaining sample items in the same manner (point to each word as the item is read to the subject):

One is to two as three is to . . . (pause). (*four, six*)
He is to she as boy is to . . . (pause). (*girl*)
Grass is to green as snow is to . . . (pause). (*white*)

dog—walks	bird—
one—two	three—
he—she	boy—
grass—green	snow—

**WORD ATTACK SAMPLE ITEM—
DO NOT RECORD ON RESPONSE FORM**

Say: **I want you to pronounce some words that are not real words. I want you to tell me how they sound.** Point to "tat." **How does this word sound?**

Sample: **tat**

If the subject incorrectly responds to "tat," point to "tat" and say it clearly. Do not pronounce any other words during the Word Attack Test.
Proceed to the next page and begin the test. Continue testing until the subject has missed five or more consecutive words, or has responded to Item 50.
How do these words sound? Point to each word if necessary. If the subject fails to respond in a few seconds, encourage a response. If the subject still fails to respond, continue the test by pointing to the next word.

1. ift	2. bim	3. ut	4. rayed	5. kak
(ift)*	(bim)	(ət)	(rād)	(kak)
6. aft	7. nen	8. ab	9. tash	10. wip's
(aft)	(nen)	(ab)	(tash)	(wips)

*Pronunciation symbols used by permission of the publishers of the Merriam-Webster Dictionaries. See test manual for further explanation.

The WRMT-R has retained many of the features of the original WRMT; however, several content and administrative changes should be noted. First, the Readiness Cluster was created. Second, the Word Comprehension test was expanded to include antonyms and synonyms, and vocabulary in the content areas of science, mathematics, social studies, and humanities can now be evaluated. Third, the number of sample items has been increased in some tests to facilitate student performance. And four, the applicability of the test has been extended to include college/university and adult groups.

Administration and Scoring

Administration of the WRMT-R requires attention to details, a thorough reading of the test manual, and general test administration experience. The WRMT-R manual provides an excellent chapter on administration with supporting self-training checklists and sample exercises.

The administration of the full scale requires, on average, 45 minutes. The test materials are well designed and feature an easel-like kit that can be positioned so that a subject can see only the stimulus items while the examiner can see both the instructions and correct answers.

The items on the test have been arranged from easiest to most difficult, except on the Visual-Auditory Learning subtest. Such an arrangement results in a power test and allows one to establish both basal and ceiling levels. By using Starting Point guidelines, an examiner tries to begin at a level of difficulty that can ensure early successes on items without seeming too simple for the examinee. The goal is to establish a Basal Level of six or more consecutive items passed and a Ceiling Level of six consecutive items failed. The use of basal and ceiling rules permits the examiner to estimate the score that would have been obtained if every item on the test had been administered to a subject. When computing the test raw score, the examiner assumes that all items below the basal would have been answered correctly, and that all items above the ceiling would have been answered incorrectly.

Each item on the WRMT-R is worth 1 raw score point. With the exception of the Visual-Auditory Learning and Word Comprehension subtests, the raw score on a subtest is the sum of the correct answers given plus a score of 1 for every item in the test below the basal. The WRMT-R provides users with an array of derived scores as a result of raw scores on the various subtests and clusters and the level of interpretation one desires. Figure 9.4 provides a picture of the four levels of interpretation for WRMT-R performances and lists the types of scores rendered. A detailed discussion of these various scores is beyond the scope of this chapter. Suffice it to say that the WRMT-R provides users with both norm-referenced and criterion-referenced results based on a large (N = 6,089) nationally representative sample of subjects from 60 communities in the United States.

Reliability and Validity

The overall reliability and validity of the WRMT-R are summarized in table 9.3. The test's manual provides good documentation of internal consistency and standard errors of measurement as evidence of the various subtest reliabilities. Median split-half reliability coefficients for all WRMT-R subtests exceed .84, with the average being in the .90 range. The validity data for WRMT-R is mostly correlations with other tests (i.e., concurrent validity) of reading and cognitive abilities. Generally, the WRMT-R correlates highly ($r > .80$) with tests such as Wide Range Achievement Test-Reading subscale, Peabody Individual Achievement Test-Reading subscale, and Iowa Test of Basic Skills-Total Reading. The author also provides a rational case for the content validity of the instrument and provides some intercorrelational data on WRMT-R subscales, which supports the instrument's construct validity. In summary, the reliability and validity of the

Figure 9.4   Hierarchy of Interpretive Information Available from the Woodcock Reading Mastery Tests–Revised

	Basis	Type of Information
Level I. Analysis of errors	Individual item responses	Description of a subject's performance on precisely defined skills
Level II. Level of development	Sum of item scores	Raw score *Rasch ability score (test W score, subtest part score, cluster W score) Grade equivalent Age equivalent
Level III. Quality of performance[a]	Performance on a reference task	*W-difference score (DIFF) Instructional range Relative Performance Index (RPI)
Level IV. Standing in a group	Deviation from a reference point in a group	Rank order *Standard score Percentile rank

Note: Scores marked with asterisks are the most suitable for statistical analysis.
[a]Another example of a Level III score is the Snellen Index for visual acuity.

Woodcock Reading Mastery Tests-Revised meets basic technical characteristics expected of tests used to make individual placement and instructional decisions.

➡ *Direct Assessment of Reading*

The materials utilized in a direct assessment of reading include norm-referenced and criterion-referenced published tests; curriculum materials; and nonstandardized devices such as checklists, informal reading inventories, and behavior observation systems. A brief review of these nonstandardized devices and their uses follows.

Checklists

Behavior checklists and rating scales frequently are used by psychologists and educators when working with children who exhibit problems. Such devices, many of which are published commercially, can help to define a problem objectively and to document the perceived strengths and weaknesses of a child. Although few commercially published checklists deal with reading problems (see, e.g., the Checklist of Instructional Needs with the Durrel Analysis of Reading Difficulty [Durrell, 1955]), there is a plethora of informal checklists (Ingram, 1980; Miller, 1974; Potter & Rae, 1981), two examples of which are displayed in tables 9.4 and 9.5. Note that these informal checklists do not define the terms used, provide administration directions, or indicate how to decide what constitutes a correct response.

The primary purposes of informal reading checklists are description and prescription. When description of an individual's current skill repertoire is the goal, any checklist that adequately covers behaviors involved in reading may be helpful. For example, the checklist in table 9.5 could be used preceding or during an initial problem-solving consultation session with a teacher or parent to help operationalize a student's strengths and difficulties, thus allowing for a more focused, skill-oriented assessment.

A prescriptive checklist goes beyond just describing by enumerating possible means for remediating an identified deficiency. Table 9.5 shows a portion of a prescriptive checklist developed by James Dunn (from Elliott & Piersel, 1982). We are skeptical of the direct remedial efficacy of such checklists, for the manner in which any given prescription is implemented would vary across instructors. In addition, there is little empirical evidence clarifying reading aptitude treatment interactions. Nevertheless, prescriptive checklists may function as general guides for brainstorming and designing alternative prescriptive interventions after assessment information has been collected and synthesized.

Table 9.4   Typical Informal Checklist of Reading Difficulties

Name _____   **Age** _____   **Date** _____

School _____   **Teacher** _____

Oral Reading

_____ Evidence of emotional tension
_____ Strained, high-pitched voice
_____ Monotonous tone
_____ Volume too loud or soft
_____ Poor enunciation
_____ Word by word reading
_____ Incorrect phrasing
_____ Eye-voice span too short
_____ Oral accuracy errors:
    _____ Hesitations
    _____ Refusals
    _____ Omissions
    _____ Repetitions
    _____ Mispronunciations
    _____ Ignore punctuation
    _____ Substitutions
    _____ Additions
_____ Inadequate oral comprehension
_____ Low oral reading rate

Silent Reading

_____ Knowledge of letter names
_____ Use of context clues
_____ Phonic analysis
    _____ Single consonants
    _____ Consonant blends
    _____ Silent consonants
    _____ Short vowels
    _____ Vowel blends
    _____ Vowel diagraphs
    _____ Phonic rules
    _____ Sound blending ability
_____ Structural analysis
    _____ Inflectional endings
    _____ Compounds

_____ Common prefixes
_____ Common suffixes
_____ Roots
_____ Auditory-visual recognition
    of syllables
_____ Syllabication rules
_____ Use of dictionary

Vocabulary Development

_____ Inadequate sight vocabulary
_____ Inadequate meaning
    vocabulary

Comprehension Skills

_____ Recall of factual detail
_____ Main idea of paragraphs
_____ Sequence of idea and events
_____ Following directions
_____ Making inferences
_____ Critical, evaluative reading

Reading Rate

_____ Lack of flexibility in rate
_____ Low silent reading rate
_____ Scanning
_____ Skimming
_____ Finger pointing
_____ Head movements

Study Skills

_____ Asks questions about readings
_____ Takes notes
_____ Reads maps and globes
_____ Reads charts, tables & graphs
_____ Uses the dictionary
_____ Uses the encyclopedia
_____ Uses other reference books
_____ Rereads difficult material
_____ Outlines difficult material

From S. N. Elliott and W. C. Piersel, "Direct Assessment of Reading Skills: An Approach Which Links Assessment to Intervention" in *School Psychology Review*, 11:274. Copyright © 1982 by the National Association of School Psychologists. Reprinted by permission of the publisher.

Table 9.5   Selected Portions of a Checklist for Planning Remedial Reading Interventions

Confusion in Letter Knowledge

Behavior Exhibited	Possible Cause	Possible Remedies
Reversals	Visual disability	Check auditory and visual acuity
Anxiety in writing and reading	Hearing disability (acuity-figure ground)	Auditory and visual discrimination training
Ineffective word analysis	Carelessness	Small group instruction at chalkboard in initial teaching
Ineffective oral reading	Neurological development	Easily confused letters taught separately
Avoidance of writing	Inadequate instruction (improper pacing)	Appropriate training in phonics by use of error avoidance strategy for mastery
Poor spelling		Kinesthetic-tactile training

Difficulty in Structural Analysis

Behavior Exhibited	Possible Causes	Possible Remedies
Poor spelling	Auditory acuity and discrimination	Precise speech—separate words in spoken language
Inability in word perception	Lack of hearing precise speech	
Stagnate vocabulary	Inadequate instruction	Training in visual and auditory discrimination
Word guessing	Lack of understanding of what a syllable is	Differentiating between words similar sounds (minimal pairs—pen, pin)
	Teacher insecurity in personal knowledge resulting in avoidance	Recognition and synthesizing elements of word (phonemic, syllabic, morphemic)
		Building memory of word form
		Teach common affixes
		Adequate listening-speaking vocabulary
		Use of directed inquiry strategy in visual clues for syllabicating
		Provide sequential procedure in analyzing unfamiliar words

Table 9.5—*Continued*

Behavior Exhibited	Regressions in Oral Reading Possible Causes	Possible Remedies
Poor oral reading	Inadequate sight vocabulary	Proper placement
Slow reading rate	Inadequate word analysis	Contextual clues
	Interruptions when reading orally	
	Inappropriate placement	Choral reading
	Inadequate listening-speaking vocabulary	Music (familiar tune, new words)
	Confusion in meaning	Read silently before orally
	Eye movement in tracking line	Build oral language facility
	Round robin reading	Build word analysis skills
		Self-evaluation of taped reading
		Do not interrupt when a word is mispronounced when reading

Informal Reading Inventories

An informal reading inventory (IRI) can be utilized to identify a student's skill level by observing reading performance on material of increasing difficulty. The most common form of an IRI is constructed by selecting short passages (60 to 200 words) from a set of graded materials that increase in difficulty. This is usually accomplished by drawing passages from each level of a basal reading series. To date, there have been several well-received attempts to "standardize" or package IRIs (Johns, 1988; McCracken, 1966; Silvaroli, 1965); however, we only discuss those made by school personnel for local use.

IRIs have been utilized in two major ways (Johnson, Kress, & Pikulski, 1987). First, they have been used by reading specialists and psychologists to identify children's independent, instructional, and frustration reading levels and to design plans for the remediation of any weaknesses. Second, IRIs have been used in the classroom for a rapid assessment of reading skills so that students can be grouped more appropriately. In both cases, IRIs have been constructed from students' curriculum materials.

The strength of an IRI is not as a test instrument but as a means for studying and diagnosing a learner's reading behavior (Pikulski & Shanahan,

1982; Powell, 1971). According to Gillet and Temple (1990), IRIs have several advantages over other methods of reading assessment because they (a) are easy to construct and include material directly from a student's curriculum, (b) document reading errors in a context identical to a classroom task, and (c) provide an opportunity to observe reading behavior. Perhaps their most frequently cited advantage is that they can reveal several levels of reading skill: independent, instructional, and frustration (Learner, 1976; Robeck & Wilson, 1974). If used intelligently, issues of readability and interest can be controlled at least as well as with a standardized test. Readability is the grade-level difficulty attributed to a passage, which is based on factors such as word length and sentence complexity. Obviously, a subject's reading level will vary with the readability of a passage. A major goal of an informal assessment of reading is to establish the readability level of material with which a student achieves successes.

Betts (1946) is usually credited with suggesting that a child has three reading levels relative to curriculum materials. The *independent level* is the highest level of difficulty of a written material that a child can cope with independently and still maintain a nearly perfect reading performance; that is, the student has almost no difficulty with word identification, understands the passage, and can remember most of the contents as evidenced by answering questions. Quantitatively, the *independent level* has been defined by Lloyd (1979) as the highest level of material with which a child can sustain approximately 98 percent word recognition and answer nearly 100 percent of the comprehension questions asked. At the other end of the skill continuum is the frustration level, or the level at which material becomes so difficult that a child cannot adequately cope because the word recognition demands or the comprehensibility of the material exceeds the skills of the reader. The *frustration level* is defined as the lowest level of reading material at which a child is able to recognize less than 90 percent of the words and can answer less than 50 percent of the comprehension questions. The *instructional level* lies between the independent and the frustration levels and is probably the level of greatest interest to teachers. This is the level of material on which a child encounters some reading difficulties, although these problems can be overcome with limited help. The instructional level is the highest level at which a child is able to recognize approximately 95 percent of the words and answer more than 75 percent of the comprehension questions posed.

IRIs usually are individually administered and may be tape-recorded so errors can be more accurately coded. A percentage score is then derived by dividing the number of errors by the total number of words in the passage and subtracting this from 100. Reading behaviors that commonly are scored by this form of error analysis include assistance needed, hesitations, insertions, mispronunciations, omissions, order reversals, regressions, self-corrections, substitutions, and disregard of punctuation. Conventions for describing and marking these 10 behaviors are illustrated in table 9.6.

Table 9.6   Typical Reading Behaviors Analyzed as Errors Using IRIs

Type of Error	Scoring Convention
External assistance needed (student is aided by another person after 5 seconds)	<u>Underline words</u> aided
Hesitations (student hesitates at a word but does not require help)	Check (✔) above words
Insertions (student adds words not on page)	Write in word(s) or word part with caret (∧)
Mispronunciation (student does not pronounce word accurately)	Write in the phonetic pronunciation above the word
Omissions (student skips a word and reads on)	Circle the (omitted) word(s)
Order reversals (student inverts word order)	Mark reversals with transpose symbol (‿)
Disregard of punctuation (student inserts or omits punctuation marks)	Circle marks (omitted) and insert and circle marks added
Regressions (student reads and then rereads a word or words)	Put a <u>wavy line</u> under the word(s) repeated
Self-corrections (student makes a mistake but corrects it spontaneously)	Write SC above word(s)
Substitutions (student reads a word as another word)	Cross out the omitted ~~word~~ and insert the substituted word above it

From S. N. Elliott and W. C. Piersel, "Direct Assessment of Reading Skills: An Approach Which Links Assessment to Intervention" in *School Psychology Review,* 11:277. Copyright © 1982 by the National Association of School Psychologists. Reprinted by permission of the publisher.

A few words of caution about IRIs are in order. Because they are not constructed rigorously, they are prone to greater measurement error than most standardized reading tests. Therefore, the results from an IRI must be carefully interpreted and should not be the sole criterion for a diagnostic placement decision. IRIs are valuable sources of information for planning a teaching or remedial program for a student; however, the construction, administration, and interpretation of IRIs require considerable clinical and technical skills. Table 9.7 lists nine of the best IRIs that we have used over the years.

Table 9.7   Published Informal Reading Inventories

Inventory and Author/ Date Published	*Publisher*
Analytical Reading Inventory Woods & Moe, 1988	Charles E. Merrill
Bader Reading and Language Inventory Bader, 1983	Macmillan
Basic Reading Inventory (4th ed.) Johns, 1988	Kendall-Hunt
Classroom Reading Inventory (5th ed.) Silvaroli, 1986	Wm C. Brown
Computer-based Reading Assessment Instrument Blanchard, 1985	Kendall-Hunt
Diagnostic Reading Inventory (2nd ed.) Jacobs & Searfoss, 1979	Kendall-Hunt
Ekwall Reading Inventory (2nd ed.) Ekwall, 1985	Allyn & Bacon
Informal Reading Inventory Burns & Roe, 1985	Rand McNally
Standardized Reading Inventory Newcomer, 1986	Pro-Ed

Behavioral Observation Systems

Assessing the prerequisite learning and basic reading skills of a student during a test is important; it is also critical to gather behavioral information in the classroom in conjunction with teacher behavior and an array of classroom stimuli.

Soli and Devine (1976), in a study of the behavioral correlation of third- and fourth-grade high and low achievers, found that (a) the observation of classroom behavior was more critical for low achievers than high achievers and (b) the best predictors of achievement for the low achievers were absence of play, paying attention, absence of self-stimulation, and complying. Thus, these findings indirectly support the need to observe the prerequisite learning skills of children experiencing reading difficulties.

The Student-Level Observation of Beginning Reading (SOBR), developed and validated at the University of Pittsburgh's Learning Research and Development Center, is a classroom observation system designed for identifying and classifying both student and teacher behaviors (Leinhardt & Sewald, 1981). The SOBR has eight categories for the classification of student behaviors. Five of the categories are nonreading related: waiting for something or someone; engaged in an academic activity other than reading; engaged in a management activity; absent from school; and out of the room. Off-task is the sixth category and is divided into two subcategories,

Focus on
Research

Dyslexia: A Confusing Term

The term "dyslexia" is commonly used to describe any reading disorder that is not the result of organic defect, low intelligence, emotional disturbance, or environmental deprivation. Knowing what dyslexia is not, however, is only half the story. Several researchers have described various subtypes of dyslexia characterized by deficits in word-analysis skills, configuration and orientation of letters and words, or a combination of these two problems. These difficulties are experienced by many developing readers and should not and cannot be reliably used to formulate a diagnosis of dyslexia because the research literature on dyslexia is replete with definitional problems. Researchers have simply chosen to define and measure dyslexia in so many different ways that the term has virtually lost a specific meaning. At best, the word "dyslexia" means a possible reading problem!

   White and Miller's (1983) research supports our position about the construct of dyslexia. They investigated the use and meaning of the term "dyslexia" by examining 45 studies reported in the *Journal of Learning Disabilities*. They concluded that a major weakness in the studies was the inadequate definition of dyslexia, which ultimately negates the generalization and often the replication of the research. Those who read such research should thus be cautioned that at this time, both research and practice concerning dyslexia should be questioned.

From "Dyslexia: A Term in Search of a Definition" by M. White and S. R. Miller, 1983, *Journal of Special Education, 17,* pp. 5–10.

reading and nonreading, depending on the situational demands. The two general reading categories are direct reading (oral and silent) and indirect reading (talking about reading and writing about reading).

   The teacher observation includes four general categories: management, no student contact, other academic, and reading instruction. The reading instruction category is further divided into cognitive (cuing and monitoring) and cognitive explanation (presentation and feedback) components.

   An examiner using the SOBR observes a target student for 10 seconds, records observations for 5 seconds, observes another student (yoked or matched control student) for 10 seconds, and again records observations for 5 seconds. Next, the examiner monitors the teacher's behavior. This student-to-teacher observation cycle is repeated several times. Leinhardt, Zigmond, and Cooley (1981) reported that interrater agreements on the SOBR ranged between 78 percent and 100 percent across nine trained observers over all students and categories during a one-hour classroom observation. In a generalizability study, both interobserver agreement and code stability coefficients were estimated to be above .95 (Lomax, 1980).

Linking Assessment to Intervention

The process of direct assessment, as described in this chapter, takes place primarily in the programming decision phase of assessment and leads directly to designing an individualized educational plan and subsequent remedial services for a student. This assessment paradigm does not reject standardized testing, nor does it hold up IRIs as the best means of testing a student's reading skills. Rather, in this paradigm, tests of all varieties are considered as measures of behavior that vary in importance relative to the decision to be made (screening, diagnostic, or programming) and to the skills required for success in a given reading curriculum in a particular classroom. In the final section of this chapter, we focus on the direct measurement and remediation of comprehension problems, an area of primary importance to secondary-level educators. A major purpose of this section is to illustrate how direct assessment can aid in the development of interventions.

➡ *Assessment for Remediation of Comprehension Problems*

The most popular method of measuring comprehension has been standardized reading comprehension tests. Usually, a student is given a passage to read and then asked a series of questions that require the selection of the main idea of the passage. A basic problem exists with most reading comprehension tests because it is not clear what they are measuring. In addition to comprehension, they may be measuring characteristics of the learner, such as attention, test-taking skills, motivation, and familiarity with the test, as well as other aspects of the reading process.

The lack of a basic understanding of the reading comprehension process makes it almost impossible to separate the preceding aspects of a student's functioning from reading comprehension ability. One way to remedy this problem is to develop better means of evaluating comprehension. However, before a refinement in test construction is undertaken, a framework of comprehension tasks is needed.

A Framework of Comprehension Tasks

What is reading comprehension? Farr (1970), and more recently Gillet and Temple (1990), compiled lists of subtests from reading tests designed to measure comprehension and believed they all attempted to measure comprehension as a "thought-getting process," although how the tests achieved such a goal varied considerably.

Carroll (1972) classified the procedures for testing comprehension. A discussion of these procedures follows, organized according to the tasks required of an individual being tested.

Subjective Reports

This category assumes the subject will attend to a task and honestly report what was not comprehended. According to Carroll, this method has been used in psycholinguistic research, but only infrequently. Such an approach could possibly be useful in an informal assessment of a subject's awareness of her or his reading problems. For example, it could reveal what elements of a message, such as particular words, clauses, or grammatical constructions, are causing a person difficulty in comprehension. Although subjective reports could yield false positive results when a subject believes comprehension exists when it actually does not, it seems unlikely they would yield false negative results. Thus, subjective reports alone do not provide enough information about a subject's difficulties, but following a standardized measure of comprehension, they may provide valuable diagnostic insights.

Reports of Truth, Falsity, or Equivalence

According to Carroll, this technique helps to measure pure comprehension because a correct response directly depends on comprehension. The subject generally listens to or reads a passage and then responds to a question with a verbalization or by pointing to a picture referent. Another variant of this technique requires a subject to evaluate whether a message is equivalent in meaning to another message. This task, however, may place too great an emphasis on memory, as the subject must remember the first meaning before comparing it to a second meaning. If a subject is able to refer back to a text or have a message repeated, the memory load is diminished.

Following Directions: Nonverbal Responses to a Message

Tests of a subject's ability to follow verbal or written directions provide reliable and convenient measures, although it may be memory more than comprehension that is assessed. Although this technique is not used widely in formal assessment, it is easily adapted to informal assessment. By itself, the ability to follow directions is not a good measure of comprehension; however, this skill is a prerequisite for successful learning and thus should not be ignored in the assessment of any learning difficulty.

Supplying Missing Elements in a Message

This technique involves altering a passage of text by deleting words according to a rule, such as every fifth word or every other noun. A subject is then presented with the passage and asked to supply the missing words. Commonly referred to as the "cloze procedure," this method is employed in the Passage Comprehension subtest of the Woodcock Reading Mastery Tests-Revised.

Answering Questions Based on a Message

On most standardized reading or listening comprehension tests, subjects are presented with a paragraph to read or listen to and then a set of multiple-choice questions to answer. According to Carroll, these questions are often not controlled for guessing. Tests designed so that subjects are unable to answer questions without first reading or listening to a passage would seem to provide a reasonable test of skill at comprehending a message. The difficult task is to design tests that cover material relatively new to a broad population of subjects without using new vocabulary. As an informal, individual method of assessing comprehension, this approach is even more valid.

Recognizing a Message on Subsequent Presentation

In this technique, which has been a traditional method of measuring learning and memory, a subject is presented with material to read and then given elements from the material along with new or modified elements and asked to identify which elements are from the original material. This approach has severe shortcomings, for the task can be successfully accomplished by memory alone without comprehension. Although the procedure may require some comprehension, it is difficult to separate the effects of comprehension from those of memory processes.

Reproducing a Message

A variety of techniques for testing comprehension involve tasks requiring reproduction of a message. As with the previous technique, memory processes may also be involved, and thus the respective roles of comprehension and memory processes may be difficult to isolate.

A wide range of recall tasks have been used to measure a student's comprehension of sentences or passages. One method, however, that deserves special consideration is the paraphrasing task (Anderson, 1972), or the reproduction of a message in a subject's own words. Generally, this task must be performed without a subject being able to refer back to the original message, but the importance of memory processes can be reduced by allowing the subject to use the original message. If paraphrasing can be objectively and validly scored, this task may be useful for measuring comprehension.

This survey of Carroll's seven categories of techniques illustrates that no one method universally gives valid and reliable information about comprehension. Carroll (1972) concluded:

> It is seldom the case that success or failure in any of these tests can unequivocally be traced to success or failure in language comprehension since there are other factors of guessing, inference, memory, reliance on prior knowledge, etc. that are operating. (p. 24)

➡ *Informal Assessment of Comprehension Skills*

Thus far we have attempted to show that comprehension (along with memory and perhaps other processes) can be measured in at least seven ways. Therefore, it is not surprising that constructors of reading tests generally have had difficulty in measuring comprehension. How can a diagnostician or teacher receive more complete information about a student's comprehension skills? An attractive alternative, which requires work and an experimental approach, is to design an informal measure of comprehension from instructional materials. In the remainder of this section, we examine the feasibility of informally assessing comprehension. More information about using one's curriculum materials in the assessment of children will be provided in a later chapter on curriculum-based assessment.

Designing an Informal Assessment

Designing an informal test requires consideration of the (a) skills or behaviors to be assessed, (b) input and output modalities necessary for success, (c) types of questions to be asked, and (d) materials to be used in the test.

Skills

Six skills or behaviors important to the process of comprehension can be identified and include two mental processes, memory and inference making, plus four means of interacting with a written or spoken message: identifying main ideas, following directions, paraphrasing, and using context.

Modalities

A student will be required to respond both orally and in writing.

Questions

A student will be required to respond to a wide variety of questions, most of which can be categorized either as open-ended or structured. Therefore, the student must both generate original responses and select the correct answers from several alternatives.

Materials

The characteristics of the materials used in the assessment of comprehension, such as readability, length, familiarity of subject, and in-text clues, play an important role in the quantity and quality of a student's response.

One would have to develop a test with hundreds of tasks to tap all possible combinations of the four dimensions listed above. Our intent is not to design a corpus of comprehension tasks but rather to outline important features that should be integrated into the construction of any comprehension tasks. To illustrate how a diagnostician or teacher can design a test of comprehension, we have developed two examples.

Example 1: Identifying the Main Idea

To assess a student's skill at identifying the main idea of reading material, one can extract five or six short passages of increasingly difficult readability from graded workbooks or classroom texts. A student is then requested to develop a one-sentence description of the main idea of each passage, plus three incorrect alternatives.

Remember that a student can and should give more than one answer for each passage. For example, have a student read a passage silently. Then, with the passage out of sight, ask (a) What is the main idea of this passage? (without the use of alternatives), (b) What would be a good title for this passage?, and (c) What is the main idea of this passage? (with the use of alternatives). If the student demonstrates comprehension of the main idea at any point, go on to the next passage. However, if the student is unable to give a satisfactory answer, reintroduce the passage and have the student read it aloud and attempt to answer the same questions with the passage present.

By using graded material and examining silent reading before oral reading, the initial emphasis is on memory (passage was taken away). Thus, the task is to be presented in the most mentally demanding form first, with a regression to a somewhat less difficult form. This design is efficient, because if a student can answer the most difficult question, one could assume he or she will also answer the easier questions correctly.

Example 2: Following Directions

Tests of following directions can be used to assess attention and memory as well as comprehension. Attention and memory factors, however, can be minimized by varying testing situations. As before, materials in various formats can be used to help identify the strengths and weaknesses in a learner's comprehension skills.

Select a game or task with which the student is unfamiliar and write directions for it that are clear and understandable. Have the student read the directions and perform the task. Next, have the student describe the task and explain the role of each step. This allows subjects to act out and verbalize their understanding of a task. The comparison between doing something and describing how to do the same thing should provide insights into a student's verbal and comprehension skills. This is a very simple example and not specific to reading comprehension; however, it can provide important information about how a person learns and solves problems.

Conclusion

Educators and psychologists presently do not have sophisticated methods of accurately measuring reading comprehension, because it seems to involve so many cognitive skills. The best one can do to evaluate students' comprehension skills is to use tests, both formal and informal, that require subjects to behave as they do in typical learning situations and systematically to attempt to isolate skills and situations in which the students can and cannot succeed. Through a systematic, personalized assessment, a diagnostician can develop interventions to refine a learner's skills or change the instructional situation (i.e., materials or teaching), or both.

Chapter Summary

In this chapter we have tried to share with you the complexities of both the reading process and the accurate assessment of children's reading skills. Many tests have been developed to simplify the assessment of reading. Two individually administered tests, the Test of Early Reading Ability and the Woodcock Reading Mastery Tests-Revised, were examined in detail, along with a psychometric overview of eight other tests. Although good reading tests exist, we also strongly advocate that educators and psychologists become proficient at directly assessing reading skills. To this end, we reviewed the use of reading skills checklists, informal reading inventories, and classroom observations and provided examples of how comprehension can be informally assessed.

Chapter 10

Math

Learning Objectives

1. Describe the uses of a scope and sequence chart.
2. Describe the use of learning hierarchies and list two differences between learning hierarchies and scope and sequence charts.
3. Describe the differences between diagnostic arithmetic testing using standardized tests and error analysis using informal assessment.
4. Explain why error analysis using standardized tests is usually inappropriate.
5. Conduct a simple error analysis with a sample of a student's work.

L ouise had *dyscalculia** or at least that is what her parents had been told by her new teacher in a meeting at school on a day less than a week ago that was filled with bewilderment and sadness. However, her twelve-year-old brother, Todd, diagnosed her as normal in less than an hour and "cured" her even more quickly. And Todd was right!

Louise, a fifth-grader, was never an outstanding student in any subject but had always "gotten by." In fifth grade she seemed to be falling behind the rest of her class and thus was referred to the school diagnostic team. The results of an evaluation indicated that she had average intelligence (i.e., she achieved a Full Scale score of 103 on the Wechsler Intelligence Scale, WISC-III and that in reading and spelling she was performing at an average level (i.e., at the 51st percentile). However, the testing in

---

*Dyscalculia is a term originally used in medicine to indicate the virtual loss of mathematical ability after head trauma and was "borrowed" by some educators to describe basic arithmetic learning disorders.

Figure 10.1 Sample Problems from Louise's Arithmetic Test

3	5	6	9
×2	×7	×6	×8
6	35	36	72

12	14	42	33
×2	×2	×3	×2
24	48	86	96

---

arithmetic suggested she was approximately two years below grade level, at the 14th percentile for her age. Based on this information, the diagnostic team recommended that Louise be given special help for her problems in arithmetic. In an attempt to involve the parents in the evaluation of their child, the school had furnished them with a copy of the arithmetic quiz on which Louise had performed so poorly.

The quiz was a norm-referenced test that contained a separate test form for each specific grade level; Louise took the fifth-grade form. One evening Todd picked up Louise's quiz and began to examine its content and her responses. He noticed that many test items required multiplication (as would be expected for a test of fifth-grade mathematics) and that Louise had missed a large proportion of these items (not to mention the division items). Eight of the multiplication problems from the test are presented in figure 10.1. From the first four problems on the test it was immediately obvious to Todd that his sister knew her multiplication facts. After all, she was capable of correctly multiplying 9 times 8. However, when she attempted to multiply anything but two one-digit numbers, she was almost always wrong.

Neither norm-referenced test scores nor the number of correct answers on a teacher-made quiz tell *why* an answer is right or wrong but only whether something *is* right or wrong. Todd, on the other hand, was a curious youngster who wanted to know what Louise was doing wrong. Maybe there was some pattern to her errors. Working under the assumption that she knew her multiplication facts, Todd decided that either she was careless or some problem existed with the process she was using to multiply. He soon discovered that there was, in fact, a problem with her process: She was multiplying digits within one factor. Thus, to get an answer of 86 from the product of 42 times 3, Louise would first multiply 3 times 2 to get 6. Then, she would mistakenly multiply 4 times 2 to get 8. Her errors and her "dyscalculia" were related to this problem.

Todd quickly called Louise into the living room and instructed her in the appropriate process of multiplication. Later, her parents shared this information with her teacher and the evaluation team members. The problem was resolved without much alteration in Louise's school routine.

This hypothetical example illustrates two important points relative to the assessment of arithmetic skills. First, it is important to go beyond test scores and examine the content of the test and the processes children use in responding to items. Second, arithmetical ability is not simply some general capacity that one has or does not have. Instead, it is composed of a series of clearly observable skills. A primary assumption of this chapter is that these skills are not only observable but they also fit into an orderly sequence. A major goal in mathematics assessment is to find exactly where in the sequence a child fails. This specific information is highly relevant, because instruction should logically be directed toward the next skill in the sequence.

➡ *The Sequence of Learning Arithmetic Skills as the Basis for Assessment*

Learning arithmetic skills follows a logical and orderly sequence. A knowledge of this sequence of skills is essential for conducting assessments in arithmetic. We will discuss two approaches by which these skills have been described and organized: (a) scope and sequence charts, and (b) learning hierarchies.

Scope and Sequence Charts

Scope and sequence charts, such as the one presented in table 10.1, list the skills students need to know (scope) along a timeline in the order according to which they are usually taught (sequence). Many teachers derive their weekly and even daily lesson plans by using scope and sequence charts to focus on specific aspects of major skills. Note that the same skills reappear at different levels for review or more sophisticated application.

Scope and sequence charts are useful in assessment in two ways. First, a norm-referenced test may suggest that a child is performing at a third-grade level, for example. By referring to a chart, it is possible to determine in general the types of skills that the child does or does not have. This information can be easily translated into instructional objectives. This whole process must be approached cautiously, because often there is not one-to-one correspondence among a test, a scope and sequence chart, and the actual curriculum being taught to a specific child.

Second, a scope and sequence chart can be used as a vehicle for informal assessment. Such charts provide abundant information about skill domains that should be assessed. One possible strategy would be to use a norm-referenced test to determine the approximate grade level at which a child is functioning and then consult a scope and sequence chart to discover the specific skills the child is expected to know. Informal tests of

Table 10.1 Scope and Sequence Chart for Mathematics

Grade	Skills Acquired
Kindergarten	Rote counting to 10 Use whole numbers in serial order Begin cardinal numbers, ordinal numbers Begin reading numerals One-to-one matching Addition as joining of sets
Grade 1: First Half	Rote counting to 100 Read and write whole numbers through 50 Place value at tens place Equivalent/nonequivalent sets Know meaning of signs −, +, and = Addition and subtraction as inverse functions Solving missing addend problems Using 0 in subtraction
Grade 1: Second Half	Rote counting beyond 100 Counting by fives, twos, tens Odd and even numbers Signs (&) Read and write to 99 Begin fractions 1/2, 1/3, 1/4 Addition combinations through 19 Addition of two-digit numbers with 2 or 3 addends through 99 (no carrying) Subtract two-digit numbers to minuends of 19 or less Multiples of 10 (2 tens = 20, 3 tens = 30)

Grade 2: First Half	Place value to hundredth place
	Addition two-digit numerals with 3 or 4 addends
	  with sums less than 100 (no carrying)
	Subtract two-digit numerals (no borrowing)
	Understand division as separation of set into
	  equivalent sets

Grade 2: Second Half	Count by ones, twos, fives, tens, hundreds,
	  through 999
	Odd-even numbers
	Read and write numerals through 999
	Write numerals in expanded notation
	Introduce carrying (regrouping)
	Subtraction involving borrowing at the tens,
	  hundreds places with numerals including 0
	Begin combination of multiples of 2, 3, 4, and 5
	  with products of 0–25.
	Know meaning of x and y
	Begin division problem with same facts as above.

Table 10.1—*Continued*

Grade	Skills Acquired
Grade 3: First Half	Count and write to 1,000 Place value for thousands Equivalent fractions for 1/2, 1/4, 1/3 Roman numerals to XII Addition of three-digit numerals with carrying Subtraction facts with combinations of 0–19 Introduce $\sqrt{}$ for division
Grade 3: Second Half	Read and write numerals with dollars and cents Rounding of numbers Fractions 1/6, 1/8 Roman numerals through XXX Addition up to seven digits Begin addition of fractions with like denominators, with sums less than 1 Subtraction of 4–7 digits with borrowing Multiplication through 9×9 Multiplication of two- or three-digit factors by one factor with or without carrying Division with combination through 9×9
Grade 4: First Half	Read and write whole numbers to 9,999 Romans numerals through C Understand concepts of 1/2, 1/4, 1/3 as equivalent sets of groups of objects, as well as congruent parts of a whole
Grade 4: Second Half	Read and write numerals to million Place value for million Learn names *numerator* and *denominator* Multiplication of two-digit numeral by two-digit multipliers Division with two-digit divisor Fractional parts, fifths, sevenths, ninths
Grade 5: First Half	Relationship between improper fractions and mixed fractions Write improper and mixed fractions Add three- or four-digit numbers of 2–6 addends Add fractions with like denominators Subtract like and mixed fractions with like denominators Multiply three-digit numbers by two-digit multipliers Two-digit divisors with 5–9 in one's place
Grade 5: Second Half	Decimals and place value Add decimal fractions Add fractions with unlike denominators Subtract five-digit numerals, fractional numbers, mixed numbers from whole numbers Multiplication with multiples of 100

Table 10.1—*Continued*

Grade	Skills Acquired
Grade 6: First Half	Learn to express numbers by using exponents Vocabulary: *power, squared, cubed* Add and subtract fractions with unlike denominators Multiplication with three-digit multipliers Multiplication of fractional numbers with proper fractions, whole numbers, and improper fractions Division of fractional numbers
Grade 6: Second Half	Relate percent to ratio, fractions, and decimals Add positive and negative numbers Multiplication with decimals and decimal fractions Division of decimal fractions

From *Informal Assessment in Education* by Gilbert R. Guerin and Arlee S. Maier, 1983, Palo Alto, CA: Mayfield Publishing Company. Copyright © 1983 Mayfield Publishing Company. Reprinted by permission.

these skills could then be constructed to determine precisely what the child knows. Based on what the child does know, recommendations for instruction would be to begin teaching with the next skill in the sequence.

Learning Hierarchies

Learning hierarchies are a second approach to organizing skill sequences. Although both learning hierarchies and scope and sequence charts list skills in an ordered sequence, they differ in that (a) learning hierarchies are typically much more detailed and specific than scope and sequence charts, and (b) learning hierarchies specify a skill that a student will be required to learn and then list the behaviors the child must acquire before successfully performing the skill in question. Table 10.2 presents a series of objectives from a learning hierarchy that was used to teach the concept of number. Note the differences between the wording and specifications of these objectives versus those in the scope and sequence chart in table 10.1.

Another difference between scope and sequence charts and learning hierarchies is that learning hierarchies do not specify the time periods for the acquisition of skills. This represents a philosophical as well as a practical difference. Scope and sequence charts are constructed in a manner consistent with many stage theories of child development in which children are thought to be ready to learn certain concepts at certain ages. On the other hand, learning hierarchies are derived from a behavioristic notion that children who have learned all the prerequisite skills for a specific learning objective are ready to learn the next objective regardless of age.

Table 10.2 Objectives of the Curriculum for Teaching the Concept of Number from a Learning Hierarchy

---

Units 1 and 2: Counting and One-to-One Correspondence

A. The child can recite the numerals in order.
B. Given a set of movable objects, the child can count the objects, moving them out of the set as he counts.
C. Given a fixed ordered set of objects, the child can count the objects.
D. Given a fixed unordered set of objects, the child can count the objects.
E. Given a numeral stated and a set of objects, the child can count out a subset of stated size.
F. Given a numeral stated and several sets of fixed objects, the child can select a set of size indicated by numeral.
G. Given two sets of objects, the child can pair objects and state whether the sets are equivalent.
H. Given two unequal sets of objects, the child can pair objects and state which set has more.
I. Given two unequal sets of objects, the child can pair objects and state which set has less.

Units 3 and 4: Numerals

A. Given two sets of numerals, the child can match the numerals.
B. Given a numeral stated and a set of printed numerals, the child can select the stated numeral.
C. Given a numeral (written), the child can read the numeral.
D. Given several sets of objects and several numerals, the child can match numerals with appropriate sets.
E. Given two numerals (written), the child can state which shows more (less).
F. Given a set of numerals, the child can place them in order.
G. Given numerals stated, the child can write the numeral.

Unit 5: Comparison of Sets

A. Given two sets of objects, the child can count sets and state which has more objects or that sets have same number.
B. Given two sets of objects, the child can count sets and state which has less objects.
C. Given a set of objects and a numeral, the child can state which shows more (less).
D. Given a numeral and several sets of objects, the child can select sets which are more (less) than the numeral: given a set of objects and several numerals, the child can select numerals which show more (less) than the set of objects.
E. Given two rows of objects (not paired), the child can state which row has more regardless of arrangement.
F. Given three sets of objects, the child can count sets and state which has most (least).

Unit 6: Seriation and Ordinal Position

A. Given three objects of different sizes, the child can select the largest (smallest).
B. Given objects of graduated sizes, the child can seriate according to size.

Table 10.2—*Continued*

C. Given several sets of objects, the child can seriate the sets according to size.

D. Given ordered set of objects, the child can name the ordinal position of the objects.

Unit 7: Addition and Subtraction (Sums to 10)

A. Given two numbers stated, set of objects, and directions to add, the child can add the numbers by counting out two subsets then combining and stating combined number as sum.

B. Given two numbers stated, set of objects, and directions to subtract, the child can count out smaller subset from larger and state remainder.

C. Given two numbers stated, number line, and directions to add, the child can use the number line to determine sum.

D. Given two numbers stated, number line, and directions to subtract, the child can use number line to subtract.

E. Given addition and subtraction word problems, the child can solve the problems.

F. Given written addition and subtraction problems in form: $\frac{x}{+y}$ or $\frac{x}{-y}$; the child can complete the problems.

G. Given addition and subtraction problems in form: $x + y = \square$, or $x - y = \square$; the child can complete the equations.

Unit 8: Addition and Subtraction Equations

A. Given equation of form $z = \square + \triangle$, the child can show several ways of completing the equation.

B. Given equation of form $x + y = \ +\ $, the child can complete the equation in several ways.

C. Given equations of forms $x + y = z + \ $ and $x + y = \ + z$, the child can complete the equations.

D. Given equations of forms $x + \square = y$ and $\square + x = y$, the child can complete the equations.

E. Given complete addition equation (e.g., $x + y = z$), the child can write equations using numerals and minus sign (e.g., $z - x = y$) and demonstrate relationship.

F. Given counting blocks and/or number line, the child can make up completed equations of various forms.

From L. B. Resnick et al., "Task Analysis in Curriculum Design: A Hierarchically Sequenced Introductory Mathematics Curriculum" in *Journal of Applied Behavior Analysis,* 6:684–685, 1973. Published by the Society for Experimental Analysis of Behavior, Inc. Reprinted with permission of the author.

Whatever one's theoretical beliefs, learning hierarchies are an invaluable asset in the assessment of children's learning problems. A detailed discussion of the hierarchies is beyond the scope of this chapter, because to present a learning hierarchy that encompasses the same range of skills as the scope and sequence chart presented in table 10.1 could require several hundred pages. The interested reader is instead referred to an excellent book entitled *The Analysis of Behavior in Planning Instruction* (Holland, Soloman, Doran, & Frezza, 1976).

➔ *Standardized Diagnostic Tests of Arithmetic*

We will examine four diagnostic arithmetic tests from the many tests now available. An expanded list of these tests is presented in the skills-by-assessment instrument matrix in table 10.3

KeyMath Diagnostic Arithmetic Test-Revised

Overview and Purpose

The KeyMath Diagnostic Arithmetic Test-Revised (Connolly, 1988) is an individually administered instrument used with children in kindergarten through ninth grade. Each of the two forms of the instrument contains 14 subtests that are categorized into three major areas: Basic Concepts, Operations, and Applications. The test is designed primarily for diagnosing difficulties in arithmetic.

The author estimates that the instrument requires approximately 30 minutes to administer. The manual is well organized and provides detailed directions for administration. In addition to the manual and an easel kit containing the test, the other major component is an individual test record form that can be used to profile subtest scores. Although this record form is relatively simple to use once you become familiar with it, at first glance it appears extremely complex and may discourage some test users.

Standardization Sample and Norms

The technical procedures utilized in the standardization of the KeyMath-R are among the best of all the diagnostic arithmetic tests. The test was normed on a sample of 1,798 children in kindergarten through ninth grade. This sample was stratified with care according to geographic region, grade, sex, socioeconomic status, and race. Item difficulty and reliability estimates are based on highly sophisticated procedures that are representative of the care with which the instrument was constructed.

Data Obtained

The KeyMath-R offers four diagnostic levels:

- Level 1—Total Test Performance. At the most general level, the KeyMath-R provides age- and grade-equivalent scores representing a child's overall test performance, which can be utilized for making placement decisions.
- Level 2—Area Performance. Relative strengths and weaknesses among the test's three broad areas of Basic Skills, Operations, and Applications can be determined.
- Level 3—Subtest Performance. The KeyMath-R provides a convenient system for profiling a subject's strengths and weaknesses across each of the 14 subtests.

Table 10.3 Diagnostic Arithmetic Tests by Skills Assessed

Instrument	Add	Subtract	Multiply	Divide	Fractions	Symbols	Money	Time	Measurement	Word Problems	Grade Equivalent	Age	Percentiles	Scaled Scores	Administration Time	Grade Range of Skills Tested
		Operations						Application				Scores			Other	
Buswell-John Diagnostic Test for Fundamental Process in Arithmetic (Buswell & John, N.D.)	X	X	X	X											15-20 min.	1-6
Diagnostic Mathematics Inventory (Gessell, 1977)	X	X	X	X												1-5-8-5
Diagnostic Test of Arithmetic Strategies (Ginsburg & Matthews, 1984)	X	X	X	X	X										80 min.	1-6
ENRIGHT® Diagnostic Inventory of Basic Arithmetic Skills (Enright, 1983)	X	X	X	X	X	X					X				not stated	1-6
KeyMath Diagnostic Arithmetic Test (Connolly, Nachtman, & Pritchett, 1976)	X	X	X	X	X	X	X	X	X		X				30 min.	K-8
Stanford Diagnostic Mathematics Test (Beatty, Madden, Gardner, & Karlsen, 1976)	X	X	X	X	X	X	X	X	X	X	X		X	X	approx. 90 min.	1-5-12
Steenburgen Diagnostic-Prescriptive Math Program (Steenburgen, 1978)	X	X	X	X	X										10-20 min.	1-6
Test of Early Mathematics Ability (Ginsburg & Baroody, 1983)	X	X	X			X	X			X		X	X		20 min.	preschool 1-3
Test of Mathematical Abilities (Brown & McEntire, 1984)	X	X	X	X	X	X	X		X	X			X	X	1 hr., 45 min.	3-12

- Level 4—Item Performance. As with most tests of arithmetic, it is possible to examine each individual item to ascertain the actual skills a student is lacking. However, a major asset of the KeyMath-R is its appendix, which states each item as a behavioral objective.

Administration

The KeyMath-R is constructed in an easel format. With the easel, a child is presented the test stimulus and the examiner is shown the test question. Administration procedures are quickly learned, and the author states that the instrument can be administered by paraprofessionals who may lack formal training in testing. Obviously, the test must be interpreted by someone who is familiar with the mathematics curricula of elementary schools and who has some background in testing and measurement.

Reliability and Validity

Reliability data reported in the manual include that derived from alternate-form, split-half, and item response theory procedures. Remarkably, the authors obtained alternate-form data on approximately one-third of the standardization sample. The correlations between alternative forms of the test ranged from .50s to .70s for subtests to approximately .90 for the total test. Split-half coefficients were even higher with reliability based on the total test in the low to middle .90s.

Although the reliability of the test as a whole is good to excellent, the reliability for some subtests, including some major ones such as fractions, addition, subtraction, and division, are well below minimal standards at some age levels. As would be expected, most reliabliity problems occur at the lower grade levels. Hence, for young children and for those with minimal skills, interpretations of specific subtests is a risky endeavor and comparisons across subtests must be made with caution.

Major improvements have been made for the KeyMath-R (over the original KeyMath) in the reporting of validity studies. Generally the KeyMath-R correlates moderately with other standardized tests of arithmetic achievement including the Comprehensive Tests of Basic Skills and the Iowa Tests of Basic Skills. The Comprehensive Tests of Basic Skills correlated .66 with the total score on the KeyMath-R and the total score for the Iowa Tests of Basic Skills correlated .76.

We judge the content validity of the test to be reasonably good for a norm-referenced mathematics test. The procedures used to develop the test resulted in a comprehensive instrument that assesses a relatively wide range of arithmetic skills.

Summary

The KeyMath-R is a well-organized test for the assessment of arithmetic skills in children in elementary and junior high school. Although some technical properties of the test are below minimal standards, it can provide useful information to teachers and other consumers. Overall this appears to be the best instrument on the market.

" I THOUGHT THERE WAS SUPPOSED TO BE SAFETY IN NUMBERS."

Testing Can Have Positive and Negative Motivational Side Effects.

Courtesy of James Warren. Reprinted by permission.

Test of Mathematical Abilities

Overview and Purpose

The Test of Mathematical Abilities, or TOMA (Brown & McEntire, 1984), is designed to assess skills in computations and story problems and to provide related information about attitudes toward math, math vocabulary, and general knowledge. The TOMA is distinguished in going beyond an assessment of the mastery of basic arithmetic skills to measure also factors that are thought to affect math performance, such as a child's attitude toward the subject. The instrument is designed for students who range in age from 8–6 to 18–11.

The TOMA has five subtests, which reflect various components of mathematical functioning and attitudes.

1. *Computation.* This test, which assesses students' mastery of arithmetical computations, consists of 25 problems ranging from addition (e.g., $5 + \_ = 8$) to simple algebra (e.g., $[x + y]\,[x - y] = \underline{\hspace{1cm}}$).

2. *Story problems.* This subtest presents verbal descriptions of 17 problems that require arithmetical solutions. For example: "Jack has a bird, a dog, and a cat. The dog is big and the bird is little. How many pets does Jack have?" The manual suggests these word

problems assess a child's reading, syntax, ability to sort relevant from irrelevant information, and basic understanding of arithmetic processes.

3. *Attitude toward mathematics.* The subtest is composed of 15 statements with which students must agree, disagree, or say they don't know. (For example: "I'd rather do math than any other kind of homework.")

4. *Vocabulary.* To assess knowledge of mathematics vocabulary, in this subtest students are asked to write definitions for words such as Celsius, coordinates, and probability.

5. *General information.* Although the items focus on mathematical concepts, this subtest is designed to assess a child's overall range of knowledge about the word. The test author apparently assumes that this subtest is roughly equivalent to a measure of general intelligence or, more specifically, the ability to learn, and indicates the rate at which a child could be expected to learn arithmetical concepts.

Very little specialized training is required to administer the TOMA. Directions for administration and scoring are clearly presented in the manual and can be followed by anyone reasonably familiar with educational and psychological tests. Each of the subtests requires from 5 to 25 minutes, with the total testing time ranging from 45 minutes to 1 hour and 45 minutes.

Standardization Sample and Norms

The TOMA was standardized on a sample of 1,560 students from Alabama, California, Washington, Wisconsin, and Vermont. Although this is not representative of the national population, the authors report a high degree of consistency between the standardization sample and the U.S. population with respect to important variables such as sex, race, and urban versus rural residence.

Data Obtained

Norms are provided in terms of standard scores and percentiles for each of the five subtests, with separate norms for each of the 13 age levels. Thus, users access the norm table for a particular child's age and determine percentiles or standard scores for each subtest. Because some subtests have a relatively small number of items and the subtests are not equal interval scales, passing or failing a single item can greatly change interpretation. For example, a 10-year-old with a raw score of 3 on the Computation subtests would be in the 37th percentile, but if the same child has one additional item correct (i.e., a raw score of 4), the percentile equivalent would be 63. The difference in meaning between these two percentiles would be highly significant in making decisions about the child even though the practical significance of a raw score of 3 versus one of 4 is hardly worth noting. Intelligent users of this test will use the standard error of measurement to help correct for this unequal interval problem.

Reliability and Validity

Two forms of reliability data, internal consistency and stability, are reported in the manual. Internal consistency coefficients are above .80 for all subtests, with many ranging into the high .90s. Figures for test-retest reliability were somewhat lower, with correlation coefficients ranging from .71 for story problems to .94 for general information. The TOMA has moderate-to-low positive correlations with the KeyMath-R, the arithmetic portions of the Peabody Individual Achievement Test, and the Wide Range Achievement Test. Most of the correlations with these tests were in the .30s and .40s. The test authors infer construct validity because test scores are correlated highly with age and grade level. Missing was any mention of content validity. Thus, we must question whether the test samples adequately the broad content of most mathematics curricula. With only 25 items on such important subtests as Computation, it is highly unlikely that the TOMA has adequate content validity.

Summary

The major use of the TOMA is as a test of computational accuracy. In this role it is only mediocre. However, if math anxiety, vocabulary, or general knowledge about the word are thought to be influencing math performance, then the TOMA may be useful in determining whether one of these factors contributes to the problem. Scores from any of the subtests should be considered only as a rough screening because of very limited sampling of skills. Should the TOMA results suggest that a problem exists, additional testing will be required before specific problems are pinpointed and remediation strategies developed. For example, if a child scored poorly on the General Information subtest, additional testing with an intelligence test would be required before deciding that the child had a learning deficiency.

The TOMA is a multifaceted examination of mathematical abilities and attitudes toward math. It can be administered quickly and conveniently by teachers or educational diagnosticians for a general indication of a student's relative strengths and weaknesses. However, the instrument is not likely to be very useful for instructional planning because it lacks the specificity required to pinpoint problems and their causes.

Diagnostic Test of Arithmetic Strategies

Overview and Purpose

One of the few math tests that takes advantage of the recent research pertaining mathematical computation and thinking in children is the

Diagnostic Test of Arithmetic Strategies, or DTAS (Ginsburg & Mathews, 1984). Unlike many other tests in this area, the focus of this test is on the identification of correct and incorrect strategies (i.e., processes) rather than correct and incorrect answers to problems. Whereas a test such as the KeyMath-R may suggest that a child has a deficiency in, for example, subtraction, the DTAS is designed to provide reasons for that weakness.

Administration of the DTAS requires a different kind of thinking by the examiner than is needed for most formal tests. The primary difference is the degree to which the examiner must be flexible, as a passage from the manual suggests:

> The identification of strategies and methods requires flexible questioning. The examiner should feel free at any time to ask questions designed to reveal how children solve particular problems. Questions like, "How did you get that answer?" or "How did you do it?" are always appropriate on the DTAS. Similarly, such techniques as telling the child, "Pretend that you are the teacher and tell me how to work the problem," may also be effective and should be encouraged. The examiner should feel free to improvise on the directions to some degree. (Ginsburg & Mathews, 1984, p. 10)

The authors suggest the test can be administered by anyone "reasonably experienced" in using tests in education, language, or psychology. We disagree. Much of the rich array of information that can be derived from the DTAS would be lost if it were administered by someone unfamiliar with testing in arithmetic. We believe that the test should be administered by a teacher, psychologist, or educational diagnostician.

The DTAS is designed for children experiencing difficulty with addition, subtraction, multiplication, or division. Thus, it is appropriate for most children in grades one through six and some older children who have deficiencies in basic arithmetic processes. The instrument is divided into four subtests, one for each basic arithmetic computational skill; each section requires approximately 20 minutes to administer. Generally, only one subtest is administered per session.

Standardization Sample and Norms

No data pertaining to the standardization sample or norms are provided with the DTAS, presumably because the purpose of the test is to identify processes, not to compare performances of children of the same age.

Data Obtained

Each of the four subtests is scored in three major areas: (a) setting up the problem, (b) written calculation, and (c) informal skills. Detailed directions and assistance are provided for scoring each area.

Within each subtest, the section devoted to setting up the problem helps the examiner determine whether a child has mastered some of the mechanics of arithmetic. These mechanics include writing digits and aligning numbers appropriately for arithmetical operations. For example, if a child were told to add 84 plus 3, each of the numbers would have to be written correctly and the 4 in 84 would have to be aligned with the 3 on the bottom.

The written calculation section examines whether the child obtained the correct answer to each problem, whether some standard method or an idiosyncratic method was used to obtain the answers, whether there were number fact errors, and whether any "bugs" (incorrect processes) or "slips" (simple errors usually involving a lack of attention) were consistently used for computation. Scoring for "bugs" is a fascinating aspect of the test. Examiners are provided with a considerable amount of instruction of "bug hunting," as table 10.4 shows.

The informal skills section assesses the specific type of strategy used by a child to obtain a particular answer. For example, a child who is asked to add 4 plus 5 may use her fingers to count the correct answer, thus using the strategy of counting rather than the preferred strategy of long-term memory of addition facts.

The DTAS does not yield traditional scores such as percentiles or grade equivalents. Instead, the test describes a child's specific skills and the computational processes and strategies used. This type of information is highly relevant for instructional planning but is less useful for placement decisions.

Reliability and Validity

Reliability data are not present in the manual, which is a serious omission and a cause for concern. The fact that the publisher suggests a flexible administration format may actually decrease reliability. In addition, scoring the test is a complex procedure, and one cannot know whether different examiners would reach the same conclusions about a particular child.

No validity data are provided. At the least, the authors should have incorporated a thorough analysis of content validity to demonstrate that the DTAS adequately samples all relevant computational processes.

Summary

Despite the lack of adequate standardization and validation data, the DTAS does hold promise for the diagnostician. Its primary advantage over virtually all other tests is the degree to which it assesses arithmetical processes. By assessing the strengths and weaknesses with such processes, it may be possible to determine why a child is failing. With reasons for the problem known, instructional remedies should not be far behind.

Table 10.4 Directions for Locating "Bugs"

The DTAS provides direct measures of key bugs. Problems 5 and 6 are designed to identify Bug A *addition like multiplication* as in the following:

$$
\begin{array}{r} 32 \\ + \ 7 \\ \hline 109 \end{array}
\qquad
\begin{array}{r} 21 \\ + \ 6 \\ \hline 87 \end{array}
$$

On problem 5 the child does: "2 + 7 = 9, and then 3 + 7 = 10 so that the answer is 109." On problem 6, the child does "6 + 1 = 7 and then 2 + 6 = 8, so the answer is 87."

Problems 7 and 8 are chiefly designed to test Bug B *zero makes zero* as in

$$
\begin{array}{r} 26 \\ +20 \\ \hline 40 \end{array}
\qquad
\begin{array}{r} 30 \\ +42 \\ \hline 70 \end{array}
$$

On problem 7 the child reasons: "6 + 0 = 0, 2 + 2 = 4, so the answer is 40." By the same logic, problem 8 gives an answer of 70.

Problems 9 and 10 are designed to identify Bug C *add from left to right*, which results in

$$
\begin{array}{r} 2 \\ 81 \\ +45 \\ \hline 18 \end{array}
\quad \text{or} \quad
\begin{array}{r} 1 \\ 81 \\ +45 \\ \hline 27 \end{array}
$$

$$
\begin{array}{r} 3 \\ 92 \\ +43 \\ \hline 18 \end{array}
\quad \text{or} \quad
\begin{array}{r} 1 \\ 92 \\ +43 \\ \hline 36 \end{array}
$$

Using this bug on problem 9 the child reasons: "8 + 4 is 12; put down the 1 and carry the 2: 2 + 1 + 5 is 8; so the answer is 18." Or on problem 9 the child may put down the 2, carry the 1, and get 27 as the answer. By the same logic, the answer to problem 10 will be 18 or 36. Of course this bug may be used on other problems.

From Ginsburg, H. P., and Mathews, S. C. (1984). *Diagnostic Test of Arithmetic Strategies.* Austin, TX: PRO–ED. Reprinted by permission.

ENRIGHT® Diagnostic Inventory of Basic Arithmetic Skills

Overview and Purpose

The ENRIGHT® Diagnostic Inventory of Basic Arithmetic Skills is described as an instrument that "thoroughly assesses, diagnoses, and analyzes 144 basic computation skills" (Enright, 1983, p. vii). The inventory has three basic functions: placement, skill assessment, and diagnosis. For placement, the ENRIGHT® Inventory provides a starting point for assessing a student's needs, the steps within skill sequences that require additional testing, and the basic arithmetic skills that have and have not been acquired. A major portion of the test is devoted to measuring basic skills in addition, multiplication, subtraction, and division. Finally, the ENRIGHT® Inventory can be used in error anal- ysis for determining why computations were inaccurately completed.

Standardization Sample and Norms
The inventory is criterion-referenced and is based upon a task analysis of basic arithmetic computation skills. The student test booklet consists of more than 125 pages of arithmetic problems, with each skill measured by at least five items. The instrument does yield grade-equivalent scores, but these are not derived from norms based upon a standardization sample. Instead, the grade levels are referred to as "text-referenced," because the grade levels were determined by examining five widely used basal mathematics series and identifying the level at which each of the 144 skills is supposed to be taught.

Data Obtained
Essentially, the process of using the ENRIGHT® Inventory involves moving from a general assessment of arithmetic skills during placement testing to specific assessment of strengths and weaknesses and finally to error analysis. The data obtained would include an approximate grade placement, arithmetic facts known and not known, computational process deficits (e.g., regrouping with subtraction problems), and the reasons why the errors are made.

Reliability and Validity
Data pertaining to reliability and validity are not provided.

Summary
The ENRIGHT® Inventory offers a comprehensive assessment of basic computational skills. The large number of arithmetic problems provided would be an asset to individuals who frequently conduct arithmetic assessments. Unfortunately, the manual gives no information concerning the test's psychometric adequacy. The fact that it is criterion-referenced does not excuse the absence of such data. Because little is known about the reliability or validity of this instrument, it would not be used in placement decisions. However, the instrument may be quite valuable in the diagnosis of arithmetic problems.

→ *Informal Assessment of Arithmetic*

"It's not whether you win or lose, it's how you play the game." Although this statement is typically applied to competitive activities, it has a great deal of relevance to assessment in mathematics. Knowing how many problems a child completed correctly is only a small part of the assessment process in arithmetic. At least as important in designing instructional strategies is an examination of the processes that the student used to obtain correct and incorrect answers. According to Brown and Burton (1978),

> a common assumption among teachers is that students do not follow procedures very well and that erratic behavior is the primary cause of a student's inability to perform each step correctly. Our experience has been that students are remarkably competent procedure followers, but that they often follow the wrong procedures. (p. 157)

If Brown and Burton are correct, and they have large volumes of research to support their claim, the task of the diagnostician is to discover the incorrect procedures children are following. One possible means of examining arithmetic difficulties would be to give a norm-referenced test to all students to determine who is having difficulty. For children identified as having problems, follow-up criterion-referenced testing could be conducted to identify general areas of weakness. Informal testing and error analysis could then be applied to determine misconceptions about arithmetic problem solving. The heart of informal assessment in mathematics is **error analysis.**

Error Analysis

Virtually anyone can determine whether the answer to a particular mathematics problem is correct or incorrect by consulting a key. To go beyond, however, requires the motivation and skill to search carefully for the types of computational and conceptual problems a child is experiencing. Error analysis thus involves an attempt to determine what a child is thinking when various errors are made. This frequently requires a careful analysis of the actual computations completed by a child. Alternatively, it is occasionally necessary simply to ask the child, "How did you do this problem?" or "Can you do this problem for me again and tell me what you did?"

Some of the most common arithmetic errors are presented in table 10.5. This list is by no means comprehensive but does illustrate the rich variety of error types. Certainly it cannot be used as a substitute for good problem-solving and detective work. Some may argue that such detective work is too time-consuming, but so is remediating children who maintain fundamental misconceptions about the process of computing arithmetic

Table 10.5 Common Arithmetic Errors

Analysis	Example
1. Lacks mastery of basic facts. a. Addition	$\begin{array}{r} 3 \\ +4 \\ \hline 7 \end{array}$ $\begin{array}{r} 2 \\ 3 \\ \hline 4 \end{array}$
b. Multiplication	$\begin{array}{r} 3 \quad 2 \\ \times \quad 3 \\ \hline 86 \end{array}$
2. Subtracts incorrectly within the division algorithm.	3) 73 rem 1 $\underline{70)}$ 3)230 $\underline{-21}$ 10 $\underline{-\ 9}$ 1
3. Does not complete addition: a. Does not write renamed number:	$\begin{array}{r} 85 \\ +43 \\ \hline 28 \end{array}$
b. Leaves out numbers in column addition.	$\begin{array}{r} 4 \\ 8 \\ 2 \leftarrow \\ +\ 3 \\ \hline 15 \end{array}$
4. Rewrites a numeral without computing.	$\begin{array}{r} \rightarrow 72 \\ +15 \\ \hline \rightarrow 77 \\ \rightarrow 32 \\ \times 3 \\ \hline \rightarrow 36 \end{array}$
5. Does not complete subtraction.	$\begin{array}{r} 582 \\ -\ 35 \\ \hline 47 \end{array}$
6. Does not complete division because of incompleted subtraction.	1)41 $\underline{40)}$ 7)397 $\underline{-280}$ 7 $\underline{\ 7}$
7. Fails to complete division; stops at first partial quotient.	$\begin{array}{r} 50 \\ 7)\overline{370} \\ 350 \end{array}$

Table 10.5—*Continued*

Analysis	*Example*
8. Fails to complete division; leaves remainder equal to or greater than divisor.	$\begin{array}{r} 80 \text{ rem } 9 \\ 9\overline{)\,729} \\ 720 \\ \hline 9 \end{array}$
9. Confuses role of zero in subtraction with role of zero in multiplication.	$\begin{array}{r} 37 \\ -\ 20 \\ \hline 10 \end{array}$
10. Subtracts top digit from bottom digit whenever regrouping is involved with zero in minuend.	$\begin{array}{r} 30 \\ -18 \\ \hline 28 \end{array}$
11. Confuses role of zero in multiplication with multiplicative identity.	$7 \times 0 = 7$
12. Lacks facility with addition algorithm: a. Adds units to units *and* tens;	$\begin{array}{r} 37 \\ +\ 2 \\ \hline 59 \end{array}$
b. Adds tens to tens *and* hundreds;	$\begin{array}{r} 342 \\ +\ 36 \\ \hline 678 \end{array}$
c. Adds units to tens *and* hundreds;	$\begin{array}{r} 132 \\ +\ 6 \\ \hline 798 \end{array}$

d. Is unable to add horizontally:
    Thinks: 3 + 7 + 1 = 11; writes 1
        4 + 3   = 7 (+ 1 carried)
          5   = 5
 	
    May add zero to make sum greater than largest addend: 1850.
	$345 + 7 + 13 = 185$
	
	$\begin{array}{r} 8 \\ 5 \\ \hline 185 \end{array}$

13. Does not regroup units to tens.	$\begin{array}{r} 37 \\ +\ 25 \\ \hline 52 \end{array}$
14. When there are fewer digits in subtrahend: a. subtracts units from units *and* from tens (*and* hundreds);	$\begin{array}{r} 783 \\ -\ 2 \\ \hline 561 \end{array}$
b. subtracts tens from tens *and* hundreds.	$\begin{array}{r} 783 \\ -\ 23 \\ \hline 560 \end{array}$

Table 10.5—*Continued*

Analysis	*Example*
15. Does not rename tens digit after regrouping.	$\begin{array}{r} 54 \\ -\ 9 \\ \hline 55 \end{array}$
16. When there are two zeroes in minuend, renames hundreds twice but does not rename tens.	$\begin{array}{r} 5 \\ 6 \\ ^{11} \\ 700 \\ -326 \\ \hline 284 \end{array}$
17. Decreases hundreds digit by one when unnecessary.	$\begin{array}{r} 3\ 7\ 1 \\ -1\ 3\ 4 \\ \hline 1\ 3\ 7 \end{array}$
18. Adds regrouped number to tens but does not multiply.	$\begin{array}{r} 35 \\ \times\ \ 7 \\ \hline 65^* \end{array}$
	$^*\ 7 \times\ 5\ =\ 35;$
	$30\ +\ 30\ =\ 60$
19. Multiplies digits within one factor.	$\begin{array}{r} 31 \\ \times\ 4 \\ \hline 34^* \end{array}$
	$^*\ 4\ \times\ 1\ =\ 4$
	$1\ \times\ 30\ =\ 30$
20. Multiplies by only one number.	$\begin{array}{r} 457 \\ \times\ 12 \\ \hline 914 \end{array}$
21. "Carries" wrong number.	$\begin{array}{r} 8 \\ 67 \\ \times\ 40 \\ \hline 3220 \end{array}$
22. Does not regroup; treats each column as separate addition example.	$\begin{array}{r} 23 \\ +\ 8 \\ \hline 211 \end{array}$
23. Subtracts smaller digit from larger at all times to avoid renaming.	$\begin{array}{r} 273 \\ -639 \\ \hline 446 \end{array}$

From *A Guide to the Diagnostic Teaching of Arithmetic* (pp. 270–276), 2nd ed., by F. K. Reisman, 1978, Columbus, OH: Charles E. Merrill. Copyright © 1978 by Fredricka K. Reisman. Adapted by permission of Fredricka K. Reisman.

problems. If we assume that most errors are systematic (i.e., not random), error analysis becomes a valuable tool. The Focus on Research in this chapter shows how researchers are using computers to help de-bug math errors.

Analyzing the errors that a child makes on a standardized arithmetic test is typically insufficient. Standardized tests, especially those that are individually administered and "wide range," usually provide only a small sample of each type of problem, making it impossible to detect patterns of errors. By using informal tests, which may be constructed through interaction with a child, it is possible to administer several problems of the same type.

Cawley (1978) has developed an excellent system that combines aspects of standardized testing, error analysis, and instructional programming. Called the Clinical Mathematics Interview, this procedure offers a process for linking assessment and instruction. Initially students are screened with the Mathematics Concept Inventory, and areas of strength and weakness are noted. Children with deficits are then administered the Clinical Mathematics Interview, which is "an intensive diagnostic procedure that integrates content, mode, and algorithm" (Cawley, 1978, p. 224).

The interview begins by having a student solve written problems. Following that, the student is asked to verbalize the process used for solving the problems. Through this process it is possible to identify the types of errors a student is making. The results of the interview are used to place a student within the Multiple Options Curriculum. Although the procedures were designed for high school students, the concept could be applied to elementary school children as well.

Chapter Summary

The most important ideas presented in this chapter focus on the process utilized in determining a student's arithmetical strengths and weaknesses. Knowing a child's grade-equivalent score or even which problems were right and wrong is not nearly as important as knowing why those problems were wrong. The situation is analogous to that of two football coaches who have different amounts of information about their opponents. One coach knows the scores of each of the opponents' games. The other has watched films of each game played by the opponents and made a detailed analysis of the strengths and weaknesses of each player on the opposing team. Which coach is better prepared for the meeting of the two teams?

Which teacher is better prepared for helping children—the one who knows the grade level at which each student is functioning or the one who knows exactly the types of errors made by each student and how to correct them? To those who have read and understood this chapter, it seems silly even to pose this question. Unfortunately, current math assessment practices lag behind research, and many teachers are operating without diagnostic road maps for improving math functioning.

Focus on
Research

Using BUGGY to Find Math Errors

Some of the work needed to analyze children's math errors has been reduced by research involving the computer. Below is an example of an interaction with a computer program developed to detect math errors, or "bugs."

WELCOME TO BUGGY.
I HAVE CHOSEN A BUG. HERE IS AN EXAMPLE OF THE BUG.

$$\begin{array}{r} 17 \\ + \ 5 \\ \hline 13 \end{array}$$

The system presents an example in which the student does not get the right answer. At present the initial examples are stored in the network linked to the buggy implementation.

NOW YOU CAN GIVE ME PROBLEMS TO DETERMINE THE BUG.

$$\begin{array}{rr} 18 & 43 \\ + \ 6 & +79 \\ \hline 15 & 23 \end{array}$$

The team generates problems that are answered by the "student." Notice that the team's test problems are similar to the initial example generated by BUGGY. This is usually a poor diagnostic strategy as it may leave other symptoms of a bug undiscovered.

Got the bug!

The team forms an initial hypothesis and tells the system they have discovered the bug. The system now asks the team to describe the bug and then tests them on their understanding. Asking for a description forces the team to verbalize their sometimes fuzzy idea of what the bug is and often makes them realize how ill-defined or vague their idea actually is. In the present system, the descriptions are saved but no attempt is made by the system to understand them.

PLEASE DESCRIBE THE BUG.

Student adds the number to be carried into the last column worked in. This cryptic description is typical of those we have observed. Describing bugs in English is surprisingly difficult. What the team is trying to say is that if a column adds to more than 9, the units digit and the carry digit are added together and the result is written as the answer. For example, in the first column of the example problem, when 7 and 5 are added, 1 (the carry) and 2 (the units digit) are added to get 3. The same with 8 + 6, 2 + 9, and 3 + 9. (This bug could easily arise if the student were using Method 2 from Fig. 1 and mistakenly wrote the carry under the same column.)

The hypothesis does account for the observed behavior. Unfortunately, it is not the student's bug. Notice the possibly humorous, probably disastrous results that would have transpired if the team had stopped at this point and tried to tutor the student on the basis of their initial belief!

HERE ARE SOME PROBLEMS TO TEST YOUR THEORY ABOUT THE BUG. WHAT IS:

$$\begin{array}{r} 21 \\ +39 \\ \hline 51 \end{array}$$

To ensure that the team has found the correct bug, the system produces several problems for the team to solve. At present, BUGGY has a heuristic problem generation program that gives a broad range of "different" problems. (For examples in which the bug is very localized, such as requiring a 0 in the top number, a special problem generator can be linked to the bug and will be used instead.) These problems are then filtered to try to get three problems which cause symptoms and two that give correct answers. This simple routine does surprisingly well at producing critical problems. So well, in fact, that a more "intelligent" routine (which determined the set of bugs consistent with the student's data and then selected the test problems which split this set) was discarded as unnecessarily time-consuming. . . .

The team's hypothesis is revealed as incorrect by the first of the five test problems. BUGGY presents its answer and then allows the team to enter more problems.

THAT'S NOT THE BUG I HAVE.
USING MY BUG:

$$\begin{array}{r} 21 \\ +39 \\ \hline 15 \end{array}$$

TRY GIVING ME SOME MORE EXAMPLES.

$$\begin{array}{rrr} 51 & 99 & 68 \\ +1707 & +99 & + 9 \\ \hline 21 & 36 & 23 \end{array}$$

After failing the test, the team gives a greater range of problems, specifically those using bigger numbers. How is it that 51 + 1707 can add up to 21? By broadening the scope of example problems they are able to reevaluate their initial hypothesis, dismiss it, and develop another one that is complete and consistent with respect to the new errors.
GOT THE BUG!

PLEASE DESCRIBE THE BUG YOU THINK I HAVE.

The student is adding all the digits together.

HERE ARE SOME PROBLEMS TO TEST YOUR THEORY ABOUT THE BUG. WHAT IS:

33	1091	8	28	90
+99	+ 60	+34	+70	+ 6
24	17	15	17	15

This time the team's hypothesis passes the test and they are given the description of the bug stored in the procedural network.

VERY GOOD. MY DESCRIPTION OF THE BUG IS: THE STUDENT ALWAYS SUMS UP ALL THE DIGITS WITH NO REGARD TO COLUMNS.

A variant of this game assigns a cost to each problem the user poses in the process of trying to discover the bug. At the same time, a much higher cost is assigned for claiming to have "discovered" the bug but then failing to pass criterion on the computer-generated test problems. A correctly structured cost algorithm encourages the user to think carefully about the diagnostic value of each problem he creates and not to jump to a conclusion too quickly or too slowly.

From J. S. Brown and R. R. Burton, "Diagnostic Models for Procedural Bugs in Basic Mathematical Skills" in *Cognitive Science, 2,* pp. 155–192. Copyright © 1978 by Ablex Publishing Corporation, Norwood, NJ. Reprinted with permission from Ablex Publishing Corporation.

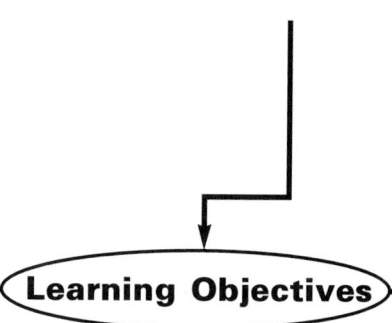

Chapter 11

Language

Learning Objectives

1. Define language and identify major developmental milestones in the acquisition of spoken language.
2. Describe areas of language functioning and list methods for informally assessing each area.
3. Identify and discriminate language disorders from speech dysfunctions.
4. Name and evaluate the strengths of five standardized tests of language functioning.
5. Conceptualize a comprehensive plan for assessing the language skills of young children.

anguage is the currency of learning. The ability to receive and send spoken messages is critical to academic and social success. Some children experience significant delays or deficits in language skills and often require special services to benefit from schooling. This chapter briefly reviews language development and documents methods for assessing basic language abilities in schoolchildren. Two previous chapters, "Preschool Screening, Kindergarten Readiness, and Early Identification of At-Risk Students" and "Reading," supplement coverage of early language skills. Interested readers are referred to sources such as Lahey (1988) or Bates, O'Connell, and Shore (1987) for more comprehensive treatments of language development and disorders.

➔ *Fundamentals of Language*

Definitions of Language

The function of language is to communicate. The essence of communication is the ability to share one's thoughts, feelings, and experiences with other people. Thus, in any communication, there is a sender and receiver who are embedded in a physical and social context. As conceptualized here, characteristics of the sender, the receiver, and the communication context influence the meaningfulness of a communication. Nevertheless, the use and understanding of language are the main factors in successful communication. Language has been defined differently by numerous investigators. Two representative definitions are:

> Language is a system of signs and the possible relations among them which, together, allow for the representation of an individual's experience of the world of objects, events, and relations. (Bloom, 1975, p. 249)
>
> Languages are composed of speech sounds, syllables and sentences, and meaning is largely conveyed by the properties and particular use of these units. (Menyuk, 1971, p. 15)

Bloom's definition emphasizes the *communication* aspect of language, whereas Menyuk's stresses the *structural* aspects of language. According to Lamberts (1979), these definitions have four components in common:

1. Language involves *symbols* which represent experiences; we must, therefore, obtain an estimate of the size of children's symbol sets (vocabulary).

2. Symbol combinations convey meaning; therefore, we must judge the child's knowledge of the *rules* for symbol combination (grammar).

3. In the case of oral language, the symbols are made up of *vocal sounds;* we must, therefore, also assess the child's knowledge of the set of phonemes (speech sounds).

4. Communication has interpersonal dimensions that are not strictly, related to knowledge of the linguistic code . . . ; [therefore] we must also assess the child's competence with regard to interpersonal *uses* of languages. (pp. 255–256)

Components of Language and Normative Development

Although numerous definitions of language exist, there is high agreement that language has four main components: phonology, morphology, syntax, and semantics.

Phonology is the sound system of language. The ability to perceive and reproduce sounds is the basis for speech. There are about 45 speech sounds, or phonemes, in English, which is why English sounds are significantly more diverse than the 26 letters in the alphabet. Children normally demonstrate mastery of the English sound system by the age of six or seven. As some guideposts, one can expect a child to master the phonemes *b, t, d, k, g,* and all vowels by age four, and *r, l, th, ar, bl, br,* and *pr* by age seven (Ulrey, 1982). By about age three, children demonstrate knowledge of which sound combinations are typical of their language (Menyuk, 1972; Ulrey, 1982).

Words are composed of phonemes and form a second basic unit of language commonly referred to as **morphology.** Thus, words, or morphemes, are the smallest elements in language that have meaning. Inflection, root words, suffixes, and prefixes are all morphological components of words. Children use morphological clues in language to derive meaning. For example, *jump* indicates the action of a child, whereas *jumped* indicates both the action and that it already happened. A good command of morphology is invaluable in analyzing words and developing comprehension skills.

Another basic component of language is **syntax,** or the rules for joining words to form sentences. Children's language learning progresses from the establishment of simple, one-proposition sentences ("Mommy come") through the gradual completion of the grammatical elements of a proposition ("Mommy is coming") to the combination of two or more propositions ("Mommy is coming home and will play") and finally to forming complex sentences ("Mommy is coming home and will play after she makes supper"). Most linguists agree that by age five children normally develop their basic oral syntactic ability.

We expect two-year-olds to verbalize approximately 150 words, to name familiar people, and to use verbs but not correctly with subjects. By the age of five, the normal child's vocabulary will have increased to approximately 1,600 words and will contain adverbs, adjectives, prepositions, and conjunctions used in sentences of six or more words.

A final component of language is **semantics,** or comprehension of the meanings and interrelationships of words as they are used in sentences and paragraphs. Besides learning a lexical, or dictionary, definition of a word, children must also learn how words derive meaning when used in a sentence. A solid understanding of syntax is essential to adequate semantic development, since the same word can often be used meaningfully as a noun, verb, and adjective. For example, the word *swimming* can be used as follows:

1. *Swimming* (noun) is one of my favorite sports.

2. He is *swimming* (verb).

3. The *swimming* (adjective) club will have a meeting on Saturday.

Given such complexity, it should not be surprising that the development of semantics is a slow, error-filled process.

Development of the major components of language (phonology, morphology, syntax, and semantics), however, is not enough for successful communication. One must also learn how to use language appropriately within context which is known as **pragmatics.** Van Hattum (1980) defined pragmatics as the "rules governing the use of language by an individual in context" (p. 300). In assessing the meaning of language within a social context, one must consider factors such as (a) the age and sex of the speaker and listener, (b) the relationship between the speaker and listener (for example, parent-to-child, sibling-to-sibling), (c) the prior knowledge or past experiences of the speaker and listener, (d) the physical setting of the communication, and, finally (e) the purpose of the message. Thus, a comprehensive evaluation of a child's language skills involves several linguistic and extralinguistic factors and provides educators and psychologists with significant challenge. In the next sections, we identify typical language and speech problems in children and outline general considerations for conducting language assessments.

Language versus Speech Disorders

Central to competently assessing any domain of behavior is knowledge of desired behaviors. Guerin and Maier (1983) developed a Spoken Language Screening form that summarizes most language skills necessary for educational success (see table 11.1). Close examination of this table shows that language functioning is characterized by three phases: receptive, inner, and expressive (see figure 11.1). The assessment of language skills within each of these phases will be discussed in a later portion of this section. Let's now briefly examine speech problems that often accompany and occasionally confound a language assessment.

Speech disorders are commonly classified as either articulation, voice, or fluency disorders. Individuals assessing children's language skills must be generally knowledgeable of speech problems so that they recognize what is and is not a language problem and can make appropriate referrals to speech and language pathologists.

Articulation is the process of producing speech sounds. **Articulation disorders,** by far the most common speech problem, include the addition, subtraction, omission, or distortion of speech sounds (see table 11.2). Functional articulation disorders result from faulty learning, whereas organic disorders are due to abnormalities of the speech mechanism. Common organic articulation disorders in children are **apraxia** (deficits in performing voluntary movements of the speech mechanism) and **dysarthria** (impairment of both the reflexive and voluntary components of the speech mechanism).

Variations in pitch, loudness, or vocal quality may be considered **voice disorders.** These characteristics of voice are influenced by the speaker's age and sex. Descriptions of voice disorders are presented in table 11.2.

Table 11.1 Spoken Language Screening Form

Category	Above Average 0	Average 1	Below Average 2
I. Receptive Language			
1. Volume of voice	____	____	____
2. Understands gestures	____	____	____
3. Remembers directions	____	____	____
4. "Reads" picture stories	____	____	____
5. Response time to questions or direction	____	____	____
6. Listening vocabulary	____	____	____
7. Enjoys listening to books	____	____	____
8. Interprets anger or teasing from others	____	____	____
II. Inner Language			
9. Amount of general knowledge	____	____	____
10. Gets "point" of story or discussion	____	____	____
11. Understands directions or demonstrations	____	____	____
12. Sense of humor	____	____	____
13. Sticks to topic	____	____	____
14. Can predict what will happen next	____	____	____
15. Can summarize story	____	____	____
16. Can do simple mental arithmetic	____	____	____
III. Expressive Language			
17. Pronunciation	____	____	____
18. Speed of speech	____	____	____
19. Speaks in complete sentences	____	____	____
20. Uses words in correct order	____	____	____
21. Uses correct word in conversation	____	____	____
22. Ability to recall names for objects or people	____	____	____
23. Can repeat a story	____	____	____
24. Participates in class discussions	____	____	____

Score:

27 or less	Satisfactory performance.
28–35	Child should be watched and language abilities checked on a periodic basis.
36 or more	Thorough evaluation needed.

From *Informal Assessment in Education* (pp. 189–190) by Gilbert R. Guerin and Arlee S. Maier, 1983, Palo Alto, CA: Mayfield Publishing Company. Copyright © 1983 Mayfield Publishing Company. Reprinted by permission.

Figure 11.1 Phases of the Language Process

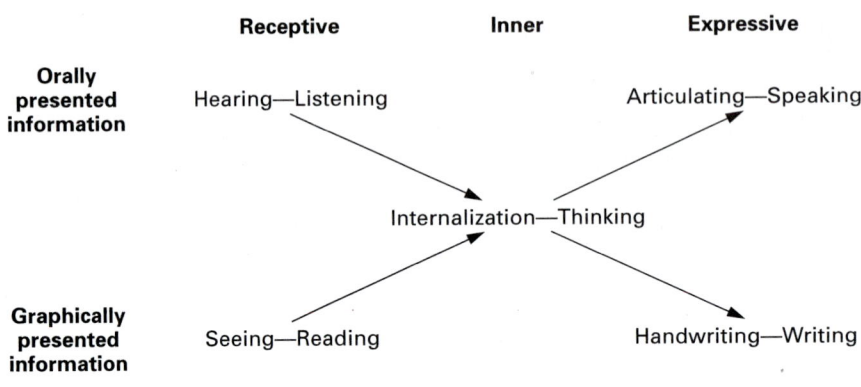

Fluency disorders of speech are characterized by difficulties of sequence, duration, rate, and rhythm. Fluent speech is a smooth synthesis of sounds. Probably the most common and obvious fluency disorder is stuttering, which is characterized by sound repetitions, sound prolongations, and broken words. Other types of relatively rare fluency errors also are summarized in table 11.2.

➡ *Language Assessment Considerations*

Formal Assessment

Both formal and informal assessment methods are available for screening the language skills of children; full speech and language examinations usually require the specialized knowledge of speech and language pathologists. Strategies for the formal assessment of language have evolved from tests of articulation and phonology to measures of language structure and content to the current emphasis on pragmatics.

Formal measures of language typically have used one or more of five types of tasks, which have been characterized by Bryen and Gallagher (1983) as:

1. elicited imitation (child repeats a list of phrases or sentences spoken by an examiner),
2. object manipulation (child moves objects as evidence of understanding a direction or a story),
3. picture identification (child points to the pictures that show a stimulus object or situation given by the examiner),

Table 11.2 Speech Disorders

Disorder	Type of Errors	Description
Articulation	Addition	Adding a sound or sounds to a word, as in *rutin* for *ruin.*
	Substitution	Substituting a sound or sounds for a sound or sounds in a word, as in *tat* for *cat.*
	Omission	Omitting a sound or sounds from a word, as in *uck* for *truck.*
	Distortion	Distorting the sound or sounds in a word.
Voice	Hypernasality	Allowing excessive air to pass through the nasal cavity.
	Denasality	Allowing too little air to pass through the nasal cavity, so the student sounds as though he or she has a head cold.
	Hoarseness	Deep, harsh voice. Student sounds as though he or she has a cold.
	Intensity	Using the inappropriate loudness of speech. This varies with situations. For example, it is appropriate to be loud at a sporting event but not in a library.
	Frequency	Using the inappropriate pitch of speech. Appropriateness varies with a person's age and sex.
Fluency	Repetitions	Repeating sounds, syllables, or words, as in *my-my-my-my-my wagon.*
	Prolongations	Prolonging sounds in a word, as in *sssssssssssing.*
	Blocks	Pausing before or after a sound, as in *b . . . all.*
	Circumlocutions	Talking around feared words, as in "I live on the avenue between First and Third Avenues" for "I live on Second Avenue."
	Starters	Using various words or phrases to start sentences or phrases in hopes of avoiding stuttering. Examples include *and then, you know,* and *I mean.*

From Linda J. Hargrove and James A. Poteet, *Assessment in Special Education: The Education Evaluation.* Copyright © 1984. Reprinted with the permission of Allyn and Bacon.

4. language completion (child supplies a missing word or otherwise finishes an incomplete linguistic structure), and

5. spontaneous language sample (child's spontaneous language is transcribed by an examiner).

An informal language assessment provides a rich source of data to supplement standardized tests and can utilize many of the preceding tasks.

An important issue in the formal assessment of language is the representativeness of language sampled. In many testing situations, it seems that language behavior is artificially separated from a meaningful context, so it is distorted or represents a very small portion of a child's repertoire of linguistic competence. When this occurs, an inaccurate evaluation can result, and thus it is desirable to supplement any formal measure of language with direct observations, teacher/parent interviews, and spontaneous language samples (i.e., informal assessment).

A second important consideration is the differentiation of **receptive** and **expressive** language. Clearly, language involves both the ability to receive messages and to express messages; however, during the assessment of a child's language skills, it is often desirable to focus on subskills such as reception and expression. Tasks that do not require a verbal response, such as picture identification or object manipulation, stress comprehension or receptive language, whereas elicited imitation and language completion tasks primarily are measures of expressive language. Of course, expressive skills require some foundation of receptive skills, but there is much controversy among linguists about the degree to which children's receptive language is more advanced than their expressive language (Ingram, 1974; Lahey, 1988). We have set forth three pragmatic points that are relevant to the assessment of children's receptive and expressive language, regardless of the outcome of the theoretical controversy:

1. Assessment of language abilities should consider both receptive and expressive skills. Tasks in which a child is required to perform an action (e.g., pointing to a picture) are tapping receptive abilities, whereas tasks in which the child describes something or repeats or completes a statement tap expressive abilities.

2. Many standardized language tests assess only receptive or only expressive abilities. Thus either multiple tests or informal methods should be used to achieve a balanced assessment of both types of skills.

3. Teachers often overestimate a child's linguistic abilities because of correct responses to instructions and classroom verbalizations. This occurs because the classroom provides a rather predictable context with many models and nonverbal cues that enhance some receptive skills; when removed from such a setting, the child's receptive skills may suffer. Therefore, in any assessment of receptive and expressive language, it is desirable to minimize extralinguistic cues such as teacher gestures or facial expressions, written instructions, and peer models.

Informal Assessment

Before reviewing several standardized tests of language, let us focus on some informal methods and tasks that can and should supplement any

Focus on
Practice

Assessment of the Language Proficiency of Hispanic Students

At present, 9 percent of the U.S. population is estimated to be Hispanic. By the year 2020, the Hispanic population is expected to surpass the Black cohort to become the largest minority group in the nation (Bouvier & Davis, 1982). Presently, many Hispanic children have limited English proficiency.

Because language proficiency is so intimately linked to academic success, the question of differentiating Hispanic students experiencing a language disorder from a bilingual, cross-cultural difference is a crucial one for educators and language specialists. For example, a Hispanic student functioning adequately in Spanish but poorly in English is qualitatively different from a Hispanic student who is functioning poorly in both languages. The latter case is indicative of an actual language or communication disorder for which speech or language services are probably needed.

Several English- and Spanish-language proficiency tests are available, including the Woodcock Language Proficiency Battery-English Form (Woodcock, 1980) and its Spanish version, the Bateria Woodcock de Proficiencia en el Idioma-Version en Espanol (Woodcock, 1981); the Expressive One-Word Picture Vocabulary Tests in Spanish and English (Gardner, 1983); and the Test for Auditory Comprehension of Language, also in Spanish and English (Carrow-Woolfolk, 1973).

As observed by Langdon (1989), one must go well beyond standardized tests in the assessment of Hispanic students. She points to the need to rule out the effects of numerous factors that influence language. For example, Langdon suggests it is important to know the length of residence in the United States, a student's attendance record at school, the types of classrooms a student has been instructed in, the student's health and development, and how the student uses language. To facilitate the assessment of Hispanic students in California, Langdon developed an assessment protocol. This protocol is reprinted here and should help you conceptualize an assessment plan that will more fairly and effectively facilitate your work with Hispanic students who may be experiencing language difficulties.

A Model Speech and Language Assessment Protocol for Students With Limited English Proficiency

I. Reason for Referral: A brief description of the teachers' and parents' concerns and perceptions about the language problem.

II. Background Information:
   - Family: Child's place of birth; number of siblings; sibling position; languages spoken at home, by whom, and for what proportion of the time; parental occupation; parents' education; whether parents have language problems; whether child is any different from his or her siblings; child's level of comprehension and expression at home; storytelling or story reading at home; language of media programs; family activities during free time; child activities at home; length of residence in country.
   - Health: Gestational, birth, neonatal history; developmental milestones; medically related conditions, hospitalizations; hearing; vision.
   - School History: Impressions from previous teachers; attendance; results from academic testing; types of programs attended; grades and performance; modifications of regular program; any other test results.

III. Testing: Description of discrete-point tests in both languages; language samples taken in a variety of contexts (familiar topics, explaining rules of games, retelling stories, creating hypothetical situations), and interacting with a variety of people; complete assessment of language proficiency in each language; full description of where testing and language samples were done.

IV. Discussion:
   - Language Proficiency: Comparisons between languages in different areas; which areas are stronger in each language; the influence of the student's experiences in each language; the impact of all this on academic performance; the degree and impact of primary or secondary language loss.

   - Language Development: Status of basic interpersonal communication skills (BICS) and cognitive academic language proficiency (CALPS) in each language; status of CALP in the primary language when English was introduced (see Mercer, 1983); breaks in language exposure; integration of language data with intellectual and academic data; comparison of student with peers who have similar linguistic and school-based experiences.

- Language Samples: Transcribed excerpts in both languages; descriptions of contexts where these were taken; fluency variables (pauses, hesitations, and repetitions); pragmatic skills (turn-taking and staying on topic); code switching patterns; dialect; articulation; syntax, grammar, and complexity of sentences; voice quality and resonance; status of oral peripheral mechanism.
- Behaviors: Observations on the one-to-one interactions across contexts.

- Eligibility: Rationale for determining eligibility or noneligibility.

V. Goals and Objectives:
- School Based: How each is linguistically appropriate; in which language the intervention should take place; answer to the "reason for referral"; suggestions for teachers on how to help the student.
- Home Based: Summarize these to parents in a letter (in the primary language); specific suggestions for helping the student at home.

Readers interested in the development and assessment of English language skills in Hispanic children are referred to a comprehensive review by Wilen and Sweeting (1986) and to an entire issue of *Exceptional Children* focusing on "Meeting the Multicultural Needs of the Hispanic Students in Special Education" guest edited by Fradd, Figueroa, and Correa (1989).

---

assessment of language competence. Approaches to informal language assessment can be divided into two categories: structured, nonstandardized tasks and spontaneous samples of language.

Structured, Nonstandardized Tasks

A wide variety of structured, nonstandardized tasks of informal assessment have grown out of research on language. These include tasks to assess (a) means-ends relations, (b) sentence imitation, (c) egocentric listening, (d) grammatical structures, and (e) comprehension of temporal relations, anomphoric pronouns, and questions. Leonard, Perozzi, Prutting, and Berkley (1978) outlined strategies by which informal assessment methods can be reliably developed with many such tasks. Bryen and Gallagher (1983) also provided excellent guidance to an examiner of young children's language. Samples of their work in developing structured, nonstandardized assessment procedures from the literature is illustrated in table 11.3.

Spontaneous Samples of Language

Informal assessment through spontaneous samples of language involves transcribing and analyzing episodes of communication. This method has two advantages over more formalized, structured approaches to assessment, namely, the availability of both a sizable body of normative data on

Table 11.3 Structured, Nonstandardized Assessment Procedures

Target Language Aspect	Materials Needed	Response Paradigm[a]	Procedures
Object use/play (Chappell & Johnson, 1976; Sinclair, 1970)	Common objects (e.g., cup, doll, pillow, hairbrush, ball, mirror, spoon, plastic phone)	OM	1. Place objects in groups of three in front of the child. Observe interaction. Does child interact with the object exploratively, functionally, or symbolically? 2. If child does not spontaneously interact with objects, hand the child one object at a time. Observe and note quality of interaction, as above. 3. Follow-up with verbal directives at a symbolic level (e.g., *Make dolly sleep on the pillow.*)
Early language comprehension (Bloom, 1973; Brown, 1973; Weiss & Lillywhite, 1976)	Contexts of commonly occurring activities	NC	1. Using commonly occurring activities, present simple sentences or words that relate to the context (e.g., at the door say, *bye-bye*). Observe and note child's response. 2. Use same procedure as in 1, but *not* in the context in which that activity typically occurs (e.g., at a table say, *Want to go bye-bye?*). Observe and note the influence of context on language comprehension.
Early language production (Bloom, 1973; Brown, 1973)	Familiar objects or toys	S & A	1. Place familiar toys/objects in front of child, one at a time. Engage child in play. Record any utterances child makes and the context. Analyze the semantic categories used by child (e.g., agent, action, location, recurrence).

Target Language Aspect	Materials Needed	Response Paradigm[a]	Procedures
			2. If no spontaneous utterances, try eliciting utterances by asking early wh- questions (e.g., *What's this? What's the ball doing? Where's the ball?*).
Reference descriptions semantic features (Clark, 1973a; Katz & Fodor, 1963)	Common objects (e.g., nail, envelope, ball) and a list of words without a specific reference (e.g., *animal, toy, hungry, arithmetic*)	D	1. Ask the child to "tell you all about" the object presented. Probe, saying *"Tell me more."* 2. After using the referent words, ask child to tell you about the words without referents. Probe. 3. Record responses and analyze semantic features used to describe each word (function, name, attributes, class inclusion).
Semantic features at the sentence level (Clark, 1973a; Katz & Fodor, 1963)	List of sentences, some of which are anomalous (violate semantic categories): 1. *She is my brother.* 2. *My mother has no children.* 3. *The candy eats Carol.* 4. *My dog writes nice stories.* 5. *The liquid became an odorless audience.* 6. *The sun danced lightly through the clouds.*	J,A,D	1. After reading each sentence, ask whether sentence is a good (makes sense) or bad sentence; then ask why it is a good (or bad) sentence. Have child correct "bad" sentences. Record all responses. 2. Note what factors influenced child's explanations. Note child's explanations and ability to correct anomalous sentences. Note differences, if any, between tacit and explicit language knowledge.
Specific grammatical structures (Bliss et al., 1977; Menyuk, 1969; Potts et al., 1979)	Short stories, with or without accompanying pictures, which focus on particular grammatical structures. Example 1—copula and deletion of past tense marker in main verb; *Carol*	SC	Construct or obtain short stories that tap structures of interest. Where appropriate, have pictures which provide needed content clues. Read each story, having the child complete

Table 11.3—Continued

Target Language Aspect	Materials Needed	Responses Paradigm[a]	Prodecures
	got a rag, and what she did next ___ (was wipe it up versus wiped it up) (Potts et al., 1979, p. 33) Example 2—count or mass nouns; Look at this sandbox. There's lots of sand and lots of toys on it. Joe said, "There's no room for me in my sandbox, there's so many ___ (toys, things). And there's so much ___ (sand, junk)." (Potts et al., 1979, p. 69)		it. Note the child's response for semantic relevance, correctness of syntactic structures, and awareness of the rules for dialogue.
Comprehension of anaphoric pronoun it (Chipman & deDardel, 1974)	Flattened cake of clay, one box containing 5 marbles, one with 20 marbles, one clear box (empty), one tray on which is displayed chocolate divided into demarcated squares on bar of plasticine	OM	Present appropriate materials saying: (1) There is the clay. Give it to me. (2) There is a box with five marbles. Give it to me. (3) The chocolate is there. Give it to me. Note the child's comprehension of the pronoun it.
Comprehension of temporal connectives before, after, until (Barrie-Blackley, 1973)	Dolls and dollhouse; sentences containing various subordinate clauses beginning with before, after, or until (e.g., Daddy lies down after he comes in. Mommy sits down before Daddy comes in. Daddy stands up until Mommy sits down.)	OM	Sentences are said to the child who acts them out using the toys.
Comprehension of connectives and propositional logical relations (Paris, 1973)	Paired pictures (e.g., Developmental Learning Materials (DLM). Sequential Picture Cards) related to accompanying sentences in four different truth forms: true-true, true-false, false-true, false-false. Compound sentences containing the following connectives: and (conjunction), but (conjunction), both— (conjunction), but (conjunction), both—	A	Picture pairs are displayed and the descriptive sentence is read. The child must decide if the description was true or false (e.g., The boy is riding the bicycle and the dog is lying down.)

Target Language Aspect	Materials Needed	Responses Paradigm[a]	Prodecures
Comprehensions of *wh-questions—who, why, when,* and *how* (Cairns & Hsu, 1978)	*and* (conjunction), *neither—or* (disjunction), *either—or* (disjunction), *if—then* (conditionality), *if—and only if then* (biconditionality) Brief videotapes or films of family life, including a father, a mother, a teenage sister, a 6-year-old brother, and a dog. Questions of the following six types: *Who* subject (e.g., *Who bugged the boy?*) *Who* object using progressive aspect (e.g., *Who was the Daddy feeding?*) *Who* object using *do* support (e.g., *Whom did the boy feed?*) *Why* (e.g., *Why did the dog eat the sandwich?*) *When* (e.g., *When did the girl feed the dog?*) *How* (e.g., *How did the girl feed the dog?*)	A	After being introduced to each character by a photograph which remains on display, the child watches a taped segment and then is asked the six types of questions.
Comprehending ongoing discourse (Glucksberg & Krauss, 1967)	Crayons and drawing paper or paste and cut-out construction paper of different sizes, colors, and shapes. A "make pretend" script of a fantasy story which the child will draw following your directions of the script or dictation of the script; or directions about the cut-out shapes that the child will follow to construct a design, mask, or scene. Script sentences should vary in complexity, have an ongoing coherent theme, and utilize, where appropriate, anaphoric pronouns.	OM	Administer directions or the made-up scripts to the child in two or three sentences at a time. Encourage the child to make his picture story (or design) exactly like the story you tell. If possible, have child retell the story or design. Analyze child's picture to determine if he was able to accurately process elaborate ongoing language. This includes expanded NP's, anaphoric pronouns.

Table 11.3—Continued

Target Language Aspect	Materials Needed	Responses Paradigm[a]	Prodecures
	Example 1: *Hi, I'm Mary Martian from Mars. As you know, I'm a little purple Martian with red, round eyes, a square head, and green pointed ears.* Example 2: *Through the window of my spaceship I can see your planet earth. It has a big round yellow sun and blue clouds. It has trees, flowers and birds.*		

From Diane N. Bryen and Diane Gallagher, "Assessment of Language and Communication" in *The Psychoeducational Assessment of Preschool Children*, edited by Kathleen D. Paget and Bruce A. Bracken. Copyright © 1983 Allyn and Bacon. Reprinted with permission of Allyn & Bacon.
[a]Response paradigms: A, answers to stimulus questions; D, descriptions; J, judgments about grammaticality; NC, natural context; OM, object manipulations; PI, picture identification; S, spontaneous langauge; SC, story completion.

spontaneous language production and more natural, less artificial, language samples (e.g., Kretschmer & Kretschmer, 1978). The potential features for analysis include phonological production, vocabulary, sentence length and structure, word uses, and pragmatics such as turn-taking, initiation of conversation, and listening skills. (For detailed systems for analyzing spontaneous language samples, see Engler, Hannah, & Longhurst, 1973; Miller, 1981; and Whitehurst & Sonnenschein, 1985.) Engler, Hannah, and Longhurst provided a method for analyzing patterns of language used by children to determine linguistic constructions. This analysis determines deviant or absent linguistic structures and can be used to plan specific remedial interventions. Informal assessment is also important because it allows the examiner to assess how a child uses language in the natural context. Increasingly, an understanding of how a child uses language in his or her normal daily routine appears essential to understanding whether a child has a language disability and what should be done about it if she or he does (Damico, 1985). Readers interested in a more comprehensive coverage of informal language assessment are referred to Bryen and Gallagher (1983), Damico (1985), and Guerin and Maier (1983). We will now evaluate six commonly used standardized measures of language. Other popular standardized tests of language skills are listed in table 11.4.

➡ *Standardized Language Tests*

Fluharty Preschool and Language Screening Test

Overview and Purpose

The Fluharty Preschool and Language Screening Test, or FPLST (Fluharty, 1978), is designed to identify preschool children (two to six years of age) in need of comprehensive speech and language evaluations. The test is individually administered and generally takes less than 10 minutes to complete. Thirty-five items compose the total test and are divided into three sections:

1. Section A—requires the identification of 15 common objects and is designed to assess vocabulary and articulation

2. Section B—measures receptive language abilities through nonverbal responses to 10 sentences

3. Section C—requires the oral repetition of 10 short sentences and is an attempt to measure expressive language

Standardization Sample and Norms

The FPLST was standardized on 2,147 children from four racial and ethnic backgrounds, three socioeconomic classes, and several geographic areas.

Table 11.4 Other Frequently Used Language Tests

Test Name	Date	Author	Publisher
Arizona Articulation Proficiency Scale	1970	J. Fudala	Western Psychological Services
Carrow Elicited Language Inventory	1974	E. Carrow	Learning Concepts
Expressive One Word Picture Vocabulary Test	1979	M. Gardner	Academic Therapy Publications
Illinois Test of Psycholinguistic Abilities	1968	S. Kirk, J. McCarthy, & W. Kirk	University of Illinois Press
Northwestern Syntax Screening Test	1971	L. Lee	Northwestern University Press
Phonological Process Analysis	1979	F. Weiner	University Park Press
Test of Adolescent Language-2	1987	D. Hammill, L. Brown, S. Larsen, & L. Wiederholt	Pro-Ed
Test for Auditory Comprehension of Language-Revised	1985	E. Carrow-Woolfolk	DLM Teaching Resources
Test of Written Spelling, 2	1986	S. Larsen & D. Hammill	Pro-Ed

More specific data on the exact composition of the standardization sample are included in the manual in tabular form, although no mention is made of its representatives of the population at large.

Data Obtained

Children receive four scores (identification, articulation, comprehension, and repetition). A child "fails" the test if any of the four scores falls below the cutoff scores, which, according to the manual, were determined by correlating scores from the FPLST with scores from the Peabody Picture Vocabulary Test (Dunn, 1965), the Goldman-Fristoe Test of Articulation (Goldman & Fristoe, 1972), and the Northwestern Syntax Screening Test (Lee, 1971). However, the derivation of the cutoff score is not explained.

Reliability and Validity

Test-retest reliability coefficients were obtained by retesting 50 of the children in the standardization sample six weeks after the initial testing. Pearson correlations ranged from .95 to .99 for the four scores. Five speech pathologists estimated interrater reliability. Ten children from the standardization sample were retested and the five speech pathologists scored their responses. Interrater reliability ranged from .87 to 1.00 for the four scores.

Validity is reported in the test manual by indicating the correlation between a child's performance on the FPLST (pass/fail) and the outcome of a more comprehensive speech evaluation (needs therapy/does not need therapy). A Pearson correlation was calculated on the basis of data from 211 children and equaled .90. At one level the validity data can be criticized, because the Pearson Product Moment correlation statistic is not the appropriate procedure for estimating the relationship between two dichotomous variables. More importantly, it is necessary to have the specific figures on the number of children who were correctly identified as needing therapy to evaluate the efficacy of the test as a screening measure. Finally, no information is provided on how the determination of whether a child needed speech therapy was made (e.g., what test was used and who made the determination).

Summary

The FPLST is a simple screening instrument. Reliability and validity data are not known because the procedures used to determine them are not well explained and seem inappropriate. Thus, the ultimate value of the test must be questioned. Other screening instruments provide more information with only a little extra commitment of time.

Goldman-Fristoe Test of Articulation

Overview and Purpose

More than a decade after its initial development the Goldman-Fristoe Test of Articulation, or GFTA (Goldman & Fristoe, 1986), remains very popular. Designed to evaluate a child's ability to articulate or produce the sounds of speech, the GFTA is divided into three sections: Sounds-in-Words, Sounds-in-Sentences, and Stimulability. Consonant sounds and blends are elicited in words and sentences (Sounds-in-Words and Sounds-in-Sentences), followed by an attempt to stimulate correct pronunciation of all misarticulated sounds (Stimulability). The first two sections of the GFTA help to determine the content of any remedial activity, and the final section aids in the assessment of a child's receptivity and ability to profit from instruction. The GFTA is individually administered and best used by examiners interested in obtaining a rapid assessment of a child's general articulation skill (Mowrer, 1989).

Standardization Sample and Norms

The major difference between the current and previous version of this test was the addition of normative data for the 2- to 6-year-old population. Eight hundred and fifty-two children (200 in each of four age groups) comprised the standardization sample of 2- to 6-year-olds and the sample appears representative of the larger population (Mowrer, 1989). Norms from the school-aged group (6 to 16) were derived from 38,802 subjects who had participated in the National Speech and Hearing Survey (Hull et al., 1971), although the exact process used to develop normative data is not clear (Mowrer, 1989).

Data Obtained

Percentile ranks are available for the Sounds-in-Words section. The most appropriate use of the GFTA, however, is as a criterion-referenced measure of children's ability to produce different sounds.

Reliability and Validity

Reliability for the GFTA is reported as percentage of agreement. For example, to assess interrater reliability, eight speech pathologists evaluated 37 children on two separate occasions (one-week interval) and reliability was reported as the number of times they agreed divided by the number of times they agreed plus the number of times they disagreed. Interrater reliability for presence or absence of an error on the Sounds-in-Sentences subtest is reported as 94 percent and for the Sounds-in-Words subtest the figure is 89 percent. Interrater comparisons for the specific type of error were also made and here the percentage of agreement figures are 86 percent and 89 percent, respectively. Unfortunately, the percentage-of-agreement method of calculating interrater agreement tends to yield spuriously high percentages. The use of the median as a measure of central tendency, which tends to discount the value of extreme scores, has also been criticized. Similar agreement values (88–91%) were obtained for interrater and intrarater reliability estimates; however, these figures are subject to the same criticisms as above. No data on age or backgrounds of subjects in the reliability studies was provided.

No validity data are presented. No attempt was made to relate the GFTA scores to other standardized measures of articulation. For a test that is often used in criterion-referenced assessment such as the GFTA, content validity is most critical. The test seems to include a thorough sampling of speech sounds, but documentation of content validity by the test authors would be helpful.

Summary

The GFTA seems best used as a criterion-referenced measure of children's ability to articulate sounds in a variety of word positions and contexts (in words and sentences). Interrater reliability data appear adequate (barely), and the test seems to sample thoroughly the content it purports to measure, although evidence in the manual for both reliability and validity is sketchy.

Peabody Picture Vocabulary Test-Revised

Overview and Purpose
The Peabody Picture Vocabulary Test-Revised, or PPVT-R (Dunn & Dunn, 1981), is a revision of the original Peabody Picture Vocabulary Test. The PPVT-R is a measure of receptive vocabulary and, according to its authors, "it is not, however, a comprehensive test of general intelligence, instead it measures only one important facet of general intelligence: vocabulary" (p. 2). This statement is important, because the original PPVT was described as a test of intellectual ability and yielded "IQ" scores. The PPVT-R is untimed and generally takes between 10 and 15 minutes to complete. There are two forms of the test (Form L and Form M), both containing 175 test items and 5 training items. It can be administered to individuals between the ages of 2 1/2 and 40. During administration, the examiner reads a stimulus word aloud, and subjects are required to pick the picture (from four choices) that best depicts that word. Members of minority cultures and women appear in nonstereotypical roles in the pictures of the PPVT-R (McCallum, 1985).

Standardization Sample and Norms
The PPVT-R was standardized on a national sample of 4,200 children and youths (ages 2 1/2 to 18) and 828 adults (ages 19 to 40). The sampling procedure was based on data from the 1970 U.S. census. Stratification variables for the younger sample included age, sex, geographic region, occupation of major household wage earner, ethnicity, and community size. Stratification variables for the older sample included age, sex, geographic region, and occupation. Although both of the standardization groups appear to be representative when compared to 1970 census data, the standardization for the younger group was clearly more comprehensive.

Data Obtained
Raw scores (number correct between basal and ceiling) may be transformed to stanines, age equivalents, standard scores (with a mean of 100 and a standard deviation of 15), or percentile ranks.

Reliability and Validity
Split-half, immediate test-retest with alternate forms, and delayed test-retest with alternate forms reliability data are presented in the test manual. Median split-half reliabilities of above 80 are reported for both forms. Median

reliabilities during immediate retests ($N = 642$) are reported as .82 for raw scores and .79 for standard scores. Median delayed retest reliabilities ($N = 962$) equal .78 for raw scores and .77 for standard scores.

No data on the validity of the PPVT-R are included in the manual. Published data confirm that the alternate forms are equivalent and that the PPVT-R generally yields lower scores than did the original PPVT (see, e.g., Bracken & Prasse, 1981). The PPVT-R also tends to yield lower scores than frequently used measures of cognitive ability such as the Wechsler Intelligence Scale for Children-Revised (Bracken, Prasse, & McCallum, 1984; Davis & Kramer, 1985).

Summary

The PPVT-R is an easy-to-use, well-developed, and appropriately standardized test of receptive (or hearing) vocabulary. Reliability data suggest that it is appropriate for screening purposes, although this instrument does assess a narrow range of language skills. Furthermore, recent data indicate that the scores on the PPVT-R tend to be lower than those for either earlier versions of this test or commonly used measures of intellectual ability.

Test of Early Language Development-2

Overview and Purpose

According to its manual, the Test of Early Language Development-2, or TELD-2 (Hresko, Reid, & Hammill, 1991), is a device for assessing the early development of oral language in the areas of expressive and receptive language, syntax, and semantics. Administration of the test is simple and explained well in the manual. It includes 136 items divided into two alternate forms of 68 items and is administered individually in approximately 15 to 40 minutes. Children are required to repeat words and sentences, answer questions, and respond to a set of pictures.

Standardization Sample and Norms

The TELD-2 was standardized on a sample of 1,329 children in 30 states. The sample was stratified on the basis of age, sex, geographic region, race, ethnicity, rural versus urban residence, and occupation of parents. Data presented in the manual support the authors' contention that this sample compares favorably with national census figures.

Data Obtained

Raw scores can be converted to percentiles, age equivalents, and two types of standard scores: quotients with a mean of 100 and a standard deviation of 15 and NCE scores. The authors correctly caution users against an overreliance on age-equivalent scores due to the psychometric shortcomings of age-equivalent scores.

Reliability and Validity

Reliability data are reported in terms of internal consistency and test-retest estimates. All internal consistency figures (coefficient alpha) exceed .90. Test-retest reliability for immediate (.98) and delayed (.97) retesting are excellent.

Content, criterion-related, and construct validity of the TELD–2 are discussed in the test manual. Data on item selection, sampling, and discrimination appear to support the claim of content validity for the TELD–2. Criterion-referenced validity was established by correlating TELD–2 scores with (a) similar language measures and (b) the original TELD. Correlations with similar tests yielded moderate correlations .47 to .66, suggesting that the TELD–2 may measure similar, but not completely overlapping, content. As might be expected the TELD and TELD–2 scores are highly correlated (.96/.97 between the TELD and two forms of the TELD–2). Construct validity was established by correlating TELD–2 scores with scores from tests of intelligence and academic achievement. These comparisons indicate that the TELD–2 does appear to be more closely related to language measures than to other types of tests.

Summary

The TELD–2 appears to be a useful, quick, easy-to-administer overall measure of language ability in young children. The manual provides a clear and detailed explanation of the rationale and appropriate use of the test. Psychometric characteristics are strong and a significant improvement over the previous edition.

Test of Written Language–2

Overview and Purpose

The Test of Written Language–2, or TOWL–2 (Hammill & Larsen, 1990), was designed to provide a comprehensive assessment of written language skills in children from 7 to 19 years of age. Subtests are Vocabulary, Spelling, Style, Logical Sentences, Sentence Combining, Thematic Maturity, Contextual Vocabulary, Syntactic Maturity, Contextual Spelling, and Contextual Style. The TOWL–2 is designed for either group or individual administration and requires 90 to 120 minutes to complete. Administration and scoring are difficult but are well explained in the manual. The results of the TOWL–2 are described as appropriate for identifying students who perform below their peers, determining specific strengths and weaknesses, documenting progress, and conducting research.

Standardization Sample and Norms

The TOWL–2 was standardized on 2,216 students in 16 states. A comparison between the normative group and 1985 data in terms of gender, place of residence, race, ethnicity, and geographic distribution is presented in the manual. The sample does appear representative in these areas. As with the previous edition, no mention is made of any attempt to control for socioeconomic status, educational level of parents, or the inclusion of handicapped children in the sample.

Data Obtained

Raw scores on the TOWL–2 may be transformed to percentile ranks or standard scores. Subtest standard scores have a mean of 10 and a standard deviation of 3, whereas the composite scores (Contrived Writing, Spontaneous Writing, and Overall Written Language) have a mean of 100 and a standard deviation of 15. No grade or age equivalents are reported in the manual because "the problems associated with the use of grade norms are serious enough that we have decided to omit them from the TOWL–2 manual" (Hammill & Larsen, 1990, p. 67). Although the authors realize that educators often like to be able to report grade- or age-level scores, they feel the potential for misuse outweighs any benefits of these scores.

Reliability and Validity

Internal consistency, test-retest, and interscorer figures are reported. Coefficient alpha and split-half measures of internal consistency are all at acceptable levels. Test-retest with alternate forms was undertaken by testing 77 children in grades 1 to 7 from Austin, Texas. The average period of time between being tested with the two forms of the test was two days and the test composite and most subtests appear to yield stable scores (above .80). The reliability evidence for the Sentence Combining (.75), Syntactic Maturity (.77), and Contextual Spelling (.59) scores is less convincing, however. Unfortunately, the one reported test of interscorer reliability involved only two scorers, the test author and someone who helped develop the test for the test publisher. Although these estimates of interscorer reliability are high, this comparison is not a good measure of whether professionals in the field will be able to score the test in a reliable manner.

Information on content, criterion-related, and construct validity is reported in the test manual. Under content validity, the manual thoroughly discusses the rationale for the test content and the manner in which it was selected. Correlations between the TOWL–2 and a variety of other tests were used as an index of criterion-related and construct validity. These comparisons appear to support the authors' claim that the test does measure skills related to written language.

Summary

Our opinion, as well as that of others (e.g., Benton, 1992), is that the TOWL–2 remains one of the best instruments for the comprehensive assessment of written language skills. The test takes a long time to administer and is more difficult to learn to score than some other tests, but the manual does provide thorough instructions. In fact, the manual serves as an excellent model in its description of what the test does and does not accomplish.

Woodcock Language Proficiency Battery-Revised

Overview and Purpose

The Woodcock Language Proficiency Battery, or WLPB (Woodcock, 1991), contains 13 tests organized into three areas: oral language, reading, and written language. The battery can be administered to individuals from 2 to 90 years of age and requires about an hour-and-a-half for an experienced examiner. In reality, the WLPB-R is a portion of the Woodcock-Johnson Psychoeducational Battery-Revised (WJ-R; Woodcock & Johnson, 1989) that has been repackaged and distributed as a separate test of language ability. According to the manual, the WLPB-R can be used for evaluating English as a Second Language, diagnosis, program placement, individual program planning, guidance, evaluating gains in language development, program evaluation, training students about testing, and research.

Standardization Sample and Norms

The normative sample for the WLPB-R included 6,359 subjects stratified on the basis of sex, race, occupation, geographic location, and type of community. It should be noted that this norm group is the sample that participated in the norming of the WJ-R and is not a separate norming of the WLPB-R. As was indicated in the review of the WJ-R (see chapter 7), the process of subject selection was excellent.

Data Obtained

Raw scores on the WLPB-R may be converted into a number of other scores, including percentile ranks, age equivalents, standard scores, normal curve equivalents, and relative mastery indexes. If an examiner has not tired of the scoring process after calculating all of these scores, intra-English discrepancy scores can be completed that allow for an assessment of the degree of difference between the three areas of English assessed with this test: oral language, broad reading, and broad written language. Calculating scores on the WJPB-R is no easy matter and can take a great amount of time.

Reliability and Validity

Internal consistency, interrater reliability, and test-retest reliability are reported in the test manual. As with the original WJ-R from which it was developed, the WJPB-R appears to yield reliable scores and to be internally consistent.

Development, selection, and sequencing of items for the WJPB-R was exemplary. In addition, a number of criterion (i.e., concurrent) validity studies are presented in the manual. The inclusion of these studies is a significant improvement over the original edition of the WJPB when the user was simply referred to the validity studies on the original Woodcock-Johnson Psychoeducational Battery as evidence of the validity of the WJPB. The criterion validity studies with tests like the Boehm Basic Concept Scales, the PPVT-R, the K-ABC, Stanford-Binet IV, and various other achievement and special ability tests support the general contention that the WLPB-R measures what it purports to measure. These studies involved few subjects and restricted age ranges and a more definitive statement about the test's value will be possible following the collection of additional validity data.

Summary

The major value of the WLPB-R appears to be its comprehensiveness. It includes a variety of skill areas, assesses these areas in a thorough manner, and covers a wide age range. Examiners will find the administration, scoring, and interpretation of this test somewhat more cumbersome than most standardized tests. The WLPB-R appears psychometrically sound; however, a clear indication of its potential awaits the collection of more comprehensive validity data. It is fair to say that the WJPB-R appears to have a great deal of promise for a wide range of applications.

Chapter Summary

In this chapter, we have tried to convey both the complexity and richness of children's spoken language and the methods commonly used to assess it. Language is a complex skill involving many different components and many different factors should be assessed before making judgments about a child's language skill (Sommers, 1989). Major points were that (a) components of spoken language targeted for assessment include phonology, morphology, syntax, semantics, and pragmatics, (b) both receptive and expressive phrases of language should be assessed, and (c) both formal and informal approaches to the assessment of language are necessary to enhance the meaningfulness and representativeness of a language sample. In both formal and informal assessments, the measurement of a child's ability to use language in natural contexts is being emphasized more and more (e.g., Damico, 1985). Speech deficits and language proficiency (e.g., in English versus Spanish) were noted as critical factors to consider when assessing a student's language performance. Educators must keep abreast of advances in language research to be useful and dependable evaluators of children's language. We hope you are now better prepared to undertake a language assessment and acknowledge the need for involving speech and language pathologists when confronted with complex problems.

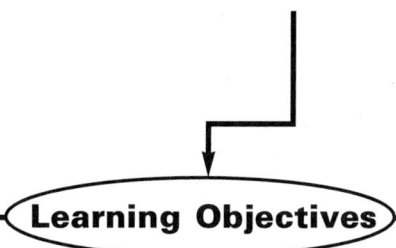

Chapter 12

Perceptual-Motor Skills and Abilities

Learning Objectives

1. Describe the relationship between perceptual-motor skills and the development of academic skills.
2. Explain the "level of inference" problem in assessing perceptual-motor skills.
3. List and explain the basic principles of perceptual organization.
4. Evaluate the psychometric properties of tests of perceptual-motor skills and abilities.
5. Explain why tests of perceptual-motor skills are among the most frequently administered tests in existence today.
6. Outline a process for directly assessing perceptual-motor skills.
7. List and explain the cautions in administering and interpreting tests of perceptual-motor skills.

Perceptual-motor skills are viewed by many persons as being important prerequisites to the acquisition and performance of academic skills. These skills are termed "perceptual" because they involve the attention to and interpretation of information gained from the senses (e.g., vision, hearing, touch, etc.). These skills are called "motor" because they involve the execution of physical movements involved in the performance of either fine motor (writing, drawing, etc.) or gross motor (e.g., walking, skipping, jumping, etc.) behaviors. An individual's ability to translate perceptual information into motor responses is known as **perceptual-motor integration.**

Children who perform poorly on tests of perceptual-motor skills are sometimes labeled as having a "perceptual-motor dysfunction" and are placed in specialized curricula designed to remediate these dysfunctions. As such, some educational programs focus on teaching or remediating perceptual-motor skills rather than academic deficits.

The practice of teaching perceptual-motor skills, or what is called **perceptual-motor training,** is questionable given that research has not shown that such training is effective in enhancing basic academic skills (Kavale & Mattison, 1982; Myers & Hammill, 1982). It appears from a careful review of the literature that improving a child's performance on perceptual-motor tests may improve perceptual-motor functioning, but it does not improve reading, arithmetic, or language skills. This holds true regardless of the child's characteristics (e.g., sex, race, and socioeconomic status), the types of perceptual-motor programs used, the grade levels trained, or the quality of the research designed to investigate perceptual-motor training programs (Kavale & Mattison, 1982).

Another use of perceptual-motor tests is in the diagnosis of brain dysfunction or neurological damage. **Neuropsychologists,** psychologists specializing in the assessment of brain-behavior relationships, believe that poor performances on tests of perceptual-motor tests indicate some sort of damage or dysfunction to the central nervous system (Haak, 1989; Reynolds & Fletcher-Janzen, 1989; Telzrow, 1989). These neurological dysfunctions are thought to be reflected in perceptual-motor test performances. For the neuropsychologist, many causes of children's poor academic performances can be traced to brain dysfunction, which is assessed by perceptual-motor tests.

Performance on perceptual-motor tests may be influenced by factors other than neurological dysfunction (unreliability, sensory deficits, motor dysfunctions, etc.). More importantly, there is little justification for using tests of perceptual-motor skills to diagnose brain damage or other forms of neurological dysfunction (Reschly & Gresham, 1989). The simple fact is that *there is not a one-to-one correspondence between perceptual-motor test performance and neurological status.*

If the research does not support the practice of assessing and training perceptual-motor skills and if the research concerning neuropsychological interpretations of perceptual-motor test performance is questionable, then why do we devote an entire chapter to this area? Our rationale is simple: *Perceptual-motor tests are among the most frequently used, misused, and abused tests in school settings.* Surveys have consistently shown that certain perceptual-motor tests rank only second in their frequency of use in the schools (Goh, Telzrow, & Fuller, 1981; Reschly, Genshaft, & Binder, 1987). We believe that readers of this text should become intelligent consumers of this frequently practiced form of assessment and question misinterpretations of perceptual-motor test results.

The purposes of this chapter are to: (a) provide an overview of basic principles of perception; (b) review selected tests of perceptual-motor skills; (c) discuss the relationships among perceptual impairments, learning, and neurological status; (d) review research regarding perceptual-motor training programs; and (e) provide an alternative strategy for assessing perceptual-motor skills.

➡ *Fundamentals of Perception*

In this section, we provide a context for understanding perceptual-motor assessment and describe how this type of assessment came to prominence in the evaluation of children with learning problems. Perceptual-motor assessment, like most other forms of assessment, relies heavily on theoretical and conceptual underpinnings. Therefore, knowledge of these issues is a prerequisite for understanding perceptual-motor assessment techniques.

Perception is the meaning or interpretation of information received through our senses. The way we perceive something depends primarily on two things: (a) the physical features of a stimulus and (b) the way we organize information (Woolfolk, 1987). Because there are five senses, there are theoretically five types of perception. In school settings and in perceptual-motor testing, two types of perception are emphasized: **visual perception** and **auditory perception.**

Physical features of visual stimuli can vary across the dimensions of size, shape, color, clarity, and complexity. Physical features of auditory stimuli can vary along dimensions of pitch, loudness, complexity, and similarity/dissimilarity of sounds. Organization of sensory information depends on the quantity and quality of stored information and concepts as well as an individual's level of cognitive development.

Familiar stimuli are perceived more readily than unfamiliar stimuli. When confronted with an unfamiliar stimulus, we tend to classify that stimulus into a category that is closest to our stored information and concepts. For example, if we have never seen a crocodile, but are familiar with alligators, we would probably classify crocodiles as alligators. Similarly, young children familiar only with horses might classify donkeys, mules, and zebras as horses.

➡ *Perception and Attention*

A critical aspect of perception is **selective attention.** Selective attention refers to the ability to select from an array of competing stimuli those stimuli that are relevant to the task at hand. Another way of defining perception is the selective attention to sensory input and the interpretation of that information as a function of stored information and concepts and the current qualitative level of cognitive development (Wyne & O'Connor, 1979).

Selective attention becomes crucial in learning tasks because the typical classroom has a variety of competing and often confusing stimuli, such

THE FAR SIDE    By GARY LARSON

Perceptual-Motor Skills Are Important to Survival, Yet the Way They Have Been Traditionally Assessed in Schools Has Not Yielded Valuable Instructional Information.

---

as noise from other classrooms, whispering, and sounds from the heating system. Obviously, if one could not ignore these distractions, it would be difficult to learn.

Attention is a complex concept, although teachers frequently refer to attention during instruction. When a teacher says, "Frank, pay attention!" because Frank is looking out of the window during reading instruction, how do we know that he is paying attention if he redirects his eyes to his book? The only way to know is to ask him a question regarding the task in which he is supposedly engaging. If he answers correctly, he must be paying attention. However, he could answer correctly because he had learned the answer earlier. Alternatively, Frank could answer incorrectly because the question was unclear or poorly asked. It should thus be apparent that attention is a complex, difficult construct because it describes an unobservable process that cannot be directly observed; it must be inferred by observing changes in behavioral performances. Similarly, the only way we can measure perception is by the same process of inferring it through observable behaviors.

➡ *Principles of Perceptual Organization*

The assessment of perceptual-motor skills began in the early 1900s with the work of gestalt psychologists such as Max Wertheimer, Kurt Koffka, and Wolfgang Kohler (McConnell, 1989). The gestalt school of psychology can be defined by the statement, "The whole is greater than the sum of its parts." That is, a perceived stimulus has greater meaning to an individual than its component parts. The basic assumptions of gestalt psychology are called **principles of perceptual organization.** The three basic laws most relevant in the assessment of perceptual-motor skills are (a) the law of proximity, (b) the law of similarity, and (c) the law of closure.

The **law of proximity** states that groups of objects are formed by elements close to one another in space or time. For example, separate notes played in rapid succession compose a melody in music. Similarly, separate printed stimuli on a page compose words that in turn compose sentences and paragraphs. Figure 12.1a depicts the law of proximity.

The **law of similarity** states that similar items tend to be perceived in groups. For example, a football team wearing orange jerseys and white pants would be perceived as one group and another team wearing white jerseys and yellow pants would be perceived as another group. Figure 12.1b illustrates this principle, with filled circles and the open circles each being perceived as separate groups.

Finally, the **law of closure** states that parts of a stimulus that are not presented will be filled in by the perceptual system. For example, if static on your radio interrupts a familiar song at random intervals, your perceptual system will tend to fill in or complete the missing melody and lyrics. Figure 12.1c shows an example of this law using the word *boy*.

➡ *The Relationship Between Perceptual Impairments and Learning*

The work of the gestalt psychologists set the stage for the clinical application of gestalt principles in the assessment of perceptual impairments. Kurt Goldstein (1939, 1948) was a pioneer in the assessment of brain-injured adults. Goldstein based much of his work on soldiers with demonstrable

Figure 12.1 Examples of the Law of Proximity (a), the Law of Similarity (b), and the Law of Closure (c)

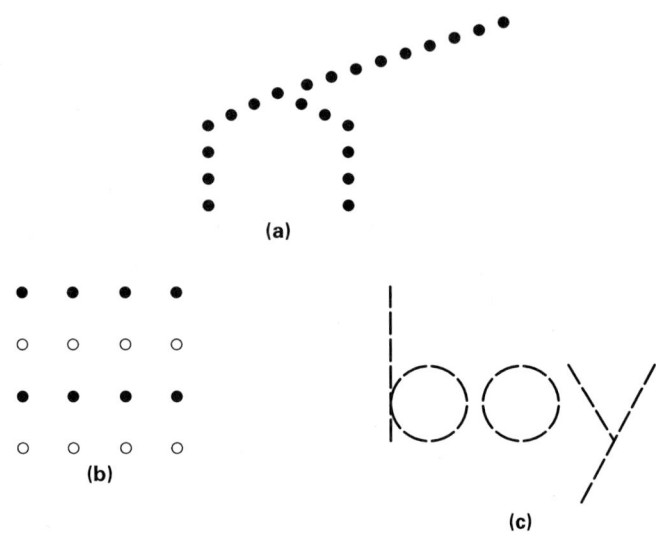

brain injuries acquired during World War I. Further application of these principles was evident in the work of Heniz Werner and Alfred Strauss, who worked with mentally retarded, autistic, and brain-injured children in the 1940s (Strauss & Lehtinen, 1947).

Central of Werner's and Strauss's assumptions regarding learning problems were **perceptual disorders,** particularly **figure-ground disturbances.** A figure-ground disturbance refers to the tendency to confuse an object with its background. Normally, when we perceive a stimulus (e.g., a painting), we tend to focus on the main object and its details and tend to ignore much of the background. In a figure-ground disturbance, some individuals will focus on or be distracted by details of the background and ignore the figure. In other words, a figure-ground disturbance is "not being able to see the tree for the forest." This relates back to the idea of selective attention discussed earlier in this chapter. That is, persons with a figure-ground disturbance tend to focus on irrelevant aspects of a stimulus (the ground) and not upon relevant aspects of that stimulus (the figure).

In the 1960s a new term was introduced to describe children who had no demonstrable sensory impairments and were not mentally disabled but still had difficulty learning. Kirk (1963) labeled these children **learning disabled,** and many of their characteristics were similar to those first described in the 1940s by Werner and Strauss in discussing brain-injured children. Assessment procedures that focus on the measurement of perceptual functioning were stimulated by and continue to be fueled by concern for children with learning disabilities.

➡ *Tests of Perceptual-Motor Skills*

The majority of tests of perceptual-motor skills on the market today do not merit review because of their psychometric inadequacy (reliability, validity, and normative samples). The following discussion is limited to a small sample of commonly used tests of perceptual-motor functioning.

Our position, which is supported in the following test reviews, is that tests of perceptual-motor skills should *never be used to diagnose or to develop remediation strategies*. There are other ways of collecting more useful information than perceptual-motor tests currently available on the market. Table 12.1 depicts some relevant questions developed by Hammill and Bartel (1975) that should be asked before assessing perceptual-motor skills in the schools. These questions are important because, unfortunately, many professionals administer tests of perceptual-motor skills more out of habit than out of thoughtful consideration of what is assessed and why.

**Table 12.1   Questions to Be Asked Before Assessing
Perceptual-Motor Skills**

---

1. Do I wish to assess perception, perceptual-motor integration, or both?
2. Am I interested in a particular perceptual skill (e.g., discrimination, figure-ground, closure, or in overall perceptual ability?
3. Is the measure appropriate for the prospective sample (i.e., are the children physically able to respond, and is the test too easy or too difficult)?
4. Is the measure reliable enough to be used for educational purposes (i.e., as the basis for an educational classification decision)?
5. Are the data derived from the test worth the time and effort of administering and scoring the test?
6. Are there any data that support the relationship between performance on the test and academic performance in the classroom? If so, how strong is this relationship and to what extent can it be generalized across samples (i.e., the external validity of the data)?
7. Are there more direct ways of assessing the skill (e.g., through the use of curriculum-based assessment methods)?

Source: Adapted from D. Hammill and N. Bartel, *Teaching Children with Learning and Behavior Problems*. Allyn & Bacon, Boston, MA, 1975.

Bender Visual Motor Gestalt Test

Overview and Purpose

The Bender Visual Motor Gestalt Test (Bender Gestalt) was developed by Loretta Bender, a physician, to differentiate brain-damage from non-brain-damaged adults. Bender (1938) used nine geometric designs published by Wertheimer in 1923 to illustrate the principles of gestalt psychology. Each design is printed on a 4-by-6-inch white card and presented in a specified sequence to an examinee, who is asked to copy all nine designs on a sheet of 8-1/2-by-11-inch white paper. The accuracy of the reproduced design is evaluated by relatively objective scoring criteria.

According to Koppitz (1975), the Bender Gestalt is a test of **visual-motor integration** because it requires the examinee to integrate what is perceived visually with the fine motor responses required to reproduce the designs. It should be noted that some persons may perform poorly on the Bender Gestalt yet not have a visual perception problem. For example, someone who has extremely poor fine motor coordination may be misdiagnosed as having difficulty in visual perception when the problem is simply one of fine motor coordination; Koppitz warns against such simple-minded misinterpretations. This is particularly problematic with individuals with cerebral palsy and children with developmental disabilities.

Standardization Sample and Norms

The most frequently used normative sample and scoring system for children was developed by Koppitz (1975). The Bender Gestalt was originally standardized on 975 children between the ages of 5 and 11. The sample was not geographically representative of the United States population, since 83 percent were from the Northeast, 15 percent from the West, and only 2 percent from the South. Koppitz's standardization sample was somewhat more representative with respect to race, with 86 percent being white, 8.5 percent black, 4.5 percent Hispanic, and 1 percent Oriental. Koppitz did not attempt to stratify the sample according to socioeconomic status (SES) and suggests that SES may not be an important variable in performance on the Bender Gestalt. This claim, however, is not substantiated by other research, which suggests that Bender Gestalt performances do vary by SES level (Buckley, 1975).

Data Obtained

In school settings, the most commonly used scoring is a relatively objective system known as the Koppitz Developmental Bender Scoring System (Koppitz, 1964). Four types of errors (Koppitz, 1975) are scored with this system:

1. *Distortion of shape.* Distortion of the figure by drawing parts in disproportionate size or substituting angles for curves or circles for dashes or dots. Distortion of shape is scored for Figures A, 1, 3, 5, 6, 7, and 8 for a total of 10 points.

2. *Rotation*. Rotation of any part of the figure by 45 degrees or more. Rotation errors are also scored if the subject draws the figure correctly but rotates the stimulus card. Rotation errors are scored for Figures A, 1, 2, 3, 4, 5, and 8 for a total of 8 points.

3. *Integration*. The failure to connect two parts of a figure, the crossing of two lines at an incorrect place, the failure to cross two lines, or the omission or addition of rows or dots. Integration errors are scored for Figures A, 2, 3, 4, 5, 6, and 7 for a total of 9 points.

4. *Perseveration*. The increase, prolongation, or continuation of the number of units in the design. Perseveration is scored for Figures A, 1, 2, and 6 for a total of 3 points.

A total of 30 errors can be made on the nine designs. The total number of errors a child makes is compared to the appropriate age-level norms in the Koppitz (1975) manual. The error score is then converted into a percentile ranking, which can be used to interpret the child's test performance.

Reliability and Validity

Koppitz (1975) reported both interrater and test-retest reliability, or stability, for the Bender Gestalt. Interrater reliability studies reported in the manual (N = 23) show that the reliabilities range from .79 to .99 with a median of .90. These high reliabilities suggest that raters agreed in the total number of errors they scored on the test. The objective scoring criteria probably account for these high agreement estimates.

The manual reports nine test-retest reliability studies, with stability coefficients ranging from .50 to .90 and averaging .71. Unfortunately, more than half of these studies were conducted with kindergarten children. The mean reliability of .71 suggests that the Bender Gestalt is not stable enough to use in making important decisions for children.

Convincing empirical evidence is not presented in the manual to support Koppitz's (1975) claim that the Bender Gestalt is a measure of visual motor integration. In other words, there is little evidence for the construct validity of the test, although the manual does report the results of correlational studies between the Bender Gestalt and measures of achievement, intelligence, and visual perception.

Evidence for the test's criterion-related validity is presented in the manual, mostly in the form of correlations between the total test score on the Bender Gestalt and measures of academic achievement. The manual lists 54 studies in which the Koppitz-scored Bender Gestalt has been compared with measures of school achievement. Fifty of these studies have been conducted with children in kindergarten through third grade. The validity coefficients in the 54 studies ranged from −.13 to −.58, with a median concurrent validity coefficient of −.23. The direction of these correlations is negative because Koppitz scores are based on the number of errors (i.e., the lower the number of errors, the higher the achievement score). Based on the data presented in the manual, the Bender Gestalt is not a strong predictor of academic achievement; on the average, it accounts for only 5 percent of the variance in academic achievement.

The manual also reports eight correlations between the Bender Gestalt and various measures of intelligence. Validity coefficients in these studies ranged from −.19 to −.60, with a median validity coefficient of −.22, which indicates poor prediction of intellectual functioning, and thus directly contradicts Koppitz's (1975) claim that "the Bender Gestalt can be used with some degree of confidence as a short nonverbal intelligence test for young children" (p. 47). By definition, a correlation of −.22 does not inspire a high degree of confidence and indicates that the Bender Gestalt (scored according to Koppitz) does not adequately measure the construct of intelligence in even the broadest and most liberal interpretation of that concept. As discussed in chapter 6, there are more valid ways of measuring intelligence than the Bender Gestalt.

Summary

The Bender Gestalt is by far the most frequently used test of perceptual-motor functioning, and, because of its simplicity and ease of administration, it is also one of the most frequently misused and abused tests. The reliability of the Bender Gestalt is too low for making any kind of placement decision, yet the test is often inappropriately used to diagnose children as brain damaged, perceptually handicapped, or emotionally disturbed (Salvia & Ysseldyke, 1991). Validity of the Bender Gestalt is likewise not well established. It has not been demonstrated that the test measures the construct of "visual-motor integration," and it has been found to be a very poor predictor of academic achievement and intelligence. In summary, the Bender Gestalt is, in the words of Koppitz (1975), "one of the most overrated, most misunderstood, and most maligned tests currently in use" (p. 2).

Developmental Test of Visual-Motor Integration

Overview and Purpose

Like the Bender Gestalt, the Developmental Test of Visual-Motor Integration (VMI) (Beery, 1982) is a test that requires a child to copy geometric designs from stimulus cards and is scored on a correct/incorrect basis for each design. The VMI is designed for children between the ages of 4 and 13 years and is similar in many respects to the Bender Gestalt.

Standardization Sample and Norms

The VMI was standardized in 1981 on approximately 3,000 children between the ages of 3 years and 19 years. Like the Bender Gestalt, little data are reported in the manual to suggest that the normative sample for the VMI was representative of the U.S. population on variables such as race, geographic region, socioeconomic status, or occupational status of parents.

Data Obtained

The VMI utilizes four types of scores: raw scores, standard scores, age equivalents, and percentile ranks. Standard scores for the VMI are expressed as scale scores having a mean of 10 and a standard deviation of 3.

Reliability and Validity

The VMI manual reports data on three types of reliability: *interrater reliability, test-retest reliability,* and *internal consistency reliability.* Unfortunately, all reliability data reported in the manual are based on an earlier edition of the VMI (1964). Interrater reliabilities for the VMI are similar in magnitude to those of the Bender Gestalt, ranging from approximately .60 to .99 with a median interrater reliability coefficient of .93. Test-retest reliability, or stability, coefficients ranged from about .60 to .90 with a median stability coefficient of approximately .80. The median internal consistency reliability for the VMI was approximately .79.

Few data are reported in the manual to support the validity of the VMI as a test of visual-motor integration. Like the reliability data, all validity data reported in the 1982 VMI manual are based on the 1964 version of the test. The VMI does show a higher correlation with academic achievement (reading) than does the Bender Gestalt ($r = .50$) and intelligence (median $r = .48$).

Summary

The VMI is designed to be a test of visual-motor integration like the Bender Gestalt. There are many similarities between the VMI and the Bender Gestalt in terms of administration, scoring, and interpretation. The VMI shares with the Bender Gestalt the dubious honor of having an inadequately described and represented standardization sample and a paucity of empirical data attesting to the validity of the test. One advantage the VMI has over the Bender Gestalt is its reliability which tends to be somewhat higher.

Goldman-Fristoe-Woodcock Test of Auditory Discrimination

Overview and Purpose

The Goldman-Fristoe-Woodcock Test of Auditory Discrimination, or GFW (Goldman, Fristoe, & Woodcock, 1970), was designed as a measure of speech-sound discrimination skills in persons between the ages of four years and adulthood. The GFW has two subtests: (a) Quiet Subtest and (b) Noise Subtest. Both are individually administered by tape recordings. A subject is presented with four pictures and must select the one that corresponds to the word spoken on the tape. Pictures depict items with names that have some sound similarity but at least one major sound difference.

Standardization Sample and Norms

The GFW was standardized on 745 subjects ranging from 3 to 84 years of age. The standardization sample was not geographically representative of the U.S. population, with subjects coming from only three states (New Jersey, Minnesota, and Tennessee). The manual presents no information regarding their ethnicity, socioeconomic status, or other important demographic characteristics. In short, the GFW norms are based on an unrepresentative sample.

Data Obtained

Scoring is straightforward and consists of counting the number of errors made by the examinee. Error scores are converted to T scores, which have a mean of 50 and a standard deviation of 10 for each subtest. The manual also reports a supplementary method scoring that differentiates errors by certain kinds of words, such as voiced and unvoiced sounds. Separate norms using this method are not presented.

Reliability and Validity

The manual reports internal consistency reliability coefficients of .79 for the Quiet Subtest and .68 for the Noise Subtest. Coefficients of this magnitude suggest some problem in internal consistency, which in turn suggests that error contributes a great deal to scores obtained on the GFW.

The manual indicates that these low coefficients are due to the relatively few number of items on each subtest. Although this is a statistically viable explanation, it does not increase confidence in the test. Furthermore, the small number of items calls into question the adequacy of content sampling, which then leads one to question the content validity of the test. Validity evidence for the GFW reported in the manual shows correlations of .60 (Quiet Subtest) and .52 (Noise Subtest) with the Stanford Binet Intelligence Scale, but lower correlations with measures of receptive language such as the Peabody Picture Vocabulary Test (.15 for the Quiet Subtest and .00 for the Noise Subtest). In our opinion, the GFW does not adequately discriminate individuals who have good or poor auditory discrimination abilities.

Summary

The GFW is a poorly standardized, technically inadequate measure of auditory discrimination abilities under quiet and noise background conditions. Although a noise subtest does represent a more ecologically valid condition for testing learning because most classrooms have some background noise at most times, the background noise for the GFW appears to be a school cafeteria. The GFW should not be used to make classification or placement decisions because of poor normative characteristics, low reliability, and a dearth of validity data.

Illinois Test of Psycholinguistic Abilities

Overview and Purpose
The Illinois Test of Psycholinguistic Abilities (ITPA) (Kirk, McCarthy, & Kirk, 1968) is designed to measure the ability to understand, process, and produce verbal and nonverbal language in children between the ages of 2 years, 4 months, and 10 years, 3 months. Although it was partially designed to represent a linguistic theoretical model, Caroll (1972) stated that "it requires some stretching of meaning to call the ITPA a measure of psycholinguistic abilities" (p. 42).

The ITPA is composed of 10 regularly administered individual tests and two optional subtests. According to the technical manual (Paraskevopoulos & Kirk, 1969), the psycholinguistic model on which the test is based attempts to relate those functions whereby the intentions of one person are transmitted either verbally or nonverbally to another person (expressive language) and the other person receives and interprets these intentions (receptive language). Specifically, the ITPA was designed to measure an individual's ability to comprehend, remember, and express stimuli that are presented visually or auditorily. The ITPA is presented in this chapter because its 11 subtests represent a number of abilities measured by many other tests of perceptual-motor functioning. The 11 ITPA subtests and examples of items from each are presented in table 12.2.

Standardization Sample and Norms
The ITPA was standardized on 963 children between the ages of 2 years, 7 months, and 10 years, 1 month. The standardization sample was not geographically representative of the United States because all subjects came from around Urbana, Illinois, and Madison, Wisconsin. The authors stated in the technical manual that children were primarily selected on the basis of "the practical requirements of accessibility and because of suitability to the requirements of being middle class communities" (Paraskevopoulos & Kirk, 1969, p. 57). This lack of representation is a serious problem because curriculum emphasis in local schools can easily affect ITPA scores, and research indicates that ITPA scores are clearly modified by instruction.

The standardization sample included only those children demonstrating "average intellectual functioning," "average school achievement," and "average characteristics of personal-social adjustment." This is perplexing, however, because the ITPA was designed as a diagnostic instrument primarily for children encountering learning difficulties. Yet because these

Table 12.2   Description and Examples of the ITPA Subtests

Auditory Reception: This test assesses the child's ability to derive meaning from verbally presented material. Since the receptive rather than the expressive process is being sampled, the response throughout is kept at the simple level of a "yes" or "no," either verbally or with a nod or shake of the head. The test contains 50 items.

Typical Items

"Do dogs eat?"

"Do dials yawn.?"

"Do carpenters kneel?"

Auditory Association: This test taps the child's ability to relate concepts presented orally. In this test, the requirements of the auditory receptive process and the vocal expressive process are minimal, while the organizing process of manipulating linguistic symbols in a meaningful way is tested by verbal analogies of increasing difficulty. There are 42 orally presented sentence completion items.

Typical Items

"I cut with a saw; I pound with a _____."

"A dog has hair; a fish has _____."

Visual Association: The organizing process in this channel is tapped by a picture association test with which to assess the child's ability to relate concepts presented visually. The child is presented with a single stimulus picture surrounded by four optional pictures, one of which is associated with the stimulus picture. The child is asked, "What goes with this?" (pointing to the stimulus picture). "Which one of these?" (pointing to the four optional pictures). The test contains 20 items of the simpler form and 22 visual analogies.

Verbal Expression: The purpose of this test is to assess the ability of the child to express his [sic] own concepts vocally. The child is shown four familiar objects, one at a time (a ball, a block, an envelope, and a button), and is asked, "Tell me all about this." The score is the number of discrete, relevant, and approximately factual concepts expressed.

Manual Expression: This test taps the child's ability to express ideas manually. This ability is assessed by a gestural manipulation test. In this test, 15 pictures of common objects are shown to the child one at a time and he [sic] is asked to, "Show me what to do with a _____." The child is required to pantomime the appropriate action, such as dialing a telephone or playing a guitar.

Grammatic Closure: This test assesses the child's ability to make use of the redundancies of oral language in acquiring automatic habits for handling syntax and grammatic inflections. There are 33 orally presented items accompanied by pictures which portray the content of the verbal expressions. The pictures are included to avoid contaminating the test with difficulty in the receptive process. Each verbal item consists of a complete statement followed by an incomplete statement to be finished by the child. The examiner points to the appropriate picture as he [sic] reads the given statements.

Typical Items

"Here is a dog; here are two _____."

"This dog likes to bark; here he is _____."

Table 12.2—*Continued*

Auditory Closure: This is basically a test of the organizing process at the automatic level. It assesses the child's ability to fill in missing parts which were deleted in auditory presentation and to produce a complete word. There are 30 items ranging in difficulty from easy words to more difficult ones.

Typical Items

"airpla /"

"ta / le / oon"

" / ype / iter"

Sound Blending: This test provides another means of assessing the organizing process at the automatic level in the auditory-vocal channel. The sounds of a word are spoken singly at half-second intervals, and the child is asked to tell what the word is. At one end of the scale it has been made applicable to younger children by including pictures, thus making the task less open-ended. At the upper levels the test has been extended by including nonsense words.

Typical Items

"type(pause)wri(pause)iter"

"ta(pause)ble"

"wa(pause)ter(pause)me(pause)llon"

Visual Closure: This test assesses the child's ability to identify a common object from an incomplete visual presentation. There are four scenes, presented separately, each containing 14 or 15 examples of a specified object. The objects are seen in varying degrees of concealment. The child is asked to locate and point to all examples of a particular object within 30 seconds.

Typical Items

"Find as many fish as you can."

"Find as many hammers and nails as you can."

Auditory Sequential Memory: This test assesses the child's ability to reproduce from memory sequences of digits increasing in length from two to eight digits. This test differs from the Digit Span subtest from the WISC-R in that the digits are presented at the rate of two per second instead of one per second. The more rapid presentation makes the task easier, which is necessary for two- and three-year-old children.

Typical Items

"4-2"

"3-1-7"

"7-4-8-5-1-3-6-2"

Visual Sequential Memory: This test assesses the child's ability to reproduce sequences of nonmeaningful figures from memory. The child is shown each sequence of figures for five seconds and then is asked to put corresponding chips of figures in the same order. The sequences increase in length from two to eight figures.

Source: Adapted from J. N. Paraskevopoulos and S. A. Kirk, *The Development and Psychometric Characteristics of the Revised Illinois Test of Psycholinguistic Abilities,* 1969, University of Illinois Press, Urbana.

children were systematically excluded from the standardization sample, there are no scores in the sample with whom the scores of children with learning problems can be compared. In fact, children's learning problems may well be diagnosed as being more serious than they actually are because their scores are being compared to a sample with atypically high achievement scores and cognitive functioning. In addition, because only middle class children were included in the standardization sample, the test is vulnerable to claims of bias against lower class and minority children.

In summary, the ITPA norms are based on a sample that is highly restrictive in terms of geographic region, socioeconomic status, minority group representation, and the inclusion of the full range of scores for comparison purposes, particularly of children with learning difficulties. The ITPA is a poorly standardized test. In fact, the standardization of the ITPA could serve as a handy compendium for violations of virtually every principle of standardization and norms construction discussed in chapter 5 of this text.

Data Obtained

Three types of derived scores can be obtained from the ITPA: (a) scale scores for each subtest, with a mean of 36 and a standard deviation of 6; (b) the psycholinguistic ages (PLAs) for each subtest, which are similar to a mental age or age equivalent; and (c) psycholinguistic quotients (PLQs), which are ratio scores (PLA/CA $\times$ 100), similar to ratio IQ scores. There are a number of statistical problems with the use of PLAs and PLQs, including unequal standard deviations at each age group, which render scores incomparable from one age to another. For example, a PLQ of 90 at age 4 represents the 50th percentile, whereas this same score at age 10 years is at the 31st percentile. Chapter 4 of this text provides a more comprehensive discussion of the problems in using age and grade equivalents and ratio IQ scores.

The technical manual also provides tables for *intraindividual* comparisons in which performances on a given subtest can be compared to the median performance over all ITPA subtests. However, the reliabilities of the subtests are so low that it is unwise to make comparisons among or between them and the total score.

Reliability and Validity

The manual extensively presents reliability data, including test-retest, internal consistency, and interscorer reliability. Table 12.3 shows median internal consistency and five-month test-retest reliability coefficients across all age levels for all subtests. As can be seen in this table, the stability of the majority of subtests for the scale is less than adequate. The internal consistency reliabilities are, for the most part, below acceptable standards, with Verbal Expression (r = .65), Visual Closure (r = .60), and Auditory Closure (r = .65) the least internally consistent subtests. In sum, the ITPA

Table 12.3   Median Internal Consistency and Five-Month Test-Retest Reliability Coefficients for ITPA Subtests[a]

Subtest	Internal Consistency	Test-Retest
Auditory Reception	.88	.46
Visual Reception	.80	.29
Auditory Association	.80	.67
Visual Association	.79	.45
Verbal Expression	.65	.47
Manual Expression	.76	.46
Grammatic Closure	.67	.61
Auditory Closure	.65	.44
Sound Blending	.85	.47
Visual Closure	.60	.63
Auditory Sequential Memory	.82	.74
Visual Sequential Memory	.74	.31
Composite	.90	.77

Source: Adapted from J. N. Paraskevopoulos and S. A. Kirk, *The Development and Psychometric Characteristics of the Revised Illinois Test of Psycholinguistic Abilities,* 1969, University of Illinois Press, Urbana.
[a]Coefficients are collapsed across age levels and are not corrected for restriction in intelligence range.

does not possess an adequate level of reliability on which to base either diagnostic or placement decisions for children. Most subtests are neither internally consistent nor sufficiently stable to ensure accurate measurement of the skills purportedly assessed by the scale.

The ITPA technical manual is virtually devoid of validity data. Thus, little evidence exists to support the statement that the test measures the construct of psycholinguistic abilities. As Caroll (1972) pointed out, almost half of the subtests could be completed by individuals who had never acquired *any* language system. Calling the ITPA a measure of psycholinguistic ability is a misnomer, because it measures only a small fraction of skills that might be considered linguistic. For example, reading, writing, and spelling are clearly language (linguistic) skills, but they were excluded from the ITPA on the premise that the scale was designed to measure basic cognitive skills not attained through schooling.

The technical manual presents no evidence for the criterion-related validity of the ITPA in predicting academic achievement. The ITPA has moderately positive correlations with Stanford-Binet IQ scores, although these correlations may be depressed because of the restricted range of the sample tested.

Summary

The ITPA is a poorly standardized and questionable instrument for measuring psycholinguistic abilities of children. The subtests have relatively low reliabilities and the test's validity has not been clearly established. The unrepresentative standardization sample creates a problem analogous to a situation in which one wishes to define shortness on the basis of a group of persons who are of average height or tall. If you only measure persons who are of average height or tall (relative to the general population), then average height persons will be defined as short. Given this fallacious means of norms construction coupled with the unreliability of ITPA subtests and the paucity of validity data, the ITPA should not be used for placement or diagnostic decisions for children with learning problems.

➲ *Perceptual-Motor Training*

As mentioned at the beginning of this chapter, many educators and psychologists believe that a direct relationship exists between perceptual-motor development and academic achievement. Between 1936 and 1970, perceptual-motor programming unquestionably became the most widely used method of assessing and teaching children with learning problems (Hallahan & Cruickshank, 1973). A spate of tests were developed to diagnose perceptual-motor problems and to generate perceptual-motor training programs to remediate these problems (Wallace & Larsen, 1978).

A basic tenet of perceptual theory is that impairment in perceptual-motor skills will significantly interfere with learning, especially learning to read. Underlying this assumption is the hypothesis that there is a strong relationship between measures of perceptual-motor skills and academic achievement. In fact, however, there is *not* a strong relationship between perceptual-motor skills (as measured by tests of perceptual-motor functioning) and academic achievement (as measured by tests of academic achievement) (Wallace & Larsen, 1978).

Studies investigating the relationships between auditory perception skills (Hammill & Larsen, 1974b), visual perception skills (Larsen & Hammill, 1975), and psycholinguistic processes (Hammill & Larsen, 1974a) with academic achievement have been extensively reviewed. Collectively, these studies provide little empirical data to support the assumption that perceptual ability is related to academic achievement (see Focus on Research).

Myers and Hammill (1976) reviewed 105 studies and found little support for the continued use of perceptual-motor training to facilitate academic achievement of school-age children. We must therefore ask what problem one is trying to solve when perceptual-motor tests are administered? We have no simple answer to this question, although we have several hypotheses. Perhaps the use of perceptual-motor tests is promulgated by the testing industry. A basic principle of marketing is that as long as a product is kept before the public's eye, it will be consumed. A brief perusal of testing catalogues suggests that testing companies are not decreasing their marketing of perceptual-motor tests.

Another hypothesis is that some individuals want to attribute learning difficulties to causes intrinsic to the person (e.g., a perceptual-motor dysfunction). Using this logic, one is able to assign a label to a problem that becomes an explanation for the existence of the problem. Thus, if the inability of some children to read, compute, or use language appropriately is attributed to "perceptual-motor deficits" or "psycholinguistic processing dysfunction," assessment of these children will focus upon perceptual and processing abilities that are the presumed "causes" of poor achievement. Perceptual-motor assessment, therefore, continues in spite of what we consider to be overwhelming empirical evidence to the contrary (for a review, see Myers & Hammill, 1976).

Finally, we believe many persons are simply unaware of the research findings regarding perceptual-motor and psycholinguistic training programs. The conceptual appeal of these programs coupled with the simplicity of assessing certain perceptual-motor skills may lead many into pseudoexplanations of a child's poor achievement. In this sense, saying something (even though it may be inaccurate) about the cause of Johnny's inability to read is less aversive than saying "I don't know."

➡️ *The Level of Inference Problem in Assessment*

Our review of perceptual-motor assessment has been negative for what we consider to be obvious reasons that pertain to the poor normative samples of most perceptual-motor tests, the relatively poor reliability and validity evidence for these measures, and the lack of a demonstrated relationship between perceptual-motor skills and academic achievement. A major problem with all of these measures, in our opinion, is the high **level of inference** required to interpret performance on these instruments. Level of inference refers to the relationship between behavior actually observed and the interpretation or meaning attributed to that behavior. The level of inference can range on a continuum from simple, straightforward, precise descriptions of what was seen or observed (no inference) to quite abstract and remote interpretations of the meaning of that behavior (high inference).

Figure 12.2 provides examples of the different levels of inference that might be used with Danny's copying of a design from the Bender Gestalt. Each of the interpretations has appeared in the literature on the Bender Gestalt or similar perceptual-motor assessment devices. The level of inference varies from a straightforward description, "Danny could not accurately copy these geometric figures" (Level I), to a suggestion of underlying personality dynamics or conclusions about emotional status, "Danny's psychosexual stage of development appears to be primitive . . ." (Level V).

Focus on
Research

Recent Attempts at Ability Training

Special educators have experienced a great deal of difficulty in deciding how best to teach problem learners. Logic would appear to indicate that if one could identify the learner's strengths and weaknesses, one could teach to the strengths and avoid the weaknesses. Unfortunately, research has not supported this process.

Educators and psychologists attempting to identify learner strengths and weaknesses began to talk about underlying learning processes or abilities such as visual sequential memory, auditory discrimination, and visual closure. However, these and other, similar so-called abilities merely represent reifications of constructs. That is, these terms do not represent anything concrete but are merely abstractions. When used often enough, these abstractions begin to be discussed and used as if they were real entities (e.g., "she is an auditory learner," or "he needs training to increase his auditory discrimination").

This approach to assessment and teaching is called the ability training model. It rests on the assumptions that learning "abilities" exist, that they can be reliably measured, and that they can be enhanced by training. Extensive research over the past fifteen years, however, offers little support for these assumptions (Hammill & Larsen, 1974b; Myers & Hammill, 1982; Ysseldyke, 1973; Ysseldyke & Mirkin, 1982). First, there is little evidence that these so-called abilities even exist. Second, attempts to measure these "abilities" have resulted in some of the most psychometrically inadequate tests on the market today (see the test reviews in this chapter). Thus there is little proof that these "abilities," even if they do exist, can be reliably measured. Finally, there is little evidence that training these "abilities" can improve school performance.

A basic assumption of the ability training model is the existence of aptitude by treatment interactions (ATIs) (Cronbach & Snow, 1979). ATI research has focused on the notion that individuals with certain aptitudes will behave differently in certain treatments (i.e., teaching strategies) than in others. For example, the statement that a student is a "visual learner" is a statement about a student's aptitude. The statement that the child needs a "whole-word" reading program is a treatment statement. The statement that visual learners will learn more in a whole-word reading program than in a phonics-based program is a statement about an aptitude by treatment interaction.

In special education there is widespread popular belief in the presence of ATIs. Although logic would seem to indicate that ATIs exist, empirical research on teaching has not supported this. Cronbach and Snow (1979) comprehensively reviewed ATI research and concluded that there are no solidly established ATI relations. Thus the age-old adage applies here: "I am an empiricist because logic is only as strong as its assumptions." The assumptions on which ATIs are based are faulty. As such, teaching strategies based upon ATIs will necessarily be faulty as well.

It would be difficult to find a special educator or school psychologist who does not talk in terms of "aptitudes" or "abilities." The use of these terms is widespread to the point of being epidemic. Although this terminology is a convenient way to label behavior, the terms represent mentalistic fictions used as pseudoexplanations of a child's difficulty in learning academic materials.

There are a number of problems with highly inferential interpretations of performance on perceptual-motor tests. One, little empirical data supports the inferences made from such tests (Reschly & Gresham, 1989). Two, the alleged variables involved (such as processing and perceptual dysfunctions) cannot be directly observed nor is there hard evidence that the presumed condition actually exists. Three, in virtually all instances there are no treatments or interventions that directly deal with underlying problems of academic deficiencies. We do not deny that individuals with severe neurological problems may draw "poor" Bender designs, but we cannot find any clear-cut evidence that knowing about Bender errors helps one to teach children with learning difficulties.

➡️ *Direct Assessment of Perceptual-Motor Skills*

Tests of perceptual-motor functioning have a number of conceptual and empirical problems and rely upon the use of highly inferential interpretations, which are often unjustified. What are the alternatives to this type of assessment? Our recommendation is relatively simple and straightforward. We suggest the direct assessment of skills with stimuli or materials that the child must use in the classroom setting. We also suggest that the child's performance using these stimuli or materials be interpreted using Level I inference depicted in figure 12.2. For example, we may be interested in whether Danny has adequate visual-motor ability. We could assess this in basically two ways. One, we could present geometric figures (e.g., Bender Gestalt designs) and ask him to copy them from cards. Two, we could present numerals and letters and ask Danny to copy them either from the board or from a workbook. Which strategy would have the most direct relevance for classroom performance? We would obviously opt for the latter, because numerals and letters, not irrelevant geometric designs, are the stimuli with which children must become proficient.

Another example may be instructive. We have heard interpretations of perceptual-motor performance such as this: "Danny had difficulty in

---

Figure 12.2 Five Levels of Inference for Danny's Bender

Danny's Bender

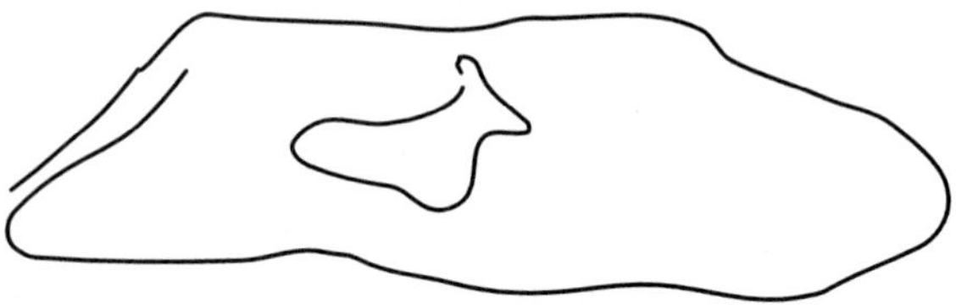

Level I: A straightforward description of behavior (e.g., "Danny could not accurately copy these geometric figures.")

Level II: Naming the skill that presumably underlies the behavior (e.g., "Danny has poor visual-motor skills.")

Level III: Suggestion of immaturity or developmental lag (e.g., "Danny's drawing appears to be immature, suggesting that his overall pattern of development is uneven.")

Level IV: Conclusions about underlying neurological status (e.g., "Danny appears to have neurological dysfunction, particularly in the right parietal lobe of the brain.")

Level V: Indication of underlying personality dynamics or conclusions about emotional status (e.g., "Danny's psychosexual stage of development appears to be rather primitive in view of his inability to correctly reproduce a relatively simple geometric figure that is believed to evoke information on psychosexual status or development.")

---

reproducing the Bender designs as he achieved a developmental age of only five years. His scale score on the Coding subtest of the WISC-III corroborates his poor visual-motor abilities. Taken together, these performances would suggest Danny will have great difficulty in copying from the board and in performing written work at his desk such as reading and math skill sheets.''

We consider this type of interpretation to be superfluous. If one wanted to make a prediction about Danny's ability to (a) copy from the board and (b) complete reading and math skill sheets, it would seem logical to assess these behaviors directly. To do this, we might take Danny into his classroom (after school or at recess), have him sit in his assigned seat, and ask him to copy from the board. We could also ask Danny's teacher for representative reading and math skill sheets and ask him to complete these tasks in his classroom. If Danny performed these tasks adequately, what would be the point of knowing his scores on the

Bender Gestalt or the WISC-III Coding subtest? Our interest in Danny is not whether he can copy meaningless designs but whether he can perform the tasks required of him in the classroom.

Suppose that Danny could not copy from the board or complete the skill sheets. Does this mean that the Bender Gestalt and WISC-III performances support the conclusion that a visual-motor problem exists? Not necessarily. Our interpretation would be consistent with the Level I inference presented in figure 12.2. That is, "Danny had difficulty in copying geometric designs, copying from the board, and completing reading and math skill sheets." Of course, one will never have to deal with the problem of inconsistencies in performances on perceptual-motor tests and direct assessment if one utilizes only one type of assessment strategy. We strongly prefer to use direct assessment of academic skills in the classroom setting, using the stimuli and materials that the child confronts daily.

The potential of direct assessment of so-called perceptual-motor skills is virtually limitless and depends on the nature of the materials being used in the classroom for a particular child. The chief advantage of this form of assessment is that it has direct relevance for that child in the classroom. We provide a much more detailed discussion of direct assessment approaches in chapter 17, "Curriculum-Based Assessment."

Chapter Summary

The available research suggests that assessment based on a traditional perceptual-motor model has neither high reliability nor validity and has little to do with diagnosing or remediating learning problems. Moreover, better methods of assessment have been developed to accomplish the same goals that perceptual-motor tests purportedly fulfill. This chapter has addressed the widespread use of tests of perceptual-motor functioning and the belief that direct assessment using lower inference techniques is preferable.

Tests of perceptual-motor functioning have little or nothing to do with the problem-solving process. That is, stating that a child has a deficit in visual-motor perception, auditory discrimination, or psycholinguistic processing does not lead to the design, implementation, or evaluation of interventions to solve a child's academic difficulties.

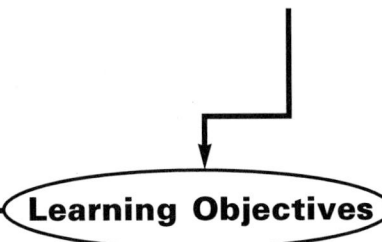

Chapter 13

Behavior Rating Scales and Inventories

Learning Objectives

1. To know the various behavior rating scales available for assessing the social skills and problem behavior for children and adolescents.

2. To be familiar with the psychometric and normative characteristics of various behavior rating scales.

3. To know the similarities and differences among behavior rating scales and the content that is assessed.

4. To understand the role of situational influences on behavior and the effects these influences have on the agreement among various informants.

5. To synthesize diverse information from multiple informants to identify children in need of intervention services and to isolate target behaviors.

Teachers' judgments of students' classroom social behavior and academic competence are among the primary bases for referrals for psychoeducational services (Hoge, 1983). Teacher and parent judgments are summary, evaluative conclusions based on samples of behavior observed over a period of time. Behavior rating scales and inventories are the most common methods for quantifying teacher and parent judgments (Carlson & Lahey, 1983; Edelbrock, 1988; Gresham, 1985).

This chapter presents the rationale behind the use of behavior rating scales and inventories to assess children's social and academic behaviors. Specific behavior rating scales will be discussed and advantages and disadvantages of each will be described. More importantly, the intelligent use of behavior rating scale information in the problem-solving process will be described with specific recommendations regarding how to get the most information out of behavior ratings from parents and teachers. Before discussing the rationale and method of behavior rating scale assessment, we present a list of assumptions that should be kept in mind when using and interpreting behavior rating scale information.

➡ *Assumptions Regarding Behavior Rating Scales*

Assumption 1: Ratings are summaries of observations of the relative frequency of specific behaviors.

One student may exhibit cooperative behavior three times a day, whereas a second student performs the same behavior once a day. Although these students exhibit different rates of behavior, when their teacher is asked to rate how often the behavior occurs, the teacher may characterize both students on a rating scale as exhibiting the behavior with equal frequency. In short, the precision of measurement with rating scales is relative, not absolute, and needs to be supplemented by more direct methods of assessment such as direct observation procedures discussed in chapter 15.

Assumption 2: Ratings of behavior are evaluative judgments affected by the environment and a rater's standards for behavior.

An individual's behavior may change depending on the situation. Such variability has led researchers to characterize many behaviors as situationally specific rather than as traits or permanent characteristics of the individual (Achenbach, McConaughy, & Howell, 1987; Kazdin, 1979). In addition to environmental influences, behaviors deemed important in one setting may be largely determined by the standards of behavior established by the adult or adults who regulate the setting. Because both the rater's standards for behavior and the situation will influence the actual rating, one should use multiple raters (e.g., teachers, parents, and students) in the assessment process. These multiple raters observe the student's behavior in many situations and settings. The composite picture of a student given two or three raters may be clearer and more accurate than the picture obtained by a single rater.

Assumption 3: The social validity of behaviors assessed and possibly treated should be understood.

Socially valid behaviors are those behaviors that society considers important, encourages, and reinforces. The social validity of a behavior is reflected in the *importance* attributed to it by society or adults who regulate specific settings in which the child functions. Social validity can also refer to the *tolerance* of a given behavior in a given setting. Problem behaviors such as fighting, inattention, disruptive behavior, shyness, and so forth are tolerated to different degrees by different persons in different settings. For example, being quiet and shy may be tolerated in church but not in situations requiring verbal communication and social interaction. Being assertive may be tolerated by parents at home but not by teachers at school. Thus, in interpreting and using behavior ratings, it is important to consider the tolerance levels of certain behavior held by raters in specific settings.

Assumption 4: Multiple raters of the child's behavior may agree only moderately.

This statement is based on three facts. First, many behaviors are situationally specific. Second, all measures of behavior are made with some degree of error. Third, rating scales use rather simple frequency response categories for quantifying behaviors that may vary widely in their frequency, intensity, and duration. The work of Achenbach et al. (1987) provides empirical support for this position. Moderate agreement should not be taken as an indictment of the use of multiple raters. Rather, it suggests that different raters perceive behaviors in various settings differently. Collectively, such ratings may tell us more about a child than only one rater from one setting.

These four assumptions regarding behavior rating scales represent important considerations in using this type of assessment methodology. It is important to recognize that the results one obtains from behavior rating scales are joint reflections of actual child behavior and the behavior standards and tolerance levels of persons completing the ratings (Edelbrock, 1988; Gresham & Elliott, 1990).

➡ *Technical Considerations in Behavior Rating Scales*

How are behavior rating scales constructed? The construction of behavior rating scales varies according to a number of factors, including what is to be assessed, response scaling, how items are selected, scoring, and standardization (Edelbrock, 1988). Each of these technical considerations will be described briefly to give readers a flavor of how behavior rating scales are constructed and the various criteria used in constructing different scales.

Content Assessed

Behavior rating scales assess a variety of content areas, including childhood psychopathology, social skills, depression, hyperactivity, anxiety, and many others. Some behavior rating scales assess a number of the aforementioned areas and other scales focus on only one or two content areas.

Items for behavior rating scales may come from a variety of sources. These sources might include clinical case records, experts (e.g., psychologists, psychiatrists, mental health professionals, etc.), school records, and the research literature. These items may be revised, rewritten, or discarded based on the readability and clarity for rating purposes. Edelbrock (1988) indicated that good items for behavior rating scales are written in terms of overt, easily observable events, behaviors, or characteristics.

Scaling

Behaviors on behavior rating scales must be quantified in some way to have some meaning. Response scaling may include 2-point (e.g., Yes/No; Agree/Disagree; Present/Absent), 3-point (e.g., Never/ Sometimes/Frequently), 4-point, and even 5-point scales.

As mentioned earlier, behavior rating scales attempt to measure behavior *relatively* rather than in *absolute* terms. Raters are typically not asked to report on the specific number of times a given behavior occurs or an estimate of its duration or intensity.

Building a Behavior Rating Scale

There are two basic approaches to constructing or building behavior rating scales. The first approach is called the **empirical** approach because the final items appearing on the scale are selected on empirical or quantitative grounds. Most behavior rating scales are constructed on the basis of a statistical procedure known as **factor analysis.** In factor analysis, items belonging to a factor (or scale) are retained if they correlate highly with that factor or scale. Items showing little or no correlation with a particular factor or scale are either deleted from the final version or are moved to another factor with which they highly correlate.

The second approach to building a behavior rating scale is termed the **rational** approach. In a rational approach, behaviors on rating scales are selected on the basis of theoretical notions of what behaviors tend to co-occur. There is no basis, other than rational considerations, for including or excluding specific behaviors from behavior rating scales constructed in this manner. Edelbrock (1983) indicated that behavior rating scales constructed using a rational approach have less descriptive validity and less predictive power than empirically derived behavior rating scales.

Normative Characteristics

There is a great deal of variability in the standardization and normative characteristics of behavior rating scales. Some behavior rating scales have no normative data and, as such, are limited in the types of comparisons that can be made. Behavior rating scales that do have normative data vary in terms of how the norms are stratified. For example, scales may be stratified according to sex, age, disability group membership, or a combination of demographic characteristics.

The decision of whether to stratify behavior rating scales according to certain demographic variables depends on whether the variable influences the scores obtained from behavior rating scales. Thus, if sex, age, or disability status influence scores derived from behavior rating scales, then the scale is typically stratified according to these variables. Chapter 5 provides a more complete discussion of norming and standardization of tests.

Informant Considerations

A key issue in using behavior rating scales is who the informant should be in completing the rating scale. Typically, informants are teachers, parents, and children themselves. Some behavior rating scales are for teachers only, others for parents only, others for children only, and still others utilize all three informants.

Some informants are in a better position to rate certain behaviors than others. For instance, teachers are in a better position to rate attention span, classroom behaviors, social interactions in school settings, and the like. Parents, on the other hand, are likely to be more knowledgeable about behaviors such as sleep disturbances, sibling interactions, mealtime behaviors and so forth.

The best practice in using behavior rating scales is to employ multiple informants to rate the same child's behavior (Achenbach et al., 1987; Edelbrock, 1983; Gresham & Elliott, 1990). Multiple informants can provide a more complete view of a child's behavior across situations and settings. By using multiple informants, one can discern which behaviors tend to occur across a variety of situations and which behaviors appear to be situationally specific. This information can be of use in classification decisions as well as for intervention planning.

➡ *Review of Selected Behavior Rating Scales*

Social Skills Rating System

Overview and Purpose

The Social Skills Rating System (SSRS) (Gresham & Elliott, 1990) provides a broad, multirater assessment of student social behaviors that can affect teacher-student relations, peer acceptance, and academic performance. The SSRS documents the perceived frequency and importance of behaviors influencing the student's development of social competence and adaptive functioning at school and at home.

The SSRS components include three behavior rating forms (teacher, parent, and student versions) and an integrative assessment and intervention planning record. Teacher, parent, and student forms elicit information about a student from the viewpoint of the informant. Teacher and parent forms are available for three developmental levels: preschool, grades K through 6, and grades 7 through 12.

The SSRS uses teacher, parent, and student rating scales to sample three domains of *social skills, problem behavior,* and *academic competence.* There are five subscales within the Social Skills Scale:

1. *Cooperation,* which includes behaviors such as helping others, sharing materials, and complying with rules and directions;

2. *Assertion,* which includes behaviors such as asking others for information, introducing oneself, and responding to the actions of others;

3. *Responsibility,* which includes behaviors that demonstrate ability to communicate with adults and regard for property or work;

4. *Empathy,* which includes behaviors that show concern and respect for others' feelings and viewpoints; and

5. *Self-Control,* which includes behaviors that emerge in conflict situations, such as responding appropriately to teasing and in nonconflict situations that require taking turns and compromising.

There are three subscales on the Problem Behavior Scale:

1. *Externalizing Problems,* which are inappropriate behaviors involving verbal or physical aggression toward others, poor control of temper, and arguing;

2. *Internalizing Problems,* which are behaviors indicating sadness, anxiety, and poor self-esteem; and

3. *Hyperactivity,* which are those behaviors involving excessive movement, fidgeting, and impulsive reactions.

The Academic Competence domain concerns student academic functioning. This domain, as measured by the SSRS, consists of a small, yet critical, sample of relevant behaviors. Items are rated on a 5-point scale that corresponds to percentage clusters (1 = lowest 10%, 5 = highest 10%). This domain includes items measuring reading and mathematics performance, motivation, parental support, and general cognitive functioning. This scale appears on the teacher form at the elementary and secondary levels. Table 13.1 summarizes the scales and subscales of the SSRS across different informants and levels.

Standardization Sample and Norms

The SSRS was standardized on a national sample of 4,170 children using their self-ratings as well as ratings of children made by 1,027 parents and 259 teachers. The sampling plan was designed to obtain approximately equal numbers of male and female students and a sufficient number of

Table 13.1 SSRS Scales and Subscales across Forms, by Level

	Teacher Form			Parent Form			Student Form	
	Preschool Level	Elementary Level	Secondary Level	Preschool Level	Elementary Level	Secondary Level	Elementary Level	Secondary Level
Social Skills								
Cooperation	X	X	X	X	X	X	X	X
Assertion	X	X	X	X	X	X	X	X
Responsibility	–	–	–	X	X	X	–	–
Empathy	–	–	–	–	–	–	X	X
Self-Control	X	X	X	X	X	X	X	X
Problem Behaviors								
Externalizing	X	X	X	X	X	X	–	–
Internalizing	X	X	X	X	X	X	–	–
Hyperactivity	–	X	–	–	X	–	–	–
Academic Competence								
(No subscales)	–	X	X	–	–	–	–	–

X = Included on the form indicated.

From *Social Skills Rating System (SSRS)* by Frank M. Gresham and Stephen N. Elliott © 1990 American Guidance Service, Inc., 4201 Woodland Road, Circle Pines, Minnesota 55014–1796. All rights reserved.

students at each grade level to ensure response stability. Grade placement was used throughout the statistical analyses as a convenient and practical substitute for age.

The SSRS standardization sample was stratified according to sex, grade, ethnic representation, geographic region, and community size. The standardization sample contained 50.6 percent females and 49.4 percent males. Approximately 27 percent of the sample consisted of minority students (black, Hispanic, etc.) compared to about 31 percent minority population based on the U.S. Census. Approximately 12.4 percent of the sample was from the Northeast, 29.3 percent from the North Central region, 44.3 percent from the South, and 14 percent from the West. About 35 percent of the sample came from the central city, 47 percent from suburban or small town areas, and 18 percent from rural areas.

Data Obtained

Four types of scores are available from the SSRS: raw scores, descriptive behavior levels, standard scores, and percentile ranks. Raw scores are based on the results of 3-point ratings of social skills and problem behavior (0 = Never occurs, 1 = Sometimes occurs, and 3 = Very Often occurs) for the Social Skills and Problem Behavior Scales. All social skills items are rated on two dimensions: frequency and importance. The inclusion of an importance dimension allows raters to specify how important each social skill is for classroom success (teacher ratings), for their child's development (parent ratings), and for the student's relationships with others (student ratings). Figure 13.1 shows how these dual frequency and importance ratings are made on the SSRS. Raw scores for the teacher ratings of Academic Competence are based on 5-point ratings of students relative to his or her classmates (1 = Lowest 10%, 2 = Next Lowest 20%, 3 = Middle 40%, 4 = Next Highest 20%, and 5 = Highest 10%).

Subscale and scale raw scores are translated into behavior levels for the Social Skills and Problem Behavior Scales and Subscales. These behavior levels for each scale and subscale are labeled *Fewer* (one standard deviation or greater below the mean raw score of the standardization sample), *Average* (within one standard deviation above or below the standardization sample mean), and *More* (greater than one standard deviation above the standardization sample mean). Since each item on the Social Skills and Problem Behaviors Scales represents a specific behavior, the words Fewer, Average, and More can be directly interpreted as referring to amounts, or frequencies of behavior.

For the Academic Competence Scale, students who are viewed by teachers as more academically capable than the majority of students in the standardization sample are assigned an *Above Average* behavior level, whereas students who are viewed by teachers as less academically capable than the majority of students in the standardization sample are assigned a *Below Average* behavior level.

Figure 13.1 Portions of the Teacher Elementary Questionnaire Showing Frequency Ratings and Scoring of the Social Skills Subscales for Andrew, a Hypothetical Case

FOR OFFICE USE ONLY How Often?				Social Skills	How Often?			How Important?		
C	A	S			Never	Sometimes	Very Often	Not Important	Important	Critical
		1	1.	Controls temper in conflict situations with peers.	0	(1)	2	0	1	2
	1		2.	Introduces herself or himself to new people without being told.	0	(1)	2	0	1	2
	1		3.	Appropriately questions rules that may be unfair.	0	(1)	2	0	1	2
		0	4.	Compromises in conflict situations by changing own ideas to reach agreement.	(0)	1	2	0	1	2
		1	5.	Responds appropriately to peer pressure.	0	(1)	2	0	1	2
	1		6.	Says nice things about himself or herself when appropriate.	0	(1)	2	0	1	2
	1		7.	Invites others to join in activities.	0	(1)	2	0	1	2
1			8.	Uses free time in an acceptable way.	0	(1)	2	0	1	2
1			9.	Finishes class assignments within time limits.	0	(1)	2	0	1	2
	1		10.	Makes friends easily.	0	(1)	2	0	1	2
		0	11.	Responds appropriately to teasing by peers.	(0)	1	2	0	1	2
		0	12.	Controls temper in conflict situations with adults.	(0)	1	2	0	1	2
		1	13.	Receives criticism well.	0	(1)	2	0	1	2
	1		14.	Initiates conversations with peers.	0	(1)	2	0	1	2
1			15.	Uses time appropriately while waiting for help.	0	(1)	2	0	1	2
1			16.	Produces correct schoolwork.	0	(1)	2	0	1	2
4	6	3		SUMS OF HOW OFTEN COLUMNS						
C	A	S								

FOR OFFICE USE ONLY How Often?				Social Skills (cont.)	How Often?			How Important?		
C	A	S			Never	Sometimes	Very Often	Not Important	Important	Critical
	0		17.	Appropriately tells you when he or she thinks you have treated him or her unfairly.	(0)	1	2	0	1	2
		1	18.	Accepts peers' ideas for group activities.	0	(1)	2	0	1	2
	0		19.	Gives compliments to peers.	(0)	1	2	0	1	2
1			20.	Follows your directions.	0	(1)	2	0	1	2
2			21.	Puts work materials or school property away.	0	1	(2)	0	1	2
		1	22.	Cooperates with peers without prompting.	0	(1)	2	0	1	2
	1		23.	Volunteers to help peers with classroom tasks.	0	(1)	2	0	1	2
	2		24.	Joins ongoing activity or group without being told to do so.	0	1	(2)	0	1	2
		1	25.	Responds appropriately when pushed or hit by other children.	0	(1)	2	0	1	2
0			26.	Ignores peer distractions when doing class work.	(0)	1	2	0	1	2
1			27.	Keeps desk clean and neat without being reminded.	0	(1)	2	0	1	2
1			28.	Attends to your instructions.	0	(1)	2	0	1	2
1			29.	Easily makes transition from one classroom activity to another.	0	(1)	2	0	1	2
		1	30.	Gets along with people who are different.	0	(1)	2	0	1	2
6	3	4		SUMS OF HOW OFTEN COLUMNS						
C	A	S								

Standard scores with a mean of 100 and a standard deviation of 15 are available on the SSRS for the Social Skills, Problem Behaviors, and Academic Competence Scales. No standard scores are computed for the SSRS subscales. In addition, national percentile ranks are available for the SSRS scales (Social Skills, Problem Behaviors, and Academic Competence). Separate norms are used for males and females, for preschool, elementary, and secondary students, and for disabled and nondisabled students at the elementary level.

Reliability and Validity

The SSRS manual presents extensive evidence for the reliability and validity of the scales. Internal consistency estimates for the SSRS across all forms and levels yielded a median coefficient alpha for the Social Skills Scale of .90, whereas it was .84 for the Problem Behaviors Scale, and .95 for the Academic Competence Scale. Overall, these coefficients indicate a relatively high degree of scale homogeneity.

Subscale internal consistency estimates were lower and showed more variability across forms. Median correlations for the Social Skills and Problem Behaviors Subscales were all between .78 and .84. The median subscale internal consistency estimate was .81.

Test-retest reliability of the SSRS was measured by having samples of teachers, parents, and students from the elementary standardization sample rate the same students four weeks after their original standardization ratings. The temporal stability of teacher ratings was .85 for Social Skills, .84 for Problem Behaviors, and .93 for Academic Competence. Parent stability estimates were .87 for Social Skills and .65 for Problem Behaviors. The test-retest estimate for Student Social Skills ratings was .68.

The SSRS manual presents a number of studies investigating the construct, criterion-related, and content validity of the scale. For example, the SSRS Social Skills Scale and Subscales correlate highly with other measures of social skills such as the Walker-McConnell Scale of Social Competence and School Adjustment (Walker & McConnell, 1988) and the Social Behavior Assessment (Stephens, 1978). The SSRS Problem Behaviors Scale and Subscales show moderate to high correlations with the Child Behavior Checklist (Achenbach & Edelbrock, 1983) and the Harter Teacher Rating Scale (Harter, 1985). In addition, the SSRS Social Skills, Problem Behaviors, and Academic Scales reliably differentiate mildly disabled (e.g., learning disabled, behavior disordered, and mildly mentally disabled) students from nondisabled students.

Summary

The SSRS is a well-designed, well-constructed, and well-researched multi-rater approach for measuring social skills, problem behaviors, and academic competence for children between the ages of 3 to 18 years. The SSRS has a representative national standardization and extensive evidence

---

**Table 13.2 Examples of Narrow-Band Factors Under Broad-Band
Factors of the Child Behavior Checklist**

Externalizing Problems

Aggressive
Delinquent
Hyperactive
Sex Problems
Cruel

Internalizing Problems

Depressed
Social Withdrawal
Somatic Complaints
Uncommunicative
Schizoid
Obsessive Compulsive

---

for reliability and validity. One of the most attractive features of the SSRS is its utility in selecting target behaviors for intervention purposes, a feature uncommon to most behavior rating scales.

Child Behavior Checklist and Profile

Overview and Purpose

The Child Behavior Checklist (CBCL) (Achenbach & Edelbrock, 1983) is a 138-item scale designed to record the behavioral problems and social competencies of children ages 4 through 16 years. The CBCL is a multi-rater behavior rating scale that utilizes teacher, parent, and child ratings.

The CBCL consists of 118 items covering specific behavior problems that are rated by teachers, parents, and children (ages 11–18 years) on a 3-point scale (0 = Not True, 1 = Somewhat or Sometimes True, 2 = Very or Often True). Twenty additional items are not included on the CBCL, assessing social competence with respect to school performance, social relations, and the amount and quality of the child's participation in hobbies, activities, and sports. These later items will provide a global sense of school/community adjustment. The CBCL is scored as The Child Behavior Profile that provides a graphical representation of item responses across domains.

The CBCL assesses two *broad-band* domains of childhood and adolescent behavior problems and a number of *narrow-band* behavior problems contained within these broad-band domains. The broad-band factors are *Externalizing Problems* and *Internalizing Problems*. The various narrow-band factors under each of these broad-band domains are contained in table 13.2 and the Child Behavior Profile is presented in figure 13.2.

Standardization Sample and Norms

The CBCL was standardized on more than 1,300 children and adolescents between the ages of 4 to 16 years. Separate norms are available for boys and girls within three broad age groups: (a) 4 to 5 years, (b) 6 to 11 years, and (c) 12 to 16 years. The normative sample for the parent version of the CBCL, however, is based on a geographically restrictive sample as virtually all cases came from Washington, D.C., Maryland, and Virginia. For the parent version, 80 percent of the sample were white, 19 percent were black, and 2 percent other.

For the teacher version of the CBCL (N = 1,100), the sample came from three geographic regions (East, South, and Midwest). In this sample, 77 percent were white and 23 percent were black.

Sex and age were the two variables that accounted for the most variance in CBCL scores and, as such, norms were stratified according to these two variables. Socioeconomic status, occupation of head of household, type of community, and other demographic variables accounted for little variance in CBCL scores.

Data Obtained

The parent, teacher, and youth self-report versions of the CBCL yields three types of scores: raw scores, T scores (M = 50, s = 10), and percentile ranks. As mentioned earlier, separate norms and scores are available for males and females in three broad age groupings (4–5 years, 6–11 years, and 12–18 years).

T scores and percentile ranks are calculated for the broad-band domains of Externalizing and Internalizing problems and each narrow-band factor with the Externalizing and Internalizing domains.

Reliability and Validity

The CBCL has extensive evidence for reliability and validity. Test-retest reliability estimates for the parent and teacher versions of the CBCL were .91 and .89, respectively (median). Interrater reliabilities between teachers were .57 and between mothers and fathers .64, respectively. The relatively lower interrater reliabilities between teachers and parents is most likely a function of the situational specificity of behavior rather than the unreliability of the rating scales (Achenbach et al., 1987).

Validity evidence for the CBCL is based on numerous investigations using both the parent and teacher versions. The CBCL correlates with observational measures of children's behavior in classroom settings, behavior ratings using other behavior rating scales, and it reliably differentiates among regular and special education students, clinic-referred and nonreferred students, and among diagnostic subgroups of emotionally disturbed children (Edelbrock, 1988).

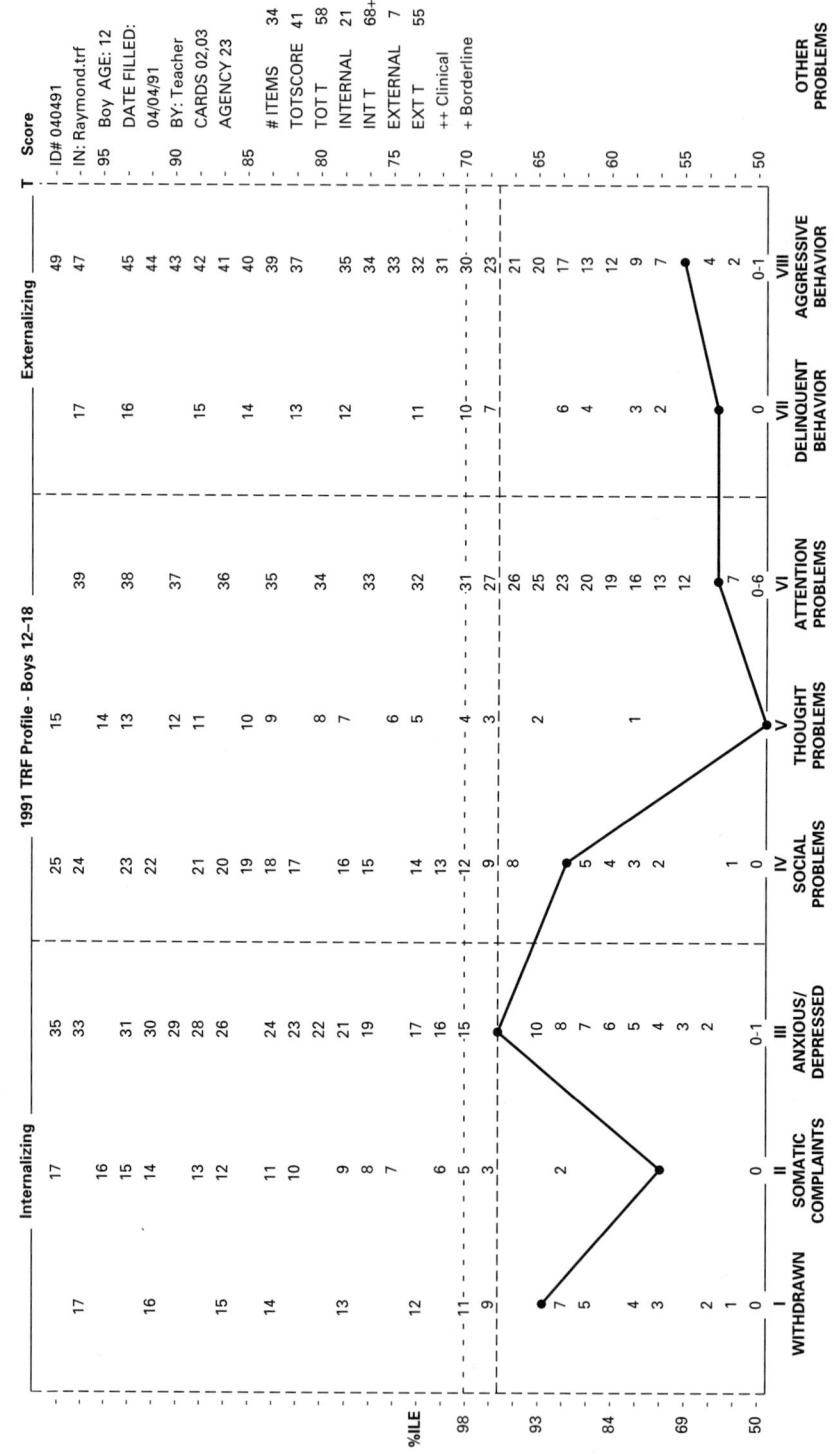

Figure 13.2 Behavior Problem Portion of a Hand-scored Teacher Profile Completed for 12-Year-Old Raymond

338

I — WITHDRAWN

- 2 42. Rather BeAlone
- 0 65. Won't Talk
- 0 69. Secretive
- 2 75. Shy
- 0 80. Stares
- 0 88. Sulks
- 1 102. Underactive
- 2 103. Sad
- 1 111. Withdrawn
- **8 TOTAL**
- **65 T SCORE**

II — SOMATIC COMPLAINTS

- 0 51. Dizzy
- 1 54. Tired
- 0 56a. Aches
- 0 56b. Headaches
- 0 56c. Nausea
- 0 56d. Eye
- 0 56e. Skin
- 0 56f. Stomach
- 0 56g. Vomit
- **1 TOTAL**
- **57 T SCORE**

III — ANXIOUS/DEPRESSED

- 2 12. Lonely
- 0 14. Cries
- 0 31. FearDoBad
- 0 32. Perfect
- 0 33. Unloved
- 1 34. OutToGet
- 1 35. Worthless
- 1 45. Nervous
- 1 47. Conforms*
- 0 50. Fearful
- 0 52. Guilty
- 2 71. SelfConsc
- 1 81. HurtCrit*
- 0 89. Suspic
- 2 103. Sad
- 1 106. AxPleas*
- 1 108. Mistake*
- 1 112. Worries
- **14 TOTAL**
- **69 T SCORE**

IV — SOCIAL PROBLEMS

- 1 1. Acts Young
- 0 11. Clings
- 2 12. Lonely*
- 0 14. Cries*
- 0 25. NotGet Along
- 0 33. Unlove*
- 1 34. OutTo Get*
- 1 35. Worthless
- 0 36. GetHurt*
- 0 38. Teased
- 0 48. NotLiked
- 1 62. Clumsy
- 1 64. Prefers Young
- **7 TOTAL**
- **64 T SCORE**

V — THOUGHT PROBLEMS

- 0 9. Mind Off
- 0 18. Harms Self*
- 0 29. Fears*
- 0 40. Hears Things
- 0 66. Repeats Acts
- 0 70. Sees Things
- 0 84. Strange Behav
- 0 85. Strange Ideas
- **0 TOTAL**
- **50 T SCORE**

VI — ATTENTION PROBLEMS

- 1 1. Acts Young
- 2 2. Hums*
- 0 4. Finish*
- 0 8. Concentr
- 0 10. SitStill
- 0 13. Confuse
- 0 15. Fidget*
- 0 17. DaDream
- 0 22. Direct*
- 0 41. Impulsv
- 1 43. Nervous
- 0 49. Learng*
- 0 60. Apath*
- 0 61. Poor School
- 1 62. Clumsy
- 0 72. Messy*
- 1 78. Inatten*
- 0 80. Stares
- 0 92. UnderAch*
- 0 100. Tasks*
- **9 TOTAL**
- **53 T SCORE**

VII — DELINQUENT BEHAVIOR

- 0 26. NoGuilt
- 0 39. Bad Compan
- 0 43. LieCheat
- 0 63. Prefers Older
- 0 82. Steals
- 0 90. Swears
- 1 98. Tardy*
- 0 101. Truant
- 0 105. Alcohol Drugs
- **1 TOTAL**
- **53 T SCORE**

VIII — AGGRESSIVE BEHAVIOR

- 1 3. Argues
- 0 6. Defiant*
- 0 7. Brags
- 0 16. Mean
- 0 19. DemAttn
- 0 20. DestOwn
- 0 21. DestOthr
- 0 23. DisbSchl
- 0 24. Disturbs*
- 0 27. Jealous
- 0 37. Fights
- 0 53. TalksOut*
- 0 57. Attacks
- 0 67. Disrupts*
- 0 68. Screams
- 1 74. ShowOff
- 0 76. Explosive*
- 0 77. Demanding
- 1 86. Stubborn
- 1 87. MoodChng
- 0 93. TalkMuch
- 0 94. Teases
- 0 95. Temper
- 0 97. Threaten
- 2 104. Loud
- **6 TOTAL**
- **55 T SCORE**

OTHER PROBLEMS

- 0 5. ActOppSex
- 0 28. EatNonFood
- 0 30. FearSchool
- 1 44. BiteNail
- 1 46. Twitch
- 0 55. Overweight
- 0 56h. OtherPhys
- 1 58. PickSkin
- 0 59. SleepClass
- 0 73. Irresponsb
- 1 79. SpeechProb
- 0 83. StoresUp
- 0 91. TalkSuicid
- 0 96. SexPreocc
- 0 99. TooNeat
- 0 107. DislkSchl
- 0 109. Whining
- 0 110. Unclean
- 0 113. OtherProb

*Not on Cross-Informant Construct

Copyright 1991, T.M. Achenbach

Summary

The CBCL represents a norm-referenced, reliable, and valid measure of childhood psychopathology. The major advantage of the CBCL, like the SSRS, is its incorporation of a multirater approach to assessing children's behavior. One drawback of the CBCL is its length (i.e., 118 items for the parent version and 113 items for the teacher version).

The CBCL is used primarily to identify and classify children's behavior problems. Individual behaviors on the CBCL may be targets of intervention, but the technical manual provides little discussion of how the CBCL can be linked to intervention strategies.

Revised Behavior Problem Checklist

Overview and Purpose

The Revised Behavior Problem Checklist (RBPC) (Quay & Peterson, 1983) is an 89-item behavior rating scale for children between the ages of 6 to 18 years. The RPBC represents a revision and extension of the original 55-item Behavior Problem Checklist (Quay & Peterson, 1983), which has been used in more than 100 published studies with a variety of populations (for a comprehensive review see Quay, 1983). The scale was designed to be completed by adults familiar with a target child or adolescent and may include parents, teachers, or direct service child-care workers.

The RPBC comprises six factors or dimensions of problem behaviors: (a) Conduct Disorder, (b) Socialized Aggression, (c) Attention Problems/Immaturity, (d) Anxiety-Withdrawal, (e) Psychotic Behavior, and (f) Motor Excess. A child receives a weighted raw score on each factor, which may then be compared to data derived from empirical investigations of the scale. Examples of behaviors for each dimension are given below:

1. *Conduct Disorder:* Child is disruptive, annoys others, fights, and blames others.

2. *Socialized Aggression:* Child stays out late at night, has bad companions, and is loyal to delinquent friends.

3. *Attention Problems-Immaturity:* Child has short attention span and poor concentration, is distractible, and has trouble following directions.

4. *Anxiety/Withdrawal:* Child feels inferior, self-conscious, fearful, and anxious.

5. *Psychotic Behavior:* Child uses repetitive speech, parrots others' speech, and expresses far-fetched ideas.

6. *Motor Excess:* Child is restless, hyperactive, squirms, fidgets, and unable to relax.

Standardization Sample and Norms

According to the manual, four samples were used to generate item statistics and factor analyses of the RBPC. Sample I consisted of 276 cases in two private psychiatric residential facilities. This sample consisted of males (72%) and females (28%) between the ages of 5 years, 5 months and 22 years, 11 months, with a mean of 15 years and a standard deviation of 3 years. Sample II consisted of 198 cases who were rated by their parents (mostly mothers) at the time of their admission to either an inpatient or outpatient psychiatric facility. The ages ranged from 3 to 21 years with a mean age of 11 years, 6 months and a standard deviation of 4 years. Sample III included 172 students in a special school for children with developmental disabilities. No ages were reported for this sample. Sample IV consisted of 114 students attending a private school for children with learning disabilities. They had a mean age of 10 years with a standard deviation of 2 years.

In sum, the available standardization data were based on 760 cases, which were exclusively "clinical" or pathological groups. The manual does provide some data from 566 "normal" children in public schools in New Jersey and South Carolina in grades 1 through 5. This sample, however, is inadequately described in terms of raters, demographic characteristics, and other relevant criteria for standardized tests and rating scales. Further, the manual does not provide standard scores or percentile ranks, but instead relies on weighted raw scores. Given the nature of the standardization sample, the RBPC is inappropriately used as a norm-referenced instrument to identify behavior problems of the general school-age population.

Data Obtained

Each item on the RPBC is scored on a 3-point scale (0 = Not a Problem, 1 = A Mild Problem, and 2 = A Severe Problem). The maximum score on any scale is twice the number of items on that scale, whereas the minimum score is zero. For example, the Conduct Disorder Scale, with 22 items, has a maximum raw score of 44 and a minimum score of zero. The Motor Excess Scale, with five items, has a maximum raw score of 10 and a minimum score of zero. All scores of the RBPC are weighted raw scores that are summed for each scale or factor. Standard scores cannot be derived from the RBPC in its current form.

Reliability and Validity

The manual provides evidence for internal consistency and interrater reliability. The coefficient alphas for each of the six scales are as follows: (a) Conduct Disorder = .94, (b) Socialized Aggression = .84, (c) Attention Problems/Immaturity = .92, (d) Anxiety/Withdrawal = .82, (e) Psychotic Behavior = .72, and (f) Motor Excess = .75. The only interrater reliability evidence was based on staff members in residential facilities and ranged from .85 (Conduct Disorder) to .52 (Anxiety/Withdrawal), with a median interrater reliability coefficient of .58. No data concerning test-retest reliability are reported.

Quay (1983) states that "it is, of course, reasonable to assume that much of the concurrent, predictive, and construct validity already established for the Behavior Problem Checklist (Quay & Peterson, 1983) can be generalized to the RBPC" (p. 247). However, this is not necessarily true because the RBPC represents a new scale and as such must establish reliability and validity in its own right. The only validity evidence provided for the RBPC is factorial validity and group differentiation in which "normal" children were differentiated from "clinical" samples. To date, the RBPC has a paucity of validity data to support its use.

Summary

The RBPC is a poorly standardized behavior rating scale that has limited evidence for reliability and validity. The fact that the original Behavior Problem Checklist has extensive reliability and validity evidence does not necessarily ensure that the RBPC will assume the same psychometric features. However, the RBPC can be used to identify teachers' behavioral concerns for individual students, particularly from a criterion-related framework. In addition, teachers may be asked to rate several students in their classroom, and these ratings can be compared.

Systematic Screening for Behavior Disorders

Overview and Purpose

The Systematic Screening for Behavior Disorders (SSBD) (Walker & Severson, 1992) is a multiple-gating screening device for the identification of children with behavior disorders. The SSBD is known as a "multiple-gating" device because it contains a series of progressively more expensive and precise assessments or "gates." The SSBD utilizes a combination of teacher nominations, teacher rating scales, and direct observations of classroom and playground behavior to identify children for placement in programs for the behaviorally disordered.

The first gate of the SSBD uses teacher nominations, in which teachers are asked to identify three students in their classes that match two profiles or types of behavior patterns. The first pattern is known as *externalizing,* which refers to all behavior problems that are directed outwardly, by the child, toward the external social environment. Externalizing behavior problems are "behavioral excesses" in that they occur too often. Examples of externalizing behavior problems are defying teachers, aggressive behavior, noncompliance with teacher directions, arguing, and so forth (Walker & Severson, 1992). The second pattern is known as *internalizing,* which refers to all behavior problems that are directly inwardly and that represent problems with self. Internalizing behavior problems are known as "behavioral deficits" (i.e., they refer to behaviors that occur too infrequently). Examples of internalizing behavior problems are not talking with other children, not participating in games or activities, being shy, having low or restricted activity levels, and so forth.

The second gate of the SSBD involves the use of teacher ratings of externalizing and internalizing behavior patterns. Teachers are asked to rate the three children ranked the highest on externalizing problems and three children ranked the highest on internalizing problems (for a total of six students). Teachers rate these children on a Critical Events Checklist that assesses whether a student has exhibited any of 33 externalizing and internalizing behavior problems within the past six months.

The second rating involves the Combined Frequency Index, which measures how often the student exhibits specific adaptive and maladaptive behaviors. Those students exceeding the normative criteria in the second gate of the SSBD are then independently assessed in gate three.

In gate three of the SSBD, a school professional (e.g., school psychologist, guidance counselor, social workers, etc.) assesses students on two measures of school adjustment using direct observation procedures. The first measure is known as *academic engaged time* (AET), which is recorded during independent seatwork periods. The second measure is the *peer social behavior observation,* which measures the quality and nature of students' social behavior during recess periods. Students exceeding normative criteria on these two measures are considered to "pass" gate three and are referred for a formal assessment of behavior disorders. Figure 13.3 presents a graphical display of the multiple-gating procedure used by the SSBD.

Standardization Sample and Norms

The SSBD was nationally standardized on 4,500 cases on the Stage Two measures and approximately 1,300 cases on the Stage Three measures. These cases were collected from 18 school districts in eight states, which included Oregon, Washington, Utah, Illinois, Wisconsin, Rhode Island, Kentucky, and Florida.

The standardization sample included both white and nonwhite students and a broad representation of students from low socioeconomic statuses. The SSBD appears to have an adequate standardization sample for the purposes for which it is to be used.

Data Obtained

The SSBD uses raw scores, T scores, and percentile ranks for the various measures. These scores are based on separate norms for males and females, grade levels (e.g., Grades 1–6 and Grades 4–6, depending on the measure), internalizers, externalizers, and nonranked students. Explicit criteria based on these normative data are used to "pass" a student through a particular gate.

Figure 13.3 Multiple-Gating Assessment Procedure for Identification of Behavior Disordered Students

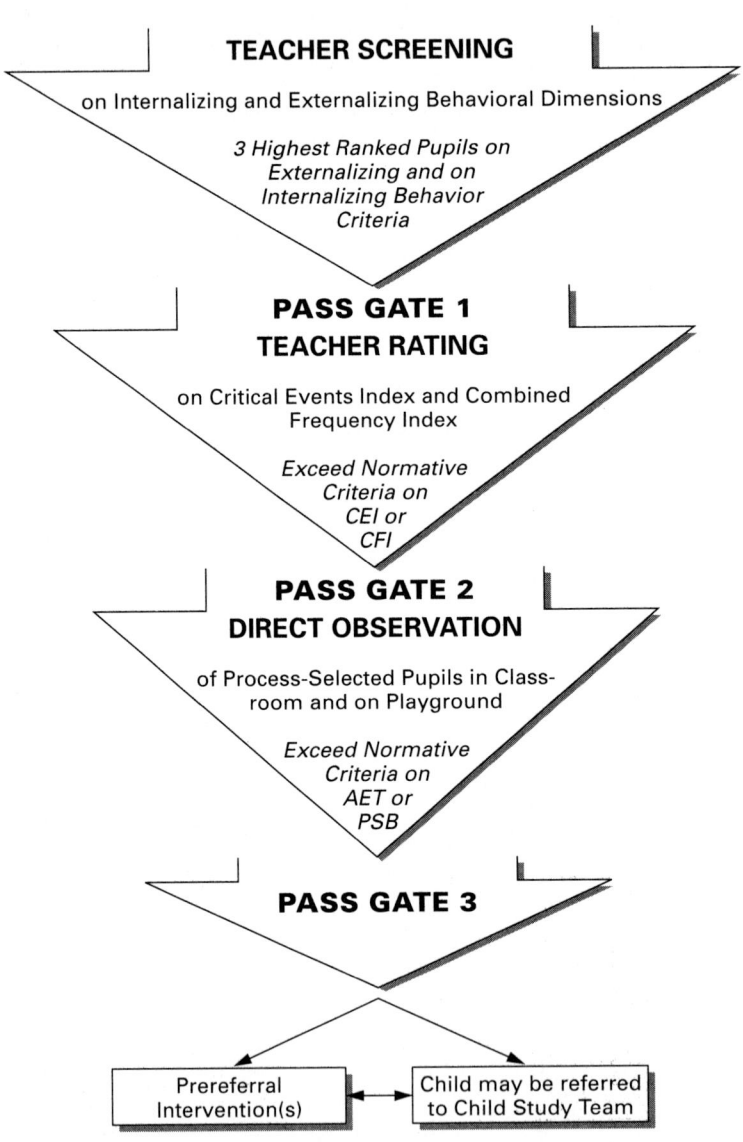

SSBD Screening Process

Pool of Regular Classroom Students

TEACHER SCREENING

on Internalizing and Externalizing Behavioral Dimensions

3 Highest Ranked Pupils on Externalizing and on Internalizing Behavior Criteria

PASS GATE 1

TEACHER RATING

on Critical Events Index and Combined Frequency Index

Exceed Normative Criteria on CEI or CFI

PASS GATE 2

DIRECT OBSERVATION

of Process-Selected Pupils in Classroom and on Playground

Exceed Normative Criteria on AET or PSB

PASS GATE 3

| Prereferral Intervention(s) | Child may be referred to Child Study Team |

Reliability and Validity

The SSBD has extensive evidence for reliability and validity. Three types of reliability are presented: test-retest, internal consistency, and interrater. The mean one-month test-retest reliability for Stage One measures (i.e., teacher nominations) was .79 for externalizers and .72 for internalizers. Test-retest reliabilities for Stage Two measures were .81 for the Cumulative Frequency Index (CFI) (adaptive behavior rating scale) and .90 (maladaptive behavior rating scale).

Internal consistency estimates of the CFI adaptive and maladaptive behavior rating scales were .94 and .92, respectively. The average interitem correlations for the adaptive and maladaptive behavior rating scales were .59 and .49, respectively.

Interrater reliability was not established for the Stage Two measures; however, interrater reliability for the Academic Engaged Time measure ranged from 90 to 100 percent. For the Peer Social Behavior observation, the interrater reliabilities ranged from 80 to 90 percent.

The SSBD technical manual presents a large amount of data supporting the validity of the measure. Included in this discussion is evidence for content, construct, concurrent, and discriminant validity. For example, the SSBD correlates with measures of behavior problems, social skills, and sociometric status. It reliably differentiates behaviorally disordered students from nondisordered students as well as distinguishes among externalizers, internalizers, and nonreferred students.

Summary

The SSBD is a well-conceptualized and well-researched instrument designed for the identification of students with behavior disorders. Its multiple-gating procedure represents an efficient method of identifying students with behavior problems and is designed to save time and money in the assessment process.

We feel that the SSBD serves as one of the best examples of how assessment methods (teacher nominations, teacher ratings, and direct observations of behavior in naturalistic settings) can be combined to identify students in need of special services and to identify target behaviors for intervention. In our opinion, there is no better instrument for the screening and identification of students with behavior disorders.

Student Self-Concept Scale

Overview and Purpose

The Student Self-Concept Scale (SSCS) (Gresham, Elliott, & Evans-Fernandez, 1993) is a 72-item group or individually administered multidimensional measure of self-concept. The SSCS provides a norm-referenced measure of self-concept for children and adolescents in grades 3 through 12 and documents the perceived *confidence* and *importance* of specific behaviors influencing the development of students' self-concepts.

The SSCS conceptualizes self-concept as being multidimensional in nature in that individuals categorize their self-perceptions into facets or domains (e.g., academic, social, etc.). The SSCS defines self-concept as an individual's perception that he or she can perform certain behaviors that will result in certain outcomes. Self-concept is multidimensional and is determined by an individual's feelings of efficacy in performing certain behaviors and the importance of these behaviors for that individual.

The following subscales and composite scales are measured on the SSCS:

1. *Academic Self-Concept Subscale.* This subscale measures students' confidence in being able to perform behaviors that are academic in nature (e.g., reading, math, etc.) or academically related (e.g., listening to the teacher, following directions, etc.).

2. *Social Self-Concept Subscale.* This subscale measures students' confidence levels in the social domain (e.g., playing with others, sharing with others, etc.).

3. *Self-Image Self-Concept Subscale.* This subscale measures general self-concept and taps students' global perceptions of who they are (e.g., proud of self, well liked by others, etc.).

4. *Confidence Composite Scale.* This scale is a composite obtained by adding the Academic, Social, and Self-Image Subscales.

5. *Outcome Academic Subscale.* This subscale measures students' perceptions that certain academic behaviors will result in certain academic outcomes (e.g., "If I study hard, I will make good grades in school").

6. *Outcome Social Subscale.* This subscale measures students' perceptions that certain social behaviors will result in certain social outcomes (e.g., "If I take turns in games, others will want to play with me").

7. *Outcome Self-Image Subscale.* This subscale measures students' perceptions that certain self-perceptions will result in certain outcomes (e.g., "If I am proud of who I am, I will get along better with others").

8. *Outcome Composite Scale.* This scale is a composite obtained by summing the Academic, Social, and Self-Image Subscales.

9. *Lie Scale.* This scale measures the degree to which students are attempting to present unrealistic levels of social desirability or "faking good" responses (e.g., "I like everyone I know," "I never get mad," etc.). Importance scores are also available for Academic, Social, and Self-Image Subscales.

Standardization Sample and Norms

The SSCS was standardized on a national sample of 3,586 elementary and secondary school students from 19 states. The standardization sample closely approximated the U.S. student population in terms of gender, race, geographical region, and urbanization, with a special emphasis on obtaining sufficient representation of special education students. Males and females were evenly represented both across the sample and within each grade level, with 49 percent being males and 51 percent being females. Approximately 16 percent of the standardization sample were students with disabilities (e.g., learning disabilities, behavior disorders, mild mental disabilities), which represents a slightly higher percentage of students with disabilities than the U.S. student population (i.e., 11%).

Norms were stratified by broad age groupings (elementary and secondary) and by gender. Gender was a particularly important stratification variable as females obtained higher scores in academic and social domains across virtually all grade levels, whereas males obtained higher scores in self-image across virtually all grade levels.

Data Obtained

Three different types of normative scores were derived for the SSCS. One is the percentile rank, the other is a standard score with a mean of 100 and a standard deviation of 15, and the last is a descriptive behavior level score. Both percentile rank and standard scores are derived for the Confidence Subscales (Academic, Social, and Self-Image), the Composite Self-Concept, and the Outcome Composite Scales. Descriptive behavior levels are available for the three Outcome Subscales (Academic, Social, and Self-Image).

Descriptive behavior levels consist of three levels labeled *High, Average,* and *Low.* These levels were determined by the means and standard deviations of the subscales. For instance, the Average category lies within the range one standard deviation around the mean, whereas the High and Low categories fall beyond one standard deviation above and below the mean, respectively. Descriptive behavior levels, like percentile ranks and standard scores, are computed separately by gender and grade level.

Reliability and Validity

The SSCS technical manual provides extensive evidence for reliability and validity. In terms of reliability, both internal consistency and test-retest reliability evidence is reported. Internal consistency estimates range from .89 to .92 for the Composite Confidence ratings and .79 to .82 for the Composite Outcome ratings. The median coefficient alpha reliability was .90 and .81 for the Composite Confidence and Composite Outcome Scales, respectively.

Subscale internal consistency estimates were lower, based largely on the fewer numbers of items on which these estimates were based. These subscale coefficient alphas ranged from .72 to .84 with a median internal consistency estimate of .78 for elementary students and .81 for secondary students.

Test-retest reliability estimates were based on samples of students at elementary and secondary levels completing the SSCS on two separate occasions separated by approximately four weeks. For SSCS Confidence Subscale ratings, the median stability coefficient was .68 for elementary students and .77 for secondary students. Composite Confidence ratings were slightly more stable with coefficients of .73 and .84 for elementary and secondary students, respectively.

The SSCS technical manual provides a large number of studies supporting the content, construct, social, and criterion-related validity of the scale. The SSCS correlates moderately to highly with other established measures of self-concept such as the Piers-Harris Children's Self-Concept Scale (Piers, 1984) ($r = .40$), Tennessee Self-Concept Scale (Roid & Fitts, 1988) ($r = .59$), Self-Description Questionnaire-1 (Marsh, 1988) ($r = .76$), and Coopersmith Self-Esteem Inventory (Coopersmith, 1981) ($r = .54$).

The SSCS also correlates with the Social Skills Rating System (SSRS) (Gresham & Elliott, 1990) with correlations between the SSCS Composite Confidence score and SSRS subscales ranging from .37 to .48. SSCS scores also showed moderate negative correlations with the Child Behavior Checklist–Self-Report Form (CBCL) (Achenbach & Edelbrock, 1987). The correlation between the SSCS Composite Confidence score and CBCL Total Problems scores was –.60, suggesting that self-concept is inversely related to behavior problems in children.

The SSCS also reliably differentiates between children with learning disabilities and children without learning disabilities. For example, significant differences were found between these groups on the Academic and Social Subscales using both Confidence and Outcome ratings as well as the Composite Scales.

Summary

The SSCS provides users several unique features to facilitate more comprehensive assessment and intervention services for children experiencing difficulties in self-concept. One, the SSCS provides norms based on a large, representative sample for boys and girls in grades 3 to 12. Two, the SSCS is theoretically based, which provides more specific, behavioral information regarding a child's self-concept. Three, consistent with recent theoretical advances in the study of self-concept, the SSCS provides a multidimensional measure of self-concept. Four, the SSCS represents the first self-concept scale to utilize joint ratings of confidence and importance for each behavior on the scale. The inclusion of importance ratings facilitates intervention planning for children and adolescents having problems in self-concept.

The SSCS offers a useful means for assessing and treating self-concept problems. The multidimensional nature of the scale allows users to distinguish self-concept problems across important domains such as academic and social and to separately assess students' levels of outcome expectations. Finally, unlike many self-concept scales, the SSCS provides an empirical means of detecting invalid profiles by the inclusion of a Lie Scale to measure social desirability of responding to items.

Other Behavior Rating Scales

Far too many behavior rating scales are available to conduct a comprehensive review of each scale. In the foregoing sections, we have reviewed what we believe to be the most well-researched and/or most frequently used behavior rating scales used with school-aged children and adolescents. The following paragraphs review other behavior rating scales used with special children to assess a variety of problem behaviors and social competencies.

Conners Rating Scales

The Conners Parent Rating Scale and Conners Teacher Rating Scale (Conners, 1985) represent two rating scales designed to identify behavior problems in school-age children and adolescents between the ages of 3 and 17 years. The Conners Parent Rating Scale (CPRS) is a 93-item scale that assesses eight domains of problem behavior: Fearful-Anxious, Hyperactive-Immature, Restless-Disorganized, Conduct Disorder, Antisocial, Obsessional, Psychosomatic, and Learning Problem-Immature.

Each behavior is rated on the CPRS on a 4-point scale and these raw scores are transformed into T scores (M = 50, s = 10). A brief version of the CPRS called the Abbreviated Parent Questionnaire is based on 10 items/behaviors that assess hyperactivity. This "Hyperactivity Index" is used frequently as part of an assessment of Attention Deficit Hyperactivity Disorder.

The Conners Teacher Rating Scale (CTRS) (Conners, 1985) is designed to measure problem behavior in children between the ages of 4 and 12 years. The CTRS is a 39-item behavior rating scale, which was standardized only on Canadian children. The CTRS measures six domains of problem behaviors: Daydreams-Attendance Problem, Asocial, Overindulgent, Conduct Problem, Emotional-Overindulgent, and Anxious-Passive. Behaviors on the CTRS, like the CPRS, are rated on a 4-point scale. T scores (M = 50, s = 10) are calculated from the raw scores of each of the six factors on the scale.

Like the parent version, the CTRS has a 10-item "Hyperactivity Index" called the Abbreviated Teacher Questionnaire. Normative data are available for this scale for children ages 3 to 17 years.

The CPRS and CTRS are used less frequently than other behavior rating scales discussed in this chapter. However, the Abbreviated Parent and Teacher Questionnaires that assess hyperactivity are used often in research and clinical practice to assist in the diagnosis of Attention Deficit Hyperactivity Disorder. Research with the Conners Scales suggests that they have adequate reliability and validity for use as screening devices to identify behavior problems in children and adolescents. Unlike the Social Skills Rating System and the Child Behavior Checklist, the Conners Scales were standardized on separate normative samples, thus not allowing for direct comparisons between parent and teacher ratings of the same children.

Walker-McConnell Scale of Social Competence and School Adjustment

The Walker-McConnell Scale of Social Competence and School Adjustment (W-M) (Walker & McConnell, 1988) is a 43-item teacher rating scale that assesses children's social skills in grades kindergarten through sixth grade. The W-M assesses three domains of social skills: teacher-preferred social skills, peer-preferred social skills, and school adjustment.

The W-M scale was standardized on a sample of more than 1,800 children from 18 states. The technical manual provides extensive evidence for reliability (e.g., internal consistency, test-retest, and interrater) and validity (e.g., content, construct, discriminant, factorial, and criterion-related). This scale covers a much narrower age range than the Social Skills Rating System (Gresham & Elliott, 1990) and utilizes only one type of rater (i.e., the teacher). In spite of this, the W-M scale is a reliable and valid measure of elementary-aged children's social skills.

Walker Problem Behavior Identification Checklist

The Walker Problem Behavior Identification Checklist (WPBIC) (Walker, 1983) is a 50-item checklist designed to identify behavior problems in children in grades 4 through 6. It is composed of observable, operational statements about classroom behavior that were furnished by a representative sample of elementary school teachers.

The WPBIC assesses five categories of problem behavior: Acting Out, Withdrawal, Distractibility, Disturbed Peer Relations, and Immaturity. Each behavior on the scale is rated on a 4-point scale and yields a weighted raw score. These weighted raw scores are transformed to T scores (M = 50, s = 10).

The WPBIC manual provides evidence for internal consistency and test-retest reliability. However, internal consistency data are provided only for the total score and not the five subscales. Validity evidence includes predictive, content, construct, and content validities. The greatest drawback of the scale is that it was not standardized on a representative sample of children and therefore scores obtained may not be comparable to other samples.

Focus on
→ Research ←

Is Behavior Situationally Determined or Cross-Situational? Implications From Research Using Behavior Rating Scales

Different schools of thought exist regarding whether behavior is determined by situational factors or by internal personality characteristics that are cross-situational. For example, certain psychodynamic theories (e.g., psychoanalysis) suggest that behavior is determined by personality traits that remain constant across a variety of situations. On the other hand, environmental theories (e.g., applied behavior analysis) maintain that behavior is determined largely by situational and setting factors and, thus, is situationally specific.

To help answer this age-old question, Achenbach, McConaughy, and Howell (1987) reviewed 119 studies that used multiple informants completing behavior rating scales to assess the degree of consistency among informants' ratings of emotional/behavioral problems of children between the ages of 1 1/2 and 19 years of age. These authors computed correlations between different pairs of informants to assess the level of agreement or consistency in ratings. Specifically, ratings from parents, teachers, mental health workers, observers, peers, and self-reports of children were compared.

Achenbach et al. (1987) sought to answer the following questions in their analysis:

1. Is there any consistency between and among informants?

2. If so, how much?

3. Does consistency among informants vary with the type of informant of child characteristics such as age, sex, type of problem, and severity of problem behavior?

4. What are the implications for assessment practice in data showing high or low levels of consistency among different informants?

Findings

1. Correlations among informants playing similar roles with respect to children (e.g., pairs of parents, pairs of teachers, pairs of mental health workers, etc.) were higher than correlations between informants playing different roles with respect to children (e.g., parents and teachers, teachers and mental health workers, peers and observers, etc.).

2. Based on 119 studies, the mean correlations between informants were as follows:

Similar Role Corrrelations

a. Parents/Parents: r = .59

b. Teachers/Teachers: r = .64

c. Mental Health Worker/Mental Health Worker: r = .54

d. Observer/Observer: $r = .57$

e. Peer/Peer: $r = .73$

Mean $r = .61$

Different Role Informants

a. Parent/Teacher: $r = .27$

b. Parent/Mental Health Worker: $r = .24$

c. Teacher/Mental Health Worker: $r = .34$

d. Observer/Teacher: $r = .42$

e. Observer/Parent: $r = .27$

f. Peer/Teacher: $r = .44$

g. Self/Peer: $r = .26$

h. Self/Teacher: $r = .20$

i. Self/Parent: $r = .25$

j. Self/Mental Health Worker: $r = .27$

Mean $r = .30$

3. There was no significant difference between correlations obtained from mothers versus fathers' ratings of boys versus girls and clinical versus nonclinical samples.

4. Higher correlations were found between informants for externalizing problems than for internalizing problems. Mothers and fathers, however, showed no differences in their ratings of externalizing and internalizing problems of their children.

Implications for Assessment Practice

1. Different informants are needed for different settings and situations. These informants are likely to vary in their effects on children.

2. The low correlation between children's self-ratings and other informants such as parents, teachers, and mental health workers indicate that children's self-reports cannot be substituted for reports by other informants.

3. The relatively low correlations among informants *do not necessarily* suggest that the measures used to collect information (i.e., behavior rating scales) are unreliable or invalid. Rather, it may suggest that different informants contribute valid, but different information.

4. In using behavior rating scales, one must ensure that a representative sample of ratings is taken from various informants having similar and different roles with respect to children. The presence or absence of consistency in these informants' ratings may help in the design, implementation, and evaluation of interventions to change behavior.

Source: From T. Achenbach, S. McConaughy, and C. Howell, "Child/Adolescent Behavioral and Emotional Problems: Implications of Cross-Informant Correlations for Situational Specificity" in *Psychological Bulletin,* 101:213–232, 1987.

Chapter Summary

➔ Summary of Behavior Rating Scales

Behavior rating scales represent useful, economical, reliable, and valid approaches for assessing social skills and problem behaviors of children and adolescents. They can be used for screening purposes, for classification purposes, and can be of great assistance in identifying target behaviors for intervention. It should be pointed out, however, that behavior rating scales *should not* be used in isolation for any of these purposes. Like other assessment strategies discussed in this book, one must always use multiple types of assessment to get a complete picture of children and their behavior.

You will recall that many of the behavior rating scales discussed in this chapter utilized multiple informants (e.g., parents, teachers, and children). A somewhat complex question is, How is one to interpret the information from multiple informants for a single child?

One way of answering this question is based on the principle of **multiple operationalism** (Campbell & Fiske, 1959; Gresham, 1985). That is, behavior can be defined or operationalized from different perspectives. For example, a parent may define arguing with peers as a form of assertive behavior, whereas a teacher may view this same behavior as aggressive behavior. Thus, the parent and the teacher have defined or "operationalized" this behavior in different ways.

Does this mean that whatever method we used to measure behavior is invalid? The lack of agreement between the parent and the teacher in this case could be due to a variety of factors. For example, the same behavior may be viewed as assertion in one setting (e.g., a baseball game) and as aggression in another setting (e.g., the classroom). In this case, the *situation,* not the behavior, may lead adults to define behaviors differently. In using behavior rating scales, it is important to consider and assess the situational determinants of behavior.

Another commonly encountered phenomenon in using multiple informants for behavior rating scales is when one informant rates the behavior as not occurring and the other informant rates the behavior as occurring very often. For instance, a parent may rate the behavior of temper tantrums as never occurring, whereas the teacher may rate this same behavior as occurring frequently.

At first blush, this would seem to indicate complete disagreement and a lack of validity of the scale used to measure the behavior of temper tantrums. Another possibility might be that the behavior is *situationally specific* in that it never occurs in the home (perhaps because it has been punished in that setting), but occurs frequently at school (perhaps because it has been reinforced with attention from the teacher and peers). Thus, the explanation for the apparent disagreement between informants in this case has to do with situational factors and *not* any psychometric characteristics of the rating scale.

Social Validity

One type of validity that is important to the use of behavior rating scales is termed **social validity** (Gresham, 1985). Social validity (Wolf, 1978) refers to the determination of the applied or social importance of exhibiting certain behaviors in particular situations.

Wolf (1978) has suggested that social validation occurs on three levels: (a) determining the *social significance* of behavior, (b) determining the *social acceptability* of interventions to change behavior, and (c) determining the *social importance* of the effects produced by interventions. The notion of social validity is important in the use and interpretation of data from behavior rating scales, particularly the concepts of social significance and social importance.

Social significance refers to behaviors that are considered by authoritative adults as being significant (as opposed to trivial) behaviors for children. In terms of problem behaviors, socially significant behaviors are behaviors that deviate from or occur more frequently than the typical behaviors exhibited by a child's peers. In terms of prosocial behaviors, these behaviors would occur less frequently than those of a representative sample of a child's peers.

One way of assessing whether or not a behavior is socially significant is to use social comparisons. Social comparisons involve the identification of the referred child's peers who are similar in age and demographic variables but differ in performance of certain behaviors. The behavior of the referred child can be compared to a child's peers by using well-standardized and representatively normed behavior rating scales to assess whether the behavior significantly deviates from the behavior of the child's peers. For example, if a child receives a T score of 70 (i.e., two standard deviations above the mean) on an aggression subscale of a behavior rating scale, then one can conclude that the child is significantly more aggressive than his or her peers whose mean score would be 50. This T score of 70 would indicate that 98 percent of the children on whom the scale was normed had lower scores on aggression than the referred child. As such, one might conclude that this child's aggressive behavior constituted socially significant behavior.

Social importance addresses the question, Does the quantity and quality of behavior change make a difference in the child's functioning? In other words, do the changes in behaviors subsequent to an intervention bring the behavior into tolerable/acceptable limits? Social comparisons can be used to assess the social importance of behavior change using normative data from behavior rating scales. For example, if the above child's T score of 70 on aggression was reduced to a T score of 50 by an intervention, then one could conclude that the intervention had a socially important effect on behavior. That is, the intervention brought the child's aggressive behavior into an average range.

Social validity represents an important consideration in using behavior rating scales. Without representative norms, it is difficult to establish with confidence that behaviors assessed represent socially significant behaviors. Without representative norms, one would have great difficulty in determining whether or not an intervention produced socially important effects.

Putting It Together

The following sample case report (see Focus on Practice) illustrates the principle of good assessment practice for behavior problems in the classroom. In reading this report, try to identify the important principles discussed in this chapter for using behavior rating scales. Pay particular attention to how the results of behavior rating scales are combined with other assessment methods and how an intervention plan was developed and evaluated.

Focus on
Practice

Integrating Assessment Information from Multiple Informants

Investigators of the social behavior of children have noted differences in behavior across various settings. It is not unusual, for example, for a child to demonstrate the ability to join a group of neighborhood friends, but to be quite reluctant to approach a group of classmates at school. Thus, a respect for the situationally specificity of an individual's social behavior is an important consideration when assessing a person.

The Social Skills Rating System (SSRS) (Gresham & Elliott, 1990) discussed in this chapter provides a means of integrating information from multiple raters of a child's social behavior. This is accomplished by using the Assessment-Intervention Record (AIR), which provides: (a) a format for documenting background information, (b) a means for analyzing and synthesizing multirater assessment data, (c) documentation of social behavior strengths and weaknesses, (d) a functional system for classifying social skills deficits tied to a model for developing intervention plans, and (e) a summary report to guide further assessments and interventions.

Case Illustration

To illustrate the various functions of the AIR, the information on Andrew Taylor, a nine-year-old boy living with both parents, is presented. Andrew's SSRS multirater data were summarized and integrated (see pages 2 and 3 of the AIR). Andrew's Graphic Profile Summary illustrates both agreement and disagreement among raters. Andrew's teacher and his mother both believe that Andrew has *Fewer* social skills than his peers in the comparison groups. Andrew's own ratings of his social skills were on the low side of average. A review of the Social Skills Subscales, however, reveals some disagreements.

Andrew's mother rated Andrew low in Assertion skills. Andrew's teacher did not feel that Andrew was particularly low in Assertion skills, but that he did have a lack of Self-Control skills. Andrew also rated himself low in Self-Control skills, but his mother did not. Andrew's teacher and his mother also agreed that, in general, Andrew did not have an unusual number of Problem Behaviors, although they both thought he had some externalizing problems.

The patterns of agreements and disagreements among raters provides a basis for consultation and offers direction for clarifying the apparently diverse views of some of Andrew's behaviors. For example, is the teacher trying to get Andrew to be more controlled while the mother is trying to have him become more assertive? Do these two people have contradictory goals for Andrew? These questions could be explored in discussions with Andrew's mother and teacher to assist in the identification of common behavior-change goals for Andrew.

In summary, the overall ratings of Andrew's behavior by his teacher and his mother showed below average performance of a number of important social skills when compared with a national sample of same-sex peers. These interindividual data in the form of standard scores and percentile ranks could be used alone, to identify Andrew as a child needing further evaluation, or they could be used in conjunction with other assessment information to explore the possibility of a formal classification requiring special services. Andrew's complete AIR follows. It details global ratings social skills and problem behaviors as well as specific behaviors from multiple informants. In addition, it provides specific recommendations for intervention planning to remediate Andrew's social skills deficits.

Social Skills

Teacher Form

Parent Form

Student Form

Rating System

Assessment-Intervention Record

Frank M. Gresham and Stephen N. Elliott

Student Information

Name _Andrew Taylor_   Date of Birth _6_ _22_ _80_
Month Day Year

Sex: ☐ Female ☒ Male   Ethnic Group (optional) _____   Age _9_ _6_
Years Months

Grade and School _4th / Prairieview_

Parents' or guardians' names

1. _Nelson Taylor_   Address _58 Shoeman Circle_
   Phone _603-274-8139_
2. _Ann Taylor_   Address _same_
   Phone _____
Teacher's name _Bentler_

Reason for referral _Has difficulty controlling his temper and frequently gets into arguments with a classmate. Generally, poor interactions with peers._

Social Skills Assessment

Record the SSRS forms that have been completed and by whom. Also list any other methods of assessing the student's behavior that have been completed and will be summarized on page 6 of this report.

SSRS	Date Completed	Rater
Teacher Form	_12-1-89_	_Jane Bentler_
Parent Form	_12-5-89_	_Ann Taylor_
Student Form	_12-5-89_	_Andrew Taylor_

Other assessment methods _Classroom and playground observations, Walker Problem Behavior Checklist, brief interview and role-play session with Andrew (12-10-89)._

Page 1 of the *Assessment-Intervention Record* Completed for Andrew, a Hypothetical Case

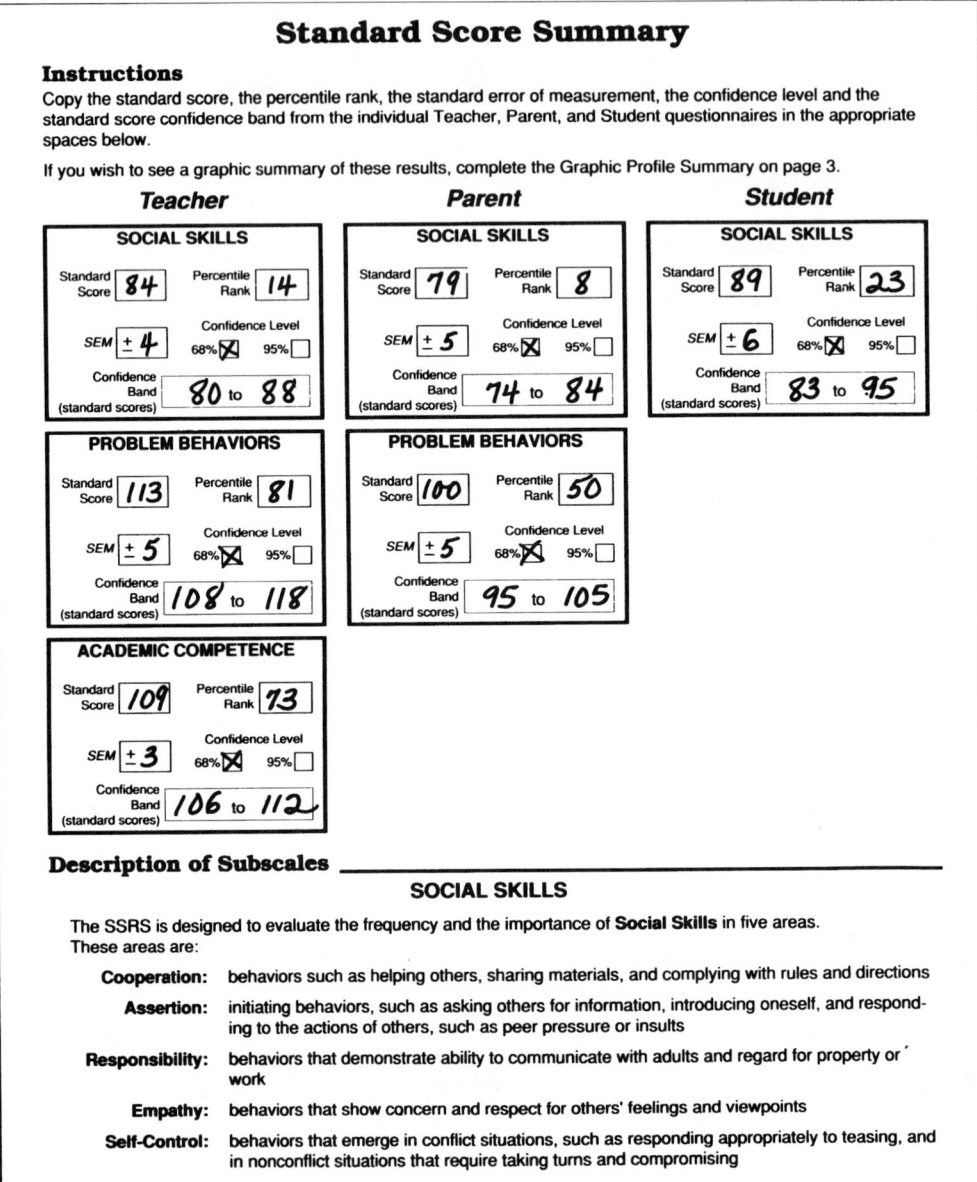

Standard Score Summary

Instructions

Copy the standard score, the percentile rank, the standard error of measurement, the confidence level and the standard score confidence band from the individual Teacher, Parent, and Student questionnaires in the appropriate spaces below.

If you wish to see a graphic summary of these results, complete the Graphic Profile Summary on page 3.

Teacher

SOCIAL SKILLS

Standard Score **84**	Percentile Rank **14**

SEM **± 4**   Confidence Level 68% ☒ 95% ☐

Confidence Band (standard scores) **80** to **88**

PROBLEM BEHAVIORS

Standard Score **113**	Percentile Rank **81**

SEM **± 5**   Confidence Level 68% ☒ 95% ☐

Confidence Band (standard scores) **108** to **118**

ACADEMIC COMPETENCE

Standard Score **109**	Percentile Rank **73**

SEM **± 3**   Confidence Level 68% ☒ 95% ☐

Confidence Band (standard scores) **106** to **112**

Parent

SOCIAL SKILLS

Standard Score **79**	Percentile Rank **8**

SEM **± 5**   Confidence Level 68% ☒ 95% ☐

Confidence Band (standard scores) **74** to **84**

PROBLEM BEHAVIORS

Standard Score **100**	Percentile Rank **50**

SEM **± 5**   Confidence Level 68% ☒ 95% ☐

Confidence Band (standard scores) **95** to **105**

Student

SOCIAL SKILLS

Standard Score **89**	Percentile Rank **23**

SEM **± 6**   Confidence Level 68% ☒ 95% ☐

Confidence Band (standard scores) **83** to **95**

Description of Subscales

SOCIAL SKILLS

The SSRS is designed to evaluate the frequency and the importance of **Social Skills** in five areas. These areas are:

Cooperation: behaviors such as helping others, sharing materials, and complying with rules and directions

Assertion: initiating behaviors, such as asking others for information, introducing oneself, and responding to the actions of others, such as peer pressure or insults

Responsibility: behaviors that demonstrate ability to communicate with adults and regard for property or work

Empathy: behaviors that show concern and respect for others' feelings and viewpoints

Self-Control: behaviors that emerge in conflict situations, such as responding appropriately to teasing, and in nonconflict situations that require taking turns and compromising

Standard Score Summary, Page 2 of the *Assessment-Intervention Record,* Completed for Andrew

Graphic Profile Summary

Instructions

The relationships among teacher, parent, and student ratings for the scales and subscales can be made readily apparent. Transfer the results from each questionnaire to the profile below. Simply make X's in each box for each form. (See sample below.) You may wish to use different colors for Teacher, Parent, and Student Forms. An example of a completed profile is shown in Chapter 3 of the SSRS Manual. If you need more specific statistical information for the scales, refer to page 2 of this Record.

Scales

SOCIAL SKILLS

(Teacher, Parent, Student — ratings: More / Average / Fewer)

PROBLEM BEHAVIORS

(Teacher, Parent — ratings: More / Average / Fewer)

ACADEMIC COMPETENCE

- Above Average
- Average (X)
- Below Average

Teacher

Subscales

Cooperation · Assertion · Self-Control · Responsibility · Empathy

(Teacher, Parent, Student — More / Average / Fewer)

Externalizing · Internalizing · Hyperactivity

(Teacher, Parent — More / Average / Fewer)

SAMPLE:

Example of Fewer, Average, and More ratings

FEWER · AVERAGE · MORE

PROBLEM BEHAVIORS

The SSRS Teacher and Parent Forms provide frequency ratings of potential **Problem Behaviors** in three areas at the elementary level and two areas at the preschool and secondary levels. These areas are:

Externalizing: behaviors involving verbal or physical aggression toward others, poor control of temper, and arguing

Internalizing: behaviors indicating anxiety, sadness, loneliness, and poor self-esteem

Hyperactivity: behaviors involving excessive movement, fidgeting, and impulsive reactions (elementary level only)

ACADEMIC COMPETENCE

The SSRS Teacher Forms also include a nine-item scale of **Academic Competence.** Ratings of reading, mathematics, motivation, and parental support are included in this scale.

Graphic Profile Summary, Page 3 of the *Assessment-Intervention Record,* Completed for Andrew

Analysis of Social Behaviors
Identifying Social Skills Strengths and Weaknesses
and Interfering Problem Behaviors

The Standard Score Summary and the Graphic Profile Summary have enabled you to identify a student's overall strengths and weaknesses. Before planning interventions for these general weaknesses, an analysis of the behaviors represented by the items in the subscales is needed. This analysis should focus on those social skills that have been identified as general strengths ("more than") or general weaknesses ("fewer than"). **Importance** ratings, as well as **Frequency** ratings must be used for this analysis. You will need to examine the questionnaires to complete this analysis. A sample case identifying a student's strengths and weaknesses is given in Chapter 4 of the SSRS Manual.

Social Skills Strengths are defined by Frequency ratings of 2 and Importance ratings of 1 or 2.

Social Skills Performance Deficits are mild deficits and are defined by Frequency ratings of 1 and Importance ratings of 2.

Social Skills Acquisition Deficits are moderate to severe deficits and are defined by Frequency ratings of 0 and Importance ratings of 1 or 2.

Problem Behaviors are those behaviors of an externalizing, internalizing, or hyperactive nature that can interfere with the acquisition or performance of social skills. Any item on the Problem Behaviors subscales that receives a Frequency rating of 2 may suggest an interfering problem behavior.

Social Skills Strengths (Frequency = 2, Importance = 1 or 2) Review the SSRS questionnaires to identify items that characterize social skills strengths. Enter a brief description of the items in the appropriate section below. List one or two behaviors rated as strengths from each subscale if that subscale is rated "More." Remember, the subscales are designated: C = Cooperation, A = Assertion, R = Responsibility, E = Empathy, S = Self-Control.

Teacher Form	Parent Form	Student Form
1 Puts materials away	Attends to speakers	Smiles, waves, nods to others
2 Joins ongoing activity	Volunteers to help with	asks others before using things
3	tasks	Feels sorry when bad things
4	Answers phone correctly	happen
5	Completes household tasks	Does homework,
		acknowledges compliments

Comments on social skills strengths _____

Andrew is attentive to most academic tasks and seems to care about his schoolwork. He also is very involved with activities and needs no help in joining others to play or work. In many ways he has good leadership skills, but often gets upset if he doesn't get his way.

Analysis of Social Behaviors, Pages 4 and 5 of the _Assessment-Intervention Record,_ Completed for Andrew

Social Skills Performance Deficits (Frequency = 1, Importance = 2) Review the SSRS question-naires to identify items that characterize social skills performance deficits. Enter a brief description of the items in the appropriate section below. If possible, list one or two behaviors rated as performance deficits from each subscale that has a Behavior Level of "Fewer."

Teacher Form	Parent Form	Student Form
1 Controls temper with peers	Keeps room clean	Makes friends easily
2 Finishes within time limits	Responds when hit or pushed	Tells others when upset
3 Receives criticism well	Makes friends easily	Disagrees with adults without fighting
4 Uses time while waiting	Avoids trouble situations	Active in school activities
5 Responds when hit by others	Controls temper when arguing Reports accidents	Controls temper when people are angry at him

Comments on social skills performance deficits Control of temper with adults, learning to communicate when he's upset, and talking out problems need improvement.

Social Skills Acquisition Deficits (Frequency = 0, Importance = 1 or 2) Review the SSRS questionnaires to identify items that characterize social skills acquisition deficits. Enter a brief description of the items in the appropriate section below. If possible, list one or two behaviors rated as acquisition deficits from each subscale that has a Behavior Level of "Fewer."

Teacher Form	Parent Form	Student Form
1 Responds to teasing by peers	Invites others to home	Ignores classmates
2 Compromises in conflict situations	Starts conversations	Tells new people name
3 Tells you when treated unfairly	Self-confident in situations	Asks friends to help with problems
4 Gives compliments		Talks over problems with classmates
5 Ignores distractions Controls temper with adults		

Comments on social skills acquisition deficits The most serious area concerns his control of his temper and his teasing of peers. Needs work on talking things out with his peers.

Problem Behaviors (Frequency = 2) Review the SSRS questionnaires to identify items that characterize problem behaviors. From those Behavior Levels rated "More," list in the appropriate section below all behaviors from each subscale that have a Frequency rating of 2. Remember, the subscales are designated as: E = Externalizing , I = Internalizing , H = Hyperactivity.

Teacher Form	Parent Form
1 Threatens or bullies others	Threatens or bullies others
2 Talks back when corrected	Talks back to adults when corrected
3 Gets angry easily	
4 Is easily embarrassed	
5	

Comments on problem behaviors Consensus is that Andrew doesn't take criticism well and often is seen as threatening or bullying others when he doesn't get his way.

Continued

Summary of Additional Assessment Information

Use this page to summarize other assessments of this student.

Direct observations—school _A 30-minute observation during Math & free time indicates 80% on task for math & appropriate behavior during free time. A 30-minute observation on playground indicates negative_ Date _12-9-89_ _peer interactions: 2 name-calling incidents & 2 pushing situations where Andrew started it._

Direct observations—home

No opportunity _____ Date _____

Sociometric measures _not done_

_____ Date _____

Teacher interview _None_

_____ Date _____

Parent interview _None_

_____ Date _____

Student interview _He acknowledges having a hard time getting along with 2 boys in his class. He recognizes that he has a "short temper" and probably argues more than he should. He doesn't think he has any_ Date _12-10-89_ _academic problems. He likes school and his teacher._

Role plays _He indicates he is aware of appropriate alternatives to pushing and arguing with peers who disagree with him. He shows he can walk away, express displeasure, and knows how to_ Date _12-10-89_ _compromise._

Other behavior ratings _Walker PBIC total score of 58; no scale scores indicative of serious problems, although Acting Out score of 64 and several behaviors identified by parents are a_ Date _12-10-89_ _concern to teachers—see forms for details._

Achievement or cognitive measures _No need to assess; doing well academically._

_____ Date _____

Self-concept or self-efficacy measures _Not assessed_

_____ Date _____

Previous intervention outcome data _None_

_____ Date _____

Summary of Additional Assessment Information, Page 6 of the
Assessment-Intervention Record, Completed for Andrew

Intervention Plan Summary

In this section, summarize your intervention plans. Describe the desired outcome behaviors, the procedures for obtaining these behaviors, the materials and personnel involved, and the method of evaluating results. Each of these components of an Intervention Plan is discussed in Chapter 4 of the SSRS Manual.

Short-Term Objectives

Target behavior(s) *(A) Respond appropriately to teasing (B) Control temper when peers disagree with him*

Desired outcome behavior(s) *(A) Politely acknowledge dislike of teasing by peers whenever teasing occurs (B) Express his position and disagreement calmly without physical threats*

Critical setting or situations for change *At school, in class and on playground*

Intervention Procedures

Procedure for maintaining strengths *Reinforce cooperation/compliance involved in the completion of tasks (both academic and at home)*

Procedure for promoting skill acquisition *Use modeling with coaching and behavioral rehearsal to teach new ways of responding to teasing and controlling temper*

Procedure for increasing skill performance *Use verbal praise to reinforce Andrew when he appropriately responds to teasing, and for each day he doesn't lose his temper*

Procedure for reducing problem behaviors *Try DRO to reduce bullying; if he doesn't respond quickly use response cost or time-out*

Procedure for facilitating generalization *Involve parents by sending a note home weekly and implement a self-monitoring report card system*

Intervention Resources

Reinforcers for target child *(1) Free time on computers at school (2) Parent-provided weekly night out (3) comic books*

Instructional or intervention materials *No special materials needed*

Intervention personnel *School psychologist and playground monitor*

Intervention Evaluation

Change in SSRS ratings *Examine Self-Control ratings by Parents, Teachers, and Andrew himself after six to eight weeks*

Mainstreamed-peer comparisons _____

Outcome interviews with significant adults *In addition to parents and teachers, interview playground monitor and school psychologist*

Intervention and Follow-up Evaluation Dates

Intervention begins __*1-7-90*__ Intervention projected to end __*3-15-90*__ Actual ending _____

Intervention evaluation completed _____ Re-evaluation of target behavior(s) _____

Intervention Plan Summary, Page 8 of the *Assessment-Intervention Record,* Completed for Andrew

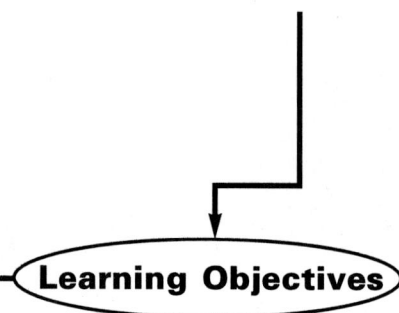

Chapter 14

Adaptive Behavior

Learning Objectives

1. Define adaptive behavior.
2. Give two major reasons why the assessment of adaptive behavior has become so widespread.
3. Describe the strengths and weaknesses of at least two major adaptive behavior assessment instruments.
4. Explain the problem of declassification and propose some solutions.
5. Discuss the relationship between adaptive behavior and intelligence.

The community of Guadalupe is located on the outskirts of Phoenix and Tempe in central Arizona. It is inhabited almost exclusively by Yaqui Indians who migrated from Mexico. For the most part, the residents live in poverty—many live in huts with dirt floors and have neither water nor electricity. Children growing up in Guadalupe often speak a mixture of Yaqui, Spanish, and English. Their cultural values encourage cooperation over competition and quality of work over speed of work. Because of economic pressures, many children drop out of school at the legal minimum age and begin working.

The culture and values of the residents of Guadalupe are quite different from those of the officials of the Tempe school district, in which Guadalupe is located. Not unlike many other suburban school systems, in the Tempe schools value is placed on achievement, timely completion of work, and preparation for college. Many middle-class children come to school knowing their English alphabet and numbers; many Guadalupe children lack these skills. Many of those who teach children from Guadalupe have white middle-class values and white middle-class expectations for their students. When children deviate markedly from these expectations, there is a good chance they will be referred for psychological and educational evaluation.

In the early 1970s large numbers of Guadalupe children were failing in the Tempe classrooms, and referrals for special education were occurring at an alarming rate. Many of these children were diagnosed after taking standardized intelligence tests administered in English. These tests often contained items that require good facility with the English language or are timed. On the basis of the teachers' referral and the testing, many of the children were diagnosed as mentally disabled and placed in special education classrooms *even though many were reported to function quite normally in their home environment.* Upon learning of this, a group of concerned citizens in Guadalupe filed suit in federal court (*Guadalupe Organization v. Tempe Elementary School District,* 1972) and successfully barred the school district from continuing these practices. Numerous similar suits were filed in other parts of the country because children, primarily those from minority cultures, who functioned well outside of school were labeled as mentally disabled because of poor performance in school. One result of these suits was a broadening of the criteria used in schools for classifying mental disabilities. Instead of relying solely on in-school behavior and performance on the intelligence test, it was mandated that the evaluation of someone suspected of having a mental disability include an assessment of out-of-school behavior as well. This out-of-school behavior has been referred to as **adaptive behavior.**

➡ *What Is Adaptive Behavior?*

Although the term applies to the behavior of children with a variety of disabilities (especially children with a behavioral disability), adaptive behavior is best understood within the context of defining a mental disability. The most commonly used definitions are those developed by the American Association of Mental Retardation (AAMR). Prior to the establishment of guidelines by the AAMR, which were formalized in 1959, mental disabilities were defined almost exclusively in terms of a score on an intelligence test. Individuals who scored significantly below were considered to have a mental disability. The AAMR definition of mental disabilities has gradually changed since first appearing in 1961 (Grossman, 1973, 1977, 1981; Heber, 1961), primarily in the use of a wider range of criteria for defining the condition. The 1961 definition broadened the previous definition based on testing. "Mental retardation refers to subaverage general intellectual functioning which originates during the developmental period and is associated with impairment in adaptive behavior" (Heber, 1961, p. 3). A subtle change in wording occurred in 1973: "Mental retardation refers to significantly subaverage general intellectual functioning existing concurrently with deficits in adaptive behavior, and manifested during the developmental period" (Grossman, 1973, p. 11). Although adaptive behavior is mentioned in both definitions, the latter made it quite clear that adaptive behavior must coexist. The 1981 AAMR definition (Grossman, 1981) suggested that mental retardation should be defined by means of a clinical process in which not only IQ but also adaptive behavior, social developmental history, and current functioning in a variety of settings are considered. Adaptive behavior thus became an integral component of the definition of a mental disability. In the most recent definition advanced by AAMR (AAMR, 1992), there has been a further deemphasis on intelligence tests and a corresponding increase in emphasis on adaptive behavior.

But exactly what is adaptive behavior? Several definitions have been offered, but perhaps the most widely accepted is the one advanced by the AAMR:

> Adaptive behavior is defined as the effectiveness or degree with which an individual meets the standards of personal independence and social responsibility expected for age and cultural group.
>
> Since these expectations of adaptive behavior vary for different age groups, deficits in adaptive behavior will vary at different ages. These may be reflected in the following areas.
>
> During infancy and early childhood in:
> 1. Sensory-motor skills development;
> 2. Communication skills (including speech and language);
> 3. Self-help skills;
> 4. Socialization (development of ability to interact with others); and
> During childhood and early adolescence in:
> 5. Application of basic academic skills in daily life activities;
> 6. Application of appropriate reasoning and judgment in mastery of environment;
> 7. Social skills (participation in group activities and interpersonal relationships); and
> During late adolescence and adult life in:
> 8. Vocational and social responsibilities and performances.
>
> The skills required for adaptation during childhood and early adolescence involve complex learning processes. This involves the process by which knowledge is acquired and retained as a function of the experiences of the individual. Difficulties in learning are usually manifested in the academic situation but in evaluation of adaptive behavior, attention should focus not only on the basic academic skills and their use, but also on skills essential to cope

with the environment, including concepts of time and money, self-directed behaviors, social responsiveness, and interactive skills. (Grossman, 1977, pp. 11–14)

This definition has two important components. First, it suggests that adaptive behavior must be evaluated relative to the social context in which it occurs. Thus, such behavior is not an immutable property of the individual, but instead differs from culture to culture. Second, an individual who behaves adaptively must exhibit skills consistent with his or her age. In younger children this requires the development of skills necessary for independent functioning (e.g., self-help and communication skills). Older children and adults must assume personal and social responsibility and maintain themselves independently, especially in an economic sense.

As noted above, AAMR has recently developed new recommendations for the assessment of mental disabilities. The definition includes a marked elaboration of the concept of adaptive behavior. Specifically, the AAMR definition of a mental disability requires the assessment of 10 subareas of adaptive behavior (see table 14.1). Although adaptive behavior has been further delineated, evaluators who attempt to follow the lead of the AAMR will be faced with new problems, not the least of which is the lack of instruments to assess all 10 areas. This will likely mean that more than one instrument would be used to assess adaptive behavior and the comparison of subtests from different instruments has numerous technical problems.

Essentially the new AAMR definition of a mental disability requires that a person have subaverage intellectual functioning and deficits in two or more areas of adaptive skills. Given the high correlation between IQ scores and academic functioning, it is a virtual certainty that anyone who has a subaverage score on an IQ test will also score low on a test of academic skills. Given that the new definition also considers subaverage intelligence to be an IQ score of less than 75, as compared to 70 in the old definition, it appears to be a definition that will allow more children to be classified.

Although the AAMR standards have never been legally binding on schools, they often do foreshadow changes in the law. Also, the standards are used frequently by school-based assessment specialists to justify actions surrounding classification and diagnosis of a mental disability. Hence, the standards merit a thorough understanding.

➡ *Reasons for Assessing Adaptive Behavior*

Although now a routine part of school evaluation of a child who may have a mental disability, the assessment of adaptive behavior was uncommon in public schools 20 years ago. There are a number of reasons that adaptive behavior assessment is now included in evaluations, and we will begin with the most important.

Table 14.1 Adaptive Behavior Subdomains of Functioning

---

1. Communication: Language development, inclusive of both nonsymbolic or preverbal and symbolic or verbal communication (speech, augmentative communication, and nonverbal symbolic communication such as manual signing or symbol use). Communicative skills include, for example, the ability to express oneself with or without the use of symbols and to communicate a request for an object or action, a greeting, a request for attention, a comment, a protest or rejection, an awareness of interrupted activity, attention to object or activity, and acceptance. Higher level skills in communication (e.g., writing a letter) would also relate to functional academics (see the following).

2. Self-Care: Skills involved in toileting, eating, dressing, hygiene, and grooming.

3. Home Living Skills: Skills related to functioning within a home, which include clothing care, housekeeping, yard maintenance, food preparation and cooking, planning and budgeting for shopping, home safety, and daily scheduling. Related skills include orientation and behavior in the home and nearby neighborhood, communication of choices and needs, social interaction, and application of functional academics in the home.

4. Social Skills: Skills related to social exchanges with other individuals, including initiating, interacting, and terminating interaction with others, receiving and responding to pertinent situational cues, recognizing feelings, providing positive and negative feedback, self-regulating one's own behavior, being aware of peers and peer acceptance, gauging the amount and type of interaction with others, assisting others, forming and fostering of friendships and love, coping with demands from others, making choices, sharing, understanding honesty and fairness, and displaying appropriate social-sexual behavior.

5. Community Use: Skills related to the use of community resources appropriately, including traveling in the community, grocery and general shopping at stores and markets, purchasing or obtaining services from other community businesses (gas stations, repair shops, doctor and dentist's offices, etc.), attending church, using public transportation and public facilities like schools, libraries, parks and recreational areas, and streets and sidewalks, and theaters and other cultural places and events. Related skills include behavior in the community, communication of choices and needs, social interaction, and the application of functional academics.

6. Self-Direction: Skills related to making choices, learning and following a schedule, initiating activities appropriate to the setting, conditions, schedule, and personal interests, completing necessary or required tasks, seeking assistance when needed, and resolving problems confronted in familiar and novel situations, and demonstrating appropriate assertiveness and self-advocacy skills.

7. Health and Safety: Skills related to maintenance of one's health in terms of eating, illness, identification, treatment and prevention, basic first aid, sexuality, physical fitness, basic safety considerations (e.g., following rules and laws, use of seat belt, street crossing, interaction with strangers, seeking assistance), regular physical and dental checkups, and personal habits. Related skills include behavior in the community, communication of choices and needs, social interaction, and the application of functional academics.

Table 14.1—*Continued*

8. Functional Academics: Cognitive abilities and skills related to learning at school that also have direct application in one's life (e.g., writing, reading, basic practical math concepts, basic science as it relates to awareness of the physical environment and one's health and sexuality, geography, and social studies). It is important to note that the focus of this skill area is not on grade-level academic achievement but rather on the acquisition of academic skills that are functional in terms of independent living.

9. Leisure: The development of a variety of leisure and recreational interests (i.e., self-entertainment and interactional) that reflect personal preferences and choices and, if the activity will be conducted in public, that reflect age and cultural norms. Skills include choosing and self-initiating interests, using and enjoying home and community leisure and recreational activities alone and with others, playing socially with others, taking turns, terminating or refusing leisure or recreational activities, extending one's duration of participation, and expanding one's repertoire of interests, awareness, and skills. Related skills include behaviors in the leisure and recreational setting, communication of choices and needs, social interaction, application of functional academics, and mobility skills.

10. Work: Skills related to holding a part- or full-time job or jobs in the community in terms of specific job skills, appropriate social behavior, and related work skills (e.g., completion of tasks; awareness of schedules; ability to seek assistance, take criticism, and improve skills; money management, financial resources allocation and the application of other functional academic skills; and skills related to going to and from work, preparation for work, management of oneself while at work, and interaction with coworkers).

From T. Oakland and D. Goldwater, "Assessment and Intervention for Mildly Retarded Children" in G. Phye and D. Reschly, *School Psychology: Perspectives and Issues*, p. 147. Copyright © 1979 Academic Press, Orlando, FL. Reprinted with the permission of Thomas Oakland and Academic Press.

The Law Requires the Assessment of Adaptive Behavior

The delivery of services to disabled children has been significantly influenced by legislation and the courts. The area of adaptive behavior is no exception. The most obvious reason for the increase in adaptive behavior assessments is the numerous lawsuits filed on behalf of children who were diagnosed as having a mental disability even though they functioned adequately outside of the classroom. Certainly, the assessment of adaptive behavior is warranted on other grounds, but without the force of law, such assessment would be far less common today. It would be easy to assume that court intervention in the educational system is an unwarranted intrusion and that educators know best how to assess and educate disabled children. However, in many instances, court decisions have taken what was simply good educational practice and made it the law.

The *Guadalupe* case provides an illustration. The apparent practice in the Tempe schools in the early 1970s was to administer highly verbal intelligence tests in English to children whose primary language was not English. The scores derived from these tests were a major determinant in whether the child was diagnosed as having a deficit in intellectual functioning, even if that child seemed normal to people in his or her community.

The plaintiffs in *Guadalupe* argued that school assessment practices were inappropriate. The court agreed and required the assessment of adaptive behavior outside of school as well. Further, the court stipulated that results of intelligence tests could not be the sole basis for classifying children as having a mental disability. From the perspective of a professional psychologist or educator, it is difficult to disagree with the court's ruling because it is consistent with good educational practice!

As cases similar to *Guadalupe* became more numerous, the assessment of adaptive behavior was incorporated into more and more federal and state legislation governing the education of disabled children. Perhaps the most important of these developments was that the assessment of adaptive behavior was incorporated into the Education for All Handicapped Children Act of 1975, P.L. 94–142 and, more recently, the Individuals with Disabilities Education Act (IDEA). The bottom line is that individuals who assess children who might be classified as mentally disabled under IDEA must incorporate an index of adaptive behavior into the assessment process.

Reduction of Bias in Assessment Processes

It is incumbent on professionals who collect and utilize test data to be as fair as possible when identifying a child with a deficit in intellectual functioning. The problems are compounded when evaluating a child from a minority culture. In many cases the content of some tests is especially difficult for such children, even though, as we have stated, the tests are unbiased. Often language problems, cultural differences, and economic factors contribute to difference among racial and ethnic groups. Including a measure of adaptive behavior in the assessment process can help differentiate children whose cultural differences account for low IQ scores. Adaptive behavior is, by definition, the ability to perform in line with *cultural* expectations. *Every* normally functioning six-year-old can reasonably be expected to take care of his or her self-care needs. However, whether the same child knows which animal gives milk or what skis are depends on a number of sociocultural factors.

Assessment Provides Information on What Skills Need to Be Taught

Intelligence tests can be used for classification and diagnostic decisions, but they are much less useful in providing a parent or teacher with information about *what* to teach. On the other hand, most adaptive behavior scales are composed of checklists or ratings, and respondents indicate whether a child can or cannot perform or how well she or he performs a particular skill. A typical item might assess the extent to which a child is capable of getting dressed without assistance. Perhaps the child can put the clothing on but cannot button buttons or snap snaps. Logically, performing these skills will be appropriate educational goals.

A slightly different approach is to view the age-appropriate skills on a measure of adaptive behavior as goals that must be accomplished before a child can be integrated into the community at a level consistent with societal expectations. Some measures of adaptive behavior provide lists of directly teachable behaviors.

➡ *Measures of Adaptive Behavior*

The selection of an adaptive behavior assessment instrument that is appropriate for a given child in a specific situation requires careful study. However, few of the scales measure all components of adaptive behavior and some are appropriate only for certain ages. Well over a hundred such instruments are available. We will describe a small sample of what we consider to be the most important. A slightly wider selection is profiled in table 14.2.

AAMD Adaptive Behavior Scale–School Edition

Overview and Purpose
Of all the instruments available for the assessment of adaptive behavior, perhaps the most widely known and used is the AAMD Adaptive Behavior Scale–School Edition, or ABS–SE (Lambert & Windmiller, 1981). Its widespread use is due to three factors. First, the ABS–SE is one of the oldest measures of adaptive behavior, with the present version representing a revision of the ABS–SE published in 1974. Second, sponsorship by the AAMR, which has assumed leadership in the development of definitions of both mental disabilities and adaptive behavior, has added to its visibility. Third, the ABS–SE is technically superior to most other measures in its standardization procedures and the degree to which it comprehensively assesses a broad range of competencies and skills.

The comprehensive nature of the ABS–SE is illustrated in table 14.3. Note that the instrument is divided into two parts. Part One consists of nine domains considered important to the development of personal independence in daily living. Part Two assesses a wide array of behaviors generally considered to be inappropriate and unacceptable. The behaviors assessed in Part One are those most commonly associated with traditional definitions of "social maturity" and adaptive behavior, such as self-help skills and language. The personality and behavior problems assessed in

Table 14.2 Measures of Adaptive Behavior

Instrument	Physical Development, Sensory Motor, and Locomotion	Self-Direction	Language and Communication	Vocational and Occupation	Economic	Social	Self-Help, Independent Functioning, and Self-Maintenance	With Peers In School	In the Family	In the Community	Mixed	Age Range	Clinical	School	Screening	Placement	Programing	Teacher (Examiner)	Diagnostician	Paraprofessional	Teacher (Respondent)	Parent/Family	Child	Reliability and Validity Data Available	Percentile	Scaled Score	Administration Time
AAMD Adaptive Behavior Scale-School Edition (Lambert & Windmiller, 1981)	x	x	x		x	x	x				x	3–17		x	x	x	x	x	x	x	x	x	x	Yes	x	x	45 minutes to 1 hour
Adaptive Behavior Inventory for Children (Mercer & Lewis, 1978)		x	x	x		x	x	x	x	x		5–11		x		x	x		x			x		Yes	x	x	1 hour
Camelot (Foster, 1974)		x	x	x	x	x	x					2–adult	x	x	x	x	x	x	x	x	x			Yes			1 hour
Children's Adaptive Behavior Scale (Richmond & Kicklighter, 1980)	x	x	x	x	x	x	x					5–10	x	x	x	x	x	x	x	x			x	Yes	x		30 minutes to 1 hour
Social and Prevocational Information Battery (Halpern et al., 1975)				x	x	x	x					junior–senior high school		x		x	x	x	x	x			x	Yes	x		1–2 hours
Vineland Adaptive Behavior Scale (Sparrow et al., 1984)	x	x	x	x	x	x	x					birth–18 yr. 11 mo.	x	x		x	x		x		x	x		Yes			20 minutes

From T. Oakland and D. Goldwater, "Assessment and Intervention for Mildly Retarded Children" in G. Phye and D. Reschly, *School Psychology: Perspectives and Issues*, p. 147. Copyright © 1979 Academic Press, Orlando, FL.

Table 14.3 Domains and Subdomains from the ABS–SE

Part One	*Domains and Subdomains*	*Part Two*	*Domains*
Domain 1	Independent Functioning	*Domain 10*	Aggressiveness
	Eating Subdomain	*Domain 11*	Antisocial vs. Social Behavior
	Toilet Use Subdomain	*Domain 12*	Rebelliousness
	Cleanliness Subdomain	*Domain 13*	Trustworthiness
	Appearance Subdomain	*Domain 14*	Withdrawal vs. Involvement
	Care of Clothing Subdomain	*Domain 15*	Mannerisms
	Dressing & Undressing Subdomain	*Domain 16*	Interpersonal Manners
	Travel Subdomain	*Domain 17*	Acceptability of Vocal Habits
	Other Independent Functioning Subdomain	*Domain 18*	Acceptability of Habits
Domain 2	Physical Development	*Domain 19*	Activity Level
	Sensory Development Subdomain	*Domain 20*	Symptomatic Behavior
	Motor Development Subdomain	*Domain 21*	Use of Medications
Domain 3	Economic Activity		
	Money Handling & Budgeting Subdomain		
	Shopping Skills Subdomain		
Domain 4	Language Development		
	Expression Subdomain		
	Comprehension Subdomain		
	Social Language Development Subdomain		
Domain 5	Numbers & Time		
Domain 6	Prevocational Activity		
Domain 7	Self-Direction		
	Initiative Subdomain		
	Perseverance Subdomain		
	Leisure Time Subdomain		
Domain 8	Responsibility		
Domain 9	Socialization		

From Lambert, N., and Windmiller, M. (1981). *AAMD Adaptive Behavior Scale—School Edition*. Austin, TX: PRO-ED. Reprinted by permission.

Part Two, which are not usually included on such instruments, offer a way to measure those behaviors that may actually *interfere* with successful adaptive functioning.

To simplify understanding and interpreting the ABS–SE, the test's domains were categorized into five clusters (see figure 14.1). These clusters were derived by evaluating statistically whether certain domains were highly interrelated. It turned out, for example, that several items in Domains 4 and 5 were highly related to each other and that each of those items seemed to be measuring some aspect of Community Self-Sufficiency. Because the statistical procedure used to determine these clusters of inter-related items is called factor analysis, the clusters are referred to as factors. In communicating information about a particular child it is much easier to interpret only the five factors than to refer to each of the 95 test items or even the 21 domains.

Furthermore, since the factors are composed of several items and the domains are composed of only a few, the factors are much more stable and reliable indicators of a child's functioning and thus more appropriate for diagnostic and classification decisions. The domain sources, which are more behavioral, may be most useful for instructional planning.

The factors can be described briefly as follows:

1. *Personal Self-Sufficiency*. This cluster reflects the degree to which a child is able to handle personal needs such as eating, drinking, and toilet use.

2. *Community Self-Sufficiency*. This factor assesses the extent to which a child can function appropriately in situations such as traveling about the neighborhood, communicating with others, and engaging in economic activity.

3. *Personal-Social Responsibility*. Items within this factor reflect relatively high-level social interaction skills, including getting to school or work on time, showing initiative in school or job settings, interacting cooperatively with others, and assuming responsibility for one's own actions.

4. *Social Adjustment*. This factor is composed of items exclusively from Part Two of the ABS–SE. The problem behaviors assessed include those in which a child is inappropriately interacting with others (e.g., being aggressive, lying, or cheating). Such behaviors are characteristic of acting-out or children with behavioral disorders.

5. *Personal Adjustment*. Items in this cluster reflect three areas of inappropriate contact with others, such as excessive hugging, touching, or kissing, and unacceptable vocal habits, such as echolalia or talking too loudly.

The first three factors are arranged in virtually a developmental progression from least complex to most complex. Skills assessed by Factor 1 are typically developed early in life and are responsive to training. By

Figure 14.1 The Five ABS-SE Factors

	Factor **1** Personal Self-Sufficiency	Factor **2** Community Self-Sufficiency	Factor **3** Personal-Social Responsibility	Factor **4** Social Adjustment	Factor **5** Personal Adjustment
ITEM 1 Use of Table Utensils	●				
ITEM 2 Eating in Public		●			
ITEM 3 Drinking	●				
ITEM 5 Toilet Training	●				
ITEM 6 Washing Hands & Face	●				
ITEM 7 Bathing	●				
ITEM 8 Personal Hygiene		●			
ITEM 10 Clothing		●			
ITEM 11 Care of Clothing		●			
ITEM 12 Dressing	●				
ITEM 13 Shoes	●				
ITEM 14 Sense of Direction		●			
ITEM 15 Public Transportation		●			
ITEM 16 Telephone		●			
ITEM 17 Miscellaneous Independent Functioning		●			
DOMAIN 2 Physical Develop	●				
DOMAIN 3 Econ Activity		●			
DOMAIN 4 Language Development		●			
DOMAIN 5 Numbers & Time		●			
ITEM 40 Job Complexity		●			
ITEM 41 School Job Performance			●		
ITEM 42 School or Work Habits			●		
DOMAIN 7 Self Direction			●		
DOMAIN 8 Responsibility			●		
ITEM 50 Cooperation			●		
ITEM 51 Consideration for Others			●		
ITEM 52 Awareness of Others			●		
ITEM 53 Interaction with Others			●		
ITEM 54 Participation in Group Activities			●		
DOMAIN 10 Aggressiveness				●	
DOMAIN 11 Antisoc vs Soc Beh				●	
DOMAIN 12 Rebelliousness				●	
DOMAIN 13 Trustworthiness				●	
DOMAIN 14 Withdrawal				●	
DOMAIN 15 Mannerisms			●		
DOMAIN 16 Appropriateness of Interpersonal Manners					●
DOMAIN 17 Vocal Habits					●
DOMAIN 18 Habits				●	
DOMAIN 19 Activity Level				●	
DOMAIN 20 Symptomatic Beh				●	

From Lambert, N., and Windmiller, M. (1981). *AAMD Adaptive Behavior Scale-School Edition*. Austin, TX: PRO-ED Reprinted by permission.

contrast, the skills assessed by Factors 2 and 3 represent more complex forms of learning that require children to generalize skills learned in one situation to new settings. Factors 4 and 5 are relatively independent of chronological age but instead represent inappropriate behaviors that can occur at almost any developmental stage.

The ABS–SE is designed for use with children aged 3 years, 3 months, to 17 years, 2 months. It is administered either by reading the items to someone who knows the child well (such as parent or classroom aide) or by someone who knows the child and who has been trained in use of the test. First-person assessments require 15 to 45 minutes, but third-party interviews can last more than an hour. The test's authors encourage users to obtain ratings from both teachers and parents whenever possible.

Figure 14.2 illustrates two items from ABS–SE. Note that both are arranged in order of difficulty, as are most items in Part One; the rater is supposed to circle the statement that describes best the most difficult task the child can perform. Items on the ABS–SE can be criticized on two counts. First, some are vague and difficult to interpret. On Item 53 (see figure 14.2), for example, what is the meaning of "a short period of time" in the second statement and "with little interaction" in the third statement? Second, an inadequate number of items assess the higher-order social interaction skills required of older children. Numerous items reflect self-care skills and self-sufficiency, but a relative lack of items measure the skills expected of adolescents.

Standardization Sample and Norms

The ABS–SE was standardized over a period of seven years (1972–79) on 6,523 subjects from 3 to 17 years of age. The sample contained children from two states (California and Florida) who were regular education, mild mental disability (formerly EMR), or moderate to severe mental disability (formerly TMR) students. Representatives from various ethnic groups (black, Spanish- surnamed, white, and others) and from cities of various population densities (urban, suburban, and rural) were included. Although the sample did not represent all geographic areas of the country, its size and diversity were admirable relative to those of most other adaptive behavior scales.

Separate norms are provided for three reference groups (regular education, mild mental disability, and moderate to severe mental disability). Depending on whether they are going to be used for classification or instructional planning, scores can be transformed into either percentiles or scaled scores.

Data Obtained

Responses to individual items are recorded in an Assessment Booklet. Following completion of the scale, total scores for each domain are calculated by summing items within the domain. Depending on the purpose for which the ABS–SE is being used, scores are transferred from the booklet to a

Figure 14.2 Sample Items from the ABS-SE

ITEM 26

Errands
(Circle only one)

Goes to several shops and
specifies different items 4

Goes to one shop and
specifies one item 3

Goes on errands for
simple purchasing
without a note 2

Goes on errands for
simple purchasing with
a note 1

Cannot be sent on
errands 0

ITEM 53

Interaction With Others
(Circle only one)

Interacts with others in
group games or activities 3

Interacts with others for
at least a short period of
time (showing or offering
toys, clothing, or
objects, etc.) 2

Interacts with others
imitatively with little
interaction 1

Does not respond to
others in a socially
acceptable manner 0

From Lambert, N., and Windmiller, M. (1981). *AAMD Adaptive Behavior Scale–School Edition.* Austin, TX: PRO–ED. Reprinted by permission.

Diagnostic Profile or an Instructional Planning Profile or both. Because these two profiles are in booklets separate from the Assessment Booklet, transferring scores is tedious.

If the ABS–SE is to be used to make a classification or diagnostic decision (e.g., Is this child's adaptive behavior consistent with a diagnosis of a mental disability?), raw scores from the Assessment Booklet are converted to scaled scores by referencing the normative tables provided. Two types of scores can be obtained. The first type is a factor score for each of the five factors. Obtaining factor scores is an eight-step process involving several score transformations and transferences from one booklet to another. The outcome is a profile of how the child compares to any one or all of the three normative groups (regular education, EMR, and TMR students).

Figure 14.3 illustrates the use of the ABS–SE factor scores. Note that factor scores have been plotted according to both regular education and the children with mild mental disability reference groups. The scores in the example appear more "average" when compared to children with mild mental disability rather than to the regular education group. Thus, the

Figure 14.3   Sample Instructional Planning Profile for Part One of the ABS-SE

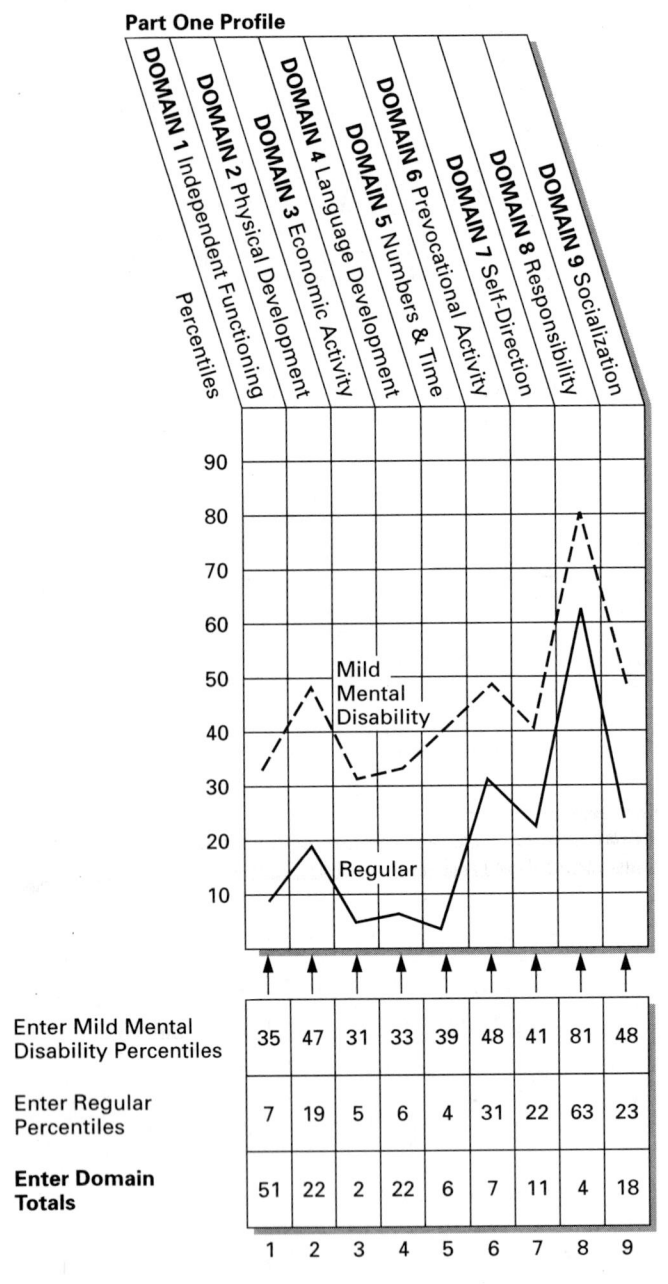

From Lambert, N., and Windmiller, M. (1981). *AAMD Adaptive Behavior Scale–School Edition.* Austin, TX: PRO–ED. Reprinted by permission.

child's adaptive behavior would be considered to be consistent with a diagnosis of mild mental disability. In general, factor scores below 7 represent a significant deviation from the reference group.

The second type of score available for classification and diagnostic decisions is the comparison score, which is derived by combining the scores from the Personal Self-Sufficiency, Community Self-Sufficiency, and Personal-Social Responsibility factors. Recall that these three scales most closely represent what has traditionally been called adaptive behavior. The comparison score is useful if an overall or summary score is needed to describe a particular child's functioning. By consulting the norm tables, the comparison score can be converted into a percentile.

If results from the ABS–SE are going to be used for instructional planning, scores from the Assessment Booklet can be transferred to the Instructional Planning Profile. Unlike the Diagnostic Profile, which contained factor scores, the Instructional Planning Profile is used to plot percentiles for each of the 21 domains (see table 14.3). The ABS–SE comes with a 90-page guide that describes a large number of commercially available instructional materials that can be used to remediate deficits in areas targeted by the test.

In sum, the effective use of the ABS–SE is thus facilitated by its comprehensive array of accompanying materials, including a 15-page Assessment Booklet that contains the items, a 90-page Administration and Planning Manual, an 83-page Diagnostic and Technical Manual, an Instructional Planning Profile, a Diagnostic Profile, and Parents Guide, which not only discusses the measure but provides information about adaptive behavior in general.

Reliability and Validity

Reliability data are extremely limited for an instrument that has had so much effort and expense put into other areas of its development. The only such information presented is for internal consistency. Although reliability is adequate with respect to this one type, it is surprising that test-retest and interrater reliabilities were not reported. Furthermore, information on reliability is available only for the factor scores and not the domain scores.

Two major types of validity data were presented by the authors: (a) data on the degree to which the scores on the ABS–SE are correlated with intelligence, and (b) data on the degree to which the ABS–SE can predict the appropriate classification for regular and mildly mentally disabled children. Scores on most domains on the ABS–SE have low to moderate correlations with IQ scores, except from those domains that overlap with intelligence test content (e.g., language development) and have a strong association with IQ scores and those domains from Part Two that have near-zero correlations with IQ scores, as would be expected.

The capacity of the ABS–SE to categorize children correctly has also been evaluated by assessing children who were already placed in classrooms for children designated as regular education, mild mental disability, or moderate to severe mental disability students. The results of several such studies suggested that children assigned to such programs were significantly different with respect to adaptive behavior as measured by the ABS–SE.

Summary

Technically, the ABS–SE is an excellent instrument that is superior to most other measures of adaptive behavior. It is a well-organized test that is accompanied by a wide array of ancillary materials. Limitations of the ABS–SE include the use of items that can be easily misinterpreted and its inadequate assessment of adolescents with mild mental disabilities. Although administration and full interpretation of the ABS–SE can be time-consuming when done by hand, the scope and depth of the data yielded by this process are impressive.

Adaptive Behavior Inventory for Children

Overview and Purpose

It is important to know that the Adaptive Behavior Inventory for Children (ABIC) was developed by a sociologist, Jane Mercer, and her colleagues (Mercer & Lewis, 1978). Her socioecological perspective is that a child's adaptive behavior can be evaluated only in relationship to the role expectations of the family, the community, the peer group, the school, and the economy and self-maintenance roles. The ABIC is an outgrowth of the research by Mercer and others into the processes used to diagnose individuals as having a mild mental disability (Mercer, 1970). Because she concluded from her data that available tests inadequately measured adaptive behavior, she developed a comprehensive assessment system—the System of Multicultural Pluralistic Assessment (SOMPA)—of which the ABIC is an integral part.

The ABIC can be best understood by reference to the unique rhetoric of Mercer (1979):

> Adaptive behavior is conceptualized as achieving an adaptive fit in social systems through the development of interpersonal ties and the acquisition of specific skills required to fulfill the task functions associated with particular roles. . . . The preschool child's experience is limited mainly to the family and neighborhood. Therefore, questions in the ABIC for young children are concerned mainly with roles in the family and in the immediate neighborhood and peer group. As the child moves into the social system of the school, there are questions concerning performance in nonacademic school roles and interaction with peers at schools. . . . As the child grows older, the child assumes more community roles, ranges over a larger geographic territory, learns to function

in earner and consumer roles, and assumes greater responsibility for protection of his or her own health and welfare. The developmental sequencing is reflected in the sequencing of ABIC items. (p. 93)

The ABIC consists of 242 questions that are administered in an interview to either a caretaker who knows the child well or, preferably, a parent. It yields scores for six scales: Family, Community, Peer Relations, Nonacademic School Roles, Earner/Consumer, and Self-Maintenance. Optimally, the interview takes place in the child's home and is conducted by someone with whom the parent or other caretaker is comfortable. Thus, interviewers are instructed to wear simple clothing that is similar to that worn by those in the same social class as the parent or caretaker. The interview should also be conducted in the primary language of the home. School districts that use the ABIC often find it useful to train paraprofessionals who already fit into a particular social system in the administration of the SOMPA.

Items are structured to assess the *frequency* with which a child performs certain activities. A typical item in terms of format and degree of vagueness of wording is: "Does [name of child] take telephone and other messages correctly and give them to the right person? 1. Sometimes; 2. Regularly; or 3. Never." Respondents are repeatedly asked to distinguish between words such as *sometimes, often, occasionally,* and *frequently.* Since these words may have different meanings to various respondents, the significance of the test results is also called into question. Another problem is that the interviewer must read *all* items appropriate for a child's age, even if the answer is known before the question is asked. Thus, an interviewer sitting in a house with a dirt floor, no electricity, and no running water may feel uncomfortable asking the parent about the child's television habits when obviously there is no television in the home.

Standardization Sample and Norms
The ABIC was standardized on a stratified random sample of 2,085 California schoolchildren. The sample was stratified according to age, gender, ethnic group (there were equal numbers of whites, blacks, and Hispanics), and community size. Sample selection appears to have been more carefully conducted than for the other measures of adaptive behavior.

Norms are provided for children aged 5 years, 0 months to 11 years, 11 months. This age span was divided into three-month intervals, with separate norm tables provided for each. The norms are used to convert raw scores into scaled scores for each of the six areas assessed by the ABIC.

Data Obtained
Scoring procedures for the ABIC contain some built-in safeguards to help ensure its validity. The most prominent of these is a Veracity Scale, which contains 24 items that involve activities performed only by older adolescents and would not be at all typical of the 5- to 11-year-old children for whom

the ABIC is designed. The validity of a child's scores are questioned if high scores are obtained on too many of these high-level skills. The number of times the respondent answered "don't know" to questions represents another validity check. It is assumed that too many responses of this type suggest that the respondent doesn't know the child well enough to give reliable results!

Raw scores for each of the six scales of the ABIC are converted to scaled scores, which correspond closely to percentiles. A more global indicator of adaptive functioning can be obtained by simply averaging the six scaled scores. The primary use for data obtained from the ABIC is to assist in diagnosis and classification decisions. It is far less useful than other instruments for the design of educational programs.

Reliability and Validity

Two types of reliability data are available for the ABIC. First, the split-half procedure was utilized to assess reliability using the entire standardization sample. This analysis indicated that reliability was generally above .75 for the six scales and above .95 for the Average Scaled Score across all age groups for which the instrument is appropriate.

Second, the interrater agreement between individuals who heard the same interview was measured at workshops designed to train people to use the ABIC. Near the end of the training, workshop participants listened to an interview conducted by the instructor. Each participant scored the interview independently, and the degree to which the scores differed was assessed. Across a series of 10 such interviews, with different parents and in different communities, there was very high interobserver agreement. The technical manual for the ABIC contains little information relevant to its validity. In fact, Mercer (1979) states that traditional psychometric methods are inappropriate for the validation to the ABIC:

> For example, it would not be logical to validate the mother's report of the child's performance in the peer group with the teacher's report of peer group performance since neither the mother nor the teacher are members of the peer group. Likewise, it would be even less defensible to "validate" the mother's report of the child's family role performance against the teacher's responses to the questions in the Family Scale. The validity of the ABIC is judged by its ability to reflect accurately the extent to which the child is meeting the expectations of the members of the social systems covered in the scales, not by its correlation with teacher judgments, school performance, or performance on measures of achievement tests, aptitude tests, or "intelligence" tests. (p. 109)

Just how to assess whether the ABIC actually reflects the degree to which the child is meeting societal expectations is not known. Lacking such a methodology, other researchers have applied more traditional psychometric criteria to the test (Oakland, 1979). Their research suggests that the correlation between cores on the ABIC and either intelligence tests or achievement tests is so low as to indicate that the ABIC is relatively independent of either intelligence or achievement. This suggests that the ABIC cannot be used in predicting progress in school. Mercer would probably not be surprised by this finding, given that the purpose of the ABIC is to predict acceptance by a social system rather than success in school. Currently, we know of no research indicating how the ABIC is related to other adaptive behavior instruments.

Because of the lack of research on the ABIC, it is impossible to determine exactly what the instrument is measuring. Studies do suggest what it is not measuring (intelligence and school achievement). Until it can be established whether it measures some aspect of adaptive behavior that would be useful in schools, its use for this purpose is highly suspect.

Summary

The ABIC was designed from a socioecological perspective to try to improve the process of diagnosing children with mild mental disabilities in elementary school children. Because its primary purpose is as a diagnostic instrument, the ABIC is less useful for developing educational plans. However, given the lack of suitable validity data, its use even for diagnostic purposes is questionable. The ABIC has the potential to be a very useful addition to the list of measures for assessing adaptive behavior, but full potential of this instrument must await additional research.

Children's Adaptive Behavior Scale

Overview and Purpose

Unlike most other measures of adaptive behavior, the Children's Adaptive Behavior Scale, or CABS (Richmond & Kicklighter, 1980) is designed to assess *directly* a child's ability to perform adaptively. Administration of the CABS is similar to the procedure used with individually administered intelligence tests in that the "testing" is conducted by a qualified examiner in a one-to-one setting. During the process the child is asked to perform various tasks and to respond to questions in five major domains:

1. *Language Development.* This area assesses "socially essential, rather than desirable, levels of development" (Richmond & Kicklighter, 1980, p. 5). Although its primary focus is oral expressive language (e.g., the child is asked to name something that can be eaten), some items require the child to read and write.

2. *Independent Functioning.* This domain measures the extent to which a child can assume responsibility for tasks encountered daily during normal living. Children are asked questions such as, "Why should you brush your teeth?"

3. *Family Role Performance*. This area assesses how well a child is capable of coping with the normal demands of a home environment. Items focus on the family ("How many people are in your family?") and duties usually performed at home (e.g., "Tell me two ways to cook an egg.").

4. *Economic-Vocational Activity*. This area assesses knowledge of working, earning, and spending. A majority of the items pertain to money concepts, money usage ("About how much does a small can of Coke cost?"), and vocational concepts ("Where does a nurse usually work?").

5. *Socialization*. This domain assesses the degree to which a child interacts appropriately with others.

The CABS is designed to be used with children from 5 to 10 years of age. Since the instrument is directly administered, third-party interviews are not required. This may be an advantage, especially in the light of indications that the information elicited from a third party may be subject to bias (Coulter & Morrow, 1978). Administration requires approximately 30 minutes, which is considerably less than is needed for many other measures of adaptive behavior.

Standardization Sample and Norms

The standardization group for the CABS consisted of only 250 mildly mentally disabled children in South Carolina and Georgia. Norms were included at each age level. Although the authors indicate that the test is appropriate for children five years of age, no five-year-olds were included in the sample.

Because the standardization inadequately represents the national population, the authors recommend that users construct local norms. A possible source of confusion in the use of the norms is that they are referenced to a group of children with mild mental disability. The instrument is interpreted by comparing an individual's domain scores with the age norms for the reference group. If there is close correspondence between the child and the reference group, the subject is presumed to display adaptive behavior consistent with a diagnosis of mild mental disability. Unfortunately, it is unclear just how close to the norms a child must be for this diagnosis. Likewise, it is not clear how far above the mean for mildly mentally disabled children a child must be for his or her adaptive behavior to be considered inconsistent with such a diagnosis.

Data Obtained

The data obtained from the CABS are in the form of age equivalent scores for each of the five major domains. The authors indicate that the domains are relatively independent and suggest using five domain scores diagnostically. Thus, a child who scores well in the Socialization domain but performs poorly on the Language domain may be a candidate for language programming.

Reliability and Validity

Internal consistency reliability coefficients were reported for a sample of 250 mildly mentally disabled children and ranged from a low of .63 for Language Development and Socialization to a high of .83 for Independent Functioning. Reliability coefficients in this range suggest that using the CABS for making important decisions is a questionable practice.

Although the CABS is designed to reflect adaptive behavior, there is some question of whether it may be more highly associated with intelligence than is desirable and to a greater degree than other measures of such behavior. Part of the problem is that because with the CABS a child is evaluated in a one-to-one setting, we must *infer* that behavior in that setting reflects how the child actually performs outside the testing situation. For example, many items on the CABS assess whether a child *knows* how to perform under given circumstances. It is thus assumed that there is a correspondence between knowing and *doing*. However, it is possible, and in fact probable, that such a relationship does not exist in many instances.

Correlations between the CABS total score and the Wechsler Intelligence Scale for Children-Revised (WISC-R; Wechsler, 1974) are .57 for Verbal IQ, .33 for Performance IQ, and .51 for Full-Scale IQ. This would suggest the CABS has a relatively strong relationship to intelligence, especially verbal intelligence. Such a relationship has disturbing implications. Recall that a primary reason for assessing adaptive behavior is to prevent children with language problems from being inappropriately labeled as having a mild mental disability. With the verbal format of the CABS, however, the true adaptive functioning of children with poor language skills may be markedly underestimated. Contrast this with the ABIC, which has near-zero correlations with IQ test scores (Mercer & Lewis, 1978).

Additional evidence that the CABS is measuring something different from other measures of adaptive behavior is that the correlations between CABS and other instruments are low to moderate; the test authors reported that such correlations were statistically significant in 42 of 60 possible comparisons. However, most of these correlations were below .40, suggesting the two instruments are not highly related.

Summary

The CABS is unique in being a *direct* measure of adaptive functioning in children. However, because of sketchy reliability data and validity studies that suggest moderate correlations with verbal IQ test scores, the CABS should be used only in conjunction with measures of adaptive behavior that rely on third-party interviews. In such cases the CABS can broaden the range of skills examined in a comprehensive assessment of adaptive behavior.

Vineland Adaptive Behavior Scales

Overview and Purpose

The purpose of the Vineland Adaptive Behavior Scales (Sparrow, Balla, & Cicchetti, 1984) (VABS) is to assess disabled and nondisabled individuals from birth to adulthood in four behavior domains: Communication, Daily Living, Socialization, and Motor Skills. Three versions of the scales exist, including the Survey Form, which has 297 items; the Expanded Form, which has 577 items; and the classroom edition, which has 244 items. Administration requires that someone familiar with the child be interviewed. The technical information pertaining to the VABS pertains primarily to the Survey Form.

Standardization Sample and Norms

The VABS was standardized on 3,000 individuals ranging in age from birth to 18 years, 11 months. The stratification of the sample is very good with respect to all major demographic variables, including age, geographic region, parental education, race or ethnic group, community size, and educational placement.

Norms are provided in a number of different forms for a wide variety of populations. A useful feature is that standard score equivalents are available for the raw scores for each behavior domain and for overall functioning. This latter score, the Adaptive Behavior Composite Standard, has a mean of 100 and a standard deviation of 15, thus facilitating comparisons with intelligence tests. Other available norms include percentile ranks and stanines, age equivalent scores, and maladaptive level scores for the optional Maladaptive Behavior domain. Supplemental norms are provided for comparison of older individuals up to age 40 as well as those who are emotionally disturbed, hearing impaired, and visually impaired.

Data Obtained

The VABS yields scores for the Communication domain (including subdomain scores for Receptive, Expressive, and Written Language), the Daily Living domain (including subdomain scores for Personal, Domestic, and Community Living), the Socialization domain (including subdomain scores for Interpersonal Relationships, Play and Leisure Time, and Coping Skills), and the Motor Skills domain (including subdomain scores for Gross and Fine Motor Skills). The Adaptive Behavior Composite Standard is based on functioning in each of the four behavior domains and reflects overall adaptive behavior. The Maladaptive Behavior domain indicates the extent to which the frequency of someone's inappropriate behavior is significantly different from that of the normative group.

Reliability and Validity

Reliability of the VABS appears to be adequate for the four behavior domains and poor to adequate for the subdomains. Median split-half reliability coefficients across ages ranged from .83 for the Motor Skills domain to .90 for the Daily Living domain. Interrater reliability for the domains were lower and ranged from .62 to .78. The reliability domains were lower and ranged from .62 to .78. The reliability of the subdomains is very questionable for some age groups, and diagnostic decisions should probably not be based on them.

Primarily because of the recent publication of the VABS, validity data are somewhat sparse. Existing data do suggest the instrument is moderately correlated with other adaptive behavior scales and predictably has relatively low correlations with intelligence tests. A large number of validation studies will no doubt appear over the next few years.

Summary

The VABS is one of the better adaptive behavior tests available. Its psychometric properties are as good or better than those of any other instrument. In addition, it is one of the more useful instruments for making intervention programming decisions.

Social and Prevocational Information Battery

Overview and Purpose

A variety of tests assess the adaptive behavior of children who are 12 years old and younger. However, the range of instruments that assess someone who is in junior or senior high school is much more limited. The Social and Prevocational Information Battery, or SPIB (Halpern, Raffeld, Irvin, & Link, 1975), is one of the most comprehensive scales available for adolescents.

Although it is not billed as an adaptive behavior scale, the SPIB comprehensively assesses the skills needed to develop personal and social responsibility. More specifically, it is designed to assess five areas widely regarded as central to the community adjustment of students with mild mental disabilities.

1. *Economic Self-Sufficiency.* Tests in this domain measure a student's ability in banking, budgeting, and purchasing. Individual items focus on understanding money, establishing a checking account, and paying bills.

2. *Employability.* This section contains items that assess job-related behaviors and job-search skills. The job-related behaviors include how to get along with a boss, how to ask for help, and how to interact with the public. Job-search skills such as completing employment applications and interviewing are also assessed.

3. *Family Living.* This area measures skills related to home management and physical health. A student is questioned about putting out accidental fires, washing clothing, and handling minor illnesses and injuries.

4. *Personal.* This domain assesses knowledge of personal hygiene and grooming, such as showering and changing clothing.

5. *Communications.* This domain exclusively tests the ability to read and interpret functional signs such as ENTER, EXIT, MEN, and POISON.

The SPIB contains a total of 277 items, which are orally administered to one or more students who mark their responses on answer sheets. Because the response format is true-false or picture selection, students are not penalized for reading difficulties. Testing requires three sessions (preferably on separate days) lasting approximately one hour each. The directions for administering the SPIB are highly structured and well organized.

Standardization Sample and Norms

The SPIB was standardized on a sample of 906 junior and senior high school students, stratified according to school size and geographic region. Unfortunately, the entire sample was taken from Oregon. The students were all diagnosed as mildly mentally disabled (mean IQ = 68) and ranged in age from 14 to 20 years. The test manual indicates that the majority of the sample group was Caucasian but does not provide actual numbers of various ethnic groups. Separate norms are provided for students in junior high (grades 7 to 9) and senior high (grades 10 to 12). Since the reference group was entirely diagnosed as mildly mentally disabled students, a student who scores at the 50th percentile is average with respect to the norm group and *not* with respect to the general population.

Data Obtained

By using the norms, raw scores can be converted into percentiles for each of the major areas measured by the SPIB. It is also possible to analyze the individual items to discover more specific areas of weakness. The results can then be translated into educational objectives.

Reliability and Validity

Two forms of reliability data are reported for the SPIB: internal consistency and test-retest. For both types, reliability was in the mid-.80s for total test scores. Such figures are slightly lower than desirable for the subtest scores but excellent for the total test score.

Several types of validity data are discussed in the manual. Predictive validity was examined by comparing the scores of graduating seniors with counselor ratings of the students one year later. The results of this comparison suggested that the SPIB predicts community adjustment reasonably well.

Correlations between the SPIB and IQ scores from both the WISC indicated a moderate positive relationship. Correlations between individual subtests on the SPIB and full-scale IQ scores ranged from .37 to .51, with a median of .49. This suggests that whatever the SPIB is measuring is somewhat similar to what IQ tests measure; in part this is to be expected, for the positive adaptive behavior of adolescents with mild mental disabilities does require some of the skills measured by intelligence tests.

Summary

The SPIB is designed to assess skills associated with the ultimate community adjustment of junior and senior high school students. It is one of the few useful measures of the adaptive behavior of adolescents, for predictive validity data suggest the instrument does adequately predict personal and social adjustment in a community setting.

➔ Problems and Issues in the Assessment of Adaptive Behavior

The strong need to assess adaptive behavior that arose during the early 1970s resulted in the proliferation of well over 100 scales and checklists (Meyers, Nihira, & Zetlin, 1979), some of which have been interviewed here. With this new technology came the inevitable need to evaluate the effects of more than a decade or research and practice. Thus, we conclude our discussion of adaptive behavior by reviewing two of the most important issues that have evolved in the assessment of adaptive behavior.

Declassification of Students

The most pressing practical problem that has resulted from the use of adaptive behavior instruments is that some children who once qualified for special education placement because of a mild mental disability are no longer eligible. Before we began assessing adaptive behavior, children needed markedly low scores on *only* intelligence tests to be placed in special programs. Now they need low scores on both intelligence tests and measures of adaptive behavior, which is less likely to occur. The declassification of students that may result can produce exceedingly difficult situations. For example, a multidisciplinary team may learn that a particular child has an IQ test score of 69, which is consistent with a diagnosis of mild mental disability, but has scored in the normal range on an adaptive behavior scale. If the IQ test score is at all predictive of functioning, the child will have difficulty succeeding in school. However, since the child has normal adaptive behavior, a diagnosis of mild mental disability may be contrary to state laws and regulations governing disabled children.

One possible outcome for a child who performs consistent with a diagnosis of mild mental disability on a measure of intelligence but who has average adaptive behavior is that no special education is provided at all. This is perhaps the most conservative legal option available. An alternative is to ignore the information concerning adaptive behavior and place the child in a special education program. Perhaps the most satisfying option is to develop and provide alternate programming for children who are comprehensively disabled rather than those who have difficulty only at school. Unfortunately, such alternatives are not widely available.

It is ironic that the declassification issue arose because of "do-gooders" on one side who wanted to provide special education services to children with mild mental disabilities and "do-gooders" on the other side who wanted to prevent abuses such as "the six-hour retarded child" (i.e., a child who is considered to have a mental disability for the six hours spent at school but functions well outside of school in his or her home and community—see President's Committee on Mental Retardation, 1970). This issue exemplifies the type of legalistic game-playing that is unfortunately all too common in current special education practice. This "hardening of the categories" often prevents the provision of services to children who really need them. The real culprit here is the education system—those administrators and school boards who believe that children must be diagnosed before receiving services. However, if children who function poorly in school can be offered a continuum of special services, there would be no need to debate the diagnosis of a particular child. Instead, the debate would center around what type of services to provide.

Relationship Between Adaptive Behavior and Intelligence

What is the optimal relationship between instruments that measure adaptive behavior and those that assess intelligence? Should there be a strong relationship or no relationship at all? Do adaptive behavior instruments actually measure some construct that everyone agrees is adaptive behavior? The answers to these questions are anything but straightforward. The problem is compounded because both intelligence and adaptive behavior are hypothetical constructs that are difficult to measure. We will approach this issue of how the two constructs are related by examining first how they are different and then how they are alike.

There are several differences between instruments that assess adaptive behavior and those that assess intelligence. First, adaptive behavior scales are most concerned with everyday behaviors, whereas intelligence tests tend to reflect thinking processes. Because of this, adaptive behavior instruments tend to focus on common or typical behaviors and intelligence tests are concerned primarily with a child's potential. Thus intelligence tests assess verbal and quantitative learning and higher-order thinking skills, whereas adaptive behavior instruments reflect the degree to which a

Focus on
Practice

Declassification—A Suggestion from Dan Reschly

How adaptive behavior is conceptualized and measured along with the available special education service options will have a significant influence on the classification/placement decisions that are made. I suggest that the adaptive behavior dimension for school-age children be conceptualized as two separate components. One component should involve performance in the public school setting with primary emphasis on academic achievement in the classroom. The other component should be role performance in social systems outside of the public school such as the home, neighborhood, and community. Separating the adaptive behavior dimension into two components is advisable because recently published data suggest that adaptive behavior in academic settings and social role performance outside of school are largely unrelated for many students. . . .

The different combinations of adaptive behavior and intelligence have implications for classification and placement decisions. Adaptive Behavior-School (AB-S) should be based on a complete educational evaluation including observation in the classroom, examination of samples of daily work, teacher interview, and the results of individually administered standardized achievement tests. Adaptive Behavior-Outside School (AB-OS) should be based on information from formal inventories . . . or informal data collection procedures.

Of particular interest are the children who exhibit the pattern of very low intelligence, very low AB-S, and normal AB-OS. A major current dilemma is whether these children should be classified and placed in special education programs. Such children are "six-hour retarded children" almost by definition. If they are classified and placed in special education programs, we will almost inevitably overrepresent minority children. In my view these children should be served in special education programs in most instances because they do, in fact, have extreme educational needs that are typically beyond the scope of regular classroom instruction. The solution of "delabelling" these children does not address these needs. However, the segregated special class for the mildly mentally disabled, which has often been the placement used because in many cases it was the only alternative, is an equally inappropriate solution.

Defining the classification system would be beneficial in resolving this dilemma. The terms "comprehensive" and "quasi" are probably as objectionable as the term "mental retardation." Using terms like "educational retardation," "educationally handicapped," or some other term that is as behaviorally descriptive as possible of the quasi-retarded pattern would be preferable. Greater refinement in the classification system is useful only if there are implications for placement decisions and educational programming. The change suggested may have such implications.

The "quasi-retarded" do need special services. However, if special education services are to be provided, the objectives should be oriented toward specific academic needs rather than broad social competencies. In most instances the resource program involving remedial and compensatory tutorial services is a more appropriate option than the special class. Special class programs for the mildly retarded have traditionally placed considerable emphasis on broadly defined social competencies and "functional" academic skills (O. Kolstoe, 1976, *Teaching Educable Mentally Retarded Children,* 2nd ed., New York: Holt, Rinehart and Winston). This emphasis is clearly appropriate for the comprehensively disabled but is probably misdirected for most of the quasi-retarded. With few exceptions the quasi-disabled, if placed in special education, should be placed in resource programs.

Using the resource option for the quasi-retarded would alleviate many of the concerns expressed by federal district courts in the placement litigation. This amount of time spent outside of the educational mainstream is minimized by the resource option, thus reducing the very proper concern about racial segregation. Placement in the resource option regardless of classification used may have the additional advantage of being less stigmatizing. Analysis of outcome data must, of course, be the ultimate criteria against which this or any other classification/placement system must be validated.

The following flowchart summarizes Reschly's recommended approach to assessing adaptive behavior and making classification and instructional placement decisions.

child can adapt to environmental demands. In sum, IQ scores are secured by a process that samples the subject's best possible performance and that interprets the results through a trait system, with a presumption of stability in the obtained scores. In contrast, adaptive behavior scales secure descriptions of everyday adaptations without necessarily determining best possible performances; in some scales, little or no regard for trait inference is intended. Further, the data on adaptive behavior measurement deny any unitary or general factor (Meyers, Nihira, & Zetlin, 1979, p. 434).

Despite the difference between instruments that assess adaptive behavior and intelligence, some adaptive behavior scales have very high correlations (up to .83) with intelligence tests. Thus, one would expect the constructs to be somewhat similar. In one review, adaptive behavior/IQ correlations ranged from a low of .09 for the ABIC to a high of .83 for the old Vineland Social Maturity Scale (Doll, 1965). Such a wide range of correlations results from the types of skills measured by various adaptive behavior instruments and the manner in which they are measured. Scales with a preponderance of items that assess communication skills and cognitive development generally have higher correlations with IQ tests than those

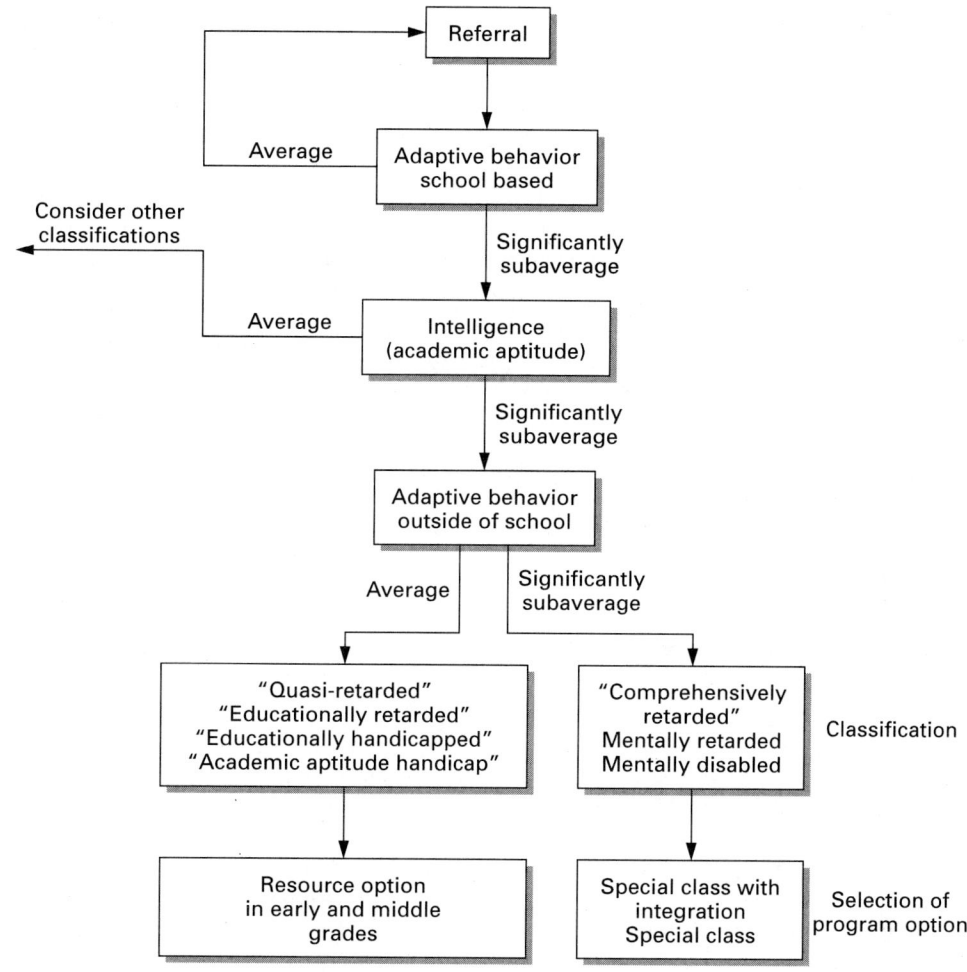

From "Assessing Mild Mental Retardation: The Influence of Adaptive Behavior, Sociocultural Status, and Prospects for Nonbiased Assessment" by D. J. Reschly in *The Handbook of School Psychology* (pp. 209–242), by C. R. Reynolds and T. B. Gutkin (Eds.). Copyright © 1982 John Wiley and Sons, Inc. Reprinted by permission of John Wiley and Sons, Inc.

that focus on self-help skills and independent functioning. Likewise, adaptive behavior instruments that are directly administered to the child rather than to a third-party informant have higher correlations with IQ tests because the format of the items, the skills assessed, and the method of administration more closely approximate those on IQ measurements.

What should be the relationship between IQ and adaptive behavior? This answer has been summarized by Lambert and Windmiller (1981):

> There is an obvious relationship between adaptive behavior and intelligence. Children with higher levels of intelligence generally learn to perform independent skills sooner, are able to assume greater responsibility, and have a greater capacity for social adjustment than children with lower levels. Yet, it is also true that there are mentally retarded and developmentally delayed children who do not have high levels of intelligence but who show potential for high levels of adaptive behavior. Such a discrepancy indicates that low to moderate correlations between adaptive behavior and intellectual functioning would be expected. An instrument designed to measure adaptive behavior should yield scores that indicate it assesses a dimension or construct that is separate from but related to intelligence since both measures provide evidence of psychological development. (p. 75)

Chapter Summary

Our review of adaptive behavior has summarized the major factors influencing assessment theory and practice in this area. However, several major issues were not resolved. For example, what is adaptive behavior? What is the *best* way to assess it? Are there reliable instruments for measuring adaptive behavior? What do we do with the declassified child? We will be better able to address these questions as research continues to accumulate.

Presently, however, measurement of adaptive behavior is difficult at best. Because of the fluctuations in their everyday adaptations, it may not be possible to develop a measure that will predict adaptive behaviors across situations and time; however, it is possible to ensure that those measures that are constructed have a truly representative norm sample and high internal consistency. Furthermore, those who use measures of adaptive behavior can be sure that they select those instruments that are in the best interest of children.

Part Four

Alternative Assessment Techniques and Approaches

This concluding section includes four chapters describing areas which go beyond traditional assessment practices. Chapter 15 describes the use of behavioral observations. This assessment technique is an essential tool for anyone seeking to truly understand problems in behavior or learning. Unfortunately this technique is underutilized and this chapter endeavors to describe how to be both effective and efficient with behavioral observations. The focus of Chapter 16 is on assessing children with low-incidence disabling conditions, including those children with hearing impairments, visual impairments, and severe or profound mental disabilities. These populations are treated separately because they often require an entirely different way of thinking about assessment. No serious textbook that concerns assessment of schoolchildren can be considered complete without a chapter on curriculum-based assessment. This practice recently has received extremely strong empirical support when compared to traditional assessment. Furthermore, curriculum-based assessment is necessary for linking assessment to intervention. The text concludes with chapter 18 on the topic of computerized assessment, which, although new to special education and psychological assessment, has already had a marked impact on the field. Since the use of computers in assessment is expected to increase, it is important to understand the issues that underlie the use of the technology.

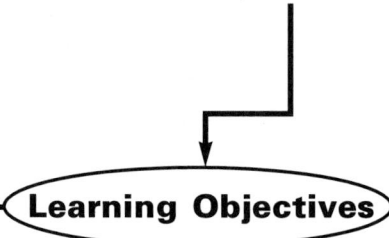

Chapter 15

Observation-Based Assessment

Learning Objectives

1. Compare and contrast observation-based assessment with other forms of assessment.

2. Understand the meaning and uses of operational definitions of behavior.

3. Describe four dimensions of behavior and their implications for observational-based assessment.

4. Describe five important considerations in using observation-based assessment.

5. Understand methods for observing and systematically recording behavior.

6. Describe methods for calculating the reliability of observational data.

7. Discuss the threats to the reliability of observation-based assessment.

O bservation-based assessment (OBA) refers to the systematic recording of observable behaviors of persons in specific situations. Any behavior that can be directly observed can be measured using observational methods. For example, running, jumping, completing math problems, and socially interacting with others represent directly observable behaviors. In contrast, thinking, paying attention, and feeling do not represent directly observable behaviors. Many tests described in this book seek to measure traits and characteristics that are not directly observable. For instance, the intelligence tests described in chapter 6 (e.g., WISC-III, Stanford-Binet, etc.) are designed to measure the trait of intelligence. "Intelligence," however, cannot be directly observed. As such, a child's responses to test items (which are directly observable) are interpreted as indications of the child's "intelligence" (which is not directly observable).

It is important to distinguish between indirect and direct assessment of behavior (Cone & Hawkins, 1977). **Indirect assessment** of behavior (e.g., intelligence tests, perceptual-motor tests, etc.) measure *indications* or *surrogates* of some hypothetical trait or characteristic (intelligence, perception, memory, etc.). Indirect assessment methods can also refer to the measurement of behavior that has already occurred at other times and in other situations. Behavior rating scales and checklists described in chapter 13 represent indirect assessment because these methods rely on a rater's evaluation of behavior that has already occurred.

Direct assessment of behavior refers to the assessment of behavior at the *time and place of its actual occurrence*. Direct assessment differs from a teacher's verbal description or rating of behavior because the teacher's description or rating is based on past performance of behavior in another situation. For example, if a teacher tells you that Frank hit Joe three times, then this represents an indirect assessment of behavior. On the other hand, if you went to the classroom and directly observed Frank hitting Joe three times, then you would have directly observed Frank's hitting behavior.

To summarize, this chapter focuses on the direct assessment of behavior using strategies and techniques that depend on the direct observation of behavior. The key distinction between indirect and direct measurement of behavior is whether the behavior is assessed at the time and place of its actual occurrence. Also, behavior assessed using observational methods is not interpreted as an indication of some hypothetical trait or characteristic. Instead, the behavior is interpreted in its own right. Frank hitting Joe would *not* be interpreted as an indication of the trait of aggression. It would be interpreted by the simple description of Frank hitting Joe.

➡ *Considerations in Observation-Based Assessment*

A number of factors must be considered before using observation-based assessment. These factors include: (a) operational definitions of behavior, (b) the dimension of behavior to be measured, (c) number of behaviors to be assessed, (d) number of observation sessions, and (e) the recording method(s) to be used. Each of these factors is discussed in the following sections.

Operational Definition of Behavior

Most of us use general descriptions of behavior that serve as a type of shorthand in talking about an individual's behavior or behavior patterns. These general descriptions, however, are not particularly useful in communicating with others about children's behavior. Terms such as "learning difficulty," "hyperactive," or "depressed" may mean very different things to different people and as such often create confusion and miscommunication.

An **operational definition** of behavior refers to defining behavior in clear, unambiguous, and explicit terms. These types of definitions are called "operational definitions" because they specify the operations that will be used in defining a behavior. For instance, an operational definition of the behavior of *noncompliance* might be as follows: *Noncompliance is defined as the student not complying with a verbal request or direction from the teacher within five seconds after the request or direction has been given. Examples of verbal requests or directions are being told to sit down, begin work, be quiet, come to the teacher's desk, etc.*

Operational definitions should be *objective, clear,* and *complete* (Kazdin, 1984). Objective means that the definition should refer to observable behaviors and/or environmental events. Operational definitions are clear if they can be read, repeated, and paraphrased by others. Observers should be able to read the definition of behavior and use it to record behavior (Kazdin, 1984). Operational definitions are complete if they specify the boundary conditions for inclusion of behaviors in the definition and delineate behaviors that are not considered part of the definition. Using our definition of noncompliance, the student is considered noncompliant if compliance with any verbal request or direction is not completed within five seconds (inclusionary criteria). However, the student would not be considered noncompliant if the teacher used hand motions or some other nonverbal request or direction (exclusionary criteria).

Dimensions of Behavior

Behavior can be described and measured along a variety of dimensions. There are four dimensions along which behavior can be measured: (a) frequency, (b) temporality, (c) intensity, and (d) permanent products.

The **frequency** of behavior refers to how often a behavior occurs. Examples of behaviors that can be measured along a frequency dimension are number of correct oral responses to questions, number of temper tantrums in a four-hour period, or number of days absent from school. Frequency measures of behavior are useful if the behavior can be categorized into discrete categories (i.e., Yes, the behavior occurred or No, the behavior did not occur).

Behavior also can vary along a **temporality** dimension. There are two aspects of temporality: *duration* and *latency*. Duration refers to how long a behavior lasts. For example, if the child began homework at 7:00 P.M. and completed homework at 8:00 P.M., the duration of homework behavior would be 60 minutes. Latency describes the amount of time that elapses between an environmental event and a behavior. Using our example of noncompliance, if the teacher instructed the child to sit down (an environmental event) and the child sat down (a behavior) after two minutes, the latency would be two minutes or 120 seconds.

Behaviors can also vary in **intensity.** Intensity refers to the amount of force with which a behavior is performed. Intensity is not as easily measured as frequency or temporality. For example, screaming in class that is heard by a teacher and children five classrooms away has a higher intensity than screaming heard only by teachers and children in adjacent classrooms. Technically, the intensity of screaming in the preceding examples could be objectively measured in decibels, which would reflect differences in the force of the behavior.

Many behaviors leave **permanent products** in the environment. These might be called *behavior by-products*. Examples of permanent products of behavior are number of worksheets completed, number of correct written responses to math problems, number of paper wads in a student's desk, and so forth. You should realize that behavioral by-products are *not* really a measure of behavior, but rather a measurement of the result of behavior. One potential difficulty with using behavioral by-products is determining the person who is responsible for a particular behavior. For example, if graffiti is written on a child's desk, then the teacher must determine which student was responsible for it. As many teachers know, this can be a source of great controversy among teachers and students.

To summarize, using observation-based assessment requires you to decide which behavioral dimension is most relevant to your purpose. These various behavioral dimensions are not unlike the type of evidence used in murder trials to determine guilt or innocence. Admissible evidence in court includes eyewitness testimony ("I saw him shoot the subject with a gun five times"). This describes a frequency dimension. Evidence could also include a duration dimension ("I saw the defendant talking with the subject for five minutes before he shot him"). It might also include a latency dimension ("The defendant stated to the subject that if he did not leave within the next 30 seconds, he would shoot him"). Finally, conviction of guilt in murder trials rely heavily on permanent products of behavior (e.g., a murder weapon, bullets, and a dead body).

Number of Behaviors Assessed

Some children display behavior problems that might be limited to only one or two behaviors. Other children exhibit multiple behavior problems and potentially display an overwhelming number of behaviors that might be observed. An important decision facing the person conducting observation-based assessment is how many behaviors should be observed. This decision is influenced by the nature and severity of the child's behavior problems and the degree of teacher concern with each behavior problem.

It has been our experience in talking with teachers about problem behaviors of children that some teachers will list as many as 5 to 10 behaviors that are problematic in their classrooms. Whereas some children may display 10 or more behavior problems, not all behavior problems are necessarily independent. Some behaviors may be subsets of a larger class of behavior. For example, *noncompliance* represents a class of behaviors that may have a number of behavioral components (e.g., defiance to teachers, cursing, throwing objects, refusing to complete assigned work, etc.).

In deciding the number of behaviors to be observed, it is useful to organize specific behaviors into larger categories for observation purposes. These larger categories containing specific behaviors are known as **response classes** because they describe a "class" or category of behaviors that share some similarities. In our example of noncompliance, we might define this response class by the specific behaviors that make up noncompliance. Thus, cursing, throwing objects, refusing to complete assigned work, and defiance to the teacher would be the behaviors making up the response class of noncompliance.

Some behaviors, however, may be independent from one another and therefore do not belong to the same response class. For instance, a child may exhibit social withdrawal, poor work completion, and temper tantrums. For some children, these behaviors may be unrelated. In these cases, persons conducting observation-based assessment would want to systematically observe all behaviors that may be of concern to teachers. If this is not possible, another strategy would be to have the teacher rank order the behaviors in terms of importance to him or her and the child.

Number of Observation Sessions

Another consideration in using observations is the issue of how many times a child should be observed. The central issue here is the *representativeness* of observations. That is, are the observations collected representative of the child's typical behavior in school? You will recall from chapter 5 that norms for standardized tests should be representative of the children being assessed by tests. In observation-based assessment, the observations you conduct should be representative of the child's behavior. Representativeness of norms for tests is based on groups of children. Representativeness of observations is based on the behavior of a single child.

Observers cannot be present in classrooms every minute of every day. As such, observers must *sample* the behavior of concern to draw valid conclusions from observational data. This sample of behavior must be representative or typical of the child's behavior in the classroom. Some behaviors may be highly atypical or unrepresentative of the child's behavior. This could be due to a variety of factors such as unusual life events (death in the family, illness, etc.). Other behaviors may occur so infrequently that it might be impossible for an observer to directly assess the behavior.

Recording Method

The type of recording method to be used depends on the dimension of behavior you are interested in measuring. A number of recording methods are designed to assess the four dimensions of frequency, temporality, intensity, and permanent products. There are four general categories of recording methods: (a) event-based methods, (b) interval-based methods, (c) time-based methods, and (d) product-based methods.

Event-based recording is designed to measure the frequency of behavior. It refers to the measurement of the number of times a behavior occurs. Event recording is best used with behaviors that are discrete in nature; they have an obvious beginning and end. Behaviors such as number of correct oral responses to questions, number of times a child hits others, or the number of positive comments to others would be examples of behaviors conducive to event recording.

Interval-based methods refer to recording behaviors as occurring or not occurring during specified time intervals. A time unit such as one minute might be divided into six 10-second intervals. The behavior would be observed as occurring or not occurring during each of the six 10-second intervals. For instance, a behavior such as *off-task* might be recorded for one minute. Suppose the student was off-task for three of the six 10-second time intervals. The student's rate of off-task behavior would be 50 percent of the intervals. Interval-based recording methods are best used for behaviors that are more continuous and do not have a specific beginning and end.

Time-based recording methods refer to the measurement of the temporal aspects of behavior such as duration, latency, or interresponse times. What is being measured in time-based recording is *not* the number of times a behavior occurs as in event recording, but rather the temporal aspects of behavior. Remember that duration refers to how long a behavior lasts and is measured in seconds, minutes, or even hours. Latency refers to the *amount of time elapsed* between an environmental event and a behavior and can be measured in time units.

Permanent product recording methods refer to the measurement of actual physical by-products of behavior. Written work, vandalized school property, messy restrooms, and the like are amenable to permanent product recording methods.

➡ *Guidelines for Using Recording Methods*

The proper use of recording methods requires familiarity with some specific information and rules for measuring behavior. In the following sections, we will present some basic information that should be helpful in using these recording methods.

Figure 15.1 Example of a Weekly Event Recording

Name: Joe   **Week of:** March 2nd

Observer: Kramer   **Teacher:** Jones

Behavioral Definition: Inappropriate talking out which includes verbalizations by the student when teacher or another student is talking.

Day	Observation Time	Frequency	Total	Rate
Monday	8:30–9:00 (30 minutes)	III	3	3/30 = .1
Tuesday	2:00–2:15 (15 minutes)	IIII	5	5/15 = .33
Wednesday	10:00–11:00 (60 minutes)	II	2	2/60 = .03
Thursday	1:00-1:20 (20 minutes)	IIIII II	7	7/20 = .35
Friday	9:20–9:45 (25 minutes)	III	3	3/25 = .12

TOTAL   **20**   **20/150 = .13**

Event-Based Recording Guidelines

There are several guidelines in using event-based recording, including the behavior or behaviors to be recorded, the number of times the student will be observed, and the length of each recording session. Event recording methods are relatively easy to design. Figure 15.1 shows an example of an event-based recording procedure designed to measure the frequency of inappropriate talking-out behavior in a classroom for one school week. Note that figure 15.1 contains a column for the day of the week, the duration of the observation session, the frequency of the behavior, and the *rate of behavior.*

The rate of behavior is simply the frequency of the behavior divided by the amount of time the behavior was observed.

Rate of Behavior = Frequency of Behavior/Duration of Session R = F/D

Rate is a more informative measure of behavior than overall frequency because observation sessions typically vary in terms of time the behavior is observed. To compare the frequency of talking-out behavior from Monday to Friday, only the behavior rates, not the daily frequencies are directly comparable.

Figure 15.2 Example of a PLACHECK Recording Method for a Classroom of 30 Students

Teacher: <u>Smith</u>   Week of: <u>October 16th</u>

Behavioral Definition: <u>Number of students engaged in academic tasks</u>
<u>such as reading, completing written assignments, copying from</u>
<u>board, etc.</u>

Time	Monday	Tuesday	Wednesday	Thursday	Friday	Median
9:30	60%	50%	48%	51%	55%	51%
10:15	75%	75%	82%	70%	71%	75%
10:45	62%	72%	70%	69%	75%	70%
11:15	71%	80%	82%	81%	80%	80%

Note: Be sure to count the number of students engaging in the behavior
at the time you observe. Divide this number by the total number of
students present in class that day and multiply by 100 to calculate the
percentage of students engaged in the behavior.

Teachers can use tally marks or check marks on the blackboard to count
the frequency of behavior. This type of event-based recording differs only in
that students are able to see a running record of their behavior. Event-based
recording used in this way can be conducted on individual students or for the
entire class. An example of using event-based recording for the behavior of an
entire classroom would be to define a behavior such as disruptive behavior. If
any student in the class exhibited disruptive behavior, a mark would be placed
on the board. The total number of marks in a specified period of time would
represent the frequency of disruptive behavior for the entire classroom.

A variation of event-based recording that is sometimes useful for teachers
is known as a Planned Activity Check (PLACHECK). In using PLACHECK,
the teacher defines a behavior such as working quietly. At periodic intervals,
the teacher looks and simply counts the number of children engaged in the
behavior. For example, if 20 out of 30 children are engaged in the behavior
at 10:30 A.M., then about 67 percent of the class would be working quietly. If
the teacher uses PLACHECK at 11:00 A.M. and finds that only 10 out of 30
children are working quietly, then only 33 percent of the class would be
considered engaging in the behavior. You should realize that PLACHECK is not
technically measuring the number of times a behavior occurs, but rather
the number of students engaging in that behavior. Figure 15.2 presents a
weekly PLACHECK monitoring form for a class of 30 students.

Keep in mind the following guidelines when using event-based recording procedures:

1. Only record discrete behaviors; that is, event-based recording should be used only with behaviors that have a discernible beginning and end.

2. Provide a clear and specific operational definition of the behavior to be recorded.

3. Design an event-based recording observation sheet that contains the following information: (a) name of student, (b) behavior to be recorded, (c) operational definition of the behavior, (d) dates and days behavior will be recorded, (e) time and duration of observation sessions, (f) frequency of behaviors, and (g) rate of behaviors. Use figure 15.1 as a guideline.

4. When recording a behavior or behaviors for an entire classroom, decide whether to use tally marks or a PLACHECK method. Use figure 15.2 as a guideline.

Interval-Based Recording Guidelines

Interval-based recording methods involve dividing an observation period into smaller time intervals and recording whether a behavior occurred during that interval. For example, an observation period of 30 minutes might be divided into 30, one-minute time intervals. The observer would record whether or not the behavior occurred during each of the one-minute intervals. It is important to remember that the length of the observation interval depends on the frequency of behavior. Thus, behaviors occurring at high frequencies should be measured with *shorter observation intervals* and behaviors occurring at low frequency should be measured with *longer observation intervals*.

The advantage of interval-based recording methods is that the observer does not have to continuously observe and record the behavior. Instead, an observer *samples* the behavior within specified time intervals.

There are four basic types of interval-based recording methods: (a) partial-interval recording, (b) whole-interval recording, (c) point-time sampling, and (d) sequential point-time sampling. **Partial-interval recording** involves an observer recording a behavior as occurring if it occurs *at any time* during a specified time interval. For instance, if an observer is recording behavior within one-minute time intervals and the behavior occurs at any time during the one-minute interval, then the behavior is recorded as having occurred during that interval. Only one occurrence of a behavior in a specified interval is recorded regardless of how many times the behavior occurred during that interval.

If a behavior occurs three or four times during a one-minute interval, it can only be counted as having occurred *once* during that interval. As such, partial-interval recording may underestimate the frequency of behavior. The purpose of partial-interval recording is to assess whether a behavior occurred during an interval, *not* to assess the overall frequency of the behavior during any particular interval.

Whole-interval recording differs from partial-interval recording in that the behavior must occur during the *entire observation interval*. Using the above example, a behavior would have to occur continuously during an entire one-minute interval to be recorded as occurring. For example, if you are measuring on-task or attending behavior of a student, the student would have to be on-task or attending for the entire one-minute interval to be considered on-task. Whole-interval recording is more of a duration method than a frequency method in that it is measuring how long a behavior lasts within a specified time interval. Whole-interval recording tends to underestimate the actual durations of behavior.

Point-time sampling recording refers to recording a behavior as occurring or not occurring at a specific point during an observation interval. Usually an observer records the behavior *at the end of an observation interval*. In the preceding example, a student would be considered on-task only if the behavior was being exhibited at the end (the 60th second) of a one-minute observation interval. Point-time sampling is less labor intensive for observers because they only have to observe behavior at specific points within observation intervals rather than the entire interval as is the case with partial-interval and whole-interval methods. Point-time sampling is not a particularly accurate method to use with behaviors that are short duration (i.e., the observation method will tend to underestimate occurrences of behavior). In addition, point-time sampling will underestimate the occurrence of behaviors if the observation intervals are too long. Figure 15.3 depicts a general example of an observation sheet that could be used with partial-interval, whole-interval, and point-time sampling recording.

Sequential point-time sampling involves the exact same method as point-time sampling, *except more than one student is observed*. Instead of observing one student at specific points within observation intervals, several students are observed sequentially over observation intervals. Figure 15.4 shows an example of a sequential-point time sampling recording of three students.

It is important to remember that students are observed *sequentially* over the entire observation session. That is, Jack is observed first and his behavior is recorded at the end of the first one-minute observation interval. Next, Joe is observed and his behavior is recorded at the end of the interval. Finally, Steve is observed and his behavior is recorded at the end

Figure 15.3 General Recording Form of Interval-Based Recording

Name: Laura   **Date:** Feb. 23rd

Observer: Witt   **Teacher:** Smith

Behavioral Definition: Off-task behavior which includes looking away from academic materials, talking to other students, out-of-seat, etc.

Minute	10 sec.	20 sec.	30 sec.	40 sec.	50 sec.	60 sec.	%
1	X	X	X	O	O	O	50
2	O	O	X	X	X	X	67
3	X	X	X	X	X	X	100
4	O	O	X	O	O	X	33
5	X	O	X	X	O	X	67
6	X	O	X	X	O	O	50
7	O	O	X	X	O	X	50
8	X	X	X	X	X	X	100
9	O	O	O	O	O	O	0
10	X	X	O	X	O	X	67

X = Behavior Occurred During Interval
O = Behavior Did Not Occur During Interval

Average % = 58.4%

of that interval. We then go to the next observation interval and observe Jack, Joe, and Steve in the same order and record their behavior. This continues for the entire observation session.

The chief advantage of sequential point-time sampling is that we can compare the rates of behavior for different students within the same classroom. Being able to make comparisons among students is sometimes useful information for evaluating students' behavioral improvement and in making referral decisions for special education assessment.

Figure 15.4 Example of Sequential Point-Time Sampling

Students: Joe, Jack and Steve

Observer: Gresham   **Observation Time:** 10:00-10:27 A.M.

Behavioral Definition: Disruptive behavior which includes talking out, bothering others, out-of-seat, etc.

X = BEHAVIOR OCCURRED   O = BEHAVIOR DID NOT OCCUR

Students	1	2	3	4	5	6	Total
Joe[1]	X	X	O	O	O	X	50%
Jack[1]	O	X	X	O	X	X	67%
Steve[1]	X	O	X	O	O	O	33%
Joe[2]	X	X	X	X	X	X	100%
Jack[2]	O	O	O	O	O	O	0%
Steve[2]	X	X	X	X	X	X	100%
Joe[3]	O	O	O	O	O	O	0%
Jack[3]	X	O	O	O	O	O	17%
Steve[3]	X	X	X	X	X	X	100%

Percent Occurrences:
Joe: 50% Jack: 28% Steve: 78%

Keep in mind the following guidelines when using interval-based observation methods:

1. Decide which interval-based method to use: partial-interval, whole-interval, point-time sampling, or sequential point-time sampling.

2. The method used will depend, in part, on the frequency of the behavior to be recorded. Point- and sequential point-time sampling methods tend to underestimate high frequency and/or short duration behaviors. For these types of behaviors, it is probably better to use event-based recording procedures.

3. Select the length of the observation interval to be used. Remember that the length of the interval is influenced by the frequency of the behavior. Therefore, high frequency behaviors should have shorter observation intervals (e.g., 10–15 seconds) than low frequency behaviors (e.g., 10–15 minutes).

4. In using sequential point-time sampling, use a criterion to select students for observation. For instance, you might have a teacher to nominate the "Best-behaved," "Average-behaved," and "Poorly-behaved" students in the classroom. Your observations of the student of concern can be compared to observations of the other three students.

Time-Based Recording Guidelines

Time-based recording methods measure the temporal aspects of behavior such as duration and latency. Whereas event and interval-based recording procedures are measuring the frequency of behavior, time-based methods record either how long a behavior lasts (duration) or elapsed times between environmental events and behaviors (latency).

Duration measures of behavior are obtained by recording the length of time elapsing between the beginning and the end of a behavior. For example, if a student begins talking at 11:00 and finishes talking at 11:05, the duration of the behavior is five minutes. Many behaviors are amenable to duration measurement, such as length of time attempting tasks before asking for assistance, length of time sitting in one's seat, and length of time engaged in academic tasks.

In using duration recording it is important to clearly record the time the behavior begins and ends. The difference between the beginning and end of a behavior is the behavior's duration. Figure 15.5 depicts an example of a duration recording sheet.

Latency recording involves recording the time elapsing between an environmental event and the initiation of a behavior. Whereas duration recording is measuring how long a behavior occurs, latency is measuring how much time elapses until the beginning of a behavior. Latency recording is appropriate for many types of behaviors in classrooms that involve instructions, directions, or commands (e.g., sit down, clean up your desk, answering questions presented orally, etc.). Figure 15.6 presents an example of a latency recording sheet.

Keep in mind the following guidelines when using time-based recording procedures:

1. Decide what temporal dimension of behavior you wish to measure: duration or latency.

2. If you are interested in how long a behavior lasts, use duration recording.

Figure 15.5 Example of Duration Recording

Name: Frank   **Date:** 10/30/92

Observer: Elliott   **Situation:** Free time

Behavioral Definition: Temper outbursts defined as yelling, crying, screaming, and/or flapping arms.

Behavior Began	Behavior Ended	Duration
8:45	9:00	15 minutes
9:30	9:35	5 minutes
10:07	10:15	8 minutes
TOTAL		28 minutes

Figure 15.6 Example of Latency Recording

Name: Steve   **Date/Day:** 4/12/Monday

Observer: Gresham   **Situation:** Reading group

Behavioral Definition: Compliance with teacher instructions or directions.

Time Instruction Given	Time Behavior Began	Latency
9:00	9:01	60 seconds
9:31	9:33	120 seconds
10:05	10:10	300 seconds
11:14	11:15	60 seconds
12:01	12:10	540 seconds
TOTAL		1080 seconds

Median = 120 seconds

3. If you are interested in compliance-type behaviors (i.e., compliance with instructions, directions, or commands), use latency recording.

4. Be sure to record the starting time and the ending time for duration or latency recording.

Permanent product recording describes the measurement of the by-products of behavior. Unlike event-based, interval-based, or time-based methods, permanent products measurement involves the measurement of actual *physical products*. Examples of physical by-products of behavior are worksheets completed, written homework, number of words written correctly, number of math problems solved correctly on written tests, and so forth.

Permanent product recording represents an easier way means of measurement than other recording procedures and products can be collected and stored for future reference. You should note, however, that permanent products are *traces* or *results* of behavior rather than behaviors themselves.

➡ *Reliability in Observation-Based Assessment*

Chapter 5 stressed that tests must be reliable to be of practical value in assessment. Recall that reliability refers to the degree to which we obtain the same result when repeatedly measuring the same thing. Reliability is just as important in observation-based assessment as it is in standardized testing.

The central meaning of reliability in observation-based assessment is the degree to which two observers viewing the same behavior at the same time agree with one another. Another term used to refer to reliability in observation-based assessment is **interobserver agreement.** Suppose you and another observer went to a classroom to observe a student's out-of-seat behavior. Using event recording, you observed the behavior as occurring 10 times and the other observer recorded it as occurring 12 times. These observations were obviously less than perfectly reliable. Does this mean you were wrong? Does this mean that the other observer was wrong? Not necessarily. For example, your recording of 10 could be accurate. On the other hand, the other observer's recording of 12 could be accurate.

Methods for Calculating Interobserver Agreement

The method used for calculating estimates of interobserver agreement depend on the type of recording method used. The following methods are recommended for calculating interobserver agreement for event, interval-based, and time-based methods. Reliability estimates are not of great concern in permanent product measurement because the actual physical products exist.

Focus on
Practice

How to Observe Classroom Behavior

Do you believe everything that everyone tells you? If not, then you might want to consider seeing things for yourself. This section describes a simple process for observing behavior in the classroom.

Why observe? First of all, you *can't* really believe everything that the teacher tells you. Teachers who refer a child tend to overestimate the severity of behavior problems. Second, a behavior, such as talking out, may function very differently depending on context, and only a highly trained specialist such as yourself can evaluate the function of the behavior. Talking out in one context may function to get peer attention and another context may function as self-stimulation for the student or to gain teacher attention. The intervention you design *must* be different in each of these cases. Third, observation is conducted not only to assess child behavior, but also *teacher* behavior or classroom conditions that may be contributing to the child's behavior. If you rely exclusively on teacher's self-report, approximately zero percent of teachers will report their own contributions to the behavior problems.

10 Steps to Conducting Classroom Observations

The conduct of classroom observation involves 10 essential components. Each of these components are described.

1. **Definition(s) of the target behavior(s).** The first step is to define the target behaviors. One good way to decide what is appropriate behavior in the classroom is to use the classroom rules posted by the teacher. However, the rules used by teachers are frequently not well operationalized. Even more frequently, teachers have no rules posted. If that is the case, then you can utilize some standard observational categories. A simple system will consist of the following:

On-task: Eye contact with teacher or task and performing the requested task.
Verbal off-task: Inappropriate verbalization or making sounds with object, mouth, or body.
Motor off-task: Student fully or partially out of assigned seat without teacher permission, or playing with objects.
Passive off-task: Student not engaged with assigned task and passively waiting, sitting, daydreaming, etc.

Occasionally, a student will exhibit unusual behaviors that would not be picked up using a standard coding system. In these cases, you will need to define the behavior yourself. For example, a child with Tourette's disorder who exhibits verbal and motor tics may require a special "tic" category.

2. **Observation of the teacher's interaction with the target student.**
Frequently, student behavior is a function of teacher reaction to the behavior. Hence, examining teacher behavior is an essential aspect of any
classroom observation. Examples follow:

Positive teacher attention: Positive comments, smiling, touching, or
gesturing directed toward target student.
Negative teacher attention: Reprimands, negative consequences, or
negative gestures directed toward target student.
Neutral teacher attention: Teacher attends to student but there is
neither negative nor positive valence associated with the attention
(e.g., teacher looks at student).

3. **Class activity.** The basic activity in which the class is engaged should
be noted on the observational form. Some examples follow:

teacher directed whole class activity
teacher directed small group activity
independent seat work
other

4. **Observation interval.** To structure the observation period, an *interval*
observational system is most often used. Hence, if you observe for 20
minutes, the entire observational period would be broken down into
many smaller intervals. The length of these smaller intervals depends on
the type and frequency of the behavior being observed. For example, if
you are observing a high frequency behavior, you would choose a small
interval (10 seconds). Alternatively, if you are observing a low frequency
behavior such as fighting, you would choose a longer interval.

5. **Alternative measures.** Although the interval recording (described
above) is useful in most cases, it is occasionally necessary to monitor
some behaviors using different methods. The two methods most commonly used as an alternative to interval recording are event and duration
systems.

Event recording allows you to note *every* instance of a behavior.
Students who are self-abusive, for example, may strike themselves 20
to 30 times in 30 seconds. An interval system would not accurately
convey the intensity of the behavior.
Duration recording allows one to note how long a behavior occurs. A
child who has trouble paying attention, for example, may be on task
and off task several times during a 30-second interval, but using an
interval system would be marked as off task only once. With duration
recording, you simply record the length of time the child is either off-
task or on-task.

6. **Observe a peer for comparison.** To determine whether the behavior you observe is a problem you can compare the target student's behavior with a "normal" peer. To accomplish this, you simply record the behavior of a peer in the classroom using the same system you chose for the target student. You should choose a same sex peer who has been nominated by the teacher as "normal." This can help you in consulting with the teacher because you can present the data for the target student and the comparison student.

7. **Class scan check.** To characterize the classroom context, it is beneficial to conduct periodic (i.e., every 3–5 minutes) classroom scans. The purpose here is to note relevant features of the classroom environment. In particular, it is important to determine the degree to which other students in the classroom are on-task, following teacher's directions, etc. The scan is an *informal* procedure that will end up later in your notes to help you characterize the classroom. It is informal in that there is no need to precisely quantify the amount of on-task activity. For example, you could provide a rough estimate of the percentage of students who are on-task.

8. **Necessary equipment.** At a minimum, classroom observations require the following equipment:

   Wristwatch—watch with second hand needed to monitor intervals and length of observation sessions.
   Observation form—see attached form, for example.
   Stopwatch—to monitor duration.

9. **Calculation of the data.** It is useful to determine the percentage of time a student is on-task. To accomplish this, you divide the number of on-task intervals by the total number of intervals observed and multiply by 100 as follows:

$$\frac{\text{\# of on–task intervals}}{\text{Total intervals observed}} \times 100$$

10. **Interpretation and report of the data.** To summarize and report the data, you should begin by describing the context of the observation. Here you can report observations from classroom scan check and you can note ongoing classroom activities during observation (e.g., teacher-directed small group activity). Next, you can report the percentage of on-task behavior for the target student and tell how this contrasts with the comparison student. The idea is to determine whether the target student exhibited behavior that is markedly different from the norm or from what would be reasonably expected in that particular classroom context.

What follows is an example of how to report data:

Kevin was observed for 30 minutes during Mrs. Wickstrom's English class. During the observation session, the class was engaged in teacher-directed large group instruction. In a classroom where students were generally very well behaved, Kevin's behavior was quite noticeable. He was off-task approximately 88% of the time. This off-task behavior consisted of mostly verbal off-task and motor off-task behaviors. That is, he was talking and out of his seat a great deal. By comparison, a peer nominated by Mrs. Wickstrom as being "normal" was only off-task 7% of the time.

For classification of a student as behavior disordered, at least three different observation sessions should be used. The reason for observing on multiple occasions and preferably multiple settings is to increase the validity of your results.

Event-Based Agreement

To assess the interobserver agreement of event recording, the following formula may be used:

Smaller Frequency/Larger Frequency × 100 = % Agreement. For example, you observed the frequency of out-of-seat behavior as occurring 10 times. Another observer recorded the frequency of the same behavior as occurring 12 times. The percentage agreement is $10/12 \times 100 = 83\%$.

Interval-Based Agreement

Interval-based reliability estimates are computed by comparing the observations of two observers on an interval by interval basis. The number of agreements and the number of disagreements are computed and entered into the following formula: **Number of Agreements/Number of Agreements + Number of Disagreements.**

For example, in 10 one-minute observation intervals there were eight agreements and two disagreements. The percentage agreement would be $8/8 + 2 \times 100 = 80\%$. This formula can be used for partial-interval, whole-interval, point-time sampling, and sequential point-time sampling methods.

Time-Based Agreement

All time-based recording methods use the same basic formula for computing interobserver agreement. This formula involves dividing the shorter recorded time by the longer recorded time and multiplying by 100 to compute percentage of agreement. The basic formula is: **Shorter Recorded Time/Longer Recorded Time × 100 = % Agreement.**

Figure 15.7 Basic Formulas for Calculating Interobserver Agreement

---

Event-Based Recording

%Agreement = Smaller Number/Larger Number × 100

Example: 15/20 × 100 = 75%

Interval-Based Recording

$$\%\text{Agreement} = \frac{\text{Number of Agreements}}{\text{Number of Agreements} + \text{Number of Disagreements}} \times 100$$

Example: 20/20 + 5 × 100 = 20/25 × 100 = 80%

Time-Based Recording

%Agreement = Shorter Time/Longer Time × 100

Example: 30 seconds/32 seconds x 100 = 93.8%

In computing duration agreement estimates, the following formula should be used: **Shorter Duration/Longer Duration × 100 = % Duration Agreement.** For computing latency agreement, the formula is: **Shorter Latency/Longer Latency × 100 = Latency Agreement.** To compute interresponse time agreement: **Shorter Interresponse Time/Longer Interresponse Time × 100 = Interresponse Time Agreement.**

Figure 15.7 presents examples of computing interobserver agreement estimates for event-based, interval-based, and time-based recording procedures.

Threats to Interobserver Agreement

There are several threats to the agreement between two observers in using observation-based assessment. Kazdin (1977) discussed three major threats to reliable measurement of behavior: (a) observer drift, (b) observer reactivity, and (c) observer bias.

Observer drift refers to the fact that observers may change the definition of behavior over time. That is, observers may tend to "drift" away from the original definition of the behavior. For example, the original definition of out-of-seat behavior may have specified that if the child's buttocks did not contact the chair, he or she would be considered out of seat. After a period of time, one observer may begin to count as out of seat only those instances when the child stands up whereas the other observer stays with the original definition. This "drifting" away from the original definition by one observer will obviously have the effect of decreasing the agreement between the two observers.

Observer reactivity describes the fact that observers will tend to be *more reliable* in their observations if they know their agreements are being checked by someone else. In this sense, observers are "reacting" to outside monitoring by improving the accuracy with which they record behavior. This might also suggest that observations are less reliable when interobserver agreements are never checked, which would make assessment data less accurate (Wolery, Bailey, & Sugai, 1988).

Observer bias refers to the effects of expectations or biases that might influence the accuracy of measurement. For example, if observers expect high rates of behavior to occur based on a teacher's verbal description, they may record higher frequencies of the behavior than if they had not talked with the teacher before the observation. Expectation biases can have a substantial influence on the reliability of measurement using observation-based methods (Kazdin, 1977).

Guidelines for Improving Observer Agreement

Several steps can be taken to improve the degree of agreement between observers. Wolery et al. (1988) offer the following guidelines:

1. Define the behavior to be counted in clear, operational terms.
2. Be sure to clearly and specifically describe the procedures to be followed in observing behavior and follow these procedures closely.
3. Practice the observation system *before* conducting the actual observations.
4. Immediately record the observational data. Do not wait until a later time to record the data.
5. Use equipment such as stopwatches, beepers, or videotapes to improve accuracy.
6. Periodically review the observation procedures and definitions of behavior.

Chapter Summary

Observation-based assessment represents a direct form of assessment in which an individual's behavior is measured at the *time* and *place* of its occurrence. Unlike standardized tests and rating scales, observational assessment evaluates ongoing behavior in the situation of interest (e.g., classrooms, playgrounds, etc.). Observational assessment requires an observer to be present in these situations to systematically observe and record behavior.

Several considerations in using observational assessment were discussed. One, it is critical that behaviors being observed are operationally defined. Operational definitions describe the operations involved in measuring behavior in clear and specific terms. Two, the dimensions of behavior to be assessed must be specified. Behavioral dimensions include frequency (how often a behavior occurs), a temporal dimension (duration or latency), an intensity dimension (the force of a behavior), and a permanent product dimension (by-products or effects of behavior). Three, the number of behaviors to be observed is an important consideration. Some behaviors are interrelated and form what is known as a response class. Specific behaviors within a response class can be used to define that response class. Four, the number of observation sessions is an important consideration because one must ensure a representative sample of a student's behavior. Five, the observation recording method used corresponds to the dimension of behavior to be assessed. Event-based and interval-based methods (e.g., partial-interval, whole-interval, and point-time sampling) are used to measure the frequency dimension of behavior. Duration, latency, and interresponse times are used to measure the temporal dimension of behavior. Behavioral by-products or behavioral effects are used to measure the permanent products dimension.

Reliability was described as being as important in observational assessment as it is in test-based assessment. Reliability was defined as the degree to which two observers viewing the same behavior at the same time agree with one another. Various methods for calculating reliability or interobserver agreement were discussed. Different methods were described for event-based, interval-based, and time-based observation methods.

Finally, three threats to obtaining reliable estimates of behavior were discussed. Observer drift referred to the tendency of some observers to change or "drift" from the original operational definition of behavior. Observer reactivity described the effects of observers being monitored for accuracy in their recording of behavior. Observer bias is the effects of expectations or preconceived biases on the reliability of observational data.

Focus on Research

Systematic Screening for Behavior Disorders: Observation Codes

The Systematic Screening for Behavior Disorders (SSBD) (Walker & Severson, 1992) was described in chapter 13 as a useful approach to measuring problem behaviors of students in grades 1 to 6. The SSBD was described as a "multiple-gating" procedure in that it contained a series of progressively more expensive and precise assessments or "gates." The first gate consists of teacher nominations and the second gate consists of teacher ratings of nominated children. The third gate utilizes direct behavioral observations of students' school adjustment.

The third gate uses two measures of school adjustment using direct observations. The first measure is Academic Engaged Time (AET), which measures the amount of time a student is academically engaged during classroom instructional periods. AET is operationally defined as follows (Walker & Severson, 1992): *AET means that the student is appropriately engaged in working on assigned material that is geared to her/his ability and skill levels. While academically engaged, the student is: (a) attending to the material and the task, (b) making appropriate motor responses, (e.g., writing, computing), (c) asking for assistance (where appropriate) in an acceptable manner, (d) interacting with the teacher or classmates about academic matters or, (e) listening to teacher instructions and directions.* Nonexamples *of AET would include such things as not attending to the assigned task, breaking classroom rules (out of seat, talking out, disturbing others, etc.) or daydreaming.*

AET represents a *duration measure* of behavior in that it assesses the amount of time a student is academically engaged. For example, if a student is observed from 9:00 to 9:15, the observer starts a stopwatch when the student meets the definition of academic engagement and stops the watch when the student is not academically engaged. The total elapsed time at the end of the 15-minute observation period represents the total amount of time the student was academically engaged. This number is converted to a percentage by dividing the elapsed time of academic engagement by the total amount of time observed and multiplying by 100. For example, if the student was academically engaged for 5 out of 15 minutes, the percentage of academic engagement would be 33 percent. Figure 15.8 presents the AET recording form.

The second observation measure in the SSBD is the Peer Social Behavior Code (PSB), which measures the quality, level, and distribution of student's social behavior during free-play settings (e.g., playgrounds). The PSB uses a partial interval recording method in which five categories of behavior are observed and coded: (a) Social Engagement, (b) Participation, (c) Parallel Play, (d) Alone, and (e) No Codeable Response. The PSB intervals are 10 seconds in length and a behavior is recorded if it occurs at any time during the 10-second interval. A total of six minutes and 40 seconds of data can be recorded per observation session. Figure 15.9 shows the PSB recording form and Figure 15.10 shows the PSB observation summary sheet. Note that the frequency of each behavior is converted to a percentage and averaged over two observation sessions. Two observation sessions are used to ensure a representative sample of behavior.

The following operational definitions are given for each of the PSB codes:

Social Engagement: Refers to an exchange of social signals between two or more children that involve either verbal or nonverbal interaction. Social engagement is coded when the target child is physically oriented toward another child (or children), is exchanging social signals of a reciprocal, purposeful nature with them, and/or produces verbal behavior in some form during the recording interval.

Systematic Screening for Behavior Disorders
ACADEMIC ENGAGED TIME (AET) RECORDING FORM[*]

Student Name _____ School _____ Grade ____

Teacher Name _____ Observer _____

Reliability Observer _____

SESSION #1

Date _____

Time Start _____ Time Stop _____ Length of Session _____

_____ ÷ _____ = _____ x 100 = _____
Time on Stopwatch   Length of Session   AET   % AET

Convert time to total # of seconds (i.e., minute equals 60 seconds) before computing. Divide time on stopwatch by total time observed.

Classroom Activity During Observation

_____

_____

SESSION #2

Date _____

Time Start _____ Time Stop _____ Length of Session _____

_____ ÷ _____ = _____ x 100 = _____
Time on Stopwatch   Length of Session   AET   % AET

Convert time to total # of seconds (i.e., minute equals 60 seconds) before computing. Divide time on stopwatch by total time observed.

Classroom Activity During Observation

_____

_____

Total Time Engaged for Sessions 1 & 2 = _____ seconds

= _____
Total AET

Total Time Observed for Sessions 1 & 2 = _____ seconds

Average Percent AET for Sessions 1 & 2 = Total AET ____ x 100 = _____
Percent AET

Figure 15.9 SSBD Recording Form for Peer Social Behavior

Systematic Screening for Behavior Disorders
PEER SOCIAL BEHAVIOR RECORDING FORM*

Student Name _____ Teacher Name _____

School _____ Grade _____ Observer _____

Reliability Observer _____ Date _____ Time Start _____

Time Stop _____ Length of Session _____

Interval Number	+ - SE	+ - P	✓ PLP	✓ A	• ✓ N	Interval Number	+ - SE	+ - P	✓ PLP	✓ A	• ✓ N
0-1						21					
2						22					
3						23					
4						24					
5						25					
6						26					
7						27					
8						28					
9						29					
10						30					
11						31					
12						32					
13						33					
14						34					
15						35					
16						36					
17						37					
18						38					
19						39					
20						40					

* © 1991 Hill M. Walker and Herbert H. Severson

Figure 15.10   SSBD Peer Social Behavior Observation Summary Sheet

Systematic Screening for Behavior Disorders
PEER SOCIAL BEHAVIOR
OBSERVATION SUMMARY SHEET*

Student Name _____

School _____ Grade _____

Dates Observed _____ and _____

Session #1   Session #2

	Number of Intervals*	Observation #1**	Number of Intervals*	Observation #2**	Average of 1 and 2
1. Social Engagement (SE)	_____	_____ %	_____	_____ %	_____ %
2. Participation (P)	_____	_____ %	_____	_____ %	_____ %
3. Parallel Play (PLP)	_____	_____ %	_____	_____ %	_____ %
4. Alone (A)	_____	_____ %	_____	_____ %	_____ %
5. No Codeable Response (N)	_____	_____ %	_____	_____ %	_____ %
6. Social Interaction (SI)	_____	_____ %	_____	_____ %	_____ %
7. Negative Interaction (NI)	_____	_____ %	_____	_____ %	_____ %
8. Positive Interaction (PI)	_____	_____ %	_____	_____ %	_____ %
9. Total Positive Behavior	_____	_____ %	_____	_____ %	_____ %
10. Total Negative Behavior	_____	_____ %	_____	_____ %	_____ %

* Enter the number of intervals recorded for each category.

** Enter the percentage of time spent for each category by dividing the total number of intervals that you observed during the observation session into the intervals recorded under different categories and multiplying by 100.

Participation: This is coded when the target child is participating in a game or activity (with two or more children) that has a clearly specified and agreed upon set of rules. Examples would be kickball, four-square, dodgeball, soccer, basketball, tetherball, hopscotch, and so forth. Nonexamples include tag, jump rope, follow the leader, and other unstructured games.

Parallel Play: This is coded when the target child is engaged in some activity within 5 feet of another child, but is not interacting (either verbally or nonverbally) with him or her. Although the activities the children are engaged in may be identical, the target child and other pupil(s) are behaving independently of each other. Examples of parallel play would include playing in a sandbox next to another child, running in a group, or sitting on a swing set with one or more students. A child engaged in self-talk (i.e., verbal behavior not directed toward anyone else) would be coded parallel play if the child met the other conditions of the Parallel Play category. Note: The target child need not be engaged in an activity similar to that of the children around him or her. For example, the child may be climbing a fence near (within 5 feet of) a sandbox where others are playing.

Alone: This is coded when the target child is not within 5 feet of another child, is neither socially involved nor socially engaged, and is not participating in a game or structured activity with other children. Examples would include sitting, standing, shooting baskets, kicking balls off walls, and so forth. A child engaged in self-talk (i.e., verbal behavior not directed toward anyone else) would be coded Alone if the child met the other conditions of the Alone category.

No Codeable Response: This is recorded when the target child's playground behavior cannot be accurately coded in one of the above five categories, e.g., the child is out of view or talking to an adult during recess. This category is coded only if there is no codeable behavior for an entire interval.

Comment on the SSBD Observation Measures

To the authors' knowledge, the SSBD, AET, and PSB observation measures represent the only well-standardized measures of behavior using observation-based assessment. Unlike the observation-based assessment measures described in this chapter, the SSBD observation measures can be compared to a representative sample of students. The SSBD measures were standardized on more than 1,200 students in six states representing the northeastern, midwestern, southern, and western regions of the United States. Percentile and T scores are available for the AET and PSB categories. The SSBD Technical Manual presents extensive evidence for the reliability and validity of the SSBD observational measures.

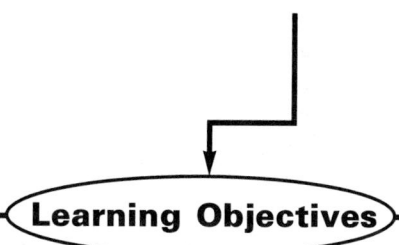

Chapter 16

Low-Incidence Disability Conditions

Learning Objectives

1. List four general considerations in the assessment of children with low-incidence disabilities.

2. Describe special preparations that can increase the validity of assessments of severely and profoundly disabled children.

3. List and describe major issues in the assessment of severely and profoundly disabled children.

4. List and describe major issues in the assessment of children with hearing impairments.

5. List and describe major issues in the assessment of children with visual impairments.

All of Colleen's undergraduate and graduate training had barely prepared her for what she was facing on the first day of her internship at a school for multiply disabled and severely disabled children. Colleen was in the process of assisting her supervisor in the evaluation of Louise. The staff had requested this evaluation because even though Louise had been diagnosed as severely disabled, they saw some "spark" in her eyes that suggested higher potential.

It was immediately obvious to Colleen that most forms of standard testing would be impossible to complete. Louise, who was eight years old, had to be strapped in a special adaptive wheelchair to sit upright. Records indicated she had spastic cerebral palsy; this meant Louise had virtually no voluntary control of her limbs, which moved in erratic, jerking movements, but she did have some head control. For many years children such as Louise were described in many psychologists' reports as "untestable." Now these children attend school, where assessments are done.

Colleen's supervisor was a good one. He asked Colleen to assume that Louise's thinking, ability to reason, and language were all normal. But how could this assumption be tested if Louise could not talk or point or communicate a correct answer in any of the usual ways? Colleen was dumbfounded. Every test she proposed to administer would be inappropriate, as her supervisor quickly pointed out. Finally, she hit upon the Columbia Mental Maturity Scale (Burgemeister, Blum, & Lorge, 1972). The response format for this test requires only that the child point to the correct answer. However, since even pointing was a problem for Louise, Colleen placed a hatlike pointer with an extended stick on Louise's head so that she could indicate her responses. Louise scored in the mildly disabled range, which was significantly above previous clinical estimates of her ability.

Colleen's story is typical in that modifications and adaptations may be needed before testing children with severe mental, physical, or sensory disabilities. The evaluation she conducted was not typical because teachers are most often not looking for an indication of cognitive functioning (such as IQ) but rather for what the child can and cannot do so that educational programs can be instituted.

➡️ *General Considerations in the Assessment of Children with Low-Incidence Disabilities*

Children with low-incidence disabilities have been diagnosed as belonging in one of five categories: (a) severely or profoundly disabled, (b) multiply disabled, (c) visually impaired, (d) hearing impaired, and (e) severely behavior disordered. Such disabilities occur relatively infrequently in the general population. In this chapter we discuss each of the low-incidence disabilities separately. We have, however, combined the severely or profoundly disabled category and the multiply disabled category because assessment procedures utilized with these two groups are quite similar. We are well aware that severely and profoundly disabled children differ from multidisabled and from each other, but part of assessment is to reveal such differences. The assessment of behavior disorders was discussed elsewhere.

Before we begin our discussion of the assessment procedures appropriate for each of the subgroups, we will specify some general considerations for assessing children with low-incidence disabilities. These guidelines are offered primarily to facilitate and encourage an approach to the assessment of severely disabled children that *qualitatively* differs from that typically used with mildly disabled children.

Use a Variety of Techniques, Strategies, and Instruments

Obtaining valid and comprehensive assessments of children with severe or multiple disabilities is extremely difficult and makes it imperative to utilize an array of assessment strategies. Three factors that contribute to assessment difficulty are (a) the possible presence of splinter skills, (b) problems in test stimuli presentation, and (c) problems in responding.

The concept of **splinter skills** refers to an unevenness in development that is sometimes seen in children with severe disabilities. Perhaps the most extreme (and rare) form of splinter skills are those present in the savant (see Focus on Practice). Other severely disabled persons may have less spectacular splinter skills, so the use of a variety of measures decreases the likelihood that splinter skills will go undetected. For three major categories of assessment strategies (standardized tests, developmental scales, and systematic observation), there are significant correlations between the measures, but the data derived from each source do make unique and nonoverlapping contributions (Diebold, Curtis, & DuBose, 1978; Simeonsson, Huntington, & Parse, 1980). A second reason for multiple assessment stems from problems in the presentation of test stimuli to some children. This point is so obvious that it hardly merits stating; nevertheless, a child must understand what is expected on a particular task while the chance of inadvertent cuing is reduced as much as possible:

> This does not pose a serious problem when assessing nonphysically handicapped children, because many language concepts found in normative-based tests utilized frequently in their natural environment. It is also not difficult to determine if they understand the examiner's language, because nonhandicapped learners will usually tell the examiner that they do not understand or have puzzled looks on their faces. Physically handicapped children may be unable to exhibit either response. The child should then be required to perform several sample tests prior to beginning the formal evaluation. (Duncan, Sbardellati, Maheady, & Sainato, 1980, p. 21)

A common problem is that test stimuli that are designed for a child's age may not be suitable for the child's developmental level (e.g., it is inappropriate to administer the Wechsler Intelligence Scale for Children-Revised, to a profoundly disabled seven-year-old because there is a very low probability of eliciting even one correct answer). One solution is to administer tests designed for infants. However, this may provide results that are not valid if disabled children were not included in the stan-dardization sample and if the norm tables do not accommodate the extreme ages and scores obtained by older disabled children (Simeonsson, 1977). One may use infant scales, however, if they have been validated for severely disabled adolescents and adults and if the literature offers reports of numerous validation studies. For assessing some

Focus on
➤ Practice ◄

The Case of Leslie Lemke

Leslie Lemke was about to play the piano before a full house at Milwaukee's Mount Carmel Lutheran Church, and he had a case of preconcert jitters. His 84-year-old foster mom, May, exuberantly steered guests over to meet her "little miracle boy," pointing to the six-footer sitting stoically in a beige wood pew. Suddenly he reached out in a frantic search to locate his foster father. "Paddy's right here," said Joe Lemke, 80, taking his son's hand. "I know Daddy's right here," repeated Leslie, who is blind, severely handicapped, and crippled by cerebral palsy. He is 32 years old.

As the audience soon learned, Leslie is also astonishingly gifted. Though his mind functions at about the level of a 3-year-old and though he has never seen a sheet of music, his foster mother long ago suspected that Leslie might be a musical prodigy. Hadn't she discovered him one day strumming rhythmically on the steel springs of his bed?

Joe and May scraped together $250 for a used piano, and to their amazement late one night, when Leslie was 16, he crawled over to the piano and started playing a Tchaikovsky concerto. He had heard Liberace play the music on television. Leslie had never played anything before, but it soon became evident that, after hearing any piece of music just once, he could unerringly reproduce it on the keyboard. Later he learned to sing as he played.

If there were skeptics in that Milwaukee audience two weeks ago, their doubts were dispelled when Leslie launched into a remarkably polished version of *Rhapsody in Blue* and a Louis Armstrong-like vocal rendition of *Hello, Dolly!* In a clear, resonant baritone, he belted out *I Believe*, his favorite song, and when he played *Somewhere My Love,* his foster parents danced together at the front of the church. Then, while many of his listeners fought back tears, Leslie tilted his head back and, with emotion, sang *Amazing Grace* and *He Touched Me.* In medical terms, Leslie exemplifies the phenomenon known as the savant syndrome, an exceedingly rare condition in which a person with severe mental disabilities demonstrates a singular, spectacular talent. Scientists can only speculate on how the Leslie Lemkes do what they do.

In medical literature only about 100 such cases of spectacular abilities have been reported since 1865, according to Dr. Darold Treffert, 51, who headed the Winnebago Mental Health Institute in Wisconsin for 15 years and is now in private psychiatric practice in Fond du Lac. Treffert is nationally recognized as an expert on the savant syndrome (the older, cruel description, "idiot savant," is now discarded). In all, Treffert has seen about a dozen people with savant characteristics, including one who could pop basketball free throws one after the other without missing and another who memorized the Milwaukee bus system. "If you told him the number of the bus that was passing and the time of day," says Treffert, "he could tell you what corner in the city you were standing on."

About one of every 2,000 severely disabled people demonstrates some savant characteristics, Treffert declares, and unaccountably, male savants outnumber their female counterparts about six to one. "There is a gradation of savant abilities, ranging from someone who may have good recall of history to one with the extraordinary talent that Leslie Lemke has."

Treffert believes that a savant possesses an idiosyncratic brain circuitry giving him "access to portions of the brain, particularly memory, that the rest of us don't have." But, Treffert admits, "we have not had the technology to find out why these people have this memory access."

Excerpted from the July 2, 1984, issue of *People Weekly Magazine*, written by Giovanna Brev/Time Inc. All rights reserved. Reprinted with permission.

skills, an examiner may be left with the options of using a checklist, creating instruments, using an inappropriate test, or making unvalidated modifications in existing instruments. Because none of these options alone is sufficient, the use of a variety of assessment methodologies helps one gain an understanding of a student.

Many children may have problems in responding. Blind children will have difficulty responding to visual stimuli, hearing impaired children may have difficulty responding to auditory stimuli, and some physically disabled children may be unable to answer questions that require motor responses. Children who are without these disabilities can be tested through a variety of modalities, and if there is a convergence of information across modalities, even if it is within the same test, one can be reasonably confident of the results. Because some children can be assessed through only one modality, an examiner cannot be as confident that the results are valid unless results from one type of assessment are supported by results of other assessment strategies.

Use a Developmental Perspective

A thorough knowledge of child development is valuable in assessing disabled children for two reasons. First, the evaluation specialist should continually ask, "What could non-disabled children reasonably be expected to do in this situation or on this task?" For example, a parent may be concerned that a five-year-old child diagnosed as brain injured is hyperactive and wants advice on how to deal with the hyperactivity. An initial observation suggests to the examiner that the child's "hyperactivity" is well within normal limits for the child's age. Thus, it was the parent's *perception* that was the problem, not the child's *behavior*. Such perceptions among family members and other caregivers may be more common for children diagnosed as disabled than for non-disabled children. A tacit assumption exists among many that any behavior that the caregiver does not like, that represents a change from the child's usual actions, or that *appears* to be deviant from the normal population is attributable to the disabling condition. Thus, a blind child who seems unusually frustrated over a period of a month may be referred for evaluation with the assumption that the frustration is caused by the blindness. Individuals who attribute this sort of blame to the disability fail to recognize that non-disabled children are hyperactive, become frustrated, and have many other problems that usually disappear without any treatment at all. A knowledge of normal development allows the specialist to determine when a "problem" really is a problem.

Second, a knowledge of child development can serve to guide assessment activities. Using developmental norms as a basis, the skills a child must acquire can be viewed as resting along a continuum from incompetent infant to competent adult. For the most part, skills along this continuum are learned in sequential order. If we can determine where a particular child falls with respect to this sequence of skills, we can provide quite relevant information to instructional specialists. For example, direct-care staff may have initiated an evaluation because an older child was not responding to toilet training. The evaluation may suggest that instruction in toilet training is likely to continue to be unsuccessful until specific skills in the sequence are learned first; that is, several skills prerequisite to toilet training still remain to be learned. The obvious recommendation would be to initiate instruction focusing on those prerequisite skills. The exact nature of the skills would be determined by referring to a good developmental skill sequence.

Use a Process Orientation to Evaluation

A major theme of this text has been that test scores are not likely to reveal a complete picture of a particular child. We have repeatedly emphasized that specific behavioral characteristics of learners can be identified by the careful observation of behavior and informal assessment. Nowhere is such a process orientation more appropriate than with children who exhibit sensory disabilities or who are severely disabled in cognition. A process orientation to the assessment of a severely or profoundly disabled child would require answers to at least the following questions:

• Does the child appear to favor certain toys, objects, or activities?

• How does the child interact with others? Does the child play? Fight? Withdraw?

• Does the child seek interaction or wait for others to initiate contact?

- Is there a difference between how the child interacts with children versus adults? Does the child, for example, play with adults but withdraw from children?

- Does the child appear to favor males over females, in adults or children?

- How does the child respond to different auditory, visual, and tactile stimuli?

- Are there certain activities the child seems particularly to enjoy? Are these directed toward the self (e.g., self-stimulatory repetitive behavior such as rocking) or outer-directed (e.g., playing with trains or coloring)?

- How long does the child generally remain with one activity or one object?

- Is the child easily distracted by various events in the room, such as voices, people passing by, school bells, or other students?

- Does the child perform certain behaviors independently, but not under adult cues? Or vice versa?

- Are there certain obvious educational programming priorities that can be identified immediately?

- Does the child demonstrate an understanding and awareness of the surroundings?

- How does the child explore the environment? Does the child primarily rely on visual, auditory, or tactile means to investigate the environment?

- How does the child respond to different reinforcers? What consequences seem to work best for inappropriate behavior? (Van Etten, Arkell, & Van Etten, 1980)

The primary advantage to a process orientation is that it broadens the scope of assessment activities and helps to ensure that the evaluation will be instructionally relevant.

Evaluations Must Have Treatment Validity

Evaluations of children with low-incidence disabilities are relatively straight-forward with respect to classification because it is usually easy to determine that the child has a problem (e.g., is blind or severely mentally disabled) and qualifies for some type of special education program. In fact, many children will already have a medical diagnosis before they enter school. Thus, when a child is referred for evaluation because of a specific problem or for a periodic reevaluation, it is not very useful to respond with only a diagnosis. The teachers who work daily in small groups with children who have severe disabilities already have a good idea of the level at which the child is functioning. What they may not know, however, is which skills to teach next and which strategies to use in teaching the skills. Evaluations that can provide such information are invaluable.

Specialists who conduct educational evaluations can often "get by" with evaluations that only categorize a child, if a primary purpose of the evaluation is to determine eligibility for special education. However, children with severe disabilities do not need relabeling. What they need are specific recommendations for treatment. Evaluations that fail to provide such recommendations are virtually worthless. Generally, standardized tests are administered primarily to obtain a "score" to fulfill legal requirements.

A primary method by which useful intervention recommendations can be developed is through the use of the **functional analysis of behavior** (see Focus on Practice). Functional analysis is important because there is no substitute for analyzing behavior in the environment in which it naturally occurs if your goal is to fully understand the behavior and to treat it. This is true whether one is attempting to increase the use of new and desirable behaviors or attempting to decrease unwanted or interfering behaviors (Wacker, Steege, & Berg, 1990).

➜ *Evaluating Severely and Profoundly Disabled Children*

Definitional Issues

Most but not all children with severe disabilities function cognitively at moderate to profound retardation levels. Until recently the severely and profoundly disabled were so classified according to definitions that utilized scores on intelligence tests as a major determining factor. The most common system of classification is that utilized by the American Association on Mental Retardation (AAMR) whereby children are classified as mildly, moderately, severely, or profoundly disabled (Grossman, 1977). In the past, American educators used a system in which children with IQs between 50 and 75 were diagnosed as educable mentally disabled (EMH) and those with IQs between 35 and 50 were referred to as trainable mentally disabled (TMH). Although IQ can no longer be used as the sole criterion for classification and adaptive behavior must be considered as well, IQ scores still carry a significant weight in decision making, in part because measures of intelligence are far more reliable than measures of adaptive behavior and in part because children are rarely referred for measurement of intellectual functioning unless they have already displayed adaptive behavior deficits.

The new AAMR definitions of mental retardation (AAMD, 1992), mentioned previously in connection with adaptive behavior in chapter 14, may further reduce the influence of IQ when classifying children as mentally disabled. As shown in table 16.1, the AAMR is now recommending a three-step process in determining the extent of disability. Very importantly, the terms mild, moderate, severe, and profound retardation are gone and have been replaced by Level 1 (mild) and Level 2 (severe) disability.

Focus on Practice

Functional Analysis of Behavior

What Is a Functional Analysis?

Functional analysis is an assessment process for gathering information that can be used to build effective behavioral support plans. A functional analysis is complete when three main outcomes can be accomplished:

1. Description of the undesirable behavior(s) operationally.

2. Prediction of the times and situations when the undesirable behavior(s) will and will not be performed across the full range of typical daily routines.

3. Definition of the function(s) (maintaining reinforcers) that the undesirable behavior(s) produces for the individual.

The general process of functional analysis assessment has many forms and many levels of precision. Anyone who has used an ABC (Antecedent-Behavior-Consequence) chart has conducted one form of functional analysis. Anyone who has observed undesirable behavior in different situations and concluded that "she does that because" has conducted an informal functional analysis. The process of functional analysis, as it was first developed in the research literature, typically involved direct manipulation of environmental variables and direct observation of changes in behavior.

The following ABC charts have been successfully used by Elliott and Gresham (1989) to help teachers and parents get started on a functional analysis. The next time you are confronted with a child's learning or behavior problem, start by filling in charts like these. They facilitate organization of assessment information and often present a set of clean hypotheses about the behavior of concern.

ABC Charts

From a list of behaviors observed, select the *one* you consider to be most important to change. This will be the Undesirable Target Behavior. Once you have briefly described this *Undesirable Target Behavior* in the space below, try to reconstruct from memory a sequential analysis of the events that occur *before* the behavior and *after* the behavior. Events that occur before the undesirable behavior are called *Antecedents* and usually involve who, what, when, and where type information. Events that follow the undesirable behavior are called *Consequences* and often involve information about what happened next and what the student received for his/her behavior. Now complete the A (antecedents), B (behavior), Cs (consequences) for the *Undesired Target Behavior* you wish to change.

Antecedents	Undesired Behavior	Consequences

Think of an alternative or incompatible behavior to the undesired target behavior above; call this the *Alternative Desired Behavior*. Even if the student doesn't presently exhibit this behavior, please complete the antecedents-behavior-consequences columns below. This should give you some ideas about what you think needs to be done before and after the alternative desired behavior to get it to occur and to continue over time.

Antecedents	Desired Behavior	Consequences

These new terms reflect more than a mere wording change and, instead, are intended to be more accurate *behavioral* descriptors within specific adaptive skill domains.

Another major change in this new AAMR definition is the third step in the process (see table 16.1), which requires the assessment team to determine the "Level of Support Needed." The three levels of support include: minimal support, substantial/extensive support, and pervasive/consistent support. The level of support thus ranges on a continuum from only occasional low-level support up through the constant (24-hour per day) support required to maintain life. Essentially this step is designed to answer the question, What type and level of support is needed for this child to live as normal a life as possible? Some children will function pretty well if provided only with a communication board in the regular class. Others will need a full-time aide to provide intensive support with self-care and other functions.

Although the AAMR standards have never been legally binding on schools, they often do foreshadow changes in the law. Also, the standards are frequently used by school-based assessment specialists to justify actions surrounding classification and diagnosis of mental disability. Hence, the standards merit a thorough understanding.

Table 16.1 1992 AAMR Diagnostic and Classification System

Step #1 Diagnosis of Mental Retardation if:
    (1) The person's intellectual functioning level is below 70–75.
    (2) The age of onset is 18 or below.
    (3) There are significant disabilities in two or more adaptive skill areas.
Step #2 Level of Disability
    (1) Level 1 (mild): if number of areas of disability is two or more and the assessed degree of the disability is the 2nd to 6th percentile in the areas of disability.
    (2) Level 2 (severe): if number of areas of disability is two or more and the assessed degree of the disability is the 1st to 3rd percentile in the areas of disability.
Step #3 Level of Needed Supports (for general planning purposes only):
    (1) Minimal
    (2) Substantial/Extensive
    (3) Pervasive/Consistent

Source: From *AAMR Diagnostic Manual,* 1992.

Issues in the Assessment of Children with Severe and Profound Disabilities

In addition to the general considerations for assessing all children with low-incidence disabilities presented earlier, there are several issues that are most important when evaluating the severely and profoundly disabled. These include special preparations for assessment and finding a reliable response mode.

Special Preparations for Assessment

It is apparent to anyone who has ever worked with severely and profoundly disabled children that one cannot typically just walk in with a test kit and launch into an assessment. Instead, it is usually necessary to obtain a considerable amount of information about the child prior to face-to-face assessment. Many children will be physically disabled and unable to respond in the usual manner. These children may require a special chair or other device to support the body. Some will not perform for strangers, and the enlistment of a familiar adult may be necessary. Other children may require primary reinforcers (such as small bits of fruit) to maintain optimal performance; however, sometimes the quickest way to lose rapport with a school or institutional staff is to give food rewards to a child whose diet is restricted. A list of other variables to consider prior to testing, as developed by Van Etten et al. (1980), is presented in table 16.2.

Hart (1977) has proposed that children be assessed in five settings that range from the informal to formal:

1. *Unstructured Setting.* The child is placed in a room with a variety of toys and/or other age-appropriate stimuli. Through a one-way mirror or from a corner of the room, the examiner observes to see with which stimuli and in what manner the child interacts.

2. *Stimulus-Oriented Setting.* Using the same room as for the unstructured setting, the examiner presents stimuli to the child to determine the child's reaction when forced to interact with various materials.

3. *Interpersonal Setting.* A familiar adult is provided with instructions for eliciting verbal interactions with the child.

4. *Task-Oriented Setting.* A familiar adult is asked to facilitate the child's display of special talents or abilities. In addition to seeing the child perform under optimal conditions, the examiner has the opportunity to determine how well the child responds to instructions and attends to the tasks.

5. *Formal Learning Setting.* With the familiar adult present, the examiner requests the child to perform specific tasks based upon strengths and weaknesses noted from observations in previous settings.

**Table 16.2 Considerations Prior to Testing Children
with Severe and Profound Disabilities**

---

1. Sensory and motor skills
   a. What sensory impairment does the student obviously display that may interfere with ability to execute test demands?
   b. Are gross and fine motor movements intact?
   c. Can the student execute bilateral movements? If not, can the student compensate adequately for testing purposes with unilateral movements?
   d. Does respiration appear adequate, or is there difficult breathing, congestion, or wheezing?
   e. What body parts can the student use most effectively to execute test demands?
2. Attentiveness
   a. Can the student make eye contact on a basis sufficient for testing?
   b. If eye contact is not in the student's repertoire, can he or she attend auditorally?
   c. Can tactile prompts be used with the student effectively for testing purposes?
   d. What is the approximate duration of attention span?
   e. Can physical or social reinforcers be effectively used for testing purposes? If so, how do reinforcers differentially affect the student's responses?
3. Communication skills
   a. Is the student verbal? To what degree are expressive and receptive language adequate?
   b. If the student is nonverbal, what is the mode of communication?
   c. Does the student respond (verbally or nonverbally) spontaneously?
   d. What prompts appear to be most effective in eliciting communication responses?

From *The Severely and Profoundly Handicapped: Programs, Methods, and Materials* (p. 45) by G. Van Etten, C. Arkell, and C. Van Etten. Copyright © 1980 by Dr. Glen Van Etten. Published by C. V. Mosby. Reprinted by permission of Dr. Glen Van Etten.

Determining and Using a Reliable Response Mode

An important prerequisite in the assessment of severely and profoundly disabled children is to determine a reliable response mode. According to Duncan, Sbardellati, Maheady, and Sainato (1980), it is essential that a child have some way "to vocalize or move as a reliable response to stimuli without any subjective interpretation on the part of the examiner" (p. 18). Children differ in their capability to respond to a question or some other stimulus. Duncan et al. (1980) presented the following hierarchy of possible responses:

1. *Expressive Language Response.* Displayed by children who possess easily understood, expressive language. They can be assessed at the recall ("From what animal do we get milk?") versus a recognition level ("Point to the picture of the animal that gives milk.").

2. *Pointing Response.* Shown by children who can reliably point to the correct answer, usually from a small array of stimuli. All too frequently, however, physically disabled children have a pointing response that is unreliable and difficult to score. For example, if two stimuli are close together, a child who has jerking hand movements may not be able to indicate reliably to which of two stimuli he or she is pointing. Also, children become extremely adept at perceiving small cues from an examiner concerning the correctness of a particular response and may switch quickly back and forth between alternatives.

3. *Using an Existing Motor Response.* Used by some children who have neither expressive language nor a pointing response, yet are nevertheless capable of answering "yes" or "no" using responses that are idiosyncratic to their own physical mobility. Usually adults familiar with the child can describe these responses, which may include small movements of some body part or noises. Such responses are usually designed to signal either "yes" or "no." Occasionally a child may have separate responses for "yes" and "no" but more often can communicate only one or the other.

4. *Training an Existing Inconsistent Response.* Occasionally it is necessary to institute a training program to increase the reliability of an inconsistent response. For example, a child may use a head movement to indicate "yes." However, the same head movement may occur when the child is angry or under stress. Thus, it becomes impossible for an examiner to interpret a child's intent. The process of teaching a consistent response usually involves placing the child on a shaping program. For example, a child who raises a finger to indicate "yes" could be taught to raise the entire arm.

5. *Teaching a Nonexistent Response.* Some children have no method of communicating or interacting with the environment. According to Duncan et al. (1980), this may result in "learned helplessness" because "their environment has been structured in such a way that they perceive no connection between their actions and the consequences they receive" (p. 20). Training a child to respond to stimuli after that child has been without such skills for *years* is exceedingly difficult. Because of the long-term nature of such training, it is best accomplished through the child's educational program.

6. *Using a Nonvoluntary Response.* At some point it may become obvious to the multidisciplinary evaluation team that a child is unlikely to develop voluntary control of responding (i.e., given a stimulus, the child does not respond in any meaningful way). An evaluation of the children may encompass the assessment of *elicited* rather than *emitted* responses. In one sense, a child has voluntary

control over emitted responses (e.g., the child points to a picture of a fork when given the appropriate verbal cue), but elicited response occurs in reaction to stimuli (e.g., smelling salts placed under the nose will usually result in an involuntary turning away from the stimulus). Thus, evaluation may include noting the types of stimuli to which the child responds, including light, vibration, heat, cold, loud noises, pinpricks, salt, and sugar. However, in certain situations it may be unethical, against institutional rules, or even illegal to utilize some of these stimuli.

Individuals who have not interacted with severely and profoundly disabled children may not anticipate the complexities of such an evaluation. Dubose (1976) has referred to such an evaluation as "the diagnostician's challenge" and suggests that as the number and severity of impairments increase, the resulting increases in the complexity of the evaluation are multiplicative.

Evaluation Methodologies for Children with Severe and Profound Disabilities

The comprehensive evaluation of children with severe and profound disabilities involves the assessment of cognitive development, adaptive behavior, communication skills, motor development, social-emotional functioning, and vocational skills. The primary assessment strategies used to yield information about these areas of functioning include: (a) interviews, (b) checklists and rating scales, (c) formal tests, (d) functional analysis, (e) observation, and (f) behavioral assessment. Since the latter two have been discussed earlier in the text, we will describe only interviews, rating scales, and formal tests in the section that follows.

Interviews

An excellent starting point for assessment is to interview individuals with whom the child has frequent interaction, such as parents and teachers. Interviews can accomplish five primary goals. First, they can yield information that clearly defines the purposes and goals of assessment. What problems prompted the assessment? How will the assessment information be used? Second, interviews can provide information about how to assess a child. Many severely and profoundly disabled children have idiosyncratic response modes or styles of interaction. Interviews with those knowledgeable of these styles can prove invaluable in conducting a comprehensive evaluation. Third, interviews not only guide other types of assessment but they are also an important form of evaluation in and of themselves. For example, many adaptive behavior scales utilize third-party interviews to obtain information about what a child can and cannot do. Fourth, interviews have been used traditionally to elicit information about a child's developmental history, family resources, siblings, and medical status. Finally, many specialists utilize interviews to conduct a functional analysis of the child's behavior, that is, an examination of the child's behavioral excesses and deficits and the environmental stimuli that control these behaviors. For example, with a child who engages in self-abusive behavior such as head banging, it is important to determine the factors that maintain this behavior (although the more remote "cause" will probably be elusive). Functional analysis is described in greater detail in the Focus on Practice (see page 433) and on page 442.

Checklists and Rating Scales

Because many children with severe and profound disabilities are difficult to evaluate through a direct question-and-answer format, a number of checklists and rating scales have emerged that minimize the amount of direct interaction with the child. These are typically completed by someone who knows the child well or through an interview with such a person. The respondent is asked to indicate either the presence or absence of a particular behavior or the degree to which the behavior is present.

Checklists and rating scales offer several advantages (Wells, 1981). They are quick, economical, and efficient, and most examine a wide range of behaviors. A primary disadvantage is that perceptions of behavior often differ markedly from actual observations (Whalen & Henkler, 1976).

The existing checklists and rating scales vary along three important dimensions: informant, scope, and structure (McMahon, 1984). The *informant* dimension pertains to who completes the instrument. The type of information desired helps to dictate the informant used. The most typical informants are teachers and parents. The *scope* of an instrument refers to the extent to which it reflects a narrow versus a wide range of behaviors. Some instruments may be useful only for self-help skills, whereas others may also evaluate vocational skills, language development, maladaptive behaviors, and a number of other domains. Finally, the *structure* dimension refers to length, format, and specificity of the scale or checklist. Some are quite global in their descriptions (e.g., the child is capable of taking care of herself), whereas others are more specific ("the child can put on a shirt without assistance"). The length can range from five to several hundred items. Formats can vary from requiring only a "yes" or "no" response for indicating the presence or absence of a skill to asking the rater to indicate on a 1 to 5 scale the degree to which a particular skill is present. A sample behavioral checklist is presented in table 16.3.

Formal Tests

Formal tests designed specifically for use with severely and profoundly disabled children are relatively rare. Tests designed for other purposes are more commonly utilized. For example, it is not uncommon to use infant intelligence tests such as the Bayley Scales of Infant Development (Bayley,

---

Table 16.3 Sample Behavioral Checklist for Drinking

1. Opens mouth when physically stimulated
2. Closes mouth when physically stimulated
3. Sucks liquid from straw
4. Takes liquids from cup/glass held by another
5. Swallows liquids when physically stimulated
6. Swallows liquids independently
7. Retains liquids in mouth without drooling
8. Touches with hands cup/glass held by adult while drinking
9. Tips cup/glass to drink held by adult
10. Holds cup/glass to drink when placed in both hands
11. Reaches for cup/glass independently
12. Grasps cup/glass independently
13. Picks up cup/glass independently with some spilling
14. Picks up cup/glass independently without spilling
15. Drinks from cup/glass held to mouth by adult, using both hands, with some spilling
16. Drinks from cup/glass held to mouth by adult, using both hands, without spilling
17. Reaches for cup/glass, grasps, brings to mouth to drink, independently
18. Reaches for cup/glass, grasps, brings to mouth, tips to drink, independently with some spilling
19. Reaches for cup/glass, grasps, brings to mouth, tips to drink, independently without spilling
20. Reaches for cup/glass, grasps, brings to mouth, tips to drink, drinks, independently with some spilling
21. Reaches for cup/glass, grasps, brings to mouth, tips to drink, drinks, independently without spilling

---

1969) with severely and profoundly disabled children. The problems of using such tests with children for whom they were not specif- ically standardized have been discussed earlier in this chapter. Bayley specifically cautions in her manual against such misuse; however, validation studies of this test have been conducted with disabled adults.

Among the formal tests that have response formats that are useful when assessing severely and profoundly disabled children is the Columbia Mental Maturity Scale (Burgemeister et al., 1972), which requires a child to select from an array of objects on a printed card the one that is different from the others. The test is intended to assess nonverbal reasoning, and all the child need do is point to the correct answer. Verbal responses are not required. The stimulus cards are large enough so that many physically disabled children with minimal muscle control can respond.

Functional Analysis of Behavior

The final, and, for this population, the most important type of assessment is the functional analysis of behavior (described in the Focus on Practice, see page 433). Underlying functional analysis is an assumption that all behaviors have a specific *function*. For example, when we say that a child has temper tantrums to get attention, we often say the child is reinforced by the adult attention. In the language of functional analysis, we would say the behavior functions to obtain reinforcement in the form of adult attention. Although many behaviors function to obtain reinforcement, others function to avoid or escape. The same behavior, for example temper tantrums, may function to gain attention in one setting and to escape work in another. Hence, a general intervention for temper tantrums would probably fail because the function of this behavior varies from person to person and setting to setting.

An example will help to illustrate the process. Assume that a severely disabled child is engaging in self-injurious behavior (e.g., head-banging, arm-scratching). Wacker et al. (1990) provided an assessment of self-injurious behavior (adapted from Iwata, Dorsey, Slifer, Bauman and Ridman, 1982) using classroom observations (see table 16.4). As can be seen, the child's rate of self-injurious behavior over a three-day period was much higher when demands were being placed on him; that is, when he was being asked to learn new skills or when asked to fold laundry. Given this result, one might hypothesize that the behavior functioned to escape the demands of the situation. An intervention designed to test this idea might be to decrease the length of time the child is placed under demands or to teach him or her to signal a teacher when a break is desired (Wacker et al., 1990).

Table 16.4   Assessment of Self-Injurious Behavior Using a Classroom Observation Approach

Time	Activity/ Instructional Domain	Condition	Average Frequency of Occurrence of SIB (3 days)
9:00–9:20	Vocational training (janitorial tasks)	Demand	40
9:30–9:45	Toileting	Alone—no activity	2
9:45–10:00	Recreation—leisure	Alone—with activity	5
10:00–10:30	Community living (folding laundry)	Demand	60
10:30–10:45	Break with peers	Social attention	3

From D. P. Wacker et al., "Best Practices in Assessment and Intervention with Persons Who Have Severe/Profound Handicaps" in *Best Practices in School Psychology-II*, edited by A. Thomas and J. Grimes. Copyright © 1990 by the National Association of School Psychologists. Reprinted by permission of the publisher.

➡ *Evaluating Children with Hearing Impairments*

Definitional Issues

To understand hearing loss one must first understand the nature of sound. Essentially, sound is measured by two primary components: intensity and frequency. In everyday language the *intensity* of sound refers to how loud it is. Assessment of intensity is generally in terms of decibels (dB), with 0 dB being the softest sound that a normal person can perceive and sounds greater than about 125 dB causing pain. Sound *frequency* refers to the degree a sound is low or high pitched. Frequency was formerly assessed in terms of cycles per second but more recently has been measured in hertz units. To understand speech sounds, we must be able to hear sounds in the 300 to 4,000 hertz range. On a piano this would correspond to approximately middle C on the low end to the highest piano note at the high end.

Degree of hearing loss is important because it is highly correlated with the acquisition of speech and is a major factor in educational placements (Spragins, 1980). Obviously the degree of loss is also important in planning and interpreting an evaluation. Children with mild to moderate hearing loss would probably be evaluated differently than children with a severe or profound loss. In addition, the interpretation of the results must be evaluated in view of the "normal" expectations within a certain degree of hearing loss. For example, expectations for the extent of language development change drastically as the extent of hearing loss increases.

Issues in the Assessment of Children with Hearing Impairments

Screening for hearing defects is done with an audiometer, usually by a school nurse; full examination is done by audiologists or medical specialists. The major problems in the educational assessment of hearing impaired children involve language competence and communications abilities that can present difficulties in obtaining a valid evaluation. If hearing impaired children are not properly evaluated and classified, they will be unlikely to receive appropriate education. Careful consideration must be given to two basis issues: (a) evaluating the impact of the impairment on other (especially cognitive) areas of functioning, and (b) determining an appropriate communication mode.

Evaluating the Impact of Hearing Impairment on Other Abilities

If a child with severe hearing loss earns a score of 88 on a verbally administered intelligence test, the prudent examiner must consider a number of alternative explanations for this below-average score. For example, how much of the low score is due to the child being penalized for having a hearing impairment? Perhaps the child missed key words in some of the questions because of poor hearing. At a more general level, the child has probably missed a considerable amount of environmental stimulation, especially in the area of language, because of the impairment and therefore may not have acquired skills that otherwise could have been learned. Spragins (1980) has listed a series of related issues:

1. What is the impact of auditory deprivation on intellectual development and functioning?

2. Is language a primary vehicle of intellectual development or is there independence of linguistic and intellectual development?

3. Is the developmental lag that hearing impaired children manifest on cognitive tasks, in actuality, a general experiential deficit?

4. Granted the fact that thinking is clearly possible without verbal language, is enculturation possible without language? (p. 58)

None of these issues is easily resolved. However, each must be raised whenever evaluating hearing impaired children. It is inappropriate to assume that hearing impaired children are otherwise normal children who are difficult to evaluate simply because of sensory deficits. This assumption would lead us to believe that if we could just find a way to communicate properly during the evaluation, we could somehow tap the child's "true" potential. Unfortunately, hearing impairment is not just a sensory deficit, for it brings with it serious linguistic limitations (Sullivan & Vernon, 1979).

Determining an Appropriate Communication Mode

Depending on the degree of hearing impairment, communication with hearing impaired children can be attempted through a variety of modalities: gesture, sign language, pantomime, vocalization, and expressive speech. Usually, the most acceptable form of communication can be determined prior to the evaluation. In the past it seems that children were evaluated in the mode that was most convenient and comfortable to the examiner. There is a growing realization, however, that the hearing impaired should be evaluated in the mode that is most useful for communication.

The most frequent problem occurs when the child is fluent in sign language but the examiner is not (Levine, 1974). Because this can lead to invalid results, it is negligent for the examiner to use the results to make important decisions about the child. As Sullivan and Vernon (1979) point out, "deaf children are linguistically proficient in the syntax, morphology, and semantics of sign language. This is their 'native' tongue which they naturally acquire. . . . English is learned as a second language by most hearing impaired children" (p. 271).

Evaluation Methodologies for Children with Hearing Impairments

Cognitive and Intellectual Assessment of Processes

So few tests have been specifically designed for children with hearing impairments that common practice has been to select instruments that require a performance rather than a verbal response format (Spragins, 1980). Accordingly, the performance sections of the WISC-III (Wechsler, 1991) have been routinely administered to hearing impaired children. According to Levine (1974), a variety of other instruments are also commonly utilized, including the Columbia Mental Maturity Scale (Burgemeister et al., 1972), Hiskey-Nebraska Test of Learning Aptitude (Hiskey, 1966), and the Leiter International Performance Scale (Leiter & Arthur, 1955), although several have problems in terms of predictive validity, norm samples, or reliability. Since hearing impaired children were not included in the standardization of many of these instruments, results must be cautiously interpreted because hearing impaired children may be disadvantaged even on perfor-mance tasks. For example, the average score for hearing impaired children on the Picture Arrangement subtest of the WISC-R is more than 2 points lower than for the normal population (Anderson & Sisco, 1977). Some tests, designed for hearing children can be adapted to the needs of hearing impaired children. For example, during test administration, children can easily learn what is expected of them through modeling and pantomime instructions, if this change in instructions has been validated.

Given that so few tests exist specifically for hearing impaired children and that the use of tests designed for other purposes is questionable, the best approach for evaluating such children would appear to be a cautious use of several formal tests. A growing research literature has assessed the effects of such an approach (cf. Sullivan & Vernon, 1979), which may make it possible to ascertain the deleterious impacts, if any, of administering various instruments to hearing impaired children. Among the cognitive measures used with these children, it appears that only the now dated WISC-R, which was restandardized on hearing impaired children (Anderson & Sisco, 1977), and the Hiskey-Nebraska, which is also becoming somewhat antiquated, have norms based on a hearing impaired population.

Assessment of Academic Achievement

The problems associated with cognitive and intellectual assessment are also applicable to the testing of academic achievement. Since reading is a language-based skill, it is not surprising that children with hearing impairments perform significantly lower in this and related areas (such as language arts and social studies) than do their nonhandicapped counterparts (Trybos & Karchmer, 1977). Informal assessment, task analysis, and test-teach-test strategies are preferred with hearing impaired children.

Assessment of Language and Communication Skills

Most children who cannot hear speech well have difficulty developing language. This area is routinely assessed in the evaluation of hearing impaired children. The two most important factors to evaluate are (a) speech intelligibility and (b) receptive and expressive manual and oral communication skills (Spragins, 1980). Speech intelligibility can be assessed by how understandable the speech is or the percent of time it is understandable. Primarily a function of degree of hearing loss, it does not improve markedly with increased age or training (Karchmer & Trybos, 1978). Communication skills can be assessed through formal tests, informal evaluation, or ongoing language curriculum.

➡ *Evaluating Children with Visual Impairments*

Definitional Issues

The three components that must be assessed to determine visual impairment in students are visual acuity, field of vision, and functional vision. Screening for visual acuity is conducted in schools by a school nurse who uses Snellen charts at a distance of 20 feet and at reading distance. Full examinations are given by ophthalmologists or optometrists. **Visual acuity** reflects the degree to which individuals can differentiate objects and discriminate details. In screening tests (e.g., Snellen charts), a child is typically presented with an eye chart placed 20 feet away and asked to identify letters printed on the chart in varied sizes. The standard criterion for ruling out visual acuity problems is 20/20 vision, meaning that one reads the line of the type size labeled 20 while standing 20 feet away. Those with visual acuity of less than 20/200 in their best eye after correction are classified as legally blind.

The second type of definition focuses on **field of vision,** or the extent to which a child can see a full range of stimuli (i.e., has peripheral vision). Some children, for example, have excellent visual acuity but their field of vision may be so restricted that they can see only one or two letters simultaneously on a printed page.

The third type of assessment for visual impairment is based on the degree to which a person has **functional vision.** Most individuals with some vision, even some classified as legally blind, can be trained to use large print and other visual materials. Using this criterion, children are classified as blind when they cannot make use of partial sight and must be educated using braille or auditory materials; those who can be educated through the visual modality are termed partially sighted. Assessment for functional vision is clinical, requiring direct observations of the child's behavior.

Issues in the Assessment of Children with Visual Impairments

Just as the educational assessment of hearing impaired children is not a matter of simply making auditory instructions and stimuli understandable, so the assessment of visually impaired children is more than avoiding the use of visual test stimuli. Visual impairments represent a disability that markedly decreases the amount and type of information available to a child during development.

Thus, in some areas, a normally functioning child with serious, uncorrected visual impairments may perform at levels below those of children with normal vision. Several problems exist with the use of psychoeducational assessment instruments designed for sighted populations. Some assessors have used verbal tests (e.g., the WISC-III Verbal section) or written tests translated into braille to evaluate visually impaired children. However, Baker (n.d.) has identified a number of problems with this approach:

1. Visually impaired children may be at a disadvantage when required to remember lengthy instructions or numerous multiple-choice responses.
2. Translations of tests designed for sighted individuals for use with the visually impaired must necessarily omit certain components such as maps and diagrams.
3. Visualization is the key component of some tests.
4. Tests may require knowledge that is only available visually and is not a part of any curriculum that would be specifically taught to a visually impaired child.

Another problem is that norms developed from a sighted population do not apply when standardized administration procedures are altered. However, many visually impaired children retain some residual sight that can be utilized through large-print materials or electronic magnification devices. It may be possible, with only very slight modification, to adapt some visual materials for use during assessment. The Focus on Practice provides some practical suggestions for establishing rapport with and evaluating visually impaired children. However, the statement that you should "expect language and motor delays" is not substantiated by research evidence.

Evaluation Methodologies for Children with Visual Impairments

A wide variety of tests have been designed or can be adapted for use with visually impaired children. It is also possible to utilize interviews and informal and behavioral assessment techniques that have been discussed elsewhere in this chapter and throughout the text.

It is the exception rather than the rule to find well-standardized and validated tests that have been normed on visually impaired populations. Because of this, Baker (n.d.) has suggested that the principle that should

Focus on Practice

Establishing Rapport with and Evaluating a Child with a Visual Impairment

When establishing rapport with a child who cannot see well, the psychologist's friendly smile will be in vain. Other techniques must be developed. A handshake, hand on shoulders, or other "hands on" approaches are quick ways to connect with that person. He may wish to be guided by holding on to your elbow. We take in a new room by looking around; allow the child to explore by touching or describing the setting, including the test equipment.

As you settle in, take a moment to discuss his vision problem. For some children, bright contrast is preferred. Others work best in diffuse, natural light and some children need dimness. Small print may be better than large print. For most blind people, minimal distraction by sounds or smell is preferred. Sounds we may ignore, such as a ticking stopwatch, a motor, or sniffling will pose a direct distraction to those who do not see. Offer to adjust the lighting, explain sounds, and ask him to let you know when he needs help. It's easiest to be frank because it allows him that privilege as well. A few people feel they need to shout or speak slowly to blind people, but obviously this doesn't help much. Use your regular vocabulary, including references to "seeing." Blind persons use these words too.

In addition, be sure your paper is off white or yellow to reduce glare. Provide a choice of pens and pencils for him to choose. A soft #2 pencil or felt tip is often desired. Then after you are both comfortable, begin to test.

Evaluating a visually impaired preschooler requires common sense and clinical skills. Remember to expect language and motor delays as well as possibly some autisticlike symptoms. One may be left wondering how to get an accurate feel for this child's potential. Unfortunately there is no magic way to find out. We have little else but several standard tests, behavioral observation, and our clinical judgment to use.

From F. H. Goldmand and D. Duda, "Psychological Assessment of the Visually Impaired Child" *Assessment of Children with Low Incidence Handicaps,* edited by R. F. Mulliken and M. Evans. Copyright © 1980 by the National Association of School Psychologists. Reprinted by permission of the publisher.

guide users of such tests is caveat emptor. The following list of potential problems (adapted from Baker) should be considered in evaluating assessment instruments for visually impaired children:

1. Overall test quality is sometimes poor because many tests were developed as part of master's theses or doctoral dissertations and may not have received the careful research and revision characteristically given to the instruments developed by major test publishing companies.

2. Norms may be based on small numbers.

3. Because institutionalized populations are readily available during standardization, these groups may be overrepresented in the normative sample.

4. Norms are typically not provided for various degrees of visual impairment (e.g., partially sighted versus blind), even though performance expectations across the range of impairments differ markedly.

5. Test instructions may be poorly standardized or difficult to interpret and introduce an unwanted source of variation in scores due to examiner interpretation (or misinterpretation!) of instructions.

6. Often there is little supporting documentation and research to establish the reliability or validity of the instrument.

The prudent test user will consider each of these factors in light of the particular information desired and the specific characteristics of an individual client. Readers wanting more information on the assessment of the visually impaired are referred to other sources (Bauman & Kropf, 1979; Goldman & Duda, 1980).

Chapter Summary

This chapter has summarized a variety of approaches for assessing children with disabilities that do not occur very frequently in the general population. For the astute reader, it will be apparent that the processes of assessing these diverse groups are more similar than different. What are the commonalities of the processes? Are the processes really that much different from those used in the assessment of children with less severe disabilities? The answers to these questions should help to put the assessment of low-incidence children in perspective with assessment in general. Our view is that all children range along a normal–abnormal continuum and that one does not necessarily adopt a completely different approach when moving from one type of assessment to another. We may use different methods but the process and the guiding philosophy remain remarkably consistent.

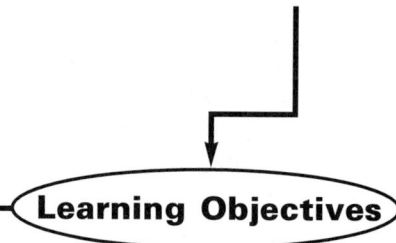

Chapter 17

Curriculum-Based Assessment

Learning Objectives

1. Define curriculum-based assessment.

2. Describe some of the concerns with traditional assessment procedures that led to the development of curriculum-based assessment techniques.

3. List the goals that led Deno and his colleagues to the development of curriculum-based measurement.

4. Describe how curriculum-based measurement would be used to monitor a child's progress in reading.

5. Describe potential uses and misuses of curriculum-based assessment data.

W anda and Ted Johnson are excited. It's a cool Tuesday evening in early February and they are on their way home after their parent-teacher conference with their son's fourth-grade teacher. Wanda and Ted learned a lot about Timmy's school behavior and his progress in reading and math. Both Wanda and Ted liked Timmy's teacher, Ms. Bailey. She answered questions thoroughly and she seemed to respect the Johnson's ideas. At the end of the meeting, she had thanked them for having Timmy ready for and interested in coming to school every day.

The Johnsons had been most impressed by the fact that Ms. Bailey had given them a series of graphs that gave very specific information about the progress that Timmy was making in reading and arithmetic. In the past (the Johnsons have had two other children attend this elementary school), they had not been given such detailed information about their children's progress (see figure 17.1 later in this chapter for an example of the type of graphs Wanda and Ted were given). Sure, they had seen worksheets and grade cards and lists of mastered objectives, but they had never been given information that so precisely charted Timmy's progress. On many past occasions they had been given results from standardized tests like the California Achievement Test; however, they were not always sure what these results meant and how these results related to their child's specific progress in their local elementary school. Ms. Bailey explained that the school had started a new program this year called "curriculum-based assessment" to help keep track of the progress of individual students in reading and math. She had been using the program since September and she wanted to share Timmy's results with his parents.

"Do you believe it?" said Wanda. "Why, Ms. Bailey was even able to show us how Timmy struggled with his math during the first few weeks of school and that after she had changed her instructional strategies his progress improved dramatically." (Ms. Bailey had changed the skills Timmy was working on when her data revealed that he had not mastered all his basic addition facts. Also, she began rewarding his improvements with free time). "I wonder," said Ted. "Do you think that a program like the one that Timmy is participating in would have helped Susan? She struggled so much with reading in school, maybe. . . ." "No sense crying over spilled milk," mused Wanda. "Let's just be thankful that Timmy's problems with math were spotted early and that he's on the right track for now."

➡ *What Is Curriculum-Based Assessment and Why Do We Need It?*

The term **curriculum-based assessment** (CBA) means simply measurement that uses "direct observation and recording of a student's performance in the local curriculum as a basis for gathering information to make instructional decisions" (Deno, 1987, p. 41). In the preceding example, Wanda and Ted were given assessment data that showed specifically how Timmy was progressing through the local reading and math curriculum. Later in this chapter we discuss a computer program that allows teachers to do curriculum-based assessment in a manner that yields information similar to that which was given to Wanda and Ted.

The process of CBA has also been referred to as direct assessment of academic skills and many different models of direct assessment have been advanced. These models all have in common the basic assumption that one should test what one teaches. Typically, these approaches have emphasized direct, repeated assessment of academic target behaviors (Lentz, 1988). In each academic area, *probes* are developed (e.g., brief reading passages, short spelling lists, samples of math items from the curriculum, etc.) and these probes are used to collect data on student performance. The probes are developed from the actual books and materials that the child is using in class. Hence, CBA provides a structured way to see how well a child performs on the materials the teacher is assigning the class. The assumption is that if we want to know whether children are progressing in reading and writing, then we should observe (or count) their behavior as they read and write in school, and we should collect this data as often as is feasible so that we quickly know whether a child is making progress or falling behind.

A child who has difficulty learning needs to be tested frequently to see if instruction is having the desired effect. Ideally, all children would be tested frequently to assess their rate of learning. If learning is not occurring, then instruction needs to be altered in some way. When a child is tested only once or twice a year (or even once every term), it is impossible to monitor accurately the effects of instruction. Since traditional norm-referenced achievement tests are not designed to be administered repeatedly, these tests should not be used to monitor a student's progress. A child would become familiar with the items and may show progress if tested again and again, but the gains in test scores would be due to familiarity with the test rather than real gains in achievement.

Despite the apparent simplicity of the notion that one should test what one teaches and test as often as is possible, the process of finding effective and useful forms of curriculum-based measures has yielded many different solutions. Investigators have had different objectives, focused on different aspects of the assessment process, collected differing amounts and types of validity data, and used somewhat different terminology to describe their approaches (see table 17.1).

In addition to those listed in table 17.1, many others (e.g., Becker, Engelmann, Carnine, & Maggs, 1982; Haring, Lovitt, Eaton, & Hansen, 1978; White & Liberty, 1976) have used curriculum probes to assess student performance, develop learning objectives, and measure student progress. The **direct instruction** model developed at the University of Oregon has been one of the most widely used and successful application of direct or curriculum-based assessment (Becker et al., 1982).

Recently, much attention has been devoted to the technology of curriculum-based measurement (e.g., Deno, 1985; Kramer, 1993; Shinn, 1989) and the use of this technology in monitoring the development of children's basic academic skills (e.g., reading, spelling, written expression, and arithmetic). Curriculum-based measurement (CBM) is the name given to a very specific approach to curriculum-based assessment that was developed during the early 1980s at the University of Minnesota. The 1980s saw a virtual explosion of research in curriculum-based measurement (Shinn, 1989). Much of the remainder of this chapter is devoted to an analysis of CBM research. Specific examples of potential use in classrooms are provided following a brief explanation of why curriculum-based assessment has become of such importance to education.

Table 17.1 Comparison of CBA Models

Comparative Features	CBM-ID (Gickling & Havertape, 1981)	CBM (Deno, 1985)	CR-CBA (Blankenship, 1985)	CBE (Howell, 1986)
Relationship to Assessment and Decision Making	Instructional Planning	Student Progress Monitoring	Instructional Planning	Instructional Planning
Evidence of Utility for Making Other Decisions	Indirect Monitoring of Student Progress	Screening, Eligibility, Program Evaluation	No	No
Timing in Instructional Planning	Ongoing, with most of assessment *preceding* initial instruction	Ongoing, with most of assessment *after* initial instruction	Pre-testing and mastery testing, with most of assessment *preceding* initial instruction	Ongoing, with most of assessment *preceding* initial instruction
Focus of Material for Monitoring Progress	Short Term	Long Term	Short Term	Short Term
Test Formats	Short Duration	Short Duration	Varies	Varies
Data on Technical Adequacy	Content Validity, Construct Validity	Reliability, Criterion-Related Validity, Construct Validity	Content Validity	Content Validity

Adapted from M. R. Shinn, S. Rosenfield, and N. Knutson, "Curriculum-Based Assessment: A Comparison of Models" in *School Psychology Review*, 18:299–316. Copyright © 1989 by the National Association of School Psychologists. Adapted by permission of the publisher.

Why Curriculum-Based Assessment

For a number of years, teachers and teacher preparation programs have been criticized for lack of attention to educational measurement (e.g., Kramer, 1993). Many believed that teachers were not well prepared to measure the educational progress of the children with whom they were working. The primary concerns have been that teachers were given little instruction in measurement principles and even less opportunity to practice effective measurement procedures while training to be a teacher. The need to better prepare teachers and to equip them with functional tools for measuring academic progress led many to explore CBA.

An additional reason for the development of CBA was that although it is true that standardized test batteries, criterion-referenced instruments, and informal assessment inventories can be used to measure student achievement and to diagnose strengths and weaknesses, these tools have not been very useful for measuring short-term change in student academic performance (Lentz, 1988). Teachers needed an effective, efficient tool for measuring whether a child's performance had improved this week, this month, this term.

Finally, there is often a mismatch between the content and sequence in which skills are introduced in a particular school district and the content of achievement tests and inventories. It does no good for an achievement test to tell you that your students have not yet mastered multiplication facts, when you know that you have just this month introduced multiplication to them. Also, it is not uncommon for someone who has tested a child with standardized tests to say something like "Susan appears to be reading at grade-level," only to have the classroom teacher say "NO WAY." How can this be? As Jenkins and Pany (1978) have shown (see table 17.2), just because a reading curriculum says that a particular reader is written at a grade 1 or 2 level does not mean that an achievement test will agree that the words used in that reader are grade 1 or grade 2 level material. Furthermore, each achievement test may give a different assessment of the difficulty of the material. Jenkins and Pany selected words from two different levels (grade 1 and 2) of different reading series and then evaluated the "difficulty" (i.e., actually, the grade level) of these words according to a series of achievement tests. As can be seen, a child's "grade level" score in reading may vary dramatically depending on the reading curriculum used in a school and the particular achievement test used to assess the child.

Although the Jenkins and Pany article is somewhat dated now and the tests and reading curriculum listed in table 17.2 have all been revised, Good and Salvia (1988) have recently found that this type of mismatch remains a problem and that reading curricula and achievement tests are no better matched today than they were a decade ago. The inability of achievement tests to match the local curriculum severely limits the ability

Table 17.2 Grade Equivalent Scores Obtained by Matching Specific Reading Text Words to Standardized Reading Test Words

Curriculum	PIAT	MAT		SORT	WRAT
		Word Knowledge	Word Analysis		
Bank Street Reading Series					
Grade 1	1.5	1.0	1.1	1.8	2.0
Grade 2	2.8	2.5	1.2	2.9	2.7
Keys to Reading					
Grade 1	2.0	1.4	1.2	2.2	2.2
Grade 2	3.3	1.9	1.0	3.0	3.0
Reading 360					
Grade 1	1.5	1.0	1.0	1.4	1.7
Grade 2	2.2	2.1	1.0	2.7	2.3
SRA Reading Program					
Grade 1	1.5	1.2	1.3	1.0	2.1
Grade 2	3.1	2.5	1.4	2.9	3.5
Sullivan Associates Programmed Reading					
Grade 1	1.8	1.4	1.2	1.1	2.0
Grade 2	2.2	2.4	1.1	2.5	2.5

From "Standardized Achievement Tests: How Useful for Special Education?" by J. R. Jenkins and D. Pany, *Exceptional Children*, 44, 1978, 448–453. Copyright © 1978 by the Council for Exceptional Children. Reprinted with permission.

of these tests to provide information of use to teachers, parents, or students. Curriculum-based approaches to assessment were designed to avoid this and the other problems noted by measuring student progress directly from the curriculum in which the student is working. Thus we become more concerned with Johnny or Susan's rate of progress through our curriculum rather than their score on an achievement test that is unlikely to match the material we're using in the regular classroom, which may yield a grade level score that is essentially meaningless.

Curriculum-Based Measurement

As indicated earlier, the term curriculum-based measurement (CBM) has been most closely associated with the research completed at the University of Minnesota (e.g., Deno, 1985). Deno and his colleagues wanted to develop a technology for assessing student achievement that was reliable and valid, simple and efficient, easily understood, and inexpensive. In short, they wanted something that would be easy to use.

The amount of research and extent of use of CBM during the last 10 years is solid evidence of how well Deno and others have succeeded in achieving these goals. This line of research has led to the existence of a technology where academic probes of 1- to 3-minute duration can be developed from the school curriculum materials, be used by teachers in a reliable manner, and provide accurate indicators of student progress (e.g., Deno, 1985). For example, simply counting the number of words read correctly from passages selected from a basal reader during brief oral reading sessions provides an excellent indication of a child's progress in reading (Deno, Mirken, Lowry, & Kuehnle, 1980). This process can be completed as little as once or twice a week and still provide reliable data.

In addition to reading, investigation of curriculum probes have been conducted across a variety of academic skill areas including spelling (e.g., Fuchs, Fuchs, Hamlett, & Allinder, 1991), written expression (e.g., Deno, Marston, & Mirken, 1982), and arithmetic (e.g., Fuchs, Fuchs, Hamlett, & Steckler, 1990). Simple measures of academic output such as number of digits (not problems) calculated correctly, letters (not words) correct in spelling, and number of words written are excellent gauges of student learning. Although most investigations have focused on the development of skills in elementary students, more recent research has focused on secondary populations and content areas (e.g., Tindal & Parker, 1989). CBM research has been disseminated widely, with applications in special (e.g., Germann & Tindal, 1985) and regular (e.g., Marston & Magnusson, 1985) education. Individuals interested in learning more about how to use this exciting technology in areas other than reading are encouraged to read about it in greater detail (e.g., Shapiro, 1989; Shinn, 1989).

Focus on
→ Practice ←

Using Curriculum-Based Measurement—
Specific Directions for Constructing Reading Probes

1. For each book in a basal reading series, the evaluator should select three 150- to 200-word passages (for first through third grades, 50- to 100-word passages)—one from the beginning, one from the middle, and one from the end. This will provide a total of three passages for each book in the basal reading series. To facilitate the scoring process, the evaluator may find it helpful to retype the passage on a separate sheet with corresponding running word counts placed in the right-hand margin.

   For preprimers and primers, shorter passages may be used. In addition, the differentiations between preprimers may not be salient enough to warrant separate probes for each individual book. In these cases, it is recommended that only the last of the preprimer books be used for purposes of assessment.

   Another issue that sometimes emerges is that a basal reading series may have more than one level assigned to a single book (e.g., parts of the Macmillan-R series). Although it is only necessary to assess by book, and not by level, some examiners may wish to create a series of probes for each level within the book. This is a perfectly acceptable practice, but may lengthen the assessment period considerably.

   Passages selected should not have a lot of dialogue, should be text (not poetry or plays), and should not have many unusual or foreign words. It is not necessary to select passages only from the beginning of stories within the text.

2. The evaluator should make two copies of each passage selected. One passage will be used for the child to read and the other copy will be used to score the child's oral reading. The evaluator may consider covering your copy with a transparency so that the copy can be reused.

3. *Optional:* For each probe, the evaluator may develop a set of five to eight comprehension questions. These questions should include at least one "who," "what," "where," "why," and inference-type question.

From E. S. Shapiro, *Academic Skills Problems: Direct Assessment and Intervention,* (pp. 92–93). Copyright © 1989 Guilford Press, New York..

Focus on
Practice

Using Curriculum-Based Measurement— Specific Directions for Reading Assessment

Setting of Data Collection

The reading measures must be administered to students individually. Prepare two copies of each passage, a numbered copy for examiner use and an unnumbered copy for the student to read.

Directions

Say to the student: *"When I say 'start,' begin reading aloud at the top of this page. Read across the page* [demonstrate by pointing]. *Try to read each word. If you come to a word you don't know, I'll tell it to you. Be sure to do your best reading. Are there any questions?"*

Say *"Start."*

Follow along on your copy of the story, marking the words that are read incorrectly. If a student stops or struggles with a word for 3 seconds, tell the student the word and mark it as incorrect.

Place a vertical line after the last word read and thank the student.

Count the number of words read correctly and incorrectly.

Scoring

The most important piece of information is the number of words read correctly. Reading fluency is a combination of speed and accuracy.

1. *Words read correctly.* Words read correctly are those words that are pronounced correctly, given the reading context.
   a. The word "read" must be pronounced "reed" when presented in the context of "He will read the book," not as "red."
   b. Repetitions are not counted as incorrects.
   c. Self-corrections within 3 seconds are counted as correctly read words.

2. *Words read incorrectly.* The following types of errors are counted: (a) mispronunciations, (b) substitutions, and (c) omissions. Further, words not read within 3 seconds are counted as errors.
   a. *Mispronunciations* are words that are misread: *dog* for *dig.*
   b. *Substitutions* are words that are substituted for the stimulus word; this is often inferred by a one-to-one correspondence between word orders: *dog* for *cat.*
   c. *Omissions* are words skipped or not read; if a student skips an entire line, each word is counted as an error.

3. *3-Second rule.* If a student is struggling to pronounce a word or hesitates for 3 seconds, the student is told the word, and it is counted as an error.

From M. R. Shinn, *Curriculum-based Measurement: Assessing Special Children.* Copyright © 1989 Guilford Press, New York.

One of the most impressive aspects of the research on curriculum-based measurement has been the collection of substantial reliability and validity data. The data obtained in the original Minnesota research, as well as subsequent investigations, suggest that curriculum-based measurement procedures are as psychometrically sound as standardized achievement tests. Deno (1985) has provided validity evidence indicating that curriculum-based measures are better predictors of short-term change than standardized tests and that a variety of CBM measures differentiate between students of different ages and ability levels (see Focus on Research). These graphs may look complex, but all they really show is that "better" students and older students do better on CBM measures. This finding is exactly what one expects, and it supports the validity of CBM as an accurate measure of reading. In addition, the final graph shows that CBM is a more sensitive measure of reading improvement than other measures.

CBM measures have been applied successfully to screening for program eligibility (e.g., Marston & Magnusson, 1985), placement in curriculum levels (e.g., Deno & Mirken, 1977), and progress monitoring (e.g., Fuchs, 1988). CBM data have been used to differentiate among exceptionalities and place children in special programs (Marston & Magnusson, 1985; Shinn & Marston, 1985). Still others have advanced methods of developing local CBM norms to assist individual school districts in the identification and placement of children in special programs (e.g., Shinn, 1988), and many school districts have moved to implement comprehensive CBM programs.

Until recently, little attention has been given to using CBM to assist classroom teachers in determining the effectiveness of instruction. Research by Fuchs and colleagues (e.g., Fuchs, 1993; Fuchs, Fuchs, & Hamlett, 1989) has changed all that and this research appears especially promising for teaching teachers measurement strategies that are both efficient and effective.

⮞ *Using Curriculum-Based Measurement in Schools*

With the explosion in research in curriculum-based assessment and curriculum-based measurement have come many attempts to apply this technology to schools, classrooms, and individual children. Below we examine five different uses of CBM data in educational decision making.

Screening for Possible Program Eligibility

One use of curriculum-based probes has been to make an initial assessment of which children should be referred for subsequent testing to determine if they are eligible for special education services. Most (Marston and Magnusson, 1985; Shinn, 1989) have advocated a cutoff that would result in any student whose performance was below the median performance for

Focus on
Research

CBM Validity Data

The graphs printed on the next pages are from a journal article prepared by Stan Deno (1985). The graphs demonstrate the potential usefulness of curriculum-based measurement data and suggest ways that these types of data might be used by teachers. The first graph provides evidence that as students get older and move through elementary school they tend to read more words correctly during a one-minute reading sample (assuming that the level of reading material is kept constant). This graph also demonstrates that regular education children do best, followed by Chapter 1 and special education students. These findings are exactly what one expects and support the contention that CBM measurement discriminates between individuals of differing ability and developmental levels.

In a similar manner, the next three graphs show that as individuals grow older they get better in reading, as well as math and spelling, as measured by CBM techniques. Although these data are averages from groups of children, these results give us confidence that when we use CBM with a particular child that our results will tell us whether the child is improving or not. Finally, the last graph demonstrates the sensitivity of CBM measures and gives us confidence that we will notice even small improvements in academic behavior if we use curriculum-based measurement. In this graph, data are presented from a 10-week period in which a child was measured weekly with CBM (words read and written correctly) while also given the SAT Reading and Language tests at the beginning and end of the 10-week period. This graph demonstrates that although the child was improving in reading and writing in the local curriculum, this change was not noticed on the standardized achievement tests. Once again, these data suggest that CBM may be a very useful tool for teachers in monitoring short-term change and for providing evidence to parents and teachers of the extent of improvement in children's academic functioning. Clearly, CBM technology is a tool unlike any tool that has ever been available to teachers. It is only a matter of time before this technology is refined and becomes a standard part of a teacher's measurement arsenal.

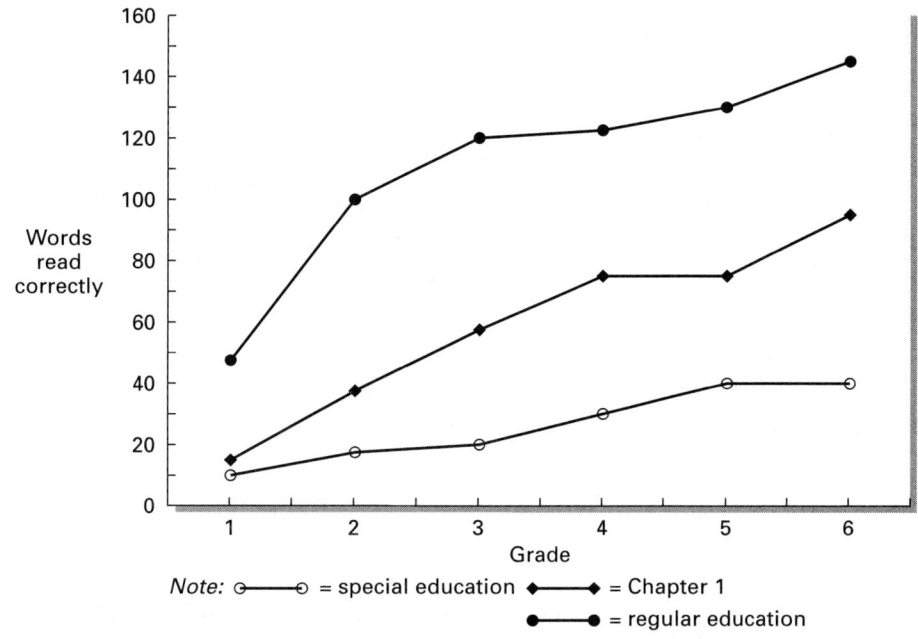

Comparison of Regular Class Chapter 1 and Special Education Students on CMB in Reading

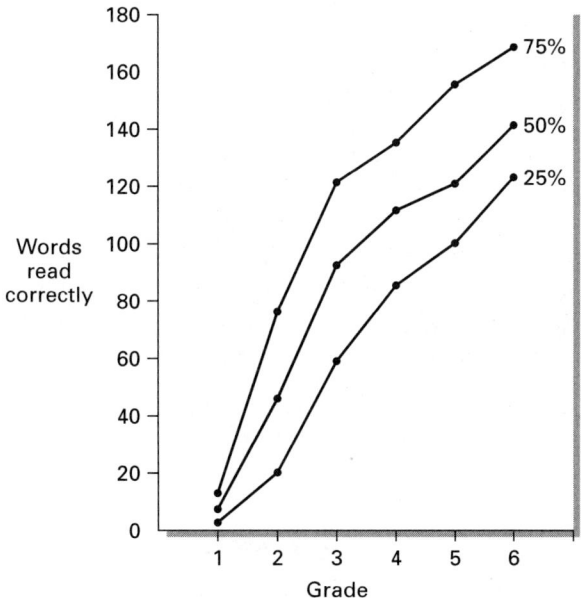

Total Number of Words Read Correctly in 1 Minute from Third Grade Oral Reading Passage

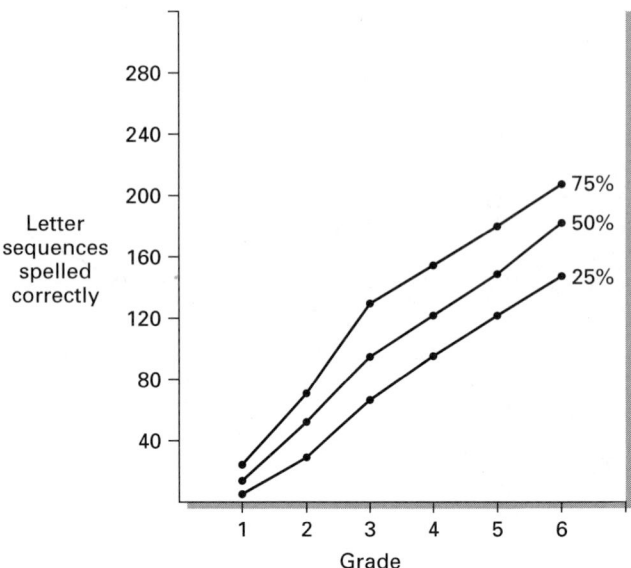

Total Number of Letter Sequences Spelled Correctly During a 3-Minute Spelling Task from Third Grade Words

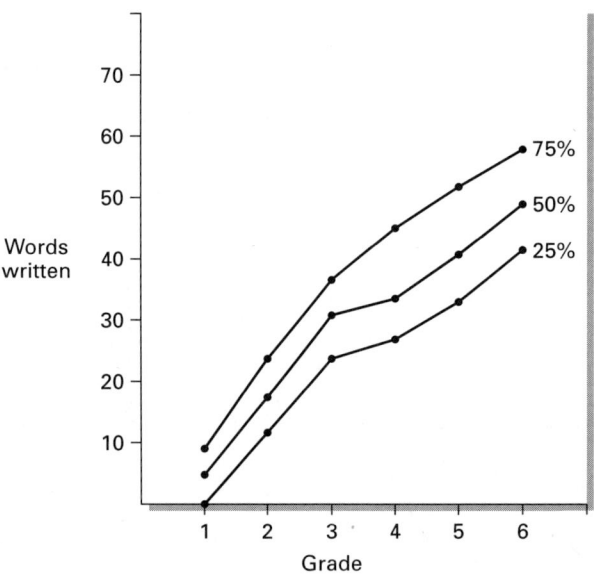

Total Number of Words Written During a 3-Minute Writing Task

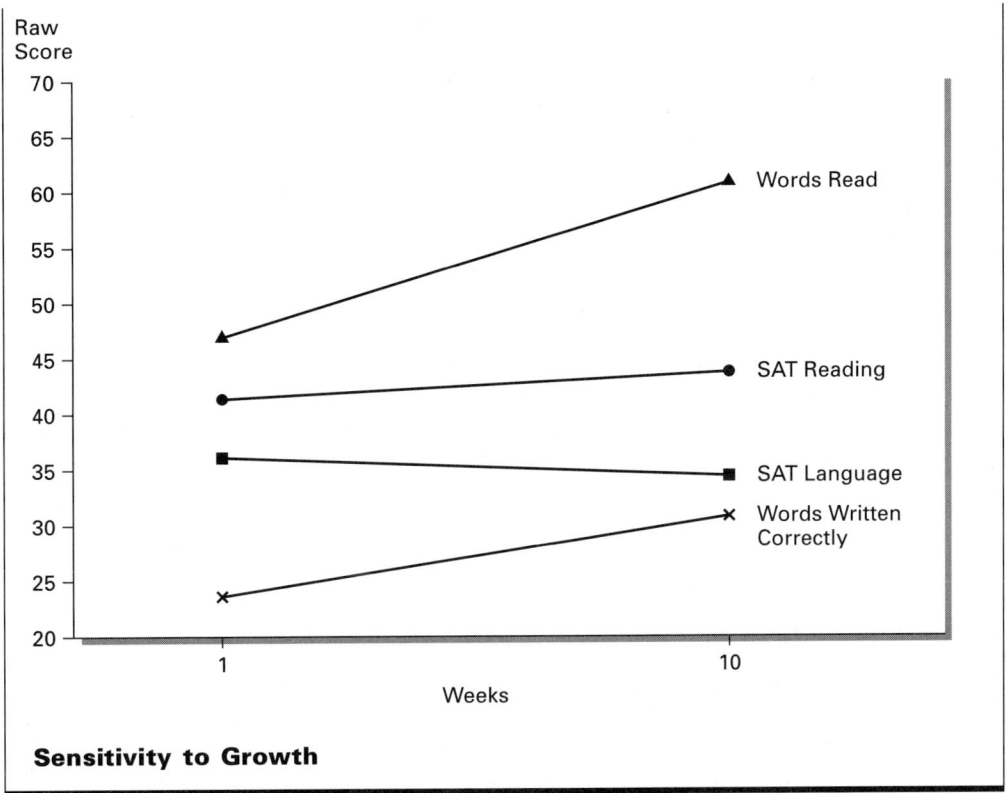

Sensitivity to Growth

her or his grade to be referred for more extensive testing. Graden, Casey, and Christenson (1985) have also reported on a prereferral system that involved the use of curriculum-based measurement.

There is much to admire in a procedure that uses the data from the local curriculum to determine possible eligibility for special programming. Lentz (1988), however, has cautioned against the use of CBM in screening, stating that "perhaps determining program eligibility for special education should not be a function for the screening phase, rather should come only after remedial efforts in the regular classroom have failed" (p. 103). Lentz is concerned that we not use CBM to refer children for special education before we try to fix the problem in the regular classroom. Further, we hope that using CBM data for screening does not divert attention from other nonstudent variables (e.g., teacher behavior, parent cooperativeness) that may need to be attended to before the child can begin to achieve in the classroom.

Placement in Curriculum

Using the curriculum that the child is about to encounter in the classroom as an assessment tool to determine the level at which the child is to be placed in the curriculum makes a great deal of sense. Criteria (e.g., correct words per minute) are established following the collection of normative data and performance on curriculum-based samples and are then used to decide where in the curriculum to begin instruction (Germann & Tindal, 1985; Marston & Magnusson, 1985). As was seen in the Focus on Research, children tend to do better on CBM measures as they move through the grades. Once normative data are established for a particular school or school system, we would be able to place a child at an appropriate level in each subject area based on our knowledge of the student's performance on those same CBM measures.

Obviously, the primary goal of placement in a sequenced curriculum is to facilitate instruction. In addition, measurement data used to determine the point at which instruction is to begin can also be used to measure individual progress toward goals, an objective that is discussed in more detail next.

Monitoring Progress

Clearly, CBA and CBM procedures have been put to many different uses. CBM differs from most other curriculum-based systems in that monitoring student progress is really what the process is all about, as Deno (1985) has stated when describing the rationale and goals of CBM: "Since the purpose of developing the measurement procedures was to place in teachers' hands a simple way to routinely monitor student achievement in the curriculum . . ." (p. 221). During the initial development stages of CBM there was little way of knowing the many different applications that CBM would have. It was clear, however, that teachers needed a more effective way to monitor student achievement.

Monitoring student progress is how CBM has been most routinely used. Indeed, all of the applications of CBM discussed here (screening, placement in the curriculum, planning, special class placement) involve progress monitoring. Because these data are simple to collect and understand, they also can be very useful in providing feedback to parents as indicated in the opening section of this chapter.

Instructional Planning

Unfortunately, teachers who collect student performance data do not always use these data to evaluate and alter instruction (Baldwin, 1976; White, 1974). Any attempt to use CBM to impact on instructional quality and student performance must take into account the need to make the system feasible for teacher use.

Lynn Fuchs and colleagues have completed much research related to these issues. For example, Fuchs, Hamlett, and Fuchs (1990) have developed and evaluated computer software applications of CBM technology "(1) to ensure standardization of the CBM monitoring, (2) to increase the feasibility of the monitoring systems, and (3) to extend the information teachers can derive from measurement" (p. 167).

This software is designed to assist teachers in monitoring academic progress in reading, mathematics, and spelling and *to facilitate student achievement*. Due to availability of Apple II computer systems in many schools across the country, the program is available currently only for these computers. Although the CBM implementation strategies vary slightly across the three academic areas, the process of using the software looks something like this:

1. In each of the three academic skill areas, teachers and students have separate disks. Following initial preparation of disks for individual students and orientation to the task, a student sits at the computer and completes a timed task ranging from 1 or 2 minutes for math to 2 1/2 minutes for reading to 3 minutes for spelling. The computer scores the responses and these data are saved to a student performance graph that is available for both teacher and student to observe.

2. Following collection of baseline data, teachers are instructed to set performance goals for each student. Specific instructions are available for teachers to guide them through the goal-setting process. Teachers may select goals based on data collected during the development of this software (e.g., an average increase of .7 word per week) or their individual knowledge of the student. Teachers are encouraged to set ambitious goals for their students. When teachers view each student's progress, they are able to see both the individual data points and the student's goal line (i.e., the student's hypothesized trend line based on the baseline data and the ultimate goal). Student graphs show data points but not the student's goal line (see figure 17.1).

3. During the school year it is recommended that students use the software once (for regular education students) or twice (for special education students) per week to provide data on the extent of their progress in whatever academic areas are being monitored. Both regular and special education students are able to use the software with little or no teacher monitoring.

4. When teachers use their teacher disk to examine individual student data, they are prompted as follows: (a) Insufficient data for analysis—this may mean that not enough data are available for a decision or that the available data do not suggest any changes; (b) Uh-oh! Make a teaching change; or (c) OK! Raise the goal. The

Figure 17.1 Teacher and Student Graphs from *Monitoring Basic Skills Progress,* by Fuchs, L. S., Hamlett, C., & Fuchs, D., 1990

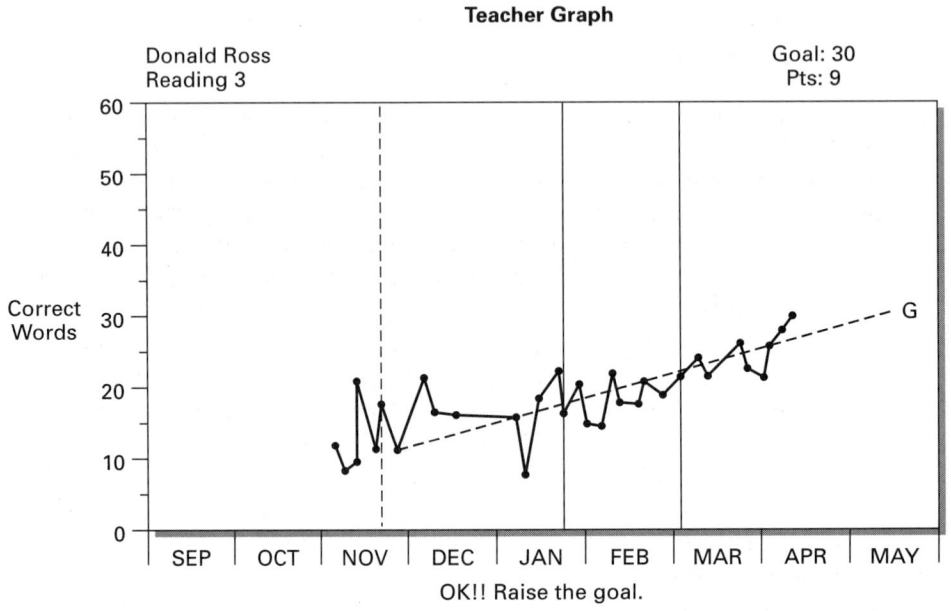

OK!! Raise the goal.

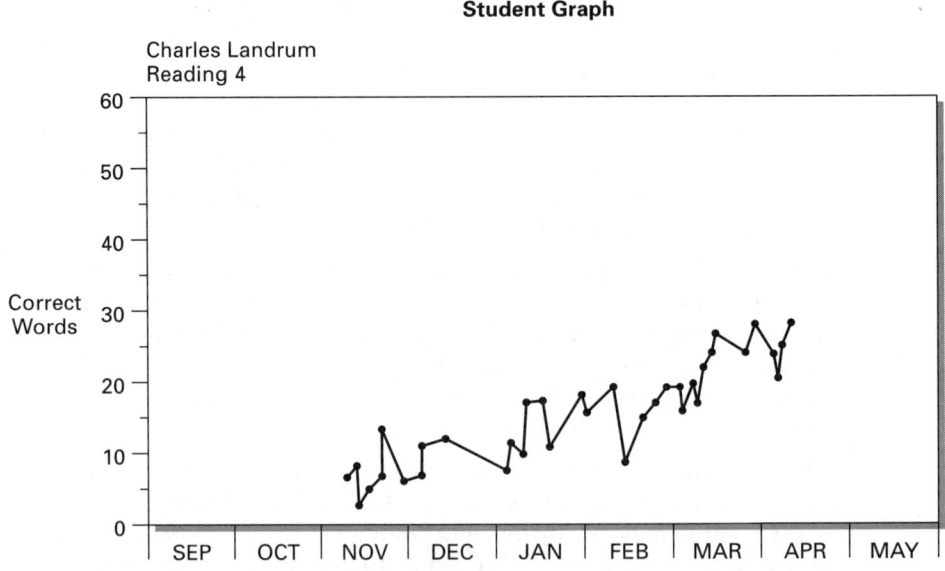

specific prompt depends on the amount of data that has been collected (e.g., Insufficient data . . .) or the match between student performance and the student's goal line. Specific numbers of data points needed to make each type of decision and a simple explanation of the specific decision rules for each type of decision are contained within the program manual.

Obviously, our review of the Fuchs et al. (1990) *Monitoring Basic Skills Progress* program has been very brief. The primary purpose in presenting this information has been as a backdrop for pointing out that the research of these investigators (e.g., Fuchs & Fuchs, 1986) has shown that the simple graphing and inspection of CBM data as described results in student achievement gains. That is, teachers who inspected the graphs of student performance were more likely to have higher levels of student improvement over the course of the study than teachers whose students' performances were not graphed.

Most importantly, requiring teachers to use standardized decision rules like those in step 4 to guide instruction results in even better outcomes than just allowing teachers to visually inspect student performance data. When teachers are required to either change instructional strategies or raise goals based on computer prompts, student achievement increases (Fuchs et al., 1989).

Placement in Special Programs

Using curriculum-based measurement to assist in the placement of children in special programs is one area where we have some concern. There is little doubt that use of CBM in placement decisions can be an improvement over use of standardized intelligence and achievement data (Salvia & Ysseldyke, 1991). Making eligibility decisions via CBM data may decrease the likelihood that children will be placed in special programs based on assumptions about underlying abilities (e.g., attention span, memory) or personality traits and increase the likelihood that children are placed in programs based on performance data relative to their peers (e.g., Shinn, 1989).

However, we must guard against CBM becoming just another method of classifying children as being learning disabled, slow learners, or mentally disabled. We must be careful that people do not stop the collection of CBM data after children are placed in special programs but continue to monitor progress following the decision to place a child in special education. The goal in making an eligibility decision about a child's qualifications for special education is not to simply place a child in a different program, but rather to provide a greater likelihood that the child will learn. We gain little if we place children in special education, but fail to change their instructional programs or monitor their progress.

Chapter Summary

The connection between direct assessment of academic behavior and effective education for children would seem obvious, but alas it has not been so. Although there can be little question that CBA is here to stay, many teachers have little or no exposure or practice with these procedures during their training to become teachers. Most educational measurement texts ignore or gloss over curriculum-based measurement, preferring instead to instruct teachers in the ways to construct good multiple-choice and essay tests. In addition, public education does not have an impressive track record of adopting efficacious procedures in a timely or comprehensive manner (e.g., Bickel & Bickel, 1986; Greer, 1983) and we are concerned CBA may be ignored, or perhaps even worse, be used in a manner that perpetuates bad practice.

Attempts to develop curriculum-based academic probes have proven very beneficial and there appears to be multiple applications of these approaches. It has been suggested that although the traditional academic achievement test has many virtues, it does not yield the most appropriate data for learning about a child's short-term progress through the local curriculum series. An alternative perspective was presented in this chapter and data from research on curriculum-based measurement (Deno, 1985) were examined. We believe that in the future a comprehensive academic assessment of a child will include standardized assessment data as well as information that is related to the child's current progress in his or her local curriculum.

Care must be taken so that new procedures are not used to support old, ineffective practices. The data indicating that CBM procedures are more efficient, as reliable and valid, and more cost effective than traditional measures of academic behavior are encouraging. These data do not suggest, however, that the use of more curriculum-based assessment procedures can be of assistance to a faulty process such as the classification of children. Classification of children into different groups has been a means by which we have attempted to get extra help to some children. CBM should not be used simply as the means to classify, but as a way to increase the potential that a student will be helped and as a way to monitor whether that assistance really does help the student.

Although many questions remain unanswered and problems loom on the horizon, there is little question that the development of CBM and other curriculum-based assessment strategies offers much to education, teachers, and students. The computer software application described in this chapter has been shown to improve student performance and to provide teachers with accurate assessment of student progress. Teachers and others preparing for careers in education or educational psychology would do well to learn all they can about curriculum-based assessment.

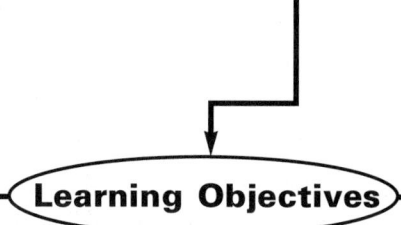

Chapter 18

Computer-Based Assessment and Test Interpretation

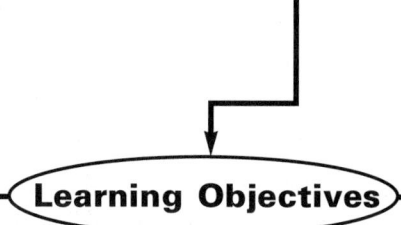

Learning Objectives

1. Distinguish between computer-based assessment and computer-based test interpretation.

2. Describe some of the concerns associated with computer-assisted testing.

3. Discuss expert systems and describe their potential applications to education.

4. List some of the concerns associated with the review and validation of computer-based test interpretation programs.

5. Describe approaches for protecting consumers from poorly developed computer-based test interpretation programs.

Audrey recently moved into the Livingston County school system. She is about to enter the second grade; however, her parents have expressed some concern about Audrey's ability "to learn as fast as the other children." Therefore they referred her for a comprehensive educational evaluation to assess her academic strengths and weaknesses as well as to help determine an appropriate educational program. Although only two weeks remain before the beginning of the school year, the school system has agreed to have a complete evaluation and feedback session prior to the first day of school. The speed with which the district has agreed to evaluate Audrey both pleases and amazes her parents, especially since her previous school had placed her on a waiting list for almost four months.

On the day of the scheduled testing, Audrey and her mother traveled to the Testing and Evaluation Center of the Livingston County Public Schools. Following a conversation with the district's school psychologist, Audrey was led to a large room containing a number of microcomputers.

Audrey was led to a large room containing a number of microcomputers. Audrey had had almost no experience with computers, but the psychologist explained that this would not be a problem, for the psychologist would give Audrey a brief, introductory lesson to learn how to respond to the computer's questions; in addition, a psychological assistant would be present at all times to assist Audrey with any questions that she might have.

During the next four hours (with a number of bathroom, water, and exercise breaks), Audrey was "tested" by the computer. She completed a general test of cognitive ability (intelligence) and an achievement battery. In addition, she took a series of academic tests in reading, spelling, and arithmetic that were specifically tailored for her. That is, based on her responses to the standardized tests, the computer was programmed to select specific types of items for administration. (This process is referred to as "adaptive testing" and is discussed in detail later in the chapter.)

When Audrey finished the testing and returned to the waiting room, she learned that her mother had also completed a number of different tasks on another computer in a room down the hallway. While Audrey's assessment had focused on general problem solving and academic skills, her mother had been asked a number of questions about Audrey's behavior and skill development. These questions had ranged from information about Audrey's early childhood (e.g., How old was Audrey when she first walked? spoke?) to information about her current behavior (e.g., How often does Audrey lose her temper? How does she get along with other children?).

Two days after the test, Audrey's parents returned to the Testing and Evaluation Center to confer with the school psychologist, two teachers (a second-grade teacher and a "resource room" teacher experienced in working with academic learning problems), and the principal from Audrey's new school. Her mother was astonished to learn that the computer that she and Audrey had worked with was programmed to analyze the results of the testing and print a long, interpretive report of her performance. Her scores were analyzed, the results summarized, and all the information carefully checked and reviewed by the school psychologist and the two teachers. According to the computer-generated report, Audrey met the federal, state, and local guidelines for assignment to a learning disability classroom. The school psychologist summarized the results and said that since the computer had done its work, she, Audrey's parents, the teachers, and the principal must discuss possible educational alternatives and plans for Audrey. As a result of this discussion it was decided that Audrey would get additional help with her reading and math in a special classroom. More importantly, specific educational goals and objectives for Audrey for the next year were identified and plans for evaluating whether she had met those goals were made.

➡ *Introduction and Background*

Does the situation described—in which a computer was programmed to test, analyze, and generate an interpretative report with specific educational recommendations, and psychologists and teachers who function primarily to check and evaluate the computer's printouts and to convey the results to parents—sound far-fetched, ludicrous, or improbable? Although the school system described exists only in our imagination, all the activities and procedures described do exist and occur in educational and clinical settings across the country every day. We know of no school system in which psychologists and teachers function *only* to check or review the computer's efforts, nor do we advocate such a system, but the possibility is not as likely as it may seem. To some, the activities described seem impressive. Others will be alarmed at the extent to which the computer can supplant the professional judgment of skilled educators and psychologists. In any case, we are about to explore the potential benefits that computer technology has to offer as well as the potential problems brought forward by this technological revolution.

As in many other areas in which the introduction of the computer has changed modern life, computer technology has the potential to alter significantly the practice of psychoeducational assessment. During the past decade the use of computers in education and psychology has become an important and pressing topic (Moreland, 1985). Entire issues of professional journals have been devoted to computer-based assessment (see, e.g., Kramer & Mitchell, 1985), computers in school psychology (McCullough & Wenck, 1984), and computer applications in counseling (Sampson, 1986). Advertisements for new computer-based assessment and test interpretation products abound. This hoopla has occurred at the same time that many professionals have decried the fact that many computer-related products are inappropriately developed and used by unqualified personnel (e.g., Matarazzo, 1983). This chapter examines some of the ways that computer technology has been applied to educational and psychological assessment and the controversy that has grown around the application of this technology. Finally, possible outcomes and solutions are discussed.

➡ *Issues and Basic Concepts*

Although we might legitimately argue with Mitchell's (1984) assertion that computer-based test interpretation is the most important problem facing psychology in the next decade, there can be little doubt that there are real problems with this new technology. Many of the specific concerns regarding the development and current status of the computer in psychoeducational assessment have been detailed elsewhere (e.g., Kramer, 1985).

" READING IS IMPORTANT, KEVIN. YOU NEED IT TO UNDERSTAND
COMPUTER MANUALS. "

Courtesy of Harley Schwadron.

We examine some of these issues with an eye toward future developments in the field of computer-based testing and their implications for the assessment of children.

To date, two types of computer systems have typically been used for assessment purposes: microcomputers (personal computers) and mainframes (very large computers such as those universities use to keep records, analyze experimental data, connect faculty and staff to a central computer system, and the like). Most professionals are likely to have access to microcomputers and the software developed for these systems; however, today many companies offer professionals access to mainframes to assist in the analysis of test results (at a price, of course!).

The computer itself (micro or mainframe) is referred to as the "hardware" of the system. "Software," usually contained on a floppy disk, refers to the programs that individuals develop to tell the computer how to handle information that is entered into the computer. These programs may be written in a variety of computer languages. Throughout this chapter we will make statements such as, "On the basis of these results the computer determines," or "The computer then decides," or "The computer analyzes." It would be more accurate to say that the computer has been told (i.e., programmed) how to determine, or to decide, or to analyze based on a series of rules (the computer "program") that someone has developed and subsequently fed into the computer.

Much software has been developed to test, score, and interpret assessment data, and the use of these products has generated many questions about the role of computer-based products in the assessment process. Currently, there is a great deal of variability in the functions that assessment-related software perform. Some programs simply administer and score tests; others perform these functions and also interpret the test scores, generate interpretive educational and psychological reports, relate the results to the research literature, and integrate data from a variety of different tests into a comprehensive report. Although the technology has generated a great deal of controversy, there can be little doubt that it is here to stay.

➡ *Computer-Based Testing*

As we have already noted, during the past few years much attention has been devoted to the use of the computer in educational and mental health settings. Much of the attention focused on the use of the computer has centered around its application to the diagnostic process and the use of computer programs in interpreting assessment results. Although less emphasis has been placed on the role of the computer in the initial assessment process, practitioners and researchers have begun to examine the use of the computer in assessment as well as interpretation (e.g., Kramer & Mitchell, 1985).

Computer-Assisted Testing

Computer-assisted testing (CAT) is the label applied to situations in which the traditional paper-and-pencil format of test administration is replaced with a computer and a monitor. The child sits in front of a computer keyboard, reads questions from the monitor, and responds by pressing a designated key. The computer has been programmed to present items in a specific manner, and responses are stored in the computer's memory for subsequent analysis.

One of the most persistent questions in the area of computer-assisted testing is what happens when a standardized paper-and-pencil test of cognitive or academic skills is transferred to the computer? Does its reliability and validity remain appropriate? Do the original norms developed under standardized testing conditions adequately represent the group taking the test on the computer?

Conventional test administration and computer-assisted test administration might differ for a number of reasons. First, the manner in which the computer presents items may differ dramatically from the way they are presented in the original test. For example, on some achievement batteries and personality tests, individuals are allowed to move through the test without regard to the order in which they answer items. In contrast, the computer can present only a few items at a time. Some subjects may also react negatively to forced interaction with the computer. Alternatively, a person may actually prefer to respond to a computer and to reveal sensitive information to this inanimate object. Moreland (1985) has examined factors that might influence performance on computer-assisted tests and concluded that although differences in individual performances sometimes occur when conventional tests are adapted to the computer, the differences are small enough to be of little consequence. Moreland also cautions that this conclusion is based on preliminary research (e.g., Hofer & Green, 1985) and that much work remains to be completed.

Test Scoring

There is little disagreement with the assertion that the computer is able to process more variables and to handle them more efficiently than even the most capable of people. One area in which these attributes of the computer have been extensively utilized is test scoring. It is clear that the computer can be very efficient in adding correct responses to yield a raw score as well as converting raw scores to standard scores, percentiles, grade equivalents, stanines, and the like, based on the normative data provided by the test publisher.

In situations in which practitioners are called upon to administer a large number of standardized tests (as in many school settings), the use of computerized scoring frees professionals from the monotonous computational procedures associated with test scoring. Furthermore, this savings in time and effort may allow the professional to become involved in other activities. Computerized test scoring has generated less controversy than any other procedure associated with computer-based assessment and test interpretation. There is little doubt that it is possible to design test scoring programs for the computer that would be more reliable than most human scorers.

Adaptive Testing

Adaptive testing refers to the process of individualizing a test based on each subject's previous responses. If programmed appropriately, the computer can immediately analyze an individual's responses and alter the sequence of subsequent items accordingly. Thus all individuals may begin at the same point in a test of, for example, academic achievement; however, subsequent items presented are based on the child's prior performance. Adaptive testing appears to be especially suited to tests that increase in difficulty as they progress and those in which specific answers result in the presentation or elimination of other items.

In the case of Audrey cited at the beginning of the chapter, the computer analyzed her performance on a number of norm-referenced measures of cognitive ability and academic achievement. Using this analysis, a pool of items was selected for further testing to obtain specific diagnostic information regarding Audrey's academic strengths and weaknesses. Based on her responses, the computer "decided" which items were to be administered next. For example, the computer quickly "realized" that Audrey was capable of completing one- and two-column addition problems with no renaming (e.g., $4 + 5 =$; $31 + 22 =$) because of her correct answers to four questions of this type. However, in three attempts Audrey was unable to answer any of the one-column addition problems with renaming (e.g., $4 + 7 =$; $9 + 16 =$); thus no two-column addition problems with renaming were administered. Had Audrey answered the renaming problems differently, however, the computer program would have selected different items to administer.

In summary, the objective of adaptive testing is to present subjects with the least redundant set of items possible by analyzing an individual's previous responses to test items. There is the potential for each subject to be administered a different set of test items based on their unique skills and abilities. In this manner, irrelevant items are omitted and testing efficiency is increased.

Behavioral/Academic Assessment

Although much of the interest in computer applications in assessment has focused on testing, individuals interested in behavioral assessment have developed a number of microcomputer applications in the behavioral field, including interviewing, modifications of traditional assessment, psychophysiological assessment, self-monitoring, and direct observation (see Kratochwill, Doll, & Dickson, 1985).

One example of a program using behavioral data is the Behavior Manager program (Tomlinson, Acker, & Mathieu, 1984), although no data are currently available regarding its efficacy. This program is designed to serve as a consultant to teachers experiencing behavior problems with their students. A teacher sits at the computer and types in information about the classroom routine, the target child, and her disciplinary procedures. The teacher than reviews a series of descriptors and is asked to identify those that describe the target child. The teacher responds to a series of forced-choice questions aimed at further delineating the problem. Ultimately the program provides a potential plan of action (as well as follow-up routines) based on the information and observations provided by the teacher. This program incorporates many features of expert systems programs described in the following section and is but one example of the potential benefits to be realized by utilizing the computer in behavioral assessment.

A recent entrant into the world of computer-based assessment is the Monitoring Basic Skills Progress program (Fuchs, Hamlett, & Fuchs, 1990). This software is designed to assist teachers in monitoring academic progress in reading, mathematics, and spelling. Adapted from the curriculum-based measurement research of Deno and colleagues (Deno, 1985; see also chapter 17 for a more detailed discussion of curriculum-based measurement and this computer program), this program has been shown to be extremely helpful in aiding teachers in monitoring student progress on a regular schedule. Perhaps most importantly, Fuchs and colleagues (e.g., Fuchs, Fuchs, & Hamlett, 1989; Fuchs, 1990) have found that use of this software promotes student learning. This software is important because it represents one of the first times that it has been shown that not only can the computer aid in collecting assessment data but also that the process of using the software actually can result in improvement in student rate of learning.

➡ *Computer-Based Test Interpretation*

Software programs developed to interpret psychological tests were originally designed for adult clinical populations, most notably to interpret the Minnesota Multiphasic Personality Inventory, a comprehensive personality test. Computer-based test interpretation (CBTI) programs for use with children in educational settings have been more slowly developed but are now available for a wide range of tests (see table 18.1 for a partial list of tests with computerized scoring or interpretation programs).

Clinical versus Actuarial Models of Prediction

The *clinical versus actuarial distinction* refers to the difference between models of prediction that are based on the research, hypotheses, and experience of skilled clinicians (clinical prediction) and those in which the computer output is determined by consistencies between that output and the input data (actuarial prediction) (Meehl, 1954). According to McDermott (1982), "a more simplistic way of explaining actuarial assessment would be to say that it is the process of making decisions about people on the basis of statistical probability" (p. 248).

Many of the systems available today for the interpretation of test scores clearly fall into the former (i.e., clinical) category. A CBTI program using clinical prediction will analyze the results obtained from a particular test (e.g., the Wechsler Intelligence Scale for Children-III [WISC-III]) in a particular fashion. The rules that guide the program as it "interprets" the test data are based on the clinician's analysis of the available research and beliefs about appropriate methods of test interpretation.

One exception to the preponderance of clinical CBTI systems is the McDermott Multidimensional Assessment of Children (M-MAC) program (McDermott & Watkins, 1985). Based on the research of Paul McDermott and his colleagues (e.g., McDermott, 1981; McDermott & Hale, 1982; McDermott & Watkins, 1979), M-MAC is an attempt to develop an actuarially

Table 18.1   A Sampling of Popular Assessment Tools with Computerized Scoring and/or Interpretation Programs

Test / Publisher	Computer Product / Publisher
Wechsler Adult Intelligence Scale-Revised (WAIS-R)/ Psychological Corporation	WAIS-R Microcomputer Assisted Interpretative Report / Psychological Corporation
Woodcock Reading Mastery/ American Guidance Service (AGS)	Woodcock ASSIST/AGS
Kaufman-Assessment Battery for Children/AGS	K-ABC ASSIST/AGS
American Association of Mental Deficiency Adaptive Behavior Scale/Publishers Test Service	ABSOFT/Publishers Test Service
Woodcock-Johnson Psychoeducational Test Battery-Revised/DLM Teaching Resources	COMPUSCORE for the WJ-R/DLM Teaching Resources
Luria-Nebraska Neuropsychological Battery/ Western Psychological Services (WPS)	WPS Test Report LNNB/ WPS
Devereux Elementary School Behavior Rating Scale II (DESBII)/Devereux Foundation	DESBII Computer Program/ Devereux Foundation
California Psychological Inventory (CPI)/Consulting Psychologists Press	Gough Narrative Report/ Consulting Psychologists Press
Parenting Stress Index/ Jastak Associates	Parenting Stress Index Computer Report/Jastak
Social Skills Rating System/ American Guidance Service (AGS)	Social Skills Rating System ASSIST/ AGS

based system for the differential diagnosis and classification of school-age children (see Focus on Practice). The M-MAC program has had a great deal of publicity; however, its long-term impact remains to be seen.

The *process* of actuarial assessment, however, offers hope that psychologists and educators will be able to improve the reliability of classification decisions. With actuarial assessment a variety of statistical procedures are used to determine the factors (such as test scores, background information, and observational data) related to the assignment of children to specific groups (e.g., mentally disabled versus learning

Focus on Practice

McDermott Multidimensional Assessment of Children

According to advertisements, the McDermott Multidimensional Assessment of Children, or M-MAC (McDermott & Watkins, 1985) is "a microcomputer system for the objective assessment of children." It is designed to accomplish two major goals: classification and program design. M-MAC materials include seven computer disks and a manual of instructions and technical data. The current version is appropriate for use with Apple II computers.

The M-MAC system is based on extensive work done by Paul McDermott and his associates on the development and validation of an actuarial system for classification of childhood problems (e.g., McDermott, 1981, 1982; McDermott & Hale, 1982; McDermott & Watkins, 1979). They have gone to great lengths to determine the factors that tend to characterize individuals who belong to certain groups such as the mentally disabled, emotionally disturbed, and attention-deficit disordered. McDermott has used this information to develop a computer program that, when provided with information about a particular child, predicts the relative likelihood that the child belongs to a specific group. Though others have criticized the classification process as being of little utility, McDermott believes that classification inevitably will be a part of the educational process and should thus be done as precisely as possible.

Exactly how does M-MAC work? First, M-MAC is not an interactive system. That is, the individual being assessed does not sit down and directly interact with the computer. Instead, the program asks for identifying information, including the child's name, age, sex, educational placement, and current date. Next, different types of background data are requested, including those related to sensory and general disabilities, general health, exceptional talents, linguistic features, cultural characteristics, environmental conditions, and educational background.

From here the computer program begins to inquire about specific assessment data. M-MAC is able to accept information from 33 different instruments related to intellectual, academic, adaptive, and social-emotional development. After these data are entered, the computer generates classifications as well as program objectives. The interpretative report ranges from 4 to 16 pages. Extensive evidence indicates that the M-MAC program does lead to consistent decision making and that experts tend to agree more with the classification decisions of M-MAC than with each other (McDermott & Hale, 1982). However, the value of the educational and behavioral objectives generated by M-MAC remains to be seen. When one considers that there are 1,111 behavioral performance objectives available in the M-MAC system, it is apparent that the validation process will be no small task.

disabled). These factors are then analyzed and translated into *decision rules,* which are used to determine whether new children qualify for inclusion in one group or another. The process of actuarial assessment ultimately results in the development of consistent rules that can be used for classification purposes. Much controversy has been generated about the efficacy and desirability of classification. However, if schools are going to group children on the basis of various factors, the process of grouping should be undertaken on the basis of clearly specified rules. Proponents of actuarial assessment claim that this process is a step in that direction and that the computer can facilitate the calculation of the complex decision rules involved in classification decisions.

Expert Systems

We have placed expert systems under the heading of computer-based test interpretations, although some might argue that this topic belongs with computer-based assessment or that these computer-based systems are a unique category that should be considered separately. Originally an outgrowth of the artificial intelligence field, expert systems (or knowledge-based systems) are computer programs that are designed to match the ability of a human expert in a particular problem area. These programs are an attempt to guide individuals in a step-by-step, commonsense manner that makes it possible to diagnose, design treatments, solve problems, or offer advice in ways that are as accurate as current knowledge allows. The basic assumption with expert systems is that "knowledge is power" (Hasselbring, 1985, p. 8).

To date, expert systems have found their greatest application in the field of medicine (e.g., Van Melle, 1977), although these programs are not limited to a restricted range of problems. The potential educational applications for these systems seems extensive. Expert systems programs aimed at facilitating the ability of classroom teachers and diagnosticians to assess learning problems have received some attention in the literature (Colbourne & McLeod, 1982; Hasselbring, 1985) and are perhaps the most obvious application of this technology within education.

In his description of expert systems applications in education, Hasselbring (1985) points out that:

> the expert system does not test the student directly, nor does it manage testing activities. Rather, at each step of the diagnosis, the system advises the user as to what to collect. The teacher or diagnostician performs the suggested task and enters the resulting information into the system. After these new data have been entered, the system analyzes the information and proposes the next step in the assessment process. When a sufficient amount of information has been gathered and entered, the system provides a report

of its diagnostic findings. The teacher can then plan a remedial program based upon the system's findings. An obvious extension of this system is to have the system prescribe appropriate remedial strategies and instructional techniques based upon the diagnostic findings. (pp. 13–14)

As with any new and powerful tool, expert systems have the potential for doing harm as well as good. Roid (1985) points out that we must be careful not to assign the label of "expert system" too quickly to inefficient or harmful computer programs. It is inevitable that many so-called expert systems will fail to live up to their advanced billing. The potential benefits of careful application of these programs, however, appear extensive.

Review and Validation of CBTI Systems

One way to ensure that consumers are protected from the use of inadequate CBTI programs is to make sure that professionals offer informed reviews of such systems. But in attempting to accomplish this goal, reviewers often face major problems not encountered when reviewing conventional tests. First, the decision rules, or instructions, that guide a CBTI program are hidden within the program itself, making it impossible for the reviewer to know how the program was constructed. This problem of inaccessibility of information is compounded by the fact that many CBTI companies are reluctant to release information regarding how their software has been developed, fearing others will misuse or copy this information for their own benefit.

Moreland (1985) suggests that the consumer wanting information about a particular CBTI program should take at least three steps to judge the value of the system. First, find out who wrote the CBTI program and investigate the author's qualifications. Does the developer have a record of scholarship with the instrument in question or any credentials that indicate special expertise as a practitioner? If the answer to this question is no, the consumer would be wise to look elsewhere. Next, it is important to examine the published documentation for the system. Specific information about decision rules for CBTI programs is rare; however, the general interpretive approach is usually documented. That is, one is usually told that the interpretation to the WISC-R is based on the work of Kaufman (1979), Sattler (1988), or whomever. Very often, the test publisher will also make available a series of references documenting the use of the CBTI system. Where do these references appear, in referred journals or in-house reports? Are validity data available and how completely are they described? Finally, the consumer should see if there are any published reviews of the system. A number of professional journals (such as the *Journal of School Psychology, Journal of Psychoeducational Assessment,* and *Computers in Human Behavior*) routinely publish reviews of assessment-related software.

Focus on Research

Man versus Model of Man

Three decades ago Kleinmuntz (1963) undertook an innovative investigation of how the computer and the clinician might interact to evaluate human behavior more efficiently.

Ten experienced clinicians were provided with the Minnesota Multiphasic Personality Inventory (MMPI) test protocols from 126 students exhibiting varying degrees of adjustment. The students' levels of adjustment were determined by a variety of factors, including the ratings of counselors and fellow students. The clinicians were required to rate each individual on a continuum ranging from well adjusted to poorly adjusted. The clinician who most accurately classified the students was asked to examine a small subsample of the 126 subjects and to verbalize his thoughts as he examined each protocol.

Following this task, Kleinmuntz translated the data that the clinician had provided into decision rules (the rules the clinician had used to make judgments). He then used this information to develop a computer program that would perform an analysis similar to that of the 10 clinicians. The program was then used to classify each of the 126 individuals according to the original adjusted/maladjusted criteria.

Not surprisingly, the computer program was more effective than the nine clinicians who were rated as less efficient than the "model" clinician. However, it is rather surprising to learn that the program outperformed even the clinician on whom it had been modeled!

Similar results have been obtained by others (e.g., Goldberg, 1970; Colbourne & McLeod, 1983), and, in general, it appears that the computerized statistical model based on the expert clinician outperforms the clinician. The model of man thus outperforms the man.

How can this be? Even the most expert, the strongest, the hardest-working clinicians occasionally tire. Everyone sometimes takes shortcuts in the hope of accomplishing a goal without expending all of one's energy. The computer, however, is not smart enough to try to get by with less effort—it can only do what it has been told to do. Thus when a program is based on an expert model, the computer will use this model every time it is asked. The computer depends on us, but we are no match for its dependability and reliability.

Although the investigative activities described might seem beyond the scope of a teacher's or psychologist's normal routine, someone must attempt to review CBTI programs in just as thorough a manner as one would review any test before recommending that it be administered to children.

CBTI: Concluding Thoughts and Needed Policies

As with the advent of any new, powerful technology, CBTI has generated enthusiasm as well as concern. If we are to maximize its potential, we must make "a sober assessment of its advantages and its problems and an effort to chart a course that will assure the former and limit or avoid the latter" (Mitchell, 1984, p. 1).

Regarding the advantages of CBTI, it is obvious that the computer can apply decision rules more consistently than even extremely accurate people and that this capability results in more accurate decision making (Goldberg, 1970; Kleinmuntz, 1963). Further, the computer can analyze information much more quickly than a person can. An additional advantage of CBTI programs is their capacity to store enormous amounts of information. Between 1938 and 1978, the *Mental Measurements Yearbook* series contained some 57,846 research references to more than 1,000 tests (Buros, 1978). During the past few years the pace of publication of new tests has quickened and there seems no end to the publication of new and revised tests (e.g., Kramer & Conoley, 1992). To remain current on the relevant research for even one test is often difficult; however, keeping track of all relevant assessment research is clearly beyond the scope of human memory. By having this information, along with frequent updates, available on a CBTI program, clinical and educational psychologists can be better able to remain current and to provide efficient services. Finally CBTI takes advantage of the computer with its penchant for speed, accuracy, and storing large amounts of information. As a result, efficient use of CBTI programs may result in an incredible savings in time and effort for professionals.

However, CBTI systems have numerous problems, some of which we have already enumerated (e.g., professional review and validation). Furthermore, CBTI systems seem to have substantial potential for validating Buros's (1961) statement that "at present, no matter how poor a test may be, if it is nicely packaged and if it promises to do all sorts of things which no test can do, the test will find many gullible buyers" (p. xxiii). Although Buros was speaking of tests rather than the computer, the statement still applies. As has been pointed out, the problem is even worse with CBTI in that much of the evidence that would substantiate (or refute) the claims of the CBTI publisher remains inaccessible to the general consumer.

The problems associated with the development of CBTI have been addressed by organizations such as the American Psychological Association (APA, 1985, 1986). According to Mitchell (1984), what is needed to protect professionals as well as consumers is a well-differentiated system of information dissemination for every CBTI system that provides data on at least three levels:

- *Level 1.* Complete discourse for professional reviewers, including all information about program development and the decision rules that guide the program.

- *Level 2.* Basic and coherent information for the CBTI user. Publishers must provide the rationale for program development as well as more than just a general notion of how interpretive statements are generated. For example, an appendix could be provided for those wanting to learn more.

- *Level 3.* Information for the test taker. These individuals need to be removed from the realm of computer myth and mystery and receive a general perspective of how the system works as well as of its weaknesses and strengths.

It would appear that this type of differentiated system offers a good deal of protection to both the CBTI publisher and consumer.

Chapter Summary

Before concluding our examination of computer-based testing and test interpretation, we would like to return to an idea that has been discussed in a number of previous chapters: treatment validity. As you may recall, treatment validity refers to the extent to which a factor, such as test result, declarative statement, or problem-solving process, results in more efficient "treatment." Do our CBTI programs help us to design more effective programs and better treatment plans? Can we teach more quickly as a result of the information provided in the interpretive report?

To date, little evidence exists that the currently available CBTI programs facilitate program development and implementation. Why should there even be such evidence? Many of the most popular programs are based on tests for which treatment validity appears to be scarce or nonexistent (see Witt & Gresham, 1985). The data accumulated to date lack convincing proof that the results of these tests can be reliably translated into instructional strategies or educational goals.

However, this lack of evidence has not deterred individuals from developing CBTI programs based on test results (see table 18.1). There appear to be few people connected with educational diagnosis who have not subjected the obtained results of various norm-referenced, general measures of cognitive or academic ability to the computer's wizardry. As we wait, the computer analyzes a bewildering array of scores and in the end prints an interpretive report summarizing the relationship among the scores and detailing the child's strengths and weaknesses. In some cases we may even receive a research summary for our subsequent analysis. It is truly amazing that the scores can be so quickly and completely analyzed, but should we not be concerned about the failure of previous researchers to document the treatment validity of the original test scores for which the CBTI program has generated a summary report? Should we not ask how the CBTI program can make something out of nothing? Have we forgotten the research showing that a scatter of intelligence test scores is rather normal (Kaufman, 1976) and relatively meaningless in the design of educational programs (Kramer, Henning-Stout, Ullman, & Schellenberg, 1987)?

Although we have some concern about the current status of CBTI in psychoeducational assessment, there is hope. The work of Hasselbring (1984, 1985) and others on expert systems as well as in areas such as adaptive testing appears to offer a great deal of promise. The Monitoring Basic Skills Progress (Fuchs, Hamlett, & Fuchs, 1990) software program discussed earlier is also a move toward effective use of the computer.

Finally, we should say that it is clear that the computer will continue to increase in importance in psychological and educational assessment. Gradually we will be able to use it to solve more and more complex problems. The process is ongoing. An incredible potential exists, but there are no guarantees that we will not misapply the technology! The best example of misapplication would be for us to continue to use the computer to analyze tests that are void of treatment validity. The widespread demonstration of computer-based programs with treatment validity awaits the talents of the skilled programmer armed with sufficient ammunition.

References

A

Aaron, P. G., & Joshi, R. M. (1992). *Reading problems: Consultation and remediation*. New York: Guilford Press.

Achenbach, T., & Edelbrock, C. (1987). *Manual for the youth self-report and profile*. Burlington, VT: University of Vermont Department of Psychiatry.

Achenbach, T., & Edelbrock, C. (1983). *Manual for the child behavior checklist and revised child behavior profile*. Burlington, VT: University of Vermont Department of Psychiatry.

Achenbach, T., McConaughy, S., & Howell, C. (1987). Child/adolescent behavioral and emotional problems: Implications of cross-informant correlations for situational specificity. *Psychological Bulletin, 101*, 213–232.

Airasian, P. W. (1989). [Review of the *California Achievement Tests*]. In J. C. Conoley & J. J. Kramer (Eds.), *Tenth mental measurements yearbook* (pp. 126–128). Lincoln, NE: Buros Institute of Mental Measurements.

Airasian, P. W (1991). *Classroom assessment*. New York: McGraw-Hill.

American Association on Mental Retardation. (1992). *Mental retardation: Definition, classification, and systems of supports*. Washington, D.C.: Author.

American Psychological Association. (1985). *Joint standards for educational and psychological testing* (3rd ed.). Washington, DC: Author.

American Psychological Association. (1986). *Guidelines for computer based tests and interpretation*. (Available from the American Psychological Association. 1200 Seventeenth Street, NW, Washington, DC 20036.)

Anastasi, A. (1981). Coaching, test sophistication, and developed abilities. *American Psychologist, 36*, 1086–1093.

Anastasi, A. (1982). *Psychological testing* (5th ed.). New York: Macmillan.

Anderson, L. M., Evertson, C. M., & Brophy, J. E. (1979). An experimental study of effective teaching in first grade reading groups. *Elementary School Journal, 79*, 193–222.

Anderson, R. C. (1972). How to construct achievement tests to assess comprehension. *Review of Educational Research, 42*, 145–170.

Anderson, R. C., Reynolds, R. E., Schallert, D. L., & Goetz, E. T. (1977). Frameworks for comprehending discourse. *American Educational Research Journal, 14*, 367–381.

Anderson, R. J., & Sisco, F. H. (1977). *Standardization of the WISC-R performance scale for deaf children* (Series T, Number 1). Washington, DC: Gallaudet College Office of Demographic Studies.

B

Bader, L. A. (1983). *Bader Reading and Language Inventory*. New York: Macmillan.

Bagnato, S. J., & Neisworth, J. T. (1990). *SPECS: System to Plan Early Childhood Services*. Circle Pines, MN: AGS.

Bagnato, S. J., & Neisworth, J. T. (1991). *Assessment for early intervention: Best practices for professionals*. New York: Guilford Press.

Bailey, D. B., & Wolery, M. (1989). *Assessing infants and preschoolers with handicaps*. Columbus, OH: Merrill Publishing Company.

Baker, R. M. (no date). *The psychological assessment of the visually handicapped*. Colorado Springs: Colorado School for the Deaf and Blind.

Baldwin, V. (1976). Curriculum concerns. In M. A. Thomas (Ed.), *Hey don't forget about me* (pp. 64–73). Reston, VA: Council for Exceptional Children.

Bates, E., O'Connell, B. & Shore, C. (1987). Language and communication in infancy. In J. D. Osofsky (Ed.). *Handbook of infant development*. New York: Wiley.

Bauman, M. K., & Kropf, C. A. (1979). Psychological tests used with blind and visually handicapped persons. *School Psychology Review, 8,* 257–270.

Bayley, N. (1969). *Bayley Scales of Infant Development.* New York: Psychological Corporation.

Becker, W., Englemann, S., Carnine, D., & Maggs, A. (1982). Direct instruction technology—making learning happen. In P. Karoly & J. Steffen (Eds.), *Advances in child behavior, behavior analysis and therapy* (pp. 151–206). Columbus, OH: Charles E. Merrill.

Beery, K. E. (1982). *Revised administration, scoring, and teaching manual for the Developmental Test of Visual-Motor Integration.* Cleveland, OH: Modern Curriculum Press.

Bender, L. (1938). *The Bender Visual Motor Gestalt Test for Children.* New York: American Orthopsychiatric Association.

Benes, K. M. (1992). [Review of the *Peabody Individual Achievement Test-Revised*]. In J. J. Kramer & J. C. Conoley (Eds.), *Eleventh mental measurements yearbook* (pp. 649–652). Lincoln, NE: Buros Institute of Mental Measurements.

Bennett, R. E., & Shepard, M. J. (1982). Basic measurement proficiency of learning disability specialists. *Learning Disability Quarterly, 5,* 177–184.

Benton, S. L. (1992). [Review of the *Test of Written Language-2*]. In J. J. Kramer & J. C. Conoley (Eds.), *Eleventh mental measurements yearbook* (pp. 979–981). Lincoln, NE: Buros Institute of Mental Measurements.

Bersoff, D. N. (1983). Social and legal influences on test development and usage. In B. Plake. *Buros/Nebraska symposium on measurement and testing* (Vol. 1. pp. 126–161). Hillsdale, NJ: Lawrence Erlbaum Associates.

Bersoff, D. N. (1983). The legal regulation of school psychology. In C. R. Reynolds & T. B. Gutkin (Eds.). *The handbook of school psychology* (pp. 1104–1138). New York: John Wiley.

Betts, E. A. (1946). *Foundations of reading instruction.* New York: American Book.

Biber, B. (1984). *Early education and psychological development.* New Haven: Yale University Press.

Bickel, W. E., & Bickel, D. D. (1986). Effective schools, classrooms, and instruction: Implications for special education. *Exceptional Children, 52,* 489–500.

Blanchard, J. S. (1985). *Computer-Based Reading Assessment Instrument.* Dubuque, IA: Kendall-Hunt.

Blankenship, C. S. (1985). Using curriculum-based assessment data to make instructional decisions. *Exceptional Children, 52,* 233–238.

Blood, D. F., & Budd, W. C. (1972). *Educational measurement and evaluation.* New York: Harper & Row.

Bloom, L. (1975). Language development. In F. D. Horowitz (Ed.), *Review of child development research* (Vol. 4). Chicago: University of Chicago Press.

Boring, E. G. (1950). *A history of experimental psychology* (2nd ed.). New York: Appleton-Century-Crofts.

Bouvier, L. F., & Davis, C. B. (1982). *The future racial composition of the United States.* Washington, DC: Demographic Information Services Center for the Population Reference Bureau.

Bracken, B. A. (1985). A critical review of *The Kaufman Assessment Battery for Children (K-ABC). School Psychology Review, 14,* 21–36.

Bracken, B. A., & Prasse, D. P. (1981). Alternate form reliability of the PPVT-R for white and black EMR students. *Educational and Psychological Research, 1,* 151–154.

Bracken, B. A., Prasse, D. P., & McCallum, R. S. (1984). Peabody Picture Vocabulary Test-Revised: An appraisal and review. *School Psychology Review, 13,* 49–60.

Brigance, A. (1977). *Diagnostic Inventory of Basic Skills.* North Billerica, MA: Curriculum Associates.

Brown v. *Board of Education,* 347 U.S. 483 (1954).

Brown, F. G. (1983). *Principles of educational and psychological testing* (3rd ed.). New York: Holt, Rinehart & Winston.

Brown, J., Bennett, J. & Hanna, G. (1981). *Nelson-Dewey Reading Test.* Chicago: Riverside.

Brown, J. S., & Burton, R. R. (1978). Diagnostic models for procedural bugs in basic mathematical skills. *Cognitive Science, 2,* 155–192.

Bruner, J. S. (1960). *The process of education.* New York: Vintage.

Bryen, D. N., & Gallagher, D. (1983). Assessment of language and communication. In K. D. Paget & B. A. Bracken (Eds.), *The psychoeducational assessment of preschool children.* New York: Grune & Stratton.

Buckley. (1978). The Bender Gestalt Test: A review of reported research with school-age subjects, 1966–1977. *Psychology in the Schools, 15,* 327–338.

Burgemeister, B. B., Blum, L. H., & Lorge, I. (1972). *Columbia Mental Maturity Scale* (3rd ed.). New York: Harcourt Brace Jovanovich.

Burns, P. C., & Roe, B. D. (1985). *Informal Reading Inventory.* Chicago: Rand McNally.

Buros, O. K. (Ed.). (1961). *Tests in print.* Highland Park, NJ: Gryphon Press.

Buros, O. K. (Ed.). (1972). *Seventh mental measurements yearbook.* Highland Park, NJ: Gryphon Press.

Buros, O. K. (Ed.). (1978). *Eighth mental measurements yearbook.* Highland Park, NJ: Gryphon Press.

C

Campbell, D., & Fiske, D. (1959). Convergent and discriminant validation by the multitrait-multimethod matrix. *Psychological Bulletin, 56,* 81–105.

Cantor, A. (1990). A new Binet and old promise: A mismatch between technology and evolving practice. *Journal of Psychoeducational Assessment, 8,* 443–450.

Carlson, C., & Lahey, B. (1983). Factor structure of teacher rating scales. *School Psychology Review, 12,* 285–292.

Carnine, D., & Silbert, J. (1979). *Direct instruction reading.* Columbus, OH: Charles Merrill.

Carroll, A. W. (1974). The classroom as an ecosystem. *Focus on Exceptional Children, 6,* 4.

Carroll, J. B. (1972). A review of the *Illinois Test of Psycholinguistic Abilities.* In O. K. Buros (Ed.), *Seventh mental measurement yearbook.* Highland Park, NJ: Gryphon Press.

Carrow, E. (1974). *Carrow Elicited Language Inventory.* Austin, TX: Learning Concepts.

Carrow-Woolfolk, E. (1973). *Test for Auditory Comprehension of Language.* Hingham, MA: Teaching Resources.

Carrow-Woolfolk, E. (1985). *Test of Adolescent Language Development-Revised.* Allen, TX: DLM Teaching Resources.

Case, R. (1974). Structures and strictures: Some functional limitations on the course of cognitive growth. *Cognitive Psychology, 6,* 544–574.

Centra, J. A., & Potter, D. A. (1980). School and teacher effects: An instructional model. *Review of Educational Research, 50,* 273–291.

Chall, J. S. (1967). *Learning to read: The great debate.* New York: McGraw-Hill.

Colbourne, M. J., & McLeod, J. (1983). Computer-guided educational diagnosis: A prototype expert system. *Journal of Special Education Technology, 6,* 30–39.

Cone, J., & Hawkins, R. (Eds.). (1977). *Behavioral assessment: New directions in clinical psychology.* New York: Brunner/Mazel.

Conners, K. (1985). *The Conners Rating Scales: Instruments for the assessment of childhood psychopathology.* Unpublished manuscript, Children's Hospital National Medical Center, Washington, D.C.

Conoley, J. C., & Kramer, J. J. (Eds.). (1989). *The tenth mental measurements yearbook.* Lincoln, NE: University of Nebraska Press.

Coopersmith, S. (1981). *Self-esteem inventories.* Palo Alto, CA: Consulting Psychologists Press, Inc.

Coulter, A., & Morrow, H. (1978). *The concept and measurement of adaptive behavior.* New York: Grune & Stratton.

Cratty, B. J. (1970). *Perceptual and motor development in infants and young children.* New York: Macmillan.

Cronbach, L. J. (1970). *Essentials of psychological testing.* New York: Harper & Row.

Cronbach, L. J., & Snow, R. E. (1977). *Aptitudes and instructional methods.* New York: Irvington.

CTB/McGraw-Hill. (1985). *The California Achievement Tests.* Monterey, CA: Author.

Cummings, J. A. (1985). [Review of *Woodcock-Johnson Psychoeducational Battery*]. In J. V. Mitchell, Jr. (Ed.), *Ninth mental measurements yearbook* (Vol. 2, pp. 1759–1762). Lincoln, NE: Buros Institute of Mental Measurements.

D

Das, J. P., Kirby, J. R., & Jarman, R. F. (1979). *Simultaneous and successive cognitive processes.* New York: Academic Press.

Davis, S. E., & Kramer, J. J. (1985). Comparison of the PPVT-T and WISC-R: A validations study with second-grade students. *Psychology in the Schools, 22,* 29–32.

deHirsch, D., Jansky, J. J., & Langford, W. S. (1966). *Predicting reading failure.* New York: Harper & Row.

Deno, S. (1985). Curriculum-based measurement: The emerging alternative. *Exceptional Children, 52,* 219–232.

Deno, S. L. (1987). Curriculum-based measurement. *Teaching Exceptional Children, 20,* 41.

Deno, S. L., Marston, D., & Mirken, P. K. (1982). Valid measurement procedures for continuous evaluation of written expression. *Exceptional Children, 48,* 368–371.

Deno, S. L., & Mirken, P. K. (1977). *Data-based program modification: A manual.* Reston, VA: Council for Exceptional Children.

Deno, S. L., Mirken, P. K., Lowry, L., & Kuehnle, K. (1980). *Relationships among simple measures of reading and performance on standardized achievement tests* (Research Report No. 20). Minneapolis: University of Minnesota Institute for Research on Learning Disabilities.

De Oreo, K. (1980). Refining locomotor skills. In C. Corbin (Ed.), *A textbook of motor development* (pp. 59–67). Dubuque, IA: Wm. C. Brown.

Diagnostic and Statistical Manual of the American Psychiatric Association, Third Edition (DSM-III-R)

Diebold, M. H., Curtis, W. S., & Dubose, R. F. (1978). Relationships between psychometric and observational measures of performance in low-functioning children. *AAESPH Review, 3,* 123–128.

Doll, E. A. (1965). *Vineland Social Maturity Scale.* Circle Pines, MN: American Guidance Service.

Dubose, R. F. (1976). Predictive value of infant intelligence scales with multiply handicapped children. *American Journal of Mental Deficiency, 81,* 388–390.

Duncan, D., Sbardellati, E., Maheady, F., & Sainato, D. (1980). Nondiscriminatory assessment of severely and physically handicapped individuals. *The Journal of the Association of the Physically Handicapped, 6,* 17–22.

Dunn, L. M. (1965). *Peabody Picture Vocabulary Test.* Circle Pines, MN: American Guidance Service.

Dunn, L. M., & Dunn, L. M. (1981). *Peabody Picture Vocabulary Test-Revised.* Circle Pines, MN: American Guidance Service.

Dunn, L. M., & Markwardt, F. C. (1970). *Peabody Individual Achievement Test.* Circle Pines, MN: American Guidance Service.

Durrell, D. D. (1955). *Durrell Analysis of Reading Difficulty.* New York: Harcourt Brace Jovanovich.

Dwyer, C. A. (1973). Sex differences in reading: An evaluation and a critique of current theories. *Review of Educational Research, 43,* 455–468.

E

Eaves, R. C., & McLaughlin, P. A. (1977). A systems approach for the assessment of the child and his environment: Getting back to basics. *Journal of Special Education, 2,* 99–111.

Ebel, R. L. (1966). Some measurement problems in a national assessment of educational progress. *Journal of Educational Measurement, 3,* 11–17.

Ebel, R. L. (1975). Educational tests: Valid? Biased? Useful? *Phi Delta Kappan, 57,* 83–89.

Edelbrock, C. (1983). Problems and issues in using rating scales to assess child personality and psychopathology. *School Psychology Review, 12,* 253–299.

Edelbrock, C. (1988). Informant reports. In E. Shapiro & T. Kratochwill (Eds.), *Behavioral assessment in schools* (pp. 351–383). New York: Guilford Press.

Education of the Handicapped Amendments, Public Law 99–457 Federal Register. (1989). *Public Law 99–457.* page 26320.

Education for All Handicapped Children Act of 1975. (1977). *Federal Register, 197,* 42474–42518.

Ekwall, E. E. (1985). *Ekwall Reading Inventory* (2nd ed.). Boston: Allyn & Bacon.

Elliott, S. N. (1991). Authentic assessment: An introduction to a neobehavioral approach to classroom assessment. *School Psychology Quarterly, 6,* 273–278.

Elliott, S. N., & Bretzing, B. H. (1980). Using and updating local norms. *Psychology in the Schools, 17,* 196–201.

Elliott, S. N., & Piersel, W. C. (1982). Direct assessment of reading skills: An approach which links assessment to intervention. *School Psychology Review, 11,* 257–280.

Engler, L., Hannah, E., & Longhurst, T. (1973). Linguistic analysis of speech samples: A practical guide for clinicians. *Journal of Speech and Hearing Disorders, 38,* 192–204.

Enright, B. E. (1983). *ENRIGHT Diagnostic Inventory of Basic Arithmetic Skills.* North Billerica, MA: Curriculum Associates.

F

Family Educational Rights and Privacy Act (FERPA), P. L. 93–380, 20 U.S.C.A., 45 C.F.R.

Farr, R. C. (1970). *Reading: What can be measured?* Newark, DE: International Reading Association.

Fenton, K. S., Yoshida, R. K., Maxwell, J. P., & Kaufman, M. T. (1979). Recognition of team goals: An essential step toward rational decision-making. *Exceptional Children, 45,* 638–644.

Fewell, R. R. (1991). Some new directions in the assessment and education of young handicapped children. In J. M. Berg (Ed.), *Science and service in mental retardation* (pp. 179–188). London: Methuen.

Fluharty, N. B. (1978). *Fluharty Preschool Speech and Language Screening Test.* Hingham, MA: Teaching Resources.

Frankenburg, W. K., & Dodds, J. B. (1967). *The Denver Developmental Screening Test.* Denver: University of Colorado Medical Center.

Frankenburg, W. K., Van Doorninck, W. J., Liddell, T. N., & Dick, N. P. (1976). The Denver Prescreening Developmental Questionnaire. *Journal of Pediatrics, 57,* 744–753.

Fry, M., & Lagomarsino, L. (1982). Factors that influence reading: A developmental perspective. *School Psychology Review, 11,* 239–250.

Fuchs, L. S. (1988). Effects of computer-managed instruction on teachers' implementation of systematic monitoring programs and student achievement. *Journal of Educational Research, 81,* 294–304.

Fuchs, L. S. (1990). Evaluating solutions, monitoring progress, and revising intervention plans. In M. R. Shinn (Ed.), *Curriculum-based measurement: Assessing special children* (pp. 153–181). New York: Guilford.

Fuchs, L. S. (1993). Enhancing instructional programming and student achievement with curriculum-based measurement. In J. J. Kramer (Ed.), *Curriculum-based assessment: Examining old problems, evaluating new solutions* (pp. 65–103). Lincoln, NE: Buros Institute of Mental Measurements.

Fuchs, L. S., & Fuchs, D. (1986). Effects of systematic formative evaluation on student achievement: A meta-analysis. *Exceptional Children, 53,* 199–208.

Fuchs, L. S., Fuchs, D., & Hamlett, C. (1989). Effects of alternative goal structures within curriculum-based measurement. *Exceptional Children, 55,* 429–438.

Fuchs, L. S., Fuchs, D., Hamlett, C., & Allinder, R. M. (1991). Effects of expert system advice within curriculum-based measurement on teacher planning and student achievement in spelling. *School Psychology Review, 20,* 49–66.

Fuchs, L. S., Fuchs, D., Hamlett, C., & Stecker, P.M. (1990). The role of skills analysis in curriculum-based measurement in math. *School Psychology Review, 19,* 6–22.

Fuchs, L. S., Hamlett, C., & Fuchs, D. (1990). *Monitoring basic skills progress* (computer program). Austin, TX: PRO-ED.

Fudala, J. (1970). *Arizona Articulation Proficiency Scale.* Los Angeles, CA: Western Psychological Services.

G

Gardner, M. F. (1979). *Expressive One-Word Picture Vocabulary Test.* Novato, CA: Academic Therapy Publications.

Gardner, M. F. (1983). *Upper-Extension Expressive One-Word Picture Vocabulary Test.* Novato, CA: Academic Therapy Publications.

Garwood, S. G., & Sheehan, R. (1989). Designing a comprehensive early invention system: The challenge of Public Law 99–457. Texas: PRO–ED.

Gaskins, R. W. (1988). The missing ingredients: Time on task, direct instruction, and writing. *The Reading Teacher, 41,* 750–755.

Gates, A. I., McKillop, A. S., & Horowitz, E. C. (Eds.). (1981). *Reading Diagnostic Tests.* New York: Teacher's College Press.

Germann, G., & Tindal, G. (1985). An application of curriculum-based assessment. The use of direct and repeated measurement. *Exceptional Children, 52,* 244–265.

Gibson, E. J., & Levin, H. (1975). *The psychology of reading.* Cambridge, MA: The MIT Press.

Gickling, E. E., & Havertape, J. (1981). *Curriculum-based assessment (CBA).* Minneapolis, MN: National School Psychology Inservice Training Network.

Gillet, J. W., & Temple, C. (1990). *Understanding reading problems: Assessment and instruction* (3rd ed.). Glenview, IL: Scott, Foresman.

Gleitman, H. (1981). *Psychology.* New York: Norton.

Goh, D. S., Telzrow, C. J., & Fuller, G. B. (1981). The practice of psychoeducational assessment among school psychologists. *Professional Psychology, 12,* 696–706.

Goldberg, L. R. (1970). Man vs. model of man: A rationale, plus some evidence for a method of improving clinical inference. *Psychological Bulletin, 73,* 422–432.

Goldman, F. H., & Duda, D. (1980). Psychological assessment of the visually impaired child. In R. K. Mulliken & M. Evans (Eds.). *Assessment of children with low-incidence handicaps.* Kent, OH: National Association of School Psychologists.

Goldman, R., & Fristoe, M. (1972). *Goldman-Fristoe Test of Articulation.* Circle Pines, MN: American Guidance Service.

Goldman, R. & Fristoe, M. (1986). *Goldman-Fristoe Test of Articulation.* Circle Pines, MN: American Guidance Service.

Goldman, R., Fristoe, M., & Woodcock, R. (1980). *The Goldman-Fristoe-Woodcock Test of Auditory Discrimination.* Circle Pines, MN: American Guidance Service.

Goldstein, K. (1939). *The organism.* New York: American Book Company.

Goldstein, K. (1948). *After-effects of brain injuries in war.* New York: Grune & Stratton.

Good, R. H., III, & Salvia, J. (1988). Curriculum bias in published norm-referenced reading tests: Demonstrable effects. *School Psychology Review, 17,* 51–60.

Good, T. L. (1979). Teacher effectiveness in the elementary school. *Journal of Teacher Education, 30,* 52–64.

Goslin, D. A. (1963). *The search for ability: Standardized testing in social perspective.* New York: Russell Sage Foundation.

Graden, J. L., Casey, A., & Christenson, S. (1985). Implementing a prereferral system, part I: The model. *Exceptional Children, 51,* 377–387.

Greer, R. D. (1983). Contingencies of the science and technology of teaching and prebehavioristic research practices in education. *Educational Researcher, 12(1),* 3–9.

Gresham, F. M. (1985). Behavior disorder assessment: Conceptual, definitional, and practical considerations. *School Psychology Review, 14,* 495–509.

Gresham, F. M. (1991). Alternative psychometrics for authentic assessment? *School Psychology Quarterly, 6,* 305–309.

Gresham, F. M. (1992). Misguided assumptions of DSM-III: Implications for school psychological practice. *School Psychology Quarterly, 7,* 79–95.

Gresham, F. M., & Elliott, S. N. (1990). *Social Skills Rating System.* Circle Pines, MN: American Guidance Service.

Gresham, F. M., Elliott, S. N., & Evans-Fernandez, S. (1992). *Student Self-Concept Scale.* Circle Pines, MN: American Guidance Service.

Gridley, B. E., & McIntosh, D. E. (1991). Confirmatory factor analysis of the Stanford Binet: Fourth Edition for a national sample. *Journal of School Psychology, 29,* 237–248.

Grossman, H. (Ed.). (1973). *Manual on terminology and classification in mental retardation* (Special Publication No. 2). Washington, DC: American Association on Mental Deficiency.

Grossman, H. (1977). *Manual on terminology and classification in mental retardation* (rev. ed.). Washington, DC: American Association on Mental Deficiency.

Grossman, H. (1981). *Manual on terminology and classification in mental retardation.* Washington, DC: American Association on Mental Deficiency.

Grossman, H. (1983). *Manual on terminology and classification in mental retardation.* Washington, DC: American Association on Mental Deficiency.

Guadalupe Organization v. *Tempe Elementary School District,* 71–435, District Court for Arizona, January 1972.

Guerin, G. R., & Maier, A. S. (1983). *Informal assessment in education.* Palo Alto, CA: Mayfield.

Guilford, J. P. (1967). *The nature of human intelligence.* New York: McGraw-Hill.

Gutkin, T. B., & Curtis, M. J. (1982). School-based consultation: Theory and techniques. In C. R. Reynolds & T. B. Gutkin (Eds.), *The handbook of school psychology* (pp. 796–828). New York: Wiley.

Gutkin, T. B., & Curtis, M. J. (1990). School-based consultation: Theory, techniques, and research. In T. B. Gutkin and C. R. Reynolds (Eds.), *The handbook of school psychology* (pp. 577–613). (2nd ed.). New York: John Wiley.

H

Haak, R. A. (1989). Establishing neuropsychology in a school setting: Organization, problems, and benefits. In C. Reynolds & E. Fletcher-Janzen (Eds.), *Handbook of clinical child neuropsychology* (pp. 489–502). New York: Plenum.

Hackola, S. (1992). Legal rights of children with attention-deficit disorder. *School Psychology Quarterly, 7,* 285–297.

Hagen, E. P., Sattler, J. M., & Thorndike, R. L. (1986). *Stanford-Binet Intelligence Scale,* 4th ed. Chicago: Riverside.

Hallahan, D. D., & Cruickshank, W. M. (1973). *Psychoeducational foundations of learning disabilities.* Englewood Cliffs, NJ: Prentice-Hall.

Halpern, A., Raffeld, P., Irvin, L. K., & Link, R. (1975). *Social and Prevocational Information Battery.* Monterey, CA: CTB/McGraw-Hill.

Hammill, D. D., & Bartel, N. R. (1975). *Teaching children with learning and behavior problems.* Boston: Allyn & Bacon.

Hammill, D. D., Brown, L., Larsen, S. C., & Wiederholt, L. (1987). *Test of Adolescent Language–2.* Austin, TX: PRO-ED.

Hammill, D. D., & Larsen, S. C. (1990). *Test of Written Language–2.* Austin, TX: PRO-ED.

Hammill, D. D., & Larsen, S. C. (1974a). The effectiveness of psycholinguistic training. *Exceptional Children, 7,* 429–436.

Hammill, D. D., & Larsen, S. C. (1974b). The relationship of selected auditory perceptual skills and reading ability. *Journal of Learning Disabilities, 7,* 429–436.

Hargrove, L. J., & Poteet, J. A. (1984). *Assessment in special education: The education evaluation.* Englewood Cliffs, NJ: Prentice-Hall.

Haring, N. G., Lovitt, T. C., Eaton, M. D., & Hansen, C. L. (Eds.) (1978). *The fourth R: Research in the classroom.* Columbus, OH: Charles E. Merrill.

Harris, A. J. (1970). *How to increase reading ability.* New York: David McKay.

Harrison, P. L. et al. (1990). *AGS Early Screening Profiles.* Circle Pines, MN: AGS.

Hart, V. (1977). Perceptual skills. In N. G. Hairing (Ed.), *Developing effective individualized education programs for severely handicapped children and youth.* Washington, DC: Bureau of Education for the Handicapped.

Harter, S. (1985). *Manual for the Self-Perception Profile for Children.* Denver, CO: University of Denver.

Hasselbring, T. S. (1984). Computer-based assessment of special needs students. In R. E. Bennett & C. A. Maher (Eds.), *Microcomputers and exceptional children* (pp. 7–19). New York: Haworth Press.

Hasselbring, T. S. (1985, August). *Computer-based assessment in the schools: Expert systems applications.* Paper presented at the American Psychological Association annual meeting. Los Angeles, CA.

Hawkins, R. P. (1979). The functions of assessment: Implications for selection and development of devices for assessing repertoires in clinical, educational, and other settings. *Journal of Applied Behavior Analysis, 1,* 97–106.

Heber, R. (1961). *A manual on terminology and classification in mental retardation.* Washington, DC: American Association on Mental Deficiency.

Hendrick Hudson District Board of Education v. *Rowley.* 347 U.S. 483 (1982).

Hendrick Hudson District Board of Education v. *Rowley,* 458 U.S. 176, 179 (1982).

Herrnstein, R. J. (1982). IQ testing and the media. *The Atlantic Monthly, 6,* 68–74.

Heward, W. L., & Orlansky, M. D. (1984). *Exceptional Children* (2nd ed.). Columbus, OH: Merrill.

Hieronymous, A. N., Linquist, E. F., Hoover, H. D., et al. (1986). *Iowa Test of Basic Skills.* Chicago: Riverside.

Hills, J. R (1976). *Measurement and evaluation in the classroom.* Columbus, OH: Charles E. Merrill.

Hiskey, M. S. (1966). *Hiskey-Nebraska Test of Learning Aptitude.* Lincoln, NE: Marshall Hiskey.

Hobbs, N. (Ed.). (1975). *Issues in the classification of children.* San Francisco: Jossey-Bass.

Hofer, P. J., & Green, B. F. (1985). The challenge of competence and creativity on computerized psychological testing. *Journal of Consulting and Clinical Psychology, 53,* 826–838.

Hoge, R. D. (1983). Psychometric properties of teacher-judgment measures of pupil aptitudes, classroom behaviors, and achievement levels. *Journal of Special Education, 17,* 401–429.

Holland, J. G., Solomon, C., Doran, J., & Frezza, D. A. (1976). *The analysis of behavior in planning instruction.* Reading, MA: Addison Wesley.

Howell, K. W. (1986). Direct assessment of academic performance. *School Psychology Review, 15,* 324–335.

Howell, K. W., Kaplan, J. S., & O'Connell, C. Y. (1979). *Evaluating exceptional children: A task analysis approach.* Columbus, OH: Charles E. Merrill.

Hresko, W. P., Reid, D. K., & Hammill, D. D. (1991). *Test of Early Language Development–2.* Austin, TX: PRO-ED.

Hull, F. M., et al. (1971). The National Speech and Hearing Survey: Preliminary results. *Journal of the American Speech and Hearing Association, 13,* 501–509.

I

Ingram, C. R. (1980). *Fundamentals of educational assessment.* New York: D. Van Nostrand.

Ingram, D. (1974). The relationship between comprehension and production. In R. L. Schieffelbusch & L. L. Lloyd (Eds.), *Language perspective—Acquisition, retardation, and intervention.* Baltimore: University Park Press.

Ireton, H., Lun, K. S., & Kampen, M. (1981). Minnesota Preschool Inventory: Identification of children at risk for kindergarten failure. *Psychology in the Schools, 18,* 193–501.

Ireton, H., & Thwing, E. (1974). *Minnesota Preschool Inventory.* Minneapolis: Behavior Science Systems.

Ireton, H., & Thwing, E. (1979). *Minnesota Preschool Inventory.* Minneapolis: Behavior Science Systems.

Iwata, B., Dorsey, M., Slifer, K., Bauman, K., & Richman, G. (1982). Toward a functional analysis of self-injury. *Analysis and Intervention in Developmental Disabilities.*

J

Jacobs, D. H., & Searfoss, S. (1979). *Diagnostic Reading Inventory* (2nd ed.). Dubuque, IA: Kendall-Hunt.

Jarman, R. F., & Das, J. P. (1977). Simultaneous and successive synthesis and intelligence. *Intelligence, 1,* 151–169.

Jastak, S., & Wilkinson, G. S. (1984). *Wide Range Achievement Test-Revised.* Wilmington, DE: Jastak Associates.

Jenkins, J. R., & Pany, D. (1978). Standardized achievement tests: How useful for special education. *Exceptional Children, 44,* 448–453.

Jensen, A. R. (1980). *Bias in mental testing.* New York: The Free Press.

Johns, J. L. (1988). *Basic Reading Inventory,* (4th ed.). Dubuque, IA: Kendall-Hunt.

Johnson, E. G. (1992). The design of the National Assessment of Educational Progress. *Journal of Educational Measurement, 29,* 95–110.

Johnson, J. H., Rasbury, W. D., & Siegel, J. L. (1986). *Approaches to child treatment: Introduction to therapy, research, and practice.* New York: Pergamon.

Johnson, M. S., Kress, R. A., & Pikulski, J. J., (1987). *Informal reading inventories.* Newark, DE: International Reading Association.

Jordon, B. T. (1980). *Jordon Left-Right Reversal Test.* San Rafael, CA: Academic Therapy Publications.

Just, M., & Carpenter, P. (1980). A theory of reading: From eye fixations to comprehension. *Psychological Review, 87,* 329–354.

K

Kamin, L. (1981). Some historical facts about IQ testing. In H. J. Eysenck & L. Kamin (Eds.), *The intelligence controversy* (pp. 90–97). New York: Wiley.

Kanfer, F. H. (1973). Behavior modification—An overview. In C. Thoresen (Eds.), *Behavior modification in education* (pp. 10–47). Chicago: University of Chicago Press.

Kaufman, A. S. (1976). A new approach to the interpretation of test scatter of the WISC-R. *Journal of Learning Disabilities, 9,* 160–168.

Kaufman, A. S. (1979). *Intelligence testing with the WISC-R.* New York: Wiley.

Kaufman, A. S., & Kaufman, N. L. (1983). *Kaufman Assessment Battery for Children.* Circle Pines, MN: American Guidance Service.

Kaufman, A. S., & Kaufman, N. L. (1985). *Kaufman Test of Educational Achievement.* Circle Pines, MN: American Guidance Service.

Kavale, K. (1990). Effectiveness of special education. In T. B. Gutkin & C. R. Reynolds (Eds.). *The handbook of school psychology* (2nd ed.) (pp. 870–900). New York: John Wiley.

Kavale, K., & Mattison, P. D. (1982). "One jumped off the balance beam": Meta-analysis of perceptual-motor training. *Journal of Learning Disabilities, 26,* 121–134.

Kazdin, A. E. (1977). Assessing the clinical or applied importance of behavior change through social validation. *Behavior Modification, 1,* 427–451.

Kazdin, A. E. (1979). Situational specificity: The two-edged sword of behavioral assessment. *Behavioral Assessment, 6,* 57–76.

Kazdin, A. (1979). Artifact, bias, and complexity: The ABC's of reliability. *Journal of Applied Behavior Analysis, 10,* 141–150.

Kazdin, A. (1984). *Behavior modification in applied settings* (3rd ed.). Homewood, IL: Dorsey Press.

Kelley, M. F., & Surbeck, E. (1983). History of preschool assessment. In K. D. Paget & B. A. Bracken (Eds.), *The psychoeducational assessment of preschool children* (pp. 1–16). New York: Grune & Stratton.

Kelly, T. L. (1927). *Interpretation of educational measurements.* Yonkers-on-Hudson, NY: World Books.

Kirk, S. A. (1963). Behavioral diagnosis and remediation of learning disabilities. *Proceedings of the annual meeting of the conference into the problems of the perceptually handicapped child* (Vol. 1). Urbana: University of Illinois Press.

Kirk, S., McCarthy, J., & Kirk, W. (1968). *Illinois Test of Psycholinguistic Abilities.* Urbana: University of Illinois Press.

Kleinmuntz, B. (1963). MMPI decision rules for the identification of college maladjustment: A digital computer approach. *Psychological Monographs, 77* (13). 1–20.

Kochanek, T. T., Kabacoff, R. I., & Lipsitt, L. P. (1990). Early identification of developmentally disabled and at-risk preschool children. *Exceptional Children, 56,* 528–539.

Koppitz, E. M. (1964). *The Bender-Gestalt Test for Young Children.* New York: Grune & Stratton.

Koppitz, E. M. (1975). *The Bender-Gestalt Test for Young Children* (Vol. 2). New York: Grune & Stratton.

Kramer, J. J. (1985). *Computer-based test interpretation in psychoeducational assessment.* Trainers of School Psychologists meeting. Los Angeles, CA.

Kramer, J. J. (Ed.). (1993). *Curriculum-based assessment: Examining old problems, evaluating new solutions.* Lincoln, NE: Buros Institute of Mental Measurements.

Kramer, J. J., & Conoley, J. C. (Eds.). (1992). *Eleventh mental measurements yearbook.* Lincoln, NE: Buros Institute of Mental Measurements.

Kramer, J. J., Henning-Stout, M., Ullman, D. L., & Schellenberg, R. L. (1987). The viability of scatter analysis on the WISC-R and SBIS: Examining a vestige. *Journal of Psychoeducational Assessment, 5,* 37–47.

Kramer, J. J., & Mitchell, J. V., Jr. (Eds.). (1985). Computer-based assessment and test interpretation: Promise, prospects, and pitfalls [Special issue]. *Computers in Human Behavior, 1* (3 & 4).

Kratochwill, T. R., Doll, E. J., & Dickson, P. (1985). Microcomputers in behavioral assessment: Recent advances and remaining issues. *Computers in Human Behavior, 1,* 277–291.

Kretschmer, R. R., & Kretschmer, L. W. (1978). *Language development and intervention with the hearing impaired.* Baltimore: University Park Press.

L

LaBerge, D., & Samuels, S. J. (1974). Toward a theory of automatic information processing in reading. *Cognitive Psychology, 9,* 111–151.

Lahey, M. (1988). *Language disorders and language development.* New York: Macmillan.

Lambert, N. & Windmiller, M. (1981). *AAMD Adaptive Behavior: School edition.* Monterey, CA: McGraw-Hill.

Lamberts, F. (1979). Describing children's language behavior. In D. A. Sabatino & T. L. Miller (Eds.). *Describing learner characteristics of handicapped children and youth* (pp. 253–291). New York: Grune & Stratton.

Lamp, R. E. & Kron, E. J. (1990). Stability of the Stanford-Binet Fourth Edition and K-ABC for young black and white children from low income families. *Journal of Psychoeducational Assessment, 8,* 139–149.

Langdon, H. W. (1989). Language disorder or difference? Assessing the language skills of Hispanic students. *Exceptional Children, 56,* 160–167.

Larry P. et al. v. *Wilson Riles et al.* (1979). United States District Court. Northern District of California. Case No. C–71–2270 RFP. Injunction in 1972 & 1974. Opinion in October 1979.

Larry P. v. *Riles.* 343 F. Supp. 1306 (N.D. Cal. 1972) (preliminary injunction). Aff'd 502 F. 2d 963 (9th cir. 1974); 495 F. Supp. 926 (N.D. Cal. 1979) (decision on merits). Aff'd (9th cir. no. 80–427 Jan. 23, 1984. Order modifying judgment, C–71–2270 RFP, Sept. 25, 1986.

Larsen, S. C., & Hammill, D. D. (1975). The relationship between selected visual skills and school learning. *Journal of Special Education, 9,* 281–291.

Larsen, S. C., & Hammill, D. D. (1986). *Test of Written Spelling–2.* Austin, TX: PRO-ED.

Learner, J. W. (1976). *Children with learning disabilities* (rev. ed.). Boston: Houghton Mifflin.

Lee, L. (1971). *Northwestern Syntax Screening Test.* Evanston, IL: Northwestern University Press.

Leinhardt, G., & Sewald, A. M. (1981). Student-based observation of beginning reading. *Journal of Educational Measurement, 18,* 171–177.

Leinhardt, G., Zigmond, N., & Cooley, W. W. (1981). Reading instruction and its effects. *American Educational Research Journal, 18,* 343–362.

Leiter, R. G., & Arthur, G. (1955). *Leiter International Performance Scale.* Chicago: Stoelting Company.

Lentz, F. E. (1988). Direct observation and measurement of academic skills: A conceptual review. In E. S. Shapiro and T. R. Kratochwill (Eds.), *Behavioral assessment in the schools: Conceptual foundations and practical applications* (pp. 76–120). New York: Guilford Press.

Leonard, L. B., Perozzi, J. A., Prutting, C. A., & Berkley, R. K. (1978). Nonstandardized approaches to the assessment of language behaviors. *American Speech and Hearing Association.* 371–379.

Levine, E. (1974). Psychological tests and practices with the deaf: A survey of the state of the art. *Volta Review, 76,* 298–319.

Levine, F. M., & Sandeen, E. (1985). *Conceptualization in psychotherapy: The models approach.* New York: Erlbaum.

Levine, S., Elzey, F. F., & Lewis, M. (1969). *California Preschool Social Competency Scale.* Palo Alto, CA: Consulting Psychologists Press.

Lewin, K. (1951). *Field theory in the social sciences.* New York: Harper & Row.

Lichtenstein, R. (1982). New instrument, old problem for early identification. *Exceptional Children, 49,* 70–72.

Lichtenstein, R. (1984). Predicting school performance of preschool children from parent reports. *Journal of Abnormal Child Psychology, 12,* 79–94.

Lichtenstein, R., & Ireton, H. (1984). *Preschool screening: Identifying young children with developmental and educational problems.* Orlando, FL: Grune & Stratton.

Lillywhite, H. S. (1958). Doctor's manual of speech disorders. *Journal of American Medical Association, 167,* 850–858.

Lindelman, R. H., & Merenda, P. F. (1979). *Educational measurement.* Glenview, IL: Scott, Foresman.

Linden, T. W. (1990). *Transdisciplinary play-based assessment.* Baltimore: Paul H. Brookes.

Lindquist, G. T. (1982). Preschool screening as a means of predicting later reading achievement. *Journal of Learning Disabilities, 15,* 331–332.

Lippmann, W. (1976). The abuse of the tests. In N. Block & G. Dwokin (Eds.), *The IQ controversy.* New York: Pantheon. (Originally published in 1922.)

Little, S. G. (1992). The WISC-III: Everything old is new again. *School Psychology Quarterly, 7,* 148–154.

Little, W. (1861). On the influence of abnormal parturition, difficult labors, premature birth, and asphyxia neonatorum on the medical and physical condition of the child, especially in relation to deformities. *Transactions of the Obstetrical Society of London, 3,* 293.

Livingston, S. A., & Zieky, M. J. (1982). *Passing scores: A manual for setting standards of performance on educational and occupational tests.* Princeton, NJ: Educational Testing Service.

Lloyd, J. (1979). Ascertaining the reading skills of atypical learners. In D. A. Sabatino & T. L. Miller (Eds.), *Describing learner characteristics of handicapped children and youth.* New York: Grune & Stratton.

Lomax, R. (1980, April). *A generalizability study of the classroom observations of learning disabled students.* Paper presented at the annual meeting of the American Educational Research Association, Boston.

Lovitt, T. C., & Fantasia, K. (1980). Two approaches of reading program evaluation: A standardized test and direct assessment. *Learning Disability Quarterly, 3,* 77–87.

M

Macmillan, D. L., & Meyers, C. E. (1980). Larry P.: An educational interpretation. *School Psychology Review, 9,* 136–148.

Mardell-Czudnowski, C., & Goldenberg, D. S. (1990). *AGS Edition of DIAL-R.* Circle Pines, MN: AGS.

Markwardt, F. C. (1989). *The Peabody Individual Achievement Test-Revised*. Circle Pines, MN: American Guidance Service.

Marsh, H. (1988): *Self-Description Questionnaire-1*. San Antonio, TX: Psychological Corporation.

Marshall et al., v. Georgia U.S. District Court for the Southern District of Georgia, CV482–233, June 28, 1984.

Marston, D. B. (1989). A curriculum-based measurement approach to assessing academic performance: What it is and why do it. In M. R. Shinn (Ed.), *Curriculum-based measurement: Assessing special children* (pp. 18–78). New York: Guilford Press.

Marston, D., & Magnusson, D. (1985). Implementing curriculum-based measurement in special and regular education settings. *Exceptional Children, 52,* 266–276.

Matarazzo, J. M. (1983, July). Computerized psychological testing. *Science, 221,* 323.

Matusiak, I. (1976). *Preschool screening for exceptional children's education needs in a large urban setting*. Milwaukee: Milwaukee Public Schools.

McCallum, R. S. (1985). [Review of *Peabody Picture Vocabulary Test-Revised*]. In J. V. Mitchell, Jr. (Ed.), *Ninth mental measurements yearbook*. Lincoln, NE: Buros Institute of Mental Measurements.

McCarthy, D. (1972). *McCarthy Scales of Children's Abilities*. New York: Psychological Corporation.

McConnell, J. V. (1989). *Understanding human behavior* (6th ed.). New York: Holt, Rinehart, & Winston.

McCracken, R. (1966). *Standard Reading Inventory*. Klamath Falls, OR: Klamath Printing.

McCullough, C. S., & Wenck, L. S. (Eds.). (1984). Computers in school

psychology [Special issue]. *School Psychology Review, 13*(4), 421.

McDaniel, E. L. (1973). *Inferrred Self-Concept Scale*. Los Angeles: Western Psychological.

McDermott, P. A. (1981). Sources of error in the psychoeducational diagnosis of children. *Journal of School Psychology, 19,* 31–34.

McDermott, P. A. (1982). Actuarial assessment systems for the grouping and classification of school children. In C. R. Reynolds & T. B. Gutkin (Eds.), *The handbook of school psychology* (pp. 243–272). New York: Wiley.

McDermott, P. A., & Hale, R. L. (1982). Validation of a systems-actuarial computer process for multidimensional classification of child psychopathology. *Journal of Clinical Psychology, 38,* 477–486.

McDermott, P. A., & Watkins, M. W. (1979). A program to evaluate general and conditional agreement among categorical assignments of many raters. *Behavioral Research Methods and Instrumentation, 11,* 399–400.

McDermott, P. A., & Watkins, M. W. (1985). *McDermott-Multidimensional Assessment of Children* [Computer program]. San Antonio: Psychological Corporation.

McMahon, R. J. (1984). Behavioral checklists and rating scales. In T. H. Ollendick & M. Hersen (Eds.), *Child behavioral assessment*. New York: Pergamon Press.

McPherson, K. S. (1985). On intelligence testing and immigration legislation. *American Psychologist, 40,* 242–243.

Meehl, P. E. (1954). *Clinical versus statistical predictions: A theoretical analysis and a review of the evidence*. Minneapolis: University of Minnesota Press.

Mehrens, W. A., & Lehmann, E. J. (1978). *Standardized tests in education*. New York: Holt, Rinehart & Winston.

Menyuk, P. (1971). *The acquisition and development of language*. Englewood Cliffs, NJ: Prentice-Hall.

Menyuk, P. (1972). *The development of speech*. Indianapolis: Bobbs-Merrill.

Mercer, J. R. (1970). Sociological perspectives on mild mental retardation (pp. 179–209). In H. Haywood (Ed.), *Social-cultural aspects of mental retardation*. New York: Appleton-Century-Crofts.

Mercer, J. R. (1979). *SOMPA technical manual*. New York: Psychological Corporation.

Mercer, J. R., & Lewis, J. (1978). *The System of Multicultural Pluralistic Assessment*. New York: Psychological Corporation.

Merwin, J. C. (1966). The progress of exploration toward a national assessment of educational progress. *Journal of Educational Measurement, 3,* 5–10.

Messick, S. (1984). Abilities and knowledge in educational achievement testing. In B. S. Plake (Ed.), *Social and technical issues in testing*. Hillsdale, NJ: Lawrence Erlbaum Associates.

Meyers, C. E., Nihira, K., & Zetlin, A. (1979). The measurement of adaptive behavior. In N. R. Willis (Ed.), *Handbook of mental deficiency: Psychological theory and research*. Hillsdale, NJ: Lawrence Erlbaum Associates.

Miller, J. (1981). *Assessing language production in children*. Austin, TX: PRO-ED.

Miller, W. H. (1974). *Reading Diagnosis Kit*. New York: The Center for Applied Research in Education.

Mills v. Board of Education of District of Columbia, 348 F. Supp. 866 (D.D.C. 1972).

Mischel, W. (1968). *Personality and assessment*. New York: Wiley.

Mitchell, J. V., Jr. (1984). *Computer-based test interpretation and the public interest*. Paper presented at the annual meeting of the American Psychological Association. Toronto, Canada.

Moran, M. R. (1978). *Assessment of the exceptional learner in the regular classroom*. Denver: Love Publishing Company.

Moreland, K. L. (1985). Computer-based psychological assessment in 1985: A practical guide. *Computers in Human Behavior, 1,* 199–206.

Mowrer, D. E. (1989). [Review of the *Goldman-Fristoe Test of Articulation*]. In J. C. Conoley & J. J. Kramer (Eds.), *Tenth mental measurements yearbook* (pp. 323–325). Lincoln, NE: Buros Institute of Mental Measurements.

Mullis, I. V. S. (1992). Developing the NAEP content-area frameworks and innovative assessment methods in the 1992 assessments of mathematics, reading, and writing. *Journal of Educational Measurement, 29,* 111–131.

Myers, P. I., & Hammill, D. D. (1976). *Methods for learning disorders*. New York: Wiley.

Myers, P. I., & Hammill, D. D. (1982). *Learning disabilities: Basic concepts, assessment practices, and instructional strategies*. Austin, TX: PRO-ED.

N

Nagle, R. J. (1979). The McCarthy Scales of Children's Abilities: Research implications for the assessment of young children. *School Psychology Digest, 8,* 319–326.

National Association of Early Childhood Educators (1989, Winter). *Resolution on testing practices*. Washington, D.C.

National Center for Fair and Open Testing. (1989, June). *Fallout from the testing operation*. Cambridge, MA.

Newcomer, P. L. (1986). *Standardized Reading Inventory*. Austin, TX: PRO-ED.

O

Oakland, T. (1979). Research on the Adaptive Behavior Inventory for Children and the estimated learning potential. *School Psychology Digest, 8,* 73–70.

Oakland, T., & Goldwater, D. (1979). Assessment and interventions for mildly retarded and learning disabled children. In G. Phye & D. Reschly (Eds.), *School psychology: Perspectives and issues* (pp. 147–169). New York: Academic Press.

P

Page, E. B. (1985). Review of the Kaufman-Assessment Battery for Children. In J. V. Mitchell, Jr. (Ed.), *The ninth mental measurements yearbook*. (pp. 357) Lincoln, NE: Buros Institute of Mental Measurements.

Paraskevopoulos, J., & Kirk, S. A. (1969). *Development and psychometric characteristics of the Revised Illinois Test of Psycholinguistic Abilities*. Urbana, IL: University of Illinois Press.

PASE (Parents in Action on Special Education) v. *Joseph P. Hannon*. U.S. District Court, Northern District of Illinois, Eastern Division, No. 74 (3586), July, 1980. Also 506 F. Supp. 831 (N.D. Ill. 1980).

Patterson, G. R. (1982). *Toddlers and delinquents: Variations on a theme of anti-social behavior*. Paper presented at the annual meeting of the American Psychological Association, Washington, DC.

Pennsylvania Association of Retarded Citizens v. *Commonwealth of Pennsylvania*. 343 F. Supp. 279 (E.D. Pa. 1972).

Pfeiffer, S. I. (1980). The school-based interprofessional team: Recurring problems and some possible solutions. *Journal of School Psychology, 18,* 388–394.

Pfeiffer, S. I. (1981). The problems facing multidisciplinary teams: As perceived by team members. *Psychology in the Schools, 18,* 330–333.

Piaget, J. (1954). *The construction of reality in the child* (M. Cook, Trans.). New York: Basic Books.

Piaget, J. (1963). *Origins of intelligence in children*. New York: Norton.

Piaget, J. (1970). *The science of education and the psychology of the child*. New York: Orion Press.

Piers, E. (1984). *Piers-Harris Children's Self-Concept Scale* (revised manual). Los Angeles, CA: Western Psychological Services.

Pikulski, J. J., & Shanahan, T. (1982). Informal reading inventories: A critical analysis. In J. J. Pikulski & T. Shanahan (Eds.), *Approaches to the informal evaluation of reading*. Newark, DE: International Reading Association.

Potter, T. C., & Rae, G. (1981). *Informal reading diagnosis: A practical guide for the classroom teacher* (2nd ed.). Englewood Cliffs, NJ: Prentice-Hall.

Powell, W. (1971). Validity of the I.R.I. reading levels. *Elementary English, 48,* 637–642.

Prescott, G. A., Balow, I. H., Hogan, T. P., & Farr, R. C. (1987). *Metropolitan Achievement Tests*. San Antonio, TX: Psychological Corporation.

President's Committee on Mental Retardation. (1970). *The six-hour retarded child*. Washington, DC: U.S. Government Printing Office.

Psychological Corporation. (1990). *Stanford Achievement Test*. San Antonio, TX: Author.

Public Law 94–142. Education for All Handicapped Children Act of 1975 (1975, November 29).

Q

Quay, H. C. (1983). A dimensional approach to behavior disorders: The Revised Behavior Problem Checklist. *School Psychology Review, 12,* 244–249.

Quay, H. C., & Peterson, D. (1983). *Manual for the Revised Behavior Problem Checklist.* Coral Gables, FL: University of Miami.

Quay, H. C., & Werry, J. (1972). *Psychopathological disorders of childhood.* New York: Wiley.

R

Reger, R. (1972). The medical model in special education. *Psychology in the Schools, 9,* 8–12.

Reisman, F. K. (1978). *A guide to the diagnostic teaching of arithmetic* (2nd ed.). Columbus, OH: Merrill.

Reschly, D. J. (1980). Concepts of bias in assessment and WISC-R research with minorities. In H. Vance & F. Wallbrown (Eds.), *WISC-R: Research and interpretation.* Washington, DC: National Association of School Psychologists.

Reschly, D. J. (1982). Assessing mild mental retardation: The influence of adaptive behavior sociocultural status, and prospects for nonbiased assessment. In C. R. Reynolds and T. B. Gutkin (Eds.), *The handbook of school psychology* (pp. 656–690). New York: Wiley.

Reschly, D. J. (1990). Best practices in adaptive behavior. In A. Thomas and J. Grimes, *Best practices in school psychology-II* (pp. 29–42). Washington, DC: National Association of School Psychologists.

Reschly, D. J., & Gresham, F. M. (1989). Current neuropsychological diagnosis of learning problems: A leap of faith. In C. Reynolds & E. Fletcher-Janzen (Eds.), *Handbook of clinical child neuropsychology* (pp. 503–520). New York: Plenum.

Reschly, D. J., Genshaft, J., & Binder, M. (1987). *The 1986 NASP survey: Comparison of practitioners, NASP leadership, and university faculty on key issues.* Washington, D.C.: National Association of School Psychologists.

Reschly, D. J., Kicklighter, R., & McKee, P. (1988). Recent placement litigation part III: Analysis of differences in *Larry P., Marshall, and S–1* and implications for future practices. *School Psychology Review, 17,* 39–50.

Reschly, D. J., & Sabers, D. (1979). Analysis of test bias in four groups with the regression definition. *Journal of Educational Measurement, 16,* 1–6.

Reynolds, C. R. (1982). The problem of bias in psychological assessment. In C. R. Reynolds & T. B. Gutkin (Eds.), *The handbook of school psychology* (pp. 178–208). New York: Wiley.

Reynolds, W. M. (1987). *Auditory Discrimination Test* (2nd ed.). Los Angeles, CA: Western Psychological Services.

Reynolds, C., & Fletcher-Janzen, F. (1989). (Eds.). *Handbook of clinical child neuropsychology.* New York: Plenum.

Reynolds, C. R., Gutkin, T. B., Elliott, S. N., & Witt, J. C. (1984). *School psychology: Essentials of theory and practice.* New York: Wiley.

Reynolds, C. R., & Mann, L. (1987). *Encyclopedia of special education.* New York: Wiley.

Richmond, B. O., & Kicklighter, R. H. (1980). *Children's Adaptive Behavior Scale.* Atlanta: Humanics.

Robeck, M. C., & Wilson, J. A. (1974). *Psychology of reading: Foundations of instruction.* New York: Wiley.

Robinson, D. Z. (1973). If you're so rich you must be smart. In C. Senna (Ed.), *The fallacy of IQ* (pp. 18–30). New York: The Third Press.

Rogers, B. G. (1992). [Review of the *Peabody Individual Achievement Test-Revised*]. In J. J. Kramer & J. C. Conoley (Eds.), *Eleventh mental measurements yearbook* (pp. 652–654). Lincoln, NE: Buros Institute of Mental Measurements.

Roid, G. H. (1985). Computer-based test interpretation: The potential of quantitative aids to test interpretation. *Computers in Human Behavior, 1,* 207–219.

Roid, G., & Fitts, W. (1988). *Tennessee Self-Concept Scale* (revised manual). Los Angeles, CA: Western Psychological Services.

Rothlisberg, & McIntosh, D. E. (1991). Performance of a referred sample on the Stanford-Binet IV and the K-ABC. *Journal of School Psychology, 29,* 367–370.

S

Salvia, J., & Ysseldyke, J. (1978). *Assessment in special and remedial education.* Boston: Houghton Mifflin.

Salvia, J., & Ysseldyke, J. E. (1991). *Assessment.* Boston: Houghton Mifflin Company.

Sampson, J. P. (Ed.). (1986). Computer applications in testing and measurement [Special issue]. *Measurement and Evaluation in Counseling and Development, 19* (1).

Sattler, J. (1988). *Assessment of Children* (3rd ed.). San Diego: Author.

Schlater, A., Fewell, R. R., & Sandall, S. R. (1987). *Seattle Inventory of Early Learning Software.* Seattle: Specialty Software, Inc.

Science Research Associates. (1987). *SRA Achievement Series.* Monterey, CA: CTB Macmillan/McGraw Hill.

Shanker, A. (1989, October 29). End standardized testing. *Washington Post.*

Shapiro, E. S. (1989). *Academic skills problems: Direct assessment and intervention*. New York: Guilford Press.

Shinn, M. R. (1988). Development of curriculum-based local norms for use in special education decision making. *School Psychology Review, 17*, 61–80.

Shinn, M. R. (Ed.). (1989). *Curriculum-based measurement: Assessing special children*. New York: Guilford Press.

Shinn, M. R., & Marston, D. (1985). Differentiating mildly handicapped, low achieving and regular education students: A curriculum-based approach. *Remedial and Special Education, 6*, 31–45.

Shinn, M. R., Rosenfield, S., & Knutson, N. (1989). Curriculum-based assessment: A comparison of models. *School Psychology Review, 18*, 299–316.

Shouksmith, G. (1970). *Intelligence, creativity and cognitive style*. New York: Wiley.

Siegel, G. M., & Broen, P. A. (1976). Language assessment. In L. L. Lloyd (Ed.), *Communication assessment and intervention strategies* (pp. 73–122). Baltimore: University Park Press.

Silvaroli, N. J. (1965). *Classroom Reading Inventory*. Dubuque, IA: Wm. C. Brown.

Silvaroli, N. J. (1986). *Classroom Reading Inventory*. Dubuque, IA: Wm. C. Brown.

Simeonsson, R. J. (1977). Infant assessment and developmental handicap. In B. M. Caldwell & D. J. Stedman (Eds.), *Infant education: A guide to helping handicapped children in first years of life*. New York: Walker & Company.

Simeonsson, R. J., Huntington, G. S., & Parse, S. A. (1980). Assessment of children with severe handicaps: Multiple problems— multivariate goals. *Journal of Association of the Severely Handicapped, 5*, 55–72.

Skinner, B. F. (1953). *Science and human behavior*. New York: The Free Press.

Soli, S. D., & Devine, V. T. (1976). Behavioral correlates of achievement: A look at high and low achievers. *Journal of Educational Psychology, 68*, 335–341.

Solomon, D., & Kendall, A. J. (1979). *Children in the classroom*. New York: Praeger.

Sommer, R., & Sommer, B. A. (1983). Mystery in Milwaukee: Early intervention, IQ, and psychology. *American Psychologist, 38*, 982–985.

Spady, W. G., & Kit, J. (1991). Beyond traditional outcome-based education. *Educational Leadership, 49 (2)*, 67–72.

Sparrow, S. S., Balla, D. A., & Cicchetti, D. V. (1984). *Vineland Adaptive Behavior Scales*, Circle Pines, MN: American Guidance Service.

Spearman, C. E. (1927). *The abilities of man*. New York: Macmillan.

Spivack, G., & Seift, M. (1967). *Devereux Elementary School Behavioral Rating Scale*. Devon, PA: The Devereux Foundation.

Spragins, A. B. (1980). Psychological assessment of the school age hearing impaired child. In R. K. Mulliken and Maryrose Evans (Eds.), *Assessment of children with low-incidence handicaps* (pp. 116–131). *Kent, OH: National Association of School Psychologists*.

Stanley, J. C. (1976). Test better finder of great math talent than teachers are. *American Psychologist, 31*, 313–314.

Stephens, T. (1978). *Social skills in the classroom*. Columbus, OH: Cedars Press.

Sternberg, R. J. (1979). [Review of "Six authors in search of a character: A play about intelligence tests in the year 2000"]. In R. J. Sternberg & D. K. Detterman (Eds.), *Human intelligence: Perspectives on its theory and measurement*. (pp. 257–268). Norwood, NJ: Ablex Publishing.

Sternberg, R. J. (1982). Who's intelligent? *Psychology Today, 16*, 30–36.

Sternberg, R. J. (1984). *Beyond IQ: A triarchic theory of human intelligence*. New York: Cambridge University Press.

Sternberg, R. J., & Davidson, J. E. (1982). The mind of the puzzler. *Psychology Today, 16*, 37–44.

Strauss, A. A., & Lehtinen, L. (1947). *Psychopathology and education of the brain-injured child*. New York: Grune & Stratton.

Sullivan, P. M., & Vernon, M. (1979). Psychological assessment of hearing impaired children. *School Psychology Review, 8*, 271–290.

Susser, M., Hauser, W. A., & Kelly, J. L. (1985). Quantitative estimates of prenatal and perinatal risk factors for perinatal mortality, cerebral palsy, mental retardation, and epilepsy. In J. M. Friedman (Ed.), *Prenatal and perinatal factors asserted with brain disorders* (Pub. No. 85–1149). Washington, DC: National Institute of Health.

Szasz, T. M. (1960). The myth of mental illness. *American Psychologist, 15*, 113–118.

T

Telzrow, C. (1989). Neuropsychological applications of common educational and psychological tests. In C. Reynolds & E. Fletcher-Janzen (Eds.), *Handbook of clinical child neuropsychology* (pp. 227–246). New York: Plenum.

Terman, L. M., & Merrill, M. (1973). *Stanford-Binet Intelligence Scale: 1973 Norms Edition*. Boston: Houghton Mifflin.

Thorndike, R. L. (1972). [Review of the *Wide Range Achievement Test*]. In O. K. Buros (Ed.), *Seventh mental measurements yearbook* (Vol. 1, pp. 67–68). Highland Park, NJ: Gryphon Press.

Thorndike, R. M. (1990). Would the real factors of the Stanford-Binet Fourth Edition please come forward? *Journal of Psychoeducational Assessment, 8,* 412–435.

Thorndike, R. L., & Hagen, E. P. (1986). *Cognitive Abilities Test.* Chicago: Riverside.

Thorndike, R. L., Hagen, E. P., & Sattler, J. M. (1986). *Stanford-Binet Intelligence Scale* (4th ed.). Chicago: Riverside.

Thurstone, L. L. (1938). Primary mental abilities. *Psychometric Monographs* (Whole No. 1).

Tindal, G., & Parker, R. (1989). Development of written recall as a curriculum-based measurement in secondary programs. *School Psychology Review, 18,* 317–343.

Tomlinson, J. R., Acker, N. E., & Mathieu, P. J. (1984). *The behavior manager* [computer program]. Minneapolis, MN: ATM.

Trachtman, G. M. (1972). Pupils, parents, privacy, and the psychologist. *American Psychologist, 17,* 32–45.

Travers, J., Elliot, S. N., & Kratochwill, T. R. (1993). *Educational Psychology: Effective teaching, effective learning.* Madison, WI: Brown & Benchmark.

Trybos, R. J., & Karchmer, M. A. (1977). School achievement scores of hearing impaired children: National data on achievement status and growth patterns. *American Annals of the Deaf, 122,* 62–69.

Turnbull, A. P., Strickland, B. B., & Brantley, J. C. (1982). *Developing and implementing individualized programs.* Columbus, OH: Merrill.

Tyler, R. W. (1966). The objectives and plans for a national assessment of educational progress. *Journal of Educational Measurement, 3,* 1–4.

V

Van Etten, G., Arkell, C., & Van Etten, C. (1980). *The severely and profoundly handicapped: Programs, methods, and materials.* St. Louis: Mosby.

Van Hattum, R. J. (Ed.). (1980). *Communication disorders: An introduction.* New York: Macmillan.

Van Melle, W. (1977). MYCIN: A knowledge-based consultation program for infectious disease diagnosis. *International Journal of Man-Machine Studies, 10,* 313–322.

Venesky, R. L. (1976). Prerequisites for learning to read. In J. R. Levin & V. L. Allen (Eds.), *Cognitive learning in children* (pp. 96–122). New York: Academic Press.

W

Wacker, D. P., Steege, M. W., & Berg, W. K. (1990). Best practices in assessment and intervention with persons who have severe/profound handicaps. In A. Thomas and J. Grimes, *Best Practices in School Psychology-II* (pp. 29–42). Washington, DC: National Association of School Psychologists.

Wadsworth, B. J. (1979). *Piaget's theory of cognitive development: An introduction for students of psychology and education.* New York: Longman.

Walker, H. (1983). *Walker Problem Behavior Identification Checklist.* Los Angeles, CA: Western Psychological Services.

Walker, H., & McConnell, S. (1988). *Walker-McConnell Scale of Social Competence and School Adjustment.* Austin, TX: PRO-ED.

Walker, H., & Severson, H. (1992). *Systematic Screening for Behavior Disorders.* Longmont, CO: Sopris West, Inc.

Wallace, G., & Larsen, S. C. (1978). *Educational assessment of learning problems: Testing for teaching.* Boston: Allyn & Bacon.

Wardrop, J. L. (1989). [Review of the *California Achievement Tests*]. In J. C. Conoley & J. J. Kramer (Eds.), *Tenth mental measurements yearbook* (pp. 128–133). Lincoln, NE: Buros Institute of Mental Measurements.

Wechsler, D. (1991). *Wechsler Intelligence Scale for Children–III.* San Antonio: Psychological Corporation.

Wechsler, E. (1974). *Wechsler Intelligence Scale for Children Revised.* San Antonio: Psychological Corporation.

Weeks, Z. R., & Ewer-Jones, B. (1983). Assessment of perceptual-motor and fine-motor functioning. In K. D. Paget & B. A. Bracken (Eds.), *The psychological assessment of preschool children* (pp. 268–269). New York: Grune & Stratton.

Weiner, F. (1979). *Phonological process analysis.* Baltimore: University Park Press.

Wells, K. C. (1981). Assessment of children in outpatient settings. In M. Hersen & A. S. Bellack (Eds.), *Behavioral assessment* (pp. 315–342). New York: Pergamon Press.

Werner, E. E., & Smith, R. S. (1982). *Vulnerable but invincible: A study of resilient children.* San Francisco: McGraw-Hill.

Whalen, C. K., & Henkler, B. (1976). Psychostimulants and children: A review and analysis. *Psychological Bulletin 83,* 1113–1130.

White, M., & Miller, S. R. (1983). Dyslexia: A term in search of a definition. *Journal of Special Education, 17,* 5–10.

White, O. R. (1974). *Evaluating educational progress* (working paper). Seattle: University of Washington Child Development and Mental Retardation Center, Experimental Education Unit.

White, O. R., & Liberty, K. (1976). Behavioral assessment and precise educational measurement. In N. Haring & R. Schiefelbusch (Eds.), *Teaching special children* (pp. 31–69). New York: McGraw-Hill.

Wiggins, G. (1989). Teaching to the (authentic) test. *Educational Leadership, 46,* 41–47.

Wiggins, G. (1990). Standards, not standardization: Evoking quality student work. *Educational Leadership, 47,* 18–25.

Williams, H. G. (1983). Assessment of gross motor functioning. In K. D. Paget & B. A. Bracken (Eds.), *The psychoeducational assessment of preschool children* (pp. 225–260). New York: Grune & Stratton.

Wise, S. L. (1985). *Determining cutoff scores for the PPST.* Unpublished manuscript. University of Nebraska-Lincoln, Lincoln, NE.

Witt, J. C., & Elliott, S. N. (1983). Assessment in behavioral consultation: The initial interview. *School Psychology Review, 12,* 42–49.

Witt, J. C., & Gresham, F. M. (1985). [Review of the *Wechsler Intelligence Scale for Children-Revised.*] In J. V. Mitchell, Jr. (Ed.), *Ninth mental measurements yearbook* (pp. 1716–1719). Lincoln, NE: Buros Institute of Mental Measurements.

Wolf, M. M. (1978). Social validity: The case for subjective measurement or how applied behavior analysis is finding its heart. *Journal of Applied Behavior Analysis, 11,* 203–214.

Wolery, M., Bailey, D., & Sugai, G. (1988). *Effective teaching: Principles and procedures of applied behavior analysis with exceptional children.* Boston, MA: Allyn & Bacon.

Woodcock, R. W. (1987). *Woodcock Reading Mastery Tests, Revised.* Circle Pines, MN: American Guidance Service.

Woodcock, R. W. (1991). *Woodcock Language Proficiency Battery.* Allen, TX: DLM Teaching Resources.

Woodcock, R. W., & Johnson, M. B. (1989). *Woodcock-Johnson Psycho-educational Battery-Revised.* Allen, TX: DLM.

Woods, M. L., & Moe. A. J. (1988). *Analytical Reading Inventory,* (4th ed.). Columbus, OH: Merrill.

Woolfolk, A. (1987). *Educational psychology,* (3rd ed.). Englewood Cliffs, NJ: Prentice-Hall.

Wright, D., & Piersel, W. C. (1987). Group administratered tests for decision making: How useful? Depends on the question. *Journal of School Psychology, 25,* 63–71.

Wyne, M. D., & O'Connor, P. D. (1979). *Exceptional children: A developmental view.* Lexington, MA: D. C. Heath.

Wyne, M. D., & Stuck, G. B. (1979). Time-on-task and reading performance in underachieving children. *Journal of Reading Behavior, 11,* 119–128.

Y

Ysseldyke, J. E. (1973). Diagnostic-prescriptive teaching: The search for aptitude-treatment interactions. In L. Mann & D. Sabatino (Eds.), *The first review of special education* (Vol. 1). Philadelphia: Journal of Special Education Press.

Ysseldyke, J. E. (1977). Aptitude-treatment interaction research with first grade children. *Contemporary Educational Psychology, 2,* 1–9.

Ysseldyke, J. E. (1979). Issues in psychoeducational assessment. In G. Phye & D. J. Reschly (Eds.), *School psychology: Perspectives and issues.* New York: Academic Press.

Ysseldyke, J. E., & Algozzine, B. (1982). *Critical issues in special and remedial education.* Boston: Houghton Mifflin.

Ysseldyke, J. E., & Christenson, S. L. (1987). *The Instructional Environment Scale.* Austin, TX: PRO-ED.

Ysseldyke, J. E., & Mirkin, P. (1982). The use of assessment information to plan instructional interventions: A review of research. In C. Reynolds & T. B. Gutkin (Eds.), *Handbook of school psychology* (pp. 395–409). New York: Wiley.

Ysseldyke, J. E., & Thurlow, M. L. (1984). Assessment practices in special education: Adequacy and appropriateness. *Educational Psychologist, 9,* 123–136.

Z

Zubin, J. (1967). Classification of behavior disorders. *Annual Review of Psychology, 18,* 373–406.

Credits

Chapter 1

Focus on Practice Adapted from J. C. Witt and S. N. Elliott, "Assessment in Behavior Consultation: The Initial Interview" in *School Psychology Review,* 1:42–49. Copyright © 1983 by the National Association of School Psychologists. Reprinted by permission of the publisher.
Figure 1.1 From S. N. Elliott and W. C. Piersel, "Direct Assessment of Reading Skills: An Approach Which Links Assessment to Intervention" in *School Psychology Review,* 11:267–280. Copyright © 1982 by the National Association of School Psychologists. Reprinted by permission of the publisher.
Figure 1.2 From J. A. Centra and D. A. Potter, "School and Teacher Effects: An Interrelational Model" in *Review of Educational Research,* 50:277. Copyright © 1980 by the American Educational Research Association.
Figure 1.3 Reprinted from *The Search for Ability: Standardized Testing in Social Perspective,* by David A. Goslin, Copyright © 1963 the Russell Sage Foundation. Reprinted with the permission of the Russell Sage Foundation.

Chapter 2

Figure 2.2 From Ysseldyke, J. E., and Christenson, S. L. (1987). The Instructional Environmental Scale. Austin, TX: PRO-ED. Reprinted by permission.

Chapter 3

Figure 3.1 From C. R. Reynolds and L. Mann, *Encyclopedia of Special Education.* Copyright

© 1987 John Wiley & Sons, New York. Reprinted by permission of John Wiley & Sons, Inc.

Chapter 5

Figure 5.1 Adapted from *Psychology* by Henry Gleitman, by permission of W. W. Norton & Company, Inc. Copyright © 1981 by W. W. Norton & Company, Inc.
Figure 5.3 From S. Jastak and G. Wilkinson, *Wide Range Achievement Test.* Copyright © 1984 Jastak Associates, Inc., Wilmington, DE.
Focus on Practice From O. K. Buros (Ed.), *Seventh Mental Measurements Yearbook.* Copyright © 1972 Buros Institute of Mental Measurements, Lincoln, NE.

Chapter 6

Figure 6.1 From Elizabeth Hagen, Jerome M. Sattler, and Robert L. Thorndike, *Stanford-Binet Intelligence Scale,* 4th edition. Riverside Publishing Company, Chicago, IL, 1986. Reproduced with permission of The Riverside Publishing Company, Chicago, IL.
Figure 6.3 From Elizabeth Hagen, Jerome M. Sattler, and Robert L. Thorndike, *Stanford-Binet Intelligence Scale,* 4th edition. Riverside Publishing Company, Chicago, IL, 1986. Reproduced with permission of The Riverside Publishing Company, Chicago, IL.

Chapter 8

Figure 8.1 AGS Edition of DIAL-R by Carol Mardell-Czudnowski and

Dorothea S. Goldenberg. Copyright © 1990 American Guidance Service, Inc., 4201 Woodland Road, Circle Pines, Minnesota 55014–1796. All rights reserved.
Figure 8.2 AGS Edition of DIAL-R by Carol Mardell-Czudnowski and Dorothea S. Goldenberg. Copyright © 1990 American Guidance Service, Inc., 4201 Woodland Road, Circle Pines, Minnesota 55014–1796. All rights reserved.
Figure 8.3 From *System to Plan Early Childhood Services* (SPECS) by Stephen J. Bagnato, John T. Neisworth, and Jean Gordon. Copyright © 1990 American Guidance Service, Inc., 4201 Woodland Road, Circle Pines, Minnesota 55014–1796. All rights reserved.

Chapter 9

Figure 9.1 From M. Just and P. Carpenter, "A Theory of Reading: From Eye Fixations to Comprehension" in *Psychological Review,* 87:329–354, 1980. Copyright © 1980 by the American Psychological Association. Adapted by permission of the publisher and the authors.
Figure 9.2 From *Woodcock Reading Mastery Tests—Revised* (WRMT-R) by Richard W. Woodcock. Copyright © 1987 American Guidance Service, Inc., 4201 Woodland Road, Circle Pines, Minnesota 55014–1796. All rights reserved.
Figure 9.3 From *Woodcock Reading Mastery Tests—Revised* (WRMT-R) by Richard W. Woodcock. Copyright © 1987

American Guidance Service, Inc., 4201 Woodland Road, Circle Pines, Minnesota 55014–1796. All rights reserved. *Figure 9.4* From *Woodcock Reading Mastery Tests—Revised* (WRMT-R) by Richard W. Woodcock. Copyright © 1987 American Guidance Service, Inc., 4201 Woodland Road, Circle Pines, Minnesota 55014–1796. All rights reserved.

Chapter 10

Focus on Practice From J. S. Brown and R. R. Burton, "Diagnostic Models for Procedural Bugs in Basic Mathematical Skills" in *Cognitive Science, 2,* pp. 155–192. Copyright © 1978 Ablex Publishing Corporation, Norwood, N.J. Reprinted with permission from Ablex Publishing Corporation.

Chapter 11

Focus on Practice From "Language Disorder or Difference? Assessing the Language Skills of Hispanic Students" by H. W. Langdon, *Exceptional Children,* 56(2), 1989, 160–167. Copyright © 1989 by The Council for Exceptional Children. Reprinted by permission.

Chapter 13

Figure 13.1 From *Social Skills Rating System (SSRS)* by Frank M. Gresham and Stephen N. Elliott Copyright © 1990 American Guidance Service, Inc., 4201 Woodland Road, Circle Pines, Minnesota 55014–1796. All rights reserved. *Figure 13.2* From Thomas M. Achenbach, *Teacher's Report Form & 1991 Profile for Ages 5–18.* Copyright © 1991 T. M. Achenbach. Reprinted with permission. *Figure 13.3* © Copyright Hill M. Walker and Herbert H. Severson (1991). *Systematic Screening for Behavior Disorders (SSBD).* Published by Sopris West, Inc., 1140 Boston Avenue, Longmont, CO 80501. Permission to reproduce these instruments must be obtained from Sopris West.

Pages 357–363 From *Social Skills Rating System (SSRS)* by Frank M. Gresham and Stephen N. Elliott. Copyright © 1990 American Guidance Service, Inc., 4201 Woodland Road, Circle Pines, Minnesota 55014–1796. All rights reserved.

Chapter 14

Figure 14.1 From Lambert, N., and Windmiller, M. (1981). *AAMD Adaptive Behavior Scale—School Edition.* Austin, TX: PRO-ED. Reprinted by permission. *Figure 14.2* From Lambert, N., and Windmiller, M. (1981). *AAMD Adaptive Behavior Scale—School Edition.* Austin, TX: PRO-ED. Reprinted by permission. *Figure 14.3* From Lambert, N., and Windmiller, M. (1981). *AAMD Adaptive Behavior Scale—School Edition.* Austin, TX: PRO-ED. Reprinted by permission. *Focus on Practice* From D. J. Reschly, "Best practices in adaptive behavior" in A. Thomas & J. Grimes, *Best Practices in School Psychology II,* pp. 29–42. Copyright © 1990 by the National Association of School Psychologists. Adapted by permission of the publisher. *Page 393* From "Assessing Mild Mental Retardation: The Influence of Adaptive Behavior, Sociocultural Status, and Prospects for Nonbiased Assessment" by D. J. Reschly in *The Handbook of School Psychology,* pp. 209–242, by C. R. Reynolds and T. B. Gutkin, eds. Copyright © 1982 John Wiley & Sons, Inc. Reprinted by permission of John Wiley & Sons, Inc.

Chapter 15

Figure 15.8 © Copyright Hill M. Walker and Herbert H. Severson (1991). *Systematic Screening for Behavior Disorders (SSBD).* Published by Sopris West, Inc., 1140 Boston Avenue, Longmont, CO 80501. Permission to reproduce these instruments must be obtained from Sopris West.

Figure 15.9 © Copyright Hill M. Walker and Herbert H. Severson (1991). *Systematic Screening for Behavior Disorders (SSBD).* Published by Sopris West, Inc., 1140 Boston Avenue, Longmont, CO 80501. Permission to reproduce these instruments must be obtained from Sopris West. *Figure 15.10* © Copyright Hill M. Walker and Herbert H. Severson (1991). summary sheet *Systematic Screening for Behavior Disorders (SSBD).* Published by Sopris West, Inc., 1140 Boston Avenue, Longmont, CO 80501. Permission to reproduce these instruments must be obtained from Sopris West.

Chapter 16

Focus on Practice 1 Excerpted from the July 2, 1984 issue of *People Weekly* Magazine. Written by Giovanna Brev/Time Inc. Reprinted with permission. *Focus on Practice 2* From O'Neill et al., "Description of Functional Analysis" in *Functional Analysis of Problem Behavior.* Copyright © 1990 Sycamore Publishing Company, Sycamore, IL. Reprinted with permission. *Focus on Practice 3* From F. H. Goldman and D. Duda, "Psychological Assessment of the Visually Impaired Child" in *Assessment of Children with Low Incidence Handicaps,* edited by R. K. Mulliken and M. Evans. Copyright © 1980 by the National Association of School Psychologists. Reprinted by permission of the publisher.

Chapter 17

Focus on Practice 1 From E. S. Shapiro, *Academic Skills Problems: Direct Assessment and Intervention,* pp. 92–93. Copyright © 1989 Guilford Press, New York. *Focus on Practice 2* From M. R. Shapiro, *Curriculum-Based Measurement: Assessing Special Children.* Copyright © 1989 Guilford Press, New York. *Page 461* From "Curriculum-Based Measurement: The Alternative" by S. Deno, *Exceptional Children,* 52, 1985,

Index